T0289660

Handbook for Strategic HR

Best Practices in Organization Development from the OD Network

Edited by

John Vogelsang, Maya Townsend,
Matt Minahan, David Jamieson, Judy Vogel,
Annie Viets, Cathy Royal, and Lynne Valek

NewYork • Atlanta • Brussels • Chicago • Mexico City • San Francisco
Shanghai • Tokyo • Toronto • Washington, D.C.

Bulk discounts available. For details visit:
www.amacombooks.org/go/specialsales
Or contact special sales:
Phone: 800-250-5308
E-mail: specialsls@amanet.org
View all the AMACOM titles at: www.amacombooks.org
American Management Association: www.amanet.org

This publication is designed to provide accurate and authoritative information in regard to the subject matter covered. It is sold with the understanding that the publisher is not engaged in rendering legal, accounting, or other professional service. If legal advice or other expert assistance is required, the services of a competent professional person should be sought.

Library of Congress Cataloging-in-Publication Data

Handbook for strategic HR : best practices in organization development from the
    OD network / edited by John Vogelsang ... [et al.].
        p.   cm.
    Includes bibliographical references and index.
    ISBN 978-0-8144-3249-5   ISBN 978-1-4002-3915-3
    1. Personnel management.   2. Organizational change.   I. Vogelsang, John.
HF5549.17.H3596 2013
658.3′01—dc23

                                                                2012017454

©2013 TheO rganizational Development Network
All rights reserved.

Thispublicationmaynotber   eproduced, stored in a retrieval system, or transmitted in whole or in part, in any form or by any means, electronic, mechanical, photocopying, recording, or otherwise, without the prior written permission of AMACOM, a division of American Management Association, 1601 Broadway, New York, NY 10019.

The scanning, uploading, or distribution of this book via the Internet or any other means without the express permission of the publisher is illegal and punishable by law. Please purchase only authorized electronic editions of this work and do not participate in or encourage piracy of copyrighted materials, electronically or otherwise. Your support of the author's rights is appreciated.

About AMA
American Management Association (www.amanet.org) is a world leader in talent development, advancing the skills of individuals to drive business success. Our mission is to support the goals of individuals and organizations through a complete range of products and services, including classroom and virtual seminars, webcasts, webinars, podcasts, conferences, corporate and government solutions, business books, and research. AMA's approach to improving performance combines experiential learning—learning through doing—with opportunities for ongoing professional growth at every step of one's career journey.

CONTENTS

Section 3   Use of Self as an Instrument of Change

Section 5   Employee Engagement

Section 6   Change Management

Section 7 Globalization, Cross-Cultural Interaction, and Virtual Working Arrangements

The Editors

David Jamieson, **PhD**, Associate Professor and Department Chair, Organization Learning & Development at the University of St. Thomas. He is also President of the Jamieson Consulting Group, Inc. He has 40 years of experience consulting to organizations on leadership, change, strategy, design, and human resource issues. He is a Past National President of the American Society for Training and Development (1984), Past Chair of the Management Consultation Division and Practice Theme Committee of the Academy of Management. He is the Associate Editor for the Reflections on Experience Section of the *Journal of Management Inquiry* and on the Editorial Boards for the *Journal of Organization Change Management* and *OD Practitioner.*

Matt Minahan, **EdD**, is president of MM & Associates, specializing in strategic planning, organization design and development, leadership development, and implementing enterprise-wide change programs, including business strategy, mission, business process simplification, new structures, and communications. He has more than 25 years' experience partnering with HR VPs and their staff. He has taught Strategic HR in the MBA programs at Johns Hopkins and the University of Maryland, and regularly offers workshops at OD Network conferences for HR staff who want to expand their skills into OD. He was the Senior Management Consultant, Institutional Change and Strategy for the World Bank. He is a member of NTL Institute, where he delivers training programs to OD and HR staff and where he does consulting projects to help strengthen the HR and OD functions in organizations.

Cathy Royal, **PhD**, is the owner and senior consultant of Royal Consulting Group. She is a System and Organizational Development professional with specialties in educational leadership, diversity, Appreciative Inquiry (AI) and organizational transformation. She presented her work on affirmative identity, gender, and Appreciative Inquiry at the 2009 AI World Summit in Katmandu, Nepal. Royal developed the Quadrant Behavior Theory (QBT)©. A dynamic theory that supports inclusion and social justice. She served as the Dean of Community Affairs and Multicultural Development at Phillips Academy, Andover, MA. She is a member of the ODN and a Ken Benne Scholar for the NTL Institute for Applied Behavioral Science (NTL). She has been honored by the US Congress for her work in gender and equality. She serves as an adjunct faculty member at Colorado Technical University.

Maya Townsend, **MSOD**, founder and lead consultant of Partnering Resources, specializes in helping leaders identify the hidden web of relationships that drive organization performance, build internal and external alignment, and reach across the "white spaces" to develop solutions that stick. She serves as an adviser to Gartner, the leading technology research and advisory company, on change management best practices. She teaches leadership, strategy, and collaboration skills through Boston University Corporate Education Group. Her articles on topics such as organizational networks, adaptability, change, and collaboration are regularly published by *CIO.Com, Mass High Tech, Chief Learning Officer,* and other industry publications. Her presentations at national conferences have been acclaimed "best in in conference" by participants. She graduated with distinction from American University/ NTL Institute Masters of Science in Organization Development program and holds a certificate in Organization Development from Georgetown University.

Lynne Valek's first career was in television where she was an award-wining art director. During those years she got an MA, MS, and PhD in organizational studies. She started her second career as a trainer, facilitator, executive coach, consultant, presenter, OD, jury consultant, and graphic facilitator. For 18 years she has taught graduate classes in organization studies at Alliant International University in change and development, organization theory, and research. She also teaches on ground and online classes at the University of Phoenix in psychology, and for the University of the Rockies.

Annie Viets, EdD, is an Associate Professor of Management at Prince Mohammad Bin Fahd University in Khobar, Saudi Arabia. Her career has included senior HR and OD positions at Ben & Jerry's Homemade, Inc., The Hay Group and Fletcher Challenge (New Zealand) Ltd. She has served on the faculties of the University of Vermont School of Business and the SIT Graduate Institute where she was Chair of the Management Degree Program. A global citizen, she has also consulted to large and small businesses, nonprofits, and government departments in the US and internationally on corporate social responsibility, sustainable leadership, conflict transformation, and management de-

velopment. Current research interests center on women and entrepreneurship in the Middle East.

Judy Vogel, MLA, partner in Vogel/Glaser & Associates, Inc., is an educator and businesswoman since 1970 as an organization development (OD) consultant, Director of both the OD and HR functions for major corporations, and adjunct faculty at several universities. She specializes in culture change initiatives, executive coaching, team development and assisting HR staffs to become skilled internal consultants and Business Partners. She has made presentations at numerous conferences and published many articles on these subjects. She is a Professional Member and trainer for the NTL Institute, including its OD Certificate Track; and she is part of the instructional staff for the American University/ NTL Masters of OD program. For many years she has been a presenter at the OD Network Conference, and she is a Reviewer for its publication, *OD Practitioner.*

John Vogelsang, PhD, is the Editor in Chief of the *OD Practitioner,* the quarterly journal of the Organization Development Network. He has been working since 1974 in the areas of leadership capacity building, board development, strategic planning, organizational and leadership transitions, conflict transformation, participatory evaluation, and strategic restructuring. He serves as a coach for executive directors, senior management teams, and boards, and he has facilitated numerous board and staff retreats and executive director peer learning groups. His clients have included foundations, human service agencies, mental health agencies, community health centers, universities, professional associations, arts organizations, advocacy and environmental organizations.

The Changing World of Human Resources

Introduction

David Jamieson and John Vogelsang

VOICES FROM THE FIELD[1]

Business leaders are actually aware of the need for HR to shed its traditional role. They want HR professionals to step up to a more value-adding contribution. They are looking to HR for help in crafting strategy, determining priorities in running the business, designing and structuring how work gets done, shaping culture, and, yes, managing people systems to give a sense of stability. Moreover, the business leaders know they need HR professionals who are credible activists who will push, prod, and even lead some discussions that chart the course for the future.

—Dave Hanna

If you [the HR leader] come to clients with a large set of tools, you will be viewed as a great craftsperson. If you come with a set of principles that help them learn and solve problems in a more sustainable way, then you will be seen as a successful Business Partner.

—Chuck Mallue

What would have been most helpful to my career as an internal, was to have done even more to accelerate the development of my colleagues OD competencies.

—Maria Ramos

HUMAN RESOURCE MANAGEMENT IS CHANGING

Since the 1990s, Human Resources (HR) has become a high-quality service provider that

plays a trusted advisory, business partner, and consultant role in strategic decision-making. While HR continues to perform the still important transactional functions, HR Business Partners are working with executives and managers to set priorities and guide change for organizations.

How has this happened? The two chapters in this introductory section give a historical perspective on this change and current opportunities. Edgar Schein (2010) in "The Role of Organization Development in the Human Resource Function" describes the four evolving roles for HR Managers:

> *Role 1: Champion of the Employees*—to be the spokesperson for the employee.
> *Role 2: Expert Administrator*—the job of managing the pay and benefits system, which requires knowledge of the relevant systems and procedures, and often requires the HR Manager to defend procedures that often appear to be too bureaucratic to the employees.
> *Role 3: Partner in Strategy*—human resources becomes important to the success of the longer range strategies, and the HR function participates in the strategy and planning process.
> *Role 4: The Professional HR Manager*—HR managers function as change agents and process consultants and bring research knowledge and practice into the organization.

---

[1] Many of the sections begin with comments from the conversations the editors had with HR and OD professionals prior to compiling resource. Information about the respondents can be found in the About the Contributors section.

Dave Hanna (2010) in "Organization Development and Human Resource Management" contends that the results of the 2007 HR Competency Study, co-sponsored by the RBL Group and the University of Michigan Ross School, urges the coming together of HR and Organization Development (OD). The study identifies six competencies that are essential for an HR professional who adds value to a business. These competencies are based for the most part on what have generally been considered OD skills.

- **The Credible Activist:** being credible (respected, listened to) and active (offering a point of view and challenging others' assumptions)
- **The Operational Executor:** flawlessly executing the operational aspects of managing people and organizations
- **The Business Ally:** contributing to the success of the business by understanding its social context, how it makes money, and how to organize its parts to make more money
- **The Talent Manager/Organization Designer:** mastering theory, research, and practice in both talent management and organization design
- **The Strategy Architect:** having a vision of how the organization can succeed in the marketplace and actively shaping the strategy to fulfill this vision
- **The Culture and Change Steward:** recognizing, articulating, and shaping corporate culture and facilitating the change processes required to keep the culture aligned with the business needs

The study also highlights the drive towards genuine integration among strategic aspects of HR functions, the role of human capital in organizational success, and the essential processes of managing change.

Making the transition to and succeeding at a Business Partner role may require some mindset shifts and a mix of core knowledge and skills, much of which have been funda-

mental to OD: consulting, action research, systems and strategic thinking, organizational design, and the competencies to partner with clients to initiate and implement change.

Mindset Shifts

The essential mindset shifts include (Jamieson et al., 2012):

- **From past-focused to future-focused.** Many of the answers to today's challenges cannot be found in the past since the issues never existed before. For example, if an organization clings to a rule that an employee needs to be in a role for two years before being promoted, and if the employee is a top talent who feels ready for the next role, the organization may lose the employee.
- **From discipline-focused to having an organization focused.** Business Partners must focus on the organization's strategic needs and use more innovation, creativity, and problem-solving to find unique solutions.
- **From authoritative to consultative.** Business Partners need to work in partnership and as equals with other business leaders and use consultative practices and influence methods to provide credible help to all parties as they strive to understand the human perspective in relation to business decisions.
- **From service provider serving internal customers to partner with other leaders.** A big shift needs to take place from being on call as services are needed or dealing with policy and compliance needs to understanding how to act in equal ways and in partnership with others that address the new organizational needs and the unprecedented challenges.
- **From being an HR professional in a business to being a business professional who specializes in OD/HR perspectives.** Some HR practitioners are highly specialized in a particular discipline and create programs, policies, and processes focused on the discipline rather than the business.

They need, however, to understand business issues and have the ability to create high impact OD/HR solutions.

- **From focus on and measurement of activities to results-based accountability.** Results must be measured in terms that relate to the bottom line rather than inputs like number of training hours, number of people completing performance evaluations, or number of new benefits offered. The new HR must relate important outcomes to business metrics.

Core Knowledge and Skills

HR Business Partners need strength in four competency areas in order to build a successful, progressive, and respected role. The areas are:

- Understanding the business of the organization
- Strategic Human Resources
- Foundational Organization Development
- Partnership

Understanding the Business

HR professionals need to be knowledgeable about the business of their organization, whether it is a corporation, a nonprofit, a school, or a hospital. This includes what it does, its products or services, customers, markets, competitors, how it works, its business model, performance and financial drivers, human resources, the mission, direction, strategy, history, culture, environment, and global influences. The Business Partner is a business person who brings the special value and perspective of an OD/HR mindset. More simply, Business Partners need to know how the business makes and spends its money so they can effectively contribute to the bottom line and organizational sustainability.

Strategic Human Resources

The second critical area of knowledge and skills is in understanding the strategic aspects of HR

work and how they differ from operational tasks. For example, understanding how to design and implement a total rewards compensation approach to support the behaviors that will meet the needs of customers is strategic; administering employee benefits is operational. Anticipating the talent needs created by a new strategy is strategic; updating employee records is operational.

Foundational Organization Development

The OD capabilities needed by the HR Business Partner help create an environment in which employees can operate at their fullest potential. They include the ability to look at organizations as systems and understand them from the individual, team, and organizational perspectives. Specifically, this understanding includes the processes of whole systems change, organization design and strategy development, leadership development, team development, organization diagnostics and assessment, coaching, facilitation, organization culture change, and the use of applied behavioral sciences to improve the effectiveness of human system dynamics.

Partnership

The fourth area has to do with understanding how to become a partner with senior leadership and management. This involves developing collaborative relationships, including understanding interpersonal relations, personality characteristics and styles, and having empathy. To be successful, the HR Business Partner must go beyond discussions at the task level to include building relationships on a personal level. Openness and trust are the foundation of a strong partnership that is strong enough to sustain frank discussions of differences and the transformation of conflicts.

Another important aspect of partnering can be learned from the sales process. In working with their customers, good sales people know how to listen, develop relationships, and identify areas where they can add significant value. Aspects of this approach can, and should be utilized by Business Partners to move from an "internal customer" mindset to a strategic business partner mindset.

Once this quality of partnership is achieved, the relationship enables the Business Partner and the internal partner to talk openly and freely, inform each other, collaborate and act authentically in jointly developing goals and executing strategies. Open discussions are necessary so the goals, projects, and initiatives necessary to add real value to the business can be *jointly* developed.

What You Will Find in This Resource

Before beginning to compile this resource, we had conversations with many HR professionals and both internal and external OD consultants. Based upon what they identified as important to their roles, we gathered key articles from the *OD Practitioner* written by seasoned OD practitioners that can provide the HR Business Partner with essential principles, creative approaches, practical tips, and proven methods to be a successful partner in crafting strategy, determining priorities, and helping shape an organization's future. HR professionals can use this resource to deepen their knowledge and skills in how to:

- Partner with senior level staff and internal or external consultants in leading a change initiative
- Think systemically and strategically identify where best to foster change in the organization
- Effectively use one's self as an instrument of change
- Put employee engagement to practical use and engage "minds, hearts, and hands" in the important work of the organization
- Operate effectively in the global market, cross-cultural situations, and virtual working arrangements

The resource is divided into six sections:

- Consulting and Partnership Skills
- Use of Self as an Instrument of Change
- Thinking Systemically and Strategically
- Employee Engagement
- Change Management
- Globalization, Cross-cultural Interaction, and Virtual Working Arrangements

Consulting and Partnership Skills

The role of the HR Business Partner is challenging and interesting with often conflicting accountabilities and allegiances to staff, management, clients, corporate headquarters, HR leadership, and consultants. As the role has shifted from personnel administration to business advisor, it has also become more complex, with multiple demands coming from multiple entry points in the system. The articles from the *OD Practitioner* in this section help explain the importance of a consultative mindset and approach, the challenges of being an internal consultant, and the steps to know in partnering with other business leaders, internal or external consultants in a change or innovation project.

Use of Self as an Instrument of Change

"Use of self" is the term OD practitioners employ to name the complex set of awareness and behaviors that make it possible to be genuinely helpful to others. Especially for the HR Business Partner, it is critical to recognize that tools and techniques are only part of the work with others. Many times, the most important influence on whether the situation changes is how HR Business Partners engage with their clients. Are they modeling the participative and collaborative principles they espouse and promote? Are they willing to listen to what is uncomfortable to hear? Are they willing to examine their own habitual behaviors and assumptions—those that serve them well and contribute to their success with others and those that may be hindering their success? The chapters in this section explain the use of self, deal with the mental maps that influence practitioners' perception of themselves and others, and encourage continued learning for greater self-awareness and behavior change that will enable more effective work with others.

Thinking Systemically and Strategically

A successful HR Business Partner needs to move beyond just a focus on the individual to understand how the larger system, including groups, the organization as a whole, and the external environment, impact work performance, the readiness for change, and the capacity for creativity. What is labeled underperformance of an individual or a group may be the outcome of many influences including: unsatisfactory supervisory/co-worker relationship, organizational policies, and resource allocation, the organizational culture, the design of the organization, and changes in the external business environment. Operating from a systemic perspective also enables the HR Business Partner to gain a sense of where best to begin fostering change—at the individual level, dyads, groups, departments, the organization (policies, practices, culture), or the market/community relationship. All are interconnected. The chapters in this section will help HR Business Partners understand the key elements of a systemic and strategic approach to fostering organizational effectiveness. The chapters explain systems thinking, describe an evolving understanding of organizational systems, and present various organizational design models and approaches for how to be strategic about improving an organization's effectiveness and ability to serve its customers.

Employee Engagement

Employee engagement is central to all of the work of HR and is often used as an overall measure of success. Engagement makes a difference in the lives and productivity of employees but also in the performance of the organization as a whole. According to a 2008 study, operating income for organizations with high employee engagement improved 19% while it declined 33% over the same period for companies with low employee engagement. The chapters in this section explore how HR Business Partners can put employee engagement to practical use and engage "minds, hearts, and hands" in the important work of the organization. This section contains case studies, data about what is effective and helpful tips and techniques for increasing employee engagement in an organization.

Change Management

HR Business Partners have a unique opportunity to lead change and the responsibility to help business leaders manage change wisely. As the business environment has experienced continuous change across sectors, the ability to help the organization adapt, anticipate, and manage changes has become essential. The chapters in this section are by experts who have led change in Fortune 50 companies, family-owned businesses, international conglomerates, nongovernmental organizations, and rural communities. The chapters describe the nature of organizational change, the three kinds of change, the experience of change from a change recipient's viewpoint, how to successfully lead change, and give examples of specific change initiatives.

Globalization, Cross-Cultural Interaction, and Virtual Working Arrangements

Organizations are globalizing at a rapid rate. The purely domestic enterprise is rapidly becoming a curiosity of the past. To be successful, even so-called "local" businesses must look beyond their own geographic areas for customers, clients, employees, information, materials, and other resources. This section contains articles that explore topics and questions faced by organizations seeking to operate successfully in the global business environment. The articles focus on alignment, the consultant role, leadership, community, and sustainability. They also provide the reader with an appreciation for the challenges and complexities of organizational integration, collaboration, and communication in global enterprises.

In addition to the articles, each section contains recommended sources for further learning about each topic.

USES OF THIS RESOURCE

This resource is designed to be both a comprehensive source of essential OD knowledge for HR Business Partners and a reference for specific OD/HR topics. The whole resource can be useful to HR professionals looking to broaden their perspective, bring tested concepts and practices to difficult situations, and identify areas for their own development. Each section can be used also as a separate document for specific situations such as:

- Pre/post reading for a skill training workshop
- A way to reinforce what is discussed in a coaching session
- Information to help an Action Learning Group deal with a work situation

- Deepening one's competence in a specific area

Reference

Jamieson, D., Eklund, S., & Meekin, B. (2012). Strategic business partner role: Definition, knowledge, skills & operating tensions. In W. Rothwell & G. Budscooter (Eds.), *The encyclopedia of human resource management, volume III: Critical and emerging issues in human resources (pp. 112–128).* San Francisco, CA: Pfeiffer/Jossey-Bass.

Acknowledgments

We express our appreciation to the many OD practitioners who contributed their knowledge, insights, and practices to the *OD Practitioner* and this collection of essential articles. We greatly benefited from our interviews with OD/HR professionals: Philip Anderson, Judith Gail, Sue Eklund, Chuck Mallue, Michael McGovern, Maria Ramos, and the many who were part of focus groups we conducted at the annual OD Network conference. We are also grateful to Peter Norlin, the former executive director of the OD Network, who suggested that we pursue this project.

CHAPTER 1

The Role of Organization Development in the Human Resource Function[1]

Edgar H. Schein

THE PURPOSE OF THIS PAPER is to explore the connection between the Human Resource Function in organizations and the evolving field of Organization Development, and to do this in a historical context with an eye toward future challenges. The connection between the field of Organization Development (OD) and the Human Resource (HR) function is complex because both OD and HR are themselves evolving in response to many global forces. We are so preoccupied with the economic factor in the organizational world, both in business and in the nonprofit sector, that we may have failed to note five important trends that are influencing both HR and OD.

First, all the organizational functions are becoming more complex and technologically sophisticated leading to the creation of subcultures based on different occupational technologies. In OD the technology of survey methodology, strategic analysis, leadership development, large systems change, group dynamics, culture change, and lean manufacturing have evolved complex processes leading to

specialized training and the licensing of practitioners. In the HR area pay systems, labor relations, management development programs, and health/environment/safety programs have become similarly specialized.

Second, the rapid evolution of information technology has changed the nature of work and the nature of organizing in dramatic ways, stimulating innovation in OD and challenging some of the most sacred cows of the HR culture. Specifically, the basic assumption that good communication, trust, and effective supervision all hinge on face to face contact has clearly been challenged by the myriad of organizations that today consist of large numbers of employees who are not co-located, who may never have met each other, yet who are required to build trusting relationships and work as teams. Increasingly organizations are becoming complex networks held together by new communication and control mechanisms that are being invented out of necessity.

Third, the world is becoming more of a global village in which the interdependencies between countries and between organizations are increasing dramatically. Through subsidiaries, joint ventures, and partnerships of various sorts more and more companies are reaching across national boundaries. The basic

---

[1]This chapter is based partly on an invited address to the Human Resource Forum, IEDC, Bled Business School, Bled, Slovenia, September 1, 2007.

driver is of course, economics. In the effort to be competitive, more and more organizations are discovering the need to go beyond their own boundaries for markets, cheaper labor, and scarce resources. Evolving policies that cut across nations and geographies is a challenge to both OD and HR.

The fourth major force is, in a sense, derivative from the others—the complexity that arises from cultural diversity. Culture is a group's learned response to the problem of survival in the external environment and the problem of internal integration. If there is no history of problem solving, there is no culture. So countries or regions of countries have cultures, organizations have cultures, and occupations develop cultures. So when sales people with a sales culture are talking to engineers with an engineering culture mentality and they come from different countries and different parent organizations, it is a wonder that they can communicate at all, much less solve problems together. Multicultural groups will become more of a fact of life (Schein, 2009a, 2010).

Fifth, the fundamental function of organizations is being reexamined around the issues of social responsibility and business ethics. As we become more multicultural we are discovering that the basic functions of organizations, their ethical systems, their rules and procedures for how to deal with each other, with customers, shareholders, employees, and the community all vary across cultures. Even the definitions of work, of career, of work-family balance, of gender roles, of rules about the age of entry and retirement are all being discovered to be highly variable. The vaunted western system, most highly evolved in the US, simply does not work in or even apply to most other countries.

The implications of these five factors for both OD and HR are staggering, but the impact is not the same on both functions. OD has always been the more innovation oriented function, while HR is typically expected to be stable and conservative. How people are paid and disciplined requires systems that are reasonably transparent and predictable. This asymmetry has important implications for the relationship between OD and HR. Let's examine each function first.

Historic Evolution of HR— Four Roles

To understand how these forces will impact the HR function, we must first look historically at the different roles that HR managers have played and see which of these roles is most relevant today and for the future. We can distinguish four basic roles:

Role 1: Champion of the Employees

One of the first and most important roles of the HR Manager was to be the spokesperson for the employee. Not all companies honored this role; but in the heyday of the human relations movement of the 1940s and 1950s, it fell to HR to show management how the employees' working conditions, wages, and benefits needed to be upgraded.

To play this role effectively required a certain set of attitudes, values, and skills. The HR Manager, usually called Personnel Manager in those days, had to have empathy for the employees, the desire to improve the lot of the worker even if this meant less profit for the company, and the skills to influence upward. Fulfilling this role effectively often put the HR manager in opposition to higher levels of management. To play this role effectively, it was useful to know something of individual psychology, and this field was rapidly evolving under the impetus of WW2 in which the need for effective selection methods stimulated industrial psychology (Schein, 1980).

The domination of psychology in HR was established early but continues to this day in the obsession with surveys, individual selection testing and interviewing, the search for competency profiles for effective leaders, and the popularity of concepts such as emotional intelligence. The basic focus of HR in this role has been and continues to be the individual, reflecting Western cultural traditions.

Role 2: Expert Administrator

The Personnel Departments of most organizations had and continue to have the job of managing the pay and benefits system, which requires efficiency and precision. The HR Manager, for whom this role is central, had to have a good knowledge of the relevant systems and procedures, must believe in the value of standardization, had to defend procedures that often appear to be too bureaucratic to the employees, and had to have the administrative skills to build and manage the pay and benefits organization. If Labor Relations is an issue in the organization, the HR Manager had to also know the laws and have the negotiating skills to deal with the contract negotiations process. Training and development in this role was typically conceived of as indoctrination of the employees in the organization's values and ways of doing things.

The individualistic psychological bias showed itself in this role as well in that administrative functions leaned heavily on individual incentives, on individualistic discipline systems, and on the assumption that economic incentives are the key to good administration.

Role 3: Partner in Strategy

As corporations became more complex and recognized the centrality of human resources to the success of their longer range strategies, they began to demand of the HR function some participation in the strategy and planning process. How many people with what talent will be needed? How are the relevant people to be found, developed, and integrated? Can career systems be designed to insure prepared people for succession in all key jobs? It was this period, sometime in the 1960s and 1970s that led to the conversion of the Personnel Manager title into Manager of Human Resources to acknowledge the importance of people in the longer run strategy of the organization.

In most organizations a problem arose since senior management wanted help from HR in strategy, but the HR Managers were not trained in that kind of thinking and, worse, often had pro-employee values that made them fight rather than help senior management. The HR manager who could play this role would have to have empathy for the strategic issues facing the CEO, would have to have the skills to think strategically and in systemic terms, would have to have a broad view of all elements of the business, and, most important, would have to share the value that the ultimate goal of the business is to increase shareholder value. The conflict with Role 1— The Champion of the Employees—is obvious. In the meantime, OD as a field of practice was evolving rapidly and creating ambiguity concerning the issue of how much OD should be part of or independent of HR.

Role 4: The Professional HR Manager

In a 1975 article for the *Journal of the College and University Personnel Association*, I outlined what at that time seemed to be the major change that the HR function was undergoing (Schein, 1975). I noted that HR Managers were, of necessity, becoming change agents and process consultants. This role shift was in part the result of the professionalization of the function. More was known about employee motivation, career development, leadership and management development, and it was often the role of the HR manager to bring the research knowledge and practice into the organization.

Instead of identifying with the employee (Role 1), the administrative functions of the company (Role 2), or the senior management (Role 3), HR managers began to identify with each other and with the profession of HR. In the other three roles, the HR manager was still an organization person. In Role 4 the HR manager was a professional whose loyalties lie outside the organization. The correct way to fulfill the HR function now was to be based on the best practices in the profession, and the HR manager became de facto both marginal in terms of the role in the company and an outside conscience to the organization, bringing knowledge, new attitudes, and new practices into the organization.

However, in order to fulfill this role, the HR manager had to have new and powerful influence and change agent skills. In particular, he or she had to be able to think of the organization in broader systemic terms and be able to get that perspective across to the executive suite. So paradoxically, as HR managers got pulled up into the strategy discussion, they also found themselves in the difficult role of influencing that discussion in value directions that the executives might not want to hear. Being both a conscience with outsider responsibilities and an effective administrator with inside responsibilities could create role conflict. The relationship to OD with its more systemic emphasis became more visible.

Some History of Organizational Development

To understand the evolution of this fourth role of the HR manager, we need first to look at some aspects of the history of OD, which was quite different from the evolution of HR. I believe that OD got its biggest stimulus from the post war problems of WW2, specifically the need to help reconstruction in war-torn countries. While Kurt Lewin and others were working on trying to understand how Nazism could have occurred in the first place, Eric Trist and others at the Tavistock Institute were helping the British Coal Mining Industry to reconstruct itself (Schein, 1980).

The Tavistock projects were more sociologically oriented and laid the foundation for what came to be seen as a new core concept—*sociotechnical* systems with which one worked in an action research model. Large-scale social projects were launched by Rice in the textile mills, Jaques in factories, and by Menzies in hospitals (Rice, 1963; Trist & Bamforth, 1951). European psychiatrists were beginning to experiment with therapeutic communities in which the helpers were not professional psychiatrists and social workers, but healthy young adults who could serve as role models for the patients and establish normal relationships with them.

In the late 1940s and early 1950s Lee Bradford and others formed the National Training Labs (now NTL Institute) that began to run group dynamics and leadership workshops in Bethel, Maine and Ojai, California (Bradford, et al., 1964; Schein & Bennis, 1965). The need to understand group dynamics and leadership led naturally to the emphasis on organizations. My book *Organizational Psychology* was first published in 1965 and pulled together in its last chapter what had evolved through McGregor, Likert, the Lippitts, Tannenbaum, Bennis and Shepard, Blake and Mouton, Dyer, and especially Richard Beckhard into the field now labeled Organization Development (Schein, 1980). One wing of Sensitivity Training became more oriented toward "therapy for normals," continuing the strong individualistic psychological focus. However, as organizations became more interested in the powerful impacts of experiential learning, they stimulated more labs, research projects, and in-house experiments that de facto created the OD field that was more oriented toward systems and group dynamics.

At the same time, applied anthropology was entering the organizational domain and creative new research approaches were spawned in places like the Western Electric Hawthorne Works. Instead of just doing psychological experiments, parts of the research program consisted of having observers just sit and observe how work groups actually functioned. Experiential learning, observation and analysis of group and interpersonal processes, and community role playing evolved in the NTL and Tavistock A. K. Rice workshops, which gave real meaning to the concept of systems.

OD as a concept and a set of practices was premised on the idea that the consultant/helper was not working with an individual or even a small group, except as a means for helping the organization or some larger segment of that organization. The concept of *client* shifted to the organizational unit (Schein, 1999). The skills required to do this could not be learned from traditional psychology. One had to attend workshops and develop one's own capacity to observe systemic processes and develop personal skills to intervene in such processes. All through the 1950s and 1960s innovations of all sorts were developed as a result of stimulus and support from large organizations such as Exxon, Union Carbide, Hotel Corporation of America, TRW Systems, and various European companies. Some of the individual innovators in the US were Blake and Mouton, Beckhard, Shepard and Bennis, Benne, Gibb, Tannenbaum and Schmidt, and Miles at the Columbia University Teachers College.

The rapid expansion of the OD field was symbolized by the Addison-Wesley series of OD books edited originally by Beckhard, Bennis, and Schein. Though integrative books were available, the feel of the OD arena was one of diversification and innovation highlighted by the fact that the OD series had more than 30 titles by the 1980s.

Connection Between the HR's Fourth Role and OD

The role of HR as a profession required some form of integration or at least alignment between HR and the growing OD field. As I have observed this over the last 50 years, there are three different patterns visible.

Pattern 1—Integration. The OD role is integrated into the job of the HR executive, which implies that the senior HR manager fulfills all four roles. Needless to say, very few HR executives have the breadth of insight, values, and skills to actually perform all four roles. It is also not clear whether the deep assumptions of the HR culture and the OD culture can be integrated because some of the HR functions are entirely driven by organizational needs while many OD functions require consideration of broader concepts of client, which may run counter to some immediate organization needs.

Pattern 2—OD Bias. The HR function is skewed toward OD by hiring an OD trained and skilled HR executive who may or may not have the administrative or strategic skills to play the other roles. I have encountered many organizations that had creative OD functions but their administrative systems were in disarray and senior management felt that the OD function was not always aligned with corporate strategy.

Pattern 3—HR Bias. The HR function is skewed toward administration and/or corporate strategy with the OD function either missing altogether or is set up as a separate function reporting to HR. This solution usually leaves the OD consultants in a compromised and sometimes frustrating position because they have to influence upward through the bureaucracy in order to get projects approved and implemented.

Pattern 4—Separate and Independent Functions. The solution that seems to me to work best is where HR and OD are treated as separate functions that report independently to senior line management. For example, when Digital Equipment Corp. (DEC) first hired Dennis Burke, they appointed him as head of management development reporting directly to founder and CEO Ken Olsen. The head of HR, who had all the administrative functions and Labor Relations, reported to Olsen separately. Burke had the independence to create a variety of developmental activities that worked very well as DEC grew (Schein, 2003).

When they later hired Sheldon Davis from TRW systems as the senior VP of HR, OD was supposed to be integrated with HR, but this solution did not work because Davis was skewed toward OD. The administrative side of HR suffered, and Davis often attempted to change Ken Olsen's behavior without success and to his own ultimate detriment.

In Procter and Gamble it was notable that the new designs of production units always had both an HR manager and an OD manager reporting to the plant manager. The OD managers were often recruited from the employment pool, often the union, because of their interest and skill in working on group and organizational process. They were then sent to workshops at NTL to learn the specific OD skills they would need, and then they joined the plant manager's staff as full time employees on the same level as the HR manager for the plant.

In Ciba-Geigy in the 1970s and early 1980s the CEO had reporting to him a Senior VP of Development whose job it was to oversee the care and feeding of the top several hundred executives (Schein, 2010). He had only a small staff but, more importantly, he reported directly to the CEO, which made him superior in rank to the VP of HR. All the work on culture that I was able to do in that organization was stimulated and supported by this executive. In fact, I never met the manager of HR, whose job was entirely to administer the bureaucratic side of the HR function such as pay and benefits.

Preliminary Conclusion and Emerging Issues

One important conclusion is that the skills and attitudes required in each HR role and the OD role are quite different, and, to some degree in conflict with each other, setting up potential role conflicts within the person occupying the HR job. Which role to treat as paramount and which sets of attitudes, skills, and values to cultivate can become a difficult psychological balancing act. As tempting as it may be to resolve these issues by looking at what has happened historically, i.e., just separate the functions because that has worked well in the past, I believe that the trends I outlined at the beginning of this paper may require new patterns and new role definitions for both HR and OD.

I previously mentioned the broad trends toward globalization, technological complexity in all areas of business, and growing cultural diversity. In addition one should note that the level of education worldwide is slowly increasing, which means that organizations will be dealing with smarter and more educated and sophisticated employees. There is also a change

in the expectations of top management as to the role that HR should play. There are growing pressures toward being able to play Role 3 (Partner in Strategy) and Role 4 (Professional HR Manager). There is clearly a change in social values around the importance of work/life balance and the psychological contract between company and employee (Bailyn, 2006). Employment security is rapidly migrating into employability security. Companies like Apple have argued that even if they fire you, you will have learned important new skills that will make you more employable elsewhere. This may not be objectively true, but many companies argue that they are, therefore, justified in hiring and firing at will.

The concept of career is itself slowly metamorphosing into a variety of concepts, especially as globalization reveals that in different cultures work and career have different meanings and are differently integrated with family and self. In the western world this shows up most clearly in the increasing mobility that employees display (as well as sometimes, the refusal to move), in the decline of company loyalty, and the growing concern for self and family. Much of this is due to the growing number of dual career families in which the family is managing two full careers. In this arena HR and OD will have to work together to shape appropriate development policies.

Research on employees has shown increasing variability in what they are good at, seek, and value. My own research on Career Anchors shows that organizations must be prepared to respond to a wide variety of employee needs and avoid the stereotype of "everyone wants to climb the corporate ladder" (Schein, 2006). This impacts HR directly because incentive, reward, and discipline systems have to become much more differentiated in order to seem fair to people with different skills, needs, and aspirations. With increasing technological complexity, work itself becomes more complex. The HR manager will have to help line and other staff managers to develop better tools for figuring out what needs to be done and how to communicate that to employees.

Around these last points I see a potential conflict between HR's need to develop standard systems and OD's view of diagnosing and working with subsystems and microcultures. What OD brings to the party is more of a process concern of how to align different individual needs and different subcultures into a functioning whole. For HR, jobs are individual sets of responsibilities and accountabilities often captured in the job description. From an OD perspective I have argued that jobs should be seen as roles that are embedded in an ever changing role set that needs to be perpetually examined and updated (Schein, 2006).

Cultural diversity is increasing and so is management's discovery of culture. Culture and sub-cultures have always been with us, but the discovery of the importance of culture in the performance of the firm is fairly recent (Denison, 1990; Denison et al., 2003; Sackman, 2006). Managers don't quite know how to deal with an abstraction like culture, so it will fall to the HR and OD functions to educate management on what culture is and does, and beyond that both functions will be involved in the implementation of culture evolution, culture change, and, in the case of subculture conflicts, culture alignment (Schein, 1996).

The dispersion of employees into networks and the loosening of organizational boundaries will be a special challenge to OD and a source of difficulty for HR. The OD function will have to evolve concepts of teamwork and collaboration in a network in which face to face contact may never take place. HR will have to develop policies that are consistent across various kinds of spatial and cultural boundaries, which will be especially difficult around pay systems since we know that money and rewards are perceived very differently in different cultures.

Organizations are increasingly catching on that people (human resources) are not an expendable resource and a cost factor in the economics of the firm but rather a capital investment to be valued and nurtured. No matter how much we automate, downsize, or break up organizations geographically, people will always, in the end, be the key to performance. The reason for this is simple—no amount of engineering and planning can predict all of the contingencies that will arise in a dynamic world. It will always fall to some people somewhere to make sense of the new data and new problems that will show up. So whether we like it or not, people will continue to be central to the organization and the HR function will continue to be central to the management of those people.

With that insight will also come the recognition that collaboration, mutual helping, leaders as providers and consumers of help will become more and more important (Schein, 2009b). OD will play a critical role in developing concepts and processes that will facilitate more mutual help and HR will have to develop administrative policies that value help and collaboration. Both functions will be needed and we can all watch with interest how they will evolve and eventually align and/or integrate.

A Final Thought—Whither Management?

Though it is beyond the score of this paper, we should consider that the biggest impact on both HR and OD might be the slowly evolving but significant growing competence of line executives in human process skills. As general managers become more aware of the value of humans and as they develop skills in handling interpersonal relationships, group dynamics, and interorganizational dynamics, and as they become more culturally sophisticated they will take on many of the roles that HR and OD play today. As managers are defined increasingly as HR and OD practitioners, it remains to be seen how the HR and OD specialists will adapt.

References

Bailyn, L. (2006). *Breaking the mold* (2nd ed.). Ithaca, NY: Cornell University Press.

Bradford, L. P., Gibb, J. R., & Benne, K. D. (Eds.). (1964). *T-Group theory and laboratory method*. Hoboken, NJ: Wiley.

Denison, D. R. (1990). *Corporate culture and organizational effectiveness*. Hoboken, NJ: Wiley.

Denison, D. R., Haaland. S., & Goelzer, P. (2003). *Corporate culture and organizational effectiveness: Is there a similar pattern around the world?* Greenwich, CT: Jai Press.

Rice, A. K. (1963). *The enterprise and its environment*. London, UK: Tavistock Publications.

Sackman, S. A. (2006). *Success factor: Corporate culture*. Guetersloh, DE: Bertelsman Stiftung.

Schein, E. H. (1975). Changing role of the personnel manager. *Journal of the College and University Personnel Association, 26*, 14–19.

Schein, E. H. (1980). *Organizational psychology* (3rd ed.). Upper Saddle River, NJ: Prentice-Hall.
Schein, E.H. (1996). Three cultures of management: The key to organizational learning. *Sloan Management Review, 38*(1), 9–20.

Schein, E. H. (1999). *Process consultation revisited*. Upper Saddle River, NJ: Prentice-Hall.

Schein, E. H. (2003). *DEC is dead; Long live DEC: The lasting legacy of Digital Equipment Corporation*. San Francisco, CA: Berrett/Kohler.

Schein, E. H. (2006). *Career Anchors* (3rd ed.). San Francisco, CA: Jossey-Bass, Pfeiffer.

Schein, E. H. (2009a). *The corporate culture survival guide* (2nd ed.). San Francisco, CA: Jossey-Bass.

Schein, E. H. (2009b). *Helping: How to offer, give, and receive help*. San Francisco, CA: Berrett/Koehler.

Schein, E .H. (2010). *Organizational culture and leadership* (4th ed.). San Francisco, CA: Jossey-Bass.

Schein, E. H., & Bennis, W. G. (1965). *Personal and organizational change through group methods*. Hoboken, NJ: Wiley.

Trist, E. L., & Bamforth, K. W. (1951). Some social and psychological consequences of the long-wall method of coal getting. *Human Relations, 4*, 1–38.

CHAPTER 2

Organization Development and Human Resources Management

Knowing Our Place for the First Time?

Dave Hanna

FOUR DECADES AGO, Herb Stokes, a pioneering change agent and my first mentor at Procter & Gamble, told me, "The organizational forces for stability are always in conflict with the organizational forces for change. [Human Resources] represents the forces for stability. Organization Development represents the forces for change. That is why [HR] and OD never should be housed in the same department."

Most of us OD practitioners in those days indeed were housed in Personnel or Industrial Relations (both known today as HR). And while we all enjoyed associating with our HR colleagues, we did have frequent disagreements with them on what to change in the organization and how to go about making those changes. If OD consultants recommended a more innovative pay system based on contribution vs. seniority or job title, HR managers would present a long list of reasons why such a change was very risky and uncertain in the benefits it would deliver. When HR would present the revised plant safety policy, OD would cry "bureaucracy" and point out how the policy failed to mesh with the empowerment initiative that was underway.

Pick the right issue in the right organization at the right time and you could find HR and OD being each other's chief antagonist.

Many years have passed since those days, but some of the enmity still persists between the two groups.

The last thing either of these players needed was someone else complicating their attempts to improve things. The HR function traditionally has fought to gain respect as a legitimate partner at the business table. Conventional wisdom said HR was supposed to take care of the people business so managers could take care of the "real" business. Accordingly, HR has been valued by its business partners as long as it could prevent people problems from landing on the calendar or inbox of the responsible manager. HR's role evolved primarily to one of conducting wage and job classification surveys, handling employee relations and union negotiations, hiring people, finding the best values in plans and benefits, managing safety and hygiene, communicating with employees, and protecting the corporate image in the community. When the era of downsizing began in the 1980s, HR was at the top of the list of those targeted to add value to the bottom line by reducing their headcount.

This traditional HR role is what Herb Stokes was talking about when he described the forces for stability. Take care of the employee systems and services; keep things stable so managers can keep their attention on the changing business needs. And find ways to do all of the above with fewer and fewer people.

The only trouble with this thinking is that the people variables always have been connected with the business variables. In recent years this connection has become more obvious to everyone. Global markets, rapidly changing technologies, and economic turmoil have led to products of shorter shelf life, unprecedented movement of people from home to foreign cultures, and traumatic measures like downsizing and outsourcing. All of these strike a dagger at the stability of people systems and practices. More and more of today's managers realize they have to handle people issues with the same level of priority as marketing, financial, or technical issues. There is a seat at the business table for HR professionals who can measure up to the partners' demanding expectations.

OD has had its own interesting journey in the past 40 years. Internal and external consultants multiplied greatly in the 1960s, 1970s, and early 1980s. The OD consultants were considered by many clients to be a bit strange in their approach, but they went along in the hope that improvements would be seen at the bottom line. Eventually the curiosity and patience subsided and by the late 1970s Japanese companies were winning more and more of the world's consumers with products of top quality and low cost. Many OD positions went away in the 1980s, but their contributions were still needed and emerged in the new Quality departments that were springing up everywhere. As the Quality tide has ebbed, the remaining internal change agents have been absorbed back into HR departments.

So today we find HR and OD back in the same homeroom, both seeking more respect and both fewer in numbers than before. I myself have experienced both sides of the homeroom. Most of my career has been on the OD side, but a number of my corporate roles, projects, and client engagements have been focused on employee relations, safety and hygiene, compensation systems, talent management, personnel research, performance management, and HR organization effectiveness. Based on my personal experiences and, with all due respect to Herb Stokes' valid observation about the conflicts between stability and change, I believe the coming together of OD and HR is long overdue.

I say coming together because OD and HR should not be content merely to be siblings living under the same roof. We need to leverage our different strengths for the greater good. In the words of noted historians Will and Ariel Durant:

> So the conservative who resists change is as valuable as the radical who proposes it—perhaps as much more valuable as roots are more vital than grafts. It is good that new ideas should be heard, for the sake of the few that can be used; but it is also good that new ideas should be compelled to go through the mill of objection, opposition, and contumely; this is the trial heat which innovations must survive before being allowed to enter the human race. (Durant & Durant, 1968, p. 36)

In other words, regardless of who is proposing what, an examination by contrary views is healthy. Diversity of thought and experience can indeed lead to the critical screening the historians say is so important for constructive, innovative breakthroughs.

The Durants' statement explains why a multifunctional business team adds value through its 360° analysis before prioritizing and implementing corporate strategies. We like to say it is synergy that makes business teams so effective—the whole being greater than the sum of its parts. But for the whole to be greater than the sum of its parts, new relationships must be forged among those parts. If all the parts do is co-exist side by side, there is no synergy. Like a business team, our different human systems disciplines, including HR and OD, could add greater value to the business through our interactions before bringing forward new organizational innovations and business solutions.

The 2007 HR Competency Study, co-sponsored by the RBL Group and the University of Michigan Ross School of Business, yielded some provocative insights into the need for synergy in HR (Ulrich, et al., 2008). This study sampled more than 10,000 HR professionals and their business clients in all regions of the world and identified six competencies as being essential for an HR professional who adds value to the business:

- **The Credible Activist:** being credible (respected, listened to) and active (offering a point of view and challenging others' assumptions)
- **The Operational Executor:** flawlessly executing the operational aspects of managing people and organizations
- **The Business Ally:** contributing to the success of the business by understanding +its social context, how it makes money, and how to organize its parts to make more money
- **The Talent Manager/Organization Designer:** mastering theory, research, and practice in both talent management and organization design
- **The Strategy Architect:** having a vision of how the organization can succeed in the marketplace and actively shaping the strategy to fulfill this vision
- **The Culture and Change Steward:** recognizing, articulating, and shaping corporate culture and facilitating the change processes required to keep the culture aligned with the business needs

The results of this study show us how much the world has changed in the last four decades. Business leaders are actually aware of the need for HR to shed its traditional role. They want HR professionals to step up to a more value-adding contribution. They are looking to HR for help in crafting strategy, determining priorities in running the business, designing and structuring how work gets done, shaping culture, and, yes, managing people systems to give a sense of stability. Moreover, the business leaders know they need HR professionals who are credible activists who will push, prod, and even lead some discussions that chart the course for the future.

Looking over the list of the six HR competencies, I am unable to choose which ones are essential only for OD and which are relevant only for HR. Our business partners in this survey said these are the competencies they expect us HR professionals to deliver if we are to add value to the issues that most concern them. If HR professionals were to become proficient in the six competencies, regardless of what their current assignment might be, where would you find "OD types" and "HR types" in the future? There would not be a meaningful distinction between the two.

So, let's face up to this scenario and its implications for us collectively and individually. First of all, regardless of our heritage, we, in both HR and OD, are all professionals today in the function known by our business partners as Human Resources Management. But this is today's HR, not the HR of yesteryear. Not the HR with OD and HR silos. Not the HR that managed the forces for stability and opposed the forces for change. It is no longer a matter of stability or change; every organization requires some of both. Today's HR needs professionals who can find the right balance between stability and change. So I am proposing that the function be called HR or HRM with centers of expertise in talent management, HR operations, OD, change management, compensation and benefits, etc.

Let us be clear that it is the global marketplace and economic fluctuations that are shaping today's HR. The marketplace requires organizations as never before to design, assess, and redesign their strategies and systems to improve the bottom line. Adding value in this complex situation represents more work than any army of HR specialists could handle (and remember the "army" is more like a "squadron" when compared to past staffing). The mere sum of our individual HR contributions won't do. A squadron of professionals, each skilled in the six HR competencies, can deploy its resources against critical business needs in a wide variety of combinations. A few true HR professionals can do the same work that many isolated specialists were required to do previously.

Come to think of it, this is precisely the same approach OD consultants have been advocating to their clients for years—tear down the silo walls, develop multiskilled flexibility and team up as required to meet the challenges of change. Now we need to apply this same process to ourselves and to our own profession.

How can we succeed at changing ourselves after all these years? There has been much discussion about why change is needed. After all is said and done, a lot more has been said than done. This is a change process as complex as any I have been involved with.

I believe each of us has to look at the big picture outside ourselves to appreciate the context for what we do in HR. I call this looking from the "outside in" and it will change the way we think about our work. Then each of us has to get centered personally and become committed to the ways we can add the most value to the big picture. This will lead us to initiate actions and work differently within our sphere of influence for the good of the business. This internal centering and commitment process I call working from the "inside out."

Looking outside in means we first have to expand our perspective. Some ways to do this:

1. Think of the business need first. We need to deeply understand the global marketplace and the business realities facing our own organization and set our priorities accordingly. This is not some nice-to-know theoretical construct. In many companies in different parts of the world, HR professionals, when asked to identify a business challenge they need to work on, invariably describe something that is valuable from an HR point of view. They identify the challenge as meeting the recruiting goals rather than building leadership capacity

for global growth. They want to build a stronger culture rather than improve flexibility and productivity to respond to changing business requirements. Are these just differences in semantics? I think not. The words we use reveal what matters most to us. If meeting the recruiting goals is on my To Do List, then I check the box and congratulate myself if we get enough people in the door. I consider that item done even if we don't yet have the leadership capacity for global growth. I have met my HR target, but may not have helped the business. Rethinking our priorities is the beginning of becoming a business ally.

2. Participate in your company's HR rotation program or work with your leaders to organize a rotation plan for yourself. Many companies have a rotation program for new HR associates. The rotation enables associates to get experience in several HR functions over a period of a few years. This may seem "beneath" you if you are a veteran in HR, but don't dismiss the concept out of hand. See if there are ways you could participate in the rotation program to build up your competencies. Or find some alternatives for short-term assignments or special projects that require you to get immersed in those areas of HR in which you have little or no experience. Learn and appreciate how these functions add value to the business. Consider how your skills and experience might synergize with these other functions.

3. Show how much you value diversity by seeking out and digesting different points of view and critiques of your own work. Remember the Durants' statement about the need for radicalism and conservatism on any major issue— how the grafted branches and roots are interdependent. If we HR professionals are truly committed to fulfilling real business needs, as opposed to merely getting approval for our individual proposals, then we ought to welcome discussions that examine any potential flaws in our plans. Approach colleagues and other associates (especially those who tend to approach things very differently than yourself) and use them as a sounding board and think tank for important initiatives you are working on. Enjoy the discussions that follow! Debate with our colleagues is not bad, different approaches are not distractions and none of us starts out with THE solution.

Having looked (and worked) from the outside in, you will see yourself, your colleagues and your work in a different light. Now internalize this outside-in perspective into personal insights and commitments that can add much more value to the business. Work from the inside out to translate personal commitments into new ways of working together that will yield much synergy. Some suggestions on how to do this:

4. Team up with those whose expertise is needed to fill the business needs. We all need improvement in some of the HR competencies. An informal, but effective way to build these competencies is to partner with someone else and learn from each other's strengths through your teamwork. Pick one of the business needs you uncovered in #1 above and identify one or more colleagues to partner with who are skilled in important areas that are your current weak spots.

For example, Marissa was the epitome of the outsider's assessment of HR: "I love my HR person, but I hate HR." Marissa was a "can do" person, who immediately volunteered to solve transactional problems involving any HR system, policy, or practice. Health insurance problem? Marissa would contact the provider and get it cleared up. Need to replace a director who just left the company? Marissa would work with the talent management system to get the replacement. The bigger business problem, however, was Marissa's research division and the company's sales and marketing division were always at war. This schism slowed down the product pipeline. Revenue targets were being missed. Relationships between the two organizations needed to improve, and the entire process needed to be redesigned to hit the targets. Marissa admitted to a close friend, "I don't know how to do any of that stuff."

Bill was an organizational consultant who prided himself on being an unorthodox, "out of the box" manager. He believed revolution, not evolution, was the only way to make change. The problem was that Bill's approach did not win much support from his clients. He had great difficulty speaking corporate language, following protocol in making a proposal and appreciating how much (or little) shock his colleagues could absorb in the process of organizational change. Clients didn't trust Bill. And Bill bemoaned how tradition bound his clients were. Bottom line: Bill changed jobs about every two to three years.

If Marissa and Bill were to team up to address a business priority, they would collectively have many of the needed skills and they could help address each other's needs for improvement. Marissa could ensure their work was practical and earned commitment from the client. Bill could provide some of the organization design expertise that Marissa lacked. If their personal commitments were aligned, each would learn from the other and as a team they would add more value than either could produce individually. This is the nature of synergy.

5. Take on a new assignment/role. Based on your new perspective from looking outside in, you may find a different assignment or role that aligns well with your current competencies, your learning needs, and the business needs. You may change assignments within HR. Or you may apply your strengths to a new client group that needs what you can provide. Or you may change members in your work group to learn from/mentor each other.

For example, Wayne had earned a PhD in organizational psychology and had applied his trade in his employer's personnel research department for many years. He was somewhat of a celebrity at national conferences and workshops because of his practical experience and adherence to professional standards. If you had an employee turnover problem, Wayne was someone you would call on the phone to explore ways of researching the issue. Then Wayne accepted a new assignment to be the HR Generalist supporting a business unit that was struggling to keep its best talent. He applied his skills against a divisional priority, but also learned a lot about the rest of the HR world through the daily issues that came to him. He was a subject matter expert and a student at the same time. The division eventually solved its turnover problem and Wayne expanded his credibility as a generalist.

6. Based on business needs, define those projects that require multifunctional resources from HR and staff them appropriately. Outsourcing initiatives require consultation that addresses operational efficiency, people policies, organization design, talent management, and change management. Union contract negotiations should be approached with a clear sense of common values, corporate strategy, high performance principles, corporate policy, and labor law. Too often we tackle such issues individually, as the generalist or as the consultant that is supposed to ensure success. The more complex the issue, the more likely it is that one HR person won't have all of the required expertise. Organizing a multifunctional HR team to address tough issues is another way to build synergy through new work relationships and expand each person's competency in the process.

I saw such synergy in one of my clients that had experienced a meltdown in HR effectiveness. The parent company was under tremendous cost pressure, the lure of business growth had left many parts of the business overextended with shrinking resources. And HR had been downsized and its transactional functions outsourced as one way of coping with the situation. But the business pressures hadn't gone away and morale among all associates was at an all time low. And just to rub salt in the wound, HR was given much of the blame for the low morale. The most senior HR leaders left the company and the HR function that was needed to regain corporate momentum was itself in a shambles.

Weeks of interviews with business unit and functional leaders as well as with many HR associates documented all of the dynamics that were now playing out. Three teams were formed, each with a mix of HR functional experts and credible leaders from different business units/functions of the company. The three teams each pursued a different target for redesigning the HR function:

- Design the leanest, most efficient HR organization imaginable.
- Design an HR organization that will deliver a talent powerhouse in the future (the company expected to lose some 6,000 employees due to retirement in the next five years).
- Design the HR organization to provide the ultimate in customer service.

Each team had to consider transactional as well as transformational issues in formulating their organizational proposals. All three had to include specific staffing headcounts, organization structures, development plans, and change management provisions in their proposals. When the three came back together, the company's General Counsel was asked to review their proposals and give feedback. This leader was impressed with what was delivered to him. He suggested that representatives of the three teams get together and combine their pieces into one package with this logic:

- The lean, mean machine option serves as the foundation.
- If the Board of Directors would like to have the foundation plus the talent powerhouse and/or customer service benefits, the cost for each addition would be $XXX and $YYY.

- The Board makes the final decision, based on the most critical needs facing the company.

In the end, the Board chose to pay for all three benefits. All board members' questions were answered in the teams' package. The case for all three options was compelling. Those in HR were shocked that the Board was willing to spend more than the bare minimum for HR resources. Such a decision could not have been reached without the coming together of all HR competencies to meet the business needs.

Putting together all the elements of this outside in and inside out process will require much exploration and collaboration. There will be moments of pain as we move out of our comfort zones and build a stronger HR community and stronger business results. In the words of T.S. Eliot, "We shall not cease from exploration. And the end of all our exploring will be to arrive where we started and know the place for the first time" ("Little Gidding," 1944).

HR and OD may have co-existed in the past, but as we discard old beliefs and habits, we will truly come together—and know the place for the first time.

References

Durant, W., & Durant, A. (1968). *The lessons of history.* New York, NY: Simon & Schuster.

Hanna, D. P. (1988). *Designing organizations for high performance.* Reading, MA: Addison-Wesley.

Hanna, D. P. (2001). *Leadership for the ages,* Provo, UT: Executive Excellence.

Hiebert, M., & Hiebert, E. (Eds.). (1999). *Powerful professionals: Leveraging your expertise with clients.* Victoria, British Columbia: Trafford Publishing.

Ulrich, D., & Brockbank, W. (2005). *The HR value proposition.* Boston, MA: Harvard Business School Press.

Ulrich, D., Allen, J., Brockbank, W., Younger, J., & Nyman, M. (2009). *HR transformation: Building human resources from the outside in.* New York, NY: McGraw-Hill.

Ulrich, D., Brockbank, W., Johnson, D., Sandholtz, K., & Younger, J. (2008). *HR competencies: Mastery at the intersection of people and business.* Alexandria, VA: SHRM.

Consulting and Partnership Skills

Introduction

Matt Minahan, David Jamieson, and Judy Vogel

VOICES FROM THE FIELD

For me, important models were joint union/management approaches and Schein's Process Consultation. Seeing the people process at work. Seeing that HR was not about transactions and simple services. Rather understanding the large context and the systems view were most useful. . . . In my highly matrixed organization, everyone has multiple interests. Getting clear about each person's role and leadership is a challenge. It is key to make a "clean" deal from the beginning. As a project proceeds, we need to stop and recontract around unexpected developments. The old HR mentality of service is not a contract.

—Chuck Mallue

We knew we needed to transform ourselves to become internal consultants vs. transactional day-to-day service providers. Our mantra was "we will become the best consulting group." The key was the support of leadership.

—Sue Eklund

What would I do differently? Talk to as many people as possible before engagement. Engage the organization at multiple levels gaining multiple perspectives.

—Judith Gail

TOPICS COVERED IN THIS SECTION

- How to successfully complete the steps involved in a consulting process.
- How to consult on group and interpersonal process issues.
- How to develop the client-consultant relationship and manage the many aspects of the relationship.
- How to act in the role of internal or external consultant.
- How to develop and maintain partnerships with leadership, staff, and an internal or external OD consultant.

WHY CONSULTING AND PARTNERSHIP SKILLS

The role of the HR Business Partner is challenging and interesting with often conflicting accountabilities and allegiances to staff, management, clients, corporate headquarters, HR leadership, and consultants. As the role has shifted from personnel administration to business adviser, it has also become more complex, with multiple demands from multiple entry points in the system. Further, it has come to include the new role of consulting and partnering with the organization's leadership and other service providers.

While there are courses and mentors to help one learn how to manage a consulting project and the skills needed to create an effective consulting partnership with managers and senior leadership, one thing is certain: the stakes can be very high and the risks can be significant. The role is complex.

There are several challenges on the road to effectiveness, and an important one is that the presenting problem is not always the *actual* problem. Further, clients are not always sure what they want, and the way to success is not always clear. For these reasons, establishing a consulting partnership relationship and contracting for the right work can be challenging and critical to results.

THE CHAPTERS IN THIS SECTION

This section includes articles from the *OD Practitioner* that help explain the steps in the consulting process, some of the challenges of being an internal consultant, and some of the strategies to develop in partnering with leaders and internal or external consultants. After an overview of a key OD process, Starting at the Beginning: Action Research, there are sections on the following subjects:

- Facilitation and the Consulting Process
- The Core Skills Needed in Consulting on Process Issues
- The Client-Consultant Relationship
- The Consultant as Person
- Partnerships Among the HR Business Partner, Leadership, Staff, and an Internal or External OD Consultant

Starting at the Beginning: Action Research

Among the highest priorities in the earliest days of scientific and psychological research was finding ways to keep the observer from influencing or contaminating the observed; the goal was to prevent any influence from the scientist on the subject of the research that could change the phenomenon under study. Rigid rules for observing events and behavior dispassionately were the norm through the early 20th century, until the Heisenberg Uncertainty Principle determined that atoms change their behavior when studied carefully. At just about the same time, Fritz Roethlis-berger and his research team at the GE Hawthorne Electric plant in upstate New York discovered the same thing happened with humans. When people believe they are being studied or observed, their behavior changes—just like the atom. This came to be known as the Hawthorne Effect.

During his research of schools and social systems in the 1930s and 1940s, Kurt Lewin confirmed the phenomena and decided to make it the cornerstone of his Action Research methodology, the core methodology of most OD consulting processes.

Action Research is the process by which managers and employees in an organization are engaged in the self-study of the organization to achieve desired changes. Data is collected and then fed back to the involved members of the system for analysis, action is determined and taken, data regarding the impact of the action is collected and fed back to the system; the cycle continues as more action is taken; and so on. Lewin describes Action Research as "comparative research on the conditions and effects of various forms of social action and research leading to social action" (1948, pp. 202-203) using "a spiral of steps, each of which is composed of a circle of planning, action, and fact-finding about the result of the action" (1958, p. 201).

Here is the spiral that is at the heart of Lewin's Action Research model. When confronted with a problem or opportunity, the organization retains a consultant or establishes an internal team (or, ideally, both). It tasks them to collect data about and, preferably by, the system itself. The problem could be about the ways of doing business in the organization, of communicating, of deciding an issue, and of working together, or the organizational climate, or the organizational culture—whatever is under study. The collected data is analyzed for patterns and themes and presented back to the organizational system. The data presents the system with information about itself which readies the system for change. The system reacts to the data, reflects on the data, and decides on a course of action, which is then implemented. Then data is collected about how well the course of action addressed the issue and about the new state of the system. Similar to the first round, this data is analyzed for patterns and themes, and presented back to the organizational system. As in the first round, the system reacts to this new data and decides on additional actions, which may trigger another round of data collection. Once the system reaches the desired future state, the Action Research cycle can end.

The values that underlie Lewin's Action Research methodology are similar to those of Brazilian philosopher and educator Paulo Freire, who proposed teaching and intervention methods that fully engaged those who were the "subjects." Freire strongly opposed traditional models of teaching and community involvement in which the teacher or wise person stands in front of the group and tells them what to do and how to think, making the participants passive recipients or receiving objects of this externally imposed knowledge. He also had a strong aversion to dividing the student and teacher roles, preferring a deep reciprocity. Replace the education references with consulting references in the following Freire quotation and you get a clear sense of the values upon which Action Research are built: "Education [Consulting] must begin with the solution of the teacher-student [consultant-client] contradiction, by reconciling the poles of the contradiction so that both are simultaneously students [clients] and teachers [consultants]" (Freire, 1970, p.72).

Facilitation and the Consulting Process

While Action Research as the core technology is a huge asset bequeathed by Kurt Lewin, it is not enough. It does not describe how consulting projects begin, get designed, get executed, get evaluated, or end. *Flawless Consulting* (Block, 2011) is probably the best known handbook for consultants, but it focuses heavily on the front end of projects, with less attention paid to the overall project cycle. For more depth on

all aspects of consultation processes, refer to Rothwell, Stavros, and Sullivan, *Practicing Organization Development and Change* (2009) and Jones and Brazzel, *The NTL Handbook of Organization Development and Change* (2006). Both have numerous chapters organized around the consultation process.

For a high-level overview of the stages of the consulting process based upon Lewin's Action Research Model, **Facilitation 101** by Matt Minahan, Judy Vogel, Lee Butler, and Heather Butler Taylor (2007) is a good start. It also contains brief synopses of tools and techniques useful in the consulting process, such as the Bridges' Transition Model, the Satir Perturbation Model, Schutz's FIRO-B group development model, the Drexler-Sibbett Team Performance Model, the RASCI tool for accountability charting, and a Use of Self-Personal assessment.

Lurey and Griffen (2002) provide a good integration of project management and social psychology approaches to the stages of a consulting project in **Action Research: The Anchor of OD Practice.**

Marv Weisbord (1973) wrote in **The Organization Development Contract:** "Clients in a bind don't get much fun out of their work. They long for something simpler, better suited to their strengths, more consistent with their values. Above all, most clients long for outcomes. They want permanent change for the better, with no backsliding." In a preview of what Chris Argyris would later flesh out into double loop learning, Weisbord identifies three levels of outcomes clients might achieve from an OD project:

1. Reducing the immediate crisis (e.g., changing structures, policies, procedures, systems, programs, relationships for the better);
2. Learning something about their own coping styles—how they deal with organizational dilemmas and how they might do it better;
3. Learning a process for continually becoming aware and making choices about whatever issue presents itself.

Connie Freeman (1995) in **Seven Deadly Sins of OD Consulting: Pitfalls to Avoid in the Consulting Practice** outlines some of the mistakes that consultants, new and old, make and advises them to avoid the following: "flight to nowhere," one size fits all, the consultant as surrogate leader, dealing with symptoms rather than causes, and several other approaches. Embedded in the ways to avoid these pitfalls are skills for data collection, analysis, and presentation; meeting design and facilitation; idea generation, option development, and decision making.

The Core Skills Needed in Consulting on Process Issues

So far, the focus has been on the consulting process. In a different order, those same words have a very different meaning: consulting on process issues, or process consulting. In the consulting role, an HR Business Partner can add value by observing and intervening on process issues in a group. Most groups are competent on the technical issues of their work, but, unless trained in the behavioral sciences, they may be blind to their own process issues and ineffective patterns. These require an outsider's perspective and a specialist's training in process observation and intervention.

Some of the best thinking in the field on process consulting has been done by Edgar Schein (*Process Consultation*, 1969; *Process Consultation Revisited*, 1999). In his 2002 **Notes Toward a Better Understanding of Process: An Essay,** Schein defines process as "not the *what*, but the *how*. It is not the final decision made by a group or individual, but the way in which that decision was reached. It is not the formal structure of the organization, but the actual behaviors that occur within that structure, what sociologists might call the 'informal organization.'" He goes on to describe the "essence of process," as

- the sequence of events,
- the interactions among components,
- the invisible forces at play,

- those things that lead toward an intervention, and
- evolving and changing as they are scaled up from the intra-personal to inter-personal to group to whole system

The job of the process consultant is to look for those invisible forces at play and skillfully to call them to the attention of the group. In her classic essay, **The Consultant as Process Leader,** Jane Moosbruker (1989) notes that groups invariably find it hard to look at their own process issues. "After a few process observations, the group would return to the content, often without knowing that that had happened. Trying to keep the focus on process, *my* agenda, not theirs, was often exhausting." Well over two decades old now, Moosbruker's chapter has a still-excellent list of interventions for the process leader. She also has a comprehensive list of things *not* to do as a process facilitator.

The Client-Consultant Relationship

The client-consultant relationship is both interesting and complex. Since each situation is different, the consultant could be working on their 20th or 200th RACI chart or SWOT diagram, but the dynamics and group process issues are completely unique to the setting, people, and personalities of those gathered around the table.

The client-consultant relationship is complex in several ways. Regardless of the problem described, clients present some combination of author, director, and main character in the saga, but they often see themselves as bit players. Clients are also the owners of the problem and are both central in the framing of the problem and in recognizing the factors in the solution. It is a challenge to create the kind of relationship with the client that enables exploring this complexity. The consultant needs to build enough trust and self-disclosure to help the client endure the level of feedback and self-reflection needed to see their own roles in the problem.

Consultants hope to be *The Trusted Advisor* (Maister, Green, & Galford, 2000) with clients who

> seek out your views and advice . . . accept and act on at least some of your recommendations, involve you in more complex, strategic issues, share more information that helps you help them, protect you when you need it, even from those in their own organization, Involve you early on when their issues begin to form, rather than later in the process, trust your instincts. (pp. 3-4)

Meanwhile, clients are looking for consultants who seem to understand them effortlessly; are consistent and truthful; always help them see things from fresh perspectives, but do not force things on them; do not panic; help clients think and clarify logic and emotions; criticize and correct gently and lovingly, but do not pull their punches; act like a real person rather than someone in a role; can be relied upon to support them and have their interests at heart; and remember everything they have ever said with or without notes. (Maister, et al, 2000, pp. 4-5)

As can be seen, the client-consultant relationship is more than just a goods-for-service exchange. There are often intense and personal feelings, in both directions. Both parties have personal and interpersonal needs that are at play. But it is still a money-for-time commercial exchange, which means the consultant must be deeply aware of her or his own personal needs, wants, and fears, and must be sure that satisfying their own personal needs does not overshadow the client's primary needs to get work done efficiently and effectively.

In **Working with the Client-Consultant Relationship: Why Every Step Is an 'Intervention,** Naomi Raab (2004) says,

> Consulting is an anxiety producing profession. Faced with what can seem like an overwhelming problem in the client organization, plus our own need to perform and succeed, it's no wonder consultants use the bravado of the expert and salesman as a defense against feelings of not really knowing what to do and perhaps even feeling a fraud.

She goes on to outline the key client-consultant issues in the various stages of the consulting project, and some of the pitfalls for the consultant to avoid to prevent colluding with the client.

A mutual dependency is built into the relationship as well. The client depends upon the consultant for knowledge and outside perspective, while the consultant depends upon the client for grounding in the system, honest guidance, and direction about the problem and its causes, curiosity about their own contribution to the problem, and willingness to make tough decisions and change their own behavior.

Obviously, there is ample room for dependency, and even co-dependency, in this most complex relationship. In a worst-case scenario, the client and consultant become dependent on each other, to their own detriment. They have difficulty in "letting go" because they have convinced themselves that they need each other to be successful and fulfilled. The mutuality of this relationship is very powerful and it can become very seductive, which requires some strong boundaries and ongoing self-awareness and reflection, especially on the part of the consultant.

Another danger of poorly defined boundaries centers on the ownership of the intervention. It is sometimes tempting for consultants to be so enmeshed in the system and to become so dependent on being needed that they can overstep their bounds and mistakenly take on ownership of the project. This is especially possible for the HR Business Partner or internal trainers who are expected to bring and deliver technical content as expert consultants. Once framed in that role, it is quite easy to be expected to ensure a particular outcome or result. Harold Mack (1974) writes about this in **Who Owns the OD Effort.**

How do you deal with a partner/client who is giving up or does not accept the power inherent in assuming responsibility for themselves and for the consequences of their own actions or inactions? Arthur Freedman (1974) offers a framework for differentiating among the roles of client and consultant in **Unraveling the "Who's Responsible?" Riddle.**

The Consultant as Person

With all of these complicated situational and relational dynamics, what is a consultant to do? First, follow the **Rules of Thumb for Change Agents** from Herb Shepard (1985). There are not many OD consultants who can say they have mastered these wise and funny rules, but most agree that the effort to learn and practice them is well worth it. These are still foundational to many of the OD courses taught in schools around the world today. Remembering and following them will be enormously helpful in keeping OD consultants focused on what is important for themselves and the work.

The last chapters in this section give a glimpse into the inner doubts and questions and turmoil that is often going on inside of the OD consultant. Geoff Bellman (2004) reveals, in **If I Knew Then . . .,** some of the truths about his own shortcomings and anxieties. He wonders aloud about how to bring a better life perspective to his work and clients, how to help himself and his clients in their aspirations and desperation, and how to help make organizations more fit places to live in, among other important questions to ponder.

How does a HR Business Partner integrate HR and internal OD consulting? Carefully. In **Who's the Client Here: On Becoming an OD Consultant,** Robert Goldberg (1991) describes how his background in HR was a detriment to his work in OD. "Little did I know in my romanticized vision of becoming a change agent that the very factors that helped me succeed in human resources would be the major obstacles in my career in organizational development."

Partnerships Between the HR Business Partner, Leadership, Staff, and Other Service Providers

Most OD projects today involve an active partnership between the HR and OD specialists, the HR business partner and the organization leadership, or the HR Business Partner/internal consultant and an external consultant, or a consulting team. In addition to all of the skills needed to manage the client-consultant relationship, there is a unique relationship involved in these kinds of consulting partnerships. Each different function —HR, OD, internals, externals—has its own set of lenses through which to see the organization and perspective on the work. Each has its own set of skills to bring to the project. Each has its own set of beliefs and values which need to be understood, acknowledged, and harmonized. In short, partnering with someone is important if these practitioners are to meet the challenge of doing the work. This section describes these challenges of partnership.

In **An Inner Blueprint for Successful Partnership Development: Putting a Relationship to Work** (2004), Peter Norlin and Judy Vogel write about partnership in general and "learning to work effectively with other colleagues or helping our customers develop their capacity to collaborate successfully." They define partnership as "a successful relationship in service of a specific task," and write that "when people chose to be partners, they are also choosing to put their relationship to work." The premise of their writing is that "becoming conscious, disciplined, and intentional is a complicated assignment when human beings are involved." They also include a model that describes phases of a consulting project and tracks those parts which are above the line, or "visible" to the other partner, and those which are below the line, or "invisible" to the other. They explore the skills and intention needed to make the important matters visible so that the partnership will thrive and be productive.

Finally, **Reflections on a Cross-Cultural Partnership in Multicultural Organization Development Efforts** (2010) by Maria Ramos and Mark Chesler is a first person account of their work together in a multicultural intervention. They write about how they deliberately use their differences in age, gender, and color as evocative interventions.

FOR ADDITIONAL LEARNING

In addition to the Peter Block and Edgar Schein resources listed in the reference section, you may find the following helpful for understanding and developing consulting and partnership strategies and practices.

- Brown, J., Isaacs, D., Vogt, E., & Margulies, N. (2002). Strategic questioning: Engaging people's best thinking. *The Systems Thinker*, 13 (9), 2002, pp. 2–6.

  When people frame their strategic exploration as questions rather than as concerns or problems, a conversation begins where everyone can learn something together. The authors describe how to construct questions that engage people's best thinking.

- Schaffer, R. (2002). *High impact consulting: How clients and consultants can leverage rapid results into long-term gains.* San Francisco, CA: Jossey-Bass.

  Schaffer describes how senior managers unwittingly collude with their consultants to perpetuate the great waste inherent in "the five fatal flaws of conventional consulting." Drawing upon his own consulting work, Schaffer identifies the key elements of an effective project design, particularly that project objectives are defined in terms of client results rather than just consultant deliverables.

- Schein, E. H. (2009). *The corporate culture survival guide* (2nd ed.). San Francisco, CA: Jossey-Bass.

  Schein presents methods for analyzing the current state and changing corporate culture.

- Schein, E. H. (2009). *Helping: How to offer, give, and receive help.* San Francisco, CA: Berrett-Koehler.

  Schein analyzes the social and psychological dynamics common to all types of helping relationships, explains why help is often not helpful, and shows what any would-be helpers must do to ensure that their assistance is both welcomed and genuinely useful.

- Schein, E .H. (2010). *Organizational culture and leadership* (4th ed.). San Francisco, CA: Jossey-Bass.

  Schein defines and describes the components of organizational culture, leadership's role in fostering culture, and processes for indentifying and changing those aspects of culture that are incongruent with the organization's vision and goals.

- Desmond, B. (2011). Effective group development: A paradoxical approach for action learning facilitators. *OD Practitioner*, 43(1), 30–34.

  Desmond outlines how a facilitator may foster the conditions necessary for co-creating a healthy and enriching group development process through each of the three phases of a relational model of group development.

- Senge, P., Kleiner, A., Roberts, C., Ross, R., Roth, G., & Smith, B. (1994). The fifth discipline field book: Strategies and tools for building a learning organization. New York, NY: Doubleday.

For more on the core skills of facilitation see:

- Justice, T., & Jamieson, D. (2012). *The facilitator's fieldbook* (3rd ed) New York: AMACOM
- Schwartz, R. (2002). *The skilled facilitator: A comprehensive resource for consultants, facilitators, managers, trainers, and coaches.* San Francisco: Jossey-Bass.
- Wilkinson, M. (2004). *The secrets of facilitation: The S.M.A.R.T. guide to getting results with groups.* San Francisco: Jossey-Bass.

References

Block, P. (2011). *Flawless consulting: A guide to getting your expertise used* (3rd ed.). New York, NY: Jossey-Bass/Pfeiffer.

Cassidy, D. (2009). *Beyond uncertainty: Heisenberg, quantum physics, and the bomb*. New York, NY: Bellevue Literary Press.

Freire, P. (1970). *Pedagogy of the oppressed*. New York, NY: Continuum.

Lewin, K. (1946, November). Action research and minority problems. *Journal of Social Issues, 2*(4), 34–36.

Lewin, K. (1948). *Resolving social conflicts*. New York, NY: Harper Row.

Lewin, K. (1958). *Group decision and social change*. New York, NY: Holt, Rinehart and Winston.

Maister, D., Green, C., & Galford, R. (2000). *The trusted advisor*. New York, NY: Touchstone

Schein, E. (1969). *Process consultation: its role in organization development*. Reading, MA: Addison-Wesley.

Schein, E. (1998). *Process consultation revisited: building the helping relationship*. Reading, MA: Addison Wesley Organization Development Series.

CHAPTER 3

Facilitation 101

The Basics to Get You on Your Feet

Matt Minahan, Judy Vogel, Leon E. Butler,
and Heather Butler Taylor

OK, I've got the agenda with me. . . good. . . . Now, get the tape . . . masking or blue tape? What kind of walls do they have at that hotel? Can I even use tape there? My notes! I need to have my interview notes for the data feedback.

. . . And, is this my new box of Mr. Sketch markers, or the old one. . . wish I'd thrown it away after the last time!

. . . and I need the pieces for the icebreaker puzzle we're doing. . . . Do I have the index cards? And, the dot vote! I forgot to pack the colored dots! What's the client's boss's name again?

ANYONE WHO HAS EVER facilitated a meeting has probably had a morning like this. Among us, we've had about a thousand! And, as indispensable as all of those things seem in that moment, the truly indispensable tools for facilitation can't be seen or touched. They are the theories and concepts that underlie our work, a few of which we'll review in this article.

So, if facilitation isn't just bringing the markers and tape, pretty drawing on chart paper, and good Powerpoint presentations, what is it?

We're defining facilitation as "The use of your self, grounded in a conceptual frame and theories rooted in the behavioral sciences, enabling groups to be effective and productive."

Facilitation occurs in the context of organization development, which we're defining as, "A body of knowledge and practice that enhances organizational performance and individual development, viewing the organization as a system or systems that exists within a larger system, each of which has its own attributes and degrees of alignment. OD interventions in these systems are inclusive methodologies and approaches to strategic planning, organization design, leadership development, change management, performance management, coaching, diversity, and work life balance" (Minahan, 2007).

So, while the facilitation *event* begins with the morning frenzy, the facilitation *work*—and our preparation for it—has been underway for some time, as we've been studying and building a theory base to support our *in the moment work* as facilitators.

Project Model

The first thing to know, and to know that you know, is a consulting project framework. We recommend a seven phase model (Figure 3.1) because it is a hybrid, combining a solid grounding in Action Research theory, OD process, and general problem solving.

FIGURE 3.1

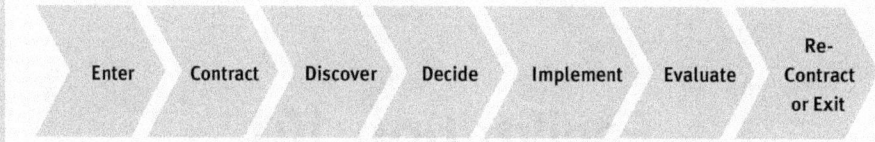

Phase 1: Enter—Getting Started

The purpose of this phase of the project is to understand the client's presenting problem or business need, communicate your understanding to the client, and establish rapport.

Theory frame and resources: The Action Research Cycle is indispensable in our work, and Arthur Freidman's chapter on it in The NTL Handbook on Organization Development and Change is a good place to start.

Phase 2: Contract

The purpose of this phase is to define a successful outcome, agree on the scope of work, establish good communication, build commitment on both sides. . . in short, construct the psychological contract for success.

Theory frame and resources: Peter Block's Flawless Consulting chapters on Entry and Contracting and Who Is the Client would probably be helpful in the Contract phase.

Phase 3: Discover

The purpose of this phase is to collect data upon which you can make your own preliminary judgments about the organization. It also helps you verify the client's perception and description of the issue and gives you data about how accurately she or he has described it to you.

Theory frame and resources: You'll want to have access to a good research methods text—and there are many good ones out there! On the quantitative side, you'll need to know basic survey design, data collection, and analysis; on the qualitative side, you'll need to know about interview protocol development, interviewing techniques, solid note taking, and qualitative data analysis. Research Methods in Organizational Behavior

by Eugene Stone provides a strong, yet easy to understand, perspective, especially on surveys and statistical measures. Qualitative Evaluation and Research Methods by Michael Quinn Patton is excellent in discussing qualitative designs, data collection, analysis, and interpretation.

Phase 4: Decide

The purpose of this phase is to jointly construct—among you, the client, and the project team—an agreed upon picture of *what is*, and a joint commitment to *what to do about it*. This demonstrates the client group's ownership of the project.

Theory frame and resources: Patton's Qualitative Evaluation and Research Methods cited has an excellent section on qualitative data presentation, and for statistical information, a breakthrough book is The Visual Display of Quantitative Information by Edward Tufte.

Phase 5: Implement

The purpose of this phase is to move the system toward the desired outcome. They may take this action without you, or use your help.

Theory frame and resources: This work involves visioning, brainstorming, problem solving, and project management, and Carter McNamara's Field Guide to Consulting and Organizational Development is an excellent resource.

Phase 6: Evaluate

The purpose of this phase is to evaluate the results of the project against its original goals.

Theory frame and resources: There is a whole body of knowledge and writing on evaluation, but for OD facilitation, we recommend Chapter 11, Evaluating and Institutionalizing Organi-

zation Development Interventions, in Worley and Cummins' Organization Development and Change (8th edition).

Phase 7: Re-Contract, Closure, Exit

The purpose of this phase is to build on your existing knowledge of the organization, leverage the contacts and relationships you've built during the first 6 phases of the project, and develop additional follow on projects that address important organizational issues.

Theory frame and resources: This is an area that is typically underexplored in our field, but Ann Van Eron and Warner Burke have done a nice job in Chapter 12, called Separation, in Practicing Organization Development: A Guide for Consultants by Rothwell, Sullivan, and McLean.

Useful Theories and Models for Facilitation

Now, what do you need to know to do the work of these stages? It helps to have a few theories, models and tools handy to cover the major elements of the work.

Four Levels of Intervention

Stay focused on the fact that the work you're facilitating is occurring at a minimum of four levels: the intrapersonal within each individual, the interpersonal among at least two people, the group, and the organization. Different tools work better, depending upon the level of your intervention, and it is important to be aware of the level on which you are working and intervening.

Change Models

A well-known and well-used model for individual change is William Bridges' (1993) three stage Transition Model (Figure 3.2). The Ending is where we begin, as we accept, let go, and mourn losses; the Neutral Zone is where we experience confusion and insecurity, as depicted by the trapeze artist between swings, but

FIGURE 3.2 Bridges Transition Model

ENDINGS

» Define:
  • Who is losing what
  • What is over and what isn't
  • Areas over which we have control

» Provide information again and again

» Acknowledge losses

» Mark the ending

» Treat the past with respect

NEUTRAL ZONE

» Reflect on
  • Differences and continuities
  • Losses and opportunities
  • Feelings

» Make temporary arrangements

» Find quiet times and stable places

» Explore and experiment

» Be present to the situation

NEW BEGINNING

» Clarify expectations

» Communicate purpose

» Identify roles and procedures

» Maintain consistency

» Ensure quick success

» Symbolize the new identity

» Celebrate the success

THE FOUR Ps

In coping with Transitions, remember the 4 Ps:

» Provide a *purpose* for the change

» Paint a *picture* of how the new outcome looks and feels

» Lay out a step-by-step *plan* for phasing in the outcome

» Give each person a *part to play* in the process

Adapted from *Managing Transitions*, Bridges, W., Addison-Wesley, 1991 also creativity, as new possibilities emerge; and the New Beginning is where we experience renewed energy, purpose, direction, and a new identity.

Another favorite can be used at the individual, group, and organizational levels. It's by well-known family systems expert, Dr. Virginia Satir (1991), and it describes what happens to people when there is perturbation, such as that which comes from change (Figure 3.3).

Group Model

You'll need to have a model that helps you understand what's going on in any group that you're facilitating. One of the simplest, and best, is Will Schutz's FIRO-B model (Figure 3.4), in which groups go through three predictable stages. The first stage is inclusion, addressing the question of who is in and who is out of this group. The second stage is control, addressing the question of who has influence, or who is up and who is down in this group. The third stage is affection or openness, or who is close and who is far. Groups cycle through these three stages over the life of the group, and every time the group convenes.

Team Model

The Drexler-Sibbet Team Performance Model (Figure 3.5) is the best researched, best docu-

mented, and best supported team model. It's a seven stage model that outlines the issues that teams must confront, and how they get resolved.

It's also helpful to have a solid grasp of the differences between groups and teams, especially as you prepare to facilitate either or both. The central difference is that the members of teams are inherently highly interdependent, and the members of groups are less interdependent. Groups can often function quite well without some, many, or even most of their members because roles are often not well differentiated. Teams, on the other hand, often have differentiated roles, and the members are dependent upon each other to get things done, which greatly increases the risk—and the potential rewards!—from working with teams. Some of the other differences are described in Figure 3.6.

Diversity Models

An important, and too often avoided dimension of group life, is the diversity of its members and the facilitator. Diversity includes many attributes, characteristics and identity group memberships, such as the following: gender, sexual orientation, physical ability, race, age, language, nationality, ethnicity, class, etc. These dimensions add both potential complexity and richness to the group's work and, if ignored, reduce the group's effectiveness by

FIGURE 3.3   Satir Perturbation Model

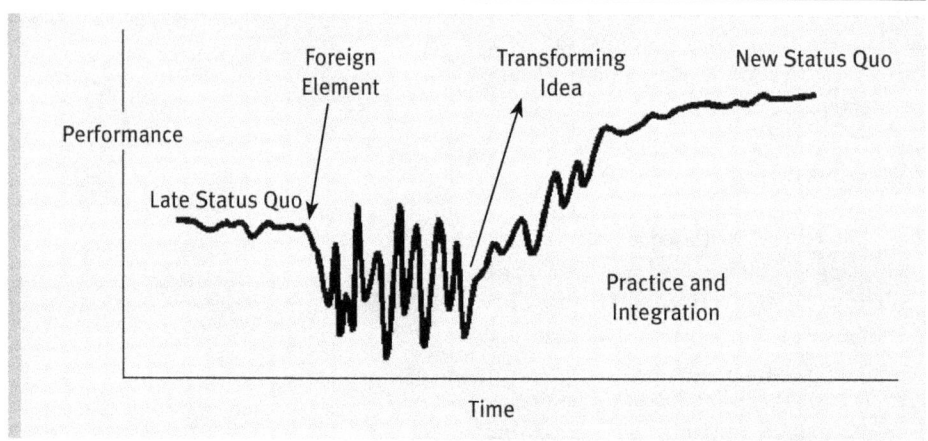

FIGURE 3.4 The FIRO-B Six Cell Model Behaviors

INCLUSION

Expressed Inclusion:

» Talking and joking with others
» Taking a personal interest in others
» Involving others in projects and meetings
» Recognizing the accomplishments of others
» Incorporating everyone's ideas and suggestions
» Offering helpful information or "tips" to new colleagues

Wanted Inclusion:

» Frequenting heavily trafficked areas (e.g., the water cooler)
» Wearing distinctive clothing
» Decorating the workspace with personal keepsakes
» Seeking recognition or responsibility
» Getting involved in high priority projects and activities
» Going along with the majority opinion

CONTROL

Expressed Control:

» Assuming positions of authority
» Advancing ideas within the group
» Taking a competitive stance and making winning a priority
» Managing the conversation
» Influencing others' opinions
» Establishing structured tasks, procedures, policies

Wanted Control:

» Asking for help on the job
» Involving others in decision-making
» Requesting precise instructions or clarification
» Deferring to the wishes, needs, and requests of others
» Asking for permission and circulating progress details
» Raising issues for others to consider

AFFECTION

Expressed Affection:

» Reassuring and supporting colleagues, both verbally and physically
» Exhibiting concern about the personal lives of others
» Being trustworthy and loyal
» Sharing personal opinions or private feelings about issues
» Coaching and developing others

Wanted Affection:

» Being flexible and accommodating
» Listening carefully to others
» Displaying an open body posture
» Sharing feelings of anxiety
» Trying to please others
» Giving others more than they want/need

Modified and reproduced by special permission of the Publisher, CPP, Inc., Mountain View, CA 94043 from *Introduction to the FIRO-B® Instrument in Organizations*, by Eugene R. Schnell and Allen L. Hammer. Copyright 1993, 2004 by CPP, Inc. All rights reserved. Further reproduction is prohibited without the Publisher's written consent.

FIGURE 3.5   Drexler-Sibbet Team Performance Model

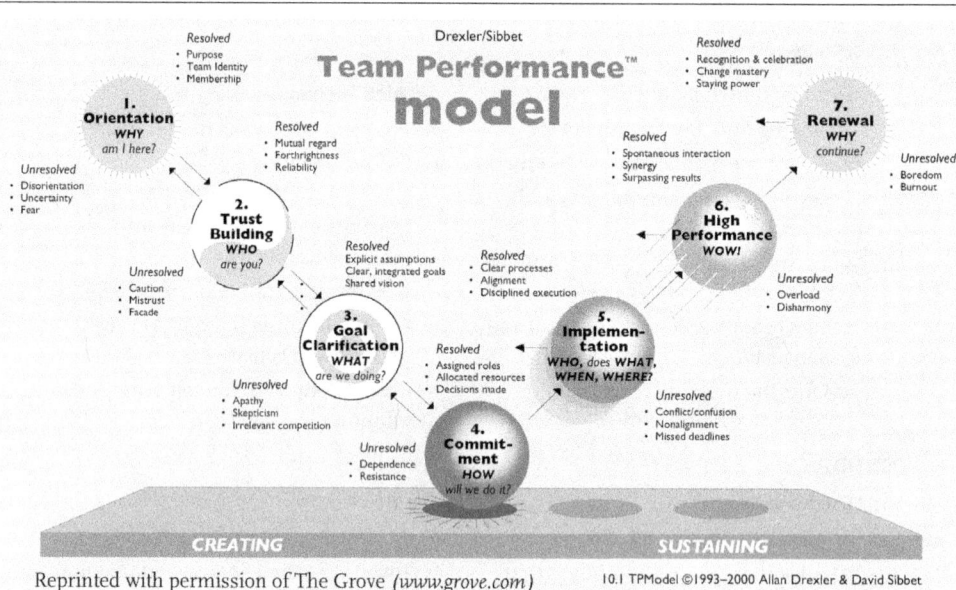

Reprinted with permission of The Grove *(www.grove.com)*   10.1 TPModel ©1993–2000 Allan Drexler & David Sibbet

creating tensions in the communications and reducing access to its members' resources.

Given this potential value to the group, why is it that such discussion is left unexplored? One reason is that facilitators are often uncomfortable and unable to explore diversity because they lack the awareness, the skills, the models or the vocabulary to guide such learning conversations in the group. The effectiveness with which we are able to recognize, name and discuss difference, work diversity issues, and use diversity models in our facilitation is directly linked to the powerful outcomes of the work we do. When worked effectively, differences in the room can be the substance of profound learning for all present.

There are several models that highlight various elements of diversity, including Quadrant Theory, Dimensions of Diversity, Path to Competence, and Dominant/ Subordinated Group Dynamics.

Group Dynamics

This topic is so large that there are several academic journals dedicated to it, but there are a few things for the facilitator to keep in mind. Wilfried Bion's work with shell-shocked soldiers revealed that there are often three "basic assumption" groups at play, and often simultaneously, behaving as if their purpose was: a) to fight with each other, or to flee; b) to rebel against the group leader; and c) to collude to anoint a new leader whom the group will ultimately remove (Rioch, 1970). These are often taken as signs of dysfunction in workplace groups, but they are normal and natural, especially when the group is lacking a clear purpose or connection to its work. When your groups start to exhibit these basic assumption group behaviors, it's a sign that it's time to revisit the group's goal, its operating procedures, and its communication patterns.

Accountability Charting

One last tool to have handy is an accountability, or RASCI chart, which identifies who is responsible for what in a project or implementation plan. RASCI is an acronym, standing for "Responsible, Approves, Supports, Consulted, Informed." The Responsi-

FIGURE 3.6   Differences Between Team and Group Functions

CRITERIA	GROUPS	TEAMS
What is the purpose?	Support and develop the principles, skills and abilities of members in a chosen domain.	Accomplish a project plan that supports organization objectives.
Who belongs?	Members from one or many organizations, or not affiliated with any organization	Members of the organization.
What makes members come together?	Self-selection based on expertise or passion.	Selected and assigned by management.
What is the glue holding it together?	The passion, commitment, and identification to the chosen cause or knowledge domain.	The organization plan or the project charter.
What is the nature of the activities?	Goals are more self-generated-best if aligned with organization.	Tasks should be aligned with organizational interests. Specific goals from organization, establishing deliverables and deadlines.
How long does it last?	As long as the members have interest in building the practice and sustaining the community.	Until the project or work is completed.
What are the resources?	Information, knowledge, experience, member commitment and collaboration, etc.	People hours and work resources.

Minahan, 2005, as originally published in *Practicing OD* (2005).

ble person owns the problem or project. The Approval person signs off and must approve the work before it can take effect. The Supportive person(s) can provide resources. The Consulted person(s) has information or capacity necessary to complete the work. The Informed person(s) must be notified of results, but need not be consulted. Using this tool with a group can greatly clarify their roles and support effective work on their task. For example, if the task were to publish the organization's newsletter, you might see a RASCI chart such as Figure 3.7.

Use of Self

In the end, your success as a facilitator is going to be based on you, and how well you use your self to connect with others, model desired behaviors, and influence people to change. That's really what our job is all about when you think about it. We establish emotional connections with people, and hopefully create an environment in which others feel comfortable connecting emotionally with each other. We have some beliefs about, and hopefully we model, how people should be treated in the workplace—that they should be given a voice in their own futures, listened to with care and grace, and respected for the differences in their backgrounds and perspectives. We bring theory and knowledge to the work, which hopefully participants find relevant and useful. Ideally, the whole package of "us" is interesting and appealing, and invites participants to consider new ways to see their worlds, change their behaviors, and accomplish important goals.

We've developed an assessment for the use of self (Figure 3.8) which identifies eight variables which determine who we are, and how we use our "self" in facilitation. Ask yourself, to what extent. . .

- Are my **boundaries** easy or difficult to penetrate, and what should they be, given the situation and the work that I'm doing?
- Am I free and open with **self disclosure**, or reluctant and closed and how should I be, given the situation and the work that I'm doing?
- Is my **intervention style** active and engaged, or passive and restrained, and what should it be, given the situation and the work that I'm doing?
- Am I **confident** and self assured, or self-doubting, and how should I be, given the situation and the work that I'm doing?
- Am I highly skilled and **competent**, or not well skilled in the context of the work that I'm doing?

FIGURE 3.7 RASCI Chart

Name	Responsible	Approves	Supports	Consulted	Informed
Charlie, the Communications Director	X				
Anne, the Communications VP		X			
Al, the Admin Assistant			X		
Functional VPs				X	
Internal Print Shop					X

FIGURE 3.8   Self as Instrument of Change: A Self Assessment

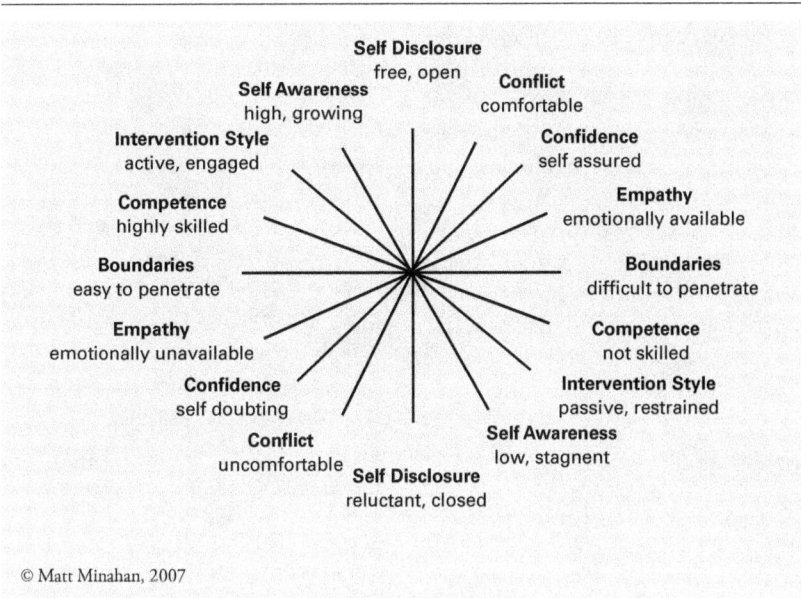

© Matt Minahan, 2007

- Am I comfortable or uncomfortable with **conflict**, and how well does that serve me, given the situation and the work that I'm doing?
- Is my **self-awareness** high and growing, or low and stagnant, and is there anything I need to do about that? Are my group memberships helping or hindering my ability to manage the group dynamics in the work I'm doing?
- Am I emotionally available and **empathic**, or emotionally distant and unavailable, and how should I be, given the situation and the work that I'm doing?

There are a thousand other questions related to facilitation, such as what to say and when and to whom when facilitating group work, and what to write on chart paper, and what to put on slides, and when to intervene, and when to call time, and when to question the process, and when to confront the leader, and when to say "yes" and when to say "no." There's no one-best answer or solution to any of them. The best way to learn how to inter-

vene in a group is to get lots of practice, especially working in partnership with a well-seasoned facilitator.

There is a huge risk—maybe even a bit of arrogance!—involved in saying that this is the body of knowledge needed for good facilitation. And, there are dozens of essential theories that we love and use every day, but could not include here, among them The JoHari Window, the Ladder of Inference, Exchange Theory, a good communications model, Difficult Conversations, the Requisite Organization, an integrative world view model such as Ken Wilber's, a good conflict resolution model, a power model, and graphic facilitation techniques. Knowing a broad range of theories gives us more options in making facilitation decisions, and we've tried to present the handful that we think are at the core of good facilitation.

For as hectic and crazy-making as facilitation mornings are, handling them well is just a small fraction of what makes as good as facilitators. The morning frenzy represents just the sizzle of our field. . . hot, frenetic, endorphin-releasing, but not very sustaining or satisfying; it is quite far from the real work that we do in facilitation. In fact, you've been collecting the truly important items for your facilitation work all of your life—a few theories, a few models, a few handy techniques, and life-long learning about yourself and your impact on others. In the end, what makes us successful at facilitation is a good strong theory base, being curious about ourselves and the world, having the patience to practice, and to practice some more, bringing our best "self" to the work, the client, and the team, always with the goal of making a contribution to a better world.

References

Adams, M., Blumenfeld, W., Castaneda, R., Hackman, H., Peters, M., & Zuniga, X. (Eds.), (2000). *Readings for diversity and social justice: an anthology on racism, antisemitism, sexism, heterosexism, ableism, and classism.* New York, NY: Routledge.

Bridges, W. (1991). *Managing transitions: Making the most of change.* Cambridge, MA: Perseus Books.

Cheung-Judge, M. (2001). The self as an instrument —a cornerstone for the future of OD. *The OD Practitioner.* 33 (3), 33–39.

Cox, T. (1993). *Cultural diversity in organizations: theory, research & practice.* San Francisco, CA: Berrett-Koehler Publishers.

Cross, E., & White, M. (Eds.) (1996) *The diversity factor: capturing the competitive advantage of a changing workforce.* Chicago, IL: Irwin professional Publishing.

Cummins, T., & Worley, C. (2005). *Organization development and change.* 8th Edition. Mason, OH: South-Western/Thompson.

Curran, K., Seashore, C., & Welp, M. (1995). Use of self as an instrument of change. As presented at the OD Network Annual Conference, November 17, 1995, Seattle, WA. Retrieved from http://www.equalvoice. com/use_of_self.pdf.

Drexler, A., Sibbet, D., & Forrester, R. (1988). The team performance model. In W. B. Reddy & K. Jamieson (Eds.) *Teambuilding: blueprints for productivity and satisfaction* (pp. 45-61). Alexandria, VA: NTL Institute for the Applied Behavioral Sciences; San Diego, CA: University Associates.

Doyle, M., & Strauss, D. (1982). *How to make meetings work.* New York, NY: Penguin-Putnam.

Freedman, A. M. (2006). Action research: Origins and applications for ODC practitioners. *The NTL handbook of organization development and change.* San Francisco, CA: Pfeiffer.

Knowles, M. (1970). *The modern practice of adult education: from pedagogy to androgogy.* Association Press Konrad, A., Prasad, P., & Pringle, J. (Eds.), (2006). *Handbook of workplace diversity.* Thousand Oaks, CA: Sage Publications.

Maslow, A. (1954). *Motivation and personality.* New York, NY: Harper.

McClelland, D. C. (1975) *Power: the inner experience.* New York, NY: Halstead.

McClelland, D.C., Atkinson, J.W., Clark, R.A., & Lowell, E.L. (1953) *The achievement motive.* Princeton: Van Nostrand McNamara, C. (2007) *Field guide to consulting and organization development.* Minneapolis, MN: Authenticity Consulting.

Minahan, M. (2005). "From groups to teams." *Practicing OD.* http://www.odnetwork.org/publications/ practicing/ practicing_od_backissues/article. php? article_id=811.

Minahan, M. (2005). "Using groups to manage change programs." Practicing OD. http://www.od network.org/publications/practicing/practicing_od_backissues/article.php?article_id=728.

Minahan, M. (2007) "What Is OD?" http://od network.org/aboutod/index.php.

Patton, M. (1990). *Qualitative evaluation and research methods.* Newbury Park, CA: Sage

Plummer, D. (Ed.). (2003) *Handbook of diversity management: beyond awareness to competency based learning.* Lanham, MD: University Press of America.

Riosch, M. J. (1970). The work of Wilfred Bion on groups. *Journal for the Study Interpersonal Processes,* 1(33), 56–66.

Rothwell, W., Sullivan, R., & McLean, G. (1995) *Practicing OD: a guide for consultants.* San Francisco, CA: Jossey-Bass/Pfeiffer.

Satir, V., et. al. (1991). *The Satir model: family therapy and beyond.* Palo Alto, CA: Science and Behavior Books.

Schutz, W. C. (1958). *FIRO: A three-dimensional theory of interpersonal behavior.* New York, NY: Holt, Rhinehart & Winston.

Speck, M. (1996, Spring). Best practice in professional development for sustained educational change. *ERS Spectrum, 33–41.*

Stone, E. (1978). *Research methods in organizational behavior.* Santa Monica, CA: Goodyear Publishing.

Tolbert, M., & Hannafin, J. (2006) Use of self in OD consulting: what matters is presence. *The NTL handbook of organization development and change.* San Francisco, CA: Pfeiffer.

Tufte, E. (2001). *The visual display of quantitative information.* Cheshire, CT: Graphics Press

Wells, M., & Pringle, V. B. (2004). Use of self-supervision model: Relational, ethical, and cultural issues. *APPIC Newsletter Online.* Retrieved from http://www2.gsu.edu/~wwwcou/wordandpdfEtc/UseofSelfSupv.pdf.

Wilber, K. (1996). *A brief history of everything.* Boston, MA: Shambhala.

CHAPTER 4

Action Research
The Anchor of OD Practice
Jeremy S. Lurey and Matt Griffin

A Tale of the Oversized File Cabinet

While working in his home office on a sunny Friday afternoon, Frank heard the doorbell ring. He went to answer the door, and as he opened it, he noticed Tom the carpenter standing outside next to a very large file cabinet.

Before Frank could even say hello, Tom eagerly greeted him with a firm handshake and said, "Hi Tom. I was so excited to get your call about the file cabinet last week that I started immediately. I designed a custom-made oversized cabinet to meet all of your current and future business needs. You're going to love it!"

With a perplexed look on his face, Frank responded, "Tom, I'm not sure what you were thinking, but my message was very clear. I asked you to come over today so we could have an initial discussion about the file cabinet and review my specific requirements. I thought we could start with the overall design of the cabinet and then determine if you were the right person for the job based on budget and time constraints."

"Yes, but I have known you for a long time Frank, and can tell you have a bright future as an OD consultant. I didn't want you to have to worry about a thing. You have enough to worry about starting your own business, that I thought I would just take some initiative," Tom enthusiastically explained as he ges-

tured to his master creation—a 20-foot high, 30-foot long, 10-drawer monstrosity with a dark maple finish. "Besides, this cabinet is perfect for you. You will have enough space in this cabinet for years of growth. You will never need another file cabinet!"

At that point, Frank was very frustrated and could feel his face burning. "Tom," he replied, "This simply isn't what I asked for, and you would have understood that if you only waited to talk with me first. "Keep in mind that organizations are complex systems, and using a mechanical approach to 'fix' a 'broken' part rarely creates effective change." I'm only planning to be in my home office for a year or two before I move into more permanent workspace with a few of my colleagues. I just need a small cabinet to hold a few important files as I get started. I'm sorry, but I can't accept the cabinet. It won't even fit in the house! I am very disappointed Tom, and think you should leave." As the door closed behind him, Frank noticed the complete bewilderment on Tom's face.

An OD Consulting Challenge

While this is a fictitious story, and an extreme exaggeration at that, it is not inconceivable that a carpenter would be so eager to please the client that initiative would be taken without fully understanding the scope of work.

Neither is it inconceivable that a skilled craftsman would be so confident in his abilities that he would jump right into the project without having more direction from the client. In fact, it even seems logical for a carpenter to take such actions after reaching a clear agreement with the client—especially if the busy client may be preoccupied with higher priority activities.

Although this story chronicles the tale of a carpenter and his client, the story speaks of an all too common event in consulting, especially organization consulting, as well. How often do we hear these stories:

- Clients who express a clear problem to a consultant, and then the consultant designs and implements his/her own solution regardless of whether or not it meets the true client need
- A consultant brings a solution to the client before the problem is understood or even discussed
- Situations where clients are completely dissatisfied with the performance of their consultants and the results they deliver simply because of a communication gap—one where the consultant implements a solution without first presenting it to the client for approval or at least discussing the possible implications in advance

What these examples indicate is that the quality and success of the project depends upon both the client and the consultant fully understanding the complexity of the issue. To illustrate this understanding, it can be helpful to think in terms of *multiple levels of awareness*. The client experiencing pain can represent the first level of awareness, and the initial client diagnosis the second level. Action taken on either of these two levels is not likely to truly address the issue. Action research is about reaching deeper levels of awareness, and thereby increasing the likelihood of addressing the issue in an effective way.

As the story suggests, it is critical for a carpenter, or an OD consultant, to develop and maintain a close working relationship with his or her client. Without this collaborative arrangement, the consultant will likely deliver an inadequate or inappropriate solution that does not meet the client's needs. In so doing, the consultant runs a great risk of alienating him or herself from the client, and more importantly causing potential harm or suffering to the client.

The story is also useful in illustrating a critical difference between the work of a carpenter and the work of an OD consultant. The "results" that a carpenter produces are tangible and cannot easily be undone. A file cabinet made from the wrong wood or with incorrect dimensions is difficult to fix without starting over from scratch, whereas a consulting project can sometimes be modified, even radically, as new information comes to the surface. Consulting projects, especially those found within the OD world, tend to be complex, subjectively perceived, and fluid. This makes it easy —if anything in OD is truly easy—to misunderstand or miscommunicate the nature of the project. At the same time, it also makes it easier to adapt your approach once you do gain a proper understanding of both the situation and the client's expectations.

The Value of Action Research

Although the origin of action research remains cloudy, and to some extent can be seen as an offshoot of the scientific method, Kurt Lewin is typically credited with bringing this methodology to the mainstream and to organizations specifically. It was the belief of Lewin and his contemporaries that in order to understand and change social conditions, those involved in creating those conditions must be involved in the process. Thus, one of the main themes of action research is enactment of social change. For this reason, action research is at the core of the OD practice. As an approach to organization consulting, it prescribes a positive and collaborative working relationship between consultant and client and therefore provides the basic foundation for the organization change process.

Using the action research process enables the consultant to better understand the system in which he/she is involved, and therefore mitigates the risk of following in Tom the Carpenter's footsteps. At the same time, an action research approach helps the clients to be more conscious of their environment and the conditions in which they live. With this heightened awareness, the consultant and client are then able to work together to realize the goals of the change process by uncovering deeper levels of awareness and understanding.

Because of the importance of client participation, this work method requires the consultant to accept more of a "facilitator" than "expert" role. It should be noted, however, that this is not an either/or choice. In addition, the choice need not be applied to the entire course of the change process. The consultant can act more as an expert in analyzing the data during one phase of the project while still being a facilitator in helping the client create the action plan during another phase. While there is often a delicate balance between the changing responsibilities of being an expert and facilitator, the process remains largely the same. The consultant creates an environment in which the client is always aware of what is happening when following an action research approach.

In this manner, the client actively participates in not only designing each step of the change process but also performing many of the required actions. One of the main reasons for this participative role is that change is usually easier to accept when those affected by the change are involved in understanding and driving the change process. This point is at the heart of action research, and therefore the client, in most cases, is involved in every aspect of the project, including:

- Establishing change priorities
- Collecting and interpreting data
- Analyzing and disseminating the results
- Creating action plans based on the results
- Implementing the action plans
- Evaluating the results

To help both the consultant and client maintain focus during the course of the change process, the action research approach consists of a standard phased methodology. The seven phases of action research are summarized below.

1. Entry—beginning to develop the client/consultant relationship and validating the fit between both parties
2. Contracting—determining whether or not to proceed with the consulting relationship and negotiating any final conditions of the engagement "contract"
3. Data Gathering and Diagnosis—collecting the necessary data and analyzing it
4. Feedback—presenting the findings, analysis, and any preliminary recommendations to the client organization
5. Planning Change—identifying specific courses of action that address the client situation and developing an action plan for implementation
6. Intervention—applying specific solution sets to the client organization
7. Evaluation—assessing project results and determining future courses of action, ranging from project closure to new contract development activities

Action Research in Action

To illustrate the value of action research to the practice of OD, the following section describes a real-life case example of how the action research approach can be used. This account details specific actions taken by both the client and consultant during each of the seven phases of a nine-month consulting engagement. The primary client group in this example was an IT organization within a regional insurance agency, and the initial presenting issue was a lack of collaboration and teaming across the organization.

Entry

After being presented with a viable business lead, the consultant arranged for an initial phone conversation with the client sponsor. While this first component of the action research approach only lasted approximately forty-five minutes, the consultant successfully gained some clarity on the presenting problems and primary concerns of the client. To summarize, the client suggested that there was a lack of collaboration and teaming across the organization. She also expressed a desire to have the consultant further assess the situation and recommend specific strategies for improving this unproductive work culture.

In conjunction with the consultant learning about the client situation, the client sponsor also took advantage of the opportunity to question the consultant about his professional background and relevant work experiences. Questions like "Can you give me an example of when you worked on a similar project?" and "What would your first step be in this situation?" helped her understand what value the consultant would bring to the organization. The client also gained a tremendous sense of confidence in the consultant's abilities due to his strong responses. As with any relationship, this is a critical step in building a positive working relationship early on in the Entry phase of the project.

While this short conference ended on a very positive note, it took approximately six weeks for the two individuals to speak again. The delay occurred for two primary reasons: first, a change in client priorities due to competing projects and second, the consultant's ongoing commitment to another client. While this may create some tension between client and consultant in some engagements, it is actually quite common within an action research framework. Both parties must be ready to move to the next stage of the relationship before any work can proceed, and in this case, the two quickly confirmed their interest in pursuing the relationship further when they did reconnect.

Contracting

The Contracting phase of action research can begin as soon as the client and consultant agree to work together. In this case, it began as soon as the two reconnected and discussed the actual scope of the project.

During a face-to-face meeting with the client, the consultant asked some probing questions to better understand the client's expectations. She repeated some of the same key phrases he heard before, namely "to help the group work better as a team" and "to help create a team identity". At this point, the consultant began clarifying the primary target audience and proposing some potential activities to get the project started. Thus, the foundation of the engagement contract included the following:

- Project objective—design and implement customized management training and development programs that improve management skills and foster stronger team leaders
- Current scope—management training and development for the seven members of the management team only
- Potential future scope—broader training programs for nonmanagers as well as organization realignment or business process redesign initiatives
- Project approach—phased approach including high-level activities, such as assessment, feedback, and intervention, over a specific timeline and with key project milestones and deliverables; requires active participation and involvement from key members of the client organization, including the client sponsor, each of the seven managers, and many of the employees during the data gathering and evaluation phases specifically

After this information was clearly documented, the consultant presented it to the client for review and approval. With a shared understanding of the project confirmed, the client then signed off on the contract. The importance of this action cannot be emphasized enough if you plan to follow an action research approach.

Data Gathering and Diagnosis

Having defined the scope of the project during Contracting, the consultant and client sponsor were now prepared to begin gathering data. In true action research form, both parties played an active role in completing this task. The client sponsor provided key organization data to the consultant to help him understand the environment, and then the consultant initiated more targeted data gathering activities.

Many members of the client organization participated in the process. All of the managers completed two different personality inventories, including the Myers-Briggs Type Indicator, and participated in a 360-degree feedback process. They also participated in one-on-one interviews with the consultant so he could learn more about their personal strengths, areas for improvements, and their beliefs about the work condition. In addition, many of the employees participated in focus group sessions to share their feelings about the organization and complete a leadership effectiveness survey.

After completing these activities, the consultant assumed more of an "expert" role during the diagnosis part of this phase. There were two primary reasons for this decision: first, the client sponsor and her direct reports were all extremely busy with other project commitments, and second, the consultant had more experience with performing such analysis, and especially with using the diagnostic tools.

Feedback

When the diagnosis was complete, the consultant actively engaged the client, and the entire management team, in the feedback process. For the change to be successful, it is vital to share these findings with the client and guide them in determining the next steps, as opposed to deciding for them. They must direct the process if they are ever going to accept the change.

Thus, the consultant presented a summary report of the findings as well as his conclusions and recommendations for moving forward. In general, the findings did support the original contention that there was a lack of collaboration and team identity within the organization. More specifically, employees indicated that there was very little teamwork

within or between units and that there was no reason to develop stronger team relations since the individual projects were so diverse in scope. One person actually stated, "I have no team . . . [This organization] is a series of fiefdoms."

Once presented with these findings, all of the managers contributed to an open dialogue about the information and possible strategies to address the situation. For the most part, the managers reacted positively, voicing their agreement with the results as if they were almost expected. Some managers, however, did react a bit more defensively and questioned whether or not specific findings were truly indicative of their units or if they were more a generalization of the rest of the organization.

For example, one manager felt that she did seek input from her employees and included them in the decision-making process. The summary results for the entire organization, however, did not suggest that employees felt they were able to contribute in such a manner. Instead, they expressed a concern that they had very limited knowledge of the long-term vision for the organization and were somewhat unclear of how their individual projects supported the future direction of the group. In the end, each of the managers agreed on the next steps of the engagement and suggested several potential activities that would address the specific areas for improvement discussed in the meeting.

In parallel to this work, the consultant also shared the results of the personal assessments with each of the managers during individual feedback sessions. The individual results, similar to the team findings, suggested that the majority of the managers did not openly communicate about the organization's future direction or inspire commitment to a shared vision, that they did not inform employees of how their work contributed to the organization's goals. The results also indicated that the managers were very weak in the areas of performance evaluation and performance management, that they did not encourage performance discussions with their employees or provide any regular feedback regarding work performance. Again, the collaborative relationship between client and consultant becomes critical if the individual managers were going to take any responsibility in addressing these concerns or promoting their own personal development.

Planning Change

The goal of the Planning Change phase is to create an action plan that will guide the next phase of the process, intervention. For this reason, planning change is not about implementing the solutions being discussed. Instead, it is an opportunity to explore the potential solutions further and determine exactly how the intervention will proceed.

In this case, the management team identified two levels of intervention: one focused on the management team and the other focused on the individuals within that team. The team-based intervention was a management training program that involved a comprehensive curriculum of courses to address their specific developmental needs. The key aspects of planning this type of change, then, were to define the curriculum and coordinate all of the logistics for delivering the training, including preparing instructor and participant training materials, scheduling the training sessions, and ultimately facilitating the training.

The second intervention was aimed more directly at the individual managers and was intended to support the team training experience. Towards this end, the consultant co-developed personal action plans that focused on one or two critical leadership skills with each manager. While these plans varied from individual to individual, many focused on addressing the concerns with performance evaluation and performance management and all specified certain developmental activities, target completion dates, as well as any resources that may be required to achieve the developmental goal.

Intervention

The Intervention phase is where the plan is executed and the solution is actually implemented within the client organization. Un-

like the Diagnosis phase where the consultant often accepts responsibility as the expert, this is one time in the engagement where the consultant can take more of a "facilitator" role. It is the consultant's goal to support the client's development, but the client must be accountable. The client organization is what must change, and only actual members of this organization (i.e., the client) can be "experts" of this environment.

During the intervention, the consultant facilitated several sessions to encourage the learning process. Topics ranged from recognizing great leadership to understanding how to become a more effective leader and were intended to help each of the managers improve in the key areas agreed to during the feedback process. As the consultant presented strategies for:

- Being a positive role model for others
- Being a coach and mentor to those you manage
- Providing the right mix of tools and resources to enable the team to achieve its goals the managers actively discussed how to apply these strategies to their organization.

Beyond the management team training, the consultant also continued to work with the individual managers on their personal development plans. Similar to the roles during training, the consultant merely supported the managers' actions, but the managers were responsible for taking the action. To understand the importance of this balanced relationship, consider those managers who did not actively pursue their plans—they did not require dedicated support from the consultant. This proves the point that both parties play a critical role in the process, otherwise the arrangement will not work.

Evaluation

In an informal manner, evaluation occurred during every phase of work during this engagement. For example, the consultant and client co-evaluated the results of the Contracting phase before moving on to Data Gathering and Diagnosis. Does the contract clearly define the scope of the project? If so, are there shared expectations between both parties as to how best to perform the work? If simple questions such as these are not adequately answered, then the individual parties must reconsider whether or not they are ready to move forward.

In addition, the consultant also performed a more formal review of the project. The consultant developed a standard protocol for measuring the success of each activity and then interviewed each of the managers to gather their thoughts and perceptions. Based on these responses, the consultant synthesized the data and presented it back to the client for review. The consultant also presented some basic recommendations for prioritizing future activities based on not only the achievement of previous goals but also the development of a more capable management team. Future scope activities may include developing a training strategy for non-managers or creating a more formal communications plan to share information more regularly across the organization. In essence, this evaluation, then, actually serves to start another iteration of the consulting process, one that begins with more advanced client problems now that the original concerns have been addressed.

Conclusions on an Iterative Process

As the "Tale of the Oversized File Cabinet" alluded, the process an OD consultant follows can be very similar to the process that a master carpenter goes through before taking hammer in hand. First, there are customer desires to be considered, then measurements to be taken, plans to be drafted and revised, and finally wood to be studied and prepared before any true action is ever taken. The consultant who is an "expert" in a particular technique is like the carpenter who can make beautiful and elaborate file cabinets. Both can provide value

to the client, but what happens when the client thinks he or she needs a customized file cabinet (or can be convinced that a customized file cabinet would solve his or problems) when what is really needed is a standard desk?

This issue gets to the core of both action research and OD. Action research and OD are about understanding the real issues and identifying what really needs to be changed. Action research and OD are about providing solutions that address the contributing factors of a problem, not simply providing a solution to the presenting problem, which may or may not be at the core.

Keep in mind that organizations are complex systems, and using a mechanical approach to "fix" a "broken" part rarely creates effective change. In this context, organizations can be thought of as a web of interacting forces, interacting individually and as a whole to produce certain outcomes. Thus, effective change entails exploring these forces and their interactions. Within a single action research cycle (Entry to Evaluation), multiple levels of awareness can and will probably be uncovered. However, it is not uncommon that there are levels of awareness that will only be uncovered in subsequent cycles, as the client's self-awareness increases and the ability to self-reflect and change develops. Thus, action research is most helpful as an iterative process, not as an event.

Action research can be a rather difficult and frustrating process to understand and use effectively. "Yes, I know *about* action research, but what do I *do*?" can be a common question for new practitioners. Understanding the process of and assumptions behind action research can make the difference between being a practitioner of OD and being someone who simply uses typical OD interventions without using the other parts of the process that make up OD. Or, to put it another way, it is like the difference between being a carpenter and being someone who knows how to swing a hammer.

CHAPTER 5

The Organization Development Contract

Marvin Weisbord

IN OD CONSULTING, the contract is central to success or failure. Most other kinds of contracts—employment, service, research, etc.—focus heavily on content, that is, the nature of the work to be performed, the schedule, and the money to change hands. Generally, these issues are negotiated through a proposal, which one party writes and the other accepts or rejects.

The consulting contract most people are familiar with takes two forms:

1. You hire me to study the problem and tell you what to do.
2. You hire me to solve the problem for you.

I call these "expert" consulting contracts. In either case, the quality of the advice and/or the solution is the focus and the *consultant* is a central figure. In OD consulting, the *clients* are central. They hire me to consult while they are working, helping them to achieve a better diagnosis of what is happening and what steps they might take to improve things. This is a form of collaboration which, if successful, helps clients also to achieve better working relationships with others, for example their peers, bosses, and subordinates.

In OD contracting, more so than in other kinds, the *process* by which content issues are pinned down is critical. Unless this negotiation is a model of the consultant's values and

problem-solving behavior, the contract, when it is tested, probably will not stand up. More about testing later. What do I mean by contract? I mean an explicit exchange of expectations, part dialogue and part written document, that clarifies for the consultant and client three critical areas:

1. What each expects to get from the relationship.
2. How much time each will invest, when, and at what cost.
3. The ground rules under which the parties will operate.

What Each Expects

Clients expect change for the better in a situation that is making their lives hard. Such situations usually have three main features:

1. Organizational issues, i.e. people leaving; excessive absenteeism; too high costs; too little budget; unmanageable environmental demands; pressure from above; conflict among individuals or work groups.
2. People problems, i.e., one or more significant relationships are singled out as particular sore spots.
3. Personal dilemma, i.e., whether this job, or this career, is what I really want.

The third component always grows in magnitude in direct proportion to the first two. Clients in a bind do not get much fun out of their work. They long for something simpler, better suited to their strengths, and more consistent with their values. Above all, most clients long for outcomes. They want permanent "change" for the better, with no backsliding. I, on the other hand, see new outcomes as evidence the client is learning a better way of coping. From my point of view the *process* for gathering information, becoming aware of deeper meanings, and making choices is my most important product.

While clients identify difficult situations they want to work on, I keep in mind three levels of improvement they might achieve:

1. Reducing the immediate crisis, e.g., changing structures, policies, procedures, systems, programs, relationships for the better.
2. Learning something about their own coping styles—how they deals with organizational dilemmas and how they might do it better.
3. Learning a process for continually becoming aware and making choices about whatever issue presents itself.

From my point of view, the existing problem is a vehicle for learning more about how to manage organizational life better. I have no preferences for the kinds of problems clients have. From my point of view, one issue will do as well as another. However, clients rarely ask my direct help in cutting costs, reducing absenteeism, raising morale, or improving services. Instead, identifying me mainly with the "people" issue, they nearly always look for guidance in taking swift, painless, self-evidently correct actions toward others who contribute to their misery.

I always ask prospective clients to name what outcomes they hope to achieve by working with me. Here are some typical replies:

- Want others to understand our goals better.

- Better communications, fewer misunderstandings.
- Getting people to shape up or ship out.
- Better meetings—more excitement, more decisions made, higher commitment.

Notice that each of these statements is somewhat abstract, self-evidently "good," and hard to measure. I am reluctant to settle for generalities as adequate statements of a client's expectations. Instead, I push hard on outcomes. What would you see happening that would tell you communications are improving? How will you know when goals are clearer, or morale has gone up? What will people do? Will you be able to watch them do it?

When I push at this level, I get more realistic statements:

- Pete will come to me with his gripes directly instead of going to Fred.
- Deadlines will be taken seriously and met more often.
- In meetings, decisions will be made, actions agreed upon, and names and dates put on them.
- I will understand how to set up the unit and will have agreement on whatever way I decide.
- We will have a new procedure for handling customer complaints.
- I will make a decision whether to keep or fire so-and-so.

These statements are good short-run indicators of change. They are realistic expectations. Are changes like these worth the investment of time and money? Is there enough in it for the clients to go ahead? It is important that they be clear they are choosing to do whatever we do together because it is worth it (rather than because it is this year's panacea or somebody else tried it and liked it). What does each client want personally out of this? Easier life? What does *that* mean? Etc.

I expect some things too. Clients know I work mainly for money and want to be paid on time. However, I try also to indicate some of my secondary motives for working with them. For example, I crave variety. I like learning about and using my skills in various "content" areas—manufacturing and service industries, medicine, law enforcement, public education. I like to try new technologies, to break new theoretical ground, to write and publish my experiences. The chance to do something new raises my incentive with any client. So does a client's ready acceptance of some responsibility for the crisis. If clients are well motivated to work on their problems, so am I—and I tell them so. In doing this, I am trying to say that each of us has a right to some personal benefits from our relationship, apart from any benefits the organization may derive.

Structuring the Relationship: Time and Money

OD, like much of life, is carried forward by a sequence of meetings among people. The central decision in any contract discussion is which people should sit in what room for how long and for what purpose. At some point it is essential to name those people, pick dates, and set a budget. The client has a right to know how much time I will invest in interviewing, or survey sampling, or whatever, and how long our meetings will require. If I need time in between to organize data, I estimate how much. Often the initial contract is diagnostic, to be completed at a face-to-face meeting where the data will be examined, a common diagnosis arrived at, and next steps decided upon.

Always, I work to clarify the costs, time, and money of each next step. Generally, this information will be written down. In addition, there are some things I will and will not do, money aside. I know what these things are and only mention them if the client does on the premise that there is no point in solving a problem I do not have. For instance, I turn down opportunities to work weekends. I will work morning, noon, and night on any scheduled day if necessary. On weekends, my contract is with my family.

I also have a strong value that *when* you work on your organization indicates how important you consider it. People get themselves into crises during the week. If they do not have time to get out during the week, they are never going to get out by working weekends. That makes me the wrong consultant for them. (Incidentally, I have never lost a client because of this policy.)

Ground Rules

Ground rules speak to the process of our relationship. Sometimes I write them down, sometimes not. In any case, I try to get an understanding that includes these explicit agreements:

1. I will supply methods, techniques, theory, etc., to help you understand and work better on your problems. You supply energy, commitment, and share responsibility for success. I do *not* study your problems and recommend expert solutions.
2. Part of my job is to raise sticky issues and push you on them. You have a right to say no to anything you do not want to deal with. If you feel free to say no, I will feel free to push.
3. Tell me if I do something puzzling or irritating and give me permission to tell you the same.
4. I have no special preferences for how you deal with others. Part of my job is to make you aware of what you do and what possible consequences your actions have for me and for the people around you. My job is also to preserve and encourage your freedom of choice about what, if anything, you should do.
5. My client is the whole organization. That means I intend not to be seen as an advocate for anybody's pet ideas, especially ones requiring your special expertise. However, I do advocate a certain process for problem-solving, and recognize that some people oppose my process. I accept that risk.

6. Any information I collect and present will be anonymous. I will never attach names to anything people tell me. However, in certain situations (e.g., team building), I don't *want* confidential information. This means anything you are unwilling for other team members to know, even anonymously.
7. All data belongs to the people who supply it. I will never give or show it to anyone without their permission.
8. Either of us can terminate on 24 hours notice, regardless of contract length, so long as we agree in a face-to-face meeting.
9. We evaluate all events together and make decisions about what to do next.

Contracting, like the seasons, is repetitive and continually renewable. If I have a long term contract (e.g., 4 days a month for a year) I also have a separate contract for each meeting, which I present on a chart pad and discuss at the outset. If I have a contract with bosses to help them build their teams, I need to extend it to each team before we go to work. If I succeed with a team, and some members want to work with *their* teams, I need to negotiate a new deal with the new people. Once, having worked with a team, I found the boss wanting to confront *his* boss. He wanted the whole team to do it with him, with me as consultant. I pointed out that that would require a temporary contract among me, him, and his boss. He set up a dinner meeting the night before the confrontation, and his boss and I made a one-day contract which stood up very well on the next morning.

In short, I'm never finished contracting. Each client meeting requires that I reexamine the contract. Does it cover everybody I'm working with? Is it clear what we are doing now? And why?

The Making of a Contract

Moreover, contracting—while it deals ostensibly with content issues—has a process side that is crucial to its success. Consider, in some detail, where and how an OD contract is made. Such contracts usually begin with a phone call or letter. Somebody has heard about what I did somewhere else. They wonder whether I can do it for (or with or to) them. If I receive a letter, I respond with a phone call to the writer. If clients call first, I return their calls at a time when I can spend 10 minutes or more discussing what they want and whether or not it makes sense to meet. This initial contact is crucial to any contract. Each of us is trying over the phone to decide whether we like one another well enough to proceed. I try not to prejudge the conversation. I want a face-to-face meeting *if* there's a chance of getting a solid contract.

Here are some questions running through my mind:

1. How open are callers with me? Me with them?
2. Is the caller window shopping, calling several consultants to find the "best deal" (whatever that means)? Does this person really want me? Perhaps—as is sometimes the case—potential clients don't know what they want. If that is so, I can consult with them on the phone, helping them clarify what they seek.
3. To which problem am I the solution? How do they name the issue?
4. What do they see as the solution? A workshop? A meeting? A series of meetings? Magic?
5. Is this person's mind made up? Has he or she done a self-diagnosis and prescribed something which I'm to administer?
6. Is there a budget? Is it adequate to the expectations? Will it be worth my while to invest in a face-to-face meeting? I don't talk price on the phone, but do test whether a budget exists or could be got together. If the answer is no, I decide not to pursue it further.
7. Assume a budget, and willingness on the client's part and mine to go forward. We need a meeting. Should anybody else be

there? Who? Is the caller in a position to enter into a contract? If not, who is? A boss? Can that person make the meeting? Is there another consultant I want to involve? If so, I ask whether I can bring an associate.

I end the phone call by clarifying that each of us intends to explore further whether there is a fit between the kinds of things my potential client needs help on and the skills and experience I have. I am investing up to a day at no fee. (If there are travel expenses involved, I test whether the client will cover those.) At the end of that day, each of us will know whether to go further.

First Meeting

I arrive, greet my prospective client(s) and introduce myself and perhaps an associate. We have coffee and exchange pleasantries. Each of us is deciding, silently, privately, perhaps unconsciously, how much we like the other. We look for cues. We give cues. Early on, we get down to Business.

The content issues might include:

1. Our backgrounds: My potential clients need to know enough about me to feel I can help before they will put out major problems.
2. Issues bothering client system: Are they symptomatic of other things, which are not being discussed. I always ask for examples in terms of observable behavior. "Communications" or "decision-making" are not issues you can see, feel, or pin down. Who needs to talk to whom? Why? What do they do now? What do people do when they disagree? What patterns of behavior do the people present see in the organization?
3. What changes would the people I am talking to like to see? What things would they observe happening that would tell them they are getting desired outcomes? This step in naming outcomes is important in

reducing the level of fantasy around OD and what I can do.
4. What first event would be appropriate to moving the system in the desired direction? Nearly always, this event should be diagnostic. It should be an activity that will heighten the awareness of the people involved about how the issues they raise are seen by others in the system, such as colleagues, subordinates, customers, students, and peers. If the system is ready, the budget exists, my reading of the client's willingness to proceed is good, and I am optimistic, I may propose workshop activity based on interviews. Sometimes I propose that the workshop start with interviews of each person as a first step in agenda building (okay if no more than 10 or 12 attend). Sometimes, it makes more sense to consult to a work group within the framework of their regular weekly or monthly meetings. Sometimes, a survey questionnaire provides a database for a diagnostic meeting. Whatever the event, we need a schedule, a place to meet, and a division of labor for organizing materials, sending out the agenda, and completing other preparations. Sometimes these things can be decided in the first meeting. Sometimes I agree to write a formal proposal and proceed from there. Always I try to close on the next step—what I will do, what the client will do, and by what date.

The above considerations focus mainly on content. However, there are several process issues surrounding this meeting which I am continually working on too:

1. First among these is, "Do I like this person?" If not a spark of fondness, or warmth, or empathy, then what am I feeling? Annoyance? Frustration? Wariness? Can I find *something* to like, respect, or admire about the other person? Until I do and until others find in me what they need, I think our work on issues, possible next steps, logistics, etc., is largely fictional. It is

a way of using the task at hand to help us get greater clarity about our relationship. Any time I am uncertain about a relationship I believe my contract is in jeopardy, no matter what fine words are spoken or written on paper. Each time the relationship question is resolved, a little spark jumps. I watch for it.

2. The client's depth of commitment is an issue for me. Does this person really want to change things? Does this person accept responsibility—at least a little bit—for the way things are? If somebody says, "I want you to change *them,*" *I* say, "Okay, but how open are you to changing?" Does the client pull back, hem and haw? Or does the client smile and admit the possibility? How open is this person to understanding how what he or she does affects other people? I value organizations improving themselves by learning together to do things better with each other. I try to test how my client feels about that.

3. Part of client commitment is resources. Clients find money to do things they want to do. If money seems to be an insurmountable problem, I look to some other process issue—anxiety about failure, a boss who's negative about OD, fear of opening up "destructive issues," etc. Helping the client get in touch with these possibilities, if I can, is valuable for both of us, whether I work with this person again or not. How do I do it? By asking such questions as: What is the risk? What's the worst thing that could happen? How much exposure can you stand? I also ask what good things might happen, and whether the possible outcomes are worth the price.

In some ways, OD is like playing the market. Every intervention is a calculated risk. There are no guarantees. Clients will have problems no matter what they do. So will I. The question I continually confront is: Which problems would you *rather* have? The ones you have now? Or the ones you *will* have if you try to solve the ones you have now? Once in a

while, potential clients decide they would rather live with what they have. I support this insight. It is better that both of us know it sooner rather than later.

More often this process leads to greater clarity and commitment on both our parts to make successful. I want to find out what is real, what the environment will support, what is possible in this relationship, and then learn how to live with the situation. Of course I want to sell my services. I want to try new interventions. More than that, I want to be successful. I am learning to spot conditions under which I fail. An unclear contract ranks high on the list.

I resist entering untenable contracts, for I know deep down that they are like airplanes without fuel. No matter how beautiful they look, they will not fly. The fuel for an OD contract is (1) client commitment, (2) a good relationship between us, and (3) a clear structure to that relationship, symbolized by our ability to agree on what services I will perform, when, and at what costs in time and money.

Structuring the Relationship

Item 3 brings us to the specific first activity. It has several criteria:

1. It is responsive to the client's perceived problem. Clients must see it as helping them gain greater clarity, insight, and control over whatever issues are bugging *them*. It is not based on my need to use any particular trick in my bag.

2. It names the people who will come together, when, for how long, and why. "Why" is generally the client's to answer. If a written statement is needed, I may help shape the language. If others balk, it's up to the client to tell others what we are doing and why. I will tell them what I see as my contract with them. It is never my job to tell people why they are there.

3. It involves some form of diagnosis. That means some systematic information is collected that will heighten the clients' aware-

ness and enlarge their freedom of choice. Sometimes this information fits a conceptual scheme, which I make explicit. (Author's note: In those days, I often used the "Six-Box Model" to good effect.) Always, I seek to collect data in such a way that the people who supply the information recognize it as critical to their lives together when I collate it and hand it back. The more interpreting or categorizing I do in advance, the less likely this is to happen. I ensure confidentiality and anonymity. Interpretation, I try to make clear, will result when people who supplied the information meet face to face to assign meaning to it. I try always to specify how much time people must give, what kinds of questions I will ask, and what will become of the answers. This structuring reduces anxiety and sets up reasonable expectations.

4. I establish that part of the contract is mutual feedback. I expect clients to confront me openly on my behavior when it doesn't make sense, to question anything I do, and to point out to me words or behavior that violate their sense of what's appropriate. In return, I expect to be open with them. It is around this clause, I think, that all contracts are tested sooner or later. In a workshop the test may come in the form of protest that the activities are irrelevant to the agenda and a waste of time. In a one-to-one relationship the test may be something I did or said that really irritated the client. It takes some risk to let me know. In opening the issue, the client is checking to see whether I'm as good at handling deeds as I am at manipulating words.

I define testing the contract as an emotion-provoking exchange between me and the client in some risky situation. As a result our relationship will become more "real," more truly experimental, more like the action research model that I advocate as an appropriate way to live. I do not expect the burden to rest entirely on the client. I test, too, whenever the time seems right, usually around some-

thing the client is doing which affects our relationship.

Once, I noticed a client would continually express disappointment in others and told him I was worried that one day—if not already—he was going to feel the same way about me. He owned up to the possibility and assured me I would be the first to know, which, when the time came, I was. The confrontation deepened our relationship and strengthened the contract. It might have ended it, too.

I welcome ending a contract explicitly by having it tested and found wanting. Better a clean death than lingering agony. It is time to test (and maybe end) a contract when:

- The client keeps putting things off.
- Agreements are made and forgotten (by either side).
- The consultant appears to have a higher emotional stake in the outcomes than the client does.
- The consultant asks for events, or activities, which intensify the feeling of crisis and pressure without much prospect for eventual relief.
- Clients look to the consultant to do things which they should be doing, such as arranging meetings, sending out agendas, carrying messages, and getting other people to do what they want them to do.
- The client is doing better and really doesn't need outside help.

For me, a crisp, clean ending remains desirable, but sometimes elusive. Going over 14 major contracts during the last four years, I find that nine ended with no "unfinished business," three ended because the boss lacked commitment to continue, and two because organizational changes left a leadership vacuum and me uncertain who the client was. Where the boss lacked commitment, the intended follow-up meetings never took place, and I let things alone, feeling, I suppose, relatively little commitment myself. In the cases of organizational changes, it became plain the interim leadership lacked either incentive or authority to keep up the contract, and I had other fish to fry.

It seems to me contracts have a natural life. Organizations eventually outgrow or tire of or cease needing a particular consultant, and vice versa. It's better for me and my client that we recognize explicitly when it's time to part.

Postscript 2011

I wrote the foregoing nearly forty years ago after a decade as a manager who used consultants and four years of consulting on my own. The world has since become a top spinning faster and the systems I work with infinitely more diverse. I was writing during the early years of a gender revolution. The original piece called everybody "he" despite my having men and women clients. Larry Porter, then ODP editor, and I could not figure out what to do. I disliked calling everybody "he or she." Worse still was the jarring distraction of "s/he," a literary contortion that had a mercifully short half life. By the mid-1970s we learned to use plural nouns, referring to "people," "clients" and "they" unless a specific person was intended. I re-edited the piece to reflect that usage.

I am struck while rereading this decades later by a few features. One is its problem focus. Today people think more in systems terms—interactions among multiple forces. Many also tend to accentuate the positive,

contracting to build on strengths rather than fix what is broken. Back then, many of us used crisis and conflict as the basis for OD and emphasized improving relationships as the linchpin. Team building and training were major tools. Yet, as I learned even then working with Paul Lawrence in medical schools, many "personality" problems could be traced to structural issues—conflict over goals, deadlines, division of labor, policy, and procedure. Give people more control of their own work and watch relationships improve.

Nonetheless, the central issues of OD contracting—task and process—remain pretty much the same. It is still a relationship business. In 40 years I never got a contract by responding to an RFP (Request for Proposal) unless I already knew the people. After a while, I learned to tell prospective clients shopping for the "best" (intervention, consultant, whatever) to talk to others first and come back to me if they could not find someone they liked. OD practice is a boutique affair. The product is you. Nobody else can do what you do. The best book on this subject is my erstwhile partner Peter Block's *Flawless Consulting*. If you want to learn more about OD's antecedents, its cousins, aunts, and derivatives, check out the 25th Anniversary edition of *Productive Workplaces* (Jossey-Bass, 2012). In it, I describe what I did and what I learned during 50 years of helping clients jockey their unstable hybrids of economics, technology, and people.

CHAPTER 6

The Seven Deadly Sins of OD Consulting

Pitfalls to Avoid in the Consulting Practice

Connie A. Freeman

I DON'T KNOW WHY the subject of sin appeals to me, but I always seem to notice articles written about it. Last year I read an article in the *Harvard Business Review* by Andrall Pearson, former president of PepsiCo, entitled "Corporate Redemption and the Seven Deadly Sins" (1992). Pearson's thoughts about how to change American organizations to be globally competitive made an impression on me. Pearson believes that "many change programs fail because they do not address the root cause of the problem (in corporate America): The negative, risk averse, bureaucratic work environments that flourished in the decades of easy growth but that now undermine the company's competitive performance" (Pearson, 1992, p. 66). He talked about management reinventing the "soft side of their organizations . . . the values and goals toward which people strive, the ways people approach their jobs, the pace of the work in the organization, how people work together" (*Ibid.*, p. 66). This is precisely where I believe OD can make a contribution.

Several months ago as a colleague and I were writing an article about the relationship between TQM and OD in managing change, I ran across another piece on sin written by Booz Allen & Hamilton (1991) that outlined the seven deadly sins of total quality management. As I read this booklet, I remember thinking about what sins apply to the consulting profession. I'd like to share with you some of my consulting experiences—successful and sometimes not so successful—in the context of the seven deadly sins of OD consulting (see Figure 6.1).

1. Change Without Direction—The Flight to Nowhere

One of the challenges I have frequently faced is working with clients who want things to be different—to change—but have, at best, only a vague idea where they want to go. What is the desired state? One of the most important aspects of the consulting process is to work with the client to determine the desired outcomes—the purpose of the change effort. Otherwise, you truly are on a flight to nowhere, and you may even end up in a worse place than you started. Furthermore, change efforts should begin with a clearly defined business problem.

Recently, the Medical Director and the Administrative Director of a 200-person laboratory department met with me and said, "We want to make some changes in the lab. We know there are some opportunities to improve things but we don't know what they are and

FIGURE 6.1 The Seven Deadly Sins of OD Consulting

1
Change without Direction—Flight to Nowhere

2
One Size Fits all

3
The Consultant as Surrogate Leader

4
Symptoms vs. Causes

5
Only Looking Up

6
Change as a Separate Activity

7
Focus on Self

---

we don't know where to begin." After some discussion about past history and recent leadership changes, we agreed that the first step was to determine the desired outcomes. We engaged in some visioning and scenario building activities to help us focus on the future and tie into the hospital's strategic goals. We then examined the present state to see where we were as compared with where we wanted to be. Only then did we have a sense of how to proceed in managing the change process because now we had some specific "targets."

Another example relates to a financial institution where, as a member of the Board of Directors, I facilitated a strategic planning process to help us determine what our key objectives—short term and long range—should be based on our assessment of the future and our members' needs. Since so many of our objectives were interdependent (i.e.,

share drafts, ATMS, new computer system), it was critical that we identify our desired state before action planning could begin.

2. One Size Fits All

Organization development is not the same thing as training or management development. Most training programs are designed to appeal to a mass audience and the program, once designed, is virtually the same for everyone. OD requires developing a relationship with the client and partnering with the client rather than working for them or doing something to them.

As an example, I've conducted team building events with numerous departments over the past few years, from the entire staff of a nursing unit to an information systems department to the management team of a surgery department. On each project, I've relied on a broad team-building framework based on a Goals-Roles-Procedures-Relationships model (Plovnick, Fry & Burke, 1982), but the process intervention was very different. In the surgery department, we spent several two-hour sessions doing some preliminary work before the group members accepted that we needed a greater block of time if we were going to accomplish our goals. Based on their recommendation, we spent two days off site working on team issues, primarily role clarification and communication issues. This was significant in that one operating room had to be closed down, additional staffing and overtime had to be arranged, and all needed the approval and cooperation of the surgeons, the Operations Vice President, and the entire department.

Team building with one nursing unit began with sessions with the charge nurses and supervisors, and then involved the entire 60-person staff. The process was facilitated in two groups because in a 24-hour-a-day, 365-days-a-year hospital setting, there are no after work or days off times. You have to be creative in applying interventions in OD. In the past, some people have argued that OD doesn't work in healthcare, but many others have found ways to apply OD to support change efforts in hospitals (Johnson & Boss, 1992).

Different situations, organizations, desired outcomes, and so on, require different approaches to OD. You may rely on the same theory, model, or specific intervention but need to tailor the process to the situation. Adopting a "one-size-fits-all" orientation to change efforts may facilitate the consultant's role but it may not adequately meet the clients' needs.

3. The Consultant as Surrogate Leader

There are times when a client truly lacks leadership abilities, and the desire to have the consultant "take charge" is quite appealing. In these instances, the consultant can be very vulnerable and may or may not be able to affect desired results. In 1991, a large service department was experiencing serious employee relations problems as evidenced in the organization's annual employee opinion survey. I was asked to support that department in improving the work environment and was told that my assistance was welcomed by the leaders in that division. I met with the Vice President and the department director, both of whom were very cooperative and interested in working with me. Unfortunately, as we began, I soon discovered that the department head had minimal management skills and was little more than a figurehead with little direct involvement or influence. In addition, the Vice President was "a very nice gentleman" but had not demonstrated leadership. To make matters worse, the supervisors were also considerably weak and ineffective leaders. In essence, these individuals were the basis for most of the problems, and there I was trying to facilitate changes at the source of the difficulties. While there was considerable awareness among the group about changes they needed to make, the problem-solving and action planning sessions were difficult and follow through was questionable. It was not until the Vice President retired and another individual assumed this position that the desired changes began to occur. The new Vice President provided the necessary leadership and guidance to direct the change effort. With training, team building, and employee participation in problem-solving and decision-making, the work climate improved dramatically in one year. In 1992, employee opinion survey results were considerably improved, and follow-up focus groups supported the positive changes. Ultimately, consulting is only as effective as the clients with whom you work. We can't work alone and sometimes the client doesn't have the skills to make necessary changes.

4. Symptoms vs. Causes

Sometimes it may appear that "everything that can go wrong ... has." This is when data collection and analysis processes are so important to help determine what are the primary issues and concerns and where can the most gains be realized. Some issues may appear trivial and/or are merely symptoms of deeper concerns. A medical records department had been experiencing major problems over the past several years. Absenteeism and turnover were high, chart completion time was growing longer and longer, physician satisfaction was declining, and employee relations were poor. At first glance, the department head and supervisor believed that the problems stemmed from employees with "poor attitudes, low skills, etc." and that changes in salaries, job descriptions, and work requirements were needed "to attract the right kind of employees." Based on initial data gathering and analysis, however, it appeared that the primary cause of these related problems was work practices that did not effectively and efficiently support the tasks. The processes that were in place to complete the tasks were inappropriate, redundant, time wasting, and served to frustrate the most dedicated and capable of employees. By refocusing on the work processes and roles rather than people's attitudes, and by involving staff in process improvement activities, significant gains were made.

5. Only Looking Up

When moving forward, if you only look up, you are more likely to stumble and fall. One of the surest ways for OD consultants to "stumble" is to involve only the management and executive level in the change process or to "take their word" that they know what is needed for the department. While management may be the primary client contact, consulting frequently involves entire departments, divisions, or organizations. To affect long-term sustainable change, people from all levels within the work unit must be involved not only in the behavioral changes, but in the planning, design, and implementation of change. Participation, empowerment, and "buy-in" are all terms that represent the difference between long-term success and failure.

I remember once proposing that a task force of employees and first-line supervisors be established to analyze preliminary flow diagrams of work processes and recommend changes. Several people were surprised at the suggestion to involve staff in such a decision-making process—historically all decisions concerning how work was completed was made at the manager level without employee input even though employees had attempted on numerous occasions to point out redundancies, weaknesses, and suggest improvements. By encouraging management to appreciate the importance of employee participation in not only designing but also accepting more appropriate work processes, desired outcomes were more quickly and easily achieved and sustained.

6. Change as a Separate Activity

Change programs are not "magic bullets" and managing change is not a separate activity. Rather, it is a leadership and management style that enables organizations to be successful in dynamic environments. In healthcare in the United States, for example, the comprehensive reform that is taking place "will favor managers who can manage resources, particularly human resources, in a rapidly changing environment" (O'Donnell, 1993, p. 68). OD consulting can be viewed as an organizational job aid. Schein's (1988) description of process consultation refers to collaborative client-consultant relationships, in which consultants function as facilitators and help clients learn to improve their internal problem-solving processes. Consultants should work *with,* not *for,* clients to help them learn how to be successful in dynamic environments. We work in partnership not just to solve problems, make decisions, or manage team difficulties, but to learn useful problem-solving and decision-making processes and to acquire skills to support team development, and so on. My aim is to move toward the client relying less and less on the consultant over time until the client feels independent. This is not always easy or welcomed because sometimes clients want consultants to "fix it" or "change it" or "take care of it" and then call them when the work is done. The challenge in these instances lies in the ability to help the client see that s/he is an integral player and that the consulting expertise is only as worthwhile as the client enables it to be.

Harvard Business Review published an article in 1990 entitled "Why Change Programs Don't Produce Change" (Beer, Eisenstat, & Spector). Several of the authors' statements have stayed with me, such as their assertion that "an approach to change based on task alignment. .. is the most effective way to achieve enduring change" (p. 159). The basic message is that successful change efforts focus on the work itself and not abstractions like "participation" or "culture." Another premise is that "individual behavior is powerfully shaped by the organizational roles that people play. The most effective way to change behavior, therefore, is to put people into a new organizational context, which imposes new roles, responsibilities, and relationships on them"

(Ibid., p. 159). In other words, OD efforts may best be focused on changing the environment in which people work rather than the people themselves.

7. Focus on Self

Finally, have you ever taken your well-reasoned, planned approach to a particular meeting and tossed it aside? If you haven't, you may want to ask yourself if you may be missing something in the process because you've planned too carefully and completely. I've experienced consultants who are so wedded to a particular technique and so thorough in their preparation that they often miss what's happening right before them. Perhaps the worst of all sins for consultants is to be too focused on what we do—on the self—that we do not see what is taking place in the present. A college professor of mine once told me to let the research question guide the methodology rather than forcing a methodology on a research question. That's good advice that I've carried into my approach to consulting. Consultants should not force favorite or familiar interventions onto the problems but rather from an analysis of the situation and desired outcomes, apply appropriate change management techniques. Having said this, I believe a thorough knowledge of theories, models, and process interventions is absolutely necessary, and utilizing various assessment instruments and diagnostic tools is appropriate. What is less appropriate is when we limit our range of knowledge and rely on the same strategy and approach in every consulting situation. Flexibility, adapt-ability, and creativity are among a consultant's most useful characteristics.

Conclusion

Obviously, my OD consulting experience has been primarily from an internal perspective. I believe, however, that my philosophy and approach is applicable in an external consulting environment as well. These seven sins are equally deadly in both consulting situations, and are pitfalls I try to avoid. Moving into an external consulting role, I'm certain there are many new "lessons" that await me. Hopefully my experiences thus far have prepared me.

References

Beer, M., Eisenstat, E., & Spector, B. (1990, Nov.-Dec). Why change programs don't produce change. *Harvard Business Review,* 158–166.

Johnson, J. A., & Boss, R. W. (1992). Organization development interventions in health services: Looking back and moving forward. *Organization Development Journal,* 10(1), 73–78.

O'Donnell, K. P. (1993, June 20). The last word. *Hospitals & Health Networks,* 68.

Pearson, A. (1992, May-June). Corporate redemption and the seven deadly sins. *Harvard Business Review,* 65–75.

Plovnick, M. S., Fry, R. S., & Burke, W. W. (1982). *Organization development: Exercises, cases, and readings.* Boston, MA: Little, Brown.

Schein, E. H. (1988). *Process consultation, Volume I: Its role in organization development* (2nd ed.). Reading, MA: Addison-Wesley Publishing.

CHAPTER 7

Notes Towards a Better Understanding of Process

An Essay

Edgar H. Schein

MANY YEARS AGO I learned about "process" from my long hours in Training Groups at Bethel, Maine, workshops. In my consulting, I felt myself focusing on process issues in groups and, in the meantime, I had learned a great deal about interpersonal dynamics, leading to several coauthored books on these "processes." In my later work on Career Dynamics, I studied the socialization "process" intensely and, most recently, the studies of Organizational Culture have again led to a focus not on structure or typologies of culture, but on cultural dynamics and "process."

In spite of this persistent focus on "process," when a layperson asks me what I mean by "process" I am still tongue tied and inarticulate. I suspect that many of my colleagues in the OD field feel the same way. Process is obvious, and we have all learned to deal with it, but it is remarkably hard to define and focus on in such a way that the layman really understands not only what it is but also why it is so very important. In this essay I want to take a stab at clarifying this mysterious yet ubiquitous concept.

The easy answer, of course, is that process is not the *what* but the *how*. It is not the final decision made by a group or individual, but the way in which that decision was reached. It is not the formal structure of an organization, but the actual behaviors that occur within that structure, what sociologists might call the "informal organization." Having said that, I am not satisfied that I have given the reader an answer that helps very much. If one wants to study *how* an organization made a decision or *how* the informal organization really works, we still do not know what to look for or why it is so important to understand.

What Is the "Essence" of Process?

Sequences of Events

One essence of process is that it is series of events that *occur over some period of time*. The "What" can be observed at a single point in time; the "How" requires observation or historical reconstruction over a period of time. One of the subtle and difficult issues in developing a "theory" or "model" of processes is to decide over what period of time to observe or how far back in history to go to get a sense of what really happened and why. This is the problem of unraveling immediate causes from ultimate causes. In each consultation we engage in we must make some decisions about how far back to go in trying to explain something or how long to observe something before we think we understand it. As far as I know, we do not clear criteria that would guide us in making this decision have in the OD field.

A good example of this kind of longitudinal process analysis is Forrester's concept of Systems Dynamics as propounded by Senge (1990), Sterman (2000) and others from MIT's Systems Dynamics Group. In a powerful exercise called The Beer Game, participants learn that a series of seemingly logical decisions of how much beer to order in terms of customer demand, can lead over time into a glut of unsalable beer unless each store learns what the sequential interactions actually do. One can show participants how their seemingly logical decisions did not take into account an understanding of others' reactions that produce ultimately dysfunctional results.

But one can further this process analysis by asking why participants come into the game with certain cognitive biases in the first place as Sterman and his team are doing to examine how managers think. In principle, then, one could study childhood education processes, occupational socialization processes, as well as the immediate systems dynamics that occur in the game.

Similarly one of the most powerful things I learned in the T-groups was how norms that were quite strong after say four to six hours of meeting could not be explained unless one carefully reconstructed the events that occurred in the first hour or two. Lets say that we observe after a couple of days that the group has a very strong leader whose suggestions are treated virtually as orders. No one speaks up in opposition even though members after the meeting will say that they disagreed. How did this state of affair arise? How did the norm form that "we do not challenge our leader"? If we have learned from the above discussion that "process" is about dynamic sequences we can probably recall or reconstruct what may have happened. I have seen such sequences frequently in groups and they go somewhat as follows:

Person A early in the life of the group asserts herself by making several suggestions of what the group should do.

Person B disagrees.

Person C reaffirms what A has suggested.

Person D supports C and A

Person A (being a good consensus tester) says: Ok, does anyone disagree?

No one says anything

Person A says: Ok this is what we will do then

Somewhat later, Person A again makes a suggestion

Person E has some doubts

Person C thinks A's suggestion is a good idea

Person A says, "what do some of the rest of you think"

Person F voices some doubts

Person A answers them

Person D supports A's suggestion

No one else says anything

Person A says: Its agreed then, lets go ahead

At this point the observer of this group process would be able to formulate a couple of hypotheses about what is going on. One hypothesis would be that a coalition is forming between A, C and D. To check this, the observer needs to wait for more examples of what happens when A makes a suggestion. Another hypothesis would be that a norm is gradually building that A is the "leader" and her ideas should be supported. She has vocal support and the rest of the group is silent, so B and F might legitimately conclude that the group has accepted A as the leader and they might as well accept it too. So the next time A makes a suggestion, B and F remain silent even if they disagree.

To test this hypothesis the observer needs to find more examples and watch what happens. Note that the inferences here are based not on projections or speculations of what is going on intra-psychically but on observed patterns of behavior that occur over time and that repeat themselves. Note, however, that if it were important to decipher why this group ended up with one leader, one might also have to go back farther in time and determine what some of the characteristics were of the members of the group, how the group was chosen, and potentially other historical factors that would only surface later.

Interactions Among Components

A *second* defining characteristic or "essence" of process is that it focuses us on *interactions* between components of a *system,* whether those be components within the head, or inter-actions among the members of a group, or inter-organizational interaction. As the above example illustrated, to explain the final state of leadership in this group one had to observe how the actual interactions occurred and what their consequences appeared to be. Process almost always deals with systemic characteristics because the events that occur over time occur within a context, never in isolation.

Process analysis thus automatically requires us to think systemically, both in terms of the many components that act at one moment in time and in terms of the temporal sequences that make up a temporal system. In the group example above, one system is the group, but another system is a given individual's pattern of behavior over a given period of time. Process analysis requires us to be able to see both of these systems.

Invisible Forces

A *third* characteristic of process, not necessarily an "essence" however, is that it is often *invisible.* In the Beer Game and in many other simulations designed to acquaint people with human processes the actual moves people make are deliberately made public and what people are thinking about those moves are also made public. In real life both the moves and the reasons for them may be hard or even impossible to observe. In the T-group example above, I tried to show what was explicit and observable, and also to speculate about the implied hidden meaning of those observables. The implicit responses could only be inferred and tested by watching how new behavior evolved.

It is this characteristic of process, its invisibility that creates a need for "process consul-tants" because the participants in the process may not be able to decipher what is happening (Schein, 1999). One way of defining the role of the consultant is that his or her function is to "uncover," to make visible things that are initially repressed, suppressed, or just out of awareness. Once things are visible, the client is in a position to act on the insight, or to work with the consultant to consider new options. This situation leads directly to the fourth characteristic.

Process Observation Is an Intervention

A *fourth* characteristic of process that leads directly to one of the central assumptions of *Process Consultation* (Schein, 1999) is that if one is going to observe it rather than histori-cally reconstruct it, one cannot make the observation without influencing the system. In other words, the presence of the observer is itself a process intervention and must be taken into account. The consultant is one of the interacting parts of the system and is therefore responsible for considering his or her own role in that system.

The same logic applies if the historical reconstruction is made with interviews or questionnaires. Doing the investigation, gath-ering the data, is a process that influences per-ceptions, feelings, and thoughts and therefore becomes an intervention in its own right. In principle the only kind of reconstruction that would not be subject to this principle would be working only with formal records.

The implications of this last point are enormous. It means that all of the models of consultation that differentiate "data gather-ing" and "diagnosis" from "intervention" are either ignoring their impact during the alleged "data gathering" stage or are denying their own role in the system. We should learn from the work of psychiatrists who work with Intra-Individual Processes, that the interac-tion with the patient which inevitably pro-duces "transference" and "counter-transfer-ence" feelings is the set of components in the situation that is richest in potential for creating therapeutic change. In the same way, the process consultant working in a group or with a larger system can produce the best results for the client by noting how his or her own interaction with the client system is both diagnostically and therapeutically central. Diagnosis and intervention are one and the same process especially when we are dealing with human systems.

If we take this point of view seriously, we must develop criteria for judging the impact of our own moment to moment behavior. We cannot imagine ourselves to be "just gathering some initial data" when we ask our client a question in the first five minutes of our meeting. We have to imagine ourselves from the beginning as an intervener, and decide how every thing we say or do can be geared to being helpful. We have to realize that from the moment of our first contact with the client we are building a relationship which includes building in the mind of the client an image of who we are, what we do, how we do it, and so on. In this sense we are creating process as well as observing it.

Processes Change with Human System Level

A *fifth* and final characteristic of process is that its nature changes as it is scaled up from intra-individual to inter-personal, group, and inter-group process. Intra-psychic processes have traditionally been the domain of psychologists and psychiatrists. They are the experts on these processes and we have more than enough theories of how things work inside the head and in our conscious and unconscious. My experience as I moved into Training Groups was that these practitioners, trained as they were in individual counseling and therapy, were remarkably blind to what I observed in the group context. The exceptions to this generalization were, of course, the family and group therapists.

Group processes add new dimensions for two reasons. First, in a group there are actor/audience effects. Second, groups often exist in the first place to solve particular problems and measure their own "health" by their degree of problem solving success or task accomplishment. By actor/audience effects I mean that the interpersonal processes that occur among a few members of the group are observed and judged by other members, and, therefore influence the behavior of these other members even though they may not have spoken at all.

Because the process field is different and more complex in groups, the interventions that consultants make when dealing with two or more people have to take into account these more complex force-fields. Even if we think we understand fairly well what goes on in the head of each individual, based on our projections of our own psychic experience, we cannot infer without a fair amount of observation and interaction what may actually be going on between two or more other people. The family therapist Edwin Friedman (1985) points out very cogently that the only relationship we can change is the one between others and ourselves. Trying to change the relationship between others presumes insight into a force field that is probably impossible to define clearly enough to know how to alter it.

Groups that have specific tasks can typically be observed at two levels of process-how they go about accomplishing their tasks and how they go about building and maintaining their group. Most groups exist within larger social systems so one can also observe how the group maintains its relationship to its environmental contexts.

Inter-group processes add still more dimensions of process—the dynamics of inter-group cooperation and competition, the processes that accompany winning and losing, the dynamics of gaining and maintaining power in a complex organizational field, and so on. Finally, on can observe at each of these levels the growth of cultural assumptions, the evolution of culture, and the dynamics of culture change (Schein, 1992, 1999).

Summary

Process is about interacting forces acting over time. Process is about the "dynamics" of human affairs. Process is about forces acting out of awareness and under the surface of things. Process is your own moment to moment behavior and the consequences of that behavior. When all is said and done, process is life in that life is forever a movement forward among the many forces that are always acting within us and among us. Process happens. The choice for us as consultants or just plain human beings is whether or not to become more aware of processes at all levels and begin to own the consequences of our own processes.

References

Friedman, E. H. (1985). *Generation to generation.* New York, NY: Guildford Press, 1985.

Schein, E.H. (1992). *Organizational culture and leadership* (2nd ed.). San Francisco, CA: Jossey Bass.

Schein, E.H. (1999). *Process consultation revisited: Building the helping relationship.* Reading, MA: Addison-Wesley-Longman.

Schein, E.H. (1999). *The corporate culture survival guide.* San Francisco, CA: Jossey-Bass.

Senge, P. (1990). *The fifth discipline.* New York, NY: Doubleday Currency.

Sterman, J. (2000). *Business dynamics systems Thinking and modeling for a complex world.* Boston, MA: McGraw-Hill.

CHAPTER 8

The Consultant as Process Leader

Jane Moosbruker

IN MY MORE THAN 15 years as an OD consultant, I often served as a process consultant to small groups attempting to accomplish one or more tasks. This role has always been problematic for me. Team Building, data collection and feedback, facilitating change efforts, third part consultation to conflict situations, even helping to improve intergroup relations have always seemed clearer, and therefore easier.

What I actually *do* as process consultant to a task team has changed over the years. It has moved in the direction of being more concrete, more direct, and more action oriented. I think of this as "working the process." My behavior contrasts, however, with the model I believe I was taught and the only model I have ever actually read about (Schein, 1969, 1987), which I will refer to as "traditional process consultation."

For the purposes of this article, "traditional process consultation" is defined as helping a small task group to learn enough about process so its members can manage an effective group process by themselves and will no longer need a consultant. This is accomplished by being a facilitator, not an expert, that is, you do not tell them what to do; even suggestions are rare. Instead you ask them to share their own observations about the group's process, adding your observations sometimes, depending on the importance of what they may be missing and on their readiness to hear it.

An example of a helpful initial intervention in traditional process consultation: "Let's go back over the meeting and see if we can reconstruct what we did the last couple of hours" (Schein, 1987). Schein does add, "Provided there is time to do it." That is just the point. In my experience working with organizational groups, there *is not* time to do it for many different reasons. Most often the group's primary focus is on task accomplishments, not on learning about process. The initiating client may want the group to learn, but is focused on success at the task. The consultant's role is perceived by most group members as helping them do it right the first time, not learning how to do it themselves. They often have enough money to keep you around to help with the process. Most important, they are under great pressure to produce.

Nor do content oriented groups take to process naturally. Unless their background was in the behavioral sciences, the groups I have worked with have invariably found it very difficult to look at their own process. After a few process observations, the group would return to the content, often without knowing that that had happened. Trying to keep the focus in process, my agenda, not theirs, was often exhausting.

Further, I think that the traditional model of process consultation to a task group is basically a clinical model. By that I mean, in part, that it is the old doctor-patient model, but with the emphasis on diagnosis rather than on giving expert advice. It has a particularly psychiatric flavor in that the major goal is to avoid dependency of a sick patient (group) on a healthy but busy doctor (consultant). There is also an expectation that the client will be defensive, not listening to or denying "correct" observation by the consultant.

I believe another role has already emerged and requires articulation. I would call it "process leader" to capture the notion that it is an action-oriented role, where the person is "working the process" more than consulting to the process. I am also aware of some dangers inherent in playing this role, and will address them after more definition.

The traditional process consultation role to a small task team may have a place with the stable management team, which believes it has time to learn about group process in order to build itself into a fully productive team. As we move away from this kind of stability in organizations I think OD practitioners will be increasingly pressured into taking more active roles.

My conversations with colleagues while preparing to write about these ideas support the notion that many of us are already operating as "process leaders" for our clients. However, I think the need exists to articulate explicitly this perhaps not-so-new role.

Forces Influencing the Development of a Process Leader Role

The need for someone to "work the process" comes in part from increasing demands on organizations due to rapidly changing conditions in their external environments. These changes include global factors, such as escalating international competition, the small-world phenomenon that causes crises occurring on the other side of the world to be reflected locally, rapidly changing financial markets, and the increasing awareness of our interdependency in keeping our planet alive and well. They also encompass the changes caused by governmental regulation and deregulation, takeovers and mergers, and rapid technological advances in some industries. Organizations are also being impacted internally by social factors such as worker participation, multicultural work forces, and increasingly demanding customers.

All of these factors combine to make life in today's industrial and business organizations far more hectic than it was even a decade ago. It is no surprise that in our books, movies, and even TV stories, business leaders are replacing doctors and scientists. It is as if this is where the battles are being fought today—inside the walls, not out on the field.

The response to these conditions includes a general speeding up of the work process, aided and abetted by computers. Task forces with short life cycles are often created to meet the needs of rapid changing business situations. Many of the groups which meet are temporary systems; therefore, they are groups that do not believe they have the time to learn about group process. However, this is just the tip of the iceberg. Today whole organizations are designed based on an awareness of these conditions.

The emphasis is on communication and innovation: authority is ambiguous, with multiple matrices that may not close until the CEO level. While these complex but loosely organized structures require an understanding of group and organizational processes, they generally believe they need someone to provide it for them, not to teach it to them.

Another factor influencing the role of process consultant is the maturation of OD as a field. Success of the general model has resulted in many companies hiring internal OD consultants. They are expected to help, but not necessarily to define the kind of help they will provide. Their status is often equal or less than the groups to which they are consulting. The internal consultant is frequently under pressure to help the group do it right, not to teach them to do it themselves.

Interventions Appropriate for a Process Leader

The following list of potential interventions are encompassed by the notion of "working the process," or moving the group along toward successful task work by impacting the structure or the process they use to accomplish the task. It is not meant to be all inclusive, just descriptive:

1. Coach the group leader before and after meetings. In particular, help in planning the agenda, suggesting needed agenda items, ordering the items, and determining what process to use and how much time will be needed for each. Help determine what decisions the group needs to make and what decisions the leader can make.
2. Ask the group members if they would like minutes, if none are being kept. In the event that they would like minutes but no one will volunteer to keep them, you volunteer. If the minutes prove useful ask at a later meeting that members take turns at writing them.
3. "Scribe" on newsprint during a group discussion in the event that no group member offers to play this role. Keeping track of the main points is helpful to the content of the discussion. You can use the easel to focus the discussion by asking people to check to be sure you are capturing their ideas. You can also invite others to perform this role, building additional skills for them.
4. Reinforce and call attention to positive processes.
5. Suggest all commit to beginning and ending on time.
6. Suggest the group discuss its operating procedures if these are posing a problem for some members, e.g., how the agenda is set, how the decisions are made.
7. Ask questions of quiet members (that you know they can answer).
8. Point out when members are not hearing or understanding each other. Help improve communication, perhaps by coaching individual members.
9. Facilitate conflict in a task-focused way; e.g., (a) when two people are engaged in a debate, decrease the polarization by asking others to state their views, (b) point out pseudo-agreements and violent agreements, (c) offer to meet outside the group with the parties involved if the issue appears to be interpersonal/personality related or pertaining to matters other than the task at hand.
10. Help keep the group on track. (This is a potential trap. If it is *ALL* the group wants you to do, you do not have a variable contract.)
11. Give "expert" opinion on organizational matters or general people issues, where theory might be useful.
12. Help the group design a process for accomplishing one of its tasks.
13. Collect data for the group on an aspect of its functioning, either from group members or from people outside the group, and report it back anonymously.
14. Suggest a "go around" for each person to give their opinion on an issue, either to help build the group or because the issue is very important, or both.
15. Ask that the decision-making process in use be articulated.
16. Suggest that the group brainstorm (when appropriate) and describe the process and when you would use it.
17. Ask questions for clarification.
18. Summarize the content (if you can) or better, ask for a summary if one seems needed.

Interventions You Do Not Make as a Process Leader

In general, time-consuming interventions which are not task focused are eliminated from the role of the process leader, but might have been a part of a traditional process consultation role.

1. Ask the group members to reflect on the process and share their observations.

2. Ask two or more people to work an inter-personal issue in the group.
3. Give feedback to an individual in the group during a meeting time (with the possible exception of the leader).
4. Ask group members to give each other feedback.
5. Ask people to fill out questionnaires about the group process.
6. Appoint process observers from the group members.
7. Make observations about interpersonal interactions, especially by naming names.
8. Encourage group members to touch each other.

The process leaders role calls for more active interventions focused on getting the task accomplished. There is some teaching involved, but it is primarily through modeling helpful behavior. Interpersonal process is only focused on when it is obviously interfering with the task.

Circumstances Influencing the Role Model Utilized

There is obviously overlap in the two models I have identified: traditional process consultant and process leader are not pure cases. Which role is most appropriate is influenced by the purpose and nature of the group, and the position of the "consultant."

The role of a process leader is closer to a member role than is a traditional process consultant. In fact, it is possible to act as process leader when you are a member of the group. My thinking for this chapter came from the roles I play in the different groups to which I devote my time, some for money and some for love. These include a computer company, a professional membership organization, and a community conservation commission. What I do as a paid consultant and as a volunteer member to help the process along in these different groups is not as varied as I would have believed several years ago.

The contracting is different, however. As a paid consultant, my initial contract is with the group's task leader. Over time the contract needs to be broadened to include all of the group members for maximum effectiveness of the role. As a member of the group I contract with the whole group about contributions I might make based on my unique background.

Dangers of Taking a Process Leader Role

Process leader is potentially a very powerful role. You are likely to be held accountable, in part, for the group's success or lack thereof. You may be taking responsibility for something you ultimately cannot deliver, because it requires a collaborative effort on the group's part. No matter how clearly you spell it out,

TABLE 8.1　Two Models

Traditional Process Consulting	Process Leadership
Group	**Group**
• Self-Study or T-Group	• Task Group
• Long term or stable	• Short term and/or changing membership
• Line organization	• Task force
Consultant	**Consultant**
• Clinical orientation	• Business orientation
• External	• Consultant or member
• Teacher or trainer	• Peer of group members
• Distant from group members	• Contract with group members as well as leader
• Contract primarily with group leader	

the result might be a perception that *YOU* fail.

"Leader" is a long-term job, while consultants work themselves out of a job. Your psychological contract with the group is different from the traditional process consultation, in that you are much more a part of the group. The group may be dependent on you to a greater extent or for longer than you may wish. Your commitment to the group may also be very strong. You may feel a psychological ownership for the process, if not the task. These are in fact the dangers of leadership.

An advantage to the process leader role is that it is less ambiguous than process facilitator or observer. You will get feedback on how you are doing, letting you know whether you are providing what the client wants, as opposed to providing what you think they need.

Conclusion

It may be that what I am really talking about is a new old role of process leadership. Remember Bales' research on task team which showed that effective problem solving groups involved not one, but two leaders, one for the task and one who was called a "socio-emotional leader?" The process leader role I am describing corresponds to this second leader.

It also may be that for many of you I have created a "straw person" because you never shared my model of traditional process consultation. In that case, perhaps I have provided a little historical perspective.

I believe that many of us in the field today are in fact doing most of the things I have described as part of a process consultant role. I believe that this role has evolved, and will continue to evolve, in the direction of more and more active leadership. I am really writing for those who, like me, have been caught with an older model which doesn't often or no longer works very well. For several years now I have been doing things which do work when I am trying to help a small task group, and it has been very useful for me to articulate the differences and make the changes explicit.

References

Bales, R.F. (1958). Task roles and social roles in problem-solving groups. In E. Maccoby, T.M. Newcomb, & E. L. Hartley (Eds.) *Readings in social psychology* (3rd ed.). New York, NY: Holt, Rinehart, Winston.

Mintzberg, H. (1979). *The structuring of organizations*. Upper Saddle River, NJ: Prentice Hall.

Schein, E.H. (1969, 1987, 1988). *Process consultation*. Reading, MA: Addison-Wesley.

CHAPTER 9

Working with the Client-Consultant Relationship

Why Every Step Is an "Intervention"

Naomi Raab

THE WORK OF AN OD consultant is often presented as a series of planned stages: entry, contracting, data gathering and diagnosis, feedback, intervention and evaluation (French, W.L. & Bell, C.H.) with discrete tasks all directed outward, at the problem. Often, I have observed, there is an assumption that the client knows what the problem is and that the consultant, "collaboratively" with the client, will address these problems and fix them. However my experience of working with clients is not like that at all; largely I think, because of three things

- I work in the here and now, i.e., I work with what ever is going on, (I don't just direct my attention to the content of a problem being outlined by the client, nor do I confine myself to the client's definition of the problem)
- I work with the client consultant relationship itself – with the dynamics of our relationship, with what's going on between us
- I don't work in a linear sequence of discrete steps which imply for example that contracting happens in the beginning, that both client and consultant are clear on what the problem is, that interventions happen after data gathering and diagnosis, etc.

It seems to me that sometimes OD consultants can hide behind the rhetoric of planned change and action research when indeed their *modus operandi* is closer to that of the salesman. Why might they do this?

Consulting is an anxiety producing profession. Faced with what can seem like an overwhelming problem in the client organization, plus our own need to perform and succeed, it's no wonder consultants use the bravado of the expert and salesman as a defense against feelings of not really knowing what to do and perhaps even feeling a fraud. Consultants get caught in the sales dynamic because they are anxious, because they don't trust their own instincts, because they fear losing the client, because they have little self insight and are frightened, embarrassed, or even unaware of their own feelings, because they want to be seen as rational and in control. They want to be the "Masters of Knowing." In trying to avoid these feelings at all costs, consultants can easily fall into the trap of Looking Good— their sales pitch is smooth and reassuring, yes, they've encountered this situation before and yes they know just what to do to fix it.

When the situation described above happens, they are at risk of colluding with client solutions to avoid a myriad of uncomfortable or difficult feelings on the part of both themselves and the client. The consequence may be that the real, or underlying, client problems are rarely confronted and worked through. To explain more, and to perhaps begin to out-line an alternative way of working, I'd like to go through the traditional consulting steps and challenge what often happens in the name of those steps.

Entry

Whilst entry in the pure OD sense is about entering the client system, I think that for many consultants it's about getting a foot in the door and selling. At the entry stage, the client tells you something about the problem, and is trying to work out whether you are the right consultant. Consultants want to look good at this stage and inspire confidence. Even though this stage often occurs over the phone, consultants, through their best paraphrasing skills, can try to convey a sense that they have a good handle on the problem. Clients, often anxious themselves, need reassurance and often venture a few interview type questions seeking to ascertain the consultant's credibility, experience and credentials. This plays right into a collusive dynamic where the anxiety of both is alleviated: the consultant gives a confident, "I can handle it" answer (and hopefully scores the job) and the client, relieved, gets a savior.

This, however, is an opportunity lost. Every contact with the client should be an opportunity to gather data, make a diagnosis on the run, and start to work. How is the client sounding on the phone? Do they sound distracted, anxious, smug? Do they sound as though they have no part in the problem? How do they talk about the problem—is their description clinical, detached, is it all over the place, panicked? How committed are they—are they prepared to make a time to talk in person about the problems they are facing?

As a consultant, you can start to work with any of this data. You can intervene, make observations on what you're hearing. You can talk about how hearing about the problem and talking with them makes you feel. You can also start to feedback your impressions of the situation or their part in it. You can raise issues that you sense have a bearing on the problem but have not been raised so far in the discussion—perhaps asking about players and relationships not yet mentioned, for example asking about the relationship the client has with her boss or her colleagues, etc. Take a risk and follow your hunches. Finally, you can try and get a sense of whether you want to and can work with this client. If you do, then you ask for a face-to-face meeting. What you're really doing is contracting for some more space in which to explore the problem.

Contracting

Contracting for me is always about getting a big enough space in which to work. I need to get my own sense of what the problem really is. However, in the way I often see contracting described, it is actually about putting forward a fairly detailed, well documented proposal of activities and interventions and getting the client to sign on the dotted line.

Contracting in this sense is about scoping a project and making sure the client will go along with you, it's a security blanket for consultants, and it holds warm a fantasy that you and the client agree, that you have client support, that they'll keep paying and hopefully not resist. The term contracting has a kind of legal feel to it in the spelling out of obligations and responsibilities… and like that other contracted relationship, marriage, a hope of safety and ever after.

But you can't contract for love. And you can't contract for what you have no idea will happen. This is why contracting can only be about space to work, and a commitment to stay with it when things get difficult. And even then, you'll need to re-contract, for contracting and re-contracting happens at every stage of the consultancy—it never stops.

An important step to make sure you take in contracting is intervening. Yet how can you be up to "intervention" when you haven't even completed data gathering, diagnosis, feedback and planning for change?! Well, you actually have a heap of data already in the way the organization contacted you, the way you were able to access entry, and your experience of the client so far. So often, and I would dare to venture, *every time,* those things that went really wrong with a consultancy later down the track were occurring right there at the start. Those first couple of interactions with a client and their organization offer a wealth of data: the way you experience the client may well be the way others experience him/her. Clues for understanding the client's contribution to the problem lie right there under your nose, or under your skin . . . is the client getting to you with her sense of self-importance and "busyness"? Does the client seem so overly in charge and impressive that you feel intimidated and are asking yourself hey, why did he ask me in if he's got it all under control? Ignore this data at your peril. This is where feedback, an intervention in itself, comes in.

Start to work with the client then and there, offering feedback and some interpretations. "I'm struck by how busy and speedy you seem, and how tightly you've narrowed down the problem . . . it's like you just want this fixed so you can go onto more important things." Tell the client what working with you will be like, and work with the response: "Look, working with me will be like this, I will be straight with you and share my reactions to what's going on and how I feel we're working . . . starting to work on this problem may well open up other issues and we may go slower not faster, things may well get worse for a while, not better."

If contracting is about getting clear on how you will work, the best way for the client to see this and understand it is in the here and now of your working with them on the spot. If you and the client can get through this, it will build your resilience to feedback and strengthen your relationship. Later on down the track when you're really working with resistance—you'll need it. In other words, you'll need a strong collaborative relationship that can withstand some straight talking. If

the client doesn't buy it, well, you've saved yourself problems later on. Sometimes I build in a rest break or thinking time. Even if the client wants to commit, I say, "Let's wait a few days to give us time to think about it." Staggering the entry/contracting process can be useful in gaining commitment, in negotiating the relationship and in beginning to work with the resistance that will always be there.

Data Gathering and Diagnosis

Data gathering and diagnosis is seen as a discrete phase often using particular tools and generating specific products or outcomes. Often however they are little more than a pre-sales warm up, generating predictable training "solutions." Also, there may be an over reliance on impressive tools and instrumentation (which cost more and require time to score and analyze) when a more low-tech anthropological approach may yield excellent results.

Data gathering and diagnosis are not neutral, scientific activities. They can in fact be more powerful intervention strategies than anything in your consultant's toolbox. Instead of just "interviewing" organization members, work with them as well. Address issues as they arise. Keep contracting, telling them how you work, and that you will share your thoughts with them along the way. It is in this phase of the consulting process that working transparently and collaboratively really has impact. Talk with people about what is emerging from your exploration of the issues, give and get feedback on what you are experiencing. Don't just leech information from them, put yourself on the line and *give* something. After all, your assessment, your opinion is your value added—that's why you're the consultant! Encourage them to talk with their colleagues, offer time to talk with you again or involve others in resolution of conflicts or issues with your assistance. Get the managers involved, feeding back to them constantly.

Feeding back does not mean being the messenger or doing others' work for them. It means working with the manager/client on issues emerging, coaching and supporting them to confront and work through emerging issues. It means creating spaces in the middle of the consultancy when different parties are brought together to address enduring and sometimes previously undiscussed problems. In this sense then, the "data gathering and diagnosis" phase is when the heat gets turned up and problems are surfaced and experienced more acutely. This is the part where things get worse, not better, as Pandora's Box reveals its terrors. This is also why the more confronting you've been earlier on in really being straight with the client and building the relationship pays off. For when it comes to feeding back your analysis, there should be no surprises—you've been talking and working with them on this all along.

Feedback

This stage is sometimes run as a show and tell "presentation" to the client where consultants can demonstrate the astuteness of their skills and the accuracy of their instrumentation. Consultants often get nervous at this stage, a kind of stage fright that is understandable if you are in performance mode, up front, "presenting" rather than grounded in your own sense of self. Working as a consultant you need to have a sense of personal authority (Gould, 1993) in that your feelings, needs and thoughts can be acknowledged and brought to the consulting encounter. This means that the consultant feels entitled to have and bring to the work his or her own feelings. This is linked to the notion of "bringing who you are to what you do" (Bellman, 1990). A consultant is not just a cardboard cut out playing a role but is able to bring who she is and all that she is into that role. In this sense you are not "performing" —you are being you and saying it as you see it.

Consultants get nervous about resistance or worry that their results are not spectacular enough because they confirm what everybody knew anyway. Yet feedback should never solely be delivered in one "presentation"—it should have been happening all along the way, there should be no surprises, only continuous re-contracting and further interventions.

If your investigations have shown that, for example, the staff is weak in areas of performance evaluation and management, then ask where does that come from? Work with the senior managers in feedback meetings around their own skills and relationships with their own bosses and staff. If the data shows a lack of openness and willingness to confront conflict, work with that in the meeting itself and their neutral or lukewarm response to the feedback. The purpose of feedback meetings should always be to bring the responsibility right back to where it belongs. This needs to be done in a strong and supportive way, not as a blaming exercise. Generating some real work in these meetings and addressing some difficult issues in the here and now can be very energizing and releasing for a management group.

Feedback should be about managers facing their dragons and actually working with them; it should generate a dynamic of empowerment not an "audience" response of applause and approval for the consultant's "results." The feedback meetings need to be focused very close to home and not quickly directed outward towards a package of solutions up the consultant's sleeve. Working with resistance is a critical task of the feedback meeting.

Intervention

This phase is usually written about as the outcome of a planned change process and is represented as "the solution" which is to be implemented. Often it represents the consultant's "product," (e.g., a training package) and in fact has often been pre-empted or presold. That is it has been "contracted" at the start of the consultancy—that's why it's the result of a "planned" change.

However the most powerful change can come from an awareness of dysfunction in existing relationships and an enhanced capacity to take up one's responsibilities more strongly. Sometimes the most radical change comes *not* from replacing something with some new process or people, but rather *from standing still and working with what's right under the client's nose.* By this I mean working with what's there currently: the conflicts, the not to be discussed issues, the game playing. Powerful change occurs as a result of enhanced understanding and insight into the nature of group and organizational level dynamics.

Having an understanding of the unconscious dynamics that are played out in organizations is an important aspect of the consultant's repertoire. A psychodynamic approach frees people up to explore the less rational aspects of organizational life in a way which acknowledges the hard to talk about tensions in organizations, for example around power, dependence, shame, authority, sex, gender, aggression, love, envy, competition and scapegoating.

It means that you can work with clients on, for example, how this group seems to work like a family with an absent father and abandoned children, or like a group of martyred women competing with each other for most victimized status, etc. For me working as a consultant with organizations it is just not that useful to see organizations, only as rational, goal driven, and problem solving entities and then to berate them for not being more so. I have found that using an approach which acknowledges the other, less visible, but arguably more powerful unconscious forces in organizations is both more forgiving, providing different options and is more reparative.

By incorporating this approach in an understanding of how organizations work I am not only addressing the pathological in organizations. Nor am I using the approach to look only at individuals, for indeed this approach enhances our understanding of organizations at the group, intergroup and organization- as-a-whole levels, providing a deeper understanding of many features of organizations, even those that appear straight forward and ordinary. In fact that can be its biggest strength—helping us understand why ordinary things surprise us when they work, or frustrate us when they clearly should work, because everyone agreed they would, but in fact, they didn't.

Instead what I often see consultants doing is pitching too many "interventions" at the rational, individual skill level, i.e.,"It's because you don't have the skills/knowledge on performance management that we have this problem, and so we will teach you." New products, like training, 360-degree feedback inventories, job analysis, etc. are easier to identify and talk about as interventions than the current dynamics, processes and relationships.

Finally, I want to say that the main intervention can in fact be you, the consultant, and the way you work in the client consultant relationship. The Client Consultant Relationship is the place where working in role and emotions come to the fore. It is often in the relationship between the client and consultant that the same problems and dynamics plaguing the client get played out in the relationship between them (Bain, 1976; Czander, 1993). This is no coincidence; the client represents part of the problem. This is not to say that training and other "product" solutions cannot make a valuable contribution to the change effort but rather that their success is dependent on a less tangible process of change that is to do with the existing nature of relationships and organizational dynamics themselves.

Evaluation

Whilst on the one hand it makes sense to have an evaluation phase at the close of a consultancy, how often is it characterized by a final show and tell in which consultants can show they've addressed the problem and which also provides an excellent opportunity to sell? Just who is the evaluation in the service of? Sometimes, an evaluation is used as a closing off and termination device, with a good dash of public relations thrown in.

Informally, evaluation should have been going on all along, especially if the consultant has been using an action research frame to the work. It should become evident, through the collaboration between client and consultant, when enough is enough, when sufficient progress has been made. I offer that a staggered entry and contracting process is useful in the beginning of the consultancy, just like a staggered ending. A series of final interventions emerge naturally as successes can be acknowledged and celebrated. Where things aren't going well, there can be a re-contracting process, or a built in time out or trial period.

Like all relationships, there are many ways to leave and make an ending or a new start. Transfer of learning is not a separate phase when working in this way. Client learning has been occurring all along, with the evaluation phase really representing collaborative reflection on the work you've been doing together. Transfer is thus embedded in the client system that is better equipped to deal with problems in the future.

Conclusion

Organizational consulting is a complex and dynamic process. Trying to understand what's really going on can be a challenge, however having the courage to work with it is an even greater one. Too often we as consultants don't trust our own instincts or are too fearful of losing the client. Other times, we are afraid to address the emotional aspects of the work and relationship, fearing we won't be seen as rational, objective and credible. (Beeby, M. et al., 1998) Yet these dynamics are integral to our understanding of what is going on in the consultancy and we ignore them at our peril (Stapley, D.F., 1996; Hirschhorn, L., 1990). We forget that we are in fact ourselves the best consulting instrument and that in bringing ourselves fully to the client consultant relationship, we are in the true service of the client. The Client Consultant Relationship provides an excellent vehicle for understanding what's going on in the consultancy, but it's often the last place we want to look.

This way of working means two things. It creates a client-consultant relationship which is intense and intimate, one in which both client and consultant see each other, and experience each other fully as whole people. But it also means that the consultant's role may mean at times that you have the courage to tell the emperor he has no clothes. Working strongly and fearlessly in role, with personal authority,

is how you add value and avoid the kind of dereliction of duty seen most starkly in the recent sagas of corporate collapses (Enron, HIH) in which consultants' absolute collusion meant they "yielded to their clients in virtually every instance of controversy and . . . failed to respond with appropriate diligence and resolve" (Ellas 2003).

Working as an organizational consultant is a very different prospect than working as a salesman. The difference is, you are working in the client's best interests in a way in which you too, as a consultant, can work with integrity, authority and meaning. You are working in a way in which *every step is an intervention.*

References

Bain, A. (1976). Presenting problems in social consultancy: Three case histories concerning the selection of managers. *Human Relations,* 29 (7), 643–657

Beeby, M. L. (1999). Consulting to a 'hurt' or 'upset' organization. *Leadership & Organization Development Journal,* 20 (2), 61–68.

Bellman, G. (1990). *The consultant's calling: Bringing who you are to what you do.* San Francisco, CA: Jossey-Bass.

Czander, W.M. (1993). *The psychodynamics of work and organizations: Theory and application.* New York, NY: Guilford Press.

Ellas, D. (2003, Jan. 14). *The Age.*

French, W.L., & Bell, C.H. 1990. *Organization development, behavioural science interventions for organization improvement.* Upper Saddle River, NJ: Prentice-Hall International.

Gould, L. (1993). Contemporary perspectives on personal and organizational authority: The self in a system of work relationships. In L. Hirschhorn & C. K. Barnett, (Eds), *The Psychodynamics of organizations.* Philadelphia, PA: Temple University Press.

Hirschhorn L. (1990). *The workplace within: Psychodynamics of organisational life.* Cambridge, MA: MIT Press.

Stapley, L.F. (1996). *The personality of the organisation —A psycho-dynamic explanation of culture and change.* London, UK: Free Association Books.

CHAPTER 10

Who Owns the OD Effort?

Harold Mack

AT A RECENT "Consultation Skills" seminar, the following question was posed to the forty conferee-consultants at the opening meeting: "What are your personal objectives for this seminar?" The group was divided into ten subgroups of four each to discuss the question and then post their lists of objectives. On six of the ten lists, concern was expressed in one way or another about "getting the client to own OD," "transferring OD ownership," "passing the baton to the client," or related statements. The large number of groups concerned about the "ownership issue" indicates that it is a real issue and a very serious one and warrants a considerable amount of attention by consultants.

Realistically, the effort can only be owned by the client. The major thrust of this paper will be to provide a framework whereby the consultant can look at the overall consultation effort and to point out some of the pitfalls where the ownership becomes confused. In addition, guidelines will be offered, that when followed will minimize the chances of ownership becoming confused. Finally, since I believe this to be an especially important problem for *internal* consultants, I will focus on the issue from that point of view.

What Is Ownership?

The word ownership as it applies to OD efforts indicates who's in charge, who has control, who makes the decisions, and who has the ultimate responsibility for success or failure of the effort. This description can only fit the client. The consultant works with the client in the client organization on client problems and has a high personal investment in and commitment to the effort. But ownership, as described and defined here, can only belong to the client.

A Model for Clarifying Ownership

One way of exploring the ownership issue and understanding how it gets confused would be to step back and look at the overall client-consultant relationship. Most client-consultant relationships follow a standard model or series of steps that provide a sequence and establish a discipline. In exploring the ownership issue, I would like to use the five-step OD model that consists of Entry, Diagnosis, Action, Evaluation, and Termination. Each step in the model will be described and examined from the point of view of ownership, pointing out danger signals and critical times when it is very easy for ownership to move from the client to the consultant or at least to move into an area of confusion.

Entry

One of the points at which ownership is probably more of an issue for the internal consultant than the external consultant is Entry—because of the way the initial contact is made.

External consultants are generally sought after, that is, the client has a problem and is actively pursuing the help of a consultant. The internal consultant, on the other hand, is often in transition, moving from a trainer role to a consultant role, and is seen by the organization as a trainer or instructor and as a provider of programs. In addition, internal consultants, when attempting to establish or plant themself as a consultant, must solicit business and pursue clients. The point is a fine one but one that begins to establish the consultant's role in the eyes of the client. If clients pursue consultants, they acknowledge that they need and want help to work on their problems. If clients are pursued by consultants, they perceive the consultant as someone who has something to sell or "lay" on them. This Entry item of "pursuer" vs. "pursuee" very early in the life of the relationship begins to establish a norm regarding ownership.

The internal consultant's role and status is strengthened when the client initiates the contact. And ownership may never become an issue if both client and consultant accept and understand why and how they came together.

An important phase of the Entry step is developing and agreeing on a contract that will set the stage and establish some guidelines for the work ahead. The contract should broadly define what the consultant is going to do, when it is going to be done, how, where, and so on. The contract, in addition, should state what the client's obligations are, the goals, the time frame, how the client is going to work with the consultant, and so on. It's also important that both parties consider the relationship to be voluntary and temporary. This understanding tells both parties that they are there because they want to be and that the relationship will terminate when the problem is solved or when some other reason arises. This temporary/voluntary idea tends to fix in clients' minds that they have contracted for some *outside* help to work on their problems, even though the consultant is actually *internal.*

Consultants should continue to remind themselves that they are not the manager, their role is to help the manager see the situation more clearly, discover alternative solutions, and find and use appropriate resources. Consultants are not the owner of the effort, they are a helper to the owner, and care must be taken by consultants that they are not—in this initial relationship setting—stage trapped into a telling role.

The Entry stage offers many opportunities for the ownership issue to become confused, but if care is taken by consultants when negotiating the contract and establishing their role, chances for confusion will be minimized. It will also help *internal* consultants to try to see themselves as *outside* consultants and to operate from that stance whenever possible, especially in this early stage of the relationship.

Diagnosis

Once the Entry and contract issues have been settled, most OD efforts move to data collection. This can be as simple as the Entry interview between client and consultant or may take the form of interview feedback, survey feedback, observation and feedback, confrontation meeting, or a problem census. Alternatives should be discussed with the client, explaining why and under what conditions various methods of collecting data are employed. The consultant, after client's input, should be in a position to suggest to the client what method he thinks would be most appropriate. Final selection however should be a joint one.

This process of mutually examining and selecting of work methods will continue to establish roles and help keep the OD effort's ownership where it belongs. The ideal relationship between client and consultant is one in which there is a high amount of joint exploration and joint decision-making. Mutuality is probably the best single word to relationship.

However, consultants should periodically make judgments as to the *quality* of the mutuality. It's important that consultants be more than a mirror. If they stay in the role of only reflecting client's opinions and wishes, they may be out looking for a new client. At different times, consultants will have to be educator, listener, advisor, and evaluator and this is proper as long as consultants know what role they are in.

Action

The Action step of our OD model has two major parts: first, the planning stage; second, the action or intervention. In terms of ownership, this particular part of the process presents another temptation for consultants to step out of role, cross a boundary, and begin to own the effort. They may assume that once the data has been collected and the diagnosis made it is time for them to step in and do their thing. After all, are not they the interventionist? Yes they are, but if they use this opportunity to display their knowledge by calling the action shots, they may unconsciously begin to absorb ownership of the effort.

This is the time when consultants earn money by helping the client set meaningful change goals that are based on the data. Once goals are set, consultants continue to earn money by offering and evaluating alternative courses of action. Consultants do not tell clients what to do—consultants present a range of actions, all of which address the problems uncovered. *Clients,* with knowledge of the organization and with the consultant's help, decides on a course of action. This mutual goal setting and action planning tends to place the ownership in proper perspective.

There are often other opportunities for consultants to indicate to clients that clients are responsible for the effort. One example would be when the action plan calls for off-site meetings and special arrangements have to be made for rooms, meals, transportation, and so on. These duties should be the responsibility of clients or someone in the organization. Here again, in operating like an *external* consultant, the *internal* consultant helps keep the confusion out of ownership.

Another opportunity for reinforcing the client ownership idea may present itself when a block of time has to be selected for meetings

or sessions. Whenever possible, OD action meetings should be conducted during regular working hours—this establishes OD activity as a legitimate part of every manager's job, not as something "extra." Getting managers involved during regular hours, and using their resources to work on their problems, helps maintain their ownership of the OD activity.

Evaluation

If consultants have been successful in maintaining their role as helper and not doer, the evaluation responsibility will be seen as that of the client system. Again, consultants should be ready to offer alternatives that will assist in evaluation. (The latter will be easier to accomplish if evaluation plans were made at the beginning of the effort.)

The evaluation stage of the effort is probably the last place to expect confusion of ownership. The focus of the effort is to solve problems and/or bring about changes, and the client is in the best position to determine the extent and value of the solutions and/or changes.

Termination

Similar to the Evaluation step, ownership should not be an issue this late in the process if both consultant and client have continued to clarify roles as the relationship moved ahead. The key words that the contract is built on are "temporary" and "voluntary" and if both parties have been able to buy into this and maintain this kind of relationship, ownership should not be an issue.

By agreeing to these clauses, each party recognizes and accepts the freedom to terminate at a specified time or when either of the parties wants out. To repeat, this provision tends to establish the fact that the client has "hired" a resource to help solve problems and when this is the case, ownership is never in doubt.

Summary

Ownership is more of an issue for the internal consultant than it is for the outside consultant.

This is because most internal consultants are also trainers and are seen by the organization as people who organize and conduct seminars that teach people to do certain things, e.g., motivate, delegate, etc. This trainer role tends to establish certain expectations in the eyes of the client. The internal consultant probably will see OD as an extension of training rather than a specific effort focused on the organization. To combat this, the consultant very early in the process may have to spend some time educating the client as to what OD is all about. This is time well spent and should not be overlooked in favor of "getting started" on OD.

Some writers have suggested that a consultant's objective in an OD effort is to work himself or herself out of a job. This makes a lot of sense in as much as OD efforts are often described as change or renewal efforts. Part of consultants' task is to help the client understand and accept this challenge. They can help

do this by regulating the amount of their time and the degree of their effort in the change process.

Consultants should be heavily involved in the early stages of the effort, (diagnosis) but, as the process moves forward (intervention), consultants may become less involved while the client becomes more involved. When this pattern is established and can be followed, it provides an easy avenue to evaluation and termination as well as establishing in clients' minds that Change or renewal (ownership) is their responsibility.

One final comment: consultants have the primary responsibility for defining ownership and for communicating to the client their role as a consultant. In addition, they have the responsibility for helping the client define the client's role. When this is done and accepted by both, ownership should never become an issue.

CHAPTER 11

Unraveling the "Who's Responsible?" Riddle

Arthur M. Freedman

AS AN INTERNAL and external consultant to a fairly diverse range of decision-making client groups, I have time and again encountered the situation in which the members of the client system *depotentiate* themselves. That is, they *give up* or *do not accept* the power inherent in *assuming responsibility for themselves* (and for the consequences of their own actions or inactions.

A classic story I heard—which may or may not be true—illustrates depotentiation and its consequences: A new PR person at an (unnamed) electronic component manufacturing subsidiary of an international corporation decided that he would like to quote the President of the parent organization in the $5.00 ad the subsidiary plant placed in the local high school yearbook. He had the *authority* but didn't want to assume the *responsibility* for departing from a PR "tradition"—the same out-of-fashion ad had been used for the past 12 years. So he wrote up a proposal and sent it to his boss, the Personnel Manager, for approval. *He* had the authority but, like his subordinate, did not want responsibility. He passed the proposal up to *his* boss, the Plant Manager, who referred the proposal to the District Manager, who referred it to the Regional Director, who passed it on and on and on until it found its way to the desk of the President of the parent organization, who read it, approved it, and passed it back down the line

to the PR person. The consequences of this sequence were that an estimated $32,000 of executive time was spent on the $5.00 ad and, by the time someone had approved it, the deadline for including it in the yearbook had passed.

Too often, decision-makers neglect to focus on these questions:

1. What authority do I have with regard to this particular decision?
2. What are my responsibilities and obligations regarding this issue?
3. Do I need to *check* with anyone else before I initiate any action?

What follows is a description of one way I have found to expedite decision-makers' awareness of these kinds of questions and to facilitate their using their time to achieve optimal personal satisfaction and organizational advantage.

1. I ask the client group of decision-makers to *list* all of the issues that they confront in their daily operations. (Many of these turn out to be issues about which the decision-makers tend to debate, among themselves, whether or not they have the responsibility and/or the authority to act on. Such debates generally absorb so much of their on-the-job time that they wind up avoiding any

definitive decision, passing the buck up to their boss instead).

2. I then ask the decision-making group members to categorize each of the listed items under one of three headings: (a) Policies; (b) Action Plans; and (c) Implementation Activities. Depending on where the particular decision-making group is located within their own organizational hierarchy, one list is usually very long, one very short, and the third somewhere in between.

3. Then, taking each of the three lists in order, I ask the group of decision-makers to determine where each listed issue fits according to the "Decision Matrix" shown in Figure 11.1. I ask the group of decision-makers to place a particular listed issue only after they have achieved a consensus decision as to where it goes, as conditions within the organization *currently exist.*

4. After looking over and analyzing the results of their work (a sort of organizational tea-leaf reading process), I raise the question as to whether this picture of their decision-making is satisfactory to them. That is, do the decision-making group members believe that decisions are made by the people who *should* be making them? Are they being made the *way* they should be made.

5. a. If the answer to one or both of these questions is "no," I invite the group to move into a problem-solving phase with the explicit intention of: (1) developing some clear and explicit statements as to how things *should* be (objectives); (2) analyzing the current situation so as to identify the obstacles preventing achievement of the desired objectives; and (3) developing a strategic plan of action to remove or reduce the potency of the identified obstacles (restraining forces).

b. If the answer to these questions is "yes," this process is terminated, with the major accomplishment being that the group members generally have acquired a clear and explicit understanding as to just *who* is responsible for *what* with regard to making decisions on different types of issues. This results in an enormous reduction of unproductive debating and a corresponding reduction in unnecessary and inappropriate buck passing.

FIGURE 11.1

List A: Policies	List B: Actions Plans	List C: Implementation Activities	Locus of Decision Making Authority
			1. Decision made by (my/our) superiors on a unilateral basis.
			2. Decision made by (my/our) superiors; (my/our) reactions to the decision are (solicited/listened to).
			3. Decision made by (my/our) superiors after (I/we) have had an opportunity/are requested to provide input.
			4. (I/we) make recommendations to superiors (if we choose/at their request), which are then either approved, modified, or rejected.
			5. (I/we) have delegated authority to make decisions, subject to the superior's approval or endorsement.
			6. (I/we) have delegated, irrevocable authority to make decisions

CHAPTER 12

Rules of Thumb
for Change Agents

Herbert Allen Shepard

THE FOLLOWING APHORISMS are not so much bits of advice (although they are stated that way) as things to think about when you are being a change agent, a consultant, an organization or community development practitioner—or when you are just being yourself trying to bring about something that involves other people.

Rule I: Stay Alive

This rule counsels against self-sacrifice on behalf of a cause that you do not wish to be your last.

Two exceptionally talented doctoral students came to the conclusion that the routines they had to go through to get their degrees were absurd and decided they would be untrue to themselves to conform to an absurd system. That sort of reasoning is almost always self-destructive. Besides, their noble gesture in quitting would be unlikely to have any impact whatever on the system they were taking a stand against.

This is not to say that one should never take a stand, or a survival risk. But such risks should be taken as part of a purposeful strategy of change and appropriately timed and targeted. When they are taken under such circumstances, one is very much alive.

But Rule I is much more than a survival rule. The rule means that you should let your whole being be involved in the undertaking. Since most of us have never been in touch with our whole being. It means a lot of putting together of parts that have been divided, of using internal communications channels that have been closed or were never opened.

Staying alive means loving yourself. Self-disparagement leads to the suppression of potentials, to a win-lose formulation of the world, and to wasting life in defensive maneuvering.

Staying alive means staying in touch with your purpose. It means using your skills, your emotions, your labels and positions, rather than being used by them. It means not being trapped in other people's games. It means turning yourself on and off, rather than being dependent on the situation. It means choosing with a view to the consequences as well as the impulse. It means going with the flow even while swimming against it. It means living in several worlds without being swallowed up in any. It means seeing dilemmas as opportunities for creativity. It means greeting absurdity with laughter while trying to unscramble it. It means capturing the moment in the light of the future. It means seeing the environment through the eyes of your purpose.

Rule II: Start Where the System Is

This is such ancient wisdom that one might expect its meaning had been fully explored and apprehended. Yet in practice the rule—and the system—are often violated.

The rule implies that one should begin by diagnosing the system. But systems do not necessarily *like* being diagnosed. Even the *term* "diagnosis" may be offensive. And the system may be even less ready for someone who calls himself or herself a "change agent": it is easy for the practitioner to forget that the use of jargon that prevents laypeople from understanding the professional mysteries is a hostile act.

Starting where the system is can be called the Empathy Rule. To communicate effectively, to obtain a basis for building sound strategy, the change agent needs to understand how the client sees himself and his situation, and needs to understand the culture of the system. Establishing the required rapport does not mean that the change agent who wants to work in a traditional industrial setting should refrain from growing a beard. It does mean that, if he has a beard, the beard is likely to determine where the client is when they first meet, and the client's curiosity needs to be dealt with. Similarly, the rule does not mean that a female change agent in a male organization should try to act like one of the boys, or that a young change agent should try to act like a senior executive. One thing it does mean is that sometimes where the client is, is wondering where the change agent is.

Rarely is the client in anyone place at any one time. That is, s/he may be ready to pursue any of several paths. The task is to walk together on the most promising path. Even unwitting or accidental violations of the empathy rule can destroy the situation. I lost a client through two violations in one morning. The client group spent a consulting day at my home. They arrived early in the morning, before I had my empathy on. The senior member, seeing a picture of my son in the living-room said, "What do you do with boys with long hair?" I replied thoughtlessly, "I think he's handsome that way": the small chasm thus created between my client and I was widened and deepened later that morning when one of

the family tortoises walked through the butter dish.

Sometimes starting where the client is, which sounds both ethically and technically virtuous, can lead to some ethically puzzling situations. Robert Frost[1] described a situation in which a consultant was so empathic with a king who was unfit to rule that the king discovered his own unfitness and had himself shot, whereupon the consultant became king.

Empathy permits the development of a mutual attachment between client and consultant. The resulting relationship may be one in which their creativities are joined, a mutual growth relationship. But it can also become one in which the client becomes dependent and is manipulated by the consultant. The ethical issues are not associated with starting where the system is, but with how one moves with it.

Rule III: Never Work Uphill

This is a comprehensive rule, and a number of other rules are corollaries or examples of it. It is an appeal for an organic rather than a mechanistic approach to change, for a collaborative approach to change, for building strength and building on strength. It has a number of implications that bear on the choices the change agent makes about how to use him/herself, and it says something about life.

Corollary 1: Don't Build Hills as You Go

This corollary cautions against working in a way that builds resistance to movement in the direction you have chosen as desirable. For example, a program which has a favorable effect on one portion of a population may have the opposite effect on other portions of the population. Perhaps the commonest error of this kind has been in the employment of T-group

[1] Robert Frost, "How Hard It Is To Keep From Being King When It's in You and in The Situation." In *The Clearing*, pp. 74–84. New York, NY: Holt, Rinehart and Winston.

training in organizations: turning on the participants and turning off the people who didn't attend, in one easy lesson.

Corollary 2: Work in the Most Promising Arena

The physician-patient relationship is often regarded as analogous to the consultant-client relationship. The results for system change of this analogy can be unfortunate. For example, the organization development consultant is likely to be greeted with delight by executives who see in his specialty the solution to a hopeless situation in an outlying plant. Some organization development consultants have disappeared for years because of the irresistibility of such challenges. Others have whiled away their time trying to counteract the Peter Principle by shoring up incompetent managers.

Corollary 3: Build Resources

Don't do anything alone that could be accomplished more easily or more certainly by a team. Don Quixote is not the only change agent whose effectiveness was handicapped by ignoring this rule. The change agent's task is a heroic one, but the need to be a hero does not facilitate team building. As a result, many change agents lose effectiveness by becoming spread too thin. Effectiveness can be enhanced by investing in the development of partners.

Corollary 4: Do Not Overorganize

The democratic ideology and theories of participative management that many change agents possess can sometimes interfere with common sense. A year or two ago I offered a course to be taught by graduate students. The course was oversubscribed. It seemed that a database process for deciding whom to admit would be desirable, and that participation of the graduate students in the decision would also be desirable. So I sought data from the candidates about themselves, and photocopied their responses for the graduate students. Then the graduate students and I held a series of meetings. Then the candidates were informed of the decision. In this way we wasted a great deal of time and everyone felt a little worse than if we had used an arbitrary decision rule

Corollary 5: Do Not Argue If You Cannot Win

Win-lose strategies are to be avoided because they deepen conflict instead of resolving it. But the change agent should build her/his support constituency as large and deep and strong as possible so that s/he can continue to risk.

Corollary 6: Play God a Little

If the change agent doesn't make the critical value decisions, someone else will be happy to do so. Will a given situation contribute to your fulfillment? Are you creating a better world for yourself and others, or are you keeping a system in operation that should be allowed to die? For example, the public education system is a mess. Does that mean that the change agent is morally obligated to try to improve it, destroy it, or develop a substitute for it? No, not even if he or she knows how. But the change agent does need a value perspective for making choices like that.

Rule IV: Innovation Requires a Good Idea, Initiative, and a Few Friends

Little can be accomplished alone, and the effects of social and cultural forces on individual perception are so distorting that the change agent needs a partner, if only to maintain perspective and purpose.

The quality of the partner is as important as the quality of the idea. Like the change agent, partners must be relatively autonomous people. Persons who are authority oriented— who need to rebel or need to submit—are not reliable partners: the rebels take the wrong risks and the good soldiers do not take any.

And rarely do they command the respect and trust from others that is needed if an innovation is to be supported.

The partners need not be numerous. For example, the engineering staff of a chemical company designed a new process plant using edge-of-the-art technology. The design departed radically from the experience of top management, and they were about to reject it. The engineering chief suggested that the design be reviewed by a distinguished engineering professor. The principal designers were in fact former students of the professor. For this reason he accepted the assignment, charged the company a large fee for reviewing the design (which he did not trouble to examine) and told the management that it was brilliantly conceived and executed. By this means the engineers not only implemented their innovations, but also grew in the esteem of their management.

A change agent experienced in the Washington environment reports that he knows of only one case of successful interdepartmental collaboration in mutually designing, funding and managing a joint project. It was accomplished through the collaboration of himself and three similarly-minded young men, one from each of four agencies. They were friends, and met weekly for lunch. They conceived the project, and planned strategies for implementing it. Each person undertook to interest and influence the relevant key people in their own agency. The four served one another as consultants and helpers in influencing opinion and bringing the decision-makers together.

An alternative statement of Rule IV is as follows: Find the people who are ready and able to work, introduce them to one another, and work with them. Perhaps because many change agents have been trained in the helping professions, perhaps because we have all been trained to think bureaucratically, concepts like organization position, representatives or need are likely to guide the change agent's selection of those he or she works with.

A more powerful beginning can sometimes be made by finding those persons in the system whose values are .s0ngruent with those of the change agent, who possess vitality and imagination, who are willing to work overtime, and who are eager to learn. Such people are usually glad to have someone like the change agent join in getting something important accomplished, and a careful search is likely to turn up quite a few. In fact, there may be enough of them to accomplish general system change, if they can team up in appropriate ways.

In building such teamwork the change agent's abilities will be fully challenged, as he joins them in establishing conditions for trust and creativity; dealing with their anxieties about being seen as subversive; enhancing their leadership, consulting, problem-solving, diagnosing and innovating skills; and developing appropriate group norms and policies.

Rule V: Load Experiments for Success

This sounds like counsel to avoid risk taking. But the decision to experiment always entails risk. After that decision has been made, take all precautions. The rule also sounds scientifically immoral. But whether an experiment produces the expected results depends upon the experimenter's depth of insight into the conditions and processes involved. Of course, what is experimental is what is new to the system; it may or may not be new to the change agent.

Build an umbrella over the experiment. A chemical process plant which was to be shut down because of the inefficiency of its operations undertook a union-management cooperation project to improve efficiency, which involved a modified form of profit sharing. Such plans were contrary to company policy, but the regional vice president was interested in the experiment, and successfully concealed it from his associates. The experiment was successful; the plant became profitable. But in this case, the umbrella turned out not to be big enough. The plant was shut down anyway.

Use the Hawthorne effect. Even poorly conceived experiments are often made to succeed when the participants feel ownership. And conversely, one of the obstacles to the spread of useful innovations is that the groups to which they are offered do not feel ownership of them.

For example, if the change agent hopes to use experience-based learning as part of his/her strategy, the first person to be invited should be those who consistently turn all their experiences into constructive learning. Similarly, in introducing team development processes into a system, begin with the best functioning team.

Maintain voluntarism. This is not easy to do in systems where invitations are understood to be commands, but nothing vital can be built on such motives as duty, obedience, security seeking or responsiveness to social pressure.

Rule VI: Light Many Fires

Not only does a large, monolithic development or change program have high visibility and other qualities of a good target, it also tends to prevent subsystems from feeling ownership of, and consequent commitment to the program.

The meaning of this rule is more orderly than the random prescription—light many fires—suggests. Any part of a system is the way it is partly because of the way the rest of the system is. To work towards change in one subsystem is to become one more determinant of its performance. Not only is the change agent working uphill, but as soon as he turns his back, other forces in the system will press the subsystem back towards its previous performance mode.

If many interdependent subsystems are catalyzed, and the change agent brings them together to facilitate one another's efforts, the entire system can begin to move.

Understanding patterns of interdependency among subsystems can lead to a strategy of fire-setting. For example, in public school

systems it requires collaboration among politicians, administrators, teachers, parents and students to bring about significant innovation, and active opposition on the part of only one of these groups to prevent it. In parochial school systems, on the other hand, collaboration between the administration and the church can provide a powerful impetus for change in the other groups.

Rule VII: Keep an Optimistic Bias

Our society grinds along with much polarization and cruelty, and even the helping professions compose their world of grim problems to be "worked through": the change agent is usually flooded with the destructive aspects of the situations he enters. People in most systems are impressed by one another's weaknesses, and stereotype each other with such incompetencies as they can discover.

This rule does not advise ignoring destructive forces. But its positive prescription is that the change agent be especially alert to the constructive forces which are often masked and suppressed in a problem-oriented, envious culture.

People have as great an innate capacity for joy as for resentment, but resentment causes them to overlook opportunities for joy. In a workshop for married couples, a husband and wife were discussing their sexual problem and how hard they were working to solve it. They were not making much progress, since they didn't realize that sex is not a problem, but an opportunity.

Individuals and groups locked in destructive kinds of conflict focus on their differences. The change agent's job is to help them discover and build on their commonalities, so that they will have a foundation of respect and trust which will permit them to use their differences as a source of creativity. The unhappy partners focus on past hurts, and continue to destroy the present and future with them. The change agent's job is to help them change the present so that they will have a new past on which to create a better future.

Rule VIII: Capture the Moment

A good sense of relevance and timing is often treated as though it were a "gift" or "intuition" rather than something that can be learned, something spontaneous rather than something planned. The opposite is nearer the truth. One is more likely to "capture the moment" when everything one has learned is readily available.

Some years ago my wife and I were having a very destructive fight. Our nine-year-old daughter decided to intervene. She put her arms around her mother and asked: "What does Daddy do that bugs you?" She was an attentive audience for the next few minutes while my wife told her, ending in tears. She then put her arms around me: "What does Mommy do that bugs you?" and listened attentively to my response, which also ended in tears. She then went to the record player and put on a favorite love song ("If Ever I Should Leave You") and left us alone to make up.

The elements of my daughter's intervention had all been learned. They were available to her, and she combined them in a way that could make the moment better.

Perhaps it's our training in linear cause-and-effect thinking and the neglect of our capacities for imagery that makes us so often unable to see the multiple potential of the moment. Entering the situation "blank" is not the answer. One needs to have as many frameworks for seeing and strategies for acting available as possible. But it's not enough to involve only one's head in the situation; one's heart has to get involved too. Cornelia Otis Skinner once said that the first law of the stage is to love your audience. You can love your audience only if you love yourself. If you have relatively full access to your organized experience, to yourself and to the situation, you will capture the moment more often.

CHAPTER 13

If I Knew Then . . .

An Essay

Geoff Bellman

WHEN THE OD NETWORK began in 1964, I was beginning too, fresh out of graduate school, newly married, and off to conquer the corporate world. I did not yet know that organization development would soon begin emerging as my life's work. OD was to be another marriage for me beginning with chance meetings, followed by frequent dates, engagement, commitment, and a shared life journey. This article describes that journey from one scenic viewpoint; it looks back for direction forward, offering nine points of wisdom.

I'm imagining that you, dear readers, are between 25 and 45 years old, and would love some affirmation or guidance on your own journey. I've written what would have been useful to me then—had I been ready to read it—and hope it's useful to you now. I've done good work, and could have done better work, had I held these nine points in my mind and heart.

Our Clients Are Not Crazy

Hear me talk about my clients twenty or thirty years ago: "What is *wrong* with her? . . . Is she *crazy*? . . . Let me tell you about the *stupid* thing she did last week . . . or . . . I *told* him what to do, then he goes out and *screws* it up! . . . or . . . Do you think they *even care* whether this place works or not?" I thought it was entirely about them, what an obvious mess they had made—and how lucky they were to have me.

Notice my distance from clients while ranting. Notice the "knowing better than" and the "it would never happen to me" implied in the criticism. All that is the opposite of what I now do—when I am doing my better work. Here's what I try to do when working with a client organization that is in some distress:

- Move toward the client mentally, physically, emotionally. Show through action that I respect them. Lean toward them, listen to them, empathize with them . . . all that good interpersonal stuff that OD has taught us so well.
- Seek to understand their situation as they understand it—and show them to their satisfaction that I understand it. Be willing to get lost in their problems along the way.
- They have reasons for the difficulties they are caught in; they make their own sense of the difficulties. Discover why and how it makes sense to them. This is their starting point.
- If they knew how to make better sense of their difficulties, they would have done it. Start with that assumption; they occasionally disprove it, but start there.
- Deal with them as capable people presently caught up in a difficult problem. Recall how often this has happened to you. Remember that your life is not as sensible and orderly as you often present it.

All of the above results are a rollicking ride with someone else in control. No longer the distant, expert analyst: you become engaged and confused; you wonder whether you will ever escape, much less do any good. You feel like you've removed your protective consulting attire and are rolling naked in the mud with the client. And, you are getting paid for this! Whoopee! Now *that's* exciting!

OD is "action research"; so get in on the action while you do the research. We've learned that our mere presence influences the system so let's become more present. Much of my past distance from clients was not about effective consulting, it was about self-protection. With my high control needs, I was afraid to get close. I might lose myself; I would no longer know who I am or what I bring. If I were starting my consulting career over, I'd wade in sooner. I'd find the "craziness" of my clients in myself and embrace it as the place to begin our work together.

A last point about these "crazy" clients: Many of them become friends; some are among my closest friends. I just made a quick list: I stay in touch with at least two dozen clients that I haven't worked with for many years. What better way to forge a friendship than to wade in and work together? Now, instead of working, we have lunch, or talk, or camp, or walk together. And, of course, we reminisce about the work we did . . . the days we faced the dragon.

Embrace Organizations as They Are

Organizations don't work. Well, at least not for very long or predictably. They are always trying to work, and occasionally do. When I got into OD, I thought organizations could, should, and will work. Give a company the right values, direction, structure, systems, culture, and this place will hummmmm! I worked at making them work. I applied myself to getting them designed, tooled, oiled, and . . . they regularly frustrated me. No sooner than people step into their new roles, they start changing things! They don't do what "we" designed this place to do. Instead, they start taking down walls, digging tunnels, hanging wall paper, and getting tattoos—all before the paint is dry on what their design team, management, and I so carefully created. If it weren't for those . . . *people* . . . organizations would work!

When it comes to organizations, our reach exceeds our grasp. We can imagine societies, communities, corporations, and agencies that fulfill our grand OD fantasies. But we cannot create them today. When I joined OD, I expected to feel the organizational earth move under my feet in some seismic way in this lifetime. That's not going to happen.

OD work becomes more fulfilling to us and useful to our clients when we embrace organizations *as they are.* We've got too much riding on this to only love organizations for what they might become. That's like marrying someone you plan to change; it doesn't work. Face and embrace organizations as they are. And how might that happen?

- Continue to be a student of organizations. Look at how complex they are. Dive into the complexity; appreciate the mystery; expect unpredictability. Delight in them!
- Consider your own paradoxical, conflicted, exciting, contradictory, and occasionally weird life. Consider the twists and turns of your career. Look at your love life. Notice your fascination with it all. That's a step toward doing the same with organizations. Quit asking them to make more sense than you do!
- Imagine 547 people living fascinating lives. . . . Now imagine those people attempting to join in a common purpose while also meeting their own individual needs. . . . Now imagine they are in fourteen cities across six countries. Of course, it's very difficult to get anything done! Of course, it's often worth trying! Of course, the organizational potential holds huge human potential!
- What if you saw yourself as an explorer of organizations, more like Columbus? There

you are, crawling up the face of the organizational monolith, looking in the windows, trying to make sense of it, trying not to fall, trying to figure out what you are going to tell the Queen. Now *that's* exciting work!

This is what keeps me looking into organizations. Not so much my immediate contribution, but how my work might be contributing to new forms of organizations. Yes, I hold evolutionary dreams while carrying few illusions about the difference I'm making. Three decades, centuries, or millennia from today, no one will notice my work. And . . . what else is there to do?

Searching, Not Finding

This work is most compelling to me when I am exploring, not when I am all-knowing. After all these years, I still experience delight (and a sense of privilege) seeing the innards of an organization—the guts, the juices, the odors, and the colors. I love looking even when I don't understand . . . *Especially* when I don't understand! The intrigue, the mystery, draws me. It's not as much about solving organizational puzzles as it is about encountering them. When I was newer to this work, my excitement was almost entirely about making a difference. That has changed; I've become less of a problem-solving world-fixer and more of a life searching choice-provider.

If I'm expert at anything, it's searching. Not finding, but searching. I am a jungle guide . . . get me a pith helmet! I accompany people into their organizational jungles. They've been living on the edge of their jungle while I've been traveling the world, exploring many jungles. I know how to enter and get around; I can read the signs, sense the danger and the opportunity. The organizational jungle attracts me, still more unknown than known. People ask me to guide them as they enter their jungle and make their way through it to . . . treasure. Often it's gold; sometimes it's happiness. But there's always treasures. Otherwise, it's not worth the risk.

When an organization calls forth my curiosity, the work goes better. When I act expert (which sometimes I do), clients act respectful, sit back, listen, and try to do what I want. They feed my ego; I go home, self-satisfied, inflated, and unengaged. When I quash my curiosity, I die a little. When I step into the mysteries of the organizational jungle, I live.

Look for Life

What gives life to this place? That question provides a great lens for seeing a person, a community, a department, or a society. My early OD questions focused on training, or planning, or people dynamics. Those questions told others what I stood for and gave me back what I wanted. If I asked about their need for training, sure enough, they needed it. When I asked about problems people had working with each other, sure enough, they told me about their problems. My questions highlighted what was important to me, not necessarily to the client.

Now, organizational life is my priority. Without life . . . well, you know. Life is where the energy is, energy vital to sustaining an organization and renewing it. Don't just interview: View! See where the life is—and it's not primarily in the management. Look for life among those deeply committed out of belief, duty or necessity. Their finest expression of life does not come out in an interview; it comes out in their work. Watch them do it, talk with them about it. Don't just be seduced by the powerful people at the "top." Also join with the powerful people at the "bottom."

Perception and Reflection

Years ago, I thought I brought clients new skills, methods, tools, systems, and structures. Now, I bring perspective. I bring that other stuff too, but it's not what my clients value most. The people I work with are pretty smart. When I help them see their world in a different way, they often act on their new insight. They rely primarily on abilities they already possess; they don't learn everything new.

How might my early consulting years have been different if I'd focused more on helping clients step back and see, rather than step in and do. The contrast is clear: Earlier, I was more often like a door-to-door sales person, pulling brushes and cosmetics from a bag, seeing what the client might like to buy. Today, I'm more like a tribal healer using incantations and medicines to help others see their world differently. The stark difference between those two roles conveys how I feel about my older and newer work. In reality, I'm probably a melding of the extremes . . . a door-to-door healer perhaps.

Reflection entwines with perspective. If you want to see your world differently, you must make time to step back. Stepping- back time is hard to come by nowadays. Many of us work with clients demanding results in hours instead of days. Much of our OD technology was designed in less hurried times and does not fit with today's pace.

How do I help organizations value reflection enough that they will create time to do it? When will they study what they have been doing and learn from that? How will they deeply connect with each other? When will they exhale? My yesterdays did not prepare me for the pace of today and tomorrow. Reflection is essential to organizations, and I'm not prepared to do it well. I'm hoping you will learn what I haven't.

Progress, Not Perfection

Aspirations to live my life and work perfectly do not serve me. My research shows I invariably fail. For individuals and organizations, this life is about progress, not perfection. This world needs residents and consultants who will live in its imperfect reality while leaning toward positive possibilities. My early consulting years focused on getting it right according to OD, blaming myself and others for getting it wrong. Hidden beneath my insistence was a lack of acceptance of myself.

Now, show me progress! Good enough! When I help clients progress on their terms, they accomplish more than when I insist on OD

perfection. If they just understood their world the way I do, they would find my ideas compelling. But that's just the point: They don't. We bring them guidance, not law. For our work to continue, our clients must see movement forward that meets their standards. Insisting on the "right way" doesn't work nearly as well as discovering "a way" forward together. We ask them to be flexible, and so must we be flexible. We ask them to risk, and so must we risk.

Know Yourself

Like you, I invested years learning about change, leadership, and organizations—all important to being an effective OD consultant. I piled up workshops, seminars, tools, and theories; I built my expertise in the fresh fads sweeping through OD. Much of my effort was rooted in anxiety: Somebody might discover I'm not really an OD consultant so I must learn to act like one! Though my learning was protective, I filled my OD toolbox with ideas useful to my work. My early learning apparently assumed that knowledge was out there and I needed to soak in it or inject and inflate myself with it to become a consultant.

How do you choose among the tools? When do you design your own models? What shall I do now? These are the questions that get past my shelves lined with books and the drawers full of articles. These are questions of the designer, the artist, and the architect, who confidently uses the resources available. These questions come closer to the self. For some reason, we find it easier to deploy ourselves at work when we regularly consider questions like these:

> Who am I?
> Where am I going?
> What's important to me?
> How might I best contribute to this world?
> Where can I find love and friendship?
> How can I make a difference?
> What work might I best do?
> What do I need to learn?

Common questions lurking behind our every action. As common as the questions are, the answers are still emerging—at least for me and for you. If OD work is to be near the center of your life, it will be part of the answers to these questions. I make better consulting choices about what to do next in this design, or this moment, or with this method, when I attend to my prevailing life questions. My choices in how to do OD work are more informed by intuition than logic, and I am more artist than mechanic.

Love Yourself

In my early consulting years, I had no notion of how my difficulties with myself interfered with my effectiveness as a consultant. I thought it was those S.O.B.s out there when, in fact, it was usually this S.O.B. in here! I saw the world through a lens clouded by low self-esteem. I believed that my issues with my clients were all about them, what they should do to change. I used their struggles to elevate myself. I "knew" that in their situation, I would handle it better.

I didn't know that my irritation with them had to do with unlit corners in myself. I did not want to know that their problems were my problems! Why am I lying awake at three in the morning in a torment about a client that irritates the hell out of me? Chances are my pattern of pain with a client is a pain with myself. Years have shown me that when I am shining some light into my dark corners, it leads to learning about and acceptance of myself. Self-acceptance leads to acceptance of others. I still struggle with this—and not just at work—but now I have quite a different sense of what to do about it than I did 20–40 years ago.

This is not as easy as finding what's wrong with me and fixing it. I need to accept, forgive, embrace, and love myself for who I am now, not for who I might become eventually. Right now—warts and all! When I am able to do this, barriers between me and my clients melt. The practical implications of this:

- I am more at ease with myself, and therefore am more at ease with clients, reducing unnecessary tension between us. I convey

my respect for them with seldom a hint of disdain.

- I am more interested in and attracted to clients. I lean toward their work and lives rather than pulling back in disgust at what they are doing.
- I ask wider and deeper questions; my inquiry is less sharply problem-focused.
- I expect that the client has probably done the best they know how, even if it's gotten them into a fix. They feel that acceptance as I work with them so they, in turn, work with me more readily.
- I share struggles from my own life that parallel their own. I do not condemn them.
- I help them with a larger perspective; I help them see how they can live through this.
- I remind them of what they are doing well. I rely on their strengths to lift them up out of the mud, rather than focusing entirely on what is wrong with them.
- My questioning or criticism of their work is more readily accepted because they know that I care about them.

Reward Yourself

The commercial marketplace has just called to tell you: "We are full of wonderful rewards! Rewards you should receive! Rewards that will make you more of whatever-you-want than you are today! You should reach for those rewards! Everybody should! Pass it on!"

The OD marketplace holds out its own rewards. There's the work others could give you . . . the recognition they could offer . . . the money you could make . . . the trip you could take. Everyone holding out a reward knows we human beings need rewards. And they are right.

In my early years, I sought my primary recognition from clients, increasing my dependence on them. I shaped myself to gain their approval; it often mattered more than effectiveness. A client saying sweet words can still charm me; I watch myself falling off my self-directed track to bask in client approval. This happens less often than years ago, but I'm still vulnerable . . . something to do with my childhood, no doubt.

I've spent years leaping for gold rings held by others. Not that those rings are unimportant, but notice: Who designed the rings? Who holds the rings? And, who is leaping? Being dependent on others to decide all your rewards is not the likely path to fulfillment. The challenges: Decide your own rewards, design your own gold rings, and reduce leaping for others' rings. And how might you do that?

- Imagine what you might be contributing to the larger world and future generations. Do something about it and see how it feels. Find a small bit of world work that engages you and return to it regularly.
- Meet with people who share your aspirations, maybe even your work . . . maybe they are in the OD Network! See them, talk with them, email them, regularly. Talk with them about why you do your work, not just how you do it.
- Read books, magazines and websites of people who are on paths like yours. Always be in the middle of a related book because it will help maintain your excitement and the sense that what you are doing is rewarding.

- Notice what you find rewarding in your work. Notice your patterns of satisfaction.
- Ask others to join you in your work—and your celebrations of what you have done. Get a license to brag about what you have done—and ask them to cheer you on.
- In small and large ways, celebrate often.
- Read this article looking for ideas that might lead to greater fulfillment in your life. Convert one idea to action.
- Put your life aspiration on equal footing with some of your common work plans. In other words, get it on your calendar. Dignify your life purpose with plans and actions.

Close

Throughout this article, I've felt the constraint of creating a short list of consulting wisdom. I focused on nine points, when actually there are 213 . . . or . . . is it 437? Living a life informed by purpose means wisdom will come to you from many sources and directions. Our wisdom is unlimited—when we pay attention. And it hovers over us like a guardian angel—when we pay attention. That's the clue: paying attention to your wisdom, to what your wiser self is telling you . . . and . . . what is your wiser self telling you right now?

CHAPTER 14

Who Is the Client Here?

On Becoming an OD Consultant

Robert Goldberg

I CAME TO ORGANIZATION Development by way of human resource management and management training. In those areas, I was considered a person with a lot to offer. From recruitment to compensation to performance management to leadership and communications skills training, I delivered services and programs relevant to most of the human resources issues that managers faced. I truly gave at the office.

I shifted into OD for what I thought were good reasons. For one, I was discovering the major issues individuals faced were seldom resolved through programs impose from the outside. OD interventions seemed an excellent way to use the energy of the group to successfully resolve its own issues. Also, I would often receive feedback that I was perceptive about organizational issues and a good listener, so I felt equipped to help people better understand their motivations and relationships at work.

Little did I know in my romanticized vision of becoming a change agent that the very factors which helped me succeed in human resources would be the major obstacles in my career in Organization Development. And I surely did not realize when I entered the field that those stumbling blocks would provide some of the most important lessons about myself in my adult life.

The seeds of my learning were planted during my earliest intervention, though at the time I was oblivious to it. I was assigned to help a division Vice President, a seasoned, crusty fellow with twenty or more years of experience at the large company where I was recently employed as an internal OD/Management Development consultant.

Armed with technologies ranging from action research and team building to instrumented learning and role clarification interventions, I began the interview. I could not wait to help. Midway through, when I had dropped what I considered only a modest amount of OD lingo, he asked, "So, what can I do for you?"

Considering that I was there to ask him the same question, I was at a loss to respond. After I stammered that I was actually there to help him, he explained that he did not need any help, but "thanks for stopping by."

I slinked away knowing only that I was through with OD and going back to management training. My "ah-ha" came after a few other episodes that strongly resembled this earlier experience—I was persuaded to not give just yet. I had to try to impress the client with my OD knowledge and skills, and had assumed that the client needed help before I found out what the situation really was. I came to realize that I was projecting; it was me that needed help. I needed an OD consultant.

So, I became one for myself. I began the long term assignment of observing myself interacting with others at work and at home, and I reflected, read, experimented, and reflected some more. I asked for tons of feedback from people I trusted; the more painful to hear, the better.

Two points kept coming back at me no matter how I tried to dodge them. First, I learned that my attempts to impress others were an indirect way of asking for recognition as a professional and as a person. This was how I masked feeling insecure.

Second, I learned I was trying to control my client-consultant relationships so I could be looked upon more as hero than as helper—an attempt to disguise my anxiety about being rejected and to hide my fear that I would not be invited back if I was not perceived as a "savior."

I gradually began to recognize that when I pontificated or tried to impress others with my command of OD technologies, I must have been feeling insecure about something, and needed to examine what and why. I realized an important paradox of security: the more I attempted to portray a secure, impregnable facade to others, the less capable and secure I was perceived. Yet the more I permitted myself to be openly spontaneous and uncertain, without all the answers, the more I was perceived as someone who might be capable of helping.

As I began to understand how and why I responded to situations that made me uncomfortable, I also began to see that I was not alone in building facades. While I worked out my control and security issues on clients' time, clients were also acting out their own anxieties indirectly. In others, this was often manifested in expressions of invulnerability or haughtiness; attempts to mask a fear of losing control or of helplessness. I realized that my clients and I had more in common than I had thought. This made even the "crustiest" of clients seem more human.

Recognizing this, I felt freer to listen more closely to clients' and to my own reactions. I developed more confidence to give feedback about what I was experiencing there and then, which often became a point of departure for a client to disclose his· or her own feelings.

Clients could sometimes see in our interactions elements of relationships that existed with people with whom they worked regularly, e.g., feeling cut off or criticized, feeling angry or frustrated, being "deified," or some other emotional reaction. Through these interactions clients had the opportunity to practice being more direct about what they were experiencing. In turn, they could model these behaviors in other situations with other people. By feeling safer to disclose to others what they truly believed or how they felt, more opportunities for building trust could occur and fewer costly misunderstandings were possible. For instance, this could prove especially important when indirect expressions of anger (such as the exclusion of a key person at an important meeting) might have the potential to spiral into long term negative consequences for an entire organization.

I also learned that it takes time to develop a relationship to the point where honesty is not threatening. Rushing to candor is another way people express being afraid of not being in control.

As time went on and I felt more comfortable with not "contracting" upfront with a client for a specific service, I realized I was able to stay focused on the client's, and not on my concerns. And when I began to wean myself from the notion that I could control the way someone felt about me I became a little less anxious to make a good impression; now I promise less, hear more, and feel capable of helping clients reach beyond surface issues.

Now, when I "hear" myself trying to impress someone I usually recognize my control/dependency issues are at work. Not that these issues are ever ultimately resolved, but dealing directly with the deeper issues often provides greater awareness and understanding for the client and for myself.

I am still working on letting go of my stubborn needs for control and on my ability to help clients become more aware through our direct contact. But I think I am pretty well recovered from the need to be the hero, or even the need for "OD technique." These days all I find myself caring about is continuing to learn and helping others to learn, "simply" by being myself (which is a paradox in itself).

CHAPTER 15

An Inner Blueprint for Successful Partnership Development

Putting a Relationship to Work

Peter F. Norlin and Judy Vogel

INTERESTING THINGS HAPPEN when two people attempt to work together for a common purpose. From earliest history, whether hunting for food, raising children, or living in a community, partnering has allowed new things to happen that would not have emerged if people were working separately. Many wisdom traditions explore the generative force of collaboration; for example, the Tao Te Ching says that "first, there is oneness. Then the one begat two. Two begat three. And three begat the myriad things." Commenting on this dynamic unfolding, Julia Measures says, "When you and I begin speaking . . . there is a 'space' between us. Then as we're together, suddenly something starts to move between us that doesn't belong to you and doesn't belong to me—the three. It can move in any direction; we can nudge it this way and that way. It's life on the move, and we are totally participating in it" (Measures, 2003). The "three," that striking manifestation of "life on the move," can be observed and experienced in a partnership relationship, and it reflects the unpredictable and exciting potential at hand.

As we have worked in the field of organization development, we've often found ourselves facing the professional challenges of learning to work effectively with other colleagues or helping our customers develop their capacity

to collaborate successfully to accomplish their goals. In both of these situations, the reasons for "working with" are usually clear: something significant needs to get done, and more than two hands are needed. In many cases, people simply pitch in informally, contribute their skills, and finish the job—and sometimes, in the process, learn something about how to work together.

In other situations, as people consider what tasks need to be accomplished and who might be best suited to accomplish them, they may decide to define this working relationship explicitly and formally. They begin to think of themselves as *partners* in an ongoing relationship, a collaboration that requires the creation of a special interpersonal connection, one that enables the full sharing of their resources in a challenging environment of customer expectations and opportunities. Choosing to partner begins a rich and complex journey and one that sometimes fails.

So why do people undertake the challenge to create successful conditions for "working with"? In *Turning to One Another,* Margaret Wheatley identifies and explores the deep human hunger to live and work in close connection with others (Wheatley, 2002). We share her interest and have gathered data from consultants and clients about their motivation to work in partnership. People report the following experiences and beliefs about the benefits of partnering

- It offers greater potential for professional effectiveness, personal learning, and creative synergy.
- It builds more credibility with customers through combined reputations and name recognition.
- It meets affiliation needs and counteracts professional loneliness.
- It provides a more comprehensive perspective through the resources of difference (i.e., gender, race, experience, etc.).
- It provides an opportunity to model partnership for customers.
- It's simply more fun.

This article offers our latest thinking about how to build and sustain a satisfying, successful partnership. We begin by outlining a model for partnership development, including some thoughts about how to "nudge" the prospective partner in order to create a resilient and productive relationship. We offer a few typical pitfalls and breakdowns in this process, and suggest strategies and key skills that can help partners to avoid or resolve these troubles. We conclude by applying our model to some familiar pairings, including consulting partnerships between internal and external, two internal, and two external colleagues.

Considering Partnership: Our Core Assumptions

We define *partnership* as a *successful relationship in service to a specific task*—we believe that when people choose to be partners, they are also choosing to *put their relationship to work*. Their achievements will be the result of both their willingness to see their relationship as the key to their effectiveness and of their ability to use it as such. People are drawn to partner for diverse and often unexpressed reasons. While intuitive "chemistry" may provide a sound initial impulse, we propose that building a suc-

cessful partnership is more predictable if conscious, disciplined, and intentional strategies are used from the very beginning.

Becoming conscious, disciplined, and intentional is a complicated assignment when human relationships are involved. First, individual behavior is driven by personal mindsets—beliefs and assumptions—that are, in turn, created by the ongoing, intricate interplay between one's own perception and experience. We assume that people are often unaware of these inner connections, of the specific nature of their own "realities," and of their own personal behavioral styles. This means that *consciously* developing a relationship depends on their ability to use a critical building block of emotional intelligence: self-awareness (Goleman, 1998; Goleman, Boyatzis, and McKee, 2002).

We also assume that even if people have a high level of self-awareness, they may be unwilling, for many reasons, to discuss their personal beliefs and the impact of their behavior openly with one another. Marshak and Katz, as they explore "covert processes," suggest that people will typically express to others—and make overt—what they believe to be "acceptable proper, reasonable and legitimate" (Marshak and Katz, 2001). Based on our observations of both successful and troubled partnerships, our last core assumption then is that partners face two key challenges. They must accept the value of self-awareness and seek to expand it, *and* they must be willing to openly explore personal information with one another. If they are not, then personal positions and reactions will remain covert and undiscussable, leading inevitably to a disabled partnership that is unable to develop strategically, efficiently, and creatively.

Putting a Relationship to Work: An Inner Blueprint for Partnership Development

The development of a successful partnership involves two sequential phases, the initiation of an *Exploratory Phase* and the emergence of an explicit *Partnership Phase*. As shown in Figure 15.1, we separate the steps in this unfolding process in another way as well. We have created a demarcation between inner, personal activity that is conducted privately by each partner, and behavior that is expressed directly as a consequence of this interior work. This boundary between inner and outer work is called the *Line of Visibility*, and it represents a point of decision for each partner, since once a person has identified personal perceptions, hopes, wants, and concerns, this material is available to be explored and negotiated with the other. Like the JoHari Window, a construct for understanding what is known to self only and what is known to others, our *Line of Visibility* identifies the moment when partners must make choices in the service of the relationship and simultaneously in the service of the work that they engage in together.

In Stage 2 of our model, the behavior that one person presents to another person is the manifestation of both predetermined and environmental factors, and these will be integrated and expressed in both clear and subtle ways. Research over the last few decades, for instance, demonstrates that one's genetic material plays a significant role in shaping self-specific character and temperament; in addition, experiences in one's family-of-origin and in subsequent personal biography will also shape personality and behavior. Further, there is the influence from messages received as a member of different identity groups, according to gender, race, age, social class, sexual orientation, and so on. And finally, since people live in a social and cultural context, mindsets and hence behavior will also be affected by experiences in school, religious settings, neighborhoods, and geographic cultures. Thus, when two individuals begin to know one another, they are each bringing to the conversation layers of personal characteristics and experience, and some of this information will be visible to the other person, through both appearance and behavior.

However, in the case of potential partners, as people talk with one another about themselves (Stage 3), we propose that they will also begin to pay attention to three specific and deeply significant qualities in the other person. They will be influenced strongly by what they see or assume to be the *status, motive,* and *competence* of the "other" (Stage 4). These factors are critical because they identify important interpersonal concerns that play a powerful role in the development of *working relationships.*

As Stage 4 indicates, when people assess differences in *status,* for instance, the underlying relationship issue is *power and control.* They make comparisons with the "other," based on assumptions about where they stand in terms of personal power and how any perceived differences in power might emerge during a relationship. The question they must answer is, "Will I have a sufficient amount of influence and control in this working relationship?"

At the same time, a second concern relates to perceptions of the other person's underlying *motives* both for considering a partnership and later for making the many decisions that they will face. Here, people are paying careful attention to behavioral cues that help them judge another's integrity and authenticity, since the underlying relationship issue is *trustworthiness.* In this case, the question to be answered is, "Will I be able to trust this person as we work together?"

The third concern, *competence,* is also of vital importance to potential partners because it relates to the actual work. Obviously, since the purpose of partnership is accomplishing tasks together, at the very least each person wants to be sure that the "other" has the skills and experience to do "the job." For example, sometimes people with similar skill sets decide to join together to intensify the impact of their individual effort. In other situations, people become partners because putting sets of different and complementary skills to work broadens the impact of their effort or creates a new synergy of quality or creativity. Regarding this third relationship issue, the concern is, "Will we be able to work together in a *positive interdependence?*"

FIGURE 15.1 An Inner Blueprint for Partnership Development

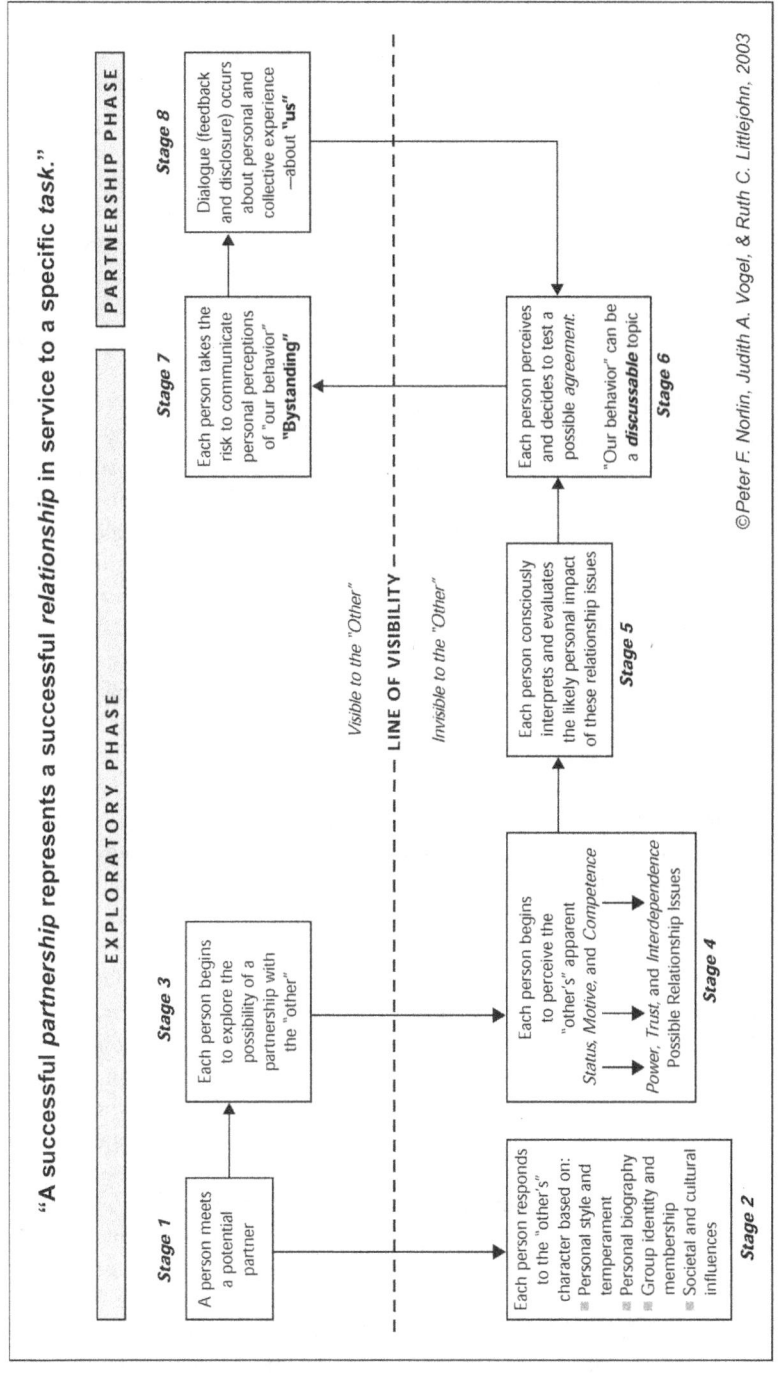

"A successful *partnership* represents a successful *relationship* in service to a specific *task*."

EXPLORATORY PHASE

PARTNERSHIP PHASE

Stage 1
A person meets a potential partner

Stage 2
Each person responds to the "other's" character based on:
- Personal style and temperament
- Personal biography
- Group identity and membership
- Societal and cultural influences

Stage 3
Each person begins to explore the possibility of a partnership with the "other"

Stage 4
Each person begins to perceive the "other's" apparent
Status, Motive, and Competence
Power, Trust, and Interdependence
Possible Relationship Issues

Stage 5
Each person consciously interprets and evaluates the likely personal impact of these relationship issues

Stage 6
Each person perceives and decides to test a possible *agreement*.
"Our behavior" can be a *discussable* topic

Stage 7
Each person takes the risk to communicate personal perceptions of "our behavior"
"Bystanding"

Stage 8
Dialogue (feedback and disclosure) occurs about personal and collective experience —about **"us"**

Visible to the "Other"
- - - LINE OF VISIBILITY - - -
Invisible to the "Other"

©*Peter F. Norlin, Judith A. Vogel, & Ruth C. Littlejohn, 2003*

Of these three important, underlying relationship issues, *trustworthiness* presents an interesting paradox. On the one hand, each potential partner requires a certain threshold of information, both assumed and observed, about the other's apparent motives in order to experience enough trust to make an explicit agreement about partnership. On the other hand, trustworthiness is a phenomenon that requires active testing through real experience to be confirmed. Tension thus emerges from the need to feel enough trust to risk living more fully into a relationship in which trust can be tested—to be confirmed, shaken but renewed, or finally denied. This paradox recalls the old chicken or the egg question. In this case, both people need to act "as if" sufficient trust exists in order to create the conditions to test trust. Only through that cycle of risk can trust deepen to a level that supports a genuine partnership. And only if trust develops can the other two key relationship issues be handled successfully.

Several key points are important during this initial period of observation, assessment, and reflection. First, we see this series of early steps as a developmental process. This means that potential partners will feel comfortable moving toward a more open conversation about an actual partnership when they have decided that they feel "good enough" with their assumptions about the other's *status, motive,* and *competence.* Next steps in the *Exploratory Phase* are possible because the questions about the relationship concerns have been satisfactorily answered—for the moment. Nonetheless, these specific concerns will persist for both; as a working relationship develops, each partner will monitor new information that accumulates and integrate it with past assumptions. At stake is whether people will continue to pursue a partnership based on what they continue to learn about the "other."

Throughout this process of generating and testing hypotheses about another person, they are also generating several kinds of informal feedback about themselves in relation to the "other." The yardstick they are using is

ultimately their perceptions of their own *status, motive,* and *competence* as compared to the "other's" (Stage 5). When people feel "good enough" about the other person's behavior, it is also because they have decided that, in some satisfying way, there is a "good fit" between their evaluation of themselves and their evaluation of the other person. Further, each person makes assumptions about how they themselves are seen through the other person's eyes. The question arises, "Will we be a good match?" If the answer is, "Hmmm, could be," then the possibilities for an actual partnership to develop increase.

Finally, during this *Exploratory Phase,* there is a continual interplay between internal process and external conversation, which means that people must decide whether they will share their thoughts aloud across the *Line of Visibility.* As people grow more familiar with each other, whether in a single conversation or over months of initial relationship, they find themselves building a database about the other person either by asking questions directly, or using informal cues, or both. The crucial issue, we've observed, is whether both people are able and willing to use this information in the service of the relationship. When two potential partners consciously reach the point of making a decision about whether to comment openly about their personal thoughts and feelings about the other person and the possibility of relationship, then they have moved into the realm of process observation, a step (Stage 7) we refer to as "bystanding."

As people stand on the edge of this choice, they are teetering on the brink of entering the *Partnership Phase,* because as they demonstrate the *ability* to talk about their interpersonal process, they are also demonstrating their *willingness* to do so. In other words, their relationship becomes a "discussable" topic (Stage 6). We believe this is the "moment of truth" for partnership development because it means that in addition to dealing openly with task issues, two people will be able to openly negotiate and resolve issues in their relationship— to talk about "us" (Stages 7 and 8). Obviously this is not a one-time decision. To ensure that a partnership endures, both people must value "bystanding" and "discussability," and over and over again, they must talk about the behavior that they observe in their *working relationship* in an ongoing process that hopefully deepens trust and supports successful collaboration.

Taking Practical Action: Some Conditions for Success

What, then, are the implications of this model? Formal partnerships rarely dissolve because of the technical incompetence of one or both individuals. In our experience, partnerships typically fail because partners don't value or access their own self-awareness and because they ignore emotional issues in their working relationship. There are some telltale signs of partnership disintegration. On a continuum of gradual personal disengagement, these include

- Open competition—an ominous sign, but we are most hopeful when partners are still competing with each other because this means they're still engaged in the relationship
- Unresolved, continuing power struggles
- Dysfunctional, triangular communication —here a third person is used to absorb feelings that are judged to be undiscussable with the "other"
- Broken promises
- Silence
- Absence—the most damning indication that a partnership is irreparably fractured

To avoid this depressing cycle, the most important first step two potential partners can take is to initiate a conversation during the *Exploratory Phase.* Specifically, to begin their relationship in a solid way and to ensure its sustainability, both partners must have the appetite and the skill to recognize—and talk about—what they notice about each other's *status, motive,* and *competence,* and how this awareness is likely to affect their working relationship in the future.

Successful partnerships are thus based on a special blueprint of relationship requirements. Beyond the *Exploratory Phase* and throughout a *Partnership Phase,* to maintain a successful partnership, individuals must also consciously monitor both competitive and collaborative *impulses* in themselves and in their relationship and then also consciously balance competitive and collaborative *behaviors.* Achieving this balance is critical, because if people in partnership begin to compete with one another more than they collaborate, then the dynamics of winning will consume their working relationship. And unfortunately, if one or both partners concentrate on winning as they work with each other, with colleagues, and with customers, then both will ultimately lose the partnership. The answer? To make a key agreement: to mutually *increase* behavior that both partners experience as collaborative, and to mutually *manage* behavior that they experience as competitive.

We need to be clear here. The urge to compete, to win, is a useful, powerful force in most business situations; the desire to win seems to be a core component of human nature; and we don't believe that we can eliminate it from human interaction. We also know that competition has some unintended consequences that can influence human emotions and behavior in unfortunate ways (Kohn, 1986). By definition, a partnership is created to capitalize on the synergies unleashed by "working with." When people begin to compete with one another, the focus shifts from relationship performance to individual performance, and people are concerned about themselves, not about their relationship. Thus, if people are not willing or able to control their competitive impulses and behaviors in the best interest of their working relationship, a partnership may limp along, but it will never be truly successful or stable.

Once partners recognize the need to operate within this balance, they are free to use their collaboration as a strategy to win externally, to dominate whatever external competition they face together. Fortunately, one of the effective and efficient ways to achieve this dynamic balance is to design work structures that will increase collaboration and manage competition, since in systems dynamics, "structure determines behavior." Fortunately, too, such structural options come in a variety of shapes and sizes. For instance, people can adopt formal or informal agreements about the way they will work together, and these "rules of the road" can be tested and revised until partners feel comfortable. Based on shared values of mutual respect, these "rules" can effectively guide "difficult conversations" during the likely times of conflict (Stone, Patton, and Heen, 1999). Other examples include regular meetings, explicit procedures for managing task requirements, agreements about budget allocations and professional fees, metrics for tracking and measuring partnership performance and reports for documenting it, technology to enable communication, and the co-location of partner's offices and work spaces. We believe that it is less important how people choose to create the correct balance between competition and collaboration than the fact that they recognize the need to create it and work to do so.

Managing Familiar Partnerships: The Impact of Context and Boundaries

The *Blueprint for Partnership Development* and its associated competencies provide a roadmap to guide the successful formation of any partnership. For organization development professionals there are some predictable opportunities for partnership that arise in work contexts and that create interesting challenges for their collaboration. Three such possibilities arise for many consultants during their careers. These are pairings of internal and external consultants, of two internals, and of two externals. Each pairing offers the potential for valuable service to clients and satisfying collaboration with each other, and each challenges the partners in several important ways.

In the case of an internal and external consultant pair, an important added structural issue arises from the generic concerns regarding *status* that were described earlier. Since frequently an external consultant is hired to provide additional experience, wisdom and credibility, the challenge to each partner is to clarify and monitor the resulting power balance in the relationship. It is common for each partner to collude, with or without awareness, in a process of assigning "guru" status to the external consultant. Several common versions of this projection include the "Invited Guest," the "Magical Outsider," and the "Detective" (Norlin & Vogel, 2002). It can be highly functional for partners to recognize differences in their expertise and utilize these effectively; however, it is important that the internal not abdicate power to or become overly dependent on the external. The corollary is that the external must be vigilant to avoid taking over, functioning rather as coach and shadow consultant when appropriate, and generally supporting the long term effectiveness and status of the internal who will, after all, remain as the ongoing resource in the organization. In any continuing collaboration, these issues need to be discussable and the resulting behaviors negotiated to the satisfaction of each and to the benefit of clients.

For the external partner, a second and related consideration is to manage consciously and ethically the normal interest in generating more work; the potential pitfall is to increase the likelihood of continued engagement at the expense of the internal's role. Inherent in this pairing is the different structure of earnings, and we believe that the external consultant is primarily accountable for consciousness and self-management on this matter.

Unique to the partnership of two internal consultants is the handling of the "sibling" relationship that arises from their shared "residence" in the organization. Specifically, they are both imbedded in the cultural context in which competition for promotions, salary increases and bonuses, and reputation may be intense. They need to handle the inevitable anxiety of whether a project will succeed or fail and who gets credit or blame. Further, as two internals, they share the challenge to be simultaneously both insiders *and* conscious managers of the marginal role and boundaries required of OD practitioners; specifically, they need to each be aware of and to assist the other to maintain objectivity, courage and perspective regarding this balance—no small challenge!

When two externals become partners, the dynamics in their relationship are both similar and different to those generated during internal partnerships. In this final pairing, the externals also need to handle "sibling rivalry" for approval of the client but from outside the margin of the organization. In addition, they must carefully monitor the allocation of their fee-based time in order to ensure that the client receives the most for their money.

Finally, whether internal or external, for OD consultants to fulfill the promise of their partnership, they need to develop a regular, high level practice of giving and receiving feedback, thus becoming professional buddies in the ongoing commitment to growth of skills and "use of self." These are the keys to long-term success. In this way, they will be able to fulfill the formal goals of their consulting engagements and also model partnership, an intervention in itself.

A Final Thought

In our work with partnership development, it is our experience that successful work partnerships have something in common with other intimate, collaborative performances like trapeze artists, jazz groups, and committed love relationships. When they're really good, they look easy. But this appearance belies the truth: partnering requires courage, superior interpersonal skills, and ongoing commitment to explore deep levels of the self and the other. The process is filled with challenge, but a map such as our *Inner Blueprint for Partnership Development* can serve, we hope, as a useful guide. The payoff when a "working relationship" *works* is worth the effort.

References

Goleman, D. (1998). *Working with emotional intelligence.* New York, NY: Bantam Books.

Goleman, D., Boyatizis, R., & McKee, A. (2002). *Primal leadership: Realizing the power of emotional intelligence.* Boston, MA: Harvard Business School Publishing.

Kohn, A. (1986). *No contest: The case against competition.* Boston, MA: Houghton-Mifflin.

Marshak, R.J., & Katz, J.H. (2001). Keys to unlocking covert process. *OD Practitioner, 33* (2), 3–10.

Measures, J. (2003). The healing relationship. *Meridians,* 10, (2/3), 8–16.

Norlin, P., & Vogel, J. (2002). Making "house calls": Whom do our clients expect to see when the doorbell rings? *Practicing OD,* 1 (1).

Stone, D., Patton, B., & Heen, S. (1999). *Difficult conversations: How to discuss what matters most.* New York, NY: Penguin Books.

Wheatley, M. (2002). *Turning to one another: Simple conversations to restore hope to the future.* San Francisco, CA: Berrett-Koehler.

CHAPTER 16

Reflections on a Cross-Cultural Partnership in Multicultural Organizational Development Efforts

Maria C. Ramos and Mark A. Chesler

THERE IS CERTAIN NEATNESS to theories and models that seek to explain human interaction and organizational behavior. The practice of organizational development (OD) and multicultural organizational development (MCOD) is, however, not very neat. We address these issues in the context of our long-term partnership as activist practitioners and generators of scholarship in OD and MCOD. In so doing we discuss: (1) the development and dynamics of our own cross-cultural partnership, particularly our race, gender, and professional orientation as scholar-practitioners, (2) how we used our partnership as an intervention and clients' reactions to it, and (3) the implications for cross-cultural partnerships in MCOD work in general. As we illustrate these issues in MCOD, we draw from three extended consultations with two corporations in different industries and a major university.

Many organizations have engaged over the past two decades in large systems OD or MCOD change efforts. While some of the challenges confronted in MCOD work are similar to those in the practice of OD, others are quite different. The reality is that most organizations have diverse work forces, but most do not behave as or aim at becoming truly multicultural or inclusive (Jackson & Hardiman, 1994; Miller & Katz, 2002). Moreover it might seem obvious that OD practitioners are committed to the eradication of social oppression, it is not so in practice. MCOD differs from more traditional forms of OD in several respects: (1) it focuses directly on issues of social identity and attendant oppression, (2) it assumes that organizational cultures and practices reflect the dominance of White male elites, (3) it assumes that attitudinal change is a minor, albeit important, element in organizational change (Chesler, 1994). In addition, MCOD differs from most traditional diversity efforts in its systems approach that goes beyond concerns with climate, management training in cross-cultural relations, or policy-level innovations.

An essential element of all MCOD change efforts is the development of staff that understands oppression and discrimination, organizational development and change, adult learning theory and practice, and their own attitudes and behavior toward themselves and others different from themselves (Cross, 2000). A critical initiative in the selected MCOD system change efforts we worked with involved the development of internal MCOD change agents and consultants. The initiatives, differing by organization, included nurturing a core internal change team, developing inter-group dialogue facilitators, and grounding diversity champions in MCOD theory and practice. We demonstrated the power of cross-cultural collaboration, while simultaneously transferring our knowledge and coaching internal practitioners in creating their own innovative interventions. Since the three organizations and interventions differed, the ways in which we played out our roles with one another and with these organizations differed as well: context matters!

The Nature and Power of Our Collaborative, Cross-Cultural Relationship in MCOD

The preferred consultant team in MCOD practice reflects diverse social identity memberships, particularly race and gender, often sexual orientation, as well as others. Consulting in cross-cultural teams can establish credibility and build trust by reflecting the social identities of different organizational members and giving authentic voice to their experience. It also can demonstrate the hoped-for outcomes of MCOD interventions by modeling an effective cross-race, cross-gender collaborative working partnership. The partnership role demands a personal willingness to work on one's own issues and dedicating oneself to continued personal growth in diversity and social justice. It is based on an agreement to courageously work the social justice issues within the consultant partnership, in the work and with the clients. The common ground shared in the MCOD consulting partnership is mutual and sustained support for grappling with the ongoing challenges confronted in doing the work.

The collaborative MCOD consulting partnership that we established was initially based on our most apparent social identity differences of race and gender, our professional affiliation as scholar-practitioners, and our bond as social

justice activists. Our work together permits us to act on our values and deepens our personal friendship by witnessing each other's good work and relying upon one another in some tough situations. Maria is a woman of Color and Mark is a White man. Maria is a second generation American born, Black woman of Cape Verdean descent. Cabo Verde is an African nation colonized by the Portuguese, hence the Latin name. Within the subordinate racial group of Blacks, she is a member of a minority ethnic-cultural group. Mark is an older White man of European-Jewish descent, second generation American born. Within the dominant racial group of Whites, he is a member of a subordinate religious-cultural group. We often observed how people of our own racial group put us through "special tests" because of our minority ethnic-cultural identities. As one example, Maria was asked to explain her race and ethnicity to a group of African-American leaders who had French or English names so they could understand how she belonged in that affinity group. In another situation, Mark was given at best a lukewarm reception into a predominantly White group because he had missed the first day of a session because it fell on Yom Kippur. These tests also led to our conversations about intraracial dynamics that furthered appreciation for and trust in one another.

Professionally, we both identify as scholar practitioners or practical theorists. The owner of a consultant firm, Maria is OD/MCOD practitioner who is also a scholar, teaching in universities regularly but secondarily. In contrast, as a professor of sociology at University of Michigan, Mark is a scholar who practices OD/MCOD regularly but secondarily. We recognized and appreciated building synergistically from each other's backgrounds and strengths with complimenting perspectives. Some examples of our collaboration include translating academic jargon into corporate language, using corporate cases to illustrate academically derived concepts, bringing the realities of external underrepresented constituencies to burst the corporate and academic privilege bubbles, and challenging the one-up perspectives of leaders with action research results from their own organization's membership.

Our collaboration has not been without struggles relative to the demands of our primary work contexts (Wasserman & Kram, 2009). Mark has suggested to Maria that she write more, although it meant taking time from consulting and perhaps not meeting clients' and associates expectations and needs. Maria has asked Mark to consult more frequently, though doing so encroached on his time for teaching, writing, and research. Managing the tension between scholar and practitioner roles can be a difficult balancing act.

We share a common ground of social justice activism. Separately each of us has been a community organizer to eliminate discriminatory practices, an initiator of social affinity groups for personal growth, and a developer of emerging social justice change agents. We belong to common professional and personal support networks of colleagues and friends dedicated to eradicating social oppression. Our race and gender identities and the difference in our generations meant that the sociopolitical environments of our activism differed. Mark's activism was shaped by the civil rights, voter-rights, and desegregation era of his youth and his experience organizing advocacy groups for families of children with cancer. The U.S. and international Black liberation, student, women's, and Pan African movements of her youth shaped Maria's activism. Mark channeled his activism into conducting action research and creating models useful to social justice change agents, including himself as he consulted. Maria channeled her activism into translating social justice change models and practices into change movements in organizations, writing about and for her consulting practice.

Early in our work relationship and continually deepening over time, we developed a high degree of personal, as well as professional trust, affection, and respect for one another. This deep relationship was facilitated by Maria's appreciation of Mark as a White male colleague who could support her without being protective and who could join forces with her in response to inappropriately personalized racial or gender attacks. Mark appreciated Maria's willingness to work with his embedded racism and sexism, his lack of corporate experience and her support when working with people acting out their prejudice and pain inappropriately with him. As we let each other do our own thing around an agreed upon agenda we also debriefed in ways that took issues, but not ourselves, seriously. Sometimes when reflecting on our presentations and interventions we found humor in each other's perspective and whether we said or did what we intended. Our freedom to joke with one another in public and obvious enjoyment in working with one another positively affected organizational members' level of trust and engagement.

The common ground and trust we developed also provided the security to challenge each other's style, interventions, and thinking. Thus, we have had an on going dialogue that has been a productive incubator for emerging models for practice and for encouraging greater client engagement and challenge. Our reflections on this partnership have revealed that:

- Each of our social identities brought to the partnership and the workplace different experiences, outlooks, and ways of relating to MCOD practice.
- Each of our professional standpoints brought some particular strengths and weaknesses. While in most contexts these standpoints are disrespected by the other, in our partnership they fueled a higher order integration of both scholarship and practice. As one organizational member commented, "Maria was more the therapist and Mark more the professor—a good team."
- Both of us saw one another as scholars and knowledge generators (although perhaps different types of scholars) and as practitioners or activists (although perhaps as different types of practitioners).

We discuss some of these differences and commonalities in the following descriptions of the consultations.

The Scope of the Consultations and Client/Organizational Reactions

The multicultural organizational development change work in all three client organizations was contracted with Ramos Associates as the primary consultant. The overriding goal of these system-wide MCOD efforts was the creation of inclusive, supportive work environments for all members (Chesler, Lewis & Crowfoot, 2005; Cox, 1991; Jackson & Hardiman, 1994; Miller & Katz, 2002). This approach involved: a core organization-wide change team of top level executives, managers, formal and informal leaders; an organizationwide human resources leadership change team; and change teams for each line of a business (LOB) and/or departments. Our MCOD consultation to those charged with planning and implementing organizational change efforts included (in different degrees in different consultations):

- Organizational assessments
- Strategic planning toward an inclusive environment
- Alignment of MCOD mission, values and performance expectations
- Diversity training, development, and coaching

We experienced many reactions to our partnership over the years and across client groups, particularly some frequent patterns of reactions to our cross-cultural pairing. While we shared power within the context of specific interventions, overall the primary power, for reasons of relevant expertise, experience, and primary contractor relationships, rested with Maria. For some participants, this was a very welcome and even inspiring experience. As two African American women noted, "Having Maria take the lead made me feel good. I iden-

tified with you and was proud of you," and "I saw Maria as a strong leader and Mark as second in command." At times, the reality of a woman of Color as the primary power, and the role of a White man as secondary, was confusing or challenging to organizational members, especially to those steeped in traditional race/gender assumptions and stereotypes. As a White man said, "I struggled with the differences in their styles—Maria took up space and Mark stayed more quiet." The power reversal was not confusing to us because we both had experience as leaders and subordinates in cross-race and cross-gender teams and coalitions. In the planning and design sessions as well as in public presentations described here, we deliberately alternated leadership roles.

The particular interventions referenced in this article occurred in three very different organizations. A brief description of each and the highlights of the corresponding intervention are provided.

A USA-based science and technology company operating in many countries was a long standing client. In response to an ever-increasing demand for tailored training and consultation from geographically disbursed businesses centers, Ramos Associates created a curriculum for internal MCOD consultants, with participants from all lines of business (LOB) and corporate functions, not just HR. Three phases of the program included use of self as an instrument of change, MCOD models/theories, and organizational practice. The self-selected participant group in the MCOD consultant training was demographically and professionally diverse. All were change agents engaged in corporate-wide or LOB valuing people/diversity efforts, including organizational assessments, upward mobility planning, critical incident investigations and intervention, and internal or external constituency relationship building. Our work was to transfer our academic approach about social justice and develop their skills as multicultural organizational consultants. Maria's identity as a corporate-related woman of Color opened the doors to certain privileges, especially among corporate leaders and members of underrepresented social identity groups. Mark's identity as a White man opened some doors of privilege, yet in this corporate sector some doors seemed stuck at half-open, as his knowledge was seen as interesting but not necessarily to the point.

The final stage of this MCOD internal consultant development program included one-on-one debriefing and advising sessions with each of the participants. We gave the internal consultants targeted feedback on what we saw as their strengths and areas for further development and offered follow-up coaching upon request. In an event that highlighted the nature of our cross-cultural partnership, Mark received a call from a Black woman HR manger who sought his advice on handling a unique problem. A group of White men leaders had taken a gender-mixed group of employees out for a celebration dinner. Towards the end of the celebration, fueled by libations, one of them yelled "hog run," followed by several of them dropping on their hands and knees to the floor and scrambling under the tables to look at the women's legs, etc. The HR manager wanted to share her personal reactions and professional concerns with a trusted white man consultant. Mark checked in with Maria about the issues for this Black woman manager, subordinate to the leaders in question, that he might not have considered, and whether there were any precedents for dealing with this type of incident (No—it was a totally unique situation at the adult level). Also, given its bizarre nature he needed to share it with her.

We worked with a large, Tier 1, national, public university with multiple undergraduate and graduate programs to implement a new MCOD effort. Maria and Mark consulted to an internal change team of representative leadership from all departments on an ongoing basis to support the President's MCOD initiative. The demographically diverse internal change team included faculty, students, union and non-union managers, and professionals.

Organizational members and representatives responded in particular ways to Maria and Mark's social and professional identities. Mark's identity as university-related, White, man opened doors to certain privileges especially among the faculty. Although there was a great interest in corporate best practices in MCOD, Maria's "business approach" was seen at times less applicable.

Some particular race and gender dynamics during this work with the university highlight the way our own identities played out with organizational members. For instance, some White men faculty members were so intent on demonstrating their own expertise, and so threatened by our leadership, that their responses started to become a distraction to others.

We agreed that Mark would move close to them and try to neutralize their negative impact and suggest behavioral alternatives. In another circumstance, some African-American women administrators appeared to be unintentionally but constantly buffering or mitigating team members' progress. We agreed that Maria would work closely with them, providing coaching in a more effective set of behaviors. Finally, we switched leadership roles in the execution of a critical preliminary step with the client organization. In meetings to discuss the assessment of campus climate it was clear that a few White women bypassed Maria and spoke primarily to Mark. Our debrief of the meetings identified two underlying factors in these interactions. The overt factor was the understandably high regard they had for Mark as a social scientist who had done this work on other campuses. The covert factor was racial privilege expressed by White women toward Black women as a pattern of treating them as invisible or competing with them regardless of the apparent status or experience differential. Rather than confront it straightforwardly, on this occasion Maria asked Mark to take the lead in following up with this group on the development of a campus climate survey. Maria's goals were to avoid getting caught up in this dynamic and to expeditiously execute the climate survey. All MCOD consultants have to choose which tests they take on and we knew the consultation would provide other opportunities to work these intragender racial dynamics.

We also worked with a USA based pharma company operating in many countries. In an effort to sustain corporate sponsored initiatives, Ramos Associates created an inter-group dialogue facilitator development program for human resource professionals employed at many facilities. The development included four components: inter-group dialogue participation, theory and models of intergroup dialogue, individual assessment with personal and group coaching, and practice of intergroup dialogue co-facilitation in cross-cultural pairs (Huang-Nissen, 2005; Zuniga, Nagda, Chesler & Citron-Walker, 2007; Ramos & Mitchell, 2001).

Our agenda was to demonstrate how to work as collaborative cross-cultural facilitators, build a common ground of knowledge about intergroup dialogue, and coach individuals and pairs of facilitators. Individuals' reactions to us were based on their personal awareness and understanding of social identity and justice issues. Some People of Color and especially women of Color, bonded or attempted to bond deeply with Maria and distanced from Mark. Some other women of Color openly challenged Maria's power. Some White men sought racial validation from Maria; others evaded or avoided deep contact with Mark. Some White men bonded, or attempted to bond with Mark and distanced or hid from Maria. Some other White men saw Mark as a "race traitor" and as a danger to the hidden knowledge of White male power. Some People of Color tested Mark to see if he was a true ally. Clearly, both race and gender dynamics played a role all the time.

Generally Mark responded to overt challenges by relaxing and letting them develop, seeing how others in the group reacted; sometimes he was "triggered" and temporarily re-

treated. Usually he was able to refer to and use these incidents to illustrate general principles in race and gender interactions in later work with the group. When White men or women bonded with him, he tried to respond empathically by entering into deeper challenge and support, and by exposing enough of himself to make it safer for them as White people to make (and grow from) racial mistakes. He did not immediately respond to individual White people who avoided or distanced from him, but over time used these incidents as examples of broader racial and gender dynamics. And facing the caution or distance from People of Color Mark sought to do the work and show himself to them. Indeed, as one man of Color stated, "I appreciated Mark's point of view as a White man."

Maria generally responded to People of Color who bonded with her, especially women of Color, by developing supportive and challenging relationships. When men or women of Color challenged her, she often used their actions as an opening for moving them to the edge of their comfort zone and into learning. When White men challenged her, she first dealt with the surface issue, often turning it back onto them in an inquiring mode. She then engaged the covert message or concern that underlay their behavior or statements, referencing conceptual models to help them understand the meaning of their behavior.

We always talked after these sessions about these interactions, and our responses to them, discussing whether we thought each of us had handled a specific situation effectively and planning how to surface and make use of the event in future work with individuals or the group. For instance, during one dialogue session, an internationally-based Latino man described to the group how he had been banned from school dances because of his dark skin color, while his light-skinned cousin had been allowed to enter. The reaction by a White woman who held an international HR business partner position was tears and shame, because she had lived in that country totally unaware of the colorism that existed. With a quick look of acknowledgement towards each other, we each took our roles: Maria with support and affirmation to the Latino man, providing the space for him to tell his story, Mark with support to the White woman as she struggled with her naiveté and acknowledged her shame, both of us facilitating others' reflections to move the learning around the group.

The Cross-Cultural Collaborative Pair as an Intervention

We quite deliberately used our pairing as an evocative intervention in these collaborations. Our mere presence as a pair generated a rich mine of content and process relative to cross-race, gender, age, and professional identity issues, particularly relative to power and privilege. We were able to experiment with different ways of unveiling these covert processes through our interactions, as the following examples suggest.

- Anticipating the challenge posed by our apparent reversal of race and gender primacy, we planned interventions to deliberately use such confusions or challenges as "learning moments"—to deepen conversation concerning race and gender stereotypes about power.
- When our perspectives, related to our social identities, differed or were unclear, we sometimes explored them in front of clients—modeling how a cross-cultural partnership works through issues.
- We publicly used our own social identities, and clients' reactions to them, as examples of broader patterns of power, privilege, and oppression in intragroup and intergroup relationships.
- We utilized our relative competencies in both scholarship and practice to avoid the clients' easy trap of expecting (and seeing) most of the conceptual inputs being made by Mark and most of the practical conduct of experiential exercises being made by Maria.

- Above all, we operated as a pair, a team, and we were aware of participants' potential to demand race/gender loyalty or to diminish our power by separating us.

Lessons for Others and Ourselves

Based on our experience and conversations with organizational members and colleagues, we make the following recommendations to cross-cultural collaborative teams.

- Be open and authentic with each other, acknowledge mistakes, and continue your learning, and above all stay fresh and alive (Shepard's "first rule of thumb") in the midst of challenge and contradiction (Brazzel, 2007; Shepard, 1985).
- Trust, respect, and admire the differential expertise and experience of both partners and generate affection for their personages, because expertise and experience does not exist apart from other personal dynamics and characteristics of the partnership.
- Acknowledge and continue to inquire about the meaning (personal and professional) of different social identities/ backgrounds and their impact on the partnership and on organizational members.
- Challenge organizational members to think and act beyond concerns for diversity itself and to focus on their own and others' privilege and oppression, the existence of structural inequality and oppression, and the ways in which the organization and society sustain and might alter these patterns.
- Be willing to model for others how to challenge the stereotypes that only credentialed scholars working in the academy have theoretical or conceptual knowledge and that only consultants with corporate experience have practical or activist knowledge and ability.

Finally, we encourage OD practitioners to work in cross-cultural, collaborative partnerships reflecting the diversity of the world and the workplace. MCOD requires such collaboration and challenges the numerical dominance of White people in the field. Demonstrating multicultural theory and practice must be a core competency of our profession. MCOD work that involves acting on the commitment to social justice, acknowledging the things we have learned from and shared with one another, and enjoying our friendship and colleagueship, has valued benefits for ourselves and our clients.

We have been on the cutting (perhaps bleeding) edge of consultants working in inter-racial and inter-gender teams with organizations on issues which have been called at various times, diversity, MCOD, multiculturalism, pluralism, inclusion, etc. We have seen the change efforts morph over the years: the expected changes in the work population have occurred; the globalization of industry has become reality; and some People of Color and women have expanded their life opportunities. Even though the need for diversity is so inescapable that the business case seldom has to be made, much more change is required to lessen the level of structural inequality in major corporate or educational organizations and in the society at large.

References

Brazzel, M. (2007). Diversity and social justice practices for OD practitioners. +*OD Practitioner,* 39(3), 15–21.

Chesler, M. (1994). OD is not the same as MCOD. In E. Cross, J. Katz, F. Miller, & E. Seashore (Eds.), *The promise of diversity* (pp. 240-251). New York, NY: Irwin & NTL.

Chesler, M., Lewis, A., & Crowfoot. J. (2005). *Challenging racism in higher education: Promoting justice.* New York, NY: Rowman & Littlefield.

Cox, T. (1991). The multicultural organization. *The Executive,* 5(2), 34–47.

Cross, E. (2000). *Managing diversity: The courage to lead.* Westport, CT: Quorum Books.

Huang-Nissen, S. (2005). *Dialogue groups: A practical guide to facilitate diversity conversations.* Los Altos, CA: Corner Elm Publications.

Jackson, B., & Hardiman, R. (1994). Multicultural organizational development. In E. Cross, J. Katz, F. Miller, & E. Seashore (Eds.), *The promise of diversity* (pp. 231-239). New York, NY: Irwin & NTL.

Miller, F., & Katz, J. (2002). *The inclusion break-through: Unleashing the real power of diversity.* San Francisco, CA: Berrett-Koehler.

Berret-Koehler. Ramos, M., & Mitchell, C (2001). Dialogue throughout an organization. In D. Schoem, & S. Hurtado (Eds.), *Intergroup dialogue: Deliberative democracy in school, college, community, and workplace* (pp. 210–221). Ann Arbor, MI. The University of Michigan Press.

Shepard, H. (1985). Rules of thumb for change agents. *OD Practitioner,* 17(4), 93–98.

Wasserman, I., & Kram, K. (2009). Enacting the scholar practitioner role: An exploration of narratives. *Journal of Applied Behavioral Sciences,* 45(1), 12–38.

Zúñiga, X., Nagda, B., Chesler, M., & Citron-Walker, A. (2006). *Intergroup dialogue in higher education: ASHE Higher Education Report.* 32(2). New York, NY: Wiley Periodicals.

Use of Self as an Instrument of Change

Introduction

John Vogelsang and Matt Minahan

VOICES FROM THE FIELD

To be effective I need to understand people's different value systems, be open to new ideas, stay with what is uncomfortable, and understand the dynamics and consequences of choosing to stay or not stay with what is uncomfortable.

—Michael McGovern

I was influenced less by material and more by people. Having colleagues and mentors to learn from was really important. You can read *Flawless Consulting* by Peter Block but not know how to do the work unless you see it in action. It is great to see people practicing the models.

—Chuck Mallue

TOPICS COVERED IN THIS SECTION

- How effective use of self is key to influencing change in an organization.
- How effective use of self depends upon understanding how assumptions and other mental constructs influence behavior.
- How to foster a well functioning diverse workplace.
- How to encourage ethical leadership.
- How to counter covert dynamics in the workplace that undermine productivity and collaborative work relationships.
- How to continue learning about effective and appropriate use of self in the workplace.

WHY USE OF SELF AS AN INSTRUMENT OF CHANGE

"Use of self" is the term OD practitioners employ to name the complex set of awareness and behaviors that make it possible to be genuinely helpful to others. Especially for the HR Business Partner, it is critical to recognize that tools and techniques are only part of the work. Many times, the most important influence on whether the situation changes is how HR Business Partners engages with clients. Are they modeling the participative and collaborative principles they espouse and promote? Are they willing to listen to what is uncomfortable to hear? Are they willing to examine their own habitual behaviors and assumptions—those that serve them well and contribute to their success with others and those that do not serve them well and may be hindering their success?

What people bring as a person, how they partner with others, how they see the situation as assumption-free as possible, how they model what they advise, and how they provide a clarity and mindfulness to what is occurring and what is being communicated—all this helps others to take risks to learn and change. When people operate from a clear sense of who they are and from a personal authority and integrity, they invite others to do likewise.

THE CHAPTERS IN THIS SECTION

After defining use of self, this section deals with the mental constructs that influence perception of oneself and others, explores examples of ethical leadership, and finally describes ways to encourage continued learning about use of self. The five parts to this section are:

- Use of Self: The Most Important Instrument of Change
- The Mental Realities People Construct
- Ethical Leadership
- Counteracting Covert Dynamics

Use of Self: The Most Important Instrument of Change

In **Managing Use of Self for Masterful Professional Practice,** David Jamieson, Matthew Auron, and David Shechtman (2010) offer a way of understanding use of self and making it more actionable for those in professional helping roles. They define the use of self as the conscious use of one's whole being in the intentional execution of one's role for effectiveness in whatever the current situation is presenting.

Jamieson, Auron, and Shechtman also describe what using oneself involves—a life-long process of developing self-awareness and certain core competencies. The competencies include: *seeing* self, others, and the context; *knowing* by making sense of what one sees; and *doing* by having a full range of options and the courage to deliver what is most helpful for a given situation.

Managers and executives are dealing with increasingly complex and fluid environments. More people at different levels of an organization are being encouraged to be more self-managing. Lawrence Gould (1997) explores in **Personal and Organizational Authority: Bringing the Self into a System of Work Relationships** the personal guiding principles that will govern self-managed initiative and accountability. He defines the nature of personal authority, highlights its links to organizational authority, examines

through clinical cases how personal authority shapes organizational authority, and concludes with some key hypotheses about the kind of organizational culture that facilitates effectively taking up and exercising mature organizational authority.

The Mental Realities People Construct

The constructed inner realities people bring to their work are suffused with assumptions about "the way things are and are done" and learned habitual responses. Someone wants to discuss how to proceed with a project. The consultant or HR professional may immediately assume the person wants advice and begins operating from a helping role, taking them through a series of questions and suggestions that they have used many times to develop and execute projects. Only when they take in the strained look on the person's face do they stop to realize that they do not know what the person really wants, and they are operating out of a comfortable power role of being the expert.

Understanding inner realities or mental maps, as Chris Argyris (1977; Argyris & Schon, 1995)[1] calls them, helps to explain why employees are reluctant to report to top executives that one of their company's products is a "loser" and why the vice presidents of companies cannot reveal to their president the spectacular lack of success of one of the company's divisions. Such habits and attitudes, which allow a company to hide its problems, can lead to rigidity and decline.

Mental maps guide people's perceptions and actions, as well as the types of learning that either reinforce people's maps or lead to their examining and changing assumptions, implicit theories, values, and beliefs. Mental maps include *espoused theories*—how people describe what they do, why they do it, and what they would like others to think about what they do, and *theories in use*—the assumptions, beliefs,

[1]Argyris and Schon's theory is summarized here; the article is not included in this resource.

values, and learned responses that actually govern their actions. Often there is incongruence between espoused theory and theory in use. The process of learning is how to align the two.

However, according Argyris, there are two types of learning—single loop and double loop. When something goes wrong or there is a gap between our espoused theory and the results, people may use single-loop learning and seek to detect and correct the error by looking for another technique that will help them achieve some resolution (often a quick fix). The focus is on finding the right technique to affirm their espoused theory, even if each of their solutions continues to fail over the long run. If they stop to examine the assumptions, the problem-solving methods they use, their theory in use versus their espoused theory, and, in the case of the organization, the underlying norms, policies, and objectives, they are doing double-loop learning. They may find that the "problem" has more to do with their approach and the gap between their espoused theory and their theory in use.

In their research, Argyris and Schon also found that there were two theories in use that influence whether individuals and organizations practice single-loop or double-loop learning. People operating with Model 1 theory in use, which depends upon single-loop learning, make inferences about another person's behavior without checking whether they are valid. People advocate their own views abstractly without explaining. Their aim is to win and avoid embarrassment. They want unilateral control and unilateral protection of self, which leads to developing defensive routines that impair the potential for growth and learning. They may deliberately leave potentially embarrassing facts unstated in order to save face; and they resist public testing of their ideas and espoused theory.

People operating with Model II, which is fostered by double-loop learning, look to include the views and experiences of others. They want to test their inferences, gather valid and quality information and data about the situation. They are willing to make their own theory in use explicit to test it in dialogue with others. They want to share control and participate in designing and implementing solutions to problems. They are willing to surface conflicting views and engage in open and constructive conversation about those differences.

As Argryis and Schon indicate it is not easy to operate with Model II and double-loop learning and people often retreat to Model I single-loop learning. The transition to Model II often takes willingness of management to invite participation of others in the decision-making process, to demonstrate openness to inquiry and different viewpoints, and to be committed to examining their inferences, assumptions, and theories in use.

Another of Chris Argyris' helpful tools, the Ladder of Inference, is a simple model of how people process their experiences, create inferences about them, and take action at lightning speed without noticing that they are responding to the inferences and not the situation. Neil Samuels (2003), in **Diversity, Inclusion, and the Ladder of Inference,** describes how the Ladder of Inference provides a way to understand how people shape, interpret, and create a story about what they experience through the lens of their mental maps, beliefs, values, and assumptions. Based upon the story, people draw conclusions and take actions. It is important to be aware of how people jump quickly to assumption informed conclusions and actions. People need to learn how to slow down to understand how their assumptions, values, and beliefs, mental maps, influence their actions in order to connect with how others see the situation and how they have filtered out data that may lead to different preferable actions. This understanding will also help people to narrow the gap between their espoused theories and theories in use.

Mindfulness is an age-old practice that can also help people to slow down and understand how routinized approaches and mental maps are shaping their experiences. In a world of flux and rapidity, living mindlessly can result in a host of problems including but not limited to: tunnel vision, increased stress, reduced physical health, reduced creativity, and difficulty navigating complex systems. Empirical studies are now finding statistical support for what many have known for two millennia: that practicing mindfulness enhances mental and physical health, creativity, and contextual learning. Bauback Yeganeh and David Kolb (2009) discuss in **Mindfulness and Experiential Learning** how mindfulness techniques can enhance experiential learning. They also provide tools for practicing mindfulness in organizations.

How can HR business partners help others address their limiting assumptions and beliefs and the gap between their espoused theories and their theories in practice? Robert Marshak (2004) introduces in **Generative Conversations** a method that coaches can use to help clients address limiting assumptions and create new possibilities. Generative conversations are based on the premise that the way people see and respond to the world is determined by out-of-awareness cognitive structures that may be identified and addressed during everyday conversations. Marshak provides ways to listen for these unspoken but powerful organizing structures and how to intervene to challenge or change them.

While the words "diversity" and "social justice" are familiar, many managers can still be uncomfortable with diversity when it comes up and they may seek ways to address organizational issues without having to directly take on diversity issues. Michael Brazzel (2007) examines in **Diversity and Social Justice** ten diversity and social justice practices that support addressing diversity and social justice issues and dynamics as an integral part of OD practice.

Judith Katz and Karon Moore (2004), in **Racism in the Workplace: OD Practitioner's Role in Change,** encourage people to see the potential role they can play to both identify and address issues of racism in the organization within which they work. Blatant racism —overt hiring discrimination, denial of promotions, discriminatory policies and actions— is illegal and has become the exception versus

the rule in many organizations. Yet racism has not gone away. The top levels of management at most organizations are overwhelmingly White. The disparity of income between white people and people of color—a direct reflection of career opportunity—is still growing. Katz and Moore offer a way to look at group patterns in order to identify and work with untested assumptions and perceptions, people's often unconscious treatment of people, and the resulting actions that allow racism to permeate organizations.

What would happen if behavior could be clearly/systematically tracked, categorized, and analyzed? Recognizing the fact that race and gender are always present in just about everything people do and especially in relationships, how would it shift the conversation on partnering and other relationships if race and gender dynamics are talked about openly? What are the small and simple things that create day to day trauma and slights which build up pressure in unbalanced power relationships? To answer those and other questions, Cathy Royal (2010) developed a method to name and work through structural inequalities of privilege, exclusion, power, and oppression in the work place. She describes her theory in **Quadrant Behavior Theory: Edging the Center** as an approach that changes the landscape of the dialogue on power, privilege, and oppression and identifies language that reshapes the world and behavior of the change agent.

Ethical Leadership

Wendell Nekoranec (2009), in **Ethics and Leadership: OD Practitioner's Role in Change,** highlights recent research on ethical leadership among CEOs. He shares stories from two CEOs about how they believed they acted ethically in tough situations and analyzes their actions. The first story looks at how a CEO dealt with individuals in a time-sensitive situation. The second story examines how a CEO managed the complexity of a potential home office relocation and the steps he took to maintain support and influence in the organization.

Counteracting Covert Dynamics

Something is likely to become covert when untested assumptions, beliefs, or constructs are limiting either reasoning or choice; the basis of the covert dynamic is in the unconscious or shadow of the individual, group, or organization; or, behaviors, thoughts, or feelings are defined by the prevailing rules, norms, and/or culture as inappropriate, unacceptable, or out of place. It is important to be aware of covert processes and how they impact any change effort. Robert Marshak and Judith Katz (1997), in **Diagnosing Covert Processes in Groups and Organizations,** discuss how to identify and work with the three dominant types of covert processes in individuals, groups, and organizations: (1) blind spots and blocks, (2) unconscious or shadow dynamics, and (3) conscious disguises and concealments.

FOR ADDITIONAL LEARNING

For more information about use of self, you may want to read the following resources.

- Beck, D., & Cowan, C. (1996). *Spiral Dynamics: Mastering values, leadership, and change.* Malden, MA: Blackwell Business.

  Beck and Cowan posit that human nature is not fixed. Humans are able, when forced by life conditions, to adapt to their environment by constructing new, more complex, conceptual models of the world that allow them to handle new problems. Each new model includes and transcends all previous models. According to Beck and Cowan, these conceptual models are organized around so-called *Memes*: systems of core values or collective intelligences, applicable to both individuals and entire cultures.

- Block, P. (1993). *Stewardship: Choosing service over self-interest.* San Francisco, CA: Barrett- Koehler.

  Block explains how to integrate the management of work and the doing of work to redistribute purpose and power within an organization. He talks about how this can affect work flow, quality control, performance appraisal, pay systems, supervisory methods, job design, and human resources.

- Cady, S. (2004). Live with passion! Your first best alternative in life. *OD Practitioner,* 36(3), 47-52.

  Cady explores the Six Ways of the Passionate Soul and integrates his findings with social cognition, positive psychology, and motivation and develops a passion framework that lends itself to inspiring people, from all walks of life, to live their first best alternative.

- Cheung-Judge, M. (2001). The self as an instrument: A cornerstone for the future of OD. *OD Practitioner,* 33(3), 33–39.

  Cheung-Judge demonstrates the importance for OD consultants of establishing effective relationships with clients and the use of self as an instrument in their work. She explores key practices in owning and refining the use of self, and offers a partial list of activities relating to owning, refining, and integrating our self-knowledge and personal development.

- Kaplan, K. (2010). Enduring wisdom from women in OD. *OD Practitioner,* 42(1), 10–14.

  Kaplan investigated what the journey was like for women practitioners of OD by hearing their stories in their own words. In order to capture the diverse voices of women, not in comparison to men, but grounded in their own experiences and perceptions, 32 women from across the United States were interviewed. Described as the "second generation" of women OD consultants, they defined themselves as the first generation of women to get formally trained in the field.

- Martinez, E. (2010). The air up there: Tiptoeing through the halls of power. *OD Practitioner,* 42(2), 14–18.

  According to Martinez the major shortcoming of Affirmative Action Programs is failing to address the natural follow-up question: "Now what?" Martinez emphasizes the need to address both this question and group and system-level dynamics of power.

- Patterson, K., Grenny, J., McMillan, R., & Switzler, A. (2005). *Crucial confrontations.* New York, NY: McGraw Hill. (2009).

Patterson, et al. present tools for working with difficult conversations. The tools include how to prepare for the conversation, to transform anger and hurt feelings into powerful dialogue, to establish a safe space to talk, and to be persuasive.

- Scharmer, C. O. (2009). *Theory of U: Leading from the future as it emerges.* San Francisco, CA: Barrett-Koehler.

Our current times require a new consciousness and a new collective leadership capacity. Scharmer provides compelling stories,

exercises, and practices that help leaders shift awareness, connect with the best future possibility, and gain the ability to realize it.

- Winslade, J., & Monk, G. (2008). *Practicing narrative mediation.* San Francisco, CA: Jossey-Bass.

Winslade and Monk offer narrative approaches to conflict transformation and explore recent research on discursive positioning and the factors that influence conflict situations.

References

Argyris, C. (1977, October). Double loop learning in organizations. *Harvard Business Review*, 115-125.

Argyris, C., & Schon, D. (1995). *Organizational learning II: Theory, method, and practice* (2nd ed.). Englewood, NJ: Prentice Hall.

CHAPTER 17

Managing Use of Self for Masterful Professional Practice

David W. Jamieson, Matthew Auron, and David Shechtman

THROUGHOUT THE DEVELOPMENT of the OD field "use of self" or "self as instrument" has always been talked about or taught as important for the role of the change agent. Emphases ranged from self-awareness and personal growth to developing better skills in aspects of consulting. Interpretations spanned simply knowing more about your "self" to deeper recognitions of consciousness, choice, shadows, agency, behavior patterns, developmental theories, and intentionality. The National Training Laboratory's T-group movement during the 1950s and 1960s brought considerable attention to self-awareness, feedback, and interpersonal and group dynamics, helping to solidify use of self in understanding one's behavior and impact. While many education programs have pursued the theme or actual course work, our conceptual grounding and literature on this topic has remained sparse. Consequently, the idea of use of self has often been ambiguous, vague, and difficult to convert into action; and has mostly been a mentored skill or shared tips and techniques to aid understanding and behavior.

Concurrently, other professional helping disciplines have also pursued the same central concept and have created their own literatures. Perhaps the introduction of the term "use of self" came from Frederick Alexander who developed The Alexander Technique in the 1890s

which ultimately enjoyed an expansive adoption across numerous disciplines. His work was focused on the integration of the mind/body system and the relationships among psychological and physical functioning and the role of consciousness (Alexander, 1932). The professional or therapeutic use of self has also been discussed over many years in the education of counselors, psychotherapists, nurses, clinical social workers, occupational therapists, and teachers (e.g., Miller, 1962; Baldwin, 2000; Chitty, 1993; Rogers, 1961). As early OD pioneers came from many of these same disciplines, it is easy to understand how the concept could have entered OD.

The topic of use of self is critical in the daily interactions of any helping professional role and especially impactful in change since the responsibilities, ethics, and outcomes affect other's lives. Situations involving use of self are continuous in our lives as helping professionals. The greater our awareness of these situations, the better chance we have to effectively manage ourselves for the benefit of our clients or others. To the extent we are unaware when these situations occur, they go unmanaged and may potentially be unhelpful or do harm. We must see beyond our tools and techniques, as many times the only instrument we have is ourselves as we engage with our clients in dealing with their situations.

Our ability to see a client's situation as bias-free as possible, interpret it, and act on it may be the most foundational concept for OD practice. In the confusion, anxiety and emotions that permeate the dynamic of helping others and facilitating change, the process ultimately begins and ends with our internal landscape of characteristics, values, beliefs, and assumptions. In short, the structures that makes up our consciousness and "self."

Fundamentally, as we are the users of theory, processes, and concepts, they are only as useful as our ability to understand and use them helpfully and appropriately.

Effective use of self includes not only our self awareness, but also our ability to interpret what's going on as clearly as possible, and take action appropriate to the situation. Because OD work (and many other helping roles) require human interaction and relationships in their conduct, use of self will always be a critical factor in the effective execution of both help and change. By being a variable in a set of human equations, what we see, understand and do affects all the other variables as each cycle of work and interaction occurs. For these reasons, the study of use of self is foundational to both the field of OD and to each of us as human beings. This article is our establishment of a new way of understanding use of self and making it more actionable for those in professional helping roles.

What Is Use of Self?

Use of self is *the conscious use of one's whole being in the intentional execution of one's role for effectiveness in whatever the current situation is presenting.* The purpose is to be able to execute a role effectively, for others and the system they're in, without personal interference (e.g., bias, blindness, avoidance, and agendas) and with enough consciousness to have clear intentionality and choice. Our use of self should always be thought of in a specific context, exercised through some role, in service of something helpful and aligned with one's personal intentions (i.e., mission, vision, goals, and values).

"Who we are" always goes with us into each of our roles and situations. Our collective knowledge, thoughts, feelings, experiences, and vulnerabilities inform all that we do. Our understanding and beliefs about ourselves are continually evolving based on our independent assessments and what is socially constructed from our interactions with others (Shotter, 1997; Arnd-Caddigan & Pozzuto, 2008).

Our use of self shows up in several ways:

- In how we appear, talk, and present ourselves (both our physical and personal presence)
- In the invisible, but operable, parts of ourselves and our personalities, such as attitudes, values, motivations, biases, fears, assumptions, anxieties, feelings, habits, self-esteem, and hidden selves
- In the actions we take, decisions we make, choices we pursue, and styles and preferences we use
- In the strengths, experience, intelligences, knowledge, and skills we bring to each situation

Our use of self is further influenced by:

- Race, ethnicity, national culture, gender, age, and social identities
- Life and family histories
- Intentions, personal agency, and self-efficacy, and
- Levels of consciousness, self-awareness, and defensiveness

Managing our use of self begins with awareness, requires conscious sensing and interpreting, and takes form as a result of our intentional and unconscious actions. Learning to manage our use of self is a lifelong process as we are constantly receiving new and updated feedback on ourselves and our work.

In a 1995 presentation for the OD Network National Conference, Curran, Seashore, and Welp (1995) offered a model and concepts that provided a useful grounding for our work. They stressed the importance of developing awareness of one's impact and ability to have choice in behaviors. Their work discussed many concepts for understanding how we can manage presence, congruence, influence, and contact and how our ability to choose gets compromised by our own issues that serve as "hooks" in interaction with others and our inability to stay centered in the present situation.

The Use of Self Framework

To help understand and work with use of self, we have found it useful to think of the "self" as a collective portfolio of who we are, what we know, and what we can do as developed over a lifetime in both known and unknown realms. The "use" of self is organized around three core competencies and three levels of development (Figure 17.1). Organizing use of self into a basic framework is a critical step in both under-

standing and applying the concept with more concrete behaviors and multiple levels of skill. This framework advances work on this concept by: (1) building on and incorporating what has been shared before, both within and outside of OD; (2) including and emphasizing action-taking, as part of managing, which has often been lacking in the overemphasis on self-awareness; (3) focusing on concrete competencies for which a practitioner can develop skills; and (4) including developmental levels to provide ways to talk about how to improve or get better in use of self.

This framework captures the essence of what using ourselves involves over time. It includes two dimensions: (1) horizontal, represented as core competencies, and (2) vertical, represented as levels of development. Competencies describe the critical capabilities that practitioners use, in every situation, and throughout all stages of development. Levels of development describe the ability of practitioners to apply these competencies in helping

FIGURE 17.1 Managing Use of Self Framework

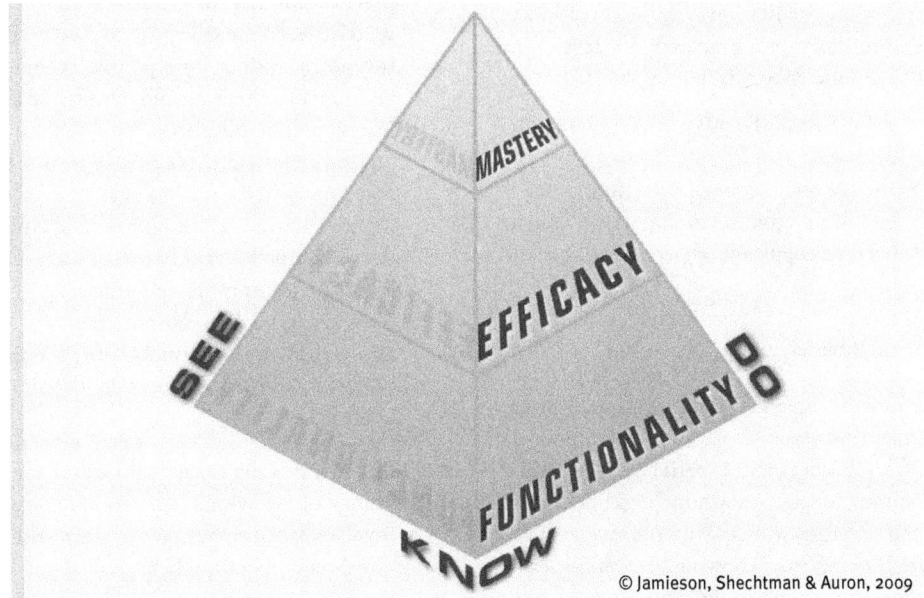

© Jamieson, Shechtman & Auron, 2009

situations. Competencies are how practitioners help. Levels of development are how well practitioners do their work.

Core Competencies

- **See**ing involves what practitioners are able to take in using the six senses. It is the competency of being aware of the world around us and the ability to take in as much data as possible. In developing the "seeing" competency we need to pay attention to seeing self, seeing others, and seeing context. Social sensitivity to the surrounding system is a way to understand this competency. This sensitivity can be compromised by our biases, personal frames, operating metaphors, and habitual assumptions. Core to this competency is the ability to see "reality" as others see it and as free of our own biases as possible, which includes both what is visible to us and what we can take in. It's also critical to learn over time to see both what is on the surface and what is below the surface or covert (Marshak, 2006). Maintaining a spirit of inquiry and openness is critical to leveraging effective seeing. This is often deepened through reflection, meditation, or other practices of getting quiet and centered. In developing this competency it is helpful to:

  - expand breadth and depth of inquiry and openness
  - enlarge one's scope of awareness
  - be able to recognize multiple types of data
  - become cognizant of personal filters and blocks
  - identify one's own individual and cultural biases

- **Know**ing involves making sense of what practitioners see. It is using a combination of knowledge and experience to organize information and draw hunches, conclusions, and interpretations. This process includes multiple ways of knowing (e.g., empirically, rationally, somatically, and socially constructed); practitioners may use a combination of many methods to give them meaning and confidence. In human systems work, the knowing phase often requires making meaning from limited data quickly and confidently. Knowing also comprises two key interpretive domains: learned theories (more objective) and internal mental models (subjective) developed through life experience. Both domains are crucial to the knowing process. The more objective domain contains theories, models and frameworks and allows practitioners to gain insights based on commonly held existing knowledge. The subjective domain, often understood as personal maps or mental models (Senge, 1990), allows practitioners to make use of internal belief systems, deeply held values, tacit knowledge, and profound life experiences. By combining the best external knowledge with one's internal understanding, practitioners improve their ability to gain insight, leverage the right data, and use proper discretion. At higher levels of development, knowing is executed through deeply internalized knowledge which often actualizes as intuition. In developing this competency it can be helpful to:

  - practice different ways of knowing
  - exercise learning agility
  - inventory various interpretive schemes and practice theories study academic research and publications work on integrating theory and experience into useable knowledge
  - develop awareness of cognitive and emotional components of knowing
  - identify meaning-making processes
  - recognize one's foundational values
  - raise one's consciousness of personal preferences and influences in decision-making

- **Do**ing involves the capacity for executing a full range of behavioral and action choices. It involves practitioners recognizing their options, demonstrating behavioral flexibility, and exercising personal skill and courage in a manner that delivers whatever is most helpful for a given situation. This capability executes the results of the previous two competencies. It is the culmination of the data intake and interpretation process that allows for the enactment of appropriate behavior. In developing this competency it can helpful to:

* develop one's skill repertoire
* develop a portfolio of action alternatives
* enhance one's ability to use will and courage
* develop the ability to execute, implement, and follow through
* enhance the ability to manage resistance
* raise one's patience and perseverance
* gain understanding of habitual preferences

This framework is intentionally simple. It represents the basic aspects of managing use of self. The competencies often operate within seconds of each other and should be understood as a dynamic representation of a practitioner's capacity to help. Competencies are constantly changing and evolving. Levels of development may be different for practitioners depending upon the topic and situation. One can move up and down the levels due to a variety of internal and external factors.

Levels of Development

Seeing human functionality through a developmental lens is critical to understanding use of self. Developmental theory states that human beings evolve through various levels of functionality, understanding, and outlook throughout their lives as they learn and grow. Persons must be seen as neither bad nor good, but in evolution through various phases of cognition, perception, individuation, and other categories that comprise the self (Kegan, 1982; Wilber, 2000). This developmental context, as applied to self, allows us to understand the various facets of the self that are growing throughout our lives. Thus, part of our work is to realize and integrate them as we grow.

In each competency there are levels of effectiveness that one can progress through. Each competency requires its own focus of attention and specific practice to improve. Below are the three stages that comprise the developmental component in the use of self framework.

Functionality is a stage of knowing "how to do it." One has learned what to do and how to operate in terms of basic aspects of seeing, knowing, and doing. One must concentrate and pay attention to doing it right, following appropriate steps or running through some criteria to determine use. One is starting to trust the material, method, technique, or concept. This may look like "doing it by the book" or applying theory to practice in a step by step fashion. This is similar to the phrase "conscious incompetence" or knowing what we are not sure of.

Efficacy is a further stage of development marked by increased flow and less concentration. Seeing, knowing, and doing become less challenging. The range of data available to work with, the knowledge available for sense-making and the behavioral flexibility of options and skills for taking action are expanded. It is marked by higher levels of confidence and agency in execution. We begin to operate from the inside and understand our role in what happens. The sequence of taking in, making meaning, and taking action become more seamlessly integrated. One begins to trust one's self in use of data, meaning-making, and action. This is similar to the phrase "conscious competence" or we are clear about what we know and are good at.

Mastery is the highest stage of development and is characterized by fully integrated and seamless work. One's presence has greater impact. Seeing, knowing, and doing have become simultaneous, back and forth activities with little conscious decision-making. One's own self-awareness has opened up ego-free space for professional work. Intentionality and end purpose are intertwined and unencumbered. One ultimately trusts in the process, outcome, and their role in it. This stage is marked by effortless action and sometimes "magical" occurrences that appear to come out of deep intuition. The three competencies blend together and operate in one fluid motion (Csikszentmihalyi, 1990). The actions of the individual are marked by an internal drive versus an external reliance on material. At this stage, one's presence—the deliberate living out of one's values—becomes the greatest technique for impacting change in an environment. It is similar to the phrase "unconscious competence" or we are no longer aware of what we do exceptionally well.

While we may gradually progress upwards, even masterful practitioners will sometimes operate at a functional level. How well we are functioning as an instrument, in any competency, will determine what level we can perform at in the present situation. Additionally, it is possible to operate at a level of mastery for seeing, while a functional level for doing. In this way, the model is fluid, with movement up and down the pyramid in any given situation or day.

Role and Importance of Self-Awareness

Our use of self engages cognitive, emotional, physical, and spiritual aspects at different moments and in different situations. Consequently, it requires development along all of these dimensions. The development process is a journey, mixing knowledge acquisition, self-awareness, and practice. Content knowledge provides concepts, frames of reference and technical requirements for taking action. Self-knowledge helps to illuminate the emotional, physical, and spiritual aspects of ourselves with greater understanding of feelings, triggers, strengths, limitations, values, personality traits, personal meaning, preferences, sensitivities, and vulnerabilities. Through self awareness, we gain greater consciousness, leading to greater intentionality and choice, and grow out of the confines of limited frames, biases, skills, and habits.

Self-inquiry and personal growth is critical to successful use of self. Who we are and

the work we do are inter-related and provide the milieu for our development. Thus, the development of self is a holistic practice where the human being and the work roles improve together. We can learn about ourselves and our internal landscape in many ways, including feedback, instruments, therapy, journals, and self assessment. Many times, we are thrown out of the nest early, utilizing unplanned opportunities to test our use of self. These situations offer significant opportunities, since the nature of growth is often an emergent phenomenon. The process of self-learning engages multiple cycles of awareness, interaction, and practice.

Self awareness has dominated much of the work in use of self and has overshadowed the importance of turning awareness into new behaviors or managing the use of self. This is especially limiting when considering the importance of the whole self in human systems work.

Finding Our Whole Self

Wherever we show up, our whole self comes along! We are always more than we present, more than we know, and more than we can control. The Johari Window (Luft, 1963; Luft & Ingham, 1955) provides a way to navigate what is known and unknown and what is open and hidden. What we don't know can surprise us or hurt us or others. Learning about "blind" areas can help us act with greater integrity. Journeys into the "unknown" may uncover new capabilities or talents. Ironically, learning more about ourselves is not a solo endeavor, as Culbert once wrote, "It Takes Two to Know One" (Culbert, 1967).

Without whole self-awareness, we only enter situations with knowledge of part of who we are and may not have the consciousness and choice to manage or leverage how we use our self for the welfare of the situation. We may also become victims of our own behavior, routines or blind spots, and under-optimize what we ultimately do. So part of the journey is a discovery of our different parts, selves, voices and messages, those we love and those we wish didn't exist, and accepting and integrating them into our whole being (Barry, 2008). By identifying, accepting, and re-integrating parts of who we are, we bring awareness and voice to these various selves, which allows us to not only understand them, but also to choose more fully when they arise and how we want to use them.

Use of self is founded in part in OD's humanistic lineage, through an understanding and acceptance of our inherent human-ness. Bob Tannenbaum, building on the work of Carl Rogers and other humanistic psychologists was an early advocate of the whole-self concept and of personhood, which embraces growth as reclamation of our full humanity (Tannenbaum & Eisen, 2005; Tannebaum, 1995). Likewise, the Gestalt perspective (Perls, Hefferline & Goodman, 1951) includes embedded and unresolved messages within us which have been split off during early life and now live mostly in our unconscious. Gestalt theory teaches us that parts that have been split off, like any system, inherently strive for wholeness and re-integration. Shapiro (1976) highlighted how split parts of our selves can act like additional "personalities" that need to be acknowledged and integrated for self realization and personal growth. Similarly, Seashore, Shawver, Thompson and Mattare (2004) describe the various conscious and unconscious "selves" inside of us that compete for attention and come to the forefront at various times, depending on the trigger or type of interaction.

One difficulty in this self-discovery journey is that some of what we don't know about ourselves resides in the unconscious. Jung refers to these parts as the "Shadow" (Jung, von Franz, Henderson, Jacobi & Jaffe, 1964; Jung & Storr, 1983), representing the inherent split in consciousness occurring from aspects that we hide, repress, and deny. The shadow operates as dark to light creating a polarity to be managed. If unaware, we tend to project these shadow aspects of ourselves onto others- turning a personal inferiority into a deficiency in

someone else. Our inner polarities operate similar to Argyris and Schon's (1974) espoused theory vs. theory in use-while one part of us is actively seeking one result, there can be repressed aspects seeking the opposite. Zweig and Abrams (1991) further elaborate on the many faces and powers of the dark side in our whole being.

Finally, another aspect of whole self, from sociology, is the "masks" individuals wear in society. Goffman (1955; 1959) explored the concept that humans will attempt to guide or control impressions of others, behaving and acting differently in different scenarios. Masks represent who we want to be or hide some aspect of who we are. And while a person is managing their impressions, they may also attempt to place various masks on others as well. Our authenticity is often compromised by the use of masks.

A whole-self approach would seek to acknowledge the masks, selves, and parts that make up our inner landscape and operate authentically. The whole-self approach is the acceptance and reclamation of our personhood (Palmer, 2004), of our humanity, and owning the polarity of our beings. By owning and accepting these aspects we can become more in charge of how we show up, begin to drop our masks and shields, and use our selves more authentically as agents of change.

The Role and Importance of Action-Taking

Using self awareness knowledge to influence behavior, intention, choice, and outcomes in service of another is where the "use of" comes into play. Doing something with self-knowledge is ultimately what counts! Action-taking represents the final stage in the use of self. It is the "Do," as referenced in the See, Know, and Do framework. Taking action is also likely the most complex and risky aspect of the use of self for a number of reasons.

• Helpful doing involves the culmination of effective seeing and knowing.

- Having role clarity is key to determining effective, intentional action
- The effectiveness of our work is mostly judged by others through our role execution

Though taking action requires a requisite amount of personal courage, even the most daring practitioner will encounter problems if the first two competencies are not executed properly. For example, a practitioner may be extremely skilled at confronting dysfunctional client behaviors. Yet this courageous act may do little-to-no good if it is employed in a client situation in which critical information has been missed or it has not been adequately understood.

The practitioner's choice of role is critical in determining effective action steps. Schein describes three main consulting roles: pair-of-hands, expert, and process consultant (Schein, 1998). When considering action options, one must be clear about the intended role. Often the best action to take in a client situation is not completely clear. The practitioner needs to bring their will and skill to bear in conjunction with the array of options they believe are relevant to the situation and both make a choice and act in accordance with their role intentions.

Most practitioners earn their reputation and make their living based on the results that they achieve through their work. This can create high stakes for many, including their esteem, public identity, and valued rewards. The action decisions a practitioner makes can therefore be encumbered with extra anxiety, confusion, and consternation.

Action taking can also become challenged by falling into habitual patterns, becoming stuck in comfort areas, or choosing options that are self-serving. The client's needs, the situation requirements, and the welfare of the system are the higher purposes in helping roles. Expanding one's behavioral repertoire helps to provide more options and greater confidence to act.

Self as Instrument of Change or Helping

Self as Instrument has often been used synonymously with use of self (Cheung-Judge, 2001; Smith, 1990; Glavas, Jules, & Van Oosten, 2006; McCormick & White, 2000). Technically, every use of self is instrumental in executing our role. Most often, this phrase has been raised in conjunction with change or helping, but could be just as relevant with other terms such as leading, healing, or learning. Because our use of self is so critical in professional relationships, we become instruments of the process we are trying to execute and of any changes we intend (Jamieson, 1991; Freshwater, 2002). If what we take in, understand, and do is related to any outcomes we achieve in our role, then our being becomes an instrument for seeing, knowing, and doing. That instrument can therefore be either highly effective across many situations, be of limited value in some situations, or stop working. It can become slow or inaccurate if we become unhealthy, emotionally knotted, or cognitively blocked. We can add functionality and advanced capabilities to our instrument over time and occasionally need to consider ways to renew and tune-up our instrument to maintain its usefulness (Heydt & Sherman, 2005). Our professional roles, including our ability to add value and do no harm, are helped or hindered by the instrumentality of our strengths and limitations, presence and movements, awareness and blind spots, cognitive and emotional intelligence, and fears and courage.

Managing Use of Self

In summary, we hope you take away these essential elements to understand and be able to manage your use of self:

- Self-awareness leads to knowledge and consciousness about one's self, allowing for better management of intentionality, choice, and impact.
- The desired end result is to perform our role(s) in service of help for others or a system (the situation). When we are able to manage our use of self, we are instrumental in the effectiveness of processes and outcomes.
- We use ourselves in all aspects of our work. We become the instrument for the core com-

petencies of seeing, knowing, and doing. We take in data in order to understand what "reality" faces us. We use all we have learned (theory, experience, tools, etc.) to assess or make sense of what we see and to identify action alternatives and strategies. We choose what to do and how to use our skills and will to take action.

- Like any instrument, we need development, calibration, tuning, and maintenance. Developing use of self is a lifelong journey. We can start anywhere in our life movie. Some of who we are is known, some is not and is discoverable, and some will elude us forever. The whole self journey pursues what's in and out of consciousness, what's presenting and shadow, what selves and voices have residence in our inner landscape, what's authentic and merely facework (Goffman, 1955). Over time, we are confronted with struggles for acceptance, integration, and better management.

- Development of use of self works on multiple dimensions such as, cognitive (theory, models, concepts, and tacit knowledge), emotional/interpersonal (EI, SI, CI, feelings, relations), spiritual (deeper meaning, higher powers, natural connections), and physical (somatic sensations, body-mind connections). Some dimensions operate simultaneously such as when we learn and use skills, methods, and tools and engage cognitive, emotional, and physical aspects. Reflection takes us singularly inside for some development, but social interaction (it takes two!) provides invaluable feedback from other perspectives.

- In pursuing the best in everything we do, we will work through levels of development starting with functionality, growing into efficacy, and ending with mastery. At each level, our work looks, and feels different. As we progress in effectiveness, execution becomes more seamless, there is greater flow and integration, one uses less conscious concentration, and we move from being directed by outside forces to being guided internally, from working with others ideas (outside theories and tools) to

our own (inside guidance, principles and choices).

And on any given day we will operate the best we can wherever we are, as humans participating in human systems!

References

Alexander, F. (1932). *The use of the self.* London, UK: Methuen & Co, Ltd.

Argyris, C., & Schon, D. (1974). *Theory in practice.* San Francisco. CA: Jossey-Bass.

Arnd-Caddigan, M., & Pozzuto, R. (2008). Use of self in relational clinical social work. *Clinical Social Work Journal*, 36, 235–243.

Baldwin, M., (Ed.) (2000). *The use of self in therapy* (2nd Ed). Binghamton, NY: Haworth Press.

Barry, A. (2008). *Practically shameless: How shadow work helped me find my voice, my path, and my inner gold.* Longmont, CO: Practically Shameless Press.

Cheung-Judge, M. (2001). The Self as an instrument-A cornerstone for the future of OD. *OD Practitioner*, 33(3), 11–16.

Chitty, K. (1993). *Professional nursing: Concepts and challenges.* Philadelphia, PA: W. B. Saunders & Co.

Csikszentmihalyi, M. (1990). *Flow: The psychology of optimal experience.* New York, NY: Harper and Row.

Culbert, S. (1967). The interpersonal process of self-disclosure: It takes two to know one. In J. Hart & T. Tomlinson (Eds.), *New directions in client-centered therapy.* Boston, MA: Houghton Mifflin.

Freshwater, D. (2002). The therapeutic use of self in nursing. In D. Freshwater (Ed.), *Therapeutic nursing: Improving patient care through self awareness and reflection* (pp. 1–16). Thousand Oaks, CA: Sage Publications.

Glavas, A., Jules, C., & Van Oosten, E. (2006). Use of self in creating a culture of collaboration. In S.Schuman (Ed.), *Creating a culture of collaboration* (pp. 304–321). San Francisco, CA: Jossey-Bass.

Goffman, I. (1955). On face-work: An analysis of ritual elements in social interaction. *Psychiatry*, 18, 213–231.

Goffman, I (1959). *The presentation of self in everyday life,* University of Edinburgh Social Sciences Research Centre. Garden City, NY: Anchor Books.

Heydt, M., & Sherman, N. (2005). Conscious use

of self: Tuning the instrument of social work practice with cultural competence. *Journal of Baccalaureate Social Work,* 10(2), 25–40.

Jamieson, D. (1990). You are the instrument. *OD Practitioner,* 23(1), 20.

Jung, C., & Storr, A. (1983). *The essential Jung.* Princeton, NJ: The Princeton University Press.

Jung, C., von Franz, M., Henderson, J., Jacobi, J., & Jaffe, A. (1964). *Man and his symbols.* New York, NY: Dell Publishing.

Kegan, R. (1982). *The evolving self.* Boston, MA: Harvard University Press.

Luft, J. (1963). *Group processes: An introduction to group dynamics.* Palo Alto, CA: National Press.

Luft, J., & Ingham, H. (1955). The Johari Window: A graphic model of interpersonal awareness. *Proceedings of the western training laboratory in group development.* Los Angeles, CA: UCLA Extension Office.

Marshak, R. (2006). *Covert processes at work.* San Francisco, CA: Berrett-Koehler Publishers, Inc.

McCormick, D., & White, J. (2000). Using one's self as an instrument for diagnosis. *Organization Development Journal,* 18(3), 49–61.

Miller, H. (1962). The professional use of self through group work in teacher education. *Journal of Educational Sociology,* 36(4), 170–180.

Palmer, P. (2004). *A hidden wholeness: The journey toward an undivided life.* San Francisco, CA: Jossey-Bass.

Perls, F., Hefferline, R., & Goodman, P. (1951). *Gestalt therapy: Excitement and growth in the human personality.* Gouldsboro, ME: The Gestalt Journal Press.

Rogers, C. (1961). *On becoming a person.* Boston, MA: Houghton Mifflin.

Seashore, C., Shawver, M., Thompson, G., & Mattare, M. (2004) Doing good by knowing who you are: The instrumental self as an agent of change. *OD Practitioner,* 36(3), 42–46.

Senge. P. (1990). *The fifth discipline.* New York, NY: Currency.

Schein, E. (1998). *Process consultation revisited.* Reading, MA: Addison-Wesley.

Shapiro, S. (1976). *The selves inside you.* Berkeley, CA: Explorations Institute

Shotter, J. (1997). The social construction of our inner lives. *Journal of Constructivist Psychology,* 10(1), 7–24.

Smith, K. (1990). On using the self as instrument: Lessons from a facilitators experience. In J. Gillette & M. McCollum (Eds.), *Groups in context: A new perspective on group dynamics* (pp. 276–294). Reading, MA: Addison-Wesley.

Tannenbaum, R. (1995). Self-Awareness: An essential element underlying consultant effectiveness. *Journal of Organizational Change Management,* 8(3), 85–86.

Tannenbaum, R., & Eisen, S. (2005). The personhood of the consultant: The OD practitioner as human being. In W. Rothwell & R. Sullivan (Eds.), *Practicing Organization Development: A guide for consultants* (pp. 583–607). San Francisco, CA: Pfeiffer.

Wilber, K. (2000). *Integral psychology: Consciousness, spirit, psychology, therapy.* Boston, MA: Shambhala Publications, Inc.

Zweig, C., & Abrams, J. (1991). *Meeting the shadow: The hidden power of the dark side of human nature.* New York, NY: Tarcher/Putnam.

CHAPTER 18

Personal and Organizational Authority: Bringing the Self into a System of Work Relationships

Laurence J. Gould

IN CONTEMPORARY organizations, there is an immediate need for managers and executives to function in increasingly complex and fluid environments—both internally and externally. Mergers, acquisitions, precipitous bankruptcies, massive layoffs, shifting alliances, and turbulence in the marketplace all are conspiring to make the experience of organizational stability and continuity fragile. Organizations, to be sure, were never closed systems, but in more stable times with much slower rates of change, they were experienced as self-contained and self-perpetuating. By contrast, contemporary post-industrial organizations often have quite the opposite character and consequently are now experienced as unstable, chaotic, and often unmanageable.

There are many reasons that organizational environments are changing, including the globalization of work, rapid technological advances, the increasingly diverse nature of the work-force, and last, but not least—and the subject of this article—corresponding changes in attitudes, beliefs, and values related to the nature of authority and the dilemmas encountered in its exercise. Taken together, these factors suggest that those responsible for managing organizations and for organizational change must have the requisite psychological and systems knowledge to take leadership in their roles and to function effectively under increasingly novel conditions.

Moreover, the likelihood that (1) people at every level in the organization will be encouraged to be more self-managing; (2) organizations will become increasingly "flat" as older forms of authority and influence give way to more collaborative influence-based models of work relatedness; (3) the majority of the workforce in America will be women and members of ethnic subgroups; (4) more and more managers, administrators, and executives will have a consultative orientation; and (5) what staff there are who hold the organization's center will not second guess field units or undermine their authority. This means that new and far more sophisticated skills, competencies, attitudes, and knowledge about the psychological and systemic forces that drives organizations and the people in them will be required. In addition, as the workforce becomes increasingly heterogeneous and markets more globalized and considerably more sophisticated, forms of relatedness will be needed. A major general consequence, which is the thesis of this article, is that an unprecedented level of self-management will be necessary as a basis for action in the absence of prescriptions, orders, commands, standardized routines, and well-defined hierarchical structures, and that a strong sense of personal authority will be the crucial determinant of effective self-management.

Today, it is perhaps difficult to comprehend fully how much managers must exercise a level of discretionary authority almost unheard of a decade ago. Nevertheless, the point is clear—if external authority, hierarchical command structures and agreed-upon informal conventions are no longer adequate to guide behavior, managers perforce will be increasingly thrown back on their own personal sense of authority as the basis for action. That is, delegations of authority will be more in the form of guidelines rather than in the form of specific orders and requirements. More and more, managers will have general goals set for them (and they, in turn, will set more general goals for their subordinates), but how such goals are accomplished will increasingly be determined "locally." The corollary point is that those whose sense of personal authority is inadequate or insufficiently developed will have difficulties in managing effectively, particularly as they advance to more responsible positions in the organization. It will no longer be sufficient to be simply a "good soldier." Effective management will require the constant taking of initiative and managing the corresponding anxieties of being accountable for the discretion one has been delegated. Given these requirements, a crucial question arises as to the sources and nature of those personal gyroscopes that guide purposeful action in the absence of clear external guidelines. It is in this context that the nature of personal authority and its relationship to organizational authority will become paramount.

In the following sections, I define the nature of personal authority, highlight its links to organizational authority, examine through clinical cases how personal authority shapes organizational authority, and conclude with some key hypotheses about the kind of organizational culture that facilitates effectively taking up and exercising mature organizational authority.

The Nature of Personal Authority

Since the term *authority* is used so variously, it is useful to begin with a definition and to distinguish between organizational and personal authority. *Organizational authority* is defined as the authority that is delegated to roles, which thereby gives the role occupant the "right to work." *Personal authority* is the counterpart of organizational authority. It is a central aspect of one's enduring sense of self no matter what role one may occupy. It, therefore, is defined as the "right to be"—that is, the right to exist fully and to be oneself in the role.

To elaborate further, we can say that *personal authority* is experienced when individuals feel entitled to express their interests and passions, when they feel that their vitality and creativity belong in the world, and when they readily accept the power and vitality of others as contributions to their own experience. They give themselves and others permission to be vital, or in a word, to be authentic in-role. In this context, personal authority can be thought of as existing on a continuum. At one end of this continuum are those who have a well-developed, realistic, appropriate, confident, and robust sense of personal authority. At the other end are people with serious difficulties around their sense of authority. Such difficulties can take many forms. Sometimes they are manifested and experienced as a seeming excess of personal authority—that is, a grandiose, unrealistic, unmodulated, narcissistic sense of authority, a belief that one is permitted to do and have everything. Alternatively, we see those who seem to have a weak, anxious sense of their own authority—that is, those who believe they are permitted nothing. Whatever form these difficulties take, adults will experience them when they attempt to exercise authority in their organizational roles.

A person's internal sense of authority is shaped in the crucible of family relations as parents make manifest their desires, fears, and wishes for their children. As parents legitimate or illegitimate a child's interests, curiosity, and feelings, the child feels either authorized or reauthorized to express his or her inner vitality, his or her "real self." Most children usually develop powerful feelings and fantasies of being delegated (or denied) some important authority, and these feelings may become reinforced by the parents over a long period of time. For example, a child may come to feel the responsibility for taking care of damaged family or a particular family member at the expense of his or her own pleasure, independence, and accomplishment. Similarly, a child may come to feel that his or her role is to be the family martyr, the family savior, the family "screw-up," or the fair-haired boy or girl.

To be sure, people are not simply passive receptacles. Some are innately more resilient; others are more easily influenced. A child's sense of personal authority emerges at the intersection of parental demands and the way he or she internalizes and interprets these experiences. Indeed, psychotherapists often see in their patients powerful fantasies about their own authority—what they have been or are permitted to do—that have little relation to reality. The therapist experiences these fantasies in the "transference" as patients bring all their feelings about their own authority and the therapist's presumed authority to the therapeutic relationship. Whether the patient tries to control, gratify, please, rebel against, or undermine the therapist, he or she is enacting his or her own deepest feelings about authority.

Although a person's sense of authority is shaped by early family relationships, it should be emphasized that it can and does change and develop over the course of the life cycle. New experiences with teachers, mentors, and peers can repair earlier damage to one's sense of self. Alternatively, a severe trauma later in life can lead a person with a robust sense of personal authority to feel undermined and conflicted. Survivors of catastrophic events provide an obvious example. Because they often feel profoundly guilty, they act as if they are not entitled to any pleasure, gratification, or success.

They deauthorize themselves in the sense that they no longer feel entitled to enjoy or accomplish anything.

The Exercise of and the Relationship between Personal and Organizational Authority

A sense of one's own personal authority deeply affects how individuals take up their organizational roles and how authorized they feel to take initiative and accomplish their objectives. An inhibited person who feels entitled to very little may fail to exercise the minimum amount of authority vested in his or her role. By contrast, people who are grandiose and have an inflated sense of self may exceed the maximum available authority. Moreover, as I have already suggested, increasingly, people have significant freedom to choose how they take up their roles. This means that their own personal characteristics—who they are, what they are feeling, how past and present have combined to determine their behavior—increasingly shape the resulting texture of roles in the organization.

Three Cases

Given the above, I would like to present case material illustrating in some detail how difficulties in developing an adequate sense of personal authority may originate.[1] I would then like to suggest explicitly how such difficulties are related to the ways in which one exercised one's personal authority in organizational work

[1] In presenting clinical material to illustrate dilemmas in taking up the authority of one's work roles, I do not wish to imply either that all such difficulties are "pathological" or that psychotherapy is usually required to deal with them. Rather, clinical examples of more extreme and persistent forms of these problems simply highlight their ubiquitous nature and bring them into clearer focus. That is, no one is entirely free of distortions in authority relations. However, within a quite broad range, the majority of successful people have learned—in many different ways, from lived experience and intimate relationships to high-quality management development programs—to understand better what drives their behavior and affects their role performance. As underscored in this article, such self-awareness has great value that potentially can be translated into more adequate self-management.

roles. There is one important caveat, however—namely, the reciprocal nature of personal and organization authority. While the purpose of this article, and therefore the case material, is cast in the direction of how personal authority influences the exercise of organizational authority, the converse is also true. A central assumption is that although an individual's sense of self, and hence personal authority, determines to a significant extent how he or she functions in role, important aspects of behavior and experience are critically affected by the setting. What a person is capable of doing and what parts of the self achieve expression depend on conditions that inhibit or amplify particular attitudes and potentials. In an organization, these conditions are set by its structure, group and social dynamics, culture, and operating methods.[2]

The following three therapy cases—two vignettes of Diane and Robert, respectively, and a more extended case description of Matt—highlight how issues of personal authority are inextricably linked to work. Diane experienced an inflated sense of self and thus denied others their authority.

Robert and Matt, in contrast, failed to take up the authority available to them to perform successfully in their roles. I will highlight the origins of these difficulties, how they affected each person's relationship to me as the therapist, and how they became manifested in the organizational context.

Diane

Diane entered psychotherapy complaining of depression, which she explicitly felt began with her father's death two years earlier. She said she

[2] The group relations training conferences pioneered by the Tavistock Institute (see, for example, Miller, 1989) are especially important in this connection. These conferences are aimed at illuminating how one's sense of authority is profoundly influenced by group and social processes and how individuals are "used" by the group to express underlying collective anxieties and concerns. In the context of this article, the direct implication is that one's sense of personal authority, no matter how robust, is always conditioned to some extent by the group situation.

could not understand why it was taking her so long to get over it and, if anything, she was feeling worse and worse. As a merchandising director for a large clothing manufacturer, she was extremely competent and generally appreciated but was having increasing difficulties with her boss and subordinates. She was impatient with her staff and usually dismissed their tentatively offered advice and opinions. Further, she required and often demanded "pride of place" with her boss to the exclusion of everybody else, including his wife.

During the course of therapy, important features of the familial and psychological roots of her behavior became clearer. The oldest of five siblings with two younger sisters behind her and then two brothers, Diane, as her "father's little wife," was to be the competent alternative to her scattered, incompetent, depressed and disorganized mother. Further, she felt that her mother was quite resigned to this state of affairs, which left her free to manage (quite competently, in fact) the four younger children. In her father's eyes, Diane was the antithesis of her mother. She was competent to manage all the affairs of the house and was "wise beyond her years"; her father often said to her, "You are my indispensable little girl."

In her relationship with me, she recreated many aspects of her relationship with her father, making me into a longed for substitute. She alternatively craved my admiration and attempted to take care of me. She detailed each small victory or triumph, excoriated unappreciative colleagues and friends, and with each recounting waited expectantly for my approval, agreement and support. When it was not forthcoming, she either became furious, bitter, withdrawn, and contemptuous, accusing me of insensitivity, coldness, and incompetence or became tearful, hurt, and whiny. She also tried to take care of me, was solicitous if I appeared tired, proffered recommendations about my ties, and begged to undertake having my office repainted and redecorated.

Her family history and the transference that developed paralleled her situation at work. Just as she had felt contempt for her siblings, whom she characterized as "my mother's kids," she believed that she was her boss's best subordinate. Just as she became daddy's little wife, she expected and covertly demanded the undivided attention of her boss and a special emotional relationship with him. While she was undoubtedly competent, these conflicts distorted her sense of personal authority. She felt entitled to too much. Consequently, she gave less and less psychological permission to her subordinates and peers, and demanded more and more authority. The trauma of her father's death exacerbated these already existing difficulties and diminished further her ability to take up her authority at work in a mature way.

Put in schematic terms, we would say that initially her grandiose sense of personal authority dominated her role and "spilled over" into her boss's and subordinates' roles. She knows best; the others are fools or incompetents. Her own role in the organization does not leave any room for others to make a contribution. The more authority she took for herself, the less she gave to others. As she made progress in therapy, she was able to redefine her authority so that it was appropriately expressed within the boundary of her role, leaving room for her colleagues and subordinates to make a contribution. She was also, as she came to understand herself, better able to relinquish her need for a special relationship with her boss.

Rob

Rob entered treatment at the age of 37 following a devastating performance review. In the early sessions, he told me how a reorganization and a related shift in reporting relationships "pulled the carpet out from under him." His new boss wanted him to devote all his energies to work on delayed, overbudget new products, for which he had a major R&D responsibility for several key components, or else risk being let go. As a senior engineer in R&D, Rob felt that his boss's demand was gratuitous. What else would he be doing?

As his story unfolded, it became apparent that he, in fact, was doing many other things—

many, many other things—including leading a popular company country-and-western band, participating on three task forces, voluntarily teaching an advanced computer course, and playing "counselor" to a large number of younger colleagues. To be sure, he was quite competent in each of these roles, as well as in his primary organizational role. He was liked by his staff and colleagues, widely respected, and always available. But despite his competence, his boss was correct: He was neglecting his major responsibilities. In early sessions, he angrily complained about being "reigned in," "squelched," misunderstood, and suddenly unappreciated by his new boss, despite his obvious dedication, loyalty, and devotion to the company. He also began to become extremely anxious.

In his relationship with me, Rob began to reenact his complex relationship to his work role. He was the man who knew about everything, including psychoanalysis and psychotherapy. He also tried to be helpful and enlightening, and he became concerned about other patients whose paths he crossed in my waiting room. He talked about books, movies, politics, music, mythology, and archaeology with appropriate modesty and not the slightest hint of braggadocio. He also ingenuously offered to computerize my billing system. But it was often quite difficult to get him to focus on the subject at hand—namely himself.

In reconstructing his family history, it became apparent that he was indeed cast in the role of "needing to know it all and be it all." His parents were academic and professional bluebloods, both multitalented, who shared an attitude of patronizing, intellectual noblesse oblige. To be competent at one thing was to be, in his family, a narrow "specialist," a term uttered with unconcealed disdain. He learned early that this was the fate of his older sister, who not only flagrantly rejected these lofty parental injunctions but had the bad grace to be a chronic problem child with episodes of destructive and self-destructive behavior and, later, a constant series of minor delinquent entanglements. So he became the official "good boy," manifesting his goodness by becoming a caricature of the Renaissance man he felt his parents could wholeheartedly endorse. Thus he could uphold the family's good name, as he ruefully later said, "unto the next generation."

In parallel with his therapy, Rob reproduced these family dynamics in his organizational role. As his boss's impatience suggested, he was not fully committed to his work. That is, he did not commit his passion and intelligence to the task at hand of developing the new product. Instead, afraid to be what he wanted to be, he sought to satisfy everyone else by meeting them in the realm of their interests and needs. Consequently, everybody but his boss admired and appreciated him. Paradoxically, while his many-sided interests suggested that he was an expansive person, he was in fact severely inhibited. He could do only what others wanted, not what he wanted to pursue or enjoy. This behavior mirrored Rob's earlier attempts to satisfy his parents. Not entitled to pursue any single interest or to identify his own passion, he pursued many to satisfy them. Indeed, whenever he began to immerse himself in any single activity, he became anxious and quickly diluted his involvement by doing other things. However, this always left him vaguely dissatisfied, so by the time he initially saw me, well into his thirties, he had little sense of real direction or purpose, despite a rather wide range of impressive intellectual and career accomplishments.

As treatment began to have an effect, Rob was better able to focus his energies and to recognize that he had never felt free (authorized) to have a single-minded, passionate interest. With this hard-won insight, he was able to bring more of himself into his primary work role.

Matt

Finally, in presenting the more extended case of Matt, I will try to show in greater detail how a person's early history, family relationships, course of therapy, and behavior at work are all interrelated.

Matt came to treatment at the age of 32, shortly after getting married. At that time he was a newly minted vice-president in a large financial services company, even though his boss complained that he failed to take sufficient initiative. In addition, Matt complained of anxiety and some marital difficulties, which he said shocked him so early in the marriage. His wife was already in psychotherapy, and her therapist had suggested he seek treatment for himself. As time passed, he increasingly framed his problem as being continually caught between the demands of his wife and his mother. His father, he said, played little role in the conflict, since he tended to be generally passive and complied with his mother's wishes. He could acknowledge some anger toward his father for this, but he also identified with his situation. When I inquired, in due course, why he felt it was so difficult to stand up to his mother or his wife, he became extremely disorganized and anxious.

Over the course of his psychotherapy, many aspects of this issue became clarified. He came to realize, for example, that his father's disinterest and his mother's intrusiveness and insensitivity felt like a cold, deadening shower on his budding interests and activities. As a result, to preserve his excitement and pleasure, he retreated more and more into a secret life that included elaborate games, hidden collections, and rich daydreams. While he could tell me about this, one obvious manifestation of his secrecy was that he almost never talked about his work or organizational role in any detail, and when he did, it was usually only in passing and in a self-deprecating way. I was able to interpret the anxiety that if he expressed his interests openly, I would, like his parents, also be a cold shower and thereby spoil his pleasure through ridicule or disinterest.

While we made considerable headway on this problem, I had the persistent feeling that something crucial was being missed. But I had no compelling evidence except a nagging feeling that "it didn't add up." I was particularly troubled by the strength of his inhibitions, since despite what seemed like considerable therapeutic work, he continued to display a high level of anxiety whenever the issue of getting into a tangle with his mother arose, and it came up more often as his wife was increasingly unwilling to submit to his mother's wishes.

During one session in which he was discussing a current conflict between his wife and mother, he said, "I really feel as if my mother is going to lose it— he gets so irrational. It scares the hell out of me, but it also makes me so angry I just don't know what to do." I also noted that he became increasingly agitated as the session progressed. Shortly before it ended, I asked him, once again, as I had in some version many times previously, how he imagined his mother would respond if she did not get her way. He gave his usual conventional response that she would pout and make him feel guilty. In his session the next morning, he reported the following dream:

> I was in the downstairs hallway of the house I grew up in. My mother came down from upstairs and started to yell at me. She also might have hit me . . . I'm not sure. Then I heard a loud thumping . . . like something banging against the wall, and I became very frightened. I think I ran out of the house and tried to hide.

He had few associations, at first, but said that the dream made him very edgy. He noted that, in fact, his mother seldom hit him, but that she did yell at him a lot. He also remembered that he would sometimes run out of the house when he was upset. In his spontaneous account of the dream, however, the oddest element, the "thumping," remained unmentioned. I pointed this out to him, and he responded by saying that it did not make him think of anything except the phrase, "banging your head against the wall." Maybe, he speculated, that showed how frustrated his mother made him feel. Suddenly, he became very quiet and finally said in a low voice, "I think it was my mother who was banging her head against the wall."

As we analyzed this dream further, we discovered that his mother had, indeed, been quite disturbed during his early years and, in fact, often became enraged and banged her head against the wall—episodes that he had entirely repressed. As he reconstructed these episodes, he gained considerable insight into his inhibitions, his need for secrecy, and his almost catastrophic anxiety at the thought of displeasing his mother by doing what he wanted to do rather than going along with her wishes. He did not feel authorized openly to pursue his interests, lest he enrage his mother or drive her crazy. Instead, he struck a compromise by asserting himself in the privacy of his fantasies and secret games, while expressing or achieving little in public except a quiet and workmanlike competence. In this way he could avoid the guilt and anxiety of hurting his mother. However, he also gained something emotionally from this arrangement. As the therapy progressed, we discovered that he took a great deal of secret pleasure in the power he had over his mother and, by implication, the privileged position he had with her vis-à-vis his father, who seemed unable to upset her, excite her, or offer her any solace. He believed that only he could make a decisive difference in his mother's emotional life—a position he relished, even though, psychologically, he paid a considerable price for maintaining it.

Not surprisingly, Matt enacted this fantasy about his power in relation to me. One day he raised, for the first time, the possibility of ending psychotherapy. He then quickly undid this by proclaiming that he still needed more time, since he had not fully resolved some important issues. A few moments later he blurted out, "I hope you're not upset that I'm thinking that the end is in sight." I responded by saying, "You make me feel as if you need to stay here to keep me happy, rather than my being here for you for as long as you think it useful." He immediately acknowledged that he was anxious that his wanting to leave would upset me and that, in fact, he had been having thoughts of ending for several months, but kept pushing them out of his mind. I then said, "If you become independent and don't need me anymore, you're afraid I won't be able to survive—just like you've always imagined your mother wouldn't be able to survive without your continued support, compliance, and availability."

Now that we are in the process of ending therapy, he wrestles with the anxiety of being independent of me and accepting that I, for my part, can flourish quite happily without him. He experiences the prospect of independence ambivalently. While he feels inhibited by his mother's fragility, he also feels powerful since he, rather than his father, could keep her emotionally table. While his mother's constant, self-referential demands burden him, his belief that she desperately needs him is enormously gratifying. As I have interpreted this gratification, he has become mildly depressed, but he is now groping toward a more realistic but scaled-down sense of personal authority that is both less secretly grandiose and more open and available in character.

These changes, not surprisingly, have also had a considerable effect on how he takes up his organizational work role. In the beginning, he invested little personal authority in his role. Instead, he kept his own thoughts, feelings, and desires hidden and simply did the bidding, or the perceived bidding, of his superiors. He followed his "marching orders." As the therapy progressed, the reasons became much clearer. He dealt with his boss in much the same way he dealt with his mother, and then with me. He was self-effacing to a fault, got excited only privately, and became very anxious whenever he started to feel as if he knew better than his boss or had an independent idea or perspective. This occurred despite the fact, as he came to understand, that his boss welcomed his input. While obvious self-promotion can certainly be a problem, Matt, by contrast, had difficulty showing himself sufficiently, that is, directly contributing and taking responsibility for his ideas and analyses. So he operated on a split level—publicly he was a good obedient boy, but all his vitality

and enthusiasm were kept private and hidden. Further, in casting his boss in his mother's image, Rob completely misread his boss; and although Rob got good reviews, they were far from the enthusiastic endorsements they later became when he started to contribute more openly to the unit, as he increasingly brought to his role aspects of the self that he previously had kept private.

Creating a Culture of Mature Authority Relations

Managers and executives in contemporary organizations must exercise great initiative while delegating substantial authority to those below them. It is no longer adequate simply to give and take orders. But as people experience greater freedom in their roles, they also must confront the anxieties and conflicts that bedevil them when they exercise authority. The external world of work is shaped increasingly by people's inner feelings and interior experiences. When people cannot take up authority freely, without undue conflict and anxiety, they fear that authentic self-expression, the full flowering of their resources and vitality, will hurt them. As the three cases presented above suggest, in the face of this prospect some people will behave in inhibited ways, while others will mask their insecurity and neediness by overreaching and demanding too much. In this sense, we can say that people are relying on what Winnicott (1959 [1965], 1960 [1965]) calls a "false self," as opposed to a "true self," to take up their roles. They will, as a result, lack flexibility and vitality, and instead they will often behave in repetitive, constricted, non-task-oriented, and frequently self-defeating ways.

Clearly, however, we cannot improve organizations by asking all of their members to engage in psychotherapy. But senior executives and managers can help to create a "culture of authorization" that supports the individual's wish to develop as a mature, self-initiating contributor. I suggest that such a culture would sustain the following norms and values at all levels in the organization.

Taking Behavioral Responsibility for Oneself

Principally, taking behavioral responsibility involves reclaiming one's projections of difficulties onto others and forgoing using others as repositories for one's own dilemmas or lack of clarity. If this is done, scapegoating and the pervasive sense of paranoia and suspiciousness that are the consequence of such projections will markedly diminish. Those with a mature sense of personal authority recognize that one always looks to one's own behavior first as a source of difficulty and that the best way to influence the behavior of others is to modify one's own behavior. This is an especially important consideration for those in positions of authority with regard to their subordinates, who, given their positions, are especially vulnerable to destructive projections and scapegoating.

Taking Emotional Responsibility for Oneself

Contemporary psychological requirements for managers include tolerance for and the capacity to contain powerful emotional states; tolerance for complexity, uncertainty, and ambiguity; and tolerance for anxiety. A mature sense of personal authority is marked by the capacity to tolerate and contain difficult, painful, and distressing emotional states, rather than denying them or, as noted, projecting them onto others. Since anxiety, uncertainty, and complexity are steady states in contemporary organizational life, managers without a capacity to contain their own feelings, as well as the projections of others, will be impaired in their decision making. The capacity for such containment largely depends on the acceptance of these feelings in oneself, as well as the ability to recognize that the projections of others are a function of the role that one occupies (that is, one's authority) and should not be overpersonalized. Having attained this emotional perspective, managers are then in a position to use their own internal states and such projections as vital clues about the state of the work

group, team, or the larger organization. Finally, a manager's ability to accept these projections, especially the negative ones of subordinates (e.g., dependency, hatred, envy), without retribution or retaliation helps to create what Winnicott terms a "holding environment"— that is, an environment that provides a sense of psychological safety within which work can productively be accomplished and people can grow and develop in their roles.

Taking Ethical and Moral Responsibility for Oneself

Those with a mature, robust, and well-developed sense of personal authority "metabolize" all organizational delegations of authority. That is, no delegations are uncritically accepted or taken at face value. Rather, they are internally filtered and, if necessary, modified as a basis for renegotiation with the source of the delegation. Those with a mature sense of personal authority do not simply and uncritically follow orders or abdicate responsibility for the consequences when they do so.

Fully Recognizing Interdependence

Individuals can no longer effectively guide or manage complex systems. Given contemporary levels of organizational complexity, no single manager or executive, no matter how brilliant or talented, can have a full understanding of how the organization functions or what needs to be done to make it function more effectively. At all levels, those in authority must depend on one another and on subordinates for insight, wisdom, and perspective. A corollary is that all managers, and especially senior managers, need to recognize, understand and take some responsibility for how the whole organization functions, as well as their own functional spheres.

Conclusion

In concluding, I would like to return to the quote with which I began. The peace with the sources of one's life that Lippmann suggests represents an ideal state. It is a state that under felicitous conditions we more fully approach as we develop through adulthood, but that we never fully attain. However, we can attain a certain sort of grace, and an increasingly more robust, adaptive, and refined sense of personal authority as development proceeds. T. H. White, author of the wonderful and charming *Once and Future King* (1966), in an extended aside regarding the foibles and follies of youth, comments on the development of a seventh sense—"a thing called knowledge of the world, which people do not have until they are middle-aged. It is something which cannot be taught to younger people. Only in the long years which bring one to the middle of life does a sense of balance develop. And balance—the sixth sense—is a precondition of the seventh. The seventh sense—knowledge of the world—is the means by which both men and women contrive to ride the waves of a world in which there is war, adultery, compromise, fear, stultification, and hypocrisy—and this discovery is not a matter for triumph" (White, 1966, p. 24). I would add to this a parallel knowledge of the self, similarly informed by the guilt, shame, and disappointment that one has not lived up to one's ideals. Such discovery and self-knowledge is also hardly an occasion for triumph, but if it leads, as it often does, to self-acceptance, it can be the basis for new possibilities of wholeness, vitality, and an emotionally rich and unconflicted sense of personal authority. However, this is not only a lofty human ideal in the individual and personal realm, but the core of effective management and leadership, since

mature authority relations will increasingly become the hallmark of enlightened and successful organizations.

Acknowledgment

I would like to express my thanks to W. Gordon Lawrence (1979, and personal communication) for some of the language of these perspectives, as well as for his seminal ideas regarding the management of the self. These have influenced us by thinking about the issues of personal and organizational authority in fundamental ways.

References

Lawrence, W.G. (1979). A concept for today: The management of oneself in role. In W. Gordon Lawrence (Ed.), *Exploring individual and organizational boundaries: A Tavistock open systems approach* (pp. 235–247). Chichester, UK: John Wiley and Sons.

Miller, E. J. (1989). The "Leicester" model: Experiential study of group and organizational processes. Occasional Paper no. 10, Tavistock Institute of Human Relations.

White, T.H. (1966). *The once and future king.* New York, NY: Berkeley Publishing.

Winnicott, D.W. (1959, 1965). Classification. Is there a psychoanalytic contribution to psychiatric classification? In *The maturational process and the facilitating environment* (pp. 124–139). London, UK: Hogarth Press.

Winnicott, D. W. (1960, 1965). Ego distortion in terms of true and false self. In *The maturational process and the facilitating environment* (pp. 140–152). London, UK: Hogarth Press.

CHAPTER 19

Diversity, Inclusion, and the Ladder of Inference

Neil D. Samuels

BP, LIKE MANY OTHER companies, struggles with how to transform the concepts of Diversity and Inclusion (D&I), into something tangible. Why is this important? As Lord John Browne, our Group Chief Executive says:

> Diversity and Inclusion is one of our greatest strengths—the source of new ideas and perspectives which will shape our future as a company. A global company that achieves and celebrates Diversity and Inclusion will attract better people, nurture and retain them, grow market share and deliver higher productivity at lower cost.

Because of its significance for the future of our company, we have incorporated discussions of D&I into a new development program for our 10,000 first level leaders. As those discussions have evolved, I have found the Ladder of Inference (developed by Chris Argyris, a professor at Harvard University, Figure 19.1) a very effective metaphor for explaining the concepts of D&I, because it helps people understand both the distinction and the intimate connection between the two.

At its essence, the ladder is a simple model of how we think; how we process our experiences, create inferences about them, and take action at lightning speed without noticing we are doing so. Here is how it works.

We live in an infinite pool of *data and experiences.* Because we are finite beings, we are exposed to only a very limited subset. Furthermore, based on our mental models, beliefs, values, and assumptions, we *select* an even smaller subset of data. Then, based on our beliefs, we add *meaning* to those data—we create a story to make sense of what we have let in. Based on our story, we draw *conclusions* and then take *actions* (make decisions, have conversations) based on those conclusions. And we do all of this in the blink of an eye, unaware that we have done so.

This ability to immediately "jump up our ladder" allowed us to survive as a species. Imagine one of our early ancestors taking time to incorporate and then evaluate *all* the available data on the savannah as the saber-tooth tiger approached. Unfortunately, we have retained the tendency to jump to conclusions based on limited data even though our current circumstances require that ability much less frequently.

But, as in the past, note that it is the tiny subset of data and experiences we are exposed to at the bottom of the adder that limits our range of actions (choices or decisions) at the top.

FIGURE 19.1   The Ladder of Inference

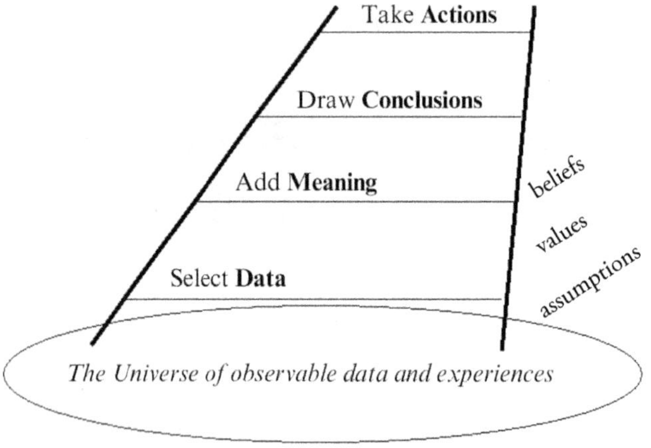

To illustrate, consider a colleague and I presenting this material to a large group. The room offers a huge data set: the sounds of air conditioning in the ceiling above, birds beyond the windows, and catering people outside the doors; the sights of flip-charts and pictures on the walls, trees outside, and sixty people with all their body language in the room. I won't go into the smells, I hope you get the image. Now, to what do I pay attention, what do I select? I notice one person sitting back in her chair, arms crossed, mouth in a bit of a scowl. I quickly infer that she is bored and from there instantaneously decide that I am doing a lousy job explaining and better do something quickly before I lose the rest of the audience. I become more animated, give more examples, do whatever it takes to "get her back" before it is too late. And it happens in less than a second and all from the tiny bit of data of one woman sitting with her arms crossed.

As we take a break, my colleague asks me; "What were you doing? Things were going great and then you started rambling, giving example after example, and running all over the room." As it turns out, my colleague was paying attention to other data. He noticed a couple of people who were leaning forward in their chairs, making eye contact with me, nodding their heads, and smiling. He inferred that the audience was getting the message and was

fully engaged. His trip up the "ladder" led to a much different interpretation than mine. Was he "right"? Was I?

Or might we both have been better served by a wider data set? What if collectively we noticed the body language of thirty, or forty, or even fifty people? Or better yet, made an observation of the body language and asked how they were feeling? What might we have inferred given more data with which to start?

Interesting, But What Does It Have to Do with D&I?

The diversity of a team defines the extent of data and experience set with which it can start —its raw material. The more diverse the data set at the bottom, the more possible options for actions at the top. Let me illustrate with the five members of a fictional leadership team managing a large business unit in Algeria. Each member's subset of data and experience is shown on Figure 19.2.

Mike is a 48-year-old, white American male from the Midwest. An engineer from a middle-class family, he has lived in a few countries outside the United States and has worked for the organization for 25 years. Jim, a white, 44-year-old Englishman, trained as a geologist and has worked for the company for 21 years. He comes from a working-class family outside

FIGURE 19.2   Diversity and the Ladder

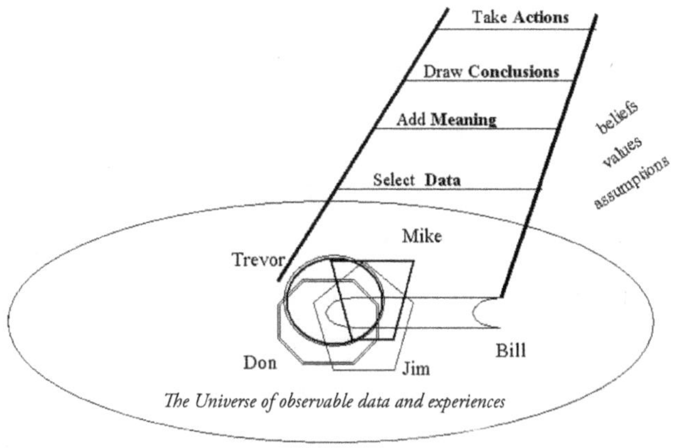

The ladder rests on a fairly narrow base when team members
have relatively little collective diversity in experiences represented
by the size and dispersion of the geometric shapes.

London, and is married with two children.
Don, another white, American male, is 49 years
old from the East coast. He trained as an engineer and has spent his entire 26-year career
working on major projects within the company. Trevor is the other Englishman on the
team. He is white, 55 years old and also comes
from the engineering discipline. He, too, had
a middle-class upbringing and was the first in
his family to graduate University. Bill was born
in Trinidad and moved to the USA for college.
He is black, Afro-Caribbean, and studied finance and accounting. Married with two children, Bill is 43 years old.

I recognize that there are many more
attributes of these men than could possibly be
discussed here. Let's assume however, that the
size and position of the labeled shapes in Figure 2 accurately depicts the sum total of data,
experiences, assumptions, beliefs, and values
each man brings to the team.

When this team is in conversation about
the Algeria Business, and they are collectively
jumping up their ladder of inference, they
are limited by the extent of the sum of their
shapes, represented by the width of the ladder at the bottom. They simply do not have
direct access to a significant part of the universe of data; it does not even enter the realm
of possibility. How might this limit the efficacy of their deliberations and decisions?

Now what happens if they bring Fatima
into the team; a younger, Algerian female
with a diplomatic background? (Figure 19.3)
Imagine they are trying to decide what kind
of pension scheme to put in place for the
Algerian staff they are trying to hire as their
business expands. Might Fatima bring some
different views about what could be effective
and meaningful into the room? Note how
much broader the range of data the team has
from which to select. It is much more diverse
in that the team now has more possibilities
with which to start.

Such breadth is a necessary, but insufficient,
condition for highly effective teams (Figure
19.4). As many young females (or any other
minority in a group) have probably experienced, being a member of the team does not
necessarily mean being truly a part of the team.
Note how (with all other factors being equal)
some diverse teams are much less effective than
their homogenous counterparts. In these teams,
members' different data sets, experiences,
beliefs, values and assumptions are ignored or
de-valued (usually unintentionally).

FIGURE 19.3   Diversity and the Ladder

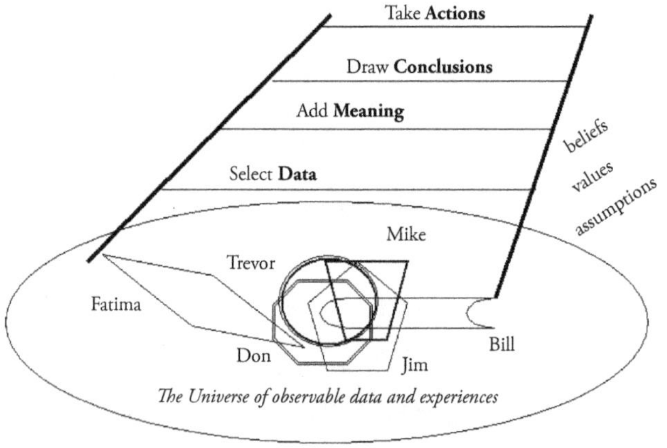

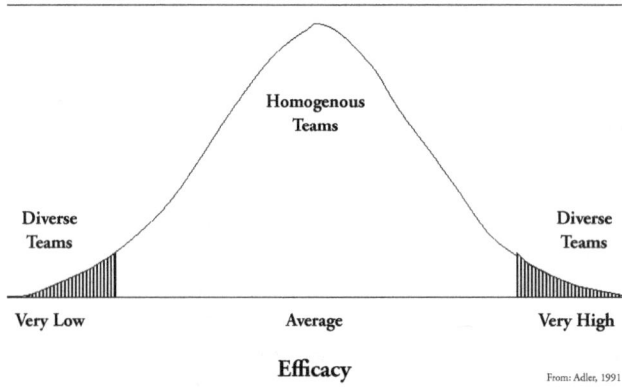

The ladder rests on a much broader base representing the wider diversity brought to the team by Fatima's significantly different set of life experiences.

FIGURE 19.4   Team Efficacy and Diversity

Diverse teams significantly outperform or underperform homogenous teams depending on how well they are able to acknowledge, explore, and value the different sets of experiences present.

Or in some cases, one aspect of the differences is highlighted at the expense of the whole data set the person offers. In our example, this may sound like well-intended questions to Fatima along the lines of: "How do you think women see this?" Or, "You're from Algeria, what reactions will it get from Algerians?" rather than truly exploring and mining Fatima's experiences to add them to their own. (For an excellent portrayal of what it's like to be different in the workplace, read "Dear White Boss", Caver and Livers, 2002)

In highly effective diverse groups, those same differences are acknowledged, explored, and valued (consciously). In short, people are included. Using our tool, that inclusion takes the form of collectively "walking down the ladder".

"Walking down the ladder" is shorthand for exploring the group's thinking. During this conversation, which requires a slower pace than many may be used to, the team inquires into each other's underlying data set and conclusions, and the logic (or beliefs and assumptions) that got them from one to the other. The higher quality of decision that results more than compensates for any delay in reaching that decision.

Observing such a group in action, one would almost certainly see the following: generous listening; adept advocacy and inquiry (laying out of reasoning and thinking, and encouraging others to question it, Ross and Roberts, 1994); and robust disagreements. Underlying these behaviors would be respect, trust, and positive relationships. And underlying all of this must be the conviction that the differences people bring into the conversations, simply by virtue of the different paths their lives have followed, are of value and therefore worth exploring.

Highly effective teams then require two attributes. First, they must have a broad enough base of data and experiences in which to plant their ladder of inference. Then, to reach the top of the ladder in a powerful way requires the individual and collective willingness and ability to slowly walk back down. Missing either aspect will relegate them to mediocrity.

References

Adler, N. (1991). *International dimensions of organizational behaviour.* Boston, MA: PWS Kent Publishing.

Caver, K. A., & Livers, A. (2002, November). Dear white boss. *Harvard Business Review,* 80(11), 76-81.

Ross, R., & Roberts, C. (1994). Balancing inquiry and advocacy. In *The Fifth Discipline Fieldbook.* New York, NY: Doubleday.

CHAPTER 20

Mindfulness and Experiential Learning

Bauback Yeganeh and David Kolb

OVER THE LAST forty years researchers from many different theoretical perspectives have discovered that individuals develop consistent, routinized approaches to learning called learning styles (Sims & Sims 2006). Of the models that have emerged, Experiential Learning Theory (ELT) has largely influenced leadership and organization development. The experiential learning cycle is one of the most well-known illustrations in management education and has become the key theoretical model to express the nature of experiential learning (Cunningham, 1994).

Experiential learning theory also forms some of the basis for notions of the learning organization (Vince, 1998; Casey, 1993; Senge, 1990). Furthermore, organizational research and practice supports the premise that when learning is defined holistically as the basic process of human adaptation, it subsumes more specialized managerial processes such as entrepreneurial learning, strategy formulation, creativity, problem solving, decision-making, and leadership.

Learning styles are used to make sense of the world and adapt to it. But what happens when learners overroutinize their learning styles? Are they missing opportunities to reach their learning potentials? This article discusses how mindfulness techniques can enhance experiential learning and provides tools for prac-

tice in organizations. Mindfulness is an age old practice used to overcome the tendency to "sleep walk" repetitively through our lives. In recent times it has been accepted into mainstream psychology, social psychology, and medicine. Empirical studies are now finding statistical support for what many have known for two millennia: that practicing mindfulness enhances mental and physical health, creativity, and contextual learning. In a world of flux and rapidity, living mindlessly can result in a host of problems including but not limited to: tunnel vision, increased stress, reduced physical health, reduced creativity, and difficulty navigating complex systems. As our sister fields of psychology and social psychology grow mindfulness research and practices, our field must as well. In this article we explore and discuss mindfulness as a tool to assist learners in unlocking their full learning potential in organizations.

Mindfulness

So what exactly is mindfulness? Any construct that has existed for thousands of years has many definitions. We would like to offer two of the most widely accepted descriptions of mindfulness. In our research with Darren Good at Case Western Reserve University, we found two predominant streams of mindfulness research and practice, meditative mindfulness and socio-cognitive mindfulness (Good & Yeganeh, 2006; Yeganeh, 2008).

Meditative Mindfulness

Although it is widely used as part of a secular mindfulness practice, mindfulness is the core of Buddhist meditation (Kabat Zinn, 1994). Thich Nhat Hanh, Gunaratana, Kabat- Zinn, and other present day authors advocate developing mindfulness through meditation techniques to help people heal themselves and live intentionally. A distinction of meditative mindfulness is that it requires a discipline of anchoring the mind in the present moment. This is often accompanied with a practice of awareness and acceptance through breathing. Kabat-Zinn (1994) defines mindfulness as "paying attention in a particular way: on purpose, in the present moment, and non-judgmentally" (p.4). Non-judgment, in mindfulness theory, is accepting the current state as part of a constant flow of changing experiences. This paradigm suggests that letting go of judgment strengthens the mind, and it challenges the illusion that overthinking something gives one control over it. Authors who discuss mindfulness within these parameters also talk about the antithesis of mindfulness which is mindlessness, or a state of autopilot and lack of intention. Are you aware of your breathing right now? Try some deep calm breaths from the diaphragm prior to reading on. Try practicing acceptance of whatever you are experiencing in the moment by letting go of evaluation and judgment.

Socio-Cognitive Mindfulness

Developed by social psychologists, this understanding of mindfulness emphasizes cognitive categorization, context and situational awareness (Langer 1997; Langer, 2000). Harvard social psychologist Ellen Langer, often relates mindfulness to learning:

> When we are mindful, we implicitly or explicitly (1) view a situation from several perspectives, (2) see information presented in the situation as novel, (3) attend to the context in which we perceive the information, and eventually, (4) create new categories through which this information may be understood. (Langer,1997, p.111)

Langer (1997) argues that our school systems largely encourage mindless learning through the accumulation of "objective" truths,

TABLE 20.1 Meditative and Socio-Cognitive Mindfulness/ Mindlessness Comparison

Socio-Cognitive Mindfulness	Similarities	Meditative Mindfulness
1. Sensitivity to context 2. Openness to new information 3. Novel distinction/New Categories 4. Multiple Perspectives	1. Awareness 2. Novelty 3. Engagement	1. Present-centered 2. Nonjudgmental 3. Purposeful
Socio-Cognitive Mindlessness	**Similarities**	**Meditative Mindlessness**
1. Autopilot 2. Following predetermined rules 3. Engaged in routinized behaviors 4. Rigid perspectives 5. Lacking capacity for variation	1. Autopilot 2. Rigid Biases 3. Predetermined Rules	1. Habitual Reactions 2. Living in past/future 3. Judgment/Evaluation 4. Autopilot

rather than mindful learning which places a value on context, uncertainty, and doubt. As with meditative mindfulness, socio-cognitive mindfulness authors contrast mindfulness with mindlessness, which is described as automatic behavior. When mindless, "we act like automatons who have been programmed to act according to the sense our behavior made in the past, rather than the present." (Langer & Moldoveanu, 2000, p.2). Mindfulness from the socio-cognitive perspective requires broadening one's repertoire of cognitive categories. The idea of creating new categories was influenced by Langer's earlier studies in bias and prejudice. Explaining the practical benefits she illustrates that "If we describe someone we dislike intensely, a single statement usually does it. But if, instead, we are forced to describe the person in great detail, eventually there will be some quality we appreciate" (Langer, 1989, p.66). One of the reasons Langer's work is so compelling is that it thoroughly supports the notion that simple labels (e.g., good and evil) do not accurately reflect the complexity of the world. Instead they allow for mindless rationalizations that justify a broad range of dysfunctional behaviors, from ineffective to criminal. Are you aware of how you are sorting and labeling what you are reading right now? Are you aware of the images, memories, and thoughts that your mind is recalling as you are reading? Try exploring one or two categories you have been using while digesting this article thus far.

One way to distinguish the two schools of thought is that meditative mindfulness, with its focus on present centered awareness, describes an internal process required to maintain a mindful state, where socio-cognitive mindfulness definitions seem to focus on cognitive applications of mindfulness (e.g. how we can more effectively sort out experiences and make sense of the world based on new mental categories/ models). Furthermore, meditative mindfulness authors offer techniques in practicing mindfulness through breathing, acceptance and present centered awareness. Socio-cognitive mindfulness deem-

phasizes meditation, suggesting supplemental practices such as placing a value on doubt, looking for disconfirming data, and producing new ways of thinking and acting. Each of these approaches offer research streams in which a person's degree of mindfulness is measured through statistically validated self-report assessments. Meditative mindfulness is often measured by Brown & Ryan's Mindful Attention Awareness Scale (MAAS) (Brown & Ryan, 2003) and socio-cognitive mindfulness is measured by the Langer Mindfulness Scale (LMS) (Bodner, 2000). A factor analyses (Yeganeh, 2006) of these two scales completed by 314 participants confirmed multiple and unique dimensions to mindfulness. Our research supports the following multi-dimensional definition of mindfulness:

Mindfulness is a state in which an individual:
1. *focuses on present and direct experience*
2. *is intentionally aware and attentive*
3. *accepts life as an emergent process of change*

Mindfulness and Experiential Learning

Building on this research, we began to explore the notion that mindfulness might increase the effectiveness of learning from experience. Specifically we designed a study to explore the learning style(s) of mindful individuals using the two mindfulness scales just described and the Kolb Learning Style Inventory (Kolb 2007) based on experiential learning theory (Kolb, 1984). By understanding the relationship between mindfulness and experiential learning styles, we could begin to design mindful experiential learning practices to be used in organizations.

Experiential Learning Theory (ELT) defines learning as "the process whereby knowledge is created through the transformation of experience. Knowledge results from the combination of *grasping* and *transforming* experience" (Kolb, 1984, p.41). The ELT model portrays two dialectically related modes of *grasping* experience— Concrete Experience (CE) and

Abstract Conceptualization (AC)—and two dialectically related modes of *transforming* experience—Reflective Observation (RO) and Active Experimentation (AE). Experiential learning is a process of constructing knowledge that involves a creative tension among the four learning modes. This process is portrayed as an idealized learning cycle or spiral where the learner "touches all the bases"—experiencing, reflecting, thinking, and acting —in a recursive process that is responsive to the learning situation and what is being learned. Immediate *concrete experiences* (*experiencing*) are the basis for observations and *reflections*. These reflections are assimilated and distilled into *abstract concepts* (*thinking*) from which new implications for action can be drawn. These implications can be *actively tested* and serve as guides in creating new experiences (see Figure 20.1).

Learning style describes the unique ways that individuals spiral through the learning cycle based on their preference for the four different learning modes— CE, RO, AC, & AE. Because of our genetic makeup, our particular life experiences, and the demands of our present environment, we develop a preferred way of choosing among these four learning modes. We resolve the conflict between being con-

FIGURE 20.1   The Experiential Learning Cycle

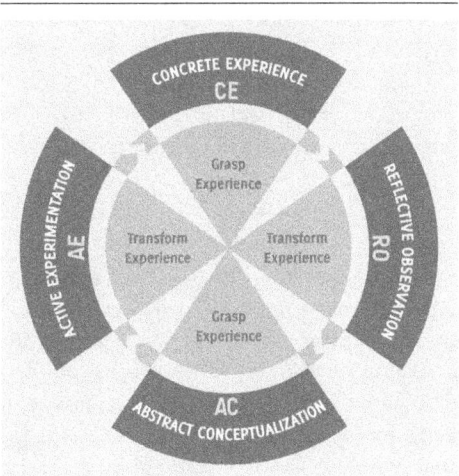

crete or abstract and between being active or reflective in patterned, characteristic ways. ELT posits that learning is the major determinant of human development and how individuals learn shapes the course of their personal development. Previous research (Kolb 1984) has shown that learning styles are influenced by personality type, culture, educational specialization, career choice, and current job role and tasks.

Our hypotheses about the relationship between mindfulness and learning style were influenced by William James, the originator of the theory of experience on which ELT is based. James (1890) stated, "no state once gone can recur and be identical with what it was before" (p.155). The mind often neglects the rich context available for observation that makes experience unique. Instead it often automatically labels stimuli based on limited exposure and moves on to the next stimulus to under-observe. To extend this further, our labels of work experiences such as productive, boring, awful, successful, urgent, relaxed, and so on are also often based in automatically categorizing experience, rather than being fully present in the unique context of the moment. James' emphasis on immediate direct sensual experience is exactly the focus on here and now experience that has been characterized by mindfulness for thousands of years. James also emphasized the importance of attention. He defines a spiral of interest-attention-selection similar to the experiential learning cycle that creates a continuous ongoing flow of experience summarized in the pithy statement— "My experience is what I agree to attend to." (1890, p. 403). This also is a central element of mindfulness.

Supporting these links between learning from experience and mindfulness, our research found that individuals who scored high on Langer's mindfulness scale emphasized direct concrete experience in their learning style (Yeganeh, 2006). We also found that individuals scoring high on mindfulness did not score high on reflective observation, suggesting that they were not "lost in thought" or rumination but were attentive to their experiences. The results suggest that the practice of mindfulness could help individuals learn from experience in two ways:

1. Encouraging a focus on here-and-now experience uncluttered by preconceptions and bias
2. Intentionally guiding their learning process by paying attention to how they are going through the phases of the learning cycle

Mindfulness becomes important when we consider *how* we choose to process and learn from events at work. Learning style determines the way we process the possibilities of each new emerging experience, which in turn determines the range of choices and decisions we see. The choices and decisions we make to some extent determine the events we work through, and these events influence our future choices. Thus, people create themselves and their learning styles through the choices of the actual occasions they live through. For many, this learning style choice has become relatively unconscious, comprised of deeply patterned routines applied globally to learning situations. Mindfulness can put the control of learning back in the learner's hands.

Practicing Mindful Experiential Learning

As it relates to mindfulness, ELT provides a grounded explanation of the learning processes of the mind when making sense of the environment (Zull 2002). The mind makes sense of complex environments by generalizing. In doing so, rules and guidelines are abstracted (AC) from experiences (CE) which are then acted (AE) and/or reflected (RO) on. Indeed this is what has enabled early civilizations to take shelter when weather worsens, use fire to ward off nocturnal scavengers, seek medicine when ill, teach right from wrong, and so on and so forth. It is clear that this propensity to generalize can be a gift, enabling us to thrive. However, the process of generalizing from experience can also result in rumination, bigotry,

fortunetelling, stress, and the like; all of which decrease learning ability. The ability to generalize is neutral; it is how we go about doing so that determines generative or degenerative outcome. Incorporating mindfulness practices into experiential learning processes will help organization members become more intentional about how and when they learn. An underlying assumption in mindful experiential learning is that the quality of experiential learning increases as organization members are more intentional. Practical examples of mindful experiential learning in organizations are limitless. For example, organizational teams can increase awareness of how individuals work with one another in specific situations, and who is best for specific kinds of work on a team. Leaders can better manage complex projects without making rash decisions based on limited information. Strategy makers can become more effective in processes by rethinking how data is collected and considered.

Mindfulness can free the mind to intentionally think and create in new ways. Those with rigorous mindfulness practices routinely practice present centered awareness. Meditation is a powerful way to discipline the mind into practicing mindfulness. However, there are also ways to practice mindfulness for those who are not dedicated to a meditation program. One thing is certain, if organization members are interested in developing mindful experiential learning skills, it is vital to begin a mindfulness routine, whether through meditation or not. For those interested in practicing mindfulness without meditation, it is important to find a way to regularly attend to one's state in order to be intentional in subsequent thoughts and behaviors. Self-monitoring when coupled with practicing acceptance creates new opportunities to think and act in learning situations. This requires a routine of "checking-in" with the self, which can be done through regular journaling, questioning, and/or taking several deep breaths from the diaphragm while accepting the present moment. Some mistakenly confuse acceptance with apathy, which it is not. In mindfulness theory, acceptance disallows the mind and body to suffer from things beyond one's control. This can paradoxically enable one to attain goals that may have otherwise been self-sabotaged by stress and attempts at overcontrolling. Working toward goals is congruent with practicing mindful experiential learning in organizations. However having an overbearing outcome-orientation in which preoccupation with a specific result hinders work effectiveness, is a classic sign of mindlessness.

Tools for Mindful Learning

Those who use the Kolb Learning Style Inventory to assess their learning style often decide that they wish to develop their capacity to engage in one or more of the four modes of the learning cycle—experiencing (CE), reflecting (RO), thinking (AC) and acting (AE). In some cases this is based on a desire to develop a weak mode in their learning style. In others it may be to increase capability in a mode that is particularly important for their learning tasks. Because of the dialectic relationships among the learning modes, inhibiting dominating modes can be as effective in developing strengths as actively developing inhibited modes. Overall learning effectiveness is improved when individuals are highly skilled in engaging all four modes of the learning cycle at contextually appropriate times.

We have created a practical model (Figure 20.2) from mindfulness and experiential learning work that answers the following question: What are various mindfulness practices that can be used to develop the capacity to engage in one or more of the four modes of the learning cycle in organizations? The next section provides some useful tools to improve specific modes of experiential learning through mindfulness. Keep in mind that the key to being mindful when learning is intentionality, as opposed to being on auto-pilot in any of the phases.

Developing the Capacity for Experiencing (CE)

This requires fully opening oneself to direct experience. Direct experience exists only in the here-and-now, a present moment of endless depth and extension that can never be fully comprehended. In fact, being heavily biased in the thinking mode (being too much "in your head") can inhibit the ability to directly sense and feel the immediate moment. Engagement in concrete experience can be enhanced by being present in the moment and attending to direct sensations and feelings. This presence and attention are particularly important for relationships. Interpersonal skills of leadership, relationship and giving and receiving, can improve by developing the experiencing mode of learning. Those who tend to be heavy in thinking and light on experiencing may wish to write out lists of everything floating around in their minds. This can include "to do's", ideas, concerns, and anything else cluttering the mind. The mind often replays these thoughts to maintain control over them. Once thoughts are written out, it is easier to practice engaging in the present moment, knowing that the list is only a glance away if something

FIGURE 20.2　Mindful Experiential Learning Practice Guide

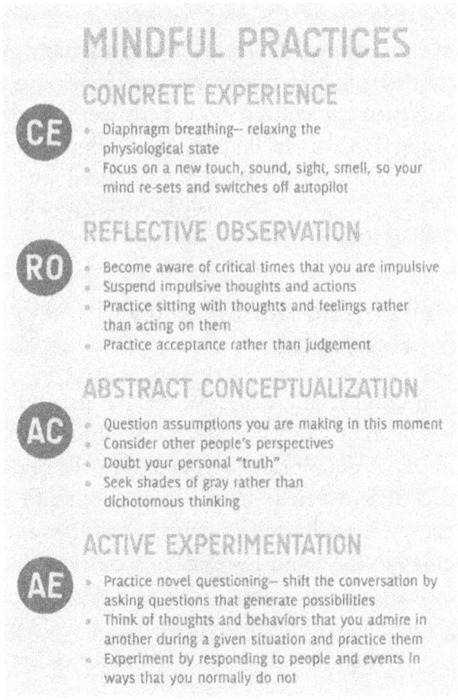

MINDFUL PRACTICES

CONCRETE EXPERIENCE

CE
- Diaphragm breathing— relaxing the physiological state
- Focus on a new touch, sound, sight, smell, so your mind re-sets and switches off autopilot

REFLECTIVE OBSERVATION

RO
- Become aware of critical times that you are impulsive
- Suspend impulsive thoughts and actions
- Practice sitting with thoughts and feelings rather than acting on them
- Practice acceptance rather than judgement

ABSTRACT CONCEPTUALIZATION

AC
- Question assumptions you are making in this moment
- Consider other people's perspectives
- Doubt your personal "truth"
- Seek shades of gray rather than dichotomous thinking

ACTIVE EXPERIMENTATION

AE
- Practice novel questioning— shift the conversation by asking questions that generate possibilities
- Think of thoughts and behaviors that you admire in another during a given situation and practice them
- Experiment by responding to people and events in ways that you normally do not

seems forgotten at a later date. Clearing the mind is a central tool for shifting from abstract thought into engaging present moment experience. Additionally, any time words are being used to think or speak, abstract thinking is happening. Words are symbols, representing only a fraction of full experience. To develop the capacity for experiencing, one can practice observing the environment while consciously shifting the mind away from words that arise, and back to the momentary observation. Taking deep breaths while doing this, anchors the mind in momentary awareness of perception: sight, sound, touch, taste, and smell, and away from abstract thought. If thoughts appear in the mind, one can gently but firmly re-focus on the breath and away from thinking in order to be more fully present. Deep breathing is a powerful intervention for strengthening the ability to experience. Most of us breathe shallowly, especially when engaged in tasks that pull us away from momentary awareness. Anchor points for creating a mindful learning routine can be as simple as routinely taking deep breaths from the diaphragm. In order to remember breathing, one can practice routine self check-ins, asking "how deeply am I breathing right now?" Creating reminder cues such as a pen dot on the hand, and/or a symbol at the desk can help as well. Because the practices suggested to engage in experience include adaptations of meditation, they often come with a host of benefits such as reduced stress, increased clarity, improved health, calmness, and creativity.

Developing the Capacity for Reflecting

Reflection requires space and time. It can be inhibited by impulsive desires and/or pressures to take action. It can be enhanced by the practices of deliberately viewing things from different perspective and empathy. Stillness and quieting the mind foster deep reflection. Information skills of sense-making, information gathering and information analysis can aid in the development and expression of the reflect-

ing mode of learning. To practice this phase of mindful experiential learning, one can actively discover critical times of impulsive action and plan to suspend action during these times through mindfulness. Focus on the physiological cues that signal when impulsivity is about to occur. When these cues arise, practicing redirecting the mind towards reflection can be a powerful tool. Those who feel quick to judge and act can routinely ask themselves "what actions have I been rushing into that I can sit with a bit longer to make sure I am being intentional?" This can be done numerous ways. One suggestion we offer clients is to program their computer calendars to announce this question on their screens every hour or few hours. Another useful practice is to hone in on one issue that requires reflection, and spend 10-15 minutes to generate new questions to answer about the issue. Create a question for yourself that you normally would not ponder, and place a value on doubt, rather than rushing into being correct. Finally, practice acceptance of the moment by identifying which actions are generative and which ones are just a way of trying to take control of an uncontrollable aspect of the environment.

Developing the Capacity for Thinking

Thinking requires the ability to cognitively represent and manipulate ideas. It can be distracted by intense direct emotion and sensations as well as pressure to act quickly. Engagement in thinking can be enhanced by practicing theoretical model building and the creation of scenarios for action. Analytical skills of theory building, data analysis and technology management can aid in the development and expression of the thinking mode of learning. From a mindfulness perspective, questioning assumptions can help to focus the mind in order to make "theories-in-use" intentional rather than automatic. Taking time to view assumptions from multiple perspectives can enrich thought. A way to do this is to experiment with how one would make sense of a situation if a current belief were untrue. Another tool is to consider the role that context plays in current mental models, and how these might differ if the context changed. Creating contextual knowledge rather than pursuing dichotomous thinking can strengthen the capacity for abstract thought. Be aware that mindlessly shifting from abstract thought to concrete experience can interfere with learning in some scenarios. Practicing a focused routine of abstract questioning and seeking shades of gray can develop the mind's ability to fully think in learning situations.

Developing the Capacity for Action

Acting requires commitment and involvement in the practical world of real consequences. In a sense it is the "bottom line" of the learning cycle, the place where internal experiencing, reflecting and thinking are tested in reality. Acting can be inhibited by too much internal processing in any of these three modes. Acting can be enhanced by courageous initiative-taking and the creation of cycles of goal-setting and feedback to monitor performance. Action skills of initiative, goal-setting and action-taking can aid in the development and expression of the acting mode of learning. Mindfulness can assist with this phase by helping learners be intentional about actions, especially when reflective observation is a more comfortable state for the learner. Asking people novel and thoughtful questions can be a safe and mindful way to begin practicing action. Another tool is having the learner envision all the ideal behaviors that he/she would like to practice. The learner then can decide which behaviors would be generative to practice in specific learning situations and begin practicing one or two of them mindfully. Learners who would like to move to action more often or more strongly will benefit from being aware of and releasing any automatic self-judgments, self-schemas, feelings and thoughts that support inaction. This can be accomplished through acceptance and breathing practices. Finally, it is important to keep in mind that acting isn't just about filling space with behavior. Intentionally suspending behavior can be a mindful act as well.

Conclusion

Everybody has learning style preferences. Cultivating mindfulness can help organization members become more intentional about how they think and behave in a given learning environment. In order to be more aware of learning processes, learners must find unique ways to engage in routines of momentary awareness. Regular practices of deep breathing can help create anchor points for learners to check in on thoughts and behaviors. In organizations it is helpful for learners to identify people who they can routinely check-in with on the degree to which they are being intentional in learning situations. These conversational anchors provide environmental cues to stay focused on a mindfulness practice and emotional support to remain optimistic. Using coaches who are well trained in mindfulness is also a powerful tool. Finally, we encourage learners not to be discouraged when facing difficulty in starting a mindful experiential learning practice. It may be best to try 1 or 2 specific mindful learning practices, and go from there. Anything more can be overwhelming and may actually inhibit progress. As techniques are mastered, additional methods can be added. In this article, we have provided mindful experiential learning practices that can improve the quality of learning in the four modes of experiential learning. These can be adapted to coaching processes, employee development programs, dialogue sessions, cultivating emotional intelligence, daily meeting practices and much more. We have presented new research and practical approaches to mindful experiential learning in organizations. We encourage others to develop innovative ways to use mindfulness in organizations and to share the results through articles and presentations so that one day using mindfulness in organizations becomes the norm. We believe it is needed more now than ever before.

Mindfulness is an age old tool to enhance life by reducing automaticity. Mindful experiential learning can be cultivated in organizations without mandating employees to commit to specific meditation practices. In many of our experiences with coaching leaders, simply presenting some of the practices discussed in this article has been enough to generate interest, resulting in self-driven exploration of mindful experiential learning. Experiential learning theory helps us understand the mental architecture of learning. Mindfulness helps us understand processes by which the mind is aware, intentional, and accepting. Using the two together unlocks a powerful tool for empowered adult learning in organizations.

References

Brown, K.W., & Ryan, R.M. (2003). The benefits of being present: mindfulness and its role in psychological well being. *Journal of Personality and Social Psychology,* 84(4), 822–848.

Bodner, T.E. (2000). On the assessment of individual differences in mindful information processing. Unpublished doctoral dissertation, Harvard University.

Casey, D. (1993). *Managing learning in organizations.* Buckingham, UK: Open University Press.

Cunningham, I. (1994). *The wisdom of strategic learning.* London, UK: McGraw-Hill.

Good, D.J., & Yeganeh, B. (2006). Mindfulness in moments of monotony. Presentation in Managerial and Organizational Cognition. Academy of Management Annual Meeting, 2006, Atlanta, GA.

Gunaratana, H. (1991). *Mindfulness in plain English.* Boston, MA: Wisdom Publications.

Hanh, T.N. (1987). *The miracle of mindfulness.* Boston, MA. Beacon Press.

Kabat-Zinn, J. (1994). *Wherever you go there you are.* New York, NY: Hyperion.

James, W. (1890). The stream of consciousness. Reprinted from *The Principles of Psychology,* I, 224–290 (Dover, 1950).

James, W. (1890). *The principles of psychology.* 2 Volumes. New York, NY: Henry Holt & Co.

Kabat-Zinn, J.(2003). Mindfulness-based interventions in context: past, present, and future. *Clinical Psychology: Science and Practice,* 10(2), 144–156.

Kolb, D. (1984). *Experiential learning: Experience as the source of learning and development.* Englewood Cliffs, NJ: Prentice Hall.

Kolb, D. A. (2007). *The Kolb learning style inventory —version 3.1: LSI workbook.* Boston, MA: Hay Transforming Learning

Langer, E.J., & Moldoveanu, M. (2000). The construct of mindfulness. *Journal of Social Issues,* 56, 1–9.

Langer, E.J. (1997). *The power of mindful learning.* Cambridge, MA: Persesus Publishing.

Senge, P. (1990). *The fifth discipline: The art and practice of the learning organization.* London, UK: Century Business.

Sims, R., & Sims, S. (Eds.). (2006). *Learning styles and learning: A key to meeting the accountability demands in education.* Hauppauge, NY: Nova Publishers.

Vince, R. (1998). Behind and beyond Kolb's learning cycle. *Journal of Management Education,* 22(3), 304–319.

Yeganeh, B. (2006). Mindful experiential learning. Case Western Reserve University. Dissertation.

Zull, J. (2002). *The art of changing the brain.* Sterling, VA: Stylus.

CHAPTER 21

Generative Conversations

How to Use Deep Listening and Transforming Talk in Coaching and Consulting

Robert J. Marshak

THE PURPOSE of this article is to introduce a subtle and powerful method that coaches and consultants can use to help clients address limiting assumptions and create new possibilities. The term *generative conversations* is used to capture the essence of this approach. Generative conversations are based on the premise that the way people see and respond to the world is determined by out-of-awareness cognitive structures that may be identified and addressed during everyday conversations. How to listen for these unspoken but powerful organizing structures and how to intervene to challenge or change them is also presented. The discussion first addresses some of the underlying premises about cognitive structures and the role of language in reinforcing and revealing what they are. The key ideas associated with generative conversations, including how to diagnose (*deep listening*) and intervene (*transforming talk*), are then discussed. This is followed by a case example to illustrate a generative conversation in action.

Premises About Cognitive Structures and Language

For many years now, I have been asked by colleagues, clients and students what I do that is special or different as a consultant or coach. Invariably I respond that, "I consult to the structure of reality of individuals, groups and organizations." Because this response is too cryptic, I'd like to elaborate here on what I mean and what is involved. I begin my work with the premise that people as individuals, groups, and organizations, experience the world through nonconscious cognitive structures that mediate or "organize" both what is experienced as well as any resulting comments, behaviors and actions. These internal structures or frameworks (in the form of assumptions, images, mindsets, metaphors, unconscious archetypes, etc.) help create and reinforce "reality" for the individual(s) by organizing how data and events are interpreted, categorized and related. This is represented in Figure 21.1.

It is further presumed that if these internal, mediating structures can be modified in some way, then transformational change may be possible. A short example will help to make the point. The classic question of whether a glass is half full or half empty is not based on the physical quantity of water and the size of the glass. Instead it is a question of meaning making or interpretation that is determined by a person's internal ways of categorizing and interpreting the world.

FIGURE 21.1   Mediating Role of Cognitive Structures

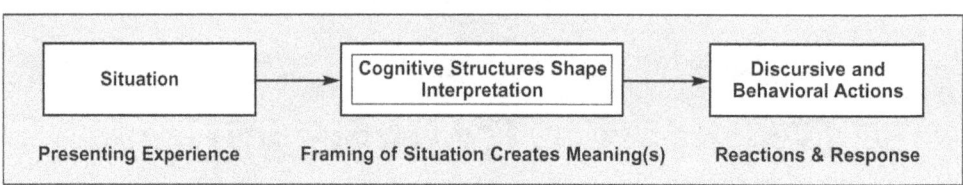

How people talk about things, the words, phrases and images they use, is further assumed to be a primary means whereby these internal cognitive structures are created, reinforced, revealed and modified. In short, what is reality for a particular person is based on a world mediated by internal structures of beliefs and ways of seeing the world that are created, conveyed and reinforced through language. Furthermore, if one listens carefully one can hear cues and clues in what is being said that may reveal the underlying cognitive structures operating in a particular situation. One may then be in a position to implicitly or explicitly challenge, reinforce and/or modify those structures, even if they remain nonconscious. Thus, when working in this mode, I address the way reality is cognitively structured for the individual or system I am working with in order to create greater awareness and options for action. I do not address what is said; I address the cognitive structures that frame what is said. These premises about cognitive structures and language are summarized in Table 21.1.

A Symbolic and Constructionist View of Language

All coaching and consulting is based in conversations carried out between two or more people. Typically participants in these exchanges don't think very much about the language they are using. Consequently, except when there are misunderstandings or confusion, the actual words and phrases are listened to less than the presumed rationally intended messages. Another view of what is going on in such exchanges, however, assumes that the words and phrases are not simply literal, but also symbolic and

TABLE 21.1   Premises About Cognitive Structures and Language

- Nonconscious cognitive structures mediate experience and response for individuals, groups and organizations.

- Cognitive structures (assumptions, images, mindsets, metaphors, archetypes, etc.) help organize how someone interprets and experiences the world.

- Changing internal cognitive structures can stimulate increased awareness, greater choice and transformation.

- How people talk about things both reinforces and reveals underlying cognitive structures.

- It is possible to listen for, address, and modify unspoken cognitive structures during normal conversations.

constructive. When we assume that language conveys implicit meanings and symbols and not just explicit, rationally intended statements, we are led to wonder what the specific words and phrases being used by a client signify about how that person is experiencing the world (Marshak, Keenoy, Oswick & Grant, 2000). We might ask ourselves:

What is the structure of beliefs, orientations, and ways of interpreting the world that is leading this person to describe things in this particular way or to use those specific word images? What words and phrases might we use in return to get "in sync with," or confront, or alter the client's inner perceptions and assumptions that may be limiting their choice(s), and are often deeply held and nonconscious?

We as coaches and consultants can use the insights provided by a symbolic and constructionist view of language to aid us with "in-the-moment" diagnosis and intervention with our clients. Our conversations with clients can be *generative* as well as informational; they have the potential to construct and reinforce meanings and therefore perceptions and possibilities (Anderson, 1995; Schön, 1993). Generative conversations are in-the-moment interactions where the coach or consultant is intentional about using the symbolic and constructionist aspects of language to help clients better assess the ways they are conceptualizing and addressing their situations, dilemmas and difficulties.

Generative Conversations in Coaching and Consulting

There are two main aspects to generative conversations between coaches or consultants and clients—Deep Listening and Transforming Talk.

Deep Listening

Deep listening is diagnostic. The coach or consultant listens to the client and develops hunches and hypotheses about unspoken mindsets, presumptions and orientations based on the explicit and implicit language used by the client. This is called deep listening because it calls for listening to overt metaphors, themes and narratives as well as unspoken, but underlying frameworks contained in unconscious and/or conceptual metaphors (Lakoff & Johnson, 1999; Siegelman, 1990). It also invites paying attention to what is emphasized and omitted in what someone is saying (Marshak & Katz, 1997).

The term deep listening emerged spontaneously several years ago during a workshop I was leading on "how to leverage language for change." The participants began referring to the way I was asking them to listen to their clients as "deep listening." The term has been used ever since. In contrast to "active listening" where the listener seeks to draw out the speaker while also acknowledging and responding to the emotions behind the words, in deep listening attention is placed on discerning and responding to the possible mindsets and cognitive frameworks behind the words and the emotions. There are four main aspects to deep listening.

First, one listens for the information the client(s) seems to be overtly trying to convey. What is the situation? What is desired? What is or is not happening? This alone would simply be *good* listening. Deep listening adds three additional aspects.

Second, one listens for *explicit* metaphors, analogies, word images, and themes in what the client is saying. For example, if he client describes a situation as "like a pressure cooker," and later that they are "under a lot of pressure" or that something got them "hot and boiling mad," then a compelling theme emerges that potentially reveals how they are experiencing their situation. This theme may be suggestive of their mindset about this and possibly similar situations even if they have not explicitly stated: "I am under intense pressure and am constrained in what I can do or where I can go. If the pressure continues, I may explode or boil over."

Third, one listens for *implicit* metaphors and images, in addition to listening for explicit expressions. In cognitive linguistics these are referred to as image schematics or conceptual metaphors and indicate the cognitively unconscious ways we tend to organize and experience the world (Lakoff & Johnson, 1980 & 1999). For example, if someone talks about their life in terms of "starting out in humble origins, getting over a number of obstacles, sometimes getting detoured, but now on the right path," then it is possible that the unconscious image schematic "Life is a Journey" is implicitly organizing their experience and therefore the choice of words for how to describe that experience: *starting, getting over obstacles, detoured, right path.* One could also listen from a psychoanalytic perspective and assume the metaphors and word images are the symbolic way the repressed unconscious expresses itself (e.g., Jung, 1964). Regardless of orientation, however, one listens for the implicit symbolic framing(s) as a potentially legitimate clue or indicator of the way the client is interpreting and experiencing the world.

Finally, one listens not only for what is said or emphasized, but also for what is not said or deemphasized. If a client leaves out seemingly relevant information or topics, this may suggest a blind spot or something hidden for presently unknown reasons. Similarly, if the client emphasizes "X" it may indicate that "Y" is being intentionally or inappropriately ignored or repressed. For example, a conflict averse client, who after describing his unit's organization structure, was surprised to discover that a key office had been omitted from the discussion. It also turned out that the head of that office and my client had a history of conflict that had never been addressed.

Deep listening requires the consultant or coach to listen simultaneously for what the client is explicitly stating, while also listening for what is being expressed implicitly and symbolically, and for what is being omitted or emphasized. This is a tall order, but deep listening can be learned and developed much like group facilitators must learn to simultaneously follow both task and process. The consultant or coach must also listen from the frame of reference of the client, in order to intuit the unspoken mindset or framework that is behind the particular word choices and expressions. A critical error of some beginning *deep listeners* is to unintentionally impose their own metaphors or framings on the situation, as if they were guessing what the client was thinking or experiencing by assuming it must be what they would think or experience in the same situation. This might be a way to empathize with the client, but it is not deep listening for the unspoken ways the client may be framing and experiencing the situation. A summary of what is involved in deep listening is provided in Table 21.2.

Transforming Talk

Based on the insights and hypotheses emerging from deep listening, the coach or consul-

TABLE 21.2   Summary of Deep Listening

In order to develop hunches and hypotheses about client mindsets and assumptions:

- Listen for the information the client is overtly conveying.
- Listen for explicit metaphors, analogies, word images, themes, and so on.
- Listen for implicit metaphors and images in addition to explicit expressions.
- Listen for what is said or emphasized and also for what is not said or is deemphasized.

tant has the opportunity to address the explicit and implicit world view(s) of the client and/or client system. This is the intervention aspect of generative conversations. Because this aspect is intended to alter or change the way a present situation is conceived by the client, it is referred to as transforming talk. Transforming talk occurs primarily through reflecting and reframing interventions.

During "reflecting interventions," the coach or consultant helps clients become more aware of their present worldview and how it may be limiting their options and choices. This is done primarily by reflecting or mirroring back to clients their own word images and themes that may be suggestive of how they are currently interpreting and experiencing a particular situation. Reflection interventions allow clients the opportunity to make conscious choices about critical and possibly limiting assumptions that might previously have been out of their awareness. For example, after hearing repeated images and phrases such as: "I am confined in what I can do," "I am watched carefully," "I better not step out of line," or "I wish they would just turn me loose," the coach or consultant might reflect back something like, "As I listen to you describe your situation it almost sounds like you are in jail. Is that true? Are you really that confined?" This form of transforming talk might help the client reflect on and modify an implicit and potentially limiting framing of a situation.

"Reframing interventions," on the other hand, go beyond reflecting back to the client hypotheses about themes and frameworks.

They also include testing out or suggesting alternative assumptions or framings with the client. Thus the consultant or coach intentionally reframes the situation to see if an alternative framing might provide greater opportunities or choice for the client. For example, a client might describe in a variety of ways that the present situation is "like going down with a sinking ship." Clearly this framing of the situation offers few positive options and invites potentially debilitating emotional associations. The coach or consultant could, in-the-moment, reframe the situation and wonder if "perhaps you are simply leaving one type of ship to get to another so as to have greater mobility and choice for your next destination?" The client can then accept or reject the reframing. Whatever the response, however, it will provide more data to the coach or consultant to develop further hypotheses to guide reflecting and reframing interventions. A summary of transforming talk is provided in Table 21.3.

Case Example

The following example is offered to demonstrate how an in the- moment, generative conversation might unfold. The example comes from a situation where the author was providing shadow consulting/coaching to an internal OD consultant. Information provided in *ital-*

ics conveys scene setting information, commentary or the internal thoughts of the consultant/author at the time.

Background: Jane is an internal OD consultant working on a difficult change initiative. Bob is working with her as a shadow consultant/coach. The following abbreviated excerpt is from a conversation they had near the beginning of their working together.

BOB: So Jane, tell me more about this new change project you are working on.

JANE: Well, it's a very challenging and difficult assignment. There isn't much support for the change; I am really out there on my own.

BOB: Is there a sponsor for the change? Who are you working for on the change?

JANE: I'm working for John C. and I don't want to let him down. I need to get out there and lead the way despite all the resistance.

BOB: You sound alone in this . . . ?

JANE: Yes, I'm very much alone. I'm kinda out there ahead of everyone else, dealing with all the resistance and attacks from everyone opposed to the change. It's a very lonely position, but someone has to do it.

Bob is now starting to hear a theme and images that sound similar to someone out on a military reconnaissance patrol deep into enemy territory and who is "on point"—out in front of everyone—in a dangerous and vulnerable position. Bob has heard military type themes many times in the past but more typically from men, so he is tentative about this initial hunch and decides to seek more background information.

BOB: By the way Jane have you ever worked in a military organization?

JANE: Well, if you count my family, then yes, of course. I come from a military family; both my father and older brother are in the army.

TABLE 21.3 Summary of Transforming Talk

- Reflect back to the client images, themes and assumptions revealed by deep listening in order to:

  - Test hunches and hypotheses.
  - Get in sync with the client's way of experiencing the world.
  - Bring to awareness ways of seeing things that may be limiting possibilities and choices.

- Reframe potentially limiting mindsets and assumptions by offering alternative ways to see and experience a situation (e.g. could the glass be half full instead of half empty?).

Knowing that Jane has some military background, Bob now seeks to draw out more information about how she is experiencing her assignment by asking questions that might elicit more insights into her ways of seeing things.

BOB: Thanks for the additional background. I understand that you are out on this difficult assignment. Tell me, how did you get this assignment?

JANE: I got it from John C.

BOB: Yes, well, hmmm, did John C. call you in and give you the assignment, were you recommended by others? Did you volunteer? How did it happen?

JANE: I knew someone needed to do it, so I went to John and told him I would be willing to take the lead to be out in front and take whatever fire or heat might happen because his change initiative is so very important.

Bob is now more confident that Jane may be operating from some kind of "on point," or "out in front of the troops" unconscious or semi-conscious organizing imagery. He begins to test this hypothesis by trying to "get in sync" with her way of seeing and experiencing the world and also to begin testing possible reframings that might give Jane more options and choices in this assignment.

BOB: Wow, it must be pretty scary to be out in front of everyone; that's a pretty vulnerable position.

JANE: *(pausing)* It is. It is very scary, but I don't think about it because it needs to be done and someone has to do it.

BOB: So you have more or less volunteered to be out on point on this assignment?

JANE: Yes, pretty much so. I just figured I was the best person to do it and I didn't want to let John C. down – that I owed him my loyalty and the change initiative is very important.

Bob decides now to be more direct and also to test one possible way the situation might be reframed to give Jane more choices or more support. He also decides that for now his approach will be to see how Jane reacts to a reframing of the possible "on point" military image without directly confronting or changing the image entirely. Bob also makes a mental note to see how extensively this image, or military images in general, may be influencing how Jane sees and experiences the world. At some future point this image may be reflected back to Jane to see if and how it may be unconsciously limiting her options and choices.

BOB: You seem to describe yourself as out in front all alone. Do you have any help or support? Have you asked for any?

JANE: Well, no, it's my job to take the lead in this.

BOB: Couldn't you ask John C. for support to back you up or provide better cover? After all you are on a mission to advance his agenda.

JANE: Well, I volunteered . . .

BOB: . . . for a suicide mission?

JANE: *(frown)* Well no . . . *(now smiling)* although sometimes it feels that way!

At this point Bob suggests a specific reframing to see if asking for support or setting up the situation in a more favorable way is a possible option for Jane in this situation.

BOB: I don't know John C., but it seems to me that if you are on an important mission for him it would be OK to ask for as much support and help as possible...

JANE: . . . even if I volunteered? Wouldn't that be "pushy" or out-of-line?

BOB: Again I don't know John C., but I think it is more than appropriate to tell him what is needed for a successful change project and ask for everything you think you need to make his change initiative a success and to ensure you are as effective as possible. You know, he has some obligation and loyalty to you too. You are advancing his initiative. If it's something he wants, then it should be something he is willing to provide strong support for.

JANE: (*tentatively*) Hmmm . . . Well, maybe I could ask him for some help. I could really use it.

BOB: If you did ask him for help or more support what would you want or need?

JANE: (*laughing*) Lots! For starters I need . . .

At this point the conversation was reframed into what was needed for a successful "mission" and that it was acceptable to request it from John C. A different and more confrontational reframing would have been to challenge the military imagery that seemed to be framing how Jane was experiencing her situation and choices. In this instance, that occurred in a later meeting when "dangerous military mission" imagery continued to pervade her descriptions of her work on the change initiative and seemed to frame how she experienced the situation and what she saw as her options and choices.

There are, of course, other possible interventions that could have occurred in this shadow consulting/coaching relationship. There are also other possible interpretations of what might have been going on with Jane and why she seemed to see the situation the way she did, including, perhaps, non-military interpretations. The purpose of presenting this case is not to suggest exactly what should be done or how certain phrases should be interpreted, but to give a realistic example of a generative conversation where deep listening is used to inform intentional transforming talk to get in sync with the client and provide more options and choices.

Concluding Comments

Consultants and coaches using a constructionist and discursive orientation always have the opportunity to enter into generative conversations with clients and client systems for the purpose of facilitating or inducing change. Interventions can occur in-the-moment and do not have to rely on or wait for more programmed or scheduled interventions. This orientation requires skills in deep listening and transforming talk to be able to hear implicit and symbolic messages indicative of internal mindsets *and* to be able to reflect back and/or reframe those messages in order to create new options and choices for the client. It also requires a good sense of timing, ability to hear the world through someone else's words, and the ethics to use this social technology with positive intent and with the ambition to always keep the client in a position of choice.

References

Anderson, H. D. (1995). Collaborative language systems: Toward a postmodern therapy. In R. H. Mikesell, D. D. Lusterman, & S. H. McDaniel (Eds.), *Integrating family therapy: Handbook of family psychology and systems theory* (pp. 27–44). Washington, DC: American Psychological Associates.

Jung, C. G. (1964). *Man and his symbols.* New York, NY: Doubleday.

Lakoff, G., & Johnson, M. (1980). *Metaphors we live by.* Chicago, IL: University of Chicago Press.

Lakoff, G., & Johnson, M. (1999). *Philosophy in the flesh: The embodied mind and its challenge to Western thought.* New York, NY: Basic Books.

Marshak, R. J., Keenoy, T., Oswick, C., & Grant, D. (2000). From outer words to inner worlds, *Journal of Applied Behavioral Science*, 36 (2) 245–258.

Marshak, R. J., & Katz, J. H. (1997). Diagnosing covert processes in groups and organizations, *OD Practitioner*, 29 (1) 33–42.

Schön, D. A. (1993). Generative metaphor: A perspective on problem-solving in social policy. In A. Ortony (Ed.), *Metaphor and thought* (2nd ed., pp. 137–163). Cambridge, UK: Cambridge University Press.

Siegelman, E. Y. (1990). *Metaphor and meaning in psychotherapy.* New York, NY: Guilford.

CHAPTER 22

Diversity and Social Justice

Practices for OD Practitioners

Michael Brazzel

THE WORDS "diversity" and "social justice" are familiar enough to Organization Development (OD) practitioners that most of us know what they mean and how they work. Many of us would say they are part of our OD practice. Yet we can be uncomfortable with diversity issues when they come up in our OD practice and we seek ways to address organizational issues without having to directly take on diversity aspects.

This is true of the OD profession as a whole. A review of the content indexes of current OD textbooks yields few listings for diversity and social justice concepts and dynamics. Bob Marshak comments that, "Given the core values of OD and the increasingly diverse and multicultural organizational settings for its practice, it is clear that all professional practitioners need to fully understand and as appropriate address multicultural and diversity issues and dynamics . . ." (Marshak, 2006, p. 25).

This article examines ten diversity and social justice practices that support addressing diversity and social justice issues and dynamics as an integral part of OD practice. They are listed in Table 22.1.

1. Understand Diversity and Social Justice Dynamics

Diversity and social justice are interrelated. Fred Miller writes, "Social justice issues must

TABLE 22.1 Diversity and Social Justice Practices

1. Understand diversity and social justice dynamics
2. Integrate diversity and social justice into OD practice
3. Work from dominant and subordinated group identities
4. Work at multiple levels of system
5. Do our own diversity and social justice work
6. Claim and use all of ourselves
7. Partner with others
8. Practice small acts of courage, irrepressible hope, and stubborn optimism
9. Stay alive
10. Create and use a guiding vision of social justice and inclusion

be addressed in order to achieve the potential of diversity." (Miller, 1994, p. xxvi.)

Diversity

Diversity includes human differences, aspects of human experience, and elements of culture. These diversity measures apply at individual, group, organization, community, nation, and world levels of human systems. Diversity also involves processes for addressing diversity at different levels of human systems: inclusion, pluralism, multiculturalism, and cultural competency. See Table 22.2.

TABLE 22.2 Diversity Measures and Processes

Diversity Measures

- Human differences: race, ethnicity, nationality, gender, sexual orientation, spiritual practice, ability, age, class, and other human differences. Human differences apply for multiple levels of human systems.
- Aspects of human experience: thinking, doing, feeling, physical sensations, values, and intuitive, spiritual and other knowing. Aspects of human experience apply for multiple levels of human systems.
- Elements of culture: authority, leadership, power, status, language, time, space, intimacy and sexuality, style, laws, regulations, rules, norms, standards, structure, values, beliefs, assumptions, ideology and ways of making meaning, individualism and collectivism, rewards and punishments, spirituality and religion, food, dress, humor, rites and rituals, and other elements of culture. Elements of culture apply for multiple levels of human systems.

Diversity Processes

- Inclusion: including people with many differences in the work of organizations.
- Pluralism: incorporating diverse groups of people in organizations, communities, and nations.
- Multiculturalism: incorporating the multiple interests, contributions, and values of diverse groups of people in the cultures of pluralistic organizations, communities, and nations.
- Cultural competency: individual ability for effective, interpersonal communication with people across cultural differences based in race, gender, sexual orientation, nationality, ethnicity, religion, age, class, and other human differences.

Diversity is often described in terms of human differences . . . race, gender, sexual orientation, physical and mental ability, ethnicity, nationality, age, spiritual practice, class, and other human differences. Diversity is also expressed in terms of human experience —Ideas, behaviors, physical sensations, feelings, values, and intuitive, spiritual, and other knowing.

These aspects of human experience are forms of intelligence and experience which are used to acquire and process information, make meaning, and define reality. Cultural differences are a third way of defining diversity. Elements of culture can include, for example, authority, leadership, power, status, language, time, space, intimacy, laws, regulations, rules, norms, standards, structure, values, beliefs, assumptions, ideology and ways of making meaning, rewards and punishments, and spirituality.

Diversity also includes processes of addressing diversity concepts in human systems. Inclusion, the process of including people with many differences, generally is used to describe organizations. Pluralism and multiculturalism are often used as characteristics of organizations, communities, and nations. Cultural competency describes the ability of individuals for effective, cross-cultural communication with other individuals.

Social Justice

Understanding and helping organizations provide for diversity and inclusion is not enough. Because organizations exist in a landscape of social identity groups, power differences among identity groups, and prejudice, social justice must also be addressed. Social justice is the elimination of oppression and development of cultures and systems that provide inclusion, equity, access, and opportunity for all people. Organizations have been unsuccessful in attempts to create a culture of inclusion without first addressing racism, sexism, and other forms of oppression and injustice. (Jackson, 2006, p. 143). Social justice concepts and processes are listed in Table 22.3.

We live in a world that is racialized, gendered, sexualized, and classed. White people, men, heterosexuals, upper- and middle-class people, and citizens of colonialist and white-settler nations receive benefits and are privileged as a result of their dominant group identities, separate from their accomplishments as individuals. People-of-color, women and transgender people, gays, lesbians and bi-

TABLE 22.3   Social Justice Concepts and Processes

- Social justice: The elimination of oppression and development of cultures and systems that provide inclusion, equity, access, and opportunity for all people.

- Oppression: Systems of inequality, privilege, and actions, behaviors, and practices institutionalized in the cultures, policies and practices of groups, organizations, communities, and nations and internalized in individuals. Oppression is based in power and prejudice about human differences. It benefits dominant group members and harms subordinated group members. The "isms" are forms of oppression, that include racism, sexism, heterosexism, classism, xenophobic oppression, colonialism, and other isms.

- Social identity groups: A group of people with common characteristics who are defined and set apart by socially-constructed boundaries, such as race, gender, sexual orientation, age, class, spiritual practice, and ability. Individuals have multiple group memberships. Most individuals are members of both dominant and subordinated groups. The concept of dominant and subordinated groups relates to group identity and not individual identity.

- Dominant groups: Social identity groups with power in groups, organizations, communities, and nations to use resources and establish sanctions, rules, norms, style, laws, policies, values and expectations. Dominant group members see themselves as normal and often better than subordinated group members, whom they view as abnormal and less-than. Dominant group power, combined with prejudice toward subordinated groups, is used to confer privilege, power, recognition and opportunity to dominant group members and deny those benefits to subordinated group members.

- Subordinated groups: Social identity groups who do not hold power and are denied privilege and subjected to harm because of subordinated group identity.

sexual people, working class people, and citizens of nations-of-color, are disadvantaged and penalized for their group identities, in spite of their accomplishments as individuals. Human differences, dominant and subordinated groups and the forms of oppression that effect them are described in Table 22.4.

2. Integrate Diversity and Social Justice into OD Practice

For the most part, the theories and models that OD practitioners use do not consider the existence and implications for organizations of dominant and subordinated identity groups, power differences among groups, prejudice, and institutionalized racism, sexism, heterosexism, and other forms of oppression. The informal assumption in OD is that racism, sexism, heterosexism and other forms of oppression are not always present and they need to be addressed only when oppression becomes an issue for the

organization. The contrasting perspective is that dominant and subordinated group memberships, power differences, prejudice, and institutionalized oppression are part of the daily experience of organizations and must be attended as an integral part of OD practitioners' work.

Consider a twelve-month experiment: Assume that dominant and subordinated identity groups, power, prejudice, and racism, sexism, heterosexism and other forms of oppression are ever-present in the organizations in which you practice OD. Incorporate the existence of dominant and subordinated identity groups, power, and prejudice into the theories and models you use in your OD practice: change, resistance, and conflict theory, systems theory, action research, use of self, values and ethics, and supplementary and practice theories, such as appreciative inquiry and emotional intelligence. Contract with your organizational clients to support their health and effectiveness,

TABLE 22.4   Human Differences, Dominant and Subordinated Groups, and Forms of Oppression

Human Differences	Dominant Groups	Subordinated Groups	Forms Of Oppression
Race	White, Caucasian	Asian descent, Black/ African descent, Latino/ Latina/Hispanic descent, First Nation/ Native People. Bi- and Multi-Racial People	Racism, Colorism
Ethnicity	White, Western European Heritage	Arab, Filipino, Gypsy/Roma, Haitian, Indian, Jewish, Mexican, Puerto Rican, Turkish, and other ethnicities	Ethnocentrism, Xenophobic Oppression, Xeno-Racism, Colorism, Anti-Semitism
Nationality	US, Canada, UK, France, Germany, Austria, Russia, Australia, other European, and white dominant and white settler nations	Panama, Afghanistan, Iraq, South Korea, Vietnam, Somalia, Malaysia, Philippines, Kenya, Zimbabwe, Guam, Granada, Puerto Rico, Bangladesh, other nations of color; refugee, legal immigrant/alien, illegal immigrant/ "alien," stateless	Nativism, Colorism, Nationalism, Xenophobic Oppression, Ethnocentrism, Colonialism
Gender	Men	Women	Sexism
Gender Identity	Gender-conforming people	Transgender, Third Gender, and other non gender-conforming people	Transgender Oppression
Sexual Orientation	Heterosexual	Gay, Lesbian, Bisexual	Heterosexism
Spiritual Practice	Christian	Agnostic, Animist, Atheist, Baha'i, Jain, Buddhist, Confucian, Hindu, Jewish, Muslim, Pantheist, Shintoist, Sikh, Taoist, Yoruba, Zoroastrian, and other spiritual practices	Religious Oppression, Anti-Semitism
Ability	Able-bodied	People with Disabilities	Ableism
Age	Adults	Children, Elders	Ageism, Child Abuse, Incest, Elder Abuse
Class	Ruling, Owning, Upper Class; Upper Middle, Professional, Merchant, Middle Class	Lower Middle Class, Working Class, Poor, Homeless	Classism

their efforts at inclusion, and their work to mitigate and eliminate racism, sexism, heterosexism and other forms of oppression.

3. Work from Dominant and Subordinated Group Identities

OD practitioners are individuals and they also have multiple dominant and subordinated group identities. These group identities affect client organizations and working relationships among OD practitioner teams and client organizations. Knowing, owning, and working from dominant and subordinated group identities opens space for being able to partner across identity groups. Paradoxically, it also reinforces the individual identity of OD practitioners.

Practitioners are more effective in working from dominant and subordinated group identities when they engage regularly in personal development work to understand and own personal bias and prejudice involving race, gender, sexual orientation, and other human differences; areas of internalized privilege, dominance, and subordination; and their effects on practitioners' actions. Working from dominant and subordinated group identities also helps with understanding and tracking the impacts of practitioner interventions and behavior at both individual and social identity group levels.

4. Work at Multiple Levels of System

Being effective in helping organizations address diversity and social justice issues can mean that practitioners have to be prepared to work at multiple levels of systems. Racism, sexism, heterosexism and other forms of oppression are interdependent and reinforcing and can show up at varying levels of system. They are manifested as internalized dominance, privilege, and subordinance in the beliefs and actions of individuals and they are institutionalized in the norms, structures, and processes of groups, units, and organizations. Practitioners can get stuck working at the individual level of

system on awareness training, internalized oppression, or interpersonal communication and not support the organization with addressing institutionalized oppression at other systemic levels of the organization. Organization may prefer to stay with, for example, coaching or one-day awareness training. Diversity and social justice work often means joining people/ groups/ organizations where they are and then helping them to explore other levels.

5. Do Our Own Diversity and Social Justice Work

As OD practitioners, we can help organizations go only as far in addressing diversity and social justice as we have gone in our own personal development. The less we attend to our own development, the more likely we will be limiting organizations as we are consulting with them. The development process around diversity and social justice is complex because OD practitioners are likely to be members of both dominant and subordinated groups.

For dominant group members, doing one's own work means coming to terms with internalized superiority, dominance, and privilege . . . the sense of entitlement that grows from embedded values and beliefs that dominant group members are normal and that the others are abnormal and less than fully human. The development process for dominant group members involves:

- Maintaining an ongoing awareness of the existence and impacts of racism, sexism, heterosexism and other forms of oppression on subordinated group members and its benefits for dominant group members,
- Being able to name and track oppression in its various forms,
- Having empathy for subordinated group members, and
- Making a commitment to interrupt oppression whenever and wherever it shows up.

Ongoing awareness is central (Hanna, Talley, and Guindon, 2000, pp. 437-439). Dominance functions by limiting the awareness and empathy of dominant group members.

For subordinated group members, development means coming to terms with internalized subordinance, identification, and collusion with dominant group members. Subordinated group members are aware of the existence, forms, and effects of oppression. Their development process includes

- Validation of their awareness and perception,
- Disidentification with harmful values and beliefs of dominant group members,
- Rightfully attributing the problem of oppression to the dominant group,
- Acknowledging the appropriateness of anger and depression that can result from the harmful effects of oppression,
- Developing self-efficacy, and
- Advocating for subordinated group members. (Hanna, Talley, & Guindon, 2000, pp. 435-437).

Again awareness is central for liberation of subordinated group members from racism, sexism, heterosexism and other forms of oppression as systems of inequality that support dominant group members and harm subordinated group members.

Personal and professional development work is a journey, not an end result. It is life's work. support for maintaining awareness and personal and professional development can be found by partnering with other practitioners; looking to the work of practitioner-elders like Elsie Y. Cross, Jack Gant, and Edie Seashore; and regularly participating in diversity and social justice labs, workshops, and certificate programs, such as NTL's Diversity Practitioner Certificate Program.

6. Claim and Use All of Ourselves

Knowing, being, and using all of ourselves as OD practitioners is an important diversity and social justice practice. Who I am includes human differences, areas of human experience,

elements of individual culture, dominant and subordinated group identities, internalized dominance, privilege, and subordination, preferred ways and styles for engaging with individuals, groups, and organizations, dreams, memories, feelings, and other inner life experience, and roles, titles, and responsibilities. Some aspects of self are listed in Table 22.5. Using

---

TABLE 22.5   Some Aspects of Self

- Human differences: race, ethnicity, nationality, gender, sexual orientation, spiritual practice, ability, age, class, and other differences,
- Human experience: thinking, doing, feeling, physical sensations, values, and intuitive, spiritual and other knowing,
- Individual culture: authority, leadership, power, status, language, time, space, intimacy and sexuality, style, laws, regulations, rules, norms, standards, structure, values, beliefs, assumptions, ideology and ways of making meaning, individualism and collectivism, rewards and punishments, spirituality and religion, food, dress, humor, rites and rituals, and other elements of culture,
- Dominant and subordinated group identities,
- Dreams, memories, body sensations, feelings, and core values of our inner beings,
- Internalized dominance, privilege, and subordination,
- Personality, culture, and history,
- Learning, resistance, conflict, risk-taking, leadership and other styles and references, skills, competencies, authenticity, strengths, and areas for development,
- Roles, titles, and responsibilities we assume in our engagement and identification with individuals, family, groups, and organizations in our environments,
- Ways we are affected by and affect others through bias, prejudice, collusion, racism, sexism, heterosexism, classism, colonialism, and other forms of oppression.

ourselves involves using all aspects of self, those about which we are proud and sorry. . . Using ourselves, with intention, to impact individuals, groups, and organizations.

Diversity and social justice work involves being imperfect and vulnerable, a willingness to make mistakes and learn from them, and forgiving oneself and others for being imperfect. It means working from both head and heart and being clear about what one stands for; identifying one's own purpose, vision, values. It means taking responsibility for ourselves and our personal and professional development, holding ourselves responsible for intentions and accountable for intended and unintended impacts, and distinguishing between intentions and effects of one-time, isolated events and the cumulative effects of successive and on-going events. It means reclaiming repressed, disowned, and projected parts of ourselves with information gained through disclosure and feedback and dreams, memories, body sensations, and feelings.

7. Partner with Others

Effective diversity and social justice work in organizations depends on the OD practitioner's ability to partner with others by building and using networks and support systems of colleagues and allies. Diversity and social justice work cannot be done alone.

Partnering has many benefits. Partnering both within and across multiple group identities brings different perspectives and experiences to the work. It provides both support and challenge for practitioners and fosters practitioner growth and development. It models working across dominant and subordinated group identities for members of client organizations and systems.

8. Practice Small Acts of Courage, Irrepressible Hope, and Stubborn Optimism

Change does not need to involve one or two big acts that change the entire world. Change

can result from one small act after another, an accumulation of acts, by people working together for social justice and inclusion. Telling the truth. Staying true to one's values. Speaking out for diversity and social justice and acting to eliminate oppression in all of its forms.

Oppression can seem insurmountable in the world. Hope, combined with optimism, is the belief that oppression, as a social construct, is not permanent and can be dismantled. Václav Havel speaks of hope as ". . . the certainty that something makes sense, regardless of how it turns out. . . . Hope . . . gives us the strength to live and continually try new things, even in conditions that seem as hopeless as ours do, here and now." (Havel, 1990, p. 182).

9. Stay Alive

In his well-known article, Herb Shepard's first rule for change agents is "stay alive" (Shepard, 1975). This is also a good diversity and social justice practice for OD practitioners.

Staying alive means helping organizations have successes, even when they are small. It means being choiceful and strategic about when and how to consult in client systems where diversity and social justice work is difficult and may not be a popular direction for the organization. It means choosing not to work in some organizations or leaving an internal position in an organization based on practitioner values and ethics.

Diversity and social justice work in organizations can be taxing, and even toxic. Not surprisingly, being healthy is the highest-priority value in a study of the values of eighty-nine diversity and social justice practitioners (Brazzel, 2007). It is important to remember practitioners who devoted themselves to diversity and social justice work and died too soon. They include Amanda Fouther, Kaleel Jamison, Marjane Jensen, Hal Kellner, Robert B. Moore, Richard Orange, Robert W. Terry, Leroy Wells, Jr. Their legacies remain with us.

In 1981, ten members of the Irish Republican Army were on hunger strike and dying in

British jails. A few weeks before my aunt Mary Brazzel died in 1981, she asked me, "Is there anything that is important enough to you that you would be willing to die for it?" Though I did not know then, I know now that social justice and the elimination of oppression are important enough to die for. They are also worth living for.

10. Create and Use a Guiding Vision of Social Justice and Inclusion

Organizations choose a path of social justice and inclusion, moving from a dominant culture to a culture that integrates the cultures of many different individuals and social identity groups . . . or they do not. When organizations do choose to address diversity and social justice issues, they do so because of business and mission-related advantages to the organization, because harmful effects of oppression are not acceptable, because of threatening legal and legislative losses, and because the course of social justice and inclusion is congruent with organizational values and is the morally right thing to do. A vision of social justice and inclusion is needed for guiding organizations on this journey.

OD practitioners support change in organizations by helping them define and be clear about both their present state and their desired future. When OD practitioners have incorporated diversity and social justice in their OD practice, they can help organizations begin to see and track the impacts of dominant and subordinated social identity groups, power differences, prejudice, and institutionalized oppression for their current situation and daily experience. The desired future for organizations is defined with a vision of social justice and inclusion. Bailey Jackson suggests a vision of social justice and inclusion in which,

The organization "has within its mission, goals, values, and operating system

explicit policies and practices that prohibit anyone from being excluded or unjustly treated because of social identity or status . . . [The organization] not only supports social justice within the organization; it advocates these values in interactions within the local, regional, national, and global communities, with its vendors, customers, and peer organizations . . . All members of the diverse workforce feel fully included and have every opportunity to contribute to the mission of the organization." (Jackson, 2006, pp. 142-143)

He reinforces this as a vision of social justice and inclusion for organizations with the observation that no organization has achieved this vision (Jackson, 2006, p. 146).

Organizations choose whether or not to address social justice and inclusion issues. . . . and that is true for OD practitioners as well. There are many reasons for OD practitioners to choose not to address diversity and social justice issues. It is hard and often uncomfortable work. The elimination of oppression in the world is unlikely to happen any time soon. The OD field and profession often treat diversity and social justice as a peripheral matter. Organizations often resist addressing diversity and social issues.

Whether OD practitioners choose to make diversity and social justice an integral part of their practice depends on what they stand for in the world: purpose, vision, and values. Creating a personal vision of social justice and inclusion can crystallize an OD practitioner's choice to stand for social justice and inclusion in their practice.

References

Brazzel, M. (2007). *Priority values of diversity and social justice practitioners.* Unpublished study.

Hanna, F. J., Talley, W. B., & Guindon, M. H. (2000). The power of perception: Toward a model of cultural oppression and liberation. *Journal of Counseling and Development, 78*(4), pp. 430–441.

Havel, V. (1990). *Disturbing the peace: A conversation with Karel Huizdala* (pp. 181–182). New York, NY: Vintage Books.

Jackson, B. W. (2006). Theory and practice of multicultural organizational development. In B. B. Jones & M. Brazzel (Eds.) *The NTL handbook of organization development and change: Principles, practices, and perspectives* (pp. 139–154). San Francisco, CA: Pfeiffer.

Marshak, R. J. (2006). Organization development as a profession and a field. In B. B. Jones, & M. Brazzel (Eds.) *The NTL handbook of organization development and change: Principles, practices, and perspectives* (pp. 13–27). San Francisco, CA: Pfeiffer.

Miller, F. A. (1994). Why we choose to address oppression. In E. Y. Cross, J. H. Katz, F. A. Miller, & E. W. Seashore (Eds.), *The promise of diversity: Over 40 voices discuss strategies for eliminating discrimination in organizations* (pp. xxv–xxix). New York, NY: Irwin.

Shepard, H. A. (1975). Rules of thumb for change agents. *OD Practitioner,* 17 (4), pp. 1–5.

CHAPTER 23

Racism in the Workplace

OD Practitioners' Role in Change

Judith H. Katz and Karon R. Moore

PEOPLE OF COLOR have often shared that they experience organizational life differently than their white counterparts. Common feedback from people of color includes that they have insufficient access to information, are given titles without real authority, or lack proper funding or compensation. Many people of color talk about feeling isolated and alone in their organization, with few people at their organizational level who are like them to interact with in their daily business routines. People of color often comment on getting busy work—or, paradoxically, the most difficult work with insufficient support.

The "comfort factor" can cause white managers and supervisors to be reluctant to give timely, appropriate, or honest feedback across racial lines. This reluctance hinders people of color from knowing where they actually stand with regard to performance or ways in which they can develop their skills, abilities, and potential for success.

In this article, we outline some of the issues of racism in organizations today and ways in which we as OD practitioners can work to address this critical issue in the organizations in which we work and the interventions we undertake.

Many OD practitioners, whose practice seems to have little to do with diversity, may be asking the question "How does this relate to us personally and professionally?" Through more fully understanding racism in all its forms, including the subtleties of racism, we will be better able to see how racism exists, rather than getting stuck in determining if it exists.

No committed practitioner would support (even unintentional) racism in a client system. Yet racism exists, and, often by our lack of awareness causing inaction and collusion, we may inadvertently be supporting its continuation. Adherence to the OD Network's "Principles of Practice" encourages all of us to see the potential role we can play to both identify and address issues of racism in the organizations within which we work. Understanding the realities of racism fully supports key values of Organization Development: Respect and Inclusion; Collaboration; Authenticity; Self-Awareness; and Empowerment.

There has been some progress in recent decades. In many (but by no means all) major corporations today there is an explicit emphasis on leveraging diversity and inclusion. Affirmative Action helped grant entry to people of color and white women, who were formerly denied access to organizations. Blatant racism—overt hiring discrimination, denial of promotions, discriminatory policies and actions—are illegal and the exception versus the rule in many organizations. As a result, people of color are more present, more visible, and more invested in organizations than ever before.

But racism has not gone away. The numbers tell the story. The top levels of leadership at most organizations are still overwhelmingly white. The disparity of income between whites and people of color remains. And in the most recent economic downturn (2008), more people of color lost their homes to foreclosure than did whites. Untested assumptions and perceptions, our often unconscious treatment of people, and the resulting actions allow racism to permeate organizations. Exclusion, disadvantage, and tokenism are still operating. In many cases, racism has merely become more subtle, more covert, and more sophisticated. How can this be at a time when so many efforts are being made to level the playing field?

We as OD practitioners must become more aware of the insidiousness of racism—particularly today, as organizations and individuals would prefer to move on and not discuss the issue. We must recognize how systems, structures, and behaviors support the pervasiveness of racism. More importantly, we need to understand the subtle ways in which many attitudes still are based in biased assumptions, and we must work to challenge and eliminate racism within our organizations. We need to be aware of the ways in which racism affects both our practice and the organizations that we serve.

What Is Racism?

Definitions of racism often include reference to power dynamics, historical inequities, and systemic biases. Here we will use a more general definition: racism includes any actions or words that have the effect of privileging some and disadvantaging others based solely or in part on race.

Under this definition, even unintentional acts or words have an effect. As a first step, we need to examine what *we* do and say—and the assumptions that underlie *our* choices—to understand how the lens of race/color affects our view of people different from ourselves. Our next step as OD practitioners must be to start seeing how racism is playing out in today's or-

ganizations. Though some believe that organizations have been sanitized by formal policies and legal guidelines designed to ensure the fair treatment of everyone, there are ways in which organizational policies as well as individual actions perpetuate racism. We must be able to recognize the subtleties of racism, so that we can move to correct it. This is one way we can focus on the effectiveness and health of client systems. See Sidebars 23.1 and 23.2.

Seeing Racial Dynamics at Play

Discrimination

The most fundamental decisions in organizations—where to recruit, whom to interview, whom to hire, whom to fire, whom to promote, how to compensate, and how to evaluate performance—are often based on subjective factors. Individuals downplay the extent to which personality, compatibility, "fit," and other subjective factors influence how they view others and perceive competence. Generally, people are most comfortable with people who are like themselves. This "comfort factor" often goes unacknowledged and ends up having great influence over who enters and who succeeds in the organization.

In another form of subtle racism, leaders give "stretch" opportunities to people with whom they feel comfortable—while others, with whom the leaders are less comfortable, must prove themselves before they get into similar positions. When stretch opportunities *are* given to people with whom leaders feel less

---

SIDEBAR 23.1 Where to Look

- Hiring for comfort or qualifications?
- Who is seen as a "risk"? A "fit"?
- Are policies and practices applied fairly?
- Competence based on past or future?
- Individual focus or focus on patterns and systemic barriers?
- Use of coded language (e.g., "qualified," "articulate")?

SIDEBAR 23.2 Some Questions for OD Practitioners

Rate yourself on a scale of 0–10 (0 not at all/10 actively pursuing)

1. To what extent have you actively pursued increasing your own knowledge about racism?
2. To what extent have you worked on your own assumptions, language, etc.?
3. To what extent are you partnering with people different from you as you work on change and other OD projects?
4. To what extent are you aware of racism – seeing it and naming it in your organization or with clients?
5. To what extent do you overtly address issues of discrimination in the projects in which you are a constituent?
6. To what extent have you discussed these issues with OD colleagues of different races?

What OD Practitioners Can Do:

1. Examine your assumptions and biases. (Do not assume that if you are a person of color, you don't have assumptions and biases.)
2. Discuss issues of racism – with the underlying assumption of asking how it exists, not if it exists in your client system or organization.
3. Be alert – pay attention.
4. Look for group patterns, not individual acts.
5. Speak up, speak out, and don't collude by avoidance or silence.
6. Form alliances with colleagues of other races.

comfortable, it is often described as "taking a risk." As OD practitioners, we can be mindful of which racial groups or populations are seen as "risky" and which populations are described as "ready" for stretch assignments; then we can help leaders identify and address the impact of their covert biases on their organizations.

On a personal level, we OD practitioners must also be aware of how, where, and when the "comfort factor" plays out for us. It can play out as we are collecting and assessing data,

focusing on systems, intervening in processes, helping leaders select teams, working with organizations in their performance review and planning, and identifying future leaders.

Many organizations describe themselves as a meritocracy or performance-based environment. Often, however, alliances and relationships ("who you know") play a major role in determining who is successful. Organizations identify rigorous policies and practices and then often apply them in their most narrow form—"just going by the book" or "just following the rules"—to people they are unsure of or with whom they feel uncomfortable. When we feel comfortable with people, we are more inclined to give them the benefit of the doubt, address conflicts and disagreements with them more easily, and feel greater trust with them. As OD practitioners working with organizations, we have an opportunity to identify policies and practices that are unfair, or unfairly applied, and help the client understand the value of having them uniformly applied to all populations.

Many leaders (both white and people of color) do not realize the extent to which their levels of confidence, trust, and definitions of "competence," "professionalism," "team player," and the like are determined by comfort and, therefore, can disadvantage people of color. In many organizations, performance evaluations skew lower for people of color on the whole. Organizations may view this as an individual phenomenon rather than considering it to be a systemic issue. The problem is compounded when those evaluations are then used to determine promotions, salary increases, or layoffs at a time of downsizing; they can have the effect of decimating the diversity of the organization. As an OD practitioner, you can help your client to look for any patterns that may surface in reviewing the results of performance evaluations.

Who is really competent to lead today's organizations? Do we ask the most important question – whether our current managers and leaders are competent to effectively interview, select, develop, coach, and lead a diverse group of people? Have we included this competency in the criteria we use to determine a person's qualifications to lead? If we were to include it now, how many individuals who have been promoted to leadership positions would no longer be able to meet this new definition of "competent?"

All too often, organizations look at what happens to people of color on an individual case by case basis, thereby missing the fact that there may be patterns of discrimination, areas or departments where discrimination exists, or patterns of behavior that adversely impact people of color. As OD practitioners, we can analyze and encourage clients to look at group level patterns. Simultaneously, while looking for group patterns, we must reinforce viewing each person as an individual.

Language

Code language that speaks to subtle racism has become prevalent in many organizations. Such statements as "we want to hire a qualified person of color" or "we want a diverse pool of qualified candidates" indicate an assumption that, without adding the word "qualified," people would recruit, hire, or promote unqualified people of color. These statements can also imply that it will take additional effort to find the "qualified" ones—an effort not needed when finding candidates who are most like the majority in the organization. Code language is also demonstrated with the use of "articulate" or "good communication skills," frequently indicating surprise at the abilities of people of color in the organization. Sometimes white colleagues tell people of color that they are "different from the rest" or "not like others" of their race.

Often when a person of color is hired for a position or receives a promotion, there are ripples of speculation throughout the organization suggesting that the move could only be attributed to their race—that it was an "Affirmative Action hire." Sometimes white women collude with this assumption of quota-filling by expressing these same speculations when,

in fact, Affirmative Action has benefited white women as well.

As OD practitioners, we need to call people on such language and assumptions when we hear them, and help people be mindful of their implications. We need to encourage leaders and managers to do the same: to consistently focus organizational communications on what individuals bring to the position, their capabilities, experiences, and qualifications.

Avoidance/Collusion of Silence

Although the above practices may exist in organizations, the hardest issues to address are those of avoidance and the collusion of silence. Many organizations would prefer not to address or even acknowledge the possibility that racism may be a part of the organization's policies, practices, and behaviors. There may be a fear of finding out the truth, which could lead to lawsuits, and therefore the organization shies away from collecting any data to learn about the current realities or gaps that may exist.

Avoidance also takes place if people of color fail in the organization or choose to leave of their own accord: organizations often avoid any analysis as to what created the situation and how to remedy it. The same companies that strictly monitor sales data and marketplace opportunities for trends and revealing information may neglect to pay attention to the attrition rates or promotion histories of people of color. The patterns that attrition and lack of promotion reveal can tell organizations a great deal about where systemic racism is impeding their performance. This lack of analysis may be an example of the organization viewing the problem as a function of the individuals who failed, not as part of a pattern or something that could be problematic in the system.

OD practitioners can work to assure that if data are collected, they will be examined in demographic groups to learn if there are different experiences for people of color, whites, and other social identity groups. In addition, we can make sure that in our recommendations and strategies, people of color and other populations are fully included in data collection and strategy generation teams with enough critical mass so that their voices, perspectives, and expertise are included and add value. We can help organizations develop the systems to monitor patterns so that they can look at the systemic issues rather than individual failings.

Collusion of silence refers to the tendency of people who witness acts of overt or covert racism (jokes, inappropriate comments, etc.) to do nothing. By not speaking out or acting against it, people tacitly approve it and allow racism to flourish. Most people in our organizations are people of good will who want to speak up against things they consider unfair. The challenge is to create safe work environments where people *can* speak up without experiencing negative consequences.

Not So Subtle After All

When we look at the ways in which organizations may operate, the conditions that people of color often experience, and the disparity that can exist in their treatment, the term "subtle racism" begins to sound like an oxymoron. What could ever be subtle about systemic exclusion, prejudice, discrimination, and unfair treatment? It is sometimes hard for people of color to know the source of the problems they encounter and exactly what or who in the system undermines their success. When the source seems invisible—or when those engaging in subtle racism have the system behind them to support their denial when

confronted—it is difficult to address disparities and perceived inequities.

Through becoming conscious of subtle and not-so-subtle racism in organizations, and through being informed by organizational data about how people of all races experience an organization, OD practitioners can identify racism, barriers that are still in place, and the ways in which they are maintained. Most importantly, we can then intervene appropriately to create a more effective, productive, and healthy organization.

The vestiges of racism are deeply rooted in our culture and therefore in our organizations. As we work with organization leaders to create effective, productive, healthy, and higher-performing workplaces that enable everyone to do their best work, we need to bring a mindset of addressing racism to every intervention we undertake. By looking at the group patterns, assumptions, and biases that may be at play, we can assure that we create more humane workplaces for all people.

References

Davis-Howard, V., & Moore, K. R. (2001). How a person of color experiences the workplace: Subtle racism in action. Available from The Kaleel Jamison Consulting Group, Inc.

Katz, J. H. (2003). *White awareness: Handbook for anti-racism training*. (2nd ed.). Norman, OK: University of Oklahoma Press.

Katz, J. H. (1995, November). A white woman writes about affirmative action, *Cultural Diversity at Work*.

CHAPTER 24

Quadrant Behavior Theory

Edging the Center the Potential for Change and Inclusion

Cathy L. Royal

Testimony, personal experience is such fertile ground for the production of libratory feminist theory—When our lived experience of theorizing is fundamentally linked to processes of self-recovery, of collective liberation, no gap exists between theory and practice. Theory emerges from . . . efforts to make sense of everyday life experiences, efforts to critically intervene in my life and the lives of others. Personal because it usually forms the base of our theory making. While we work to resolve those issues that are most pressing we engage in a critical process of theorizing that enables and empowers.

—bell hooks, 1992

FINDING MY VOICE and maintaining a strong identity as a Black woman, a woman of African descent living in the United States of America, has been and continues to be a journey of choices, consequences, and celebrations. My voice is valuable, and I have something to say. I stand by this statement as I share my work, and the circumstances that led to the development of my Quadrant Behavior Theory.

The choices that I have made have largely been shaped by a community of Black women and men living, teaching, and learning in Detroit during the sleepy 1950s and the turbulent 1960s. I am a child of the Jim Crow-Desegregation-Civil Rights era. I learned about "race pride" early in my education, and about collective work and organizing as a teenager in Detroit during the automobile strikes, the civil disobedience riots, and the amazing socially expressive music of the artists of Motown like Marvin Gaye, Stevie Wonder, and Mary Wells. I carry into my work the dedication to the work of inclusion, to continue true integration, and recognition of the importance of community, the value of the knowledge and dignity of the "common person."

As a college student at Wayne State University (WSU) living through the riots of the 1960s and the devastation these events created in cities I was very interested in the findings of the *Kerner Commission Report on Civil Disorders* and the work of Abraham Citron, *The Rightness of Whiteness* (1963). These writings addressed the role and responsibility of White America in creating the circumstances that led to the civil disobedience of the 1960s. The work of Citron discussed the implications of believing that White was right in all manner of things in our culture. I carried values and learning from my community, WSU, and my earliest social justice professor, Morel Clute, a pioneer in Urban Education and experiential learning, into my teaching career and later into my work as a social justice advocate and Organization Development practitioner. The education I received in inquiry, activism, and the importance of personal voice were beginning to fuel my desire to understand the circumstances of power and privilege.

In the 1970s, as I taught in urban schools and prestigious independent schools across the United States, learned the practice of Organization Development consulting, and lived my life, I was aware of an ache, a void, and sadness in my relationships with colleagues. I thought I had friends and colleagues across race and gender that saw and understood what I was seeing in the world. Friends who saw the indignities and inequities that Black women and girls endured on a daily basis; who understood that their *privilege credentials* were not mine. This was not the case. What was missing? What I wanted were authentic friendships and peers who were willing and able to stand firm as we explored the hidden activities and assumptions in every exchange between individuals. I wanted to believe in the power of truth; and practice the skill of "telling the truth." I wanted allies and colleagues on the path toward eliminating repetitive behaviors of power, intimidation, silence, and retribution.

Development of Quadrant Behavior Theory (QBT)

During the 1980s and 1990s while teaching and pursuing degrees at Fielding Institute, opportunities for inquiry into the climate and assumptions that are present in systems and communities about privilege, skin color, gender, and sexual orientation were plentiful. My responsibilities and experiences in these educational environments afforded me an opportunity to refine my Quadrant Behavior Theory (QBT). Lindy Sata, a wonderful colleague, psychiatrist, and a Japanese-American internment camp survivor, said to a group of NTL members during a lab that focused on clinical

incidents in training sessions that "most psychiatrists go into the field seeking to explain a phenomenon that is troubling or affecting them" (1995). He continued by framing this need for answers by telling us that they are seeking to explain the issue for themselves and to help others with healing trauma or hurt. I was Lindy's assistant for this lab and was forever changed by his brilliance and clarity about oppression and trauma. My desire to explain the heartbreak I repeatedly saw and felt personally in the Black community fueled my research. Lindy's lecture energized my desire to explain the incidents I, my friends, and my students were experiencing daily. This spirit of inquiry was present as I used Lewin's ideas to examine the intersection of race, gender, and oppression in systems.

> There is nothing so practical as a good theory.   —Kurt Lewin

Thinking about Lewin's quote and bell hooks' belief about creating theory led me to ask the following questions.

- What would happen if behavior could be clearly/systematically tracked, categorized, and analyzed?
- How would this impact the work of social justice?
- What is the purpose of identifying the behaviors of power and privilege in day to day engagements?
- Recognizing the fact that race and gender are always present in relationships, how would this shift the conversation on partnering and other relationships when race and gender dynamics are present in the relationships?
- What were the small and simple things that create day to day trauma and slights which build up pressure in unbalanced power relationships?

An expanded and revised examination of repetitive behavior, racism, sexism, retribution, and silence would lead me to a new awareness about distinguishable personal behavior, actions, and choice.

Working with Lewin's quote led to a desire to track, name, and study the impact of behavior repeated over consistent encounters with White people by People of Color. This research led to Quadrant Behavior Theory and the QBT sessions. The research was fueled by a passion in me to advance Applied Behavioral Science in the service of social justice and oppression free societies. Using the frame of critical theory, QBT provides an analysis of social dynamics present in relationships and cultural norms where identity characteristics impact an individual's or group's ability to access position or success because of the presence or absence of certain characteristics.

Quadrant Behavior Theory and Organization Development

Quadrant Behavior Theory has embedded in its structure that power, exclusion, and unearned privilege are wrong and impact all members of a society, community, or system. It assumes social change advocates and concerned citizens want skills that create open and equitable systems. QBT uses tracking and naming of repetitive and oppressive behavior to identify ways to change the behavior. The theory believes that power, a key component of oppressive systems, can be shared. QBT changes the landscape of the dialogue on power, privilege, and oppression. QBT identifies language that reshapes the world and behavior of the change agent, the OD practitioner, and QBT practitioner. Some of this new language will be *highlighted* in this article.

For example, as a critical theory on social injustice, QBT seeks to change the behavior of groups and individuals that is oppressive. The QBT formula [Db=f (d,c,a)] captures the core of the theory. *Distinguishing behavior* DB is a function of the **desire** to eliminate systemic oppression and exclusion plus **contact** with "the other"; engaging differences at the edge of one's own identity, combined with **awareness** of the impact of oppressive actions on the lives

of "the other." This awareness comes from confronting power and the misuse of power credentials, as well as hearing the stories and struggles of people who are excluded—"the other."

The new behavior is what distinguishes you and how you use your *power credentials* from other group members. Distinguishing behaviors are behaviors (actions, statements, and body language) that give the impacted or targeted group member information about an individual's commitment to social change, equity, and the dismantling of oppression. It is what creates the authentic friend, ally, or colleague in systems and personal relationships. Distinguishing behavior is a core theme in QBT.

The formula and the theory emerged as a process for shifting behavior described as predictable. "Predictable behavior" refers to repeated actions and activities that can be tracked and named across various experiences and circumstances. This behavior is displayed by those with power and unearned identity privilege over people who do not possess the same power identities.

Predictable behaviors are present across the spectrum of socially constructed identities. Predictable behavior is often unconscious to the privileged group whether the group is White, male, heterosexual, physically able, or ranking in class. An illustration of predictable behavior is the statements that are repeatedly made by men, when discussing gender bias and sexism. Men will say, "I am a man, and I experience that; it is the same for men, what is the big deal?" Or, "my boss is a woman; I work in a woman dominated group and I am the oppressed person and I don't complain." These statements are heard so often they are predictable in discussions about sexism or gender privilege. Predictable behavior severely impacts the ability to trust across what is often referred to as the "big eight."

The big eight are race (skin color), gender, sexual orientation, class, age, ability, nationalism/ethnicity, and religious beliefs and reflect the cultural norms of acceptance and value.

The big eight are the areas which create significant privilege or oppression for members of identity groups. QBT uses these social identity characteristics in the long-term learning group or cohort sessions. The more characteristics of the big eight a person has as personal attributes the more privilege is afforded him or her by the culture or system. The fewer attributes a person has that fit the "norm" the higher the oppression factor in a person's life.

This assignment of privilege and power or oppression and exclusion become group level privilege credentials. This transference of values and beliefs about human characteristic to all members of a group [Whites, men, heterosexuals, and Christians] becomes the point where group membership and privilege intersect with cultural assumptions and stereotypes. This creates the oppression/privilege factor of what is considered the "cultural membrane"[1] that influences every person in the culture. This cultural membrane that pushes and influences us is the environment f our day to day activities and contact between individual and groups. Every member of the culture participates in the activities, and they hold the norms and values that create the structures which are incubators for oppression and inequality.

Structural Inequality

In QBT *structural inequality* is defined as a combination of privilege, exclusion, power, and oppression that is present in all levels, facets, and functions of cultures, societies, systems, and organizations. These factors when exercised create preferred favor, privilege, or benefit for one group (dominant) over another or other groups. Structural inequality is supported through visible and hidden policies, programs, rules, norms, assumptions, and attitudes. It is the behavior that creates, supports, and contributes to the existence and continuation of bias, discrimination, and dominance in all areas of a society, culture, or system. Structural Inequality is the parent or umbrella structure for the presence of racism, sexism, heterosexism (homophobia), and other forms of exclusion and bias in our culture.[2]

These norms and assumptions about the other create the acceptance code. The acceptance code is embedded in every social group indicator of the QB quadrant matrix. The code lives and integrates at four levels of system. Culture and the dominant social contract is the membrane in which the entire behavior scheme is framed. The cultural membrane surrounds all areas of every system and attaches current and historical value. Systems and agencies are the second level where we begin to see the impact of the cultural construct. This level creates, implements, and enforces norms and policy. Group membership is the functional level of the cultural membrane. It is within the group that each access level or barrier is constructed and preserved. Group membership and acceptance of your identity group credentials is the strongest intersection of culture and systems. The group carries out the cultural contract. The organization is the stage for the action. The individual level is the arena of highest impact for behavior change because each of us has the power to influence and create new group behavior based on our individual and personal power. We can create a new acceptance code.

QBT uses a four square matrix to divide the two primary social indicators race and gender along a grid providing a container for the analysis of the significance of race and gender on systems, groups, and individuals (see Figure 24.1). In the matrix, eight social identity dynamics are given a value indicator attaching a positive or negative indicator to the identity. The positive indicators are given to identities that carry cultural and systemic power and privilege and the opposite or power down identity variable is given a negative value.

[1]Cultural membrane is the QBT definition that describes the norms, values, policies and rules; written and unwritten that informs members about acceptable behavior and groups.

[2]Structural Inequality definition based on work created by Cathy Royal and Susan Y. Taira at the Fielding Institute.

FIGURE 24.1   Quadrant Behavior Theory — The Big Eight

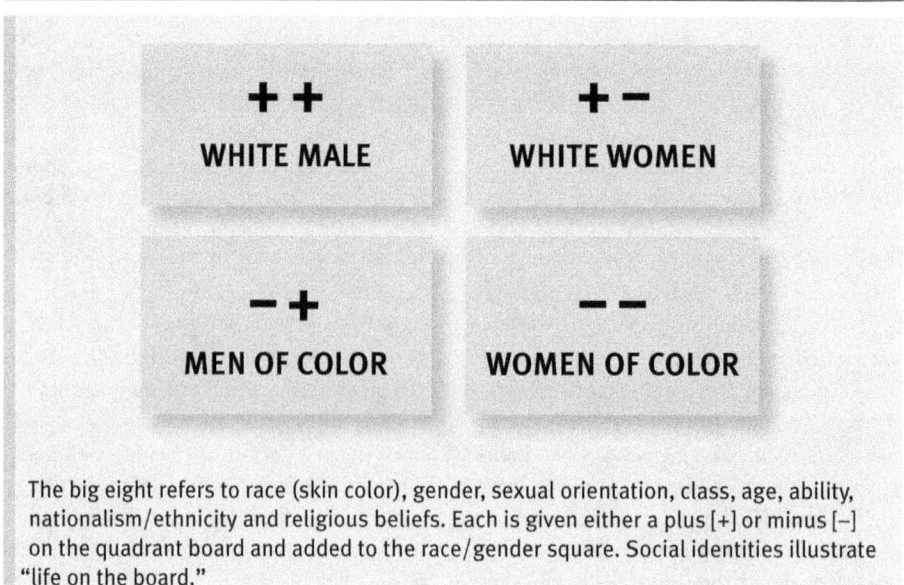

The big eight refers to race (skin color), gender, sexual orientation, class, age, ability, nationalism/ethnicity and religious beliefs. Each is given either a plus [+] or minus [–] on the quadrant board and added to the race/gender square. Social identities illustrate "life on the board."

The value valence is assigned to all members of the four quadrants and each identity variable that represents access or denial of success and opportunity is used to underscore the impact of privilege or oppression on individuals and groups.

The Quadrant Matrix

The quadrant matrix incorporates other social identities into every quadrant. The QBT frame expands and becomes a kaleidoscope of identities. A kaleidoscope of identities in QBT is present when any exchange is viewed through the multiple lenses of QBT frameworks. The presence of eight identity indicators forms an integrated model, a kaleidoscope, for working multiple areas of impact (see Figure 24.2). QBT works this kaleidoscope and measures impact of each indicator. When the frame incorporates sexual identity, class, and ability you have the presence of an intricate set of access or barrier indicators. QBT calls this construct the "abacus of oppression and privilege." The abacus, the ancient Asian counting apparatus, gives a compelling picture of how

many benefit or barrier indices QBT cohort members hold, carry, and internalize. Viewing social dynamics and interactions based on these indicators illustrates the many cases where race carries the strongest impact of impenetrable barriers to success and acceptance. In our society in 2010 race (skin color preference) is the dominant barrier to access, opportunity, goods, and services.

QBT and Experiential Process

In QBT workshops the actions of the group are discussed as well as theory. Hologram imagery is a QBT method of seeing systems and the impact of one's behavior in real time activity. Using the metaphor of the hologram we track, name, examine the actions and language present in the cohort. The tracking of actions across the cohort is defined as the "hologram of the play board."[3] The hologram metaphor is a pow-

[3]Play board refers to gaming language; first made famous by Eric Berne with Games People Play. The board is where all moves of the game take place, like a monopoly or chess board.

FIURE 24.2 The Kaleidoscope of Identity and the Big 8

Every social interaction spins the kaleidoscope for analysis and QBT behavior change.

erful tool of QBT and every member of the cohort is encouraged to become skilled at activating the hologram and examining the activity on the board. Everyone comes to understand that "the board is always in play."

QBT uses contact, dialogue. and theory to increase capacity for behavior change at the individual and group level. In experiencing the QBT dynamics a cohort is created and works together over a defined period of time. In the cohort People of Color and White people self-sort into four quadrants based on race and gender to engage in dialogue and activities that illustrate the impact of personal behavior on systems and individuals. QBT provides current and historical information that illustrates the often hidden and obscure impact of identity group influence on systems, policies, attitudes, and assumptions about social identity differences such as race, gender, sexual orientation, age and other areas of difference. The community always engages race and gender as power dynamics. Each cohort is different and engages the social identity power indicators from multiple views using the information that is in the community, as well as in the culture to deepen awareness about self and other.

The sustained contact of QBT cohorts generates opportunity for engagement, dialogue, conflict, tension, and intimacy. The power of QBT groups is the face to face intimacy that develops through truth telling **awareness],**

presence of self [**desire**] and an exploration [**contact**] of group dynamics over a defined period of time. A QBT cohort is the optimum exposure to QBT with life changing result as a deliverable from the sustained contact with the other. Behavior change requires contact, texture, witness, and support. QBT confronts the cultural membrane, the acceptance code and the assumptions of competency and value that build huge barriers to success and access.

The sessions are designed to stimulate dialogue. Members of the cohort are first asked to design their identity kaleidoscope using graphics and the big eight to bring the power grid into the community. Sitting in four quadrants divided by race and gender, each person lives the intersection of race and gender for cohort dialogue sessions. Holding the intersection of race (skin color preference) and gender (male dominance) as the framework for other attendant expressions of power and privilege the dialogue uses data in the room, from each participant, current information and historical background data to create reference points for the cohorts experiences with each other. Sharing the data and the kaleidoscope is a powerful exercise awareness of social identity impact. Kaleidoscopes are saved and used throughout the cohort experience.

An impactful illustration of QBT and growth and change is an example from our work with same gender loving cohort members. An entire cohort had to face their surprise and discomfort when Nailah (naa-ee-lah), a feminine Black, lesbian woman, quietly commented that she spent most of her life in the company of women, and did not see a need to engage with men except at work, and most of the men she worked with and supervised were same gender loving just as she was. There was a series of diverse reactions most of them inquiries directed at the lesbian of Color.

This could have easily turned into a three tiered power over interrogation. The cohort "froze the board," used the theory to engage the hologram of the quadrants and worked the dynamics real time. The result was a very different conversation for the heterosexual members of the cohort; it was also an opportunity to shift the focus of the dialogue from Nailah to what the quadrant identity group was doing, thinking, and create new behavior. It was also an opportunity to deepen the trust factors between Nailah and her allies. This example illustrates the power of the "board in play" process at the individual level.

Other illustrations demonstrate the significance of QBT dynamics at the group level. Even when individuals profess their understanding of structural inequality, racism, sexism, and other forms of oppression, it is quite possible to be oblivious to how their group memberships impact their understanding of structural inequality. In one circumstance the group energy around a woman of Color who challenged men and male behavior was creating tension in the men's quadrants. Several men wanted her to manage herself. Alicia was certain that she had allies within the men's quadrant, and felt secure in her support with the men of Color. When she continued to challenge men on their sexism and their inappropriate behavior the reaction of the group was quite surprising.

Much of the conversation in the cohort was directed toward Alicia. She should think about what she was saying before she speaks. Men interrupted her when she tried to explain her position; dismissed her data and tracking in the system. Women were silent, and only nodded when she held her ground. When she reminded them that she was feeling the push of the quadrants and watching the focus of the conversation move to the women of Color quadrant only one man backed her story. When the group moved to a simulation on sexism, the men began to instruct the women on sexism and proper dress. Alicia stopped the dialogue; engaged the hologram and began to use the definitions and QBT frame to identify the collusion and privilege in the exercise. What became clear in the dialogue was how silence and predictable group thinking were present in the cohort; even as we claimed knowledge of sexism and power. Women began to identify fear and silence in their behavior; men talked openly about anger and frustration for being challenged on their behavior.

An important action of QBT sessions is the transparent analysis of all members of the cohort, including the facilitators. Everyone receives feedback about actions, inaction, language, silence, and identity membership during the training. This close examination of individual behavior through the eyes of the group is also a time to examine how blame and punishment, even violence can be present in a quadrant identity groups' reaction to challenges to its assumed authority or position. This use of the board in play illustrates the presence of predictable behavior at the group level; provides opportunities for creating distinguishing behavior when group dynamics are pressing on the cohort and quadrant members.

When working in the Diversity Practitioner's Certificate Program where QBT is a theoretical cornerstone both faculty and participants struggle with what comes up in the dialogue and experiences. It is only through sustained contact and a desire to shift the systems at every opportunity do cohort members come to truly see each other and themselves. As cohort members develop a stronger skill at using QBT activities the expectation that they will use this skill to freeze the board becomes a norm of the community. Facing into feedback and real time dialogue about simple statements which hurt or dismiss, confronting the emergence of predictable quadrant behaviors by any member of community, and working the edges in community allow intimacy and strength of voice emerge. The cohort creates change [distinguishing behavior] that can, and should, be transferred to other relationships thereby impacting communities and systems through a network of interventions.

Quadrant Behavior Theory Is a Platform Theory

Platform theories are frameworks and models capable of being integrated into other OD theories to enhance and support their effectiveness in system interventions. QBT creates a formula and prescriptive for discovering the hidden assumptions and actions present in human relationships where exclusion and power permit unearned privilege and opportunity to exist. QBT is a platform theory and it is applicable at any or all levels of a system. In seeing QBT as a platform that other OD theories and social justice actions can build upon allows the impact of unearned privilege and power to be integrated into organizational climate review, executive decisions, and management actions. Integrating QBT language and technology into personal change processes reveals what each individual can consider as they work across race, gender, and other social identity lines. The practitioner can support the system in creating interventions that speak to the presence of historical inequities and current exclusions.

QBT practitioners are able to integrate QBT into OD activities at any level of system. For example in an Appreciative Inquiry model QBT activities become part of the AI summit, reviewing who is in the room when decisions are made. Often in oppressive systems women are absent, the poor are excluded, and people with disabilities rarely are engaged in the process of defining the topic; QBT activities are a core part of the dream, and design phases of AI. It is transferable and scalable; it works in family systems as well as for the global community.

Benefits/Contributions

QBT is part of the core curriculum in NTL's Diversity Leadership Certificate Program (DLCP) and formerly in AU/NTL's Use of Self course. I have shared the framework in several academic and organizational programs over the past 25 years. QBT is a value based social change model which believes that people can and do change and grow (Moore, 1988).

The benefit at the individual level has generated, or strengthened, true, strong, authentic friendships with White women, White men, men of Color, and women of Color. At the systems level the impact has been the integration of QBT learning into other systems and communities. Colleagues in Salvador da Bahia, Brazil collaborate with me on social justice dynamics, eco-racism, north-south nation states relations, and gender bias using QBT theory. QBT practitioners are raising their voices in systems and programs in the United States demonstrating that the learning is transferable, and that distinguishing behavior is possible across communities. Alumni of the program are networks of support for each other as they embark on large systems change interventions across the globe.

So how does working in QBT and creating theory that challenges individual behavior throughout social systems impact me and strengthen my voice? The benefit for me, as a Black woman exists on several levels. I see and live the impact of six (of the eight social identity characteristics) that are power down indicators in my life daily and constantly. QBT is my balm in Gilead; it keeps the fringes from unraveling on a daily basis. Seeing systems, global impact, and the integration of quadrant identity power into policy, behavior, and regular occurrences is an inoculation against many of the day to day indignities that I often experience as I manage personal relationships and systems.

It is comforting to know that QBT has touched the lives of hundreds of people who have benefited from this work. The importance of creating a community of practitioner scholars who understand QBT dynamics and have experienced the QBT workshops will lead to significant changes in the way we approach social justice and inclusion. People will raise their voice in everyday situations where power over is present and targeted groups are invisible in systems and communities.

As I use the theory, its language and the formula to analyze change I am more easily able to identify where and with whom to place my trust and confidence. I can make choices about raising my voice and my safety based on what behaviors I see present in the relationship. I also use my voice to identify myself as someone who is trustworthy as an ally. It has changed my life in powerful ways.

We who believe in freedom must not rest.
—Ella's song, from Sweet Honey
in the Rock

References

Citron, A. (1963). *The rightness of whiteness.* Detroit, MI: Wayne State University Press.

hooks, b. (July-Aug, 1992). Out of the academy and into the streets. *MS Magazine,* 3(1), 80.

Kerner, O. (1968). *Report of the National Advisory Commission on Civil Disorders.* Washington, DC: U.S. Government Printing Office.

Moore, R. (1988). Anti-Racism workshops. Andover, MA: Phillips Academy.

Royal, C., & Taira, S. (1994). *Diversity facilitation skills, Training manual and handbook, module 3.* Arlington, VA: NTL Institute.

Sata, L. (1995). Lecture given during the Professional Work Conference, NTL member session, San Francisco, CA.

CHAPTER 25

Ethical Leadership and OD Practice

Wendell Nekoranec

WITH THE GLOBAL economy in turmoil and questionable leadership practices pervasive, people wonder when will the economy turn around and real leadership surface in the headlines. The more I hear about companies and associated financial systems in financial trouble (Cebon, 2009), the more I ask myself what happened to cause so many good companies to become financially stressed. Having studied ethical leadership in CEOs (Nekoranec, 2007), I returned to the one-hour interviews and findings about how CEOs believed they acted ethically in tough situations. I reflected on hints about the ways successful companies during the recession weathered the economy and leadership struggles. I believe ethical leadership and success are connected.

I further pondered if ethical leadership may have been present in current financially stressed companies but for some reason failed to influence necessary business practices. Or, I questioned if ethical leadership was present at all. Trying to be a good OD practitioner, I asked these and other questions to know how to guide leaders (Nekoranec & Kusy, 2005) during tough economic times as a practitioner and coach. Leaders who practice ethical leadership can create solid financial companies that can weather tough financial times. Using these thoughts, I pondered avenues that OD practitioners can use to engage leaders in ethi-

cal conversations in order to build and maintain ethical companies.

In this article, I will highlight recent research on ethical leadership in CEOs (Nekoranec, 2007) since I believe ethical CEOs make strong statements about how leaders and staff can act to do the right thing in a situation. Next, I will share two stories from two CEOs about how they believed they acted ethically in tough situations followed with an analysis of their actions to the study's themes. As a preview, the first story looks at how a CEO dealt with individuals in a time sensitive situation. The second story examines how a CEO managed the complexity of a potential home office relocation, and the steps he took to maintain support and influence in the organization. Then, I will provide insights about working with ethical leadership in situations and within organizations. Lastly, I will offer a simple conclusion.

Acting Ethically: The Experience of Top Leaders

The content for this article comes from a research study of ethical leadership in CEOs and top leaders (Nekoranec, 2007). I chose this topic since I have worked with many top leaders in different organizations and industries, and functioned as a board president where other board members, suppliers, customers, and staff questioned and challenged my decisions. With this interest about ethical leadership, I interviewed eight top leaders (Table 25.1) and uncovered three themes and 20 subthemes (Table 25.2) that can be vital for the ways OD practitioners work with top leaders and all leaders and managers.

Using the interview transcripts from the eight top leaders and phenomenology as the research methodology, three themes and 20 subthemes surfaced that described the experience of CEOs and top leaders. I will refer to the themes and subthemes in the analysis of the two stories and the advice offered to OD practitioners. In addition, four values by which these leaders lived influenced how they acted ethically: integrity, honesty, responsibility, and trust. These values were found throughout their experience of acting ethically to do the right thing for others, the situation, and themselves, and in this order. With this brief background, I will move to the first story about Theresa and saving a newborn.

Saving a Newborn

Theresa, CEO and chairwoman of the board of a multi-billion dollar Catholic healthcare system, found herself faced with a tough ethical situation. Two doctors came to Theresa about a newborn needing a live-saving blood transfusion. The doctors wanted her help be-

cause the parents were Jehovah's Witnesses and refused to allow the blood transfusion. As an ethical focus, Theresa wanted to keep the needs of the newborn in mind since the baby could not speak for himself. What weighed heavily on Theresa was a previous experience where a 14-year old Jehovah's Witness girl required a blood transfusion. The girl agreed with her parents and their religious beliefs, and died. For Theresa, the struggle in this situation was a baby that had no one to serve directly as his objective advocate. Ultimately, Theresa permitted a blood transfusion.

To come to this conclusion, Theresa had to work through her own thoughts and feelings, gather information from the doctors and the parents, and seek insights from an outsider, all in three hours during the middle of the night. After her conversation with the doctors, she took a few minutes to quietly sit, reflect, and pray so she would be open to what people had to say. Then she talked to the parents to understand their issues, as she said, "in a way where I was really respectful of the parents and their beliefs and at the same time, share my concern about the situation." For Therese, the decision could have been a matter of fact—the newborn receives a blood transfusion. But because of her belief system and being the CEO of a Catholic healthcare system, a routine decision had to incorporate the human consideration.

Theresa next met with the doctors and the parents so both groups shared their con-

TABLE 25.1 Leadership Background of Participant Group

Name*	Title	Years As Top Leader	Age	Organization Size	Education
Theresa	CEO/Chairwoman of the Board	15	64	Multi-billion	MA
Gabrielle	Executive Director	21	52	Multi-million	JD
Dick	CEO/Chairman of the Board	17	74	Multi-billion	MBA
Paul	Catholic Bishop	13	66	Multi-million	PhD
Walter	Elected Legislator	36	69	—	JD
Tom	Executive Director	20	66	Multi-million	STD/JCD
Sally	CEO	5	39	Multi-billion	JD
Laura	CEO/Executive Director	14	45	Multi-million	MA

*Pseudonyms are used to ensure participant anonymity

TABLE 25.2   Themes for Acting Ethically

Theme I *Personifies Espoused Values*	Theme II *Builds Relationships for Harmony and Purpose*	Theme III *Works for Mutually Beneficial Solutions*
• Sees Self as Ethical Vanguard	• Supports People to Bring out Their Best	• Gets the Facts Honestly and Openly
• Acts with Integrity to Do the Right Thing	• Respects Others and Acts Out Respect	• Seeks Counsel to Clarify Thought Process
• Incorporates Reflective Intuition	• Shares Information so All Hear, Understand, and Act	• Knows the Law and Legal Operating Parameters
• Speaks Honestly and Frankly about Issues	• Instills a Sense of Trust to Guide and Lead	• Thinks through the Pieces of the Situation
• Learns from the Past to Move Forward in Positive Ways	• Maintains a Visible Profile to Remain Approachable	• Listens to Hear Others' Thinking and Feelings
• Leads Others with a "We" Inclusiveness		• Negotiates the Information-Gathering Process
• Lives Values for Others to Emulate		• Challenges Self and Others to Find a More Effective Solution
• Shows and Explains Emotions		

cerns with one another. She asked the doctors to leave so she could spend time with the parents, giving them what she considered vital time to talk to her about their grief. In this conversation, as she said, "I felt the need to just articulate what the struggle was for me" and her sense of what was right for the baby. She shared her struggles: the need for the blood transfusion, religious beliefs and how they affected her data gathering process, respect for the parents, and the gravity of the situation. She gave the parents time to talk, and she listened to them and their issues. Her ultimate personal issue was to be nonjudgmental. She finished with asking the parents what they would do if she allowed the blood transfusion, and they said they would still love the baby but knew their community would look down on the child.

Theresa shared her ethical concern: "I think the big struggle for me ethically in this was, how are you really respectful and how do you honor the beliefs and practices of other religions because that is really important to me. But at the same time, how do you act with integrity in terms of what you think should be

done, and that was the struggle I was having." After she discussed the parent's perspective with the doctor, who kept pushing their agenda, she took quiet time to talk to a confidant outside of the organization who helped her objectively work through a rational thought process. Her biggest process concern was did she really listen (the eight leaders expressed this critical leadership component). After 15 minutes alone, she shared with the parents her decision to grant the blood transfusion, and followed up with the doctors.

Analysis of Themes and Subthemes for Ethical Leadership

Theresa practiced the first and third themes and many subthemes as she handled this tough situation, which I'll highlight below. Because of the time limitation, her ability to build relationships was minimal, though she clearly showed *respects others and acts out respect.*

Theresa demonstrated the theme *personified espoused values* by living the four values identified in the study of ethical leadership: integrity, honesty, responsibility, and trust. She also showed five subthemes. First, she *acts with integrity to do the right thing* by incorporating the beliefs, thoughts, and feelings of the parents and the doctors. Next, she *incorporates reflective intuition* by taking time to think about the situation privately and by listening. Third, she *speaks honestly and frankly about issues* in that she states to the parents her position about the need for the blood transfusion and the baby having an advocate. Fourth, she *learns from the past to move forward in positive ways* since she reflected on a previous situation where the 14 year-old Jehovah Witness girl needed a blood transfusion. Lastly, she *shows and explains emotions* especially to the parent, but also to the doctor and her outside confidant.

Theresa displayed the theme *works for mutually beneficial solutions* by working intimately with the parents and doctors and gathering their thoughts and feelings as well as sharing her thoughts and feelings. She also showed three subthemes. First, she *gets the facts honestly and openly* by talking directly and honestly to the parents and the doctors. She believed she needed to know the long-term reality of the child living in the parent's religious community. Next, she *seeks counsel to clarify thought process* by using an outside confidant to discuss her situation and to have the person validate her thought process, though not make her decision. Lastly, she *listens to hear others' thinking and feelings* since both play a vital role in how a leader needs to make a decision, and a decision that all involved can respect.

Theresa was aware of the complexity of the situation, and knew there was not a definitive process to follow. She kept investigating the situation including the feelings of the parents. Her goal was to make a decision that all could live with in the short term and throughout the baby's life.

To Relocate or Not

Dick, CEO and chairman of the board of a multi-billion dollar food service company, faced a situation about moving the company's home office from one state to another for tax benefits that would enhance the bottom line. The company owned a number of manufacturing facilities that would not be affected directly because of the home office move. As a major employer in a large East Coast community, Dick was looking for tax benefits since he wanted to enhance stockholder's investment. In addition, he recognized the value of the home office staff, and worked out a plan to move the home office operation to a new state if that was the final decision.

Dick wanted to work out a deal with local and state officials for an agreement on tax breaks that would keep the home office in its present location. At the same time, other states began to offer Dick substantial tax benefits to entice him to move. Dick didn't want to move due to the magnitude of change, but he had to determine the best thing for the company, which included employees, all operations, stockholders, suppliers, and customers. He kept looking for a better solution in the current location. State and local officials were willing to talk but offered no enticements.

With his commitment to communicating to staff, Dick conducted a bi-weekly update about the process and the progress. He wanted to communicate fully with some restraint, not showing all his options. The restraint rested on communicating to staff and dispelling fear while negotiating with local and state officials. He did not want to move because of the burden on the staff and the loss to the community, and he would lose valuable staff. At the same time, he pondered ways to generate the greatest benefits for all involved. Progress with local and state officials remained slow, so he continued to explore other options.

As the decision grew closer, he called an all-company meeting for everyone in the home office, as he said, "So everyone knew what I was thinking and planning on doing." State and local officials were quick to hear about the meeting, and reporters jumped at the opportunity to report the decision. Dick called the staff meeting since he was close to a decision, and was waiting for final board approval. The company had struck up a deal with another state, so the headquarters would be moving. He wanted employees to hear the news first. He relayed his eminent decision, and said, "I want them to hear it from me before they heard it on the news or read it in the newspapers." He shared the information, and ended the meeting. As one would suspect, after this meeting state and local officials worked out a tax break plan, and the company's home office remained in its current location.

Analysis of Themes and Subthemes for Ethical Leadership

Dick lived the three themes and subthemes in handling this tough situation, which I will highlight below. The analysis of Dick acting ethically takes place in a large organizational context, so the analysis will provide higher-level comments without connections to individuals.

Dick *personifies espoused values* by living trust so his staff knew he would tell them what he could so they knew what was going on. Trust is a value experienced by others, and not prescribed by a leader. Trust surfaces because a leader is recognized for living integrity, honesty, and responsibility. Next, Dick *acts with integrity to do the right thing* by how he kept focused on a few key actions: being concerned about his staff and the financial benefits for stakeholders. In his interactions with everyone, he *speaks honestly and frankly about issues* so everyone knew his thinking and proposed actions—moving the company if he didn't receive tax benefits from state and local officials.

Dick *builds relationships for harmony and purpose* through his honesty and sharing information. To keep staff apprised of the ongoing developments, he *shares information so all hear, understand, and act* with respect to the final outcome—meeting investor's goals. In addition, he *maintains a visible profile to remain approachable*. Even though Dick could have passed as an NFL linebacker in his younger days, his friendly demeanor and desire to keep

people informed reinforced his commitment to his staff to do the right thing for them and the company.

Lastly, Dick *works for mutually beneficial solutions* for the benefit of his staff, other stakeholders, and the company. Specifically, Dick *knows the law and the legal operating parameters*, in that he suggested CEOs know the law to achieve organizational results, but, in addition, leaders know that doing the ethically right things supersedes the legal obligations by which any leader lives. For him, ethics and doing the right thing dictated how he would act with staff, and state and local officials. Finally, he *negotiates the information-gathering process* since he wanted his staff to know the progress of the potential move while keeping state and local officials calculating options and proposals and ultimately keeping the press immediately out of the picture. Dick knew that information from many sources was vital for him to make decisions and for the project to achieve a successful outcome. In addition, gathering and sharing information would help his staff remain committed and focused to a few vital goals during the imminent transition, but communicating frequently would paint a clearer picture for his staff. Dick knew there was no simple answer for the complexity of the situation. By keeping focused on his staff that was his greatest allies, he could manage the steps in the process and find an acceptable outcome.

Working with Ethical Leadership in an Organization

Acting ethically for Theresa and Dick was a critical part of their leadership styles. Many leaders and managers are aware of the ethical component and work to do the right thing and to model ethical leadership for their staff. Many leaders do not go around praising the virtues of ethical leadership; they simply and gently incorporate ethical leadership into how they interact with others, demonstrating the themes and subthemes of the study. Other ethical leaders profess their values, and they challenge themselves to meet their own ethical standards. These are ethical leaders.

Not all leaders practice their values and keep an ethical perspective. Many leaders may not want to be reminded of ethical leadership, hence, offer challenges to OD practitioners who want to help them generate ethical, and legally acceptable, outcomes. Using the findings of the study and clear ethical leadership language may be problematic for everyone involved with a questionable leader. As an OD practitioner seeking to find ethical solutions in complex situations, suggesting "Will this course of action generate the right outcome?" can elicit a positive nod from a leader along with supportive ethical behaviors. Many leaders know how to do the right thing. However, being reminded of it directly can erode the value of an OD practitioner, so finding acceptable language for the leader, the situation, and the organization becomes a requirement. Focusing actions and language on generating a positive environment can help surface an awareness of ethical leadership in the leader and for the benefit of the situation.

Two types of leadership styles can present a challenge for an OD practitioner when trying to generate ethical outcomes for situations: bad leadership (Kellerman, 2004), where leaders can be either ineffective or unethical, and ethically neutral leadership (Trevino, Brown, & Hartman, 2003). With ineffective leadership, the leader demonstrates the following types of bad leadership: incompetent, rigid, and intemperate. With unethical leadership, the leader demonstrates the following types of bad leadership: callous, corrupt, and insular. With ethically neutral leadership, the leader does not consider the ethical perspective.

Ineffective and unethical leaders exist. When a bad leader operates in an organization, people work with him or her, knowing that discussing ethics can elicit scorn and a lecture about the glories of the leader. Sadly but realistically, in these cases I would advise skirting comments about ethical leadership, provide the work and solution requested *precisely as dictated by the leader*, and move on to another

consulting engagement. Bad leaders want to hear about themselves, and a neutral approach that focuses on the work is advised. To bring about an acceptable outcome for the staff and organization, an OD practitioner works with a bad leader for the sake of others.

Ethically neutral leaders (Trevino et al., 2003) present a different challenge. Though this leadership type may support ethical leadership, the language and behaviors demonstrated may represent someone not attuned to ethical leadership. Ethically neutral leaders and managers simply forget the ethical issues and the need for ethical outcomes, and move forward as if their actions may generate acceptable (ethical) outcomes. These leaders need subtle coaching so they remember to do the right thing without directly surfacing ethical leadership topics.

Ethically neutral leaders may not want to hear about ethical leadership, and they may feel challenged by talk about principles. Focusing descriptive language on doing the right thing and generating good outcomes on the part of an OD practitioner can ultimately produce ethically acceptable outcomes. With either leadership type, direct use of ethical leadership language, as found in the themes and subthemes of the study, can be seen as a challenge and possibly viewed as a direct attack on the leader.

In the current global recession, the use of innovation without ethical considerations has led to global financial struggles (Cebon, 2009). Leaders responsible for these decisions were motivated by the call for innovation, something OD practitioners would strongly support. Yet, no one seemed to have called attention to the short-term wins (good) that can affect long-term outcomes (bad). Identifying ethical concerns along the way could have felt like crying wolf when no threat existed in any substantive form.

Here, OD practitioners can find themselves in a tough situation. If one remains involved in an initiative long term, keeping accounts of stories and a personal journal concerning what is seen, heard, and felt for future analysis can help identify patterns and raise concerns. Many times the past will come forward in the future, and reflection about clearly defined situations can identify patterns early so potential unethical or ethically neutral outcomes can be diverted. Senior leaders should appreciate this practice.

Because of the complexities involved in generating financial outcomes, citing any individual about ethical issues could have challenged people to pay attention to ethical issues (Henry, 2009). Vague hints of something strange or unsettling can present a challenge for raising alarms. To say something or not is in itself an ethical challenge. For OD practitioners keeping track of what is seen, heard, and felt can provide analysis to assist leaders in redirecting an initiative to do the right thing and to work in an ethical context (Garrett, 2008).

Preaching to the masses about ethical business practices in the recent global economic boom probably would have fallen on deaf ears. The power of innovation was too great to ignore, considering the personal financial gains. The larger ethical issues were ignored and most likely not even considered because of the potential for substantial gains. Supporting the study on ethical leadership, Cebon (2009) cites the need for greater governmental oversight, which is true but incomplete. Leaders who *personify espoused values* support his comment about the need for leaders and regulatory organizations to demonstrate integrity—the key value cited in the study. Could the current global financial situation be mitigated? Yes, and with the help of ethical leadership and leaders living the themes of the study from the value of integrity.

Conclusion

Acting ethically for an OD practitioner is imperative for the client's success and for the organizations we serve. Steering leaders to ethical actions can represent a challenge when working with bad leaders and with the more common ethically neutral leaders. Quietly living your ethical values and actions that speak volumes about doing the right thing can subtly and positively influence a leader, so a leader *gets the message* to focus on acting ethically. Yet, asking questions about ethical responsibility may be what's required when the emerging actions and potential outcomes have a sense of being either bad or ethically neutral.

With the stories we hear about unethical behaviors by CEOs and senior leaders and ethically neutral leaders, OD practitioners can call into question the potential results that challenge ethical business practices and leadership. As much as one may not want to stand in harm's way for sounding the ethical action drum, organization development theory and practice challenges its professionals to call into question actions and potential outcomes that push the ethical envelope. By standing your ground, you *can* sleep better at night.

References

Cebon, P. (2009). Innovating our way to a meltdown. *Sloan Management Review,* 50(2), 13–15.

Garrett, M. (2008). What will you do when your desires to please and ethics collide? *Leadership and Management in Engineering,* 8(1), 42–44.

Henry, K. (2009). Leading with your SOUL. *Strategic Finance,* 90(8), 44–51.

Kellerman, B. (2004). *Bad leadership: What it is, how it happens, why it matters.* Boston, MA: Harvard Business School Press.

Nekoranec, W. (2007). *Acting ethically: The experience of top leaders.* Unpublished doctoral dissertation, University of St. Thomas, Minneapolis.

Nekorance, W., & Kusy, M. (2005). Engaging executives in strategic conversations: More than a random event. *OD Practitioner,* 37(4), 20–25.

Trevino, L. K., Brown, M., & Hartman, L. P. (2003). A qualitative investigation of perceived executive ethical leadership: Perceptions from inside and outside the executive suite. *Human Relations, 56*(1), 5–37.

CHAPTER 26

Diagnosing Covert Processes in Groups and Organizations

Robert J. Marshak and Judith H. Katz

BY DEFINITION, something covert is un-dercover. It is concealed, disguised; in short, hidden from view. How then does one go about detecting the presence of a covert dynamic at work in a group or organization?

When we first began thinking about covert processes, this was a question we frequently asked ourselves. One approach we discovered is paying attention to the symbolic messages being sent by the system. We found that a dynamic which was basically covert is frequently presented more openly on a symbolic level by one or more people in the system. Earlier we presented our insights about how to use such symbolic data for group and organizational consulting (Marshak & Katz, 1992). In this article we wish to present a general way of thinking about covert processes that helps generate hypotheses about the presence of covert dynamics.

Types of Covert Processes

In our work, we began with the assumption that multiple covert processes are always present. This is true regardless of whether we are working with individuals, groups, or organizations. Everything cannot always be out in the open—i.e., "on-the-table"—all of the time. We also did not make any initial presumption about whether what is covert is hidden for good, bad, or unknown reasons.

In dealing with individuals, groups, and organizations, we believe something is likely to become covert when: untested assumptions, beliefs, or constructs are limiting either reasoning or choice; the basis of the covert dynamic is in the unconscious or shadow of the individual, group, or organization; or, behaviors, thoughts or feelings are defined by the prevailing rules, norms, and/or culture as inappropriate, unacceptable, or out of place.

The three dominant types of covert processes that develop from these circumstances are:

1. **Blind Spots and Blocks,** where some or all members of the group or organization are prevented from considering possibilities due to untested or out-of-awareness beliefs, assumptions, values and paradigms. In such cases individual, group and organizational behavior will be "controlled" by these unseen and untested constraints. Participants will not "see" the limiting impacts of these invisible boundaries. Meanwhile, observers, not similarly constrained, often will be confused as to why relatively obvious possibilities are being systematically ignored. For example, the members of a system may not be able to get their thinking "out-of-the-box." Meanwhile, to an observer, it may appear as if everyone is trying to push open

a door that is locked, while simultaneously ignoring a nearby open window.

2. **Unconscious or Shadow Dynamics,** where the behavior of the system may be influenced by collectively repressed or projected emotions, desires, needs, and so forth. Group and organizational projections, stereotypes, and compensatory behaviors are common manifestations of this type of hidden dynamics. Groups that claim everything is fine while they drive themselves relentlessly, with no acknowledgment of the emotional, psychological, or physical toll, are likely to be under the influence of shadow forces. For example, work teams operating in dangerous situations may take unnecessary risks as a show of bravado to compensate for their very real, but repressed fears. Additionally, unimagined creativity, higher values, and spiritual dimensions that could be significant sources of energy and renewal may lie untapped in the system's higher unconscious (Ferrucci, 1982).

3. **Conscious Disguises and Concealments,** where some or all members of the group or organization keep things closed to discussion because certain behaviors, thoughts, and/or feelings are defined by the prevailing beliefs, rules, norms, or culture as inappropriate, unacceptable or out of place. It's worth noting that early meanings of the word covert included *sheltered* and *protected.* There are two subcategories of Conscious Disguises and Concealments:

   a. *Protective Disguises and Concealments,* which occur when some or all members are fearful of raising or addressing certain issues. This fear may be based on real or imagined possibilities of harm. Topics and issues that the culture of the group labels as unwanted, out-of-bounds, inappropriate, and/or "punishable," are likely candidates for protective disguises and concealments. When all members have an interest in keeping something hidden for fear of the consequences, you are likely to find both explicit (overt) and implicit (covert) collusion. This type of covert process is especially common

in settings where there is little trust and/ or a high degree of suspicion.

   b. *Strategic Disguises and Concealments,* which seek to gain some advantage or realize a particular aim. These occur when some members believe that they can achieve their purposes best in situations where not everyone knows what is going on. This often occurs when there are competitive dynamics related to power, rewards, resources, and so forth. Sometimes, strategic disguises and concealments are approved. This occurs when individuals act in secret to advance commonly agreed upon goals of the group and/or organization. These include actions that require "quiet diplomacy." or must be done with little or no visibility to insure success. When acting in this capacity, individuals become the covert *agents* of the group and/or organization. Often, individuals acting in this capacity are "authorized" and protected by those "in the know." They also can occur when individuals— on their own—act in secret to advance their own goals, needs, and desires. Individuals and/or groups acting in this capacity are considered to be "out for themselves."

All three of these covert processes have four things in common: they are hidden from public discourse; they limit choices, block creativity, and trap participants in repetitive and self-defeating behavior. They are not easily identified unless one knows where to look. And they are ubiquitous.

Overt Versus Covert Processes in Groups and Organizations

In our experience, *overt processes* are task related, rational, literally communicated, and defined by the prevailing group and organizational norms as legitimate and appropriate in the context. If asked, most people would be aware of and could describe "what is going on." On the other hand, *covert processes* are relationship related, emotionally or spiritually based, symbolically communicated (often out of awareness or unconscious), and defined by the culture as inappropriate to the context (Marshak & Katz, 1990; 1991a; 1991b; 1994). If asked, some system members might have a sense that "something is going on that I can't quite put their finger on," while others might not be aware of anything at all.

Some typical covert issues in groups and organizations include:

- Feelings, emotions, and needs regarding power, inclusion, authority, intimacy, attraction, trust, hatred, anger, etc.
- Fears and taboos.
- Conflicts and disagreements.
- Aspirations, dreams, hopes, visions, and/or spiritual values that are considered "pie in the sky."
- Limiting beliefs, norms, and cultural assumptions.
- "Political" deals, arrangements and understandings that are intended to advantage some over others.
- Professional and personal biases and prejudices.
- Unaddressed or unacknowledged differences based on culture, religion, gender, race, sexual orientation, physical ability, style, or values.
- Formal and informal frameworks that guide thought and action, such as paradigms, theories, and "lessons learned."

Given the dynamics and complexity of these processes, the ability to recognize, diagnose, and/or develop good hunches becomes a critical competency for leaders, managers, and consultants.

In the next section, we introduce and discuss some of the cues and clues that can be used for "reading between the lines."

Diagnosing Covert Processes

Expressed succinctly, clues to the existence of a covert process are a function of noting relative

Emphases and/or *Omissions* to a *Pattern* framed by a particular organizational *Context*, expressed as a "formula" this would be:

Covert Process Clue(s) = Function of [(Context) • (Patterns) • (Emphases/Omissions)]

Let's look at each aspect of the formula separately and then explore how each element works together to generate hypotheses about possible covert dynamics.

Context

Paying attention to a particular context involves interpreting data, events, and interactions in terms of the milieu that "frames the situation." For example, the meaning of a particular set of behaviors could be quite different depending upon the time, place, setting, people, roles, relationships, history or assumed future involved. The context gives meaning to the behavior, but - and this is the important fact to understand - it is the context as seen *from the frame of reference of the participants* that matters. The diagnostician must be able to enter into the frame of reference of the participants to successfully "look for" covert processes. For example, knowing that the group you are observing is meeting at a time when the organization is facing the need for significant downsizing is an important contextual factor for understanding what is or is not happening in the group. Needless to say, knowing that the group is also the executive committee and/or it's their first meeting, and/or it's an emergency meeting, are all important contextual variables that need to be factored into the diagnostic equation.

Patterns

Paying attention to patterns involves noting recurring sequences, relationships, configurations and/or other regularities related to behaviors or issues. For example, a pattern observed in many groups avoiding conflict is that, whenever a discussion begins to get heated and angry, someone cracks a joke. Patterns related to possible covert processes may be observed at the individual, interpersonal, group, and/or organizational levels of behavior:

- Recurring patterns of behavior by an individual, regardless of the context, may connote *individual processes*. For example, Pat behaves in an aggressive fashion toward anyone in a position of authority, anytime, anywhere.
- Recurring patterns of behavior between the same individuals that do not occur in interactions among or with others, may connote *interpersonal processes*. For example, Lee and Leslie constantly question what each other are doing, but this behavior is specific to them. It does not occur between Lee or Leslie and anyone else.
- Recurring patterns of behavior exhibited by different individuals in the same group usually indicate *group processes*. For example, every time someone in the group attempts to initiate an idea someone else questions whether or not it will work. The persons doing the challenging may change each time; it's the pattern that remains constant.
- Recurring patterns of behavior exhibited by different individuals, in different groups, at different levels, throughout an organization, often suggest *organizational processes*. For example, regardless of the setting, the people present, or the particular task, everyone talks and behaves in a way to indicate that "top leadership" is supposed to have all the answers (e.g., people defer or refer problems "upstairs").

Paying attention to patterns like these also means being cognizant of relevant theories and models that suggest or describe how things should occur. For example, one theory concerning the pattern of team development identifies four stages: forming, storming, forming and then, performing. If this pattern is not observed it would imply, theoretically at least, that something was going on that was altering the "normal" process of team development. The same would be true of theories about organizations and organizational behavior. They all imply a rough template or pattern of what should be "normal" in a particular context. When this pattern does not unfold, a hidden dynamic may be at work.

Emphases and Omissions

Finally, paying attention to emphases and omissions involves looking for "underlines" and "holes" in a pattern. When individuals, the group, and/or the organization, place special emphasis on one thing, it may mean that something else is being consciously or unconsciously hidden and/or compensated for. For example, members of a work group might stress their competencies and past successes because they (secretly) fear their ability to handle a new problem. Thus their self doubts and fear of failure are hidden or covered-up by extra special proclamations of their skills and abilities. Likewise, emphatic denials— "me thinks thou doth protest too much"— may be another form of underline worth noting. Things can also stand out by their omission (i.e., something that is expected or would be "normal" in a particular context is absent). Such omissions may point toward a blind spot, conceptual limitation, cultural filter, concealment, disguise and/or some repressed emotion or concern. For example, not discussing or addressing group leadership when a group is "floundering," might imply unspoken fears about raising needs for power and control, or not trusting the group's leadership, or cultural prohibitions about directly challenging leaders. Alternatively, not considering a possible solution that "normally" would be raised—"Let's train them to do it better"—might imply, a hidden assumption ("You can't teach an old dog a new trick"); politics ("Don't give the initiative to Human Resources"); or, repressed self doubts ("Could I learn how to do it better?").

Diagnosis in Action

In using the Covert Processes Diagnostic Formula—Clue(s) = F [(C) • (P) • (E/O)]—the potential existence of a covert process is revealed by observing an emphasis and/or omission in an expected pattern, given the particular context. This method of diagnosis, of course, is an art form and benefits from a broad knowledge of a wide range of contexts and patterns. Thus, we have found that the wider our theory base is as to individual, group, and organizational behavior, the greater our ability to recognize holes and underlines. For example, most readers might readily recognize the holes and/or underlines in the following two examples because they are familiar with either or both the pattern and context:

- 1, 2, - , 4, 5, - , 7, 8, - , *10*
- *Forming, Norming, Norming!, Performing.*

However, most readers would likely miss or misinterpret the hidden element denoted by the question mark (?) in the following example, unless they knew the context and/or pattern

- *X, +, 10* =?

One answer, of course, is that it is an algebraic equation of some sort adding an unknown, X, to the number 10 resulting in the quantity (X + 10). This looks familiar, except for the commas after the X and the plus sign. If, however, the reader knew the context (say a cross cultural training course), and also Roman (X), Chinese (+), and Arabic (10) *numerals,* the pattern, and therefore the missing element, would be clear, that is, each is a different way of writing the quantity ten, (X, +, 10 = Ten). Thus, knowledge of context and recognition of pattern(s) is a prerequisite to both noting and interpreting the potential meaning of an emphasis or omission.

Another type of example comes from a group one of us was working with where, as part of a warm-up exercise, they listed all of the "subgroups" that made up the total group. A list of over twenty items was produced, including: "men and women," "locals and out-

of-towners," "smokers and nonsmokers," "late-niters and early-risers," and so on. Not included on this fairly comprehensive list was any mention of the very visible racial/ethnic differences represented by different members of the group. When this omission was pointed out, one white woman very quickly and emphatically asserted, "That's because we don't see them as different from us!" This was met with an even more emphatic response from an African-American woman who countered, "How can you negate me by not seeing who I really am!" Given the context of very visible demographic differences and the exhaustive pattern of the list, the omission of noting any racial/ethnic subgroups was an early and clear clue that there might be some blind spots or blocks, unconscious or shadow dynamics, and/or conscious disguises or concealments related to racial issues in the group. Sometimes what's missing says a whole lot more than what's present.

A Practice Case Example

The following case is intended to be an opportunity for diagnostic thinking about covert processes and to help further illustrate our discussion. First, a situation will be presented and then more information regarding aspects of the context, patterns, and emphases/omissions will be added to demonstrate how they help develop hypothesis and hunches. The reader is invited to review the summary of covert processes listed in Table 26.1 and think along with us as the information unfolds.

TABLE 26.1   Types of Covert Processes

1. Blind Spots and Blocks
2. Individual, Group, and/or Organizational Unconscious or Shadow
3. Conscious Disguises and Concealments to:
   a. Protect
   b. Achieve Group/Organizational Aims
   c. Achieve Individual Aims

The Situation

Six members of a team are meeting to discuss an organizational problem. One member of the team is missing. People seem to be trying to rationally address a problem, but quickly get sidetracked. There are frequent references to past successes by the team and little sense of urgency in the meeting. After about an hour the meeting ends with no decisions, other than to make sure the missing member is informed about what was discussed.

Before reading further, what are some of your initial or intuitive hunches about what may be going on in this situation? What do you think may be some specific covert processes at work in this situation: blind spots or blocks, unconscious or shadow dynamics, conscious disguises or concealments? What additional information do you believe is important for you to know?

Some Contextual Factors

This is the seven person Executive Committee of Omega Corporation. The corporation is facing a difficult financial situation and the committee has convened for the third time to address the issue. A change in the corporation's "no-lay-off" policy is needed and morale is at an all-time low. The question is no longer whether or not to downsize, but how deeply to cut. The history and culture of Omega emphasize paternalistic, top-down leadership with decisions carried out quickly and efficiently. Executives are selected for their rational problem-solving skills and ability to get things done. The missing member of the team is the CEO.

What are your hunches about what may be going on in this situation? Now that you have some contextual data what are your thoughts about some of the specific covert processes that may be at

work in this situation? What patterns do you believe would be helpful to know more about?

Some Patterns

There are a range of historic patterns for this team that might be relevant. Typically, there are one hour and three hour executive committee meetings. The one hour meetings are "business as usual" meetings. Three hour meetings usually involve major decisions and/or strategic choices. Executive committee meetings almost always result in decisions being made, along with assigned responsibilities. During discussions, people usually talk about the future, and in problem-solving ways. The members of the executive committee are task oriented and meetings have a "no-nonsense," "let's get on with it" tone. Finally, no one has ever missed a meeting in the past.

Given these historic patterns, what begins to strike you as different about this situation? How are your initial thoughts being refined and shaped by this additional information?

Some Emphases and Omissions

In observing the meeting, given the context and past patterns, several things stand out through emphasis or omission. These include:

Emphases
• One Hour Meeting (Business as Usual)
• Rationality
• Past Successes
• Little Urgency
• Inform Missing Member

Omission
• Not a Three Hour Meeting (Major Decision)
• No Emotions, re: Impending Layoffs

- No Expressed Fears, re: the Future, Possible Failure, or One's Own Competence
- Absence of Decisions
- Not Dealing with a Missing CEO

'What hypotheses are you now considering about possible covert dynamics at work in this situation? What additional data or observations do you wish you had and how might you get them? Note also how paying attention to the combined effects of context, patterns, and emphases and omissions helps in developing more focused hunches and hypotheses.

Some Hypotheses re: Covert Processes in Omega Corporation

Clearly, a wide range of interpretations could be made based on the limited data presented about the Omega Corporation. The following are some illustrative hypotheses (to add to your own) about possible hidden dynamics that may be at work given the above situation, context, patterns, and emphases/omissions:

1. In a top-down culture, team members believe no decisions can be made without the missing CEO (*Blind Spot* or *Block*).
2. Repressed fears and feelings about their failure to keep the corporation healthy are blocking problem-solving in the executive committee (*Unconscious* or *Shadow*).
3. The executives do not have the knowledge or skills to solve the downsizing problem, but cannot admit they do not know because, as executives, they are expected to have all the answers (*Protective Concealment*).
4. The executives assume there will be a win-lose political fight over cuts and no one wants to say too much too soon in order to protect their "turf" (*Concealment to Achieve Individual Aims*).
5. The executive team's anger at the CEO for not taking care of them and the workforce is being acted out through avoidance and/or passive-aggressive behavior (*Collusive Concealment to Achieve Group Aims and/or Unconscious or Shadow*).
6. Questioning or even discussing the absence of the CEO would threaten the culture of the organization, adding to the stress, anxiety, and sense of loss inherent to the downsizing situation (*Blind Spot or Block and/or Shadow and/or Concealment*).

Clearly, more information and observations as to context, patterns, and emphases or omissions might help to either narrow the list of hypotheses or increase it. We find it helpful to always generate more than one plausible hypothesis and then seek additional data, clues, and insights, both literally and symbolically, to help narrow our focus. In the end, we can't always be sure we know exactly what is going on covertly. We, however, can have some well educated hunches that can guide exploratory interventions that may help validate our hypotheses and/or help move things along.

For example, in the above situation, one reasonable hypothesis to test is that repressed emotions are blocking problem-solving. Thus, some interventions set a climate of safety where fears and concerns can be expressed, which could be a reasonable first step. If this produces clear results, additional interventions in the same vein might be pursued. If not, it may be because the feelings are deeply repressed, it still isn't safe enough, or the hypothesis is false. It may then be appropriate to test another approach or hypothesis. In diagnosing covert processes, the issue is not about being right in guessing what is hidden, but developing guided judgments about the best possible interventions to pursue. Remember, the essence of action research is to try something and see how the system responds. What we are proposing is to not intervene blindly, or be blind to intervening.

Covert Processes and Change

In our experience, most people tend to react in similar ways to the subject of covert processes. Usually they equate them with the category "conscious disguises and concealments for personal gain," which includes hidden agendas, secret deals, and politics. They also almost uniformly describe covert processes as negative and undesirable.

We have a different view. First, covert processes involve much more, and are more complex, than conscious deceptions for personal gain alone. Second and most critical, covert processes are the natural complement to overt processes. They go together. When there are overt processes, there will always be covert processes. That which is focused on obscures and hides that which is neglected. That which is legitimate and proper defines that which is illegitimate and improper, and therefore must be hidden. Third, the content of what is hidden may be considered good or bad itself, but the reason it is covert is to either protect the individual, group, and/or organization from attack, or because it is unconscious or out of awareness. Therefore, for us, covert processes are simply a given in the dynamics of individuals, groups and organizations. To ignore them is to keep their influences hidden and to be vulnerable to powerful forces outside of our awareness.

In order to speak the unspeakable and, in the quest for change, turn the covert into the overt, one first must know they are there. Then a clear understanding of the dynamics of covert processes and their manifestations in a particular context is necessary. Many times, no matter how much a system says it wants to change, often the reality is that, at the same time, covert processes have a hold on maintaining the status quo. In order to have a starting point to facilitate significant change (and *all* significant change involves covert processes), we have found it helpful to remember first that there will be covert processes existing on multi-dimensional levels and, second, to seek to understand why they exist and how they are being manifested.

Consequently, we believe it is important to develop the skills and competencies to see what is missing, hear what is not said, and feel what is not expressed when working with others. We also believe these are increasingly important skills and competencies as the scope, complexity, and rate of change escalates geo-metrically in today's organizations (Katz & Marshak, 1995). We realize that to do so will require confrontation of our own covert processes: our blind spots and blocks, shadow sides, and the disguises and concealments we use to protect our personal and professional identities and goals. Nevertheless, our role as change agents requires us to develop the understanding and skills necessary to address the full range of covert processes. We must learn how to better help groups and organizations give voice to their secret hopes and fears, create pathways for exploring untested or unimagined possibilities, and develop enough safety, support and confidence to explore the unknown. Only in this way can we help groups and organizations achieve the breakthrough changes needed to move effectively into the twenty-first century.

References

Ferrucci, P. (1982). *That we may be.* Los Angeles, CA: J.P. Tarcher.

Katz, J. R., & Marshak, R. J. (1995). Reinventing organization development theory and practice. *The Organization Development Journal*, 13(1), 63–81.

Marshak, R. J., & Katz, J.R. (1994). *The covert processes workbook: Dealing with the hidden dimensions of individuals, groups and organizations.* Unpublished manuscript.

Marshak. R. J., & Katz, J. R. (1992). The symbolic side of OD. *OD Practitioner*, 24(2), 1–5.

Marshak, R. J., & Katz, J. R. (199Ia). Keys to unlocking covert processes. In M. McDonald (Ed.), *Building ourselves . . . our work . . . our organizations . . . our world: Organization Development Network conference proceedings* (pp. 65–71). Portland, OR: Organization Development Network.

Marshak, R. J., & Katz, J. R. (199Ib). Covert processes at work. *Chesapeake Bay Organization Development Network Newsletter,* 6(2), 1, 4–5.

Marshak, R. J., & Katz, J. R. (1990). Covert processes and revolutionary change. In M. McDonald (Ed.), *Forging revolutionary partnerships: Organization Development Network conference proceedings* (pp. 58--65). Portland, OR: Organization Development Network.

THINKING SYSTEMICALLY AND STRATEGICALLY

Introduction

John Vogelsang and Matt Minahan

VOICES FROM THE FIELD

When I am asked to work on a problem, I now lead with questions, whereas in the past I would lead with directives. I learned how to think systemically and to pay attention to what are the implications of what is happening for the organization's strategy and the functioning of the organization as a whole . . . I now focus on making every interaction strategic.

—Philip Anderson

Most critical to my being successful at my role are facilitation skills, being able to build coalitions, and being able to think systemically—having a sweeping understanding of how actions and decisions in various divisions and departments connect and affect each other.

—Michael McGovern

TOPICS COVERED IN THIS SECTION

- How to move beyond a focus on the individual to understand the larger organizational and environmental systems and how the dynamics of those systems impact work performance and the readiness for change.
- How to decide where strategically to foster change—individual, dyad, group, department, the organization (policies, practices, culture, etc.), or the organization and market/community relationship.
- How to utilize the evolving understanding of approaches/models for organizational systems to discern what might be missing if there are gaps/low performance and how to

strategically foster better functioning organizational systems.

WHY THINKING SYSTEMICALLY AND STRATEGICALLY

A successful HR business partner needs to move beyond just a focus on the individual to understand how the larger system, including groups, the organization as a whole, and the external environment, impact work performance, the readiness for change, and the capacity for creativity. What is labeled underperformance of an individual or a group may be the outcome of many influences including: an unsatisfactory supervisory/coworker relationship, organizational policies, resource allocation, the organizational culture, the design of the organization, and changes in the external business environment.

Thinking systemically means understanding how certain problems recur and are often made worse by quick solutions, and projecting how one decision can impact many people and set in motion a situation that can create many unexpected outcomes for the organization. It is a way to take into account the multiple perspectives, the learned and persistent behaviors, the many formal and informal work relationships, the various organizational structures, and the pervasive organizational culture that influence a situation. It is a way to find a relationship point where change can be made that ripples through the interactions that compose the organization. Operating from a systemic perspective also enables the HR Business Partner to gain a sense of where best to begin fostering change—at the individual level, dyads, groups, departments, the organization (policies, practices, culture, design), or the market/community relationship. All are interconnected.

THE CHAPTERS IN THIS SECTION

In this section HR Business Partners will find chapters about the key elements of a systemic and strategic approach to fostering organizational effectiveness. After defining systems thinking and describing an evolving understanding of organizational systems, this section presents various organizational design models and approaches for how to be strategic about improving an organization's ability to serve its customers. The articles are divided into three topic areas:

- Systems Thinking: The Connectedness of Everything
- An Evolving Understanding of Systems Thinking
- Designing Organizations

Systems Thinking: The Connectedness of Everything

An organization may be taking too long for product development. One approach would look at this as an employee performance issue. A systems approach might look at whether there is a good fit among the production equipment, organization hiring practices, and communication and collaboration among the product developers, management, and the manufacturing division. Looking at an organization's various systems might reveal that there are similar patterns of misalignments in other divisions and departments, which might be creating chaos among the various systems to the extent that they are unable to integrate their efforts toward a common goal because they are focusing on functional objectives in

order to survive. William Becker (2005) in **General Systems Theory: What is it? Is There an Application Example for OD?** describes elements of a general systems approach that can help managers understand how to foster organizational adaptability to current and emerging environments and, thereby, survive.

Veronica Hooper Carter (2004), in **Gestalt OSD and Systems Theory: A Perspective on Levels of System and Intervention Choices,** provides key principles from a Gestalt psychology systems thinking perspective to inform how HR Business Partners position themselves as interveners, how they make meaning of what they see, and what actions they take at what level of the system. To follow these principles means that to understand a situation the HR professional enters with curiosity, reserves judgment, operates with patience and tolerance, and focuses on an ongoing process of learning. Rather than seeking a scapegoat to blame and or a hero to rescue everyone, they recognize that many aspects of the system influence what is happening and will influence what will change.

What contributes to a high performing system? Why is it that organizations do better than other similar organizations that are composed of similar people, utilize similar technologies, pursuing similar goals, or adhere to similar standards? As an answer to these questions, Peter Vaill (1977), in **Towards a Behavioral Description of High-Performing Systems,** provides a list of 44 hypotheses based upon his experience working with many different kinds of organizations. The purpose of the list is to provide a basis for determining to what extent managers are inadvertently managing organizations today in such a way as to prevent high performance.

An Evolving Understanding of Systems Thinking

Since the beginning of the 20th Century, approaches to organizational systems have gone through two major evolutions. As we proceed into the 21st Century, a third evolution with roots in the previous century is reshaping how we see the workplace and how we foster change.

For years, managers believed that organizational success was fostered by the mechanistic approach to organizational systems. Through a division of labor, hierarchical decision making and authority structures, and the scientific method (diagnosis and address the particular cause of a problem) organizations could be structured to be effective and productive.

Some of the Scientific/Mechanistic metaphors for the organizational system include:

- The Thermostat—changes in environment contributes to responses in the thermostat which returns the environment to the desired state
- The Assembly Line—each part fits together in a continuous linear assembly process to make the whole
- Cogs and Gears—each entity is part of a precise arrangement that allows transfer of energy and movement from one part to the other

The Mechanistic System is often focused on gaining maximum efficiency from workers and machines by determining through time and motion studies the best methods to perform a task in the least amount of time. Managers measure, decide, monitor, standardize, maintain control, and fix problems by finding the one underlying cause. Decision-making is maintained at higher levels and a hierarchy of control holds all the parts in place.

Fritjof Capra summarizes the basic beliefs behind this approach: the world is a mechanical system, the body is a machine, life is a competitive struggle, and unlimited progress is achieved through economic and technological growth (Capra, 1982).

Gradually, another metaphor for organizational systems developed: organizations as organic, open systems that adapt, impact, and co-evolve with other systems in a given situation. Stuart Kauffman offers an amusing example of how the patchwork of co-evolutionary changes impact each other:

The car comes in and drives the horse out. When the horse goes, so does the smithy the saddlery, the stable, the harness shop, buggies, and in your West, out goes the Pony Express. But once cars are around, it makes sense to expand the oil industry, build gas stations dotted over the countryside, and pave the roads. Once the roads are paved, people start driving all over creation, so motels make sense. What with the speed, traffic lights, traffic cops, traffic courts, and the quiet bribe to get off your parking ticket make their way into the economy and our behavior patterns. (Kauffman, 1995, p. 279)

Rather than measuring, standardizing, and controlling to develop and stabilize the organization, the organic/open system is grown and replicated by designing organizations that "respond to the environment, internal capabilities, and change while maintaining balance, a sense of stability, and clarity" (Hinrichs, 2009). The organization maintains its stability by staying true to its "genetic code": its mission, vision, values, history, and working agreements. Organic/open systems metaphors for the organization include different types of living organisms, the cell with its nuclei, and the human body with its interdependent parts. The major concerns of management include: enable and empower, foster responsiveness, growth, and change, and be the keeper and promulgator of the code: the mission, vision, values, history, and working agreements.

The organic/open system approaches emphasize team work, team management, flat organizational structures, participatory management, empowerment processes for employees, and managers acting as interdependent mentors and coaches.

Organic/open System approaches also seek to build "healthy" organizations based upon models of what has worked in other situations. Some of the models of healthy organic/open system organizations are dealt with in the organizational models section below.

In **Chaos and Complexity: What Can Science Teach?,** Margaret Wheatley **(1993)** describes a shift in consciousness and focus that is occurring:

So what is this shift in consciousness that is required of us and what is the true paradigm that needs to change? I believe that it is a simple but profound world shattering recognition that we do inhabit a well-ordered universe. It functions well, even without us. Stewart Kaufmann, a scientist working in complexity theory, has said, "This is a world where you get order for free." Order arises spontaneously when you create simple connections. If you require simple connections among thousands upon thousands of individual elements, a pattern of organization emerges. We get order for free. This discovery of order has moved most dramatically in the past twenty years in the area of science first known as chaos. Now it is a more complex science. Of course, mystics in every spiritual tradition have known about this order for a very long time.

"Order arises spontaneously when you create simple connections." The emerging approach does not see Organizations as entities controlled or encouraged to grow by senior leadership but ongoing, self-organizing constructs within the various, complex, and evolving relationships among the people involved. Ralph Stacey says,

What an organization becomes would be thought of as emerging from the relationships of its members rather than being determined simply by the global choices of some individuals... the very constitution of organizations depends on its product of local knowledge through local language practices...making sense of organizational life requires attending to the ordinary, everyday communicative interaction between people at their own

local level of interactions in the living present. (Stacy, 2001, pp. 8, 144, 163)

Duncan Watts (2003) offers two metaphors for organizations as ongoing constructs: fireflies in Papua, New Guinea, and the Internet. Fireflies will start the evening with erratic flashing but as the evening progresses thousands will pulse in synchronicity. The Internet continues to grow without a master plan but people are still able to send an email that reaches a distant country in seconds. Watts says that all this works because there are clusters—people, insects, computers—that are closely connected but across and between these clusters are a few random (sometimes planned) connections that rapidly shrink the distance between the clusters. Viewing organizations this way, management tends to encourage clusters of expertise and practices (work teams, action learning groups, etc.), cross function connections, and random informal connections to other people inside and outside the organization:

. . . it appears that a good strategy for building organizations that are capable of solving problems is to train individuals to react to ambiguity by searching through their social networks, rather than forcing them to build and contribute to centrally designed problem solving tools and databases. (p. 289)

Organizations are communication and relationship networks. Whatever design is developed in a particular organization is both born of and fosters how people are organizing, relating, and communicating to effectively carry out the mission and vision.

These newer approaches to organizational systems, variously called complex adaptive systems or dialogic systems, focus more on the processes of communicating and organizing but not at the expense of formally identified organizational designs. The role of leadership in such a system is to assure the flow of communication among the various groups; to be a broker of responsibility, a connector, and a promoter of relationships that contribute to learning and self-organization; to disturb and nurture the patterns of relationships; to hold the anxiety of constant change; to be a participant in the constructing/reconstructing of the core purpose, values, working agreements, and outcomes in the organization; and to be mindful of:

- The changes that only need to be acknowledged because they are already happening and are deepening and extending current practices
- The changes that need to be influenced because they need some support and direction to occur and they have the potential to further improve current practices and/or create new practices
- The changes that need a plan of action to happen because they are new directions, new practices or the seeds for future development[1]

As Bushe and Marshak in the *Journal of Applied Behavioral Science* expanded version (2009) of their article **Postmodern Turn in OD** (2008), that is included here, say,

First, Dialogic OD change processes emphasize changing the normal, everyday conversations that take place in the system (Barrett et al, 1995). This can be done in a variety of ways, including changing who normally takes part in these conversations, changing how people have these conversations, changing conversational patterns (Ford & Ford, 2008), changing the skills people bring to these conversations (Bushe, 2009), and by changing the framings and content of what the conversations are about (Marshak & Grant, 2008). Secondly, there may or may not be a data collection phase, but when there is, there is seldom the assumption that an objective reality or set of facts exist to be discov-

ered or discerned. Instead, processes of inquiry are used to surface, legitimate, and/or learn from the variety of realities that exist in the system. In short, there is no attempt to objectively diagnose the system per se. Third, the aim is to generate new images, stories, narratives, and socially constructed realities that affect how people in the system think and act. (2009, p. 361)

The newer approaches to organization systems are concerned with transforming the conversations and relationships in organizations in order to transform the organization.

Designing Organizations

Models of organizational designs have been very useful when operating from an Organic systems theory to analyze and strategize about what needs to change in an organization. The complex adaptive and dialogic approaches operate with the assumption that organizational designs are idiosyncratic to whatever group or organization in which they develop. Using innovations or change processes from one organization to the other may result in different outcomes. However, one organizational construct that has been useful for both Organic and complex adaptive/dialogic approaches is organizational culture.

Organizational Culture

Edgar Schein (2000), in **Corporate Culture,** defines the nature of and offers an approach for analyzing culture. Understanding organizational culture helps practitioners identify which beliefs, values, and principles are explicit and which are implicit and possibly influence all that an organization does. In other words, the explicit aspects of an organization's culture— the office layout, people working in teams, action learning groups—and an organization's espoused beliefs may express a commitment to collaboration, participation, and valuing each other's input. However, management may at

[1]This is a modification of E. D. Beinhocker (1999, Spring).

times operate from implicit, underlying assumptions and push aside team accountability and collaboration in order to effect quick decisions; thereby undermining collaboration. Understanding culture can also help transform the conversation by identifying how the work environment is an expression of the underlying values and beliefs and how what is said and done is shaped by what is assumed.

Why is it that highly mission driven organizations dedicated to serving others or to advocating social changes often function in the very way they are trying to counteract in the larger society? Why do they become a traumatized system where there are recurring conversations without resolutions, groupthink, and contagious stress? Pat Vivian and Shana Hormann (2002), in **Trauma and Healing in Organizations,** use an approach for understanding both the explicit and implicit, strengths and shadows, in an organization's culture. This approach provides a way for members of an organization to see the shadow as a starting point for systemic analysis and insight, self-awareness, and for aligning their organizational structures and processes with their mission and values.

Too often managers see the departure of skilled women and people of color as an individual situation and fail to examine the systemic nature of the workplace culture that may have influenced their departure. Many organizations see building a diverse and inclusive workplace as a distinct program to address a particular problem rather than a need for organizational culture change. Judith Katz and Fred Miller (2001), in **Diversity and Inclusion as a Major Culture Change Intervention,** offer a case study of changing an organization's culture to become a culture of inclusion that leverages diversity as a way of life. They describe the path from status quo to a culture of inclusion and the six strategic levers that help drive the culture change.

Organic/Open System Models

Gina Hinrichs (2009), in **Organic Organizational (Org²) Design,** gives an overview of

various organizational design approaches. Those approaches include Weisbord's Six Box Model, Galbraith's Star Model, Gelinas and James' Collaborative Organizational Design, Hiock and Getzendanner' Chaordic Design, and others. She then offers Org² Design as an approach that builds upon the best of that organizational design thinking and provides a guide to designing either a part of or a whole organization.

Hinrichs Org² Design has six facets:

- **Purpose** (mission) is pursuing what is deeply meaningful; the reason for being is a foundational level of purpose.
- **Principles** (values and beliefs) are clear, commonly understood and agreed upon statements of *what* will guide the behavior of the participants in pursuit of purpose.
- **Practices** (behaviors) are specific working agreements on *How* to operate and grow together.
- **Participants** are members of the organization. Participants define who is involved and how he/she or the team contributes, is valued, and valuable.
- **Processes** define the work and information flows that produce value for the customer and community.
- **Pieces** are the organizational configuration or structure. Pieces are aligned and coordinated groupings of Participants executing the Processes and utilizing resources (especially information) to further the Purpose/ strategy of the organization.

Another way to look at organizations is as circulatory systems. Art Kleiner (2007), in **Organizational Circulatory Systems,** describes four circulatory systems, how they work, and the implications for intervention in organizations. The four systems are Hierarchy (the flow of authority), the Clan (core group), the Market (flow of work), and the Network (the flow of knowledge).

Greg Vaughan (2003), in **Participative Design: An Overview,** contrasts the mechanistic model (Design Principal 1) with the organic (Design Principle 2). Design Principle 1 is a:

> . . . command and control structure where responsibility for coordination and control of work occur one level above where the work is being done . . . The other is an organizational structure where coordination and control occur by those actually doing the work. This is called Design Principle 2 (DP2) and it is the structure necessary for truly self-managing organizations

Design Principle 1 works with the assumptions that employees are interchangeable and replaceable cogs in the wheel. There needs to be concise job descriptions and layers of managers, supervisors, and specialists. Design Principle 2 assumes that:

> . . . given the right organizational conditions, employees are purposeful, ideal seeking, and can manage themselves. This paradigm views people as capable of contributing to a learning and planning community, collaborating to achieve a shared desirable future. In DP2 organizations, employees develop the capacity and accept the responsibility to perform multiple functions as needed by the work group to achieve its purposes.

Complex Adaptive and Dialogic Approaches

Complex adaptive and dialogic approaches focus on the process of organizing and communicating, and more on transforming conversations and relationships than fitting the organization to a particular model that may have been developed in another organization. Dudley Tower (2002), in **Creating the Complex Adaptive Organization: A Primer on Complex Adaptive Systems,** provides a systemic framework for the application of complex adaptive systems principles to all levels of human systems in an organization. He also lays the foundation for a way of interpreting and

practicing Organizational Development in a world growing irreversibly more complex; one that de-emphasizes traditional planned change efforts, and instead concentrates on actualizing conditions for the emergent development of an organization to increasing levels of flexibility, creativity, innovation, and overall fitness in relationship with its larger system arena.

Informal social relationships are critical levers to organizational success. Analyzing these self organizing and self managed relationships can reveal where cross-functional communication is lacking, where it is blocked, and how teams can work collaboratively to develop better communication systems. Stephen Garcia and Edward Shin (2008) in **Incorporating Social Network Analysis into Traditional OD Interventions** present a case study of how a social networking perspective can assist organizational change.

Another method for transforming the conversation and how people relate to each other in organizations is Appreciative Inquiry. David Bright (2009), in **Appreciative Inquiry and Positive Organizational Scholarship: A Philosophy of Practice for Turbulent Times,** describes the elements of an Appreciative Inquiry approach. The initial steps include asking staff, "What gives life to you and to this organization when you and it are functioning at your and its highest level?" This is the discovery phase of a four phase process: Discovery, Dream, Design, and Destiny (Whitney & Trosten-Bloom, 2003). Instead of using the traditional SWOT (Strengths, Weaknesses, Opportunities, Threats), which tends to focus on the past and the present, Appreciative Inquiry processes often use Stavros' (2007) SOAR (Strengths, Opportunities, Aspirations, Results), which tends to focus on the present and the future and which can generate more energy for change than the SWOT approach.

Finally, changed actions can lead to changes in conversation and changed conversations can lead to changes in behavior. Change agents can approach organizations with an understanding that language in its many manifestations is constructive and central to the establishment, maintenance, and change of what is and what could be. Bob Marshak and David Grant (2011), in **Creating Change by Changing the Conversation,** explore how language shapes perception, action, and the organization.

FOR ADDITIONAL LEARNING

For more information about thinking systemically and strategically, you may want to read the following articles.

- Brown, J., & Isaacs, D. (1996-97). Conversation as a core business process. *The Systems Thinker,* 7(10), 1-6.

  Brown and Isaacs describe how to develop appropriate tools and environments to support conversations that contribute to collaborative learning and breakthrough thinking.

- Eoyang, G. H. (2004, fall). The practitioner's landscape. *E-CO,* 6(1–2), 55–60.

  Eoyang presents a taxonomy for the diversity of tools and techniques available to deal with complex systems.

- Quade, K., Perme, C., Eoyang, G., Barton, K., & Holladay, R. (2004). Tried and true: How the emergent theory of human systems dynamics informs the long-term success of large group events. *OD Practitioner,* 36(3), 14-18.

  The authors explore the mechanisms that make or break large group events and those who facilitate them. One major principle of human systems dynamics is that truly transforming processes involve multiple levels of engagement and repeated cycles of data collection and intervention.

- Doolin, B. (2003). Narratives of change: Discourse, technology, and organization. *Organization,* 10(4), 751-770.

  Doolin develops an understanding of organizational change predicated on the idea of organization as a performance or an effect, rather than a stable social structure. Doolin uses the concept of "narratives of ordering" to make sense of the processes that constitute organizations and the various mechanisms of ordering and organizing employed by organizational actors. He demonstrates this through a case study of change in a New Zealand hospital during a period of public sector reform.

- Townsend, M. (2002). Lessons from the field: Applying complex adaptive systems theory to organization change. *OD Practitioner,* 34(3), 10–14.

  Townsend shares lessons from using complex adaptive systems theory to understand organization behavior and challenges conventional notions of how organizations function.

- Vogelsang, J. (2002). Futuring: A complex adaptive systems approach to strategic planning. *OD Practitioner,* 34(4), 8–12.

  Vogelsang offers an approach to strategic planning that builds upon organizational learning methods while it emphasizes mindfulness, mission and values based decision making, fostering relationships and systems of communication, and continuous construction of possibilities that contribute to an organization's self-organizing and resiliency in its immediate and distant environment.

- Yaeger, T, & Sorensen, P. (2008). Social Construction and the new OD; *OD Practitioner,* 40(4), 38–42.

  Yaeger and Sorensen describe how Social Construction has become a major influence on the practice of OD, creating new organizational realities and potential through dialogue, discourse, and stories. Social Construction has influenced a number of new approaches to OD, including Appreciative Inquiry.

References

Barrett, F. J., Thomas, G. F., & Hocevar, S. P. (1995). The central role of discourse in large-scale change:

A social construction perspective. T*he Journal of Applied Behavioral Science,* 31, 352–372.

Beinhocker, E. D. (1999, spring). Robust adaptive strategies. *Sloan Management Review,* 40(30), 95–106.

Bushe, G. R. (2009). Clear leadership: *Sustaining real collaboration and partnership at work* (2nd ed.). Palo Alto, CA: Davies-Black.

Bushe, G., & Marshak, R. (2009). Revisioning organization development: Diagnostic and

dialogic premises and patterns of practice. *Journal of Applied Behavioral Science,* 45(3), 348–368.

Capra, F. (1982). *The turning point.* New York, NY: Simon and Schuster.

Ford, J. D., & Ford, L. W. (2008). Conversational profiles: A tool for altering the conversational pattern of change managers. T*he Journal of Applied Behavioral Science,* 44(4), 445–467.

Kauffman, S. (1995). *At home in the universe.* New York, NY: Oxford University Press.

Marshak, R. J., & Grant, D. (2008). Organizational discourse and new organization development practices. *British Journal of Management,* 19(S1), S7–S19.

Stacey, R. (2001). *Complex responsive processes in organizations: Learning and knowledge creation.* New York, NY: Routledge.

Watts, D. (2003). *Six degrees: The science of the connected age.* New York, NY: W. W. Norton & Company, Inc.

Wheatley, M. J. (1992). *Leadership and the new science: Learning about organization from an orderly universe.* San Francisco, CA: Berrett-Koehler.

CHAPTER 27

General Systems Theory

What is it?
Is There an Application Example for OD?

William Becker

WE RECOGNIZE EMERGING patterns from seemingly random events. These in turn stimulate our feelings, which urge us to organize those patterns into knowledge schemes, which then allow us to create a conceptual synthesis. Armed with these syntheses we create concepts and take action.

As applied to Organization Development, the patterns we detect by looking at the interfaces or kinds of interactions between an organization and its marketplace help us to understand how the organization's internal and external relationships influence the success of the enterprise. An understanding of these patterns (that form a General System Theory—GST) may also be used to improve organization and marketplace boundary exchanges and the internal exchanges within the operations of an organization. Without either having paid attention to such patterns as part of our ongoing holistic inquiry or having made the effort to focus specific exploration of these patterns, we are unable to use a valuable tool of inquiry.

Admittedly, this is a work in progress by a "layman practitioner" as opposed to a systems theory analyst) trying to understand the fundamentals and importance of GST and its multifaceted applications for OD. Without such inquiry, there is a constraint on innovation if there is insufficient knowledge and un-

derstanding of the tools available to proceed with effective organizational interventions. For instance, the many tools we in OD use to help our clients are based on the theories and concepts resulting from the action research efforts of OD practitioners and the studies of academicians and theoreticians. As a case in point, how many of us still use Maslow and Herzberg theories to support our organization work relative to human motivation and modes of behavior? In all probability, most of us! So it is with this practitioner's inquiry into GST and its practical application to OD.

Reliance on the Quantitative

Many early organization interventions, whether provided through training, management and executive development, restructuring, strategies, tactics, and so on, have been based on the disciplined approach of those who came before us (such as the Hawthorne experiments and Taylorism). Before we can prove that our intuitive or extrapolated ideas might work, we still tend to take our cue from our predecessors and try to validate our insightful impulses with quantifiable, validated data. Further, in order to justify our worth to business enterprise, OD and individual and group development professionals have typically relied on studies that were problem-focused rather than solution-focused.

Frequently, technology has been the driver or engine that caused us to rethink and reinvent how people work. Our impulse is to provide a plethora of quantitative data through surveys, empirical observation, analysis and feedback to prove the usefulness of our change methodologies to help people adapt to new workplace technologies. We often seem driven to hit our prospective clients over the head with the results of carefully collected and quantitatively validated data in order to sell our services. In a way, this persuasive approach is a pattern of expectation that we have set up. For decades we have created the knowledge schemes and concepts in the minds of our clients and prospective clients. If we present information and conclusions in certain patterns, it feels comfortable to prospective consumers of our services and they engage us. It's a reasonable scenario, as entry into the business world for the early *average* social scientist and social practitioner was not easy; their credibility (without overwhelming evidence) left something to be desired for most prospective business clients. After all, what we work with are intangibles, therefore our effort is usually to make the intangible tangible! The old retort by the hardened line manager is, "When I see the train coming at me at eighty miles an hour, I don't want some tomfoolery theory, I want to know what to do!" Our usual response, based on the mechanistic approach, was to help the businessperson find ways to stop the trains. Today, because of our continued efforts to improve our services, we turn more to creating ideal scenarios (extrapolating what might or could be) with our clients to help them avoid building their enterprises on a railroad track!

A Shift to the Qualitative

By searching for solutions (based on the work of academicians, theorists and the action research of fellow OD practitioners) we have begun to look beyond solely linear quantifiable methods into a much more general, undefined, and intangible field of searching for common patterns that exist in all systems. By finding such patterns, even if we don't thoroughly understand the scientific underpinnings, we are better able to extrapolate what's happening in and among organizational systems. While any findings must still be tested, based on client collaboration and measuring to see if we reach desired results, we spend less time trying to prove that we know what we are talking about; and more time improving current situations and creating better futures for our clients. Marvin Weisbord at an early Future Search Conference training session said, in response to a question about the validity of the Search process, something to the effect of, "I don't worry about trying to prove that the Search Conference works when asked for quantitative data. I just say we know it works because the results speak for themselves!"

Making Sense of Things

There are times we might not feel we have a grasp of what the client's issues are, that some pieces are missing when diagnosing the needs and opportunities of an organization. It's most likely because we haven't collected enough patterns to develop knowledge schemes that will provide us with the "aha!" provided by a conceptual synthesis. The patterns may be in the data collected and resulting information. But if we are not looking for patterns we may miss the underlying causes for the dysfunction (or productive functioning) of the organization.

For example, we have learned that the behaviors of teams, groups, and individuals are pretty much the same in all settings. When certain kinds of things are said or done, one can fairly accurately predict the nature of the resulting response(s). Recognizing that there are common patterns of response whether it is in the Boardroom or on the shop floor, alerts us to the fact given certain conditions we can construct system models that help us avoid undesirable results, or at minimum, mitigate them so as to not damage the effectiveness of the organization.

How can we make effective use of GST in our work? Here is some of my experience.

What Is Systems Theory?

First, let's take a look at Systems Theory from the explorations of Laszlo, Banathy and other theorists who provide us solid reasoning and Conceptual Syntheses from which to make this inquiry.

Broadly, Systems Theory is, according to Heylighen and Joslyn (1992), a transdisciplinary study of the abstract organization of phenomena, independent of their substance, type, or spatial or temporal scales of existence. It investigates both the principles common to all entities, and the (usually mathematical) models that can be used to describe them. B.H. Banathy (1996) offers some insight into the usefulness of general systems theory in social systems by noting the following:

> By observing various types of social systems and studying their behaviors, we recognize characteristics that are common to them. Once we have identified and described a set of systems concepts that are common to social systems, and observed and discovered between them certain relationships, we can construct systems principles. A systems principle emerges from an interaction and integration of related systems concepts. Next, we can organize related principles into certain conceptual schemes called systems models. (p. 78)

We can understand his perspective through an illustration of our experiences as practitioners working in different industries. For example, based on events around us, we develop feelings. These in turn help us develop cognitive recognition of emerging patterns that we develop into knowledge schemes. We reach a state of homeostasis (a kind of satisfaction that this makes "sense" to us), which produces a conceptual synthesis. This synthesis lends itself to applications for all kinds of systems. With these new concepts we more easily understand more complex knowledge from which we can reexamine (and discover) new patterns and their relationships to what we already know, as well as to extrapolate meaning that provides us informed guesses. See Figure 27.1 for a Model I developed to demonstrate the ongoing process of Conceptual Synthesis.

Banathy (1996) also generally supports this Conceptual Synthesis Model when he says:

> Systems thinking is a property of the thinker, who organizes internalized systems ideas, systems concepts and principles into an internally consistent arrangement, using a systems way of viewing and understanding, in order to establish a frame of thinking. As we observe what is "out there," this frame of thinking enables us to reflect upon what we experience; thus we construct our own meaning. We create our own cognitive map, which is our own interpretation of the out there. As we view and work with social systems, systems think-

FIGURE 27.1 Conceptual Synthesis-An Ongoing Process

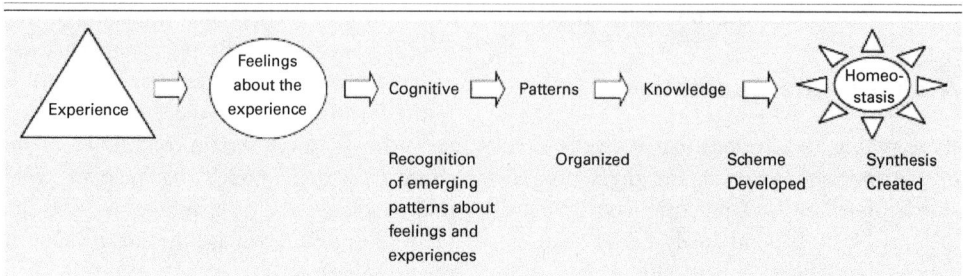

ing enables us to explore and understand those systems…(p. 156)

Conceptual Synthesis

Some of the key principles of Conceptual Synthesis therefore appear to me to be:

- Life, in all its manifestations, is made up of PATTERNS. Whatever the manifestation, biological, mathematical, or psychological, these patterns bear some commonalities in their relationships to one another.
- We build KNOWLEDGE as we collect data from our experience and SYNTHESIZE it. The greater our knowledge the quicker we accelerate the perception of patterns.
- What we FEEL about our experiences is turned into cognitive recognition of patterns, which is synthesized into knowledge that helps us understand the patterns.
- We develop understanding based on KNOWLEDGE SCHEMES instead of instinctual and random responses.
- The actions we take are behavioral choices that provide consequences and feedback to help us constantly make adjustments so that we can create an ongoing feeling of stability (EQUILIBRIUM and HOMEOSTASIS). A perception of stability enables us to avoid being overcome by the seeming chaos from whence come these patterns.
- In order to evolve, new knowledge schemes must be developed. By building upon the reiterative process of developing CONCEPTUAL SYNTHESES, we create models that further enable us to see new patterns, and so on. (In OD, an Open Systems approach offers the opportunities to keep adapting in order to survive. Closed Systems approaches become constrained and stagnate—unless no new demands are made of the system—due to the lack of new and different experiences, therefore limiting the chance to see new patterns and develop new knowledge schemes that result in adaptive behaviors.)

In some ways, the process of Conceptual Synthesis resembles how spell-checkers work in our computers. The programming picks up arrangements of letter patterns and automatically corrects misspellings. Sometimes the program "guesses" correctly and sometimes not. Without such programming, the computer obeys whatever we type in! It makes no false assumptions, nor does it offer alternatives (unless one is in Spell Check). So it is with our own experiences. Our experiences and education constitute our programming. We perceive what is happening based on preliminary data that we interpret using our previously built knowledge schemes. If we do not develop new knowledge schemes on which to base our understanding, we will most likely keep making the same type of decisions, taking the same kind of actions, and realizing the same kind of results as we have in the past.

It is not unreasonable to extrapolate that learning new things can help people develop new knowledge schemes. According to the popular press and professional journals in the 1980s, some Japanese organizations, for instance, encouraged and often required that people keep learning new things, whether it was flower arrangement or some other endeavor. They either consciously, or not, surmised (created knowledge schemes/conceptual syntheses) that by dealing with new experiences people expand their ability to keep learning on the job (construct new conceptual theories and therefore have greater ability to reason and, hence, to innovate and solve problems).

So it is with OD practitioners. We have at least two sources for developing new concepts. First, each organizational intervention allows us to build upon our past experiences. We are able to expand our knowledge schemes and therefore increase the pace at which we reach stability so that we can be more efficient and effective in the help we provide our clients. Second is the degree of variety we seek outside of our profession. The more we study and participate with other professionals who have developed knowledge schemes from their experiences the more we expand our own abilities.

The opportunity to shadow consult with colleagues is a good example. It provides us a time to identify patterns from our own experience in a context in which we have not previously applied our skills. We can develop new conceptual syntheses for our own practice and at the same time fast forward the understanding of our colleagues by sharing our observations. It is Margaret Wheatley (2001) who notes that relationships are the pathways to knowledge. Shadow consulting situations offer such a pathway. In addition, opportunities to see similar patterns in social circumstances are not restricted to our professional work. Whether it is in our church, the PTA, country clubs, or neighborhood associations, we can see and use GST as a tool to help others and at the same time expand our understanding of the universality of its application.

Conceptual Synthesis and Its Effect on Adaptation

It's not unusual to feel overwhelmed when too many new patterns are introduced too rapidly. For example when we have to learn all the variety of new technologies, and in some instance relearn, unlearn or learn several similar but different processes simultaneously. We don't have the time to assimilate the meaning of the patterns and create a moment of equilibrium.

Still greater frustration is experienced by members of stagnant or closed systems, as they find it more difficult to adapt to new situations because they lack adaptive knowledge schemes to deal with incoming new patterns. Perhaps this is why we often find that people on the front lines who deal directly with customers (and all the enablers and disablers within their own organizations) are often more ready for change than their top management. Top management has been resting in homeostasis atop the pyramid, and is not ready to make adaptive moves. They often do not see new patterns in the marketplace or in the boundary exchanges that take place daily between the organization's liaisons and the marketplace, and therefore are either unpre-

pared or unwilling to develop new knowledge schemes. (Admittedly, however, they sometimes cannot take action on new knowledge schemes because of uncontrollable happenings in the marketplace.)

General Systems Theory applied would have all organizational members experience the patterns emerging from the marketplace. Their collective intelligence is profoundly greater because there is a full spectrum of conceptual synthesis at all marketplace interfaces leading into and out of the organization.

What Has This to Do With OD Application?

Our roles as OD practitioners are enhanced when we view things from the perspective of relationships among events, processes, people, structures, domains, intention, and strategy when we look at organizations as systems.

Banathy (1996) notes Russell Ackoff's view of this approach:

> Ackoff (1981) says that systems thinking reverses the analysis-focused machine-age thinking that aimed at understanding an entity by decomposing it, explaining its behavior by its parts, and aggregating these explanations as the explanation of the whole. In contrast, systems thinking identifies the whole that contains its parts, explains the behavior of the whole, and then explains the parts in terms of their role(s) and functions within their containing whole. (p. 159)

OD needs to do both. We look from the whole to its parts and from the parts to its whole.

Why? Because a symbiotic relationship exists among various systems based on the patterns caused by their interactions.

Ervin Laszlo (2003) notes that there is a paradigm shift taking place in our 21st century. That there is a growing awareness of previously unnoticed coherence in nature, a kind of

---

A CASE EXAMPLE

A prominent food company processes and packages a variety of food products. At their main manufacturing/ processing facility, numbering some 350 employees, it was diagnosed that were two major problems. One required them to increase their degree of involvement of their employees and the other was to improve their process for decision making relative to their selection of new products to produce. How did General Systems Theory play a part in the diagnoses?

As data were collected at every level and every function by lines of business, certain bits of information began to form. These formations turned into patterns, which became themes. From these themes, based on previously stored conceptual syntheses, I was able to extrapolate their meaning into certain assumptions, feel comfortable that I had reached a state of equilibrium or balance that intellectually and affectively seemed to make sense, which enabled me to describe the situation in a conceptual way that led to recommended actions.

Some of the themes that emerged were expressed in different words, degrees of feeling, and out of a variety of circumstances. However, having had enough experiences to develop knowledge schemes that resulted in a conceptual synthesis, it allowed me to see the patterns coming from the participants of the assessment and anchor them to actions that could be taken. For instance, patterns coming from long-time frustration were expressed:

- Workers said management did not listen to them or take advantage of their suggestions.
- Workers were not empowered to make the changes that they had the ability and the resources to accomplish.
- Top management was dependent on the decisions of their corporate executives located three thousand miles away.

These patterns led to the conclusion that employees had already synthesized the patterns and knowledge into firm concepts and were ready to make positive operational changes ten years before management began to entertain the idea. Further, the patterns of chaos emanating from all parts of the operations system due to an undisciplined and political approach to selecting products that might lead to greater sustained revenue became noticed by themes that were traceable back to the marketing group. This was a clear example of how the micro system disabled four or five other systems (such as sales forecasting, production, budget management, packaging design, and resourcing) from being as effective and efficient as they might.

---

immediate synchronization between the parts that make up a system and between systems and the context in which they exist. By recognizing that all systems within an organization have the same, or at least a similar, relationship of patterns, and grasping the patterns even in just one subsystem in an organization, we can extrapolate what might be happening among other subsystems. For example, the organization that has too long a turn-around time in product development might be suffering because of the lack of investment in the size of the facility, outdated equipment or cheap hiring practices. Looking at such an organization's various systems might reveal that similar patterns of inadequacies are due to a lack of investment in those systems. Lack of investment might be creating chaos among the various systems to the extent that they are unable to integrate their efforts toward a common goal because they are focusing on functional objectives in order to survive.

Understanding the interdependency of the various systems can enable us to help organizations adapt to their current and emerging environments, and thus survive. Recognizing patterns and having the ability to see and help others see the relationship of those patterns is part of the art of OD.

In a conversation about GST with a consultant to organizations, Nancy Brown, (2003) she suggested the following:

> Concepts . . . most critical to system theory and [that] have the most import for folks thinking about OD, include:

- occurrence of patterns
- the connectedness of everything
- the concept of boundaries, permeable and impermeable
- existence of a system, in the context of a larger environment
- impact of larger environment and system on one another
- systems always transform inputs into outputs intended and unintended
- adaptive steps taken by the system to survive in its environment
- evolution and devolution of the system

Certainly awareness of linkage, connectedness, boundaries, and the like, are important factors. Being able to recognize the patterns that lead to such linkages enhances how we look at situations and influence the actions we take.

Some of us work with clients who operate primarily from the frame of reference of the mechanistic method and view humanistic approaches to OD as irrelevant or antithetical to their goals. They lack the conceptual patterns to understand the humanistic approach that would help them create such an integrative concept.

A good example of how we have yet to integrate the patterns of the mechanistic and humanistic is the struggle we have with integrating sociotechnical processes, or at least helping organizations grasp and apply the process. For instance, how many organizations have integrated their Human Resource processes into their line operations? There are far too few!

How was management brought to recognizing patterns to new knowledge schemes and on to a conceptual synthesis that helped them understand that the recommendations were legitimate? It was a matter of:

- bringing them together and introducing them to concrete examples of what we had done with other companies in similar situations
- providing them with the themes that emerged from the patterns diagnosed in their organization
- and, asking them to give us a reality check to see if what we saw indeed made sense to them

Once we had group agreement that everyone was operating from the same understanding (conceptual synthesis) we then carefully outlined the importance of their commitment and follow- through and described the kinds of results they might expect in the future if they did or did not take the recommended action.

That's *how* it was done.

Why Management decided to take the recommended action included a number of things:

- the preferred future scenarios they desired
- a motivation to get out of the pain they were in
- chagrin over the circumstances into which they had brought the company
- embarrassment that their employees saw it before they did

What We Can Apply

Responsibility for recognizing all of the basic patterns within an organization cannot alone rest upon the shoulders of the OD practitioner. With dozens, if not hundreds, of pertinent patterns, it requires the involvement of the people at all levels in the organization. It is, however, the job of the OD practitioner to provide techniques and experiences to organization members so that they may:

- recognize their feelings about the patterns they have seen
- develop some knowledge schemes to understand them
- create conceptual syntheses so that they reach states of equilibrium and are prepared to make decisions resulting in productive action to meet marketplace demands

The more we practice identifying patterns in all parts of our personal lives, and the greater opportunity we give stakeholders to experience things together and to develop feelings about those experiences, and dialog in ways that create knowledge schemes so that they may reach a state of consensus (homeostasis), the greater is the probability that they will develop conceptual synthesis that enable them to have a common understanding of how they are to work together to achieve the results they desire. We are practicing what Marvin Weisbord calls making the movie together, and the notion of Margaret Wheately of creating relationships that build pathways to knowledge. Not a bad day's work, in all!

Note

This article is based upon a paper written by Constance Hochberg, when she was my student in the graduate OD Program at the New School in New York City. I credit her as the primary catalyst for my inquiry into this subject, and for initial research into some of the fundamental systems theory descriptions.

References

Ackoff, R. L. (1999). *Re-creating the corporation: A design of organizations for the 21st century.* Oxford, UK: Oxford University Press.

Banathy, B. H. (1996). *Designing social systems in a changing world.* New York, NY: Plenum.

Brown, N. (2003). Personal conversations and collegial mentoring.

French, W., & Bell, Jr., C.H. (1975). *Organization development: Behavioral science interventions for organization improvement.* Englewood Cliffs, NJ: Prentice Hall.

Heylighen, F., & Joslyn, C. (1992). "What is Systems Theory?" Retrieved from *http://pespmcl.vub.ac .be.SYSTHEOR.html.*

Kauffman, D. L. (1980). *Systems one: An introduction to systems thinking.* Minneapolis, MN: Future Systems, Inc.

Laszlo, E. (1974). *A strategy for the future: The systems approach to world order.* New York, NY: George Braziller.

Laszlo, E. (2003). *The connectivity hypothesis: Foundations of an integral science of quantum, cosmos, life, and consciousness.* Albany, NY: State University of New York Press.

McCoy, T. J. (1996). *Creating an "open book" organization—Where employees think and act like business partners.* New York, NY: AMACOM.

Wheatley, M. J. (1993). *Leadership and the new science: Learning about organization from an orderly universe.* San Francisco, CA: Berrett-Koehler.

CHAPTER 28

Gestalt OSD and Systems Theory

A Perspective on Levels of System and Intervention Choices

Veronica Hopper Carter

AS OD PRACTITIONERS interested in working effectively with groups and individuals, it is no longer enough to simply rely on group development theory and organization change theories or individual psychology and the seat of our pants. Integrating principles of systems thinking while training ourselves to see various levels of system simultaneously at play, assures the intervener a breadth of choices and possibilities for effecting change and achieving powerful results. In this article I will describe and demonstrate using reliable developmental theory in concert with systems thinking principles and the Gestalt "compass" of levels of system.

A Systems Perspective

Faculty of the OSD Center at the Gestalt Institute of Cleveland uses an integrative perspective of systems theory and Gestalt theory as a way of describing how groups and organizations behave. We do this to more effectively use ourselves to intervene in behavioral phenomena— thoughts, feelings, actions—and to enhance the life and growth of living systems and their component parts—individuals, pairs, groups, organizations, cultures, and societies. Systems theory and systems thinking keep us mindful of the interconnectedness of these component parts, and thus cautious about hasty moves to

"correct a problem" before observing and assessing the situation from the standpoint of multiple contexts and multiple levels of the system. Upon integrating a systems thinking perspective, one returns to the practice of intervening with the capacity to work in greater depth than if otherwise unaware and untrained in these multiple and multi-level contexts.

Several key principles from a systems thinking perspective inform how we position ourselves as interveners, how we make meaning of what we see, and what actions we take. The principle of "embeddedness" states that *every part is a whole and every whole is part.* Thus in systems thinking, any aspect to be analyzed is more fully understood when viewed within the context of its larger system and explained within its role in that larger system. A well-established mathematical principle instructs us that any system can only be defined by a point outside itself. Three conclusions extend from this perspective: (a) *a system is different than the sum of its parts,* for example we can write or run, although none of our individual "parts" can; (b) *system performance depends on how well all the parts fit and work together, not on how well any one or each part performs independently;* and (c) *if the whole system is behaving the best it possibly can, none of the parts will be behaving the best they possibly can, and vice versa.* To wit, a team of superstars is not necessarily a "super team." Effective systems shuttle between maximizing the effectiveness of the whole and maximizing the effectiveness of any individual(s), depending on the demands from its internal or external environment. Finally, the holistic, embedded and interrelated nature of systems means that *issues, patterns and themes exist simultaneously across multiple levels of system.* Together these phenomena enhance the potential for the intervener to have maximum impact from any astutely and strategically placed intervention.

Gestalt theory states we see in forms, and, "The whole character (of any system) manifests itself in the relationships between parts as well as in changes produced in the parts themselves. The perceiving of relationships is an essential aspect of wholeness in experience." When applying these principles to organizational competence, we easily see the importance of the intervener's ability to discern the various levels of system and the patterns of interaction that delineate them.

Three further principles of systems thinking have implications for the stance of the intervener: (a) *any system is behaving the best it possibly can at any given moment in time;* (b) *there is always more than one way to reach a desired end or outcome;* and (c) *the refuse or products of breakdown (e.g. failures) may be used for further growth and development in any system*—the principle of negentropy. Taken to heart, these principles demand a non-judgmental stance and compel the intervener to convey a posture of patience and tolerance, and a focus on an ongoing process of learning, They place the responsibility squarely on the whole for system functioning and herald the end of both the scapegoat and the hero.

Finally, a favorite statement from Plato: *Love is the pursuit of the whole.* This and the systems thinking principles highlighted above have profound implications for the value stance of the intervener, in a sense, the spiritual dimension of the work that is carried in the intervener's overall intent and view of human efforts. Adopting a systems thinking perspective compels the intervener to bring a principled stance and a disciplined presence to the work at hand, knowing that the nature of systems is on his side.

Levels of System

The primary motivation of Gestalt OSD interventions involves "heightening awareness" in order to inaugurate and augment self-perpetuated learning in the client system. Consequently, these interventions take into account all levels of the client system and strive specifically to determine the most powerful site for any intervention, realizing that one intervention conducted at any given level of system will have an impact on all other levels of system.

Any system can be conceptually divided into component parts or subsystems. However, systems theory presumes, as does Gestalt OSD, that "the whole is *different from* the sum of its parts" — that one can only fully understand the whole by studying the arrangement and purpose of parts relative to the whole and, further, by studying the relationship of the whole to its larger, external environment. "System" can mean an organization, a team, or an individual. Which entity is perceived to be a system for intervention depends on which boundary is chosen: The chosen boundary demarcates what is "system" and what is "environment," and defines "the client." While there is an element of the arbitrary in all of this, the preferred boundary is critical in that it defines the *contact boundary*—the boundary around which awareness is raised, energy is mobilized, and change occurs. Interventions are targeted at the designated boundary since, from a Gestalt OSD perspective, change occurs when contact occurs. Hence interventions are developed to create and support contact with the designated form or figure, i.e., at the contact boundary. A contact boundary can be anything from a personal belief or value system (individual level) to success indicators for an organization change project (group or organization level) to the decision-making processes between an executive and his or her top team (group and interpersonal levels), and so on.

System principles have deeply effected Gestalt theory and methodology, and have become cornerstones in the application of Gestalt OSD to organizational change processes. Client and consultant, for example, are a two-person system (dyad). A tendency to "break the system apart" and to assess the functioning of either client or consultant individually rather than viewing the pair as an interactive system will obstruct the intervener's ability to see the system dynamics and mutual effects at work. Small system or group applications are impossible to develop without such a systemic framework. Interventions at larger, more complex levels of system (e.g., at the division or organization level) can be severely impeded if only individual or interpersonal dynamics are considered.

The goal of Gestalt OSD interveners is to find out how to most effectively influence the client system with which they work. For this the practitioner must be able to:

1. Identify and understand the unique issues related to development at each level of system, i.e.
   (a) self system, both individual and intrapsychic/intrapersonal
   (b) self and other, both dyadic and interpersonal
   (c) subgroup
   (d) group
2. Be clear regarding appropriate skills for interaction at each level
3. Understand the consequences of an intervention at one level of system on all other levels

In the design and implementation of organizational change efforts, the "level of system" is both a theoretic perspective and a choice point. The practitioner's preferences and skills, the existence (or lack) of a shared purpose, and the relationship between the intervener and the system all play a role in choosing the most appropriate and effective level for intervention. However, the goal at any and all levels of system is to heighten awareness of the individual's, subgroup's, or organization's functioning, i.e., how members are interacting and making meaning of their experience in order to define and meet their designated ends. The Gestalt OSD belief is that heightened awareness enhances contact, which in turn leads to growth, development, and productivity at all levels. Enhancing interaction —i.e., contact—between different levels of the organization is an inherent focus of the Gestalt OSD approach.

The Gestalt OSD model for organizational change thus embraces the following goals for the intervener:

- heighten awareness in the client system regarding any interactions occurring within or at the organization boundary
- support the generation of data, i.e., valid information concerning issues, problems, dilemmas, values, and ways of functioning in the organization
- establish a presence that aids awareness, data generation, and the contact process
- build on the energy of the client system in relation to a current figure, theme, or issue
- enhance contact between the parts of the system and provide learning about subsystem boundaries and opportunities for joint efforts
- position oneself effectively with a useful degree of both marginality and involvement
- further the development of client skills in finding ways to address system problems, especially regarding what is possible in the moment—that is, the value of "what is" as well as the value of "what might be"

Levels of System as Choice Points

The overall goal of intervention at a given system level within a group, for example, is to heighten awareness of how the group is interacting and "making meaning." Such heightened awareness leads to growth, development, and productivity within the group. Four primary levels of system are useful in working with groups:

- self system, both individual and intrapsychic/intrapersonal
- self and other, both dyadic and interpersonal
- subgroup
- group

No hard and fast rules exist to determine the most effective level of system within which to work. As an intervener, your choice of level will often depend as much on your personal preferences as on "objective" measures of the best point for intervention. However, several important factors do influence the choice, e.g., the stage of a system's development: The existence (or lack) of a shared sense of purpose, the extent of trust and familiarity between intervener and system, and the extent to which one level has been developed at the expense of another. Inappropriate choices, however, can hinder the system's effectiveness. For example, working at the self (individual or intrapsychic) level early on in a group could hinder building cohesiveness, lead to dependency on leadership and have repercussions for the individual. Intervening at the largest possible level of system is often more effective.

Changes at one level of system affect other levels, whether positively or negatively. An intervener must be able to perceive and differentiate between system levels, to shift attention from one level to another, and have minimal prejudice about the "best" level for intervening. All levels of system exist and function simultaneously; awareness of the interplay between levels helps the intervener understand and assess the operations of the total system. At the same time, it is often easier to perceive and assess a system from the conceptual vantage point of one particular level. Each level is a conceptual construct that provides discrete boundaries. Each brings attention to specific interactions and distinct intervention strategies.

Good News: Many Levels But Only Two Types of Boundaries for Intervening

From a Gestalt OSD perspective there are primarily two activities healthy systems participate in: A system can either *engage*, with aspects of itself or with the environment, or it can *integrate*, take in and assimilate what has been accessed or acquired from the internal or external environment. The process of engagement involves setting up an exchange between differing aspects of the system, or between one system and another. This is the process of coming into contact with a form or figure. The purpose of exchange is largely differentiation – exploring what distinguishes one aspect of the system from another. Similarities are often revealed and common figures and shared ground often result. Exchange at the boundary of one system and another often results in a new definition of the system itself. The process of integration briefly allows the system to experience itself as a unified whole. In short it experiences a momentary *definition* of itself. The net result of this definition is that the system is more fully capable of entering into the next instance of exchange, with aspects of itself or with the environment, in part or full.

Work at any exchange boundary supports system definition: Work at any definition boundary supports and enhances the system's capacity for exchange. There are multiple levels of system. Within each are two types of boundaries available for any intervention. As an intervener you are either supporting the system to be clear about itself in some respect, about the definition of the system itself, its elements and capacities, or you are trying to support the system to engage in an exchange with its internal or external environment in order to satisfy a need or achieve a desired result. Each makes the other possible (see Figure 28.1).

FIGURE 28.1

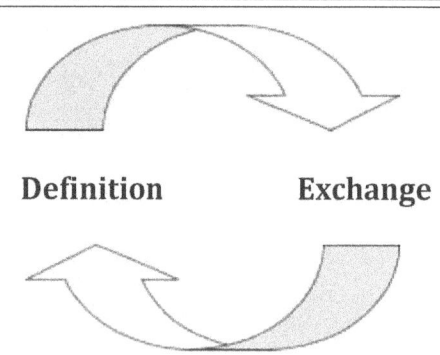

Definition   Exchange

LEVELS PROVIDE THE FOCUS FOR INTERVENTIONS

Self level of system: Individual and intrapsychic

When working with one person (the self level of system), the intervener may support the person to speak clearly about his views, experience, knowledge, thoughts or feelings — in short, about anything that would help a person say to himself and others, "This is who I am." Giving a presentation, making a speech, or making a personal statement about oneself is work at the individual level. That is, one seeks to present some definition of the self, however momentary, which does not involve seeking feedback, influence or reaction from others. An example of individual level work in groups is "checking in" or "reporting out." It is a critical skill involving a sophisticated ability to scan one's interior and to articulate the same in a public venue. It is essential for building common ground and establishing groundwork for building trust.

The second choice for work with the self system involves the possibilities of exchange between aspects of the self within a person's own interior (the intrapsychic level of system). Here an intervener supports the client to develop awareness of her sensory response, sort through inner conflicts, explore reactions and arrive at an understanding and comfort with her own experience.

Regardless of the boundary involved, individual or intrapsychic, work at the self level focuses on the client's relationship to his or her own experience of response and interaction. The goal is to heighten the client's awareness and management of sensory input, meaning-making, mobilization of energy, capacity for action, closure, and so on. Heightened awareness empowers the individual to make desired changes in his or her management of self.

Assessment at the self level remains "personal." Attention is paid to an interaction only in terms of how that interaction affects the individual in question. Nevertheless, work at the self level often benefits the other systems of which the client is a part. For example, a wish or perception regarding other team members may express an issue or theme needing resolution at the group level. Working issues at the individual level often facilitates resolution at the group level, and while the focus is on an individual's need to work through personal wishes, perceptions, and the like, the intervener might use the conflict to segue to the same issue at other system levels.

Self and Other Level of System: Dyadic and Interpersonal

I have often stated that if an intervener understands and can work effectively with a two-person system, everything else is a piece of cake. When working with one person, an intervener will enhance her effectiveness if she can view their two-person system as a dyad at work. Once one acquires the skills to work with a dyad, the basis for understanding and working within any other level of system is present. The "self and other" or two-person system is immensely more attention-grabbing and complicated than an individual. Working with one person gives you two boundaries to manage. Add a second person and the number of choices goes to six! The dyad, like the individual level, is another definition boundary. When working with a dyad the intervener helps the twosome identify qualities, processes, and so forth, which characterize their functioning as a unit.

At the interpersonal level of system, boundaries are drawn between pairs. In the dyad, the pair is individual to individual. Within a larger configuration, the interpersonal boundary is best described as system to system, i.e., individual/dyad, individual/subgroup, individual/group, subgroup/subgroup, dyad/group and so on. The goal of work at the interpersonal or system/system level is to support exchanges that clarify the nature of the boundary, i.e., how often and with whom interaction takes place, and how exchanges of influence, information and other factors, occur across that boundary (see Figure 28.2).

The successful functioning of the dyad involves skills for managing the interpersonal, individual and intrapsychic levels. An interpersonal intervention might highlight differences and or similarities, or exaggerate differences to make discernible the contribution each individual brings to the exchanges. The exchange, in turn, helps to characterize the life of the dyad involved. When working with a dyad it may be necessary to focus for periods of time on one side of the system or the other. In such cases the intervener needs to be clear with the individuals in the dyad that any deviation from working in the dyadic level is ultimately in service of returning to the dyad and supporting its overall functioning. On the other hand, the dyad should be challenged to support the capacities, when appropriate of each individual. Again we see the circularity of function and purpose between the definition boundaries and the exchange boundaries; and the dyad is a useful configuration for learning about the elements, challenges and skills needed to support any level of system.

Figure 28.2 illustrates the complexity and simplicity of seeing the multiple possibilities for intervention—the most predominant being the interpersonal boundary between the potential intervener and the dyad. The intervener uses himself as a tool. He draws upon his own intrapsychic or intrapersonal process to sense and observe the need for intervening with the dyad, between the two people (another interpersonal boundary), or with the man's or the

FIGURE 28.2

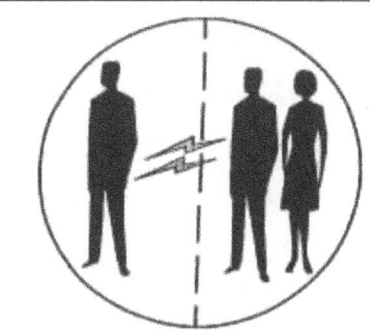

woman's interior (intrapsychic). The intent of the work determines which level he will choose. He may even use the three of them as a functional subgroup in a larger system. While the choice of level may move up and down the system as needed, it will revert back to the primary choice to close out the work and fulfill the original intent of supporting dyad as a whole.

Subgroup Level of System

The subgroup level of system, another definition boundary, is made up of three or more people existing in the context of a larger group. Work at this level focuses on the subgroup as an independently functioning whole that is different from the sum of its parts. The goal is to develop awareness of the subgroup as having "a life of its own." The emphasis of intervention is to identify and articulate the jointly-created characteristics that define the nature of this functional whole. These characteristics may be short-term (temporary), in mutual response to a current problem, or long-term (chronic), which may prove either healthy or dysfunctional in interacting with others.

Within a subgroup, as with a dyad, the intervener will inevitably find it necessary to approach the work from multiple levels. The choice of level depends in part on the intervener's judgment regarding the nature of the relationships that exist, and in part on personal skills. For example, if an individual in the subgroup is highly differentiated and in conflict with the others, the intervener may prefer to emphasize the subgroup boundary, focusing attention on how each individual contributes to the creation of a subsystem with distinctive traits. The desired effect is to heighten the cohesiveness of the subgroup. On the other hand, in a subgroup where inequality or passive agreement is problematic, the intervener may choose to intervene at the interpersonal level, emphasizing differentiation and supporting the development of each individual's boundaries. All levels of system are available to the skilled intervener to support the work at hand. Once again, however, the intent of the work is to support the subgroup understanding how it functions as a whole. Work on other levels should ultimately support this goal. Once achieved, the field is open for whatever work is needed next at whatever level of system.

Political caucuses are interesting examples of subgroups. While they are often conflict ridden behind closed doors, they are bound together by a common purpose. Their power rests in being able to define themselves as a unit and present a united front. Their definition of themselves is always in relationship to a larger level of system, which provides the ground against which their own identity more readily stands out—a good instance of the figure/ground phenomenon in Gestalt theory.

Group Level of System

The defining boundary of a group is set by the purpose of the group as well as by the membership, including the leader(s). As with the subgroup level, the goal is to heighten awareness of the group as being a whole whose sum is different from its part—as having a life of its own. The group is a system in which all members have a position and play a role and in which any individual, pair or subgroup may display the "symptoms" of the group's dilemma or problem. Even though the intervener can speak to the group as a whole, individual members will respond personally from the basis of personal experience or beliefs about "the group." However, the focus

of intervention is on perceiving and assessing the group as a whole.

Something that is true about a group may not be true of each individual member, nor true all the time. The group "speaks" through its interactive behavior, that is, through the nature and quality of the interplay between the members. The intervener may notice and articulate that the group is avoiding the inclusion/exclusion issue by forming two distinct subgroups, or that all but one member agrees to membership requirements, or that work in the group primarily gets done through two-person encounters. Such observations call for intervention strategies that focus members' attention on the fact that they are functioning within a higher level of system, not just as separate entities.

Again, when the intervener's intent is to enhance the functioning of the group as a whole, work at all other levels should be in service of that goal and framed in that context. For example, often in a group there will exist an especially chronically conflicting pair who plays out issues in the life of the group that the group has been unsuccessful in identifying and owning. Unless the group is challenged to take responsibility for how and why it allows the ongoing conflict, the benefits of the developmental issues involved in the conflict will elude the group and rob them of developing key strengths in the group. Choosing to intervene only with the conflictual pair will never completely resolve the issue since the rationale for the conflict is embedded in the group itself.

The excitement in working in a group rests in the many avenues for work available to the intervener. Training oneself to see the multiple boundaries available for work in a group is akin to training yourself in childhood to see the various animal shapes camouflaged in a tree. The more you see, the more exciting it gets and the more you help others to see, and so on.

Organizational Level of System

Most of the work in organizations occurs in subsystems comprised of one or more groups, where processes take place in face-to-face interaction at the group or interpersonal levels. However, "organization development" demands an ability to conceptualize at much larger system levels, e.g., organizational environment, total organization, division, and department. This conceptual demand requires, in turn, a familiarity with and sensitivity to boundary phenomena and boundary management relative to the differing realities, subcultures, structures, goals, and processes of the subsystems.

In designing organization-level interventions, a number of balances need to be struck between, for example, organizational goals and subgroup and individual impact, between long and short-term objectives or perspectives, between stability and change, between ideal desired outcomes and degrees of change that can be assimilated. Any and all interventions conceived and carried out at larger levels of system will have echoes, influence, and consequences upon all subsystems.

The specific goal of organizational interventions is to harness the maximum energy of the system in service of organizational need. An understanding of the inherent tensions in the system, the forms in which those tensions manifest themselves at various levels, and the implications of those tensions for all levels will support the likely success of any intervention design. Maximizing the embedding of awareness of these factors within the total system is the superordinate goal of any change initiative.

An Important Caveat

A predisposition or preference on the part of the intervener to be more aware of some system levels than of others, or to favor one level for intervention over another, tends to skew and impede the effectiveness of the work. Interventions and changes effected at one level of system impact all other levels of system. Awareness of the distinctness and importance of each level, and awareness of the substantive interplay and interdependence between all system levels, helps us understand and assess the system as a totality, and to design interventions that are appropriate, significant, and effective, and in general to find more fulfillment in simply observing and existing in the world at large.

Note

The conceptual framing of levels of system presented in this article was developed, presented, and taught in the work of the Organization & Systems Development founders and the OSD Group Track Training Program faculties between 1977 and 2004—with special mention of Frances Baker and Claire Stratford.

References

Allport, F. H. (1955). *Theories of perception and the concept of structure: A review and critical analysis with an introduction to a dynamic-structural theory of behavior.* New York: John Wiley and Sons, Inc.

Carter J., Hirsch L., Nevis, E., Kepner, E., Lukensmeyer C., (with Gestalt Institute of Cleveland Professional Staff). (1977). *Organization & Systems Development Center: Gestalt Workbook.* (Available from The Gestalt Institute of Cleveland, Organization & Systems Development Center, 1588 Hazel Drive, Cleveland, OH 44106.)

Carter, J. D. (with Gestalt Institute of Cleveland Professional Staff). (1980–2004). *Organization & Systems Development Center: Working with Groups: The Group Track Training Program Workbook.* (Available from The Gestalt Institute of Cleveland, Organization & Systems Development Center, 1588 Hazel Drive, Cleveland, OH 44106.)

CHAPTER 29

Towards a Behavioral Description of High-Performing Systems

Peter Vaill

THIS ARTICLE seeks to answer the following question: When a set of persons utilizing some collection of technologies is performing, in relation to some pre-defined goals or standards, in a way which may be described as "excellent" or "outstanding" or "high performing," what events may be observed in such systems?

This question contains a number of loosely defined terms which, for the moment, will be left undefined. An overly restrictive definition will prevent us from engaging in the acts of imaginative hypothesizing which are the main focus of this paper. Perhaps a little more clarity can be introduced, though, if it is stipulated that the focus is on systems which are "doing better" than other similar systems, composed of similar people, utilizing similar technologies, pursing similar goals or adhering to similar standards.

Before proceeding with the attempt to fashion some behavioral hypotheses about "what is happening" in such high performing systems (HPS), several key underlying assumptions should be stated. These assumptions are offered without defense or proof.

1. The first assumption is that most of what we think we know about the performance of work systems derives from research in settings where the human members of the system are not there voluntarily. We have tended to study *employees,* people who have to work for a living; and we have studied *employers,* people in a role of stewardship relative to external stockholders, whose basic responsibility is to make the organization work in the financial interest of these stockholders.

2. The second assumption is that most organizational research has been problem-oriented: the research has been done in order to throw light on the causes of *unsatisfactory* performance. Even where the research itself has been purely descriptive in purpose, the underlying motive for conducting or sponsoring it has tended to be normative, i.e., to learn how to make the organization work better.

3. A third assumption follows: that one can extrapolate from the causes of ineffective performance to the causes of more effective performance. For example, if opportunity for decision-making is found to be lacking and an effect on performance seems to exist, then it should follow that more opportunity for decision-making will produce improved performance.

4. The criteria for evaluating whether a work system is performing satisfactorily have tended to be comparative. If one system, for example, is not as profitable as another apparently similar system, then the first system can be assumed to be relatively less effective.

5. Either the human or the nonhuman (e.g., technological) components have tended to be the focus of most research, with major simplifying assumptions about the components-not-being-studied being made by the researcher.

6. A somewhat casually thought out assumption has been that the system should be studied in accord with a *priori* specifications. The internal boundaries of the organization which are used by the management for its control purposes have been permitted to define the system to be investigated. Specification of the system to be studied has tended *not* to be an empirical question.

7. A major category of research findings has been the observed discrepancy between what is supposed to be happening in the system and what actually is happening. The assumption: what is as the standard for a desirable level of system functioning.

8. At key interfaces between the system in question and entities in its environment, the assumption has been that improved coordination and integration of interests "across the boundary" are desirable.

A great deal of what we think we know about management and organizational behavior seems to rest on assumptions such as these. This list has usually been taken for granted by the bulk of studies. Occasionally a study calls one or two of these assumptions into question, but rarely has the whole list been questioned. (Assumption 4 has been questioned fairly frequently. Assumption 5's bankruptcy has been a major tenet of the so-called "sociotechnical systems" approach to organizational research and improvement. Some academic organization theorists have fastidiously avoided Assumption 2.)

This article grows originally out of questioning Assumption 5, the "man vs. machine" assumption. The concept of "joint optimization" as it has been developed by the sociotechnical systems researchers was taken seriously as an alternative assumption. However, as the phenomenon of joint optimization was considered more carefully, it became clear that all the other assumptions on the list had to be questioned as well. *It is possible that a high-performing system, as defined at the outset of this paper, cannot be fully understood so long as any of these assumptions are accepted without question.*

In the remainder of this chapter, two things are done. First, the concept of "joint optimization" is discussed more fully. Then we will ask: when joint optimization is occurring in a system, what is happening?

Joint Optimization

Recently in an informal lecture, Eric Trist (of the Tavistock Institute of Human Relations and the University of Pennsylvania's Wharton School) spelled out what joint optimization means in a work system. Basically a work system is some organized collection of people and things. The "things" may be tools and machinery, from the simplest to the most complex elements. The people may function as individuals, and/or in two's and three's, and/or in groupings of a dozen or so, and/or in large organizations. To make the system work, Trist writes, the problem is to get the things, whose behavior is governed by one set of laws, to interface effectively with the people, whose behavior is governed by another set of laws. The laws which govern the behavior of things are physical laws: for instance, laws of mechanics, thermodynamics, hydraulics, and electronics. The laws which govern the behavior of people are the laws of psychology and sociology and anthropology, as well as the perhaps-better understood laws of biology. Each set of laws (one for inanimate, one for animate) has its own limits, imperatives, and opportunities. Each is discoverable, Trist believes, and manageable by its own particular brands of scientific investigation.

We may go on to observe, from Trist's basic premise, that history has shown man's tendency to attempt to reduce one class of laws to the other. One strong pressure has been to investigate and interpret the behavior of animate entities by the laws of the inanimate. Many theorists have commented on the fascination psychology has had for physics. It is not hard to demonstrate that the psychological vocabulary owes more to physics than to any other field. But the reverse process occurs as well. The history of Romanticism is, in one sense, the history of the attempt to investigate and interpret the physical world in humanistic terms.

Joint optimization is that stream of processes in a work system where the various elements are behaving to, but not beyond the limits set by the laws which govern their behavior, and where the behavior of any particular element is not preventing some other element from behaving in accordance with the laws which govern it. A simple example: an automobile may be capable, within the laws which govern it, of going 200 mph. But a particular person may not be capable, within the laws which govern him/her, of driving it that fast. Therefore, at 200 mph a condition of joint optimization does not exist. The system is unstable and probably cannot endure at that level of performance. Conversely, the person may be capable of controlling an automobile at 200 mph, but the particular car s/he is driving may not be capable of that sustained speed. Therefore, at or near 200 mph joint optimization is again not occurring. Thus, the problem of joint optimization here would be, "what is the optimal level of performance for a particular person in a particular car under a particular set of road conditions?"

A First, Tentative Step

This somewhat abstract discussion can be brought to a concrete focus in the day-to-day conduct of organizations. The problem is seen where we find people doing well-engineered jobs which they find intolerable. And it is seen where we find well-qualified people doing work which does not call forth what they have to contribute. And it is seen where we find people "misusing" equipment and other resources because they must, in order to behave in the way that they prefer. In the first two cases, the person is asked to behave contrary to the laws governing his or her behavior in order that the technology may be operated in accordance with laws governing its behavior. In the third case, we see people behaving according to the laws of their behavior at the expense of the laws governing the technology's behavior.

The problem of joint optimization in a work system is a research issue of the greatest importance. It is no longer satisfactory to design one part of the system carefully and let the other parts fall into step. Nor is it any longer satisfactory to design the several elements of the system carefully and expect them to integrate themselves automatically.

We need some laws of joint optimization -some statements at a fairly high level of generality about the limits of people-operating-technologies. These laws are probably not fully deducible from the laws we now know of people and the laws we now know of technologies. It is, possibly, a set of laws for a new phenomenon that we seek.

A first and tentative step is to look for real-world systems of a fairly conventional and simple kind and to see if we can state what is happening in these systems when they are working well. In the list of hypotheses which follow, I have made some use of what goes on in business organizations and other formal work systems, but I have made at least as much use of what I think goes on in settings we don't often think about as relevant to management studies. I mean athletic organizations, performing arts (such as music, theater, and dance), and various craft specialties.

In the list of hypotheses that follows, it is probably possible to group the several statements in some more organized way than I have. But I have refrained from this because I think a taxonomy is premature.

Forty-Four Hypotheses

1. One may observe a great deal of experimentation and rehearsal in an HPS. Various ways of operating the system are tried. There

seems to be only temporary fixation (if at all) on "the one best way" to operate the system.

2. No one kind of human behavior dominates the system. There is a considerable amount of shifting around among various manual and mental activities.

3. One may note members of the system paying a great deal of attention to "arranging the environment" within which activity is going to occur. Things have to be "just right." Failure to achieve the right arrangement of environmental conditions is sometimes cause for system members to fail to begin the activity, or to terminate it abruptly.

4. A private language and set of symbols arise among members of the system for talking about its conduct and problems. These language systems relate to the nuances and complexities of the system's operation. These language systems are often thought to be unintelligible jargon by outside observers, 'who miss the functionality of the language.

5. Members evolve a set of indices of system performance which are system-specific and which may not relate easily to any other system, even one which is superficially identical.

6. When the system is not operating satisfactorily, relative to members system-specific performance criteria they become greatly agitated and upset. The consequences of "failure" often seem to observers to be greatly magnified. Observers may feel members "take things too seriously."

7. There may be a public, objective theory or "rule book" about how to do the thing that the HPS is doing, but there will always be discrepancies between this public recipe and what the HPS is actually doing. This may be called the "Doug Sanders backswing" hypothesis.

8. The initial involvement in the activity of the HPS will often have been voluntary for members, and have occurred at a relatively young age. At some point the member will have "turned pro."

9. Where there are three or more people involved in a particular HPS, a set of explicit values and ideologies about what the system does and why will tend to arise.

10. Communication from members to outsiders about how and why the HPS operates as it does will tend to be in platitudes and generalities, or by showing rather than telling. Members will feel and often say, "There is no way I can explain it to you."

11. Hours of work, intensities of effort, and other style variables will tend to be determined by the imperatives of Hypotheses 1, 2, 3, 4, 5, 6, and 8, rather than by external agencies which ostensibly "govern" the system.

12. Members will report "peak experiences" in connection with their participation in the HPS. They will "enthuse," "bubble," communicate "joy" and "exultation."

13. Performance breakthroughs occur in unplanned ways. Hypothesis 12 will be especially obvious on these occasions. Members will account for the event in relatively non-operational idioms, such as "we finally got it all together."

14. The inanimate elements of the system are often anthropomorphized by members of an HPS. Machines become people. Various elements are assumed to have a psychology all their own which a member feels he must relate himself to. (For example, ships are always women.)

15. A personal relationship between himself and his equipment is therefore felt to develop by a member. ("A pole is a very personal thing to a pole vaulter"—Bob Seagren)

16. Observers may come to feel that members "live, eat, sleep, and breathe" the activity. This perception on the part of observers is an important clue to the existence of an HPS in the vicinity.

17. External controls on the activity of the HPS are seen by members as at best irrelevant, and at worst as positive impediments to performance. Circumvention of the rules tends to be overt and non-apologetic.

18. Members may seem to possess general abilities which can be transferred to other systems. This assumption is often incorrect. A .350 hitter is not just a .350 hitter, typically, but a .350 in a context.

19. The system does not have a clear OFF/ON character. Members may regard it as ON when it seems OFF to observers, and OFF when it seems ON.

20. Members seek relief from the pressures of participation in the HPS according to criteria which are internal to the system-its current phase of operations and the needs and expectations of other members. External schedules for relief and breaks are usually regarded by members as inappropriate.

21. In HPS's, the activities involved in task performance and the activities involved in fellowship and the maintenance of social solidarity within the system may be the *same* activities to a much greater extent than in non-HPS's.

22. Leaders in HPS's will tend to be persons who are perceived by members as experts in the techniques of the system's basic activity. Leaders' initial status, influence, credibility, and prestige will derive from the demonstration of their expertise.

22a. Leaders of HPS's will not be "generalists"-i.e., perceived by members as no longer fully expert in performing the system's basic activities.

22b. The process of leadership in an HPS will tend to be by example and precept. Leaders will be perceived by members as "pacesetters."

23. Members of HPS's will exhibit a consciousness of the history, tradition, and lore of the system's activity and perhaps of the particular system itself (e.g., "putting on the Yankee pinstripes"). Members' consciousness of the system's lore may persist long after a particular system has ceased to be an HPS.

23a. Where there are many systems performing a similar set of activities, a "hall of fame" phenomenon will arise. Membership in the hall of fame will tend to be associated with membership in an HPS.

24. The social value of the output of an HPS is problematic. Entities in the HPS's environment will not automatically be "pleased" with its output.

24a. Efforts on the part of entities in the HPS's environment to call forth a particular kind and quality of output will tend to depress motivation in the HPS unless the function described in Hypothesis 25 is performed with extraordinary care and effectiveness.

25. HPS's will tend to evolve various boundary roles for mediating their relations with the environment: managers, handlers, advance men, press agents, etc.

26. Members of HPS's will tend to discover potentialities in their technology and their separate talents which are not predictable by observers or deducible by examining the characteristics of various elements taken singly.

27. Members will be found adding to and elaborating upon the inanimate objects of an HPS. They will invent a variety of jigs, props, fixtures, and signaling devices which function to improve their relation to the inanimate objects, make the inanimate objects work better or last longer.

28. Members tend to engage in a wide range of maintenance activities on themselves and on the inanimate elements of the system. Maintenance is co-mingled with performance and is not experienced by members as a necessarily separate function.

29. Performances may be called forth from the inanimate side of the system in an HPS which may seem to observers to be impossible. Physical laws may seem to be broken. Such is not the case; rather the true constraints of physical laws are misperceived by observers, owing to Hypothesis 30.

30. Unless an observer is a trained performer, s/he cannot detect all the actions which go into the operation of the system, and often s/he cannot detect any but the most overt and prominent actions.

30a. Some observers will be fascinated by the hidden character of system actions and will evolve research techniques (e.g., videotape instant replay) for investigating the system's operation more closely. HPS's in particular will excite such curiosity. Some observers will become knowledgeable "buffs" regarding an HPS's action and may come to play critical boundary roles with respect to the system's wider environment.

31. Members may tend to develop scenarios of desirable states for the HPS to be in. A considerable amount of apparently meaningless behavior can be explained as attempts to realize these scenarios. The function of all such attempts is to prepare members to participate in the system's operation and to sustain them through its difficult moments.

32. In terms of McLuhan's Hypothesis that some technologies are "hot" in the sense that their effect on a person requires little physical/psychological participation by him/her, members of HPS's will tend to experience the technologies of their systems as relatively "cool," i.e., that the meaning of the activity is in the doing of it.

33. Members of an HPS may tend to have a powerful esthetic experience regarding the inanimate objects of the system and/or the system's operation. As this process unfolds for members, they may acquire esthetic motivation with respect to the system and *seek* the experience rather than merely receive it.

34. Hypothesis 33 may be broadened to suggest that kinds of motivation may be found in HPS's which are not detectable in other settings. To the extent that members find participation in the HPS thrilling, they may become "thrill seekers." Activity in the HPS may provide a wide variety of sensual, affective, and cognitive experiences which, over time, members may become "motivated" to attain and re-experience. For the most part, these kinds of motivation may be relatively incomprehensible to observers, who may come to regard members-so-motivated as "weirdos" or "mystics."

35. When an HPS ceases to perform to the degree of effectiveness that it had been, members will go through various stages of feeling and behavior in reaction to the decline. One such stage will be the phenomenon of "pressing."

36. When a person has been the leader of an HPS for an extended period, s/he will become a quasi-mythical figure, embodying in her/his person much of the meaning which the work of the HPS has for members and aficionados.

37. Processes of attention in system members will have some attributes that are absent or dormant in non-H PS's:

37a. The sense of the passage of time will correlate with the perceived temporal process of system performances and will not be a set of awarenesses apart from system operation. In short, boredom and anticipatory anxiety will tend to be absent.

37b. The meaning to a member of his/her own and other members' behavior will be a function of system activities rather than a function of "personal values" or the norms of the wider culture.

37c. Many behaviors will be automatic such that members cannot account later for how or why they did them.

38. Marvin Weisbord has suggested that in HPS's people have ways of keeping track of how they're doing that may be internal and very personal, i.e., involving a highly personalized coding system that may have little meaning to anyone else.

39. HPS's exhibit a rhythm of operation which is both subjectively felt by members 'and objectively evident to observers. An argot will exist for describing this rhythm; for example, "tempo" (chess); "footing" (yacht racing); "wailing" (improvisational jazz); also, "getting it on" and "grooving"-and note that "grooving" has been extended in its application to many other activities; "taking it to . . . (the opposing team)," "traction" (term coined by W. Baldamus to account for the tendency of an assembly line job to pull the worker along); "hitting one's stride;" "having a hot hand" (basketball); and "mounting a charge" (golf). The general phenomenon that these terms refer to is that the same or improved effects are produced with substantially less effort than before the particular rhythm was achieved.

40. In every HPS, there will be observable a phenomenon, named differently depending on the system, which refers to what in sports is called "execution", i.e., an umbrella word which covers a system of actions which have to be performed with considerable precision in relation to each other.

41. HPS's will pay more attention to the initiation processes of new members than will comparable systems (i.e., engaged in the same activity) which are less successful. Initiation processes will have many non-logical components. To external observers they may appear to be silly, childish, etc.

42. Members of the HPS will become skilled real time observers of the process by which the HPS is doing whatever it is doing. RTOP will be regarded as a principal member responsibility. There may be some role differentiation around this function, i.e., certain members are expected to be especially watchful.

43. HPS's will be observed to manage with extreme care the process by which tools and personnel are changed. HPS's may appear to be quite "conservative" to observers, i.e., not readily embracing new methods, techniques, personnel, etc. There may be an overt philosophy of "do not tinker with a good thing." Members will be concerned about not disturbing the experienced equilibrium of the system. (See Hypothesis 39 about rhythm.)

44. HPS's will tend to be both aware of their dependencies on environmental elements *and* relatively uncaring of the amount of effort expended or cost incurred by these environmental elements in order to serve the HPS. In a word, HPS's will exhibit an attitude of "non-guilty exploitation" toward environmental elements which supply them with critical inputs.

A Sobering Exercise

Why speculate at such length about what is going on inside what I have called a high-performing system? The basic answer is that if I can understand such systems better, the problem of improving the performance of human or organizations may be eased. As noted in the list of assumptions with which this discussion began, social scientists and managers are presently groping forward toward improved performance levels without having in mind any norms of what is really possible. It is possible that at least some of these hypothesized properties of HPS's may provide such norms-targets, as it were, to shoot at. It is a sobering exercise to go over the list of 44 hypotheses stated above and ask in connection with each one: To what extent are we inadvertently managing our organizations today in such a way as to prevent the emergence of the particular condition the hypothesis is about? We espouse a philosophy of high performance. Our management and leadership literature is full of it. But do we *manage* and *lead* in such a way as to achieve the hypothesized conditions?

CHAPTER 30

Chaos and Complexity
What Can Science Teach?
Margaret Wheatley

Everywhere around us and within us we experience complexity and diversity.

Everywhere around us and within us we experience change, death, and renewal; order and chaos; growth and decay that becomes new life.

Everywhere around us and within us we see pattern upon pattern, ever-deepening levels of complexity and variety.

Why do we resist the vision or blind ourselves to the beauty or fail to embrace the learnings

EACH OF US lives and works in organizations designed from 17th-century images of the universe. The universe of Isaac Newton and Francis Bacon was a seductive place filled with clockwork images promising us prediction and reliability, teaching us to view everything, including ourselves, as machines. We learned to manage by separating things into parts. We engaged in planning for our future that we would determine. We sought for more and more precise and correct measures of a world we thought was objective.

For three centuries we *have* been planning, predicting, and analyzing the world. We have held on to an intense belief of cause and effect, and we have let numbers rule our lives. But at the end of the 20th century, our 17th-century organizations are crumbling. Our world grows more disturbing and mysterious. Our failures to predict and control leer back at us from many places. Yet to what else can we turn? If our world is not predictable, then our approaches cannot work. But then, where are we?

Our organizations are strong complicated structures that are resistant to change, fearful of the future, and we have built them that way deliberately. We built them that way to hold back the forces that seem to threaten their very existence. We are afraid of what would happen if we lose our grip. If we let the elements of our organizations recombine or reconfigure or even to speak truthfully to one another, we are afraid that things will fall apart. We do not trust that this is a world of growth, rejuvenation, and process. We believe we must provide the energy to hold it together. By sheer force of will, we have resisted destruction. And if we let go, the world will disintegrate.

Yet, throughout the universe, things work very well without us. Wherever we look, we see a landscape of movement and complexity, of forms that come and go, of structures that are not from organizational charts or job descriptions, but from impulses arriving out of deep natural processes of growth and of self-renewal. In our desire to control our organizations, we have detached ourselves from the forces that create order in the universe. All these years we have confused control with order. So what if we reframed the search? What if we stop looking for control and begin the search for order, which we can see everywhere around us in living dynamic systems?

It is time, I believe, to become a community of inquirers, serious explorers seeking to discover the essence of order—order we will find even in the heart of chaos. It is time to relinquish the limits we have placed on our organizations, time to release our defenses and fear. Time to take up new lenses and explore beyond our known boundaries. It is time to become full participants in this universe of emergent order.

To the early Greeks, the universe that they inhabited was peopled with many primordial beings. The first two founding parents of all that we observe in life were two gods: Chaos, the original abyss of darkness, and Gaea, the earth mother, the generative force. These two partners worked in tandem. Gaea knew that she would be unable to create anything that was alive without reaching into the dark abyss of Chaos and pulling forth what she needed from there to give form to life. These are very different assumptions about the workings of chaos and order than those that have played into our work.

To start, I would like to say that we function as a community of people who still want to make a difference. People who really want to change life in organizations for all of us. Who really want organizations to feel alive and worth working in, and adaptive and resilient; organizations that no longer worry about managing change, but instead, realize that change is a constant process of life. I assume that's who we are.

Given the assumption of our good hearts and our good intent, there are several other assumptions that, when I look at it, are severely hampering our work. I am going to list three, some of which are fading in potency already. But I also know how deep these assumptions are embedded in me personally.

Assumption 1: Organizations Are Machines

The first assumption is that organizations are, in fact, dead. They are machines. This is the 17th-century imagery of Sir Isaac Newton, that the world is a clockwork machine. We have really bought this one! Just look at our language. We have tools and techniques. We have technologies. We have methodologies. We have mechanisms. We have levers for change. We have hands-on applications. It is really hard to avoid using a machine metaphor. I have tried to avoid it and they still just creep right in. It's part of our deep thought process. From Chandler to Michael Porter, people who have made enormous contributions to organizational strategy all came from engineering backgrounds. And today, what do we have? Reengineering! I hope this is the last gasp of the machine model.

Assumption 2: Change Happens as a Result of External Influences

The second assumption that we've labored under is that change happens as a result of some external influence. Here again, our language is quite revealing. We consider ourselves to be change agents or change masters. Our whole field of organizational development says that organizations need to be developed by us—who else but us. Change, in this assumption, is something we do. We make it happen. We impose it on the organization. We have long discussions on where to intervene—do you start at the top, do you start at the bottom, or do you hope for the middle? We talk about strategies that need to cascade down throughout the whole organization. We talk about training designs in which everyone must participate. We see the change as some external force that is imposed on this inert lump of an organization.

Assumption 3: Things Fall Apart

The third assumption is the one that I personally find the hardest to let go of—it is that "things fall apart." It is the natural tendency of all living things, as our culture has taught us. We subscribe to the second law of thermodynamics (which we have misunderstood but have deeply taken into our consciousness) that the natural state of everything is to decline and die, and to turn to rust in front of our eyes.

And that the only way to avoid this tendency toward deterioration and death is to come in with our good creative energy and impose it on the system.

This has been a very fearsome and costly posture for all of Western culture. But it is this great belief that, "without me, the world doesn't work." If you talk to me about letting go of control, it means the world is going to fail. I don't know what else this is if it's not playing God, and that is a fearsome prospect.

These assumptions blind us to some very wonderful truths.

Truth 1: Organizations Are Living, Dynamic Systems

The first truth, which you have discovered in your own work, is that it is much more fun to view organizations as living, dynamic, breathing systems with a life of their own. These are wonderful beings, these organizations. We do not understand them but if we think of them as alive, a whole different approach is available to us.

Truth 2: Change Is an Inherent Capacity of Living Systems

The second truth is that change is an inherent capacity of living systems. All of us are here, no matter what we are on the planet, no matter what kind of life form we are, have a deeply embedded process to create ourselves, to maintain ourselves and to change ourselves if required, to survive. I do not think other living systems take classes on "resistance to change." But I do not know, because I do not communicate with them. We need to start observing that change is a process that we are capable of and that perhaps we even know how to handle, if we could clear away this debris of 20th-century thinking.

Truth 3: Order Is Inherent in the Universe

Lastly, our deep assumptions have prevented us from seeing that order is inherent in the universe. There is in each of us a tendency to organize toward greater and greater levels of order or complexity.

The Search for New Lenses

"Are we doing significant, authentic work? Are we not polluting organizations by our presence?" In working with other consultants, I noticed how rare it was for consultants to feel they had accomplished something of value that was going to last. There was far too much change, far too much turbulence. Nothing held long enough to see a result. And among consultants that I talked with, there was always wonder if something really worked.

Four years ago, I embarked on work that was new and interesting, which I approached very fearfully. I was intrigued by natural science. I think there are many places to look for new ways of seeing, and I realized as I entered into that inquiry, that something was required of me that I wasn't quite ready to do. What was required was moving into a state of "not knowing," to be willing to give up the tools and techniques by which I had made my bread and butter. I wrote about this need to throw everything I knew into an abyss and to face the unknown. I must say that a few years down the road now I actually find this process fun. It has gotten to the point where I can say, "Well, what else can we throwaway? Let's look for a deeper level of certainty here and let go of it." It was Voltaire, the French philosopher, who said, "Doubt is not a very pleasant status, but certainty is a ridiculous one."

Also I have had some experience now in letting go of some very tried-and-true techniques and being out there in an experimental mode. And it does take a particular kind of client to experiment. I say that as a casual offhand remark, but the whole foundation for why any of us can do anything different is that clients are willing to step into the void with us. But I have seen many encouraging signs. I have witnessed large groups engaged in a self-organizing process that did not need us as expert facilitators. I have seen people who were tired and cynical and just plain fed up, become hopeful and engaged because the work that they were engaged in was work of creation and not problem solving. I have seen learnings spread through an organization with a speed that no theory ever predicted. And I've seen people become advocates of the power of learning that is available to them when they are willing to stay in a process that is fuzzy, ambiguous and open.

Now I painted that real fast brushstroke of things that feel interesting to me and even wondrous at times. I say this only to indicate what Joel Barker has been saying for years, that "What is difficult or impossible with one paradigm may be easy with another." Einstein said something very similar. He said, "No problem can be solved from the same consciousness that created it."

So what is this shift in consciousness that is required of us and what is the true paradigm that needs to change? I believe that it is a simple but profound world shattering recognition that we do inhabit a well-ordered universe. It functions well, even without us. Stewart Kaufmann, a scientist working in complexity theory, has said, "This is a world where you get order for free." Order arises spontaneously when you create simple connections. If you require simple connections among thousands upon thousands of individual elements, a pattern of organization emerges. We get order for free.

This discovery of order has moved most dramatically in the past 20 years in the area of science first known as chaos. Now it is a more complex science. Of course, mystics in every spiritual tradition have known about this order for a very long time.

Finding Order in Chaos

One of the great gifts that chaos science provides is that order is found in chaos. A system in chaos is defined as a system that, from moment to moment, is totally unpredictable. You cannot predict where it is going next. With the creation of three-dimensional space on high-speed computers, scientists could plot the movement of a system in chaos. When plotted on a two-dimensional scale, it looked totally unpredictable-like an EKG gone berserk. But when converted into multidimensional space, you could track many variables at once. The system, from moment to moment, zoomed from one part of the screen to another. You could not predict what would happen next. But over time, you came to realize that the system conformed to a boundary. It had an inherent shape that it did not violate. It would not move out of this boundary. Plots that are simple, nonlinear equations, over much iteration and after tracking behavior over a very long time, produced symmetrical patterns. Those images have been named "strange attractors." There are many other kinds of attractors in science. These were called strange by two scientists who said, "It was a suitable and psychologically suggestive name for these objects of astonishing beauty of which we know so·little."

I think there are some very important learnings in chaos.

Lesson 1: You Cannot See Order in Chaos Moment to Moment

You cannot see the order in chaos if you are looking moment to moment. You cannot see order if you are micromanaging. You cannot see order if you are managing individual behaviors. These strange attractors draw attention to one of the great paradoxes of chaos science, which is that you get order without predictability. I urge you to think about that statement. We did not grow up believing you got order if you were not predicting it, controlling it and making it happen. So how do you get order without predictability? Through a strange combination of a rule of randomness, which at the human level is individual autonomy, and a rule of specification. There is an initial formula or equation. But you combine this initial formula with individual behavior. If you look moment to moment, you will not see a pattern. You will see what looks like a system out of control because the behavior jumps all over the place. But, if you stand back far enough, if you wait over time, scale or distance, you will observe the order that is in chaos. If we do that, then we can see the pattern.

Lesson 2: Chaos Breeds Self-Organization and Creativity

A second learning from the science of chaos is that chaos serves a function. It is in the darkness of chaos that our self-organizing processes, our creativity, comes forth. I would like you to think about a time in your life when you were confronted with a real darkness—a dark night of the soul, a time of utter confusion, a feeling you could not make sense of the world anymore in a way that you were accustomed to. Depression is a frequent companion to these events in our lives. Think about what happened to you, the other side of your own personal chaos. What was available to you in terms of your experience and self-identity, once you had passed through this dark night of chaos? Now, there are two paths that one can take. The first is the path toward destruction and death. The other is the path that moves through chaos to a greater sense of peace, of enhanced capacity, knowing you can handle life that you have survived. Some people feel quite pleased with their learning, they feel a new sense of hope. They return to a state that feels calm. That is the lesson of the uses of chaos for self-organization.

We believed in the path of the second law of thermodynamics: that any system moving into chaos was on the road to certain death. There was only one way the rough and that was pretty awful. At the end of the 1970s, Ilya Prigogene won the Nobel Prize for exploring what happens to living organic systems when confronted with high levels of stress and turbulence. He found that they reached a point in which they let go of their present structure. They fell apart, they disintegrated. But they had two choices. They could die or reorganize themselves in a self-organizing process and truly transform their ability, their capacity to function well in their changing environment.

This self-organizing process feeds on information that is new, disturbing and different. We are confronted with information we cannot fit into the present structure, and our first response to that kind of information (whether we are molecules or CEOs) is to discount it. We push it away. But the information becomes so large and meaningful that the system cannot hold it, then the system will fall apart. But it will fall apart with the opportunity to reconfigure itself around this new information in a way that is more adaptive and healthier. It can suddenly explode, grow and change.

Erich Jantsch, a systems scientist, said that "self-organization lets us feel a quality of the world which gives birth to ever new forms against a background of constant change." That giving birth to ever new forms against a background of constant change is my personal quest for organizations. How do you create the self-organizing process? I am not going to give you answers; I don't have them yet. I think this is part of our work for the next decade. But there is something about the uses of chaos that could profoundly change our work right now. If self-organization is only available through this passage into chaos, then we need to be very thoughtful about how to create chaos intentionally at the right moment in our organizational interventions. You cannot get true transformation without chaos. Because in chaos, when people are overwhelmed, confused and fed up with you as a facilitator, they let go. And what they let go of is their present construction of reality. They hate being confused, but then something happens in which the intelligence and creativity of the group comes together and what they get is a transforming result.

This is a really difficult learning for 20th century Western folks who feel so good at getting themselves out of hard spaces. But, in fact, we need to encourage more of the workings of chaos in our personal lives and in our organizational interventions. It is a very powerful force.

Lesson 3: Complexity Arises from Simplicity

The third learning of complexity science is that at the heart of complex systems is simplicity. Complexity seems to evolve from very simple patterns that build on one another. When we were all saddled with Euclidean geometry, we looked for perfect forms. We looked for perfect spheres, cubes, triangles, boxes, organization charts, etc., all of which are perfect Euclidean creations (useless as the geometry of Euclid was to explain what was really going on in real life). Benoit Mandelbrot, who coined the word "fractal," said, "Look around us. Mountains are not cones, clouds are not spheres and lightening does not fall in a straight line. How can we understand this complexity of form that we are seeing?" He concluded that if you try and look for a pattern and look deeply into the object, you will see that the pattern repeats itself at different levels of scale. But if you identify the pattern, you have identified the essence of that very complex shape.

I want to look at a few natural fractals with you. A fern is a classic object because the dominant fern pattern is repeated on the fronds. Patterns in the branches of trees are replicas of the whole tree. As you look at finer and finer levels of scale you see the patterns repeating. Look for the dominant shape in clouds and see if you can identify the shape in smaller segments. This is another way of understanding the geometry of mountains, clouds, beaches, forests and such.

This notion of looking for patterns as a way of dealing with complexity is quite profound. Instead of looking for linear solutions to problems, take a nonlinear approach. Look at behavior over time. Formulas are a process to be unfolded. Examine the behavior of an unpredictable evolving formula in the space of a computer. It reveals a deep inner creativity which is woven in the very fabric of existence. One of the great thrills of fractal observation is that it is very much like looking out into the night sky but reversing the projection. As you look deeply into a fractal, you

are exploring regions that never end. And wherever you look, you will always see the same pattern.

There is something to be said here about identifying and managing patterns in organizations rather than managing people. I hope I am laying the groundwork for years to come, moving away from a focus on individuals to a focus on what are the key behaviors, patterns that we want to have in place in this organization and in the great dream of a fractal organization, we would see that behavior everywhere we looked. If we peered deeply into the organization, we would see the same pattern in place. I have worked with senior leaders who are very intent on trying to figure out the patterns of behavior they would like in place, and help them to realize that their task is to ensure that those patterns are well known and to remove themselves from the day-to-day management of individual behavior.

Now I have gone rather quickly through some very profound sciences, but those three key sensibilities, whether you take the sciences literally or metaphorically are that, first, in the heart of chaos, order is available. When you change how you look at the system, bringing in time, distance and multiple dimensions, you can see order. Second, chaos is the root to creativity. And without the passage of chaos and letting go, we cannot hope to truly transform anybody's thinking. Third, complexity can be understood as some very simple patterns or some very simple rules of interaction, which, over time, create wonderfully complex forms.

Transformation Through Information

Ikujiro Nonaka, a Japanese theorist who has been looking at chaos and self-organization for a few years now, said, "Whether or not an order is formed depends on whether or not information is created. The essence of order is in the creation of information." This is a profound quote. What is challenging about this is that this is not the way senior executives think about information.

They do not see it as an ally in their search for order; they see it as a resource that must be carefully controlled in order to maintain their sense of order for their organization. But, if we truly want an organization to organize itself, to do it without the imposition of structures and plans and reengineering and templates and models, then we have to build a very different theory of information in organizations.

In the old model, information is power. If I choose not to reveal to you my sources, or what I know, or the timing of when I tell you something—I have power. We have used information as a way of controlling other people's behavior in organizations. We have held onto it very tightly. We have also used it to regulate behavior. To see if we are meeting plans, to see if we have met our goals, to see if our processes are up to performance standards. We have seen information as negative, as regulatory feedback that provides us with data so that we can correct our behavior and get back to where we want to be. That kind of information does not take us into the future; it does not take us into any transforming processes.

The kind of information that does create fundamental shifts in the self-organizing system is always information that it does not want to hear. It is information that is new and disconfirming, that is difficult and challenging. Chaos is a state of information richness. One of the switches we made in our understanding of chaos is that it is no longer an abyss—it is filled with information that we cannot make sense of. Self-organizing systems only change when they are confronted with information that they cannot absorb into their existing structure. Or in Senge's words, would change when we could not absorb the information into our existing mental model. Claude Shannon, one of the early information theorists, said that "Information is that which changes us." Even in his definition there is this senses that if you want change, you have to have information. You cannot change without

it. Only when we allow organizations to look at troubling information and trust people within them to reorganize around that information that we get truly transforming levels of change. Only then can we get self-organization. What self-organization is saying is that the structure will emerge to fit the situation. If people have sufficient information and sufficient knowledge and good levels of skill for thinking, they will then form around the information. Their structure will change, it will be temporary, and it will be fluid.

However, most organizations do not trust their people to act as adults. The other stumbling block to using information as an organizing element is our great fear or our great belief that you cannot have order without predictability.

The Questions We Need to Ask

I want to close by putting out a few more areas in which a lot of thinking needs to be done. David Ruelle, who is a chaos scientist (now they are known as "chaologists"), said about his work in chaos, "My answers are modest and tentative but worth knowing" I would like to say that the questions I want to leave us with are tentative but worth asking:

Question 1: If we could manage complex organizations by simple patterns then how would that shift our work?

We would probably become much more seriously engaged in looking at processes that support the creation and sustenance of patterns. We would have to make sure that the right ones are in place. How do you know they are the right ones? Well, you examine their effects over time. This is tricky stuff.

We would also need to encourage the leadership of the organization to ensure that these patterns are consistent, that their concern is to manage the pattern, not the people. This is a vast area for inquiry and experimentation.

Question 2: If chaos is the root to truly transforming organizations, then how confident and supportive can we be about processes that use chaos intentionally?

I have to admit that I have worked with chaos science for a few years and intentional chaos with organizations for a year and a half and for the first year, every time a group went into chaos, I panicked. I wanted to whip out the flip charts and the markers and structure them into feelings of security. It is a very difficult experience at the beginning to use chaos, because everything in us screams that something has gone very wrong. But each of us does have these experiences in our own lives of having seen the good effect of chaos. So we need to be, as one scientist asked managers to be, "equilibrium busters." We need to realize, as Burt Nanus said in *The Leader's Edge,* "If you're not confused, you're not thinking clearly."

Pushing for Chaos

I am pushing for more messiness, greater confusion, and greater ambiguity. We need to figure out how to create disconfirming information in our organizations and keep it present. We need scanning devises. We need to keep talking to more and more people who have a stake in the organization. We need to realize that diversity is the way in which life creates itself. Diversity is what is at the root of all life and we need to find ways to realize that it is the source of our creativity in organizations. It's a much bigger issue than we even thought.

My last assertion is that if information is the source of new order, then we need *very* different theories of information. We need to let down our barriers in organizations, and in ourselves. We need to move to a position taken by Gore Associates (manufacturers of Gortex), who use the metaphor that information is like salmon they just had to release it. Salmon find their spawning grounds. Flush them into the system and see where they go. We need a different imagery around information.

Where We Are Now

Many learnings of chaos science are new, but I also want to recognize the elders who have gone before. In the 1940s, when Eric Trist was looking into what happened in coal mines in Great Britain, he noticed what is essentially a self-organizing process. In reading about the early years of OD, people talked about the magic, the sense of discovery, and the sense of invention. When flip charts and markers were the greatest thing because of what they allowed you to do, when suddenly you were focused on human issues and process and you were building networks among human beings rather than these old rigorous, scientific management, engineering models. The beauty of being part of that discovery was what was really compelling. I believe that kind of hope is available to us again. I believe that kind of gift of new visions, which allow us to peer more deeply into organizations and make sense of them in an age where there is not a lot of sense to be had, I believe that is available to us through many different lenses.

I like new science, so I use that. We could peer deeply into organizations through many different disciplines, but we cannot peer more deeply and with more efficacy and better *resolve* if we hold on to what has made us great. Some of these pathways have been established for us in the past 50 years, and yet the new lenses are different. We are no longer just peering into groups, we are peering into the universe-a universe whose order we barely noticed and seldom trusted in our work. So, to embrace these new visions, these new learnings, I think will take years of serious inquiry that I also hope is playful. True paradigm shifts are really hard.

Joel Barker also taught us that when the paradigm shifts, we all go down to zero. Past expertise does not carryover. This is a troubling truth. But we may be at a point in our field where everything, or almost everything that has made us who we are, that has made us useful is not going to work anymore. To stand at the edge of that abyss and to throw in our tools and techniques and to know that out of that process something more wonderful, more useful, more helpful can come, I believe, is the real challenge. It's not going to be solved in one conference; this is the work of our lifetime. As organizations are letting go of bureaucracy, we need to let go of the engineering machine imagery, which, at this point, is crippling us.

My Hopes

Here are some hopes. I do not want "self-organization" to become a buzzword. We cannot just take our existing techniques and say, "OK, this is a self-organizing process." We cannot say that self-managing teams are necessarily self-organizing processes. We need to keep the lens open and peer into these learnings more seriously.

I hope we do this with care and rigor. That we just do not superficially glean onto chaos or self-organization or complexity. I hope that this community of inquiry builds on our knowledge and experience so that we truly feel in a community together. I hope that each of us is willing to throw into the abyss the tools and techniques and applications, re-engineering—all of these things that are a holdover from a metaphor that doesn't make sense of the world anymore. In the midst of these hopes that I have for the profession is the good news of chaos! And the good news of chaos is that this is a very well ordered world. In his own inquiries into the whole strangeness of quantum physics, John Archibald Wheeler, the physicist, expressed a hope that I share: "To my mind, there must be at the bottom of it all, not an equation or a formula, but an utterly simple idea. And to me that idea when finally we discover it, will be so compelling, so inevitable, that we will say to one another, 'Oh, how beautiful. How could it have been otherwise?'"

CHAPTER 31

The Postmodern Turn in OD

Gervase Bushe and Robert J. Marshak

RECENT YEARS have witnessed an emerging set of OD practices based on premises that are different from key assumptions of the founders. In this article we want to identify this new form of OD and bring the underlying assumptions into the mainstream of theory and practice.

Different Forms of OD

Many of the premises underlying the original or *classical* formulation of OD are based in modernist science. Classical OD assumes that a team or organization can be studied using empirical methods before intervening. Starting with Lewin the commitment to scientific inquiry may well be why OD is one of the few fields of consulting practice to also be recognized as a scholarly discipline. In many writings, and virtually all OD textbooks, the purpose of data gathering is described as "diagnosis"—the organization exists as an entity that needs examination prior to prescribing remedies. That formulation links with another element of classical OD, the emphasis on the organization as an open or living system. Classical OD assumes that like real living systems, if we can understand the interdependence between all parts of the organization and its environment, we can identify how it all ought to work together to produce the best outcomes.

Postmodern forms of OD think about organizations differently. Without denying the utility of open systems theory, a dialogical narrative has supplanted the organic one. Intervening into the meaning making process is the objective. In any large group there are multiple realities so any data collected is used not to identify the problem, or *the truth*, but to raise collective awareness of the multitude of perspectives at play in the system and/or the meaning making process itself. Table 31.1 summarizes some of the contrasts between what we are calling classical OD and newer forms, or postmodern OD.

Another difference to note is classical OD's focus on changing behavior. Postmodern OD practices focus on changing what people think, instead of focusing on changing behavior, with the assumption that once people change how they make sense of things they will change their own behavior. Table 31.2 provides a suggestive list of some current OD practices that might be considered, in whole or in part, to include postmodern forms of OD.

Continuing OD Values

While postmodern forms of OD have different assumptions about what can be changed and how, they continue to embrace classical OD's humanistic and democratic values. These values and ideals are reflected in the empowering and collaborative nature of postmodern OD practices, the facilitative and enabling role of the consultant, and the underlying goal of developing and enhancing organizations and broader social systems.

TABLE 31.1 Contrasting Forms of OD

	Classical OD:	Postmodern OD:
Differences	Influenced by classical science and modernist thought and philosophy	Influenced by the new sciences and postmodern thought and philosophy
	Organization as living system	Organization as meaning making system
	Reality is an objective fact	Reality is socially constructed
	There is a single reality	There are multiple realities
	Truth is transcendent and discoverable	Truth is immanent and emerges from the situation
	Reality can be discovered using rational and analytic processes	Reality is socially negotiated
	Collecting and applying valid data using objective problem-solving methods leads to change	Raising collective awareness and generating new possibilities and social agreements leads to change
	Emphasis on changing behavior and what people do	Emphasis on changing mindsets and what people think
Similarities	Strong humanistic and democratic values	
	Consultants stay out of content and focus on process	
	A concern for capacity building and development of the system	

TABLE 31.2 Examples of Postmodern OD Practices

- Practices based on social constructionism such as Appreciative Inquiry
- Practices used in large group interventions to seek and achieve common ground
- Practices intended to change the consciousness of leaders and organizations
- Practices used to recognize, work with and address multi-cultural realities
- Discursive practices such as dialog, narrative, sense-making, changing conversations, etc.

OD consultants operating from postmodern premises use methods consistent with traditional OD ideals like free and informed choice, authenticity and congruence, participative democracy, trust and collaboration. Postmodern OD processes often attempt to circumvent the power of entrenched groups to equalize the variety of interests represented in the system, giving everyone as much equal footing in the co-construction of new realities as possible. The role of the consultant in postmodern OD is also consistent with facilitating and enabling others as opposed to providing expert advice. Like the classical OD consultant, the postmodern OD consultant's expertise is in understanding human social dynamics and in offering change and decision-making processes that support organizational goals and OD values. The OD consultant, classical or postmodern, is concerned with developing the capacity of the client system and not developing client dependence on the consultant. The consultant therefore stays out of the content and focuses, instead, on processes while members of the system deal with the content.

This emphasis on the consultant's role in capacity building links to the final characteristic all forms of OD share, an interest in *de-*

velopment. There are, at a minimum, three common themes. First, a person, group, organization or network is more developed the greater awareness it has of itself—it can talk to itself about itself. Secondly, in a more developed system, emotional, reactive behavior decreases and rational, goal directed behavior increases. Third, the more developed the system, the better able it is to actualize its potential. These ideas about development are implicit in all forms of OD, although specific practices may differ.

Toward a Definition of Postmodern OD

To help define this burgeoning field of practice we offer in Table 31.3 a set of five characteristics for categorizing postmodern OD.

In brief, rather than collecting data to diagnose a system prior to intervening, postmodern OD creates events that facilitate collective inquiry into the multiple "realities" in order to generate new collective understandings and cognitive maps that will lead to a team's or organization's further self development.

Conclusion

We are witnessing the emergence of new forms of organizing that are co-evolving with the information revolution and it is not surprising that these require new forms of OD. Postmodern forms of OD will not attempt to diagnose systems in the traditional sense so much as attempt to create events where organizational members increase their awareness of the system and how social reality is being constructed by them. This can then lead to the central contribution of postmodern forms of OD: *generativity*, the creation of new possibilities based on new meanings, new ideas and new energy to do something with them.

TABLE 31.3   Basic, Shared Characteristics of Postmodern OD Practices

1. The change process emphasizes changing the conversations that normally take place in the system through changing who is in the conversation, how the conversation is run, and/or what the conversation is about.

2. The change process creates containers for greater total system awareness and self-organization.

3. The purpose of inquiry is to surface, legitimate, and/or learn from the variety of perspectives, cultures, and/or narratives in the system.

4. The change process results in new images, stories, and socially constructed realities that impact how people think and act.

5. he change process is consistent with traditional OD values of collaboration, free and informed choice, and capacity building in the client system.

CHAPTER 32

Corporate Culture

Edgar H. Schein

How to Think About and Define "Culture"

To understand corporate culture one must first understand the concept of culture. A chronic issue in conceptualizing culture is whether to think of culture as a static property of a given organization—its shared customs, beliefs, norms, values, and tacit assumptions or whether to think of culture as a dynamic human process of constructing shared meaning (Frost et al, 1985). Culture creation is one of the unique characteristics of humans, being based on our capacity to be self-conscious and able to see ourselves and others from each others' points of view. It is this reflexive capacity of humans that makes culture possible. At the same time, it is the human need for finding meaning that creates the motivation for culture stabilization. Without some predictability social intercourse becomes too anxiety provoking. Developing shared meanings of how to perceive, categorize, and think about what goes on around us is necessary to avoid the catastrophic anxiety that would result from reacting to everything as if it were a new phenomenon.

Given these human characteristics, it then becomes clear that culture is both a process and a state. In new situations shared meanings must be constructed through a social learning process. As these meanings help the participants to make sense of their world they become stabilized and can be viewed as "states." At the same time, as the members of a group interact, they not only recreate and ratify prior meanings but also construct new meanings as new situations arise.

A useful way to think about this issue is to take a cue from the anthropologist Marshall Sahlins (1985) who argues that one cannot really understand certain social phenomena without understanding both the historical events and the cultural meanings attributed by the actors to those events. While it is undeniably true that we produce and reinforce culture through perpetual enactment and sense making, it is equally true that the actors in those same social events bring to them some prior meanings, stereotypes, and expectations that can only be understood in a historical context. Culture production in the enactment sense, then, is either the perpetuation of or a change of some prior state, but that prior state can be thought of as "the culture" up to that point. And one can describe that culture as if it were a "state" of the existing system, even though one knows that the system is dynamic and perpetually evolving. The direction of that evolution will be a product of several forces: (1) technological and physical changes in the external environment; (2) changes in the internal dynamics of the social system; and (3) historical circumstances that are fortuitous or serendipitous.

For example, let me offer my oversimplified summary of Sahlins' very sophisticated analysis of the death of Captain Cook at the hand of the Hawaiians. Because Captain Cook was viewed as a God (as predicted in the Hawaiian mythology), the sexual favors offered to his sailors by the Hawaiian women were viewed as gifts and as opportunities to relate to the divine. The sailors' cultural background defined this as a version of prostitution, however, for which they felt they should pay. When they offered the women something in exchange for the sex, the women asked for something that was scarce in the society, namely metal. Once the loose metal on board the ships had been used up, the sailors began to pull nails from the ship itself, weakening it structurally. Hence, when Captain Cook set sail he discovered that the ships needed repair and ordered a return to harbor. In Hawaiian mythology a God returning under these circumstances had to be ritually killed. At the same time, Hawaiian social structure was undergoing change and became permanently altered because the subordinate role of women in the society was altered by their ability to acquire metal, a scarce resource that gave them social power.

When one contemplates this wonderful analysis it appear pointless to argue whether culture should be viewed as a state of the system or as a process of enactment. Clearly there was a culture in Hawaii and a different culture on board the British ship, and clearly the interaction of these two cultures produced events that had a profound impact on both of these cultures.

Implications for "Organizational" Culture Analysis

The major lesson of Sahlins' analysis is that when we have access to historical data we should use it. Organizations have defined histories. Therefore, when we analyze organizational cultures we should reconstruct their histories, find out about their founders and early leaders, look for the critical defining events in

their evolution as organizations and be confident that when we have done this we can indeed describe sets of shared assumptions that derive from common experiences of success and/or shared traumas. And we can legitimately think of these sets of assumptions as "the culture" at a given time. That description will include subcultures that may be in conflict with each other, and there may be subunits that have not yet had enough shared experience to have formed shared common assumptions. In other words, culture as a state, does not have to imply unanimity or absence of conflict. There can be some very strongly shared assumptions and large areas of conflict and/or ambiguity (Martin, 1992) within a given cultural "state."

At the same time, we can study the day to day interactions of the members of an organization with each other and with members of other organizations to determine how given cultural assumptions are reinforced and confirmed, or challenged and disconfirmed. We can analyze the impact of these perceptual interactive events in order to understand how cultures evolve and change. This process could be especially productive in mergers, acquisitions, and joint ventures of various sorts. Whether one chooses to focus one's cultural research on building typologies of cultural "states," categories that freeze a given organization at a given point in time, or on analyzing the moment to moment interactions in which members of a given social system attempt to make sense of their experience and, in that process, reinforce and evolve cultural elements, becomes a matter of choice. Both are valid methodologies and in practice they should probably be combined.

A Formal Definition of Culture

Culture as a property or process of any group can now be defined as: A pattern of shared basic assumptions that the group has learned as it solved its problems of external adaptation and internal integration, that has worked well enough to be considered valid and, therefore, to be taught to new members as the correct way to perceive, think, and feel in relation to those problems (Schein, 1992).

Once these patterns have been learned they function to reduce anxiety and provide moment to moment meaning and predictability to daily events. Or, as Trice and Beyer (1993) put it: "Human cultures emerge from people's struggles to manage uncertainties and create some degree of order in social life" (p. 1). Note that patterns of overt behavior are not part of the formal definition because such patterns can be caused by other causes such as common instinctive patterns (e.g., ducking when we hear a loud noise) or by common reactions to a common stimulus (e.g., everyone running in the same direction to avoid some threat). If one understands the shared basic assumptions, one can determine which regularities of behavior are "cultural" and which ones are not. One cannot, however, infer the assumptions just by observing behavior.

A Conceptual Model for Analyzing Culture

Whether one chooses to analyze culture as a state or as a process, it is helpful to differentiate the levels at which culture as a shared phenomenon manifests itself. Any group, organization, or larger social system can be analyzed in terms of: (1) its visible and feelable "artifacts"; (2) its espoused beliefs and values; and/or (3) its less visible, taken for granted shared basic assumptions (see Figure 32.1).

This model is useful in two ways: (1) it helps a novice observer of organizational culture to differentiate the superficial manifestations and espoused values that most organizations display from the cultural substrate or essence, the tacit, shared assumptions that drive the day to day behavior that one observes; and (2) the differentiation of levels is a necessary conceptual tool in helping an organization to decipher its own culture.

To further understand these distinctions, especially the distinction between espoused values and shared tacit assumptions, it is necessary to take a historical evolutionary point of view toward culture formation. If we take a typical business organization, the process starts with one or more entrepreneurs who found a company based on some personal beliefs and values. As they hire others to work with them they will either choose those others on the basis of their compatibility or will socialize newcomers to the beliefs and values that they regard as core to running the new business. The founders' beliefs and values will cause the organization to make decisions in its environment and, if those decisions are successful, the newcomers will begin to entertain collectively the idea that the founder's beliefs and values must be "correct." As the environment continues to reinforce the behavior of the organization, what were originally the

FIGURE 32.1 The Levels of Culture

ARTIFACTS

The Visible, Hearable, Feelable Manifestations of the Underlying Assumptions (e.g., Behavior Patterns, Rituals, Physical Environment, Dress Codes, Stories, Myths, Products, etc.)

SHARED VALUES

The Espoused Reasons for Why Things Should be as they are (e.g., Charters, Goal Statements, Norms, Codes Of Ethics, Company Value Statements)

SHARED BASIC ASSUMPTIONS

The Invisible but Surfaceable Reasons Why Group Members Perceive, Think, and Feel The Way They Do about External Survival and Internal Integration Issues (e.g., Assumptions About Mission, Means, Relationships, Reality, Time, Space, etc.)

founder's personal beliefs and values gradually come to be shared and imposed on new members as the organization grows. If this success cycle continues, these shared beliefs and values gradually come to be taken for granted, drop out of awareness, and can, therefore, be thought of as "taken for granted assumptions" that become increasingly non-negotiable.

This process of culture formation will occur not only in reference to the organization's primary task in its various external environments but also with respect to its internal organization as well. Those founder beliefs and values, which make life livable and reduce interpersonal anxiety, will gradually come to be taken for granted and come to be tacit assumptions about the "correct" way to organize. But in both domains the driving force is what works. Culture is the result of successful action. If things do not work out the group will disappear.

A basic need in human groups is to justify what they do. And paradoxically, the justifications often are not the same as the tacit assumptions that actually determine the behavioral regularities. Thus groups create ideologies, aspirations, visions, and various other kinds of "espoused values" which may or may not correspond isomorphically with the tacit assumptions. The most difficult aspect of deciphering organizational cultures, then, is to determine to what extent the claimed espoused values actually correspond to the behavioral regularities observed and, if not, to determine what the shared tacit assumptions are.

How to Describe Cultures

There are three approaches to describing cultures: (1) Profiling them on various pre-selected dimensions; (2) Creating conceptual typologies into which to fit given cultures; and/or (3) Clinical or ethnographic descriptions that highlight unique aspects of a given culture.

Among the profiling approaches, one of the most widely used is Hofstede's four dimensions based on factor analyzing questionnaire responses—Individualism (vs. Groupism), Mas-

culinity (the perceived gap between male and female roles), Tolerance for Ambiguity, and Power Distance (the perceived distance between the most and least powerful in the society). These dimensions were originally used to describe national cultures but have also been extended to descriptions of organizational cultures (Hofstede, 1980; 1991).

A different approach has been to use sociological dimensions developed by Parsons (1951) and elaborated by Kluckhohn and Strodtbeck (1961) as a way of creating profiles of a given organization and identifying critical value issues—universalism vs. particularism, individualism vs. collectivism, affectively charged vs. neutral, specific vs. diffuse, time orientation, and degree of control over nature (Hampden-Turner & Trompenars, 1993; Trompenars, 1993). A third version of this approach is to take one or two dimensions, consider them to be conceptually central, and create a typology based on a two by two table with those dimensions. Cameron & Quinn (1999) use (1) Flexibility vs. Stability and Control and (2) Internal Integration vs. External Differentiation to create four types of cultures—Clan, Adhocracy, Hierarchy, and Market. Goffee & Jones (1998) use the dimensions of Degree of Solidarity and Degree of Sociability to create four types—Networked, Communal, Fragmented, and Mercenary. Among the typologies we have Likert's Systems 1 to 4, Harrison and later Handy's *Gods of Management*, McGregor's Theory X and Theory Y, Ouchi's Theory Z and the more popular distinctions between "command and control" vs. "committed and empowered" (Likert, 1967; Handy, 1978; McGregor, 1960; Ouchi, 1981).

The clinical or ethnographic approach attempts to deal with any given culture as a unique pattern of shared assumptions around issues that are not known before the clinician/researcher is on the scene as an observer and active inquirer (Schein, 1987, 1992, 1999). The prime objection to questionnaires as research tools for the study of culture is that they force us to cast the theoretical net too narrowly. The advantage of the ethnographic or clinical research method is that we can consciously train ourselves to minimize the impact of our own models and to maximize staying open to new experiences and concepts we may encounter. In the end we may well sort those experiences into the existing categories we already hold. But at least we will have given ourselves the opportunity to discover new dimensions and, more importantly, will have a better sense of the relative salience and importance of certain dimensions within the culture we are studying. The issue of salience is very important because not all the elements of a culture are equally potent in the degree to which they determine behavior. The more open group oriented inquiry not only reveals how the group views the elements of the culture, but, more importantly, tells us immediately which things are more salient and, therefore, more important as determinants.

As to the categories themselves I have found it empirically useful to start with a broad list of "survival functions"—what any group must do to survive in its various environments and fulfill its primary task, and "internal integration functions"—what any group must do to maintain itself as a functioning system. This distinction is entirely consistent with a long tradition of empirical research in group dynamics that always turns up two critical factors in what groups do—1) task functions and 2) group building and maintenance functions. Ancona and others have pointed out that we must add a third set to these two—boundary maintenance functions (Ancona, 1988). Task and boundary maintenance functions are external survival issues, and group building and maintenance functions are internal integration issues. We may then construct different lists of what specific dimensions of behavior, attitude, and belief we will look for in each domain but at least we have a model that forces us to cast the net widely, and a reminder that culture is for the group the learned solution to all of its external and internal problems.

If we then look a little deeper, drawing again on anthropology and sociology, we find

broad cultural variations around deeper more abstract issues such as those developed by Kluckhohn and Strodtbeck. Also useful is the work of England (1975) on managerial values that deals specifically with how in a given culture one arrives at "truth." If one combines these dimensions with some of the dimensions identified by Edward Hall (1966, 1976, 1983) on concepts of space and spatial relationships, and with more recent concepts about the nature of the "self" in different cultures, one has a pretty good template of what culture covers at this deeper level.

Does Corporate Culture Matter?

Several claims based on various different kinds of research have tried to show a connection between the strength and/or type of culture and economic performance (Deal & Kennedy, 1982; Denison, 1990; Kotter & Heskett, 1992; Collins & Porras, 1994). The problem is that different kinds of cultural dimensions relate to different kinds of environments in ways that are not entirely predictable. The best way to summarize, then, is to say that culture certainly influences economic performance, but the manner in which this occurs remains highly variable. A culture that can be very functional in one environment or at one stage in a company's evolution can become dysfunctional and cause that same company to fail. Culture needs to be analyzed and understood but until much more research has been done, one cannot make generalizations about its impact.

References

Ancona, D. G. (1988). Groups in organizations: Extending laboratory models. In C. Hendrick (Ed.), Annual *review of personality and social psychology: Group and intergroup processes* (pp. 207–231). Thousand Oaks, CA: Sage.

Cameron, K. S., & Quinn, R. E. (1999). *Diagnosing and changing organizational culture.* Boston, MA: Addison-Wesley.

Dennison, D. R. (1990). *Corporate culture and organizational effectiveness.* Hoboken, NJ: Wiley.

England, G. (1975). *The manager and his values.* New York, NY: Ballinger.

Frost, P. J., Moore, L. F., Louis, M. R., Lundberg, C. C., & Martin, J. (Eds.) (1985). *Organizational culture.* Thousand Oaks, CA: Sage.

Goffee, R., & Jones, G. (1998). *The character of a corporation.* New York, NY: Harper Collins.

Hall, E. T. (1966). *The hidden dimension.* New York, NY: Doubleday.

Hall, E. T. (1976). *Beyond culture.* New York, NY: Doubleday.

Hall, E. T. (1983). *The dance of life.* New York, NY: Doubleday.

Hampden-Turner, C., & Trompenars, A. (1993). *The seven cultures of capitalism.* New York, NY: Doubleday-Currency.

Handy, C. (1978). *Gods of management.* London, UK: PanMacmillan.

Hofstede, G. (1980). *Culture's consequences.* Thousand Oaks, CA: Sage.

Hofstede, G. (1991). *Cultures and organizations.* New York, NY: McGraw-Hill.

Kluckhohn, F. R., & Strodtbeck, F. L. (1961). *Variations in value orientations.* New York, NY: Harper Collins.

Kotter, J. P., & Heskett, J. L. (1992). *Corporate culture and performance.* New York, NY: Free Press.

Likert, R. (1967). *The human organization.* New York, NY: McGraw-Hill.

Martin, J. (1992). *Cultures in organizations.* New York, NY: Oxford University Press.

McGregor, D. (1960). *The human side of enterprise.* New York, NY: McGraw-Hill.

Ouchi, W. G. (1981). *Theory Z.* Boston, MA: Addison-Wesley.

Parson, T. (1951). *The social system.* New York, NY: Free Press.

Sahlins, M. (1985). *Islands of history.* Chicago, IL: University of Chicago Press.

Schein, E. H. (1987). *The clinical perspective in fieldwork.* Thousand Oaks, CA: Sage.

Schein, E. H. (1992). *Organizational culture and leadership* (2nd ed.). San Francisco, CA: Jossey-Bass.

Schein, E. H. (1999). *The corporate culture survival guide.* San Francisco, CA: Jossey-Bass.

Trice, H. M., & Beyer, J. M. (1993). *The cultures of work organizations.* Upper Saddle River, NJ: Prentice-Hall.

Trompenars, A. (1993). *Riding the waves of change.* London, UK: Economist Books.

CHAPTER 33

Trauma and Healing in Organizations

Pat Vivian and Shana Hormann

THE NATURE of an organization's work directly impacts the culture of the organization. An organization that provides services to traumatized individuals, families and/or communities is susceptible to becoming a traumatized system experiencing the cumulative effects of the work itself. Although the problems are often viewed as interpersonal or intra-personal, ones that could be addressed through better communication or clarity of roles and expectations, in fact they are deeper, embedded within the organization's system.

Our ideas are based on almost thirty years of experience as managers and consultants with "highly mission-driven" nonprofit organizations across the United States. A highly mission driven organization is one whose mission is compelling and pervasive, defining not only the nature of the work but also the approach to the work and the nature of the internal relationships. We have come to believe that there is a connection between the dynamics of the organization and the heart of the organization's work. The purpose of this article is three-fold: to explore the work-culture connection, describe a set of internal dynamics that frequently result, and offer ideas for OD practice.

What Is Organizational Culture?

An organization is a living human institution whose real existence is expressed through the hearts, minds, and hands of its employees, members, and volunteers. The organizational culture is the cohesion of values, myths, heroines, and symbols that have come to mean a great deal to the people who work there. Schein (1985, p. 6) defines culture as "the deeper level of basic assumptions and beliefs that are shared by members of an organization, that operate unconsciously, and that define in a basic 'taken for granted' fashion an organization's view of itself and its environment." These assumptions are learned responses to a group's problems of survival in its external environment and its problems of internal integration (p.9). This definition sets the stage for exploring the functions of culture and the connection between an organization's work and its culture.

What Functions Does Organizational Culture Perform?

- Organizational culture makes sense of our experience and provides answers, reducing our collective and individual anxiety. The culture provides positive problem-solving approaches for external issues and anxiety avoidance strategies related to internal relationships and norms. (Schein, 1985) The taken-for-granted assumptions that influence the ways in which group members perceive, think, and feel about the world stabilize the world and the organization's place in it. (p. 312) Individuals who recognize societal issues or human needs join forces to address them. Two examples: In the mid-1970's adolescents who ran away from home were viewed negatively by the police, juvenile justice organizations, and social services. Girls could be locked up for having sexual relations, for being promiscuous, boys for incorrigibility. A group of individuals in Seattle viewed runaways differently and came together to start The Shelter, a center for runaway youth. They believed that teenagers ran away from their homes for reasons that needed to be identified and addressed, and that the youth needed a safe and supportive place to be. An organizational culture of non-coercive and respectful values emerged from that foundation. And in Seattle in the 90s, a group of people recognized the differential impact of HIV/AIDS on communities of color and the lack of resources available to address that impact. POCAAN (People of Color Against A IDS Network) was formed to address that disparity in a respectful and culturally competent way.

• Culture defines the identity of the organization and supports the experience of belonging, acceptance, and understanding. Identity rests on the core values, worldview, spirit, *raison d'être* of the organization. These elements define the boundary between what is inside and what is outside the organization and provide an identity for the members. It attracts and supports a group of committed individuals who demonstrate an emotional connection and attachment to the work.

In exchange for belonging and acceptance members take on the needs of the organization. "At the core of every culture will be assumptions about the proper way for individuals to relate to each other in order to make the group safe and comfortable" (Schein, 1985, p. 104). An internal society with its own norms develops and determines the extent to which there is room for difference.

• Culture offers a common language and way of thinking for members. The culture defines the basic framework and worldview of the work. It describes the context, purpose, and rationale, and communicates its values through its language. What outsiders might call jargon helps members understand each other quickly within a common practice framework.

What Is the Work-Culture Connection?

• We think that the work of highly mission-driven organizations directly influences the culture of those organizations. For example, crisis-response organizations tend to have crisis-oriented management, workers in victim-advocacy agencies tend to report being victimized by structure and internal dynamics, anti-oppression organizations tend to create cultures highly sensitive to any oppression dynamics within the organization. Furthermore we think that some organizations suffer from trauma and that traumatization influences the organization's culture. A women's health clinic that is bombed because it offers abortion services suffers trauma directly. Other organizations, however, experience trauma over time as the result of several factors. A traumatic beginning or history might initiate the pattern of trauma. Victims or survivors of crimes often started sexual assault service agencies, domestic violence shelters, and chapters of Mothers Against Drunk Driving. Their efforts were frequently met with the community's hostility or denial of the problem. Connected to the work itself, organizations and their members are exposed continuously to the pain and suffering of others (a phenomenon known by several names- we prefer compassion fatigue). Eventually, the dysfunctional internal dynamics, which develop from the culture, begin to reinforce the organization's trauma.

How Does the Work Influence the Culture?

- Out of the work emerges the "creation story" for the organization.

  The story of how an organization got started—who was involved, the setting and circumstances, the challenges—is usually powerfully retold in reports, orientation materials, rituals, and celebrations. That story often has an element of the heroic; that is, the organization was often started against all odds, against denial of the problem, against active resistance and disbelief in the wider community.

- The need perceived by the founders and the impetus to meet that need are the foundation for the organization's "moral narrative."

  An organization's moral narrative is its value-based story about the need for its existence and the rationale for its work. Its development begins with the creation story, forming its foundation, but it also changes over time as organizational members refine it and the refinements become part of the narrative. The moral narrative and the members' articulation of it mutually reinforce each other and solidify the story. If an organization's beginning was traumatic, its members might perceive the wider environment as an uncaring or even dangerous place.

- Both the creation story and the moral narrative communicate the expected (right) way to accomplish the work.

  Members of the organization hold values and standards that they want to see manifested in the world. They also hold an expectation that all the work of the organization exemplifies those values. For example, sexual assault centers hold strong core values related to their work. These values have been forged in response to an historical pattern and current tendency to hold the victim responsible for his/her assault or victimization. In particular these centers value expertise that comes from those who experienced the assault over expertise from other sources, such as professional training. They also value treating clients with respect, which includes being listened to, believed, and responded to in a supportive way. These core values are also reflected in the expectation that staff listen to, respond to, and support one another, setting the stage for problematic internal dynamics, which we will take up later in this article.

- The nature of the work names the struggle or challenge and creates expectations about individual identification with the work.

  The struggle or challenge is often revealed in an organization's mission. This compelling statement communicates how essential and important the work is. Frequently these mission statements communicate an uncompromising intention about social change. Here are two examples:

  > Support-Heal-Educate-Prevent:
  > Helping the Community STOP
  > Sexual assault
  > (*Sexual assault services program*)

  No More Victims. No More Victimizers.
  (*Children's anti-violence training group*)

- The work is perceived to be a higher calling and provides individual and collective identities as a result of participating in the struggle.

  Individuals are attracted to the mission and work for a variety of personal, professional, and values-based reasons. Personal reasons include a sense of belonging, connection, and affection; personal empowerment; and perhaps even an unconscious need for self-healing. Individuals also discover that their personal experiences and qualities have an important place in their professional lives. Professional reasons include knowledge and skill development, training, and an orientation to service. Values-based reasons include commitment to social change and an altruistic desire to give back to and be a part of the community or group being served.

Workers develop an intense emotional connection to their clients and to their own identity as part of the struggle. The needs of the clients and the organization become the needs of the workers. Individuals end up taking on the mission as their life work and become psychologically identified with it. Organizational identity and worker identity merge in the extreme cases, especially in highly traumatized systems. One example: A woman who helped start a rape crisis center in her mid-20s developed a life-long passion to help organizations that work on behalf of women and girls. Now in her 50s, she continues to lend her time and energy to sexual assault services programs.

- The highly mission-driven work creates an intense emotional culture, and the emotional nature of the mission seeps into that culture. The culture and work mutually reinforce each other over time.

An "emotional field" (Friedman, 1985) comes from the intense feelings individuals bring to the struggle as well as the normal development of emotional interdependency in any human system. Furthermore the essential place of empathy in the work reinforces relationships characterized by empathic concern between workers and their clients as well as between co-workers. The interplay of these factors intensifies the emotional field. In a traumatized organization the emotional intensity may reach extremes that interfere with day-today functioning.

- The creation story and moral narrative can reinforce a separation of the organization from the larger society.

When the wider community responds with denial or outright hostility to an organization's founding, organizational members experience themselves as different, apart, even marginalized, and tend to assume little or no support for their organization. A continuing gulf frequently leads to the development of protective boundaries and consequent isolation of the organization. Many times this situation is experienced as "us versus them", and sometimes the community and the organization become polarized.

What Is the Impact of Organizational Culture on Internal Dynamics?

The interaction of the above factors creates and sustains a strongly felt organizational culture. That culture in turn breeds a set of internal dynamics that are both functional and dysfunctional for the organization and its members. Culture develops explicitly and implicitly and is passed on from one generation of workers to the next through a process of socialization. Because the influence is both explicit and implicit, contradictory assumptions can become embedded in the culture without members of the organization being aware of them. If their development is implicit, their influence on internal dynamics is often hidden.

Using our model of "Strengths and Shadows" (see Figure 33.1), we explain some of these dynamics and describe three ways in which they play out in organizational life.

We use the word "Strength" to refer to values and assumptions that support an organization's successful accomplishment of its mission. We use the term "Shadow" to mean elements that are denied, rejected, hidden, and undiscussable. These elements frequently hinder either accomplishment of the mission or the organization's sustainability. Also, Strengths may be overly relied on or rigidly and/or inappropriately applied; Shadow elements often result. In addition other qualities or Strengths that might be useful to the organization remain underdeveloped. Strengths and Shadows are bound together. For example, in many service organizations *Commitment to the Work and Client-Center* (Strengths) create a susceptibility to *Over-Functioning* (Shadow).

Both Strengths and Shadows become part of the culture. Explicitly they are incorporated

FIGURE 33.1 Copyright Pat Vivian, MA and Shana Hormann, MSW, May 2002

into value statements, policies, standards of practice, and recognition and reward systems. Implicitly they develop through collective norms and interpersonal dynamics. Both Strengths and Shadows arise from choices about where to focus attention, how to respond to crises, and deliberate and/or inadvertent role modeling by leaders. Contradictions emerge, and rationales are developed to explain them. Over time both the contradictions and the explanations become part of the Shadow dynamics of the culture, what Argyris refers to as "defensive routines." (1993)

The inner circle in our diagram represents the Strengths developed by the organization to meet its mission and sustain itself. The outer circle represents the Shadow elements of organizational life. The arrows connect the related Strengths and Shadow elements. The boundary between the organization and its environment is drawn as a solid line to show its relatively closed nature; the boundary between the Strengths and Shadow elements is drawn as a dotted line to show its relatively fluid and open nature. While in our experience many highly mission-driven nonprofits experience these dynamics, traumatized systems, which tend to develop very protective boundaries between organization and environment, experience them most intensively. As we have shared this model with colleagues in nonprofits, they have responded immediately with recognition. "You are describing *my* organization."

We have noticed two general patterns related to these internal dynamics. One is a tendency to focus on Strengths alone rather than a complete picture of organizational dynamics. Little criticism of the organizational efforts to achieve its mission is allowed, and overused Strengths as well as Shadow characteristics are denied. We think this comes from organizational members' experience of the difficulty in achieving their mission, and a consequent need to affirm themselves, the work, and the struggle. The second is the tendency of other organizations to experience ONLY their Shadow side because dysfunctional dynamics have so intensified that members have forgotten their Strengths. In this case routine cynicism and apathy set in, and individuals feel little responsibility to try to make changes.

The next section identifies three specific patterns we see occurring in organizations as a result of the Strength-Shadow dynamics. *They are recurring conversations with no resolution, groupthink, and stress contagion.*

Recurring conversations with no resolution

The same conversation occurs over time between the same or different individuals, sometimes with a lack of awareness about how often the topic has been discussed. Each time the conversation occurs either no resolution is reached or resolution is reached but quickly dissipates without action being taken. Several Strengths/Shadow pairs might account for this pattern. First, the Strength, *Interdependence and Caring about Relationships* with its Shadows of *Conflict Avoidance* and *Unclear Boundaries,* predisposes those within the organization to seek harmony or at least to avoid disharmony. Limited verbal disagreements are tolerated, but the basic differences are not worked through, and no closure is reached. Members persist in their image of harmony and reaffirm their care for each other and the importance of relationships. Secondly, the Strength *Shared Power and Authority* with its Shadow *Lack of Decision-Making* encourages expenditure of group energy on process and obscures the need to reach an outcome. Progress, action, and achievement all suffer when these dynamics occur.

Groupthink

Groupthink refers to the tendency of group members to share common assumptions and worldviews. Consequently they do not realistically assess alternative perspectives or courses of action. Groupthink develops as strong norms influence and sometimes dictate internal rela-

tionships as well as relationships between the organization and its environment. The combined Strengths of *Commitment to the Work* and *Mission-Driven* and the perception that the external environment does not care about the need or those served reinforce the Shadows of *Merging Identities* and *Coercion.* Uniformity of perspective and normative behavior both interfere with healthy questioning of the organization's mission and approach. Distrust of the environment makes it easier to reject input and feedback, reinforcing the uniformity. Innovation is neither sought nor valued.

Rigidity of Approach, the Shadow of *Expertise-Based Success,* and *Suppression of Conflict,* the Shadow of *Care about Relationships* and *Interdependence,* reinforce normative behavior. Disagreements, criticism, and blame are personalized or politicized because members have no other frameworks within which to understand differences. Some suppress their dissenting views because they believe no one will agree with or support them. Other individuals say their piece but do not really expect change. Individuals who do not act according to explicit or implicit norms are isolated, marginalized, and scapegoated. When the tension of being different becomes too great, the individual leaves the organization. In some circumstances they are treated as if they have betrayed the struggle and rejected the mission and their co-workers. Traumatized organizations, often perceiving the environment as hostile, place even greater emphasis on internal support and camaraderie. This experience makes them highly susceptible to groupthink.

Stress Contagion

The Strength of *Mission-Driven* fosters its Shadow of *Merging Identities,* and the Strength of *Social Change Mandate* fosters its Shadows of *Sense of Failure* and *Internalized Guilt.* Coupled with the various motivations individuals bring to their work, these dynamics frequently lead to acute or chronic stress. The Strength of *Empathic Response* with its Shadow of *No Permission to Not Care or to Not Listen,* sets the stage for stress contagion, individuals picking up stress from each other. (Braiker, 1986)

Both *Commitment to the Work* and *Client-Centered* (Strengths) lead to *Over-Functioning* (taking on more than one's reasonable role while others take on less), which in turn increases stress. Finally the very Strength of the organization's *Expertise-Based Success* with its Shadow *Exceed Capacity Limits* causes the organization to overfunction in relation to its environment.

Stress contagion is the manifestation of these dynamics. But it is also a vehicle through which stress becomes embedded in the organization's culture and is passed on to new employees who have not been there long enough to experience their own emotional exhaustion. In this way the dynamic occurs at the individual, interpersonal and organizational levels.

Implications for OD Practice

Organizational members tend to see these patterns as interpersonal or intra-personal problems, rather than systemic dynamics. Problem solving or improvement practices focus on individuals and their behavior. Little organizational learning occurs, and the patterns persist. Individuals end up being depleted, and the organization's sustainability is threatened. New ways of understanding and addressing these dynamics can help organizations see these patterns and intervene systemically.

How Can OD Practitioners Assist Organizations?

Shine Light on the Shadows

The OD practitioner can hold the tension and anxiety in a way that helps organizations begin to feel hopeful about making changes. Organizational members become more ready to explore their experience using these frameworks, which allow for discussion of the inherent tensions without assigning blame to individuals or roles. They also help members remember their creation stories, the source of their inspiration and current strengths.

Practitioners reframe the task from problem-solving to seeing the situation in a new light. The task is not eliminating the Shadow but rather recognizing it as a starting point for systemic analysis and insight. Identification of organizational patterns helps to normalize workers' experiences and reduces their individual sense of failure and isolation. By identifying both Strengths and Shadows, organizations can achieve a more balanced perspective and rekindle hope.

Reduce Stress Contagion

Practitioners can help organizational members recognize both the inherent stress in highly mission-driven work and the stress from their own commitment and expectations. They facilitate structured experiences to help members recognize and interrupt patterns of personalizing and projection (an unconscious process of disowning one's own quality or behavior while simultaneously noticing that same quality or behavior in another person.). Practitioners help groups surface and change the norms that lead to stress contagion, and encourage boundary setting that says "No" to over-functioning. Finally they strongly encourage organization-wide conversations about the organizational capacity and limits and support realistic prioritizing.

Coach Leaders to Embrace Organizational Strengths and Shadows

Practitioners can help leaders to develop awareness of their individual Strengths and Shadows and to use that insight to notice and name organizational Strengths and Shadows. They can help leaders better understand the roles they play in shaping organizational culture and changing dysfunctional dynamics. Finally, they can coach leaders to convene and facilitate conversations about these dynamics in open and non-defensive ways. Leaders learn to ask thought-provoking questions to surface the group's deepest beliefs and assumptions.

Reflect and Learn from Experience

The more self-aware an organization is about its own Strengths and Shadows and organizational culture, the less likely it is to be trapped in polarized perspectives. The OD practitioner can facilitate exploration of the organizational values inherent in its creation story and culture. This allows organizational members to understand more fully the organization's Strengths and to create change strategies in alignment with those strengths and values. Using this self-awareness, the organization can open its boundaries to the external environment, increase information flow and energy, and move from protective to collaborative relationships.

Understanding the work-culture connection is the first step an organization can take to free itself from dysfunctional dynamics and heal from trauma. Organizational members can then be more open to change while affirming the organization's mission. Healing and sustainability emerge from a deepened respect for their values and understanding of their organizational culture. They are ready to write the future chapters of their organizational story.

References

Argyris, C. (1993). *Knowledge for action A guide to overcoming barriers to organizational change.* San Francisco, CA: Jossey-Bass Publishers.

Braiker, H. (1986). *The type E* woman How to overcome the stress of being everything to everybody.* New York, NY: Dodd, Mead and Company.

Friedman, E. (1985). *Generation to generation family process in church and synagogue.* New York, NY: The Guilford Press.

Schein, E. (1987). *Organizational culture and leadership.* San Francisco, CA: Jossey-Bass Publishers.

CHAPTER 34

Diversity and Inclusion as a Major Culture Change Intervention

A Case Study

Judith H. Katz and Frederick A. Miller

CHANGING AN ORGANIZATION'S culture is difficult work. It requires getting at the intangible aspects of an organization, as well as its overt actions and policies. A comprehensive OD approach is required for a true transformation, one which brings new values and goals to all levels of the organization and positions them not as discrete "programs" and "best practices," but as a Way of Life.

Creating a culture of inclusion that leverages diversity is radical change for any corporation. Isolated policies won't produce meaningful and lasting change. There needs to be a comprehensive, strategic, and integrated initiative that recognizes important points along the path to success. As companies move from exclusive clubs to inclusive organizations, they must identify the unique challenges and opportunities that define each step.

In our work, we have helped many clients create strategies that move them toward their goal of achieving higher performance through greater inclusion and raising the bar on diversity. Our success is based on taking an OD approach to the work and treating the initiative as a major culture change intervention. Our definition of an OD approach is a comprehensive, value-based strategy to create change within an organization that positions the organization for the future. It addresses: the leadership, management policies and practices, organizational and individual competencies, structures, quality of interactions and the overall working environment. An OD intervention touches all aspects of organizational life and process.

Combining Programs and Activities into an "Initiative"

When an organization realizes that its future success hinges on its ability to achieve higher performance through building inclusion and leveraging diversity, the "diversity work" that had previously been given piece-meal attention as a "soft," people-related activity or public relations necessity suddenly becomes an important business priority. Instead of pursuing these activities because they are "the right thing to do," a moral duty felt by a senior executive, or the current fad, the organization begins to pursue them out of strategic intent.

As part of this process, the various parts of the "diversity work" are evaluated, and those activities that fit with the strategic intent are knit together into a "Diversity Initiative." The investment in this initiative is justified through the creation of an Organizational Imperative that focuses on the mission-critical relationship of the work, including the need to retain and attract talented people and address the complex needs of today's marketplace. The investment also includes changes in people-related systems, management practices and accountabilities. The focus moves from intent and the needs of certain individuals to the needs of all the people of the organization and creating new competencies for a new culture and workplace.

To succeed, a critical mass of leaders must realize that integrating the culture change effort into the strategic work and goals of the organization is essential. This involves embedding the new competencies and practices into all the organization's other major strategies and initiatives, e.g., Leadership, Quality, Mergers/Acquisitions, Strategic Alliances, Attracting the Best & Brightest, Downsizing, Re-engineering, and/or Becoming a Preferred Stock. It also means recognizing that this work is not just internal: it has an impact on customers, suppliers, community relations, marketplace, and a host of other constituents. Leveraging diversity and creating a culture of inclusion need to be integrated into every level of the business.

The Goal: Moving Along the Path

This kind of aligned approach is crucial for moving the organization along the path of change (see Figure 34.1). This path extends from an exclusive, monocultural club, to an inclusive, diverse organization. The steps along the way are distinctive and important to understand—for organizations and for OD professionals working with them (Katz & Miller, 1995).

Exclusive Club

This is an organization that pursues monocultural norms and values. Membership is open only to people who meet a narrow range of criteria. Since there is little or no tolerance for differences, recruitment is often an exercise in hiring people just like everybody else.

Passive Club

In a Passive Club, the exclusive rules are no longer "official"; they are only spoken quietly, if at all, but they permeate the atmosphere. The policies may not be overtly exclusive but the actual practices effectively exclude anyone not in the traditional group.

Symbolic Difference

Here the organization tolerates—maybe even accepts—differences in appearance, but not in behavior. Pioneers from different identity groups are often seen as "tokens" in these organizations. Most organizations in the United States fit into this category. While the workforce is at least somewhat diverse in appearance, the decision-making responsibilities remain almost exclusively with people from the traditional group.

Critical Mass

The organization has a growing core of people who are different from the traditional group and growing support for a more diverse, inclusive culture. This is a key transition point: the old rules no longer work, but the new rules have not all been created. This is the stage at which most organizations turn back, stop where they are, bring in a different consulting team, or try a different "initiative of the month."

Welcoming

Integral to a welcoming organization is recognition of the presence of systemic barriers and discrimination. Perhaps for the first time, the organization and its people clearly see the need for a systematic effort to level the playing field so all people have equitable footing. All aspects of the organization are examined to identify the structures, procedures, and norms that impede people's ability to contribute. People find it safer to speak up about obstacles to inclusion, and the organization finds it easier to recognize and address these issues. This is the opportunity to truly redefine the organization and its operations.

As differences are welcomed, people begin finding multiple ways of connecting with each other. Instead of sticking to culturally defined

FIGURE 34.1 Path Model

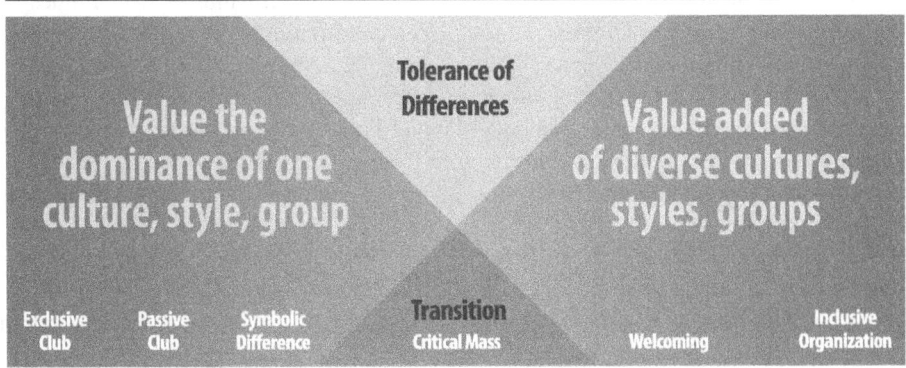

or stereotyped interactions or fear-driven avoidance, people find many areas of commonality and common ground. A mindset emerges that sees differences as normal and positive rather than something to be avoided or diminished.

Inclusive Organization

The organization actively seeks out and utilizes the full range of perspectives, opinions and skills offered by different individuals, identity groups and functional specialties. It is committed to and geared for change, continuous improvement, and a constant search for 360-degree vision. It constantly widens its bandwidth of human resources and human potential, eager to gain from the synergy that can be tapped when those differences are brought together. The people of the organization see the ability to form effective partnerships, teams and strategic alliances as mission critical for individual and organizational success and they feel a sense of ownership for the effort.

Practicing inclusive behaviors is a way of life in the workplace. The organization experiences the payoff on a daily basis through higher and higher performance, improved processes, opening of new markets, more successful retention and recruitment efforts, and a broader, deeper talent pool. People feel free to express their views and make suggestions; input and feedback is solicited constantly and

offered freely. People are encouraged and supported in efforts to learn, grow, experiment and take risks.

A Case Study: The XYX Corporation

We have worked with dozens of organizations over the past 30 years to help them achieve higher performance by creating a culture of inclusion that leverages diversity. One recent client—we'll call them the XYX Corporation —serves as a good example of a company that had imported all the "best practices" without achieving any of their goals.

The XYX Corporation is a financial organization that nets $2 billion annually. Prior to our work with them, which began in October of 1999, they had embarked on a series of programs that they hoped would enhance their diversity and therefore improve their corporate culture. They established employee networks (for women, working parents, lesbians and gays, etc.), adopted domestic partner benefits, conducted one-day education events for all people in the organization, funded a variety of community outreach programs, held diversity celebrations (e.g., events around Black History, Asian and Hispanic Months), and pursued other efforts aimed at recognizing and valuing diversity in its workforce. Located in a major metropolitan area, the company had done a good job of recruiting for diversity at entry levels in the organization.

They had also formed a Diversity Function that was well staffed. Each division within the company had its own Diversity Council, which connected to the corporate-wide body. These groups planned education and awareness events and coordinated efforts for efficiency and maximum impact.

None of these efforts added up to any change in the culture or the practices of the organization. Although there was a core group of people in the organization dedicated to moving the company forward, the efforts they were undertaking did little more than raise awareness on a surface level. In fact, the organization experienced behavior (including racist graffiti and other overt actions) that indicated a hostile environment for diversity and a non-inclusive work culture. On the path to greater inclusion, the company was stuck in the Symbolic Differences stage.

In addition, the culture was very risk-averse and slow to make important business decisions. Innovation and creativity were low. Many people were not enthusiastic about their work, some were highly discouraged. Recruitment and retention rates were suffering as a result.

What Went Wrong

A variety of factors were working against the organization in its goal to reap benefits from its diversity and inclusion efforts.

Getting the Message Right

Despite the education events provided and various corporate-wide attempts to align the diversity message, different people had different understandings of what it meant to be inclusive and why the organization was making the effort. Some thought the goal was to ensure that the company was "colorblind"—that it ignored differences among people instead of actively recognizing and embracing differences. Some did not recognize how inclusion

would benefit them; they perceived it strictly as a program for white women and people of color. A fair number of people in the organization perceived the effort as a legal compliance measure related to Affirmative Action and Equal Employment Opportunity obligations. Still others supported the effort as "the right thing to do," but saw no connection to their business objectives.

With such different understandings of the purpose for the work, people in the organization were not moving toward a common goal. They had different hopes, expectations, and fears about just what creating inclusion and leveraging diversity really meant.

Walking the Talk

Even among those who understood the main goals of the effort, there was an inconsistent approach to the behaviors associated with creating an inclusive culture that leverages diversity. This was true throughout the organization, but particularly at the management level. A relationship culture prevailed, where whom you knew counted more than how you performed your work. Our initial surveys showed that fewer than a quarter of respondents felt that promotions were based on merit. (White people were three times more likely than African Americans to feel that promotions were based on merit, but even among whites, only 24% felt this way.)

There was an obvious disconnect between the rhetoric and the reality. This is a common outcome of diversity and inclusion efforts that have no impact below the surface of an organization: people feel that all that is required of them is lip service. In the case of the XYX Corporation, where so many different "best practices" had been adopted, many people assumed that these were all "programs of the month," passing fads briefly embraced by management with no real commitment or connection to their daily work activities. They were wary of investing in the effort and taking risks on new behaviors—even ones they endorsed—for fear that the effort wasn't real and that they'd get burned by it in the end.

In addition, many in the company were blind to the ways in which diversity and inclusion issues play themselves out in the workplace. For example, many women executives had been leaving the company. Attrition statistics showed this trend clearly and led to the conclusion that something about the culture was inhospitable to women once they reached a certain level in the organization's hierarchy. As a result, there were few women in top positions and a lot of talent was opting out of the organization.

The XYX Corporation saw these women's departures as individual stories: she left for *this* reason, she left for *that* reason, and so on. They never viewed the exodus as a function of the system itself, but as a case-by-case series of departures. This, too, is symptomatic of an approach to diversity that fails to see the big picture or understand the systemic nature of the workplace culture. Even as the organization was implementing a variety of programs aimed at valuing diversity, it was not comprehending the many repercussions of their non-inclusive environment.

Making It Mission-Critical

One of the main reasons the company had the problems it did was its programmatic approach to diversity and inclusion. Instead of seeing it as a major OD intervention, they viewed it as an "add-on"—a nicety, as opposed to a necessity.

Part of this impulse came from an ideologically pure place: the CEO and some of the other senior leaders felt strongly that the impetus for a diversity and inclusion effort came from a moral imperative. They saw it as only about values and social justice. While such a perspective is laudable, separating leveraging diversity and creating a culture of inclusion from the business mission of the organization ignores its impact on higher performance and the bottom line. It keeps inclusion efforts at

the outskirts of the organization and disconnected from its core and main purpose.

For diversity and inclusion efforts to be meaningful and truly effective, they need to be woven into the very fabric of the organization itself. The behaviors and policies associated with them need to be a way of life within the organization. Figure 34.2 illustrates the stages involved in achieving this integration.

The XYX Corporation had climbed the first two rungs of this ladder. With their education sessions and imported best practices, they had developed some individual awareness throughout the company and had begun implementing programs related to building inclusion and leveraging diversity.

But they stalled at this level. Without a larger vision for what leveraging diversity and a culture of inclusion could bring them (and without a larger understanding of how these concepts work), they never sought to combine

FIGURE 34.2 Way of Life Model

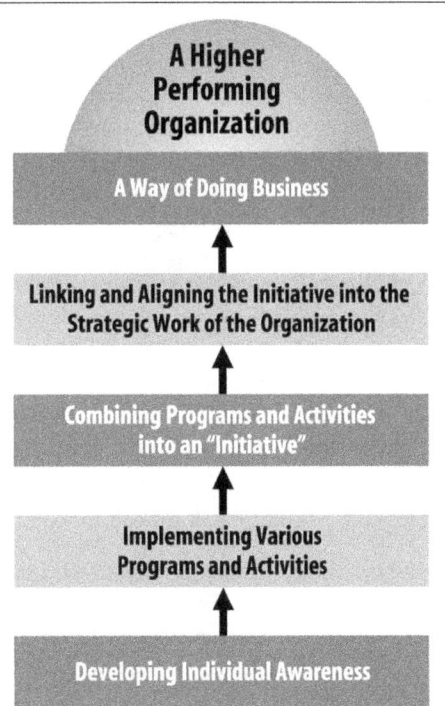

isolated programs into a larger initiative. Such an approach is essential for aligning leveraging diversity and inclusion work to the mission-critical goals of the organization—using them, for instance, to help expand the company's skill set, penetrate new markets, widen the organization's vision, attract and retain top talent, etc. Only after establishing the connection between inclusion and high performance can the initiative become a Way of Life that transforms the entire organization.

Our Intervention

In response to a request from members of XYX Corporation's Diversity Function, we conducted a series of data gathering initiatives (including surveys, focus groups, and one-on-one interviews with a cross section of the organization) to get a snapshot of the company and educate ourselves on its culture, status, and goals. We worked with senior leaders as well as all levels in the organization to construct a rounded and comprehensive view.

Six Strategic Levers

We structured our approach around Six Strategic Levers that built on the work already underway in the organization while also moving the company forward in its drive to make a culture of inclusion that leverages diversity a Way of Life.

Lever I: Create an Aligned Understanding of the Current State and the Imperative for Inclusion.

This establishes how the work of creating a culture of inclusion that leverages diversity is connected to organizational needs and competitive opportunities—the organization imperative that was missing from XYX's earlier efforts. The shared perspective, is the platform for all forthcoming activities, ensuring that leaders and others are clear at the outset about the current state of leveraging diversity and inclusion and the direction in which the organization needs to move to become higher performing.

At XYX, the introduction of this lever encountered several hurdles. First there was resistance to moving away from the strict moral imperative message. In response, we worked to educate all leaders on the increased effectiveness that comes from tying inclusion to the core mission of the organization.

Another hurdle to creating the Organizational Imperative was the perception among many leaders that leveraging diversity and inclusion held only limited benefits for their bottom line. As a company that sells to institutions in an industry based largely on financial advantage (as opposed to corporate culture), they were slow to appreciate the ways in which an inclusive environment could impact their profitability and give them a competitive edge. We worked with a variety of divisions to expand their vision and identify many areas where inclusion would make a difference (including greater innovation, better retention of talent, increased creativity and problem-solving skills, status as an Employer of Choice, etc.).

With the Imperative identified, it was then important to communicate it to everyone throughout the organization. Communications began to stress the Imperative and the CEO began including references to inclusion and leveraging diversity in all major organizational announcements. It was critical that the link between inclusion and business success be well understood and is given a high profile in every facet of the organization's daily life.

The Imperative is now included in the orientation program for new employees, in the Employee Handbook, and in company-wide communications. The Diversity Function is partnering with other divisions to ensure the message is consistent and well understood. Annual reviews will be conducted to assess movement.

Lever II: Develop Competencies of Executives, Managers, and Supervisors to Build a Culture of Inclusion that Leverages Diversity through Education and Accountability.

It is crucial to provide leaders with the essential tools and information they need to model the new behaviors and develop the new competencies for building inclusion and leveraging diversity, thus leading to higher performance.

In XYX, we helped leaders develop the competencies, knowledge and skills required to become strong supporters of leveraging diversity and inclusion—people who lead the initiative and model the values and behaviors of the new organizational culture. We held meetings and education sessions for these leaders, with specific goals in mind:

- To gain greater alignment among Senior Executives on creating an inclusive and high performing environment that leverages diversity.
- To clarify leadership roles and accountability in facilitating culture change.
- To promote a better understanding of the business imperative for leveraging diversity including linkages to critical business strategies.
- To explore issues of oppression and bias at both the individual and social identity group levels.
- To develop skills around feedback, conflict management and resolution.

In addition, education sessions for the managers enabled them to focus on seeing the connection between high performance and inclusion, understanding the ways in which inclusive practices impact all people, recognizing blind spots that hinder inclusion, and learning ways to facilitate people's ability to contribute their best work. It was especially important to create a safe environment where people could ask questions, take risks, and express a range of feelings related to their own diversity and that of other people.

After these sessions, continued support for managers was provided as they implemented what they've learned to make it A Way of Life. Such support included quarterly check-ins and the development of on-line tools that provide models and activities for managers.

Another focus was to develop a network around leveraging diversity and inclusion, whose purpose is to build community, to continue education and to link efforts across the organization. Sessions were held, designed to expand and add to the learning from the Managers' Education. Network members become either Advocates or Change Partners (*see below*).

Lever III: *Seed the Organization with Agents of Change for a Culture of Inclusion that Leverages Diversity.*

These Agents of Change comprise a network of pioneers and champions across the organization who are interested in and committed to practicing and living leveraging diversity and inclusion behaviors in their daily work interactions. By identifying, recruiting, and training these Agents of Change, the organization populates its levels and functions with people who are on-board with the new Way of Life and can stand as living testaments to the advantages of practicing the behaviors.

Education sessions were held for the Agents of Change, aimed at helping participants fully comprehend the new behaviors and concepts. We showed them the connection to higher individual and organizational performance so that they can be effective models for the rest of the organization.

Lever IV: *Link and Align the Inclusion and Leveraging Diversity Process with Corporate Initiatives and Engage Key Partners and Leaders in Moving the Process Forward.*

Such linkage is crucial to ensure that the culture change effort is proceeding in an organized and efficient manner, and is connected to all of the various initiatives that are currently being undertaken across the organization.

For example, at XYX Corporation a major business strategy team was looking at how to improve cycle times for getting products to market and responding to customers. It was critical that the culture change effort connected this team to the leveraging diversity and inclusion effort and showed how the initiative could add value to such a strategic business goal.

Meetings with key groups at XYX Corporation created synergies and strengthened partnerships. These have been critical for keeping the initiative focused, aligned, and moving forward. A summit on leveraging diversity and inclusion focused on what a successful inclusive culture looks like. Visits to other organizations allowed key leaders and the Agents of Change to learn more and share wisdom about implementing inclusive change efforts.

Lever V: *Implement Management Practices to Retain, Develop, and Attract Talent to Ensure Their Best Contribution.*

The focus of this Lever was to embed the principles, values, and behaviors that support a diverse, inclusive culture into all aspects of the people-management practices of the organization. XYX needed to develop a reputation as an Employer of Choice and be seen as a Worthy organization where people can do their best work. Building Inclusion and Leveraging Diversity had to be incorporated into all the ways the organization oriented, retained, developed, promoted, mentored, and recruited people. New practices in hiring and promoting were developed to reflect the new competencies that are being created.

In addition, HR leaders at XYX have explored the ways to enhance career progression utilizing a more diverse talent pool. Sessions for senior executives have addressed retaining, developing, and attracting talent. Specific goals and targets have been identified on the basis of these sessions. The organization is also seeking to earn recognition/awards from respected institutions that honor diverse and inclusive organizations.

Lever VI: *Communicate, Engage, and Enroll the workforce in creating a Culture of Inclusion that Leverages Diversity for Higher Performance.*

Making inclusion a "Way of Life" takes the understanding, effort, and commitment of every person in the organization. It requires new behaviors and competencies that support and enable the new culture. Every communication should be seen as an intervention. The outcome of each communication should be

that the people in the organization will know more about the effort, understand more about leveraging diversity and inclusion, and begin to learn about the desired behaviors and their responsibilities to support the new culture.

XYX Corporation has held ongoing one-day sessions designed to increase understanding and build knowledge throughout the organization. These sessions communicate the Organizational Imperative for making inclusion and leveraging diversity A Way of Life throughout the organization. The sessions also assist people in understanding their part in the process and in the achievement of a culture of inclusion that leverages diversity.

Conclusion

The work continues at XYX Corporation. The word is spreading, behaviors are changing, and people are seeing and feeling a new corporate culture. The ultimate goal is to make a culture of inclusion that leverages diversity more and more as a Way of Life within the organization.

Institutionalizing the change involves constant communication and education, establishing accountabilities for ensuring goals are achieved, and finding new methods for bringing the message to every aspect of organizational life. Senior executives, managers, and all members of the organization must continually acquire and practice new competencies, thereby enhancing the organization's skill-base and business outcomes. Companies that continue to challenge themselves and take a strategic, integrated approach to their culture change initiatives will move themselves along the path to becoming more inclusive organizations AND more successful organizations.

Reference

Katz, J., & Miller, F. (1995). Cultural diversity as a development process: The path from a mono-cultural club to inclusive organization. In J. W. Pfeiffer (Ed.), 1995 Annual V 2 Consulting (pp. 267–281). San Diego, CA: Pfeiffer & Co.

CHAPTER 35

Organizational Circulatory Systems

An Inquiry

Art Kleiner

OVER THE PAST 30 years, the idea has been floated again and again that organizations are "living systems:" they aren't mechanistic and shouldn't be thought of as machines. Among the writers who have put this idea forward are Gareth Morgan (in Images of Organizations), Arie de Geus (in The Living Company), Peter Senge (in The Fifth Discipline), and Eric Trist (in his various papers). And there's good reason to believe they're right. After all, as anyone who has ever tried to intervene in an organization can tell you, they don't react as machines would when you try to fix them.

When approached with change, in other words, they do not respond like clocks, automobiles, engines, telephones, or even computers. They do not either start working better or stop working at all. Instead, they respond like animals, plants, families, and communities. They shift course and react in unexpected ways, often rejecting the measures and approaches that you thought would be most helpful.

But if the idea that organizations are living systems makes sense, there's far less of a complete understanding about how to translate that into effective interventions. This is one reason why Elliot Jaques was right when he said, "Management is in the same state today that the natural sciences were in before the discovery of the circulation of the blood." The

fields of organizational design and effectiveness, to say nothing of organization development, are full of practitioners who apply "best practices" to fix organizational problems in the same way that barber-surgeons once applied leeches. They base their interventions on a great deal of practical experience, but they've unconsciously learned to differentiate those cases where the patient lived ("proof that my method works") from those cases where the patient died ("those just aren't significant examples.") And while there's a lot of organizational theory to draw on, most of it remains far less robust than, say, the theory of the circulation of the blood. To say nothing of an understanding of germs or DNA.

None of this is surprising. After all, large managerial organizations, separate from the state or the church, have only existed since the mid-19th century. They began with the railroad and the telegraph. We have only had 175 years or so to begin to understand them. And it took a long time to recognize that they are living systems. But if they are living systems, where would we look first to learn how they work?

Maybe the answer is to look at circulatory systems. Some of the most interesting and accessible writing (at least to a lay person like myself) about the human body has to do with circulatory systems. For example, Sherwin Nuland, the Yale University-based surgeon and writer, used the following passage to explain the uncanny responses of human physiology in his book *The Wisdom of the Body:*

> To coordinate all of the instabilities in all of the cells [of the human body] requires that the far-flung parts of an organism be in constant communication with one another, over long-distances as well as locally. . . . This is accomplished by messages sent via nerves, in the form of electrical energy we call impulses; via the bloodstream, in the form of the chemicals we call hormones; and—to nearby groups of cells—via the specialized substances we call local signaling molecules. As each of these methods of communication was discovered, researchers . . . came to recognize the inherent wisdom of the body.

Might the same be true of circulatory systems in the organizational body? For the past few years, ever since my book *Who Really Matters* was published, I've begun to think it's true. Indeed, there are probably dozens of circulatory systems through which organizations get their work done. Some of them are machine-like in many respects: Information Technology systems or supply chains. But all of them are living in some way—even the architecture of an office building is, in some vernacular way, alive.

I've been attracted to four circulatory systems in particular. In the rest of this article, I'd like to express some very preliminary ideas about these four circulatory systems, how they work, and the implications for intervention. I do this not as an OD practitioner (indeed, my consulting experience is very limited) but as a historian, writer and editor whose subject is management. I'd like nothing better than to be corrected and to adjust my perceptions based on actual empirical evidence—or based on more robust theory. And I'd be grateful to find out that, like Robinson Crusoe, I've simply been ignorant of others' explorations.

The four circulatory systems that attract me have certainly been written about elsewhere. They are the Market, the Hierarchy, the Network, and the Clan (Figure 35.1). But they have not typically been described as webs through which different types of information and other things travel. And that description may be helpful in making sense of them.

The Hierarchy

We think of hierarchies as controlling mechanisms, but actually they are circulatory systems for aggregation. They are the means through which an organization scales itself up without losing equilibrium. Alfred D. Chandler, in his studies of railroad enterprises as the first managerial organizations, noted that the most distinctive feature of them was their hierarchies. Owners needed to make sure that there were people and systems in place to manage the various far-flung parts of a railroad line, with similar systems for scheduling trains, charging fees, and keeping track of profits. Otherwise, the whole system would (literally) crash.

The hierarchy is perhaps equivalent to the limbic system of a living mammal. It is not a sophisticated conveyance, but without it, movement and growth would cease. And it resonates with primal attitudes about King, God, and authority. When the system is under stress, communication reverts to the hierarchy.

Our best theorist about hierarchies is in fact the late Elliott Jaques, who proposed that some hierarchies were "requisite"—that is, well-suited to the nature of human beings who worked within them. Jaques' proffered that hierarchical design had some qualities in common with golden mean-based designs for buildings. A good hierarchy places people at a level of authority consistent with the cognitive capabilities, and it manages them so that they rise gradually through the system as their capabilities increase.

What travels well through a hierarchy? Preliminary observations suggest that the hierarchy carries anything that can be aggregated

FIGURE 35.1   Organizational Circulatory Systems

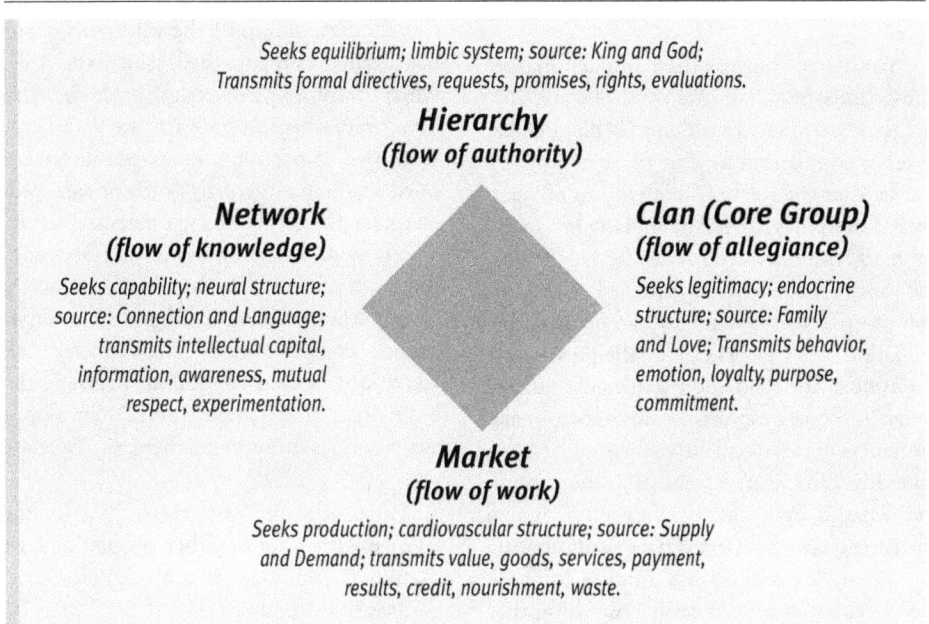

Seeks equilibrium; limbic system; source: King and God;
Transmits formal directives, requests, promises, rights, evaluations.

Hierarchy
(flow of authority)

Network
(flow of knowledge)

Seeks capability; neural structure;
source: Connection and Language;
transmits intellectual capital,
information, awareness, mutual
respect, experimentation.

Clan (Core Group)
(flow of allegiance)

Seeks legitimacy; endocrine
structure; source: Family
and Love; Transmits behavior,
emotion, loyalty, purpose,
commitment.

Market
(flow of work)

Seeks production; cardiovascular structure; source: Supply
and Demand; transmits value, goods, services, payment,
results, credit, nourishment, waste.

easily: estimates, statements of completion, evaluations, decision rights, categorization, statements of acceptance or decline, and statistical data. Fernando Flores and Terry Winograd, when they established their idea of "conversation for action," may have been actually naming types of speech that flow easily through a hierarchy: requests, promises, offers, and so on. All of these can be added up and tracked without much effort.

But some things don't travel well through a hierarchy. In my experience, these include stories, excuses, analogies, trust, open inquiry, and knowledge. These types of in-depth observations and attitudes simply can't be aggregated; they depend too much on personal contact. Therefore, the hierarchy is never the sole way to govern an enterprise; and most managers learn not to rely on this system for their communications.

The Market

Back in the 1980s, W. Edwards Deming and others wrote about seeing the "organization as a system:" or as Rummler and Brache put it, managing the "white spaces in the organization chart." Like Eric Trist and many others, they were concerned about the actual flow of work and knowledge about work through the organization: goods, services, throughput, money, and anything tangible that ultimately reached a customer. Indeed, some of the most effective organizational work of the past 50 years, from the quality movement to sociotechnical systems to reengineering (when it worked) to lean production has all been interventions in the domain of processes and workflow. People at every step of a good lean process are trained to observe, regulate, and contribute to better flow of goods and services according to the needs of the people who will ultimately use them.

It turns out that at every stage of an organization's work flow, there is an implicit market. There is a supplier, and a receiver, and always an implicit price for what is delivered. This is true at every stage of an assembly line, for instance—and it is also true for staff services. Every service delivered requires a charge code, and there is always a prevailing view of whether or not the service has been worth the price.

For better or worse, these implicit market transactions are not always allowed to be visible; they are often overridden by hierarchical or other considerations. But those companies that let them be freely visible tend to prosper. Thus, Caterpillar thrived by making its "internal markets" more explicit in the late 1980s, and Springfield Remanufacturing Corporation prospered by opening up its financial information in a process called "the great game of business." I've come to regard most process design and quality efforts as attempts to make the market-based circulatory system flow more smoothly and clearly by enlisting the supply-and-demand dynamics at every point where one person's work is passed over to another.

What flows through a market (or process) circulatory system easily? Anything that can be traded. Economists Paul Milgram and John Roberts have noted that a transaction-based system automatically tends toward co-ordination, and the same is true of a work flow in a large organization. Like a human digestive and circulatory system, there tends to be the buildup of blockages over time, and every once in a while it's helpful to try to remove the cholesterol. (It's even more helpful to keep exercising regularly to clear way for better throughput.)

If that's true, then some things would flow through this system more easily than others It would carry goods and services, contracts, statements of worth (prices), bids and trades, allocations, and efficiencies. It would have a harder time with secrets, objects of ambiguous value, emotionally charged information, controls, commands, and loyalty. After all, a price is a price, no matter who's on the other side of the transaction. It's no coincidence that the popularity of lean production has risen at the same time that the popularity of vertical integration has fallen. An enterprise which owns its suppliers and retailers is congenitally prone to hardening of the workflow arteries.

The Network

Our understanding of the value of networks has dramatically increased since the 1970s, when Stanford University professor Mark Granovetter began to research the "strength of weak ties." Since then, many people have applied mathematical analysis to contact among people, particularly in such measurable forms as phone and email contact. It turns out to matter much less what people talk about than simply who is talking to whom. In an organization, as the eminent network researcher Karen Stephenson has found, there are three basic roles that people fulfill, that pop up again and again in the mathematical analyses:

- Hubs—people who regularly communicate with a lot of other people, and who thus naturally act as central nodes for the flow of information;
- Gatekeepers—people who provide the only links into a sub-section of the organization or a body of knowledge, and thus control the flow of relevant informal information in that domain;
- Pulsetakers—people who are relied upon for their ability to offer perspective on the organization and its direction, and who thus maintain connections to a significant and select group of others.

One can create major changes in an organization's effectiveness by aligning and moving people in ways that shift habitual connections for these three key roles. The network thus becomes an equivalent to the neural network of a living mammal. What starts off as informal chatter becomes habituated, deep channels of regular communication. These in turn are the channels through which the knowledge of the organization passes. People learn how to do their work, how to advance in the company, and how to build knowledge through these types of channels. They also learn whom to trust; indeed, Karen Stephenson's book on this subject, forthcoming this year, is called *A Quantum Theory of Trust.*

287-292

All of these circulatory systems carry information, but what sorts of information does this particular circulatory system carry? Anything unstructured. Network typology depends not on the agenda of the meeting, but on who is in the meeting and how free they feel to talk. Information, ideas, gossip, news, light observations, knowledge and learning, working advice, collaboration all flow easily. It is more difficult to exchange emotionally fraught information, issues of depth, difficult conversations, commitments, or absolute truth; after all, these networks represent the strength of *weak* ties. These are the networks of acquaintanceship, not deep friendship, and they get their power more from their breadth and speed than from their depth.

The Clan

For depth, we turn to the clan. Like a community or family, the clan structure of an organization is primarily cognitive. What matters is not the actual relationships or actual people, but the images that each individual carries in his or her mind about the other people of the system. Instead of the images of mother, father, grandfather, child, or sibling, each with its emotional punch, there are images of boss. Subordinate. Peer. CEO. Customer. And rival.

In *Who Really Matters,* I suggested that in every organization there is some core group of key people, not exactly the same as the hierarchy. Every decision maker in the organization, from top to bottom, carries in his or her mind a mental image of that core group. Because life is short and many decisions are complex, we tend to take the cognitive shortcut of asking ourselves, "What would so-and-so think of this?" Or of saying to ourselves, "I don't want to walk into so-and-so's office and say this is not going to happen." The core group for each of us individually is made up of the "so-and-sos" in each of our minds. And the core group of the organization, always shifting and in motion, is made up of the amalgamated so-and-sos of everyone in the organization, weighted by the power of each person's decisions.

In other words: Enough people, enough of the time, make enough decisions based upon core group perceptions that this determines the direction of the organization more than any single factor. The core group doesn't dominate all the time; but it dominates enough. And because it dominates so much, no organization will go anywhere unless the core group is perceived to endorse that direction.

That's why "walking the talk" is so important. It doesn't matter what the CEO really thinks. It matters what he or she is perceived to think. And if the CEO changes an attitude, it will take a while for the organization to catch up. Resistance to change occurs not because people fear change, but because they fear the consequences of contradicting the perceived priorities of the Core Group. The same resistance occurs in families, where people fear contradicting the perceived priorities of the most powerful members of the family.

The core group might range in number from one person to thousands. (The larger the core group, the greater the capabilities of the organization need to be.) Its members are not necessarily people in authority (though they often are.) Some, like the gatekeepers of the network structure, are "bottlenecks" to a key part of the enterprise (a division, a function, a product, a labor union, a supply chain element. . .) Some are people known for speaking with integrity or influence. Some are representatives of a key constituency. Some organizations have one stable core group; others have many core groups in constant flux. Some core groups are good for their organizations; others are highly dysfunctional. But there is no such thing as an organization without a core group Moreover, behind every great organization, there's a great Core Group. . . . And behind every organization in trouble, there's a Core Group in crisis.

The clan (or core group) structure is like the endocrine system of an organization. If you want to change an individual person in a hurry, give them a drug. Similarly, if you want to change an organization, make a sudden and dramatic change in the Core Group. But be careful of overdoses. For what travels through a core group structure easily is emotionally charged information: legitimacy, pride, shame, misunderstanding, and loyalty. What travels with difficulty are reliable news, transactions, anonymity, and commands.

Putting It All Together

Or so it seems at first glance. For I'd be the first to admit that none of this is definitive. And the empirical evidence on which it is based is spotty. At the same time, the ideas resonate enough that challenges tend to focus on details. Few people question the premise that organizations are alive, that circulatory systems are the means by which they stay alive, and that different circulatory systems respond to different types of interventions.

Consider, for instance, two individuals shown as circles in the organization chart in Figure 35.2.

The light grey boxes and dark grey lines represent the hierarchy. The black solid arrows show the flow of work through the market. The black dashed lines show communications channels for the network. And the stars represent people in the core group.

The circle on the left depicts someone relatively high in the hierarchy, well connected in the network, solid in the core group—and relatively far removed from the flow of work or the market. This is a bureaucrat. An organization can only afford to keep a limited number of such people, or it will go bankrupt.

Meanwhile, three boxes to the right is an individual equally high in the hierarchy, thoroughly immersed in the network, crucial to the market's flow of work, but with no core group status. This individual is heading for burn-out. He or she may well be crucial to the organization's survival, but will probably flee before there is a chance to find out.

There is much to learn about all four of these organizational circulatory systems, and about others as well. The stakes could not be higher, because most of the effective change that people make in the world happens in (and through) organizations. The more effective we are as intervenors, the better our world becomes. And in the end, it may be our awareness of circulatory systems—and how we fit into them—that makes us effective as intervenors.

FIGURE 35.2   Importance of the Core Group

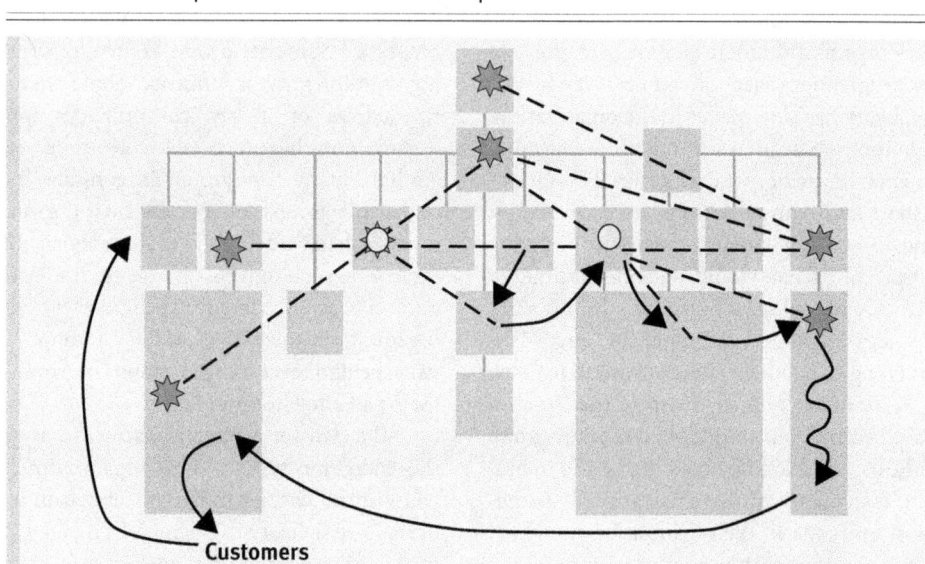

CHAPTER 36

Organic Organizational (Org²) Design

Gina Hinrichs

A CORE CONCEPT for design is form follows function. An organization, like any design challenge should be designed to effectively deliver to its function (purpose). Organizational design would be a relatively straightforward task if organizations operated in isolation or if the external environment was stable. Since organizations are open systems that exist within an ever changing and increasingly complex environment, the task of organizational design is an ongoing challenge. To add to the difficulty, organizations are in the midst of moving from an industrial age to a knowledge age (Miles, Snow, Mathews, Miles, & Coleman, 1997) that disrupts existing paradigms and structures.

Despite many approaches to organizational design a practical, multi-level framework is missing that can guide organizational designers to deal with the dynamic environment[1] and shift to the knowledge age. In this chapter, an explanation of organizational design, a case for action for a new approach, the Org² Design framework and a comparison of classic approaches are provided in Table 1. Org² Design is offered as an approach that builds upon the best of existing organizational design thinking and provides a guide to de-

signing either a part or a whole organization. An example of a social profit organization, the Positive Change Core (PCC), is provided as a case study with outcomes and implications for profit organizations.

Org Design 101

Organizations deliver exactly what they are either intentionally or unintentionally designed to deliver. If there is a lack of understanding or intentionality in the design, what is delivered may not be what is desired. Organizational design should respond to the environment, internal capabilities, and change while maintaining balance, a sense of stability, and clarity. Galbraith (1995) contends that organizational design is a key task for leaders. Leadership in an organization should be as concerned about organizational design as they are about strategic planning since the best strategy without implementation does not deliver value. Organizational design addresses the structure that delivers the strategy. By focusing on organizational design, leadership becomes decision shapers instead of decision makers (Galbraith, 1995).

Organizational design is the creative process for aligning elements of an organization to efficiently and effectively deliver the purpose of an organization. Organizational design is concerned with accomplishing the work to achieve the strategic intent. The basic design question is

---

[1] Some theorist use terms such as turbulent, dynamic, permanent whitewater, etc., to describe an environment that is both complex and unpredictable.

how to distribute the work while maintaining alignment and integration of people, processes, structures, systems, and culture.

Burns and Stalker's (1994) research identified two archetypes for structure they termed as mechanistic and organic. Mechanistic favors stable environments while organic favors uncertain environments. Most organizations still fall into these archetypes but it is no longer an "either/or" but a "both /and."

Design Elements

Many theorists have proposed methods to design organizations. Although most theories focus on a different aspect of the design challenge, there is a commonality of key elements. Most of the approaches acknowledge that strategy drives the design. Common elements to be considered for design are:

- **People**: the members of the organization, their attraction, capabilities, aspirations, development, and retention
- **Processes**: the information and workflows that deliver value to the customer, maintain the business, or enable other processes
- **Systems**: information/knowledge, communication, and measurement systems
- **Structures:** configurations and connections of roles, responsibilities, accountabilities, relationships to share knowledge, make decisions, take action, and learn
- **Culture**: shared values, assumptions, and approaches to cope with external adaptation and internal integration that are reinforced through norms, artifacts, stories, and rewards.

Design Choices

There are many points of tension in designing an organization. Finding the balance that optimizes the aligned performance of the above elements is the goal. Key design choices involve:

- Location of power and authority for decision making and resource allocation

- Task differentiation (economies of scale) vs. coordination (integration)
- Configuration- Unit form and alignment (e.g., functional, product/service, geographic, matrix, networked, self-managing teams, cellular, all of the above)
- Responsiveness vs. stability/consistency
- Perspective of the whole vs. parts

Design Approaches

A comparison chart of different organizational design approaches is provided in Table 36.1. It compares such prevalent organizational design approaches as Galbraith's 5 star, Mckinsey's 7-s, Tichy's strategic management model, Nadler's congruence model, Gelinas and James collaborative organizational design, Weisbord's 6 box model, and Hock and Getzendanner's chaordic six lens. These approaches are compared on aspects of number of design elements, the design elements, the focus of the design, and key points or differentiators of the approach. Each approach is valuable in addressing the important design elements of an organization. Org² design builds from aspects of all of these organizational design approaches but especially draws from the chaordic approach.

The situation and type of organization to be designed determines which approach would best be employed by the designer. Situations that would indicate the employment of the Chaordic approach or the proposed Org² Design is that of globalization, growth, complexity, and change. The Org² Design is suited to designing a whole or parts of the organization. Hatch (2006) observed that no organization design is perfect. Org² Design is used to complete the high level mechanistic structure by addressing gaps and overlaps. This approach is effective because it uses participation and commitment as an organizing principle to enable alignment, flexibility, and growth. Growth, as organic growth, allows for both emergence of new entities/units and the demise of units that no longer generate value.

TABLE 36.1 Organizational Design Approaches Comparison

Approach/ Theorist	# Design Elements	Design Elements	Focus/ Point	Key Points or Differentiators
Five Star Galbraith	5 Categories of decision	• Strategy • Structure • People • Rewards • Processes	Strategy	An organization is an information processing entity dealing with uncertainty as it achieves the strategy. Org. design is a critical leadership role. Matching, linking, coordinating all the categories
McKinsey 7-S Waterman & Peters	7 connected circles	• Strategy • Structure • Systems • Skills • Staff • Style • Shared Values	Strategy	Strategic focus—Super ordinate goal. Seeks sustainable competitive advantage. Most prevalent. Top down
Strategic Management Tichy	6 elements 3 X 2	*3 System aspects* • Technical • Political • Cultural *Aligned Mgmt Tools* • Mission/Strategy • Org Structure • HR Mgmt	Alignment of Systems & Tools	Multiperspective look at change and response needed. Fit of Technical, Political, and Cultural Systems to Management Tools.
Congruence Model Nadler et al.	4 Org Components	• Informal Org • Formal Org • Work • People	Fit	Organization as an effective system that transforms an input to an output through the fit of 4 components. Acknowledges the power of informal
Collaborative Organizational Design Gelinas & James	7 Integrated Circles	• Core Goals & Values • Strategy • Work Processes • Structure • Systems • People • Culture	Core Goals of Future at design team level	Design Teams use this model to both create their vision and design their organization. Goals are measurable while values are the how. It is used for unit level design.
Six Box Model Weisbord	6 Boxes	• Purpose • Structure • Relationships • Helpful Mechanisms • Rewards • Leadership	Purpose And Leadership	Clarity and balance important. The model helps the client to visualize his or her organization as a systemic whole without the use of strange terminology.
Chaordic Design Hock & Getzendanner	6 Lenses	• Purpose • Principles • Participants • Org Concept • Constitution • Practices	Purpose & Principles	High Commitment, Whole System, Growth & Change focus Iterative so all elements inform, support, and balance each other. Departure from Rationalist tradition results focus.

The Impact of Age Shifts: Industrial Age ➔ Information Age ➔ Knowledge Age

It is widely acknowledged that we are in the midst of an historic shift from the industrial age to a knowledge age. The shift is uneven at both a macro and micro level (Miles, et al., 1997). From our industrial age roots, organizations were thought to have clear boundaries and assumed an authoritarian (command and control), hierarchical organizational structure often depicted as a pyramid.

Organizational design changes as organizations change in response to the environment. As organizations grow, globalize and deal with virtuality, the structure design should alter. More attention has been given to the organizational design challenge in the last decades than previous centuries.

An important paradigm shift in the emerging knowledge age is the movement from machine metaphors to biological metaphors. Just as the basic unit of an organizational system, the human system, has both a mechanistic aspect (skeletal) and an organic system (nervous, digestive, and reproductive), an organization now needs both mechanistic and organic design elements. There should be a focus on the whole and the connection of the parts (pieces) rather than on the pieces alone.

The mechanistic model was effective for the industrial era since the need for efficiency was predominate and responding to change was not as prevalent. Access to information was not widespread nor was there a highly educated workforce. Access to information and decision making was concentrated at the top. This authoritarian, hierarchical model provided clarity, consistency, and control. It worked then and continues to work in environments that call for these characteristics.

Most organizations have a stated mechanistic structure chosen by senior leadership. This is often referred to as the formal structure that supports the strategy. Hatch (2006) provides many of the most common mechanistic structures such as: Simple, Functional, Multi-divisional, Conglomerates, Multi-national corporations, Matrix, and Hybrid.

What is not explicitly stated and deserves attention is the organic aspect that completes the mechanistic design. By following a "both/and" approach to organizational design, the organic design can address the gaps and overlaps. Org² Design can be accomplished by leadership/management at the unit, department, or team level throughout the organization for operational execution. This organic approach can guide management at different levels of an organization. It is also suited to support entrepreneurial start ups, to help organizations dealing with diverse partnerships, or to provide clarity for organizations that depend on volunteers.

In today's world, information technology, globalization, increasing customer demands, and more highly educated workforce push organizations to be more flexible, responsive, and growth oriented. In addition, there have been mindset shifts in the perceptions of the nature of organizations and communities. Some of the most prevalent mindset shifts follow:

- Nature and adaptation are better models for dynamic organizational environments than the efficient but inflexible machine models of a more stable Industrial Age.
- Centralized control is self-limiting. Diversity and innovation thrive when authority and information are located where the value creating work is done.
- Stability ⇔ change; competition ⇔ collaboration; freedom ⇔ self-governance; and individuality ⇔ community are not opposites. The greatest benefit comes when we think in terms of both/and rather than either /or.
- Communities and organizations are held together by the power of purpose, shared beliefs, and identity—commitment not force.
- Communities/organizations progress through their ability to remain coherent, make sense, and respond effectively to their environment.

The above emerging themes justify more organic organizational designs. The shift to a

TABLE 36.2 Mechanistic and Organic Organizational Factors

Mechanistic	Organic
Function driven	Purpose driven
Closed	Open
Parts	Whole
Top down– hierarchical control	Local focus & empowered
Centralized	Distributed/networked
Departmentalized	Connected
Sameness	Diversity
Stability	Growth/change

more organic metaphor that focuses on growth and sustainability for the organization and the environment is taking root.

Table 36.2 compares mechanistic and organic organizational factors. One should consider when and where the mechanistic side and/or the organic side is appropriate.

Org² Design contends that the traditional approaches in organizational design that were effective in the mechanistic, industrial age need to expand and consider the factors favoring the organic, knowledge age demands for growth and responsiveness. It has been seen that the organic side supports innovation in complex environments through empowerment in an open, whole system organization. It is especially suited for both global and local communities where members are drawn together by shared understanding and deep conviction to the purpose of the organization.

Org² Design— A Practical Approach

Org² design builds upon foundational organizational design approaches captured in the design approach comparison table (Table 36.1). It utilizes a similar approach of Chaordic Design by utilizing six lenses, albeit different lenses. These lenses (or facets) are used for perspective into the organization and must be integrated and iteratively designed. By engaging in a process of considering each of the facets of the organization, designers gain clarity that leads to decisions about how to deliver to the purpose of the organization. The process is not linear and cannot be done in one pass. Org² Design considers six facets (see Figure 36.1) somewhat sequentially (Purpose, Principles, Practices, Participants, Processes and Pieces) and absolutely iteratively. The simplified Org² Design process can be conducted in a two day workshop and refined as needed over subsequent months.

In the Org² Design process, one discovers that each facet provides clarity and raises questions for the other facets. In addition, some facets have a stable foundational aspect and a changing, responsive aspect. In a sense, the design process may be complete for a moment but it is never really finished since the organization and its environment continue to develop. The design must evolve while remaining aligned and integrated.

Org² Design Six Facets— High-Level Overview

A brief introduction of the six facets is provided below:

- **Purpose** (mission) is pursuing what is deeply meaningful; the reason for being is a foundational level of purpose. It is externally influenced but internally focused. It is sustained over time. Purpose is a clear and simple statement of the worthy pursuit that

FIGURE 36.1 Six Facets of an Org² Design™

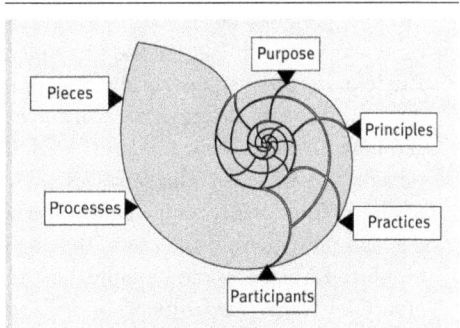

identifies and binds the organization (stable aspect). Purpose leads to commitment which is the ultimate internalized linking and coordinating mechanism. The responsive aspect of purpose that is more immediately environmentally influenced is strategy. Strategy can be considered a set of decisions to achieve the organization's goals for delivering value to stakeholders. The goals change as the environment changes but delivering value does not change.

- **Principles** (values and beliefs) are clear, commonly understood and agreed upon statements of *what* will guide the behavior of the participants in pursuit of purpose. Organizing principles and shared beliefs (the *What*) are intrinsic values that create alignment and coordinated relationships. Values like quality, integrity, and innovation are core so remain stable. Principles rarely change but can be affected by the environment and local culture (e.g., employee engagement as a principle can be impacted by culture or level of education).

- **Practices** (behaviors) are specific working agreements on *How* to operate and grow together. Practices are more observable than Principles (e.g., location of power/authority, decision making, accountability, acquiring and distributing resources, knowledge sharing, and acknowledgement). Trust is created in the organization when Participants can anticipate how others will behave. Innovation is created in the organization when there are a minimum amount of working agreements. Practices change to respond to external and internal changes. The changes must be agreed to by Participants and align with Purpose and Principles.

- **Participants** are members of the organization. Participants define who is involved and how he/she or the team contributes, is valued, and valuable. This involves roles, responsibilities, skills, competencies, learning, and movement in and out of the organization. Participants can be individuals or group in teams, departments, or units. They are the locus of distinctive skills that allows collaborative execution to the Purpose/Strategy.

- **Processes** define the work and information flows that produce value for the customer and community. There are two main types of processes: customer value creating processes and supporting processes. There is a tension in processes to provide stability/consistency yet responsiveness/flexibility. Variation is both friend and foe.

- **Pieces** are the organizational configuration or structure. Pieces are aligned and coordinated groupings of Participants executing the Processes and utilizing resources (especially information) to further the Purpose/strategy of the organization. Pieces are the nodes (units, department, teams, etc.), networks, patterns of growth, relationships, and connections to the whole. The linkages are as important as the nodes. Each Piece of the organization is a fractal in the sense that each entity contains aspects of the whole.

These high-level definitions for the six facets may not seem difficult at a theoretical level. However, the real understanding of the meaning of the facets and how they describe the organization is gained by experiencing and having conversations about each facet in context of each other and the organization that is being created, completed, or revised.

Case Study: Positive Change Core (PCC)

PCC is a global community of practice created to bring strength-focused whole systems change approaches to school communities. It began in 2001. The purpose was compelling but the organization struggled because it lacked an organizational design that could deliver the purpose. In 2005, after little progress had been made, a member suggested the possibility of applying Chaordic design to co-create the organizational design. A few members worked with Joel Getzendanner over a period of a year to learn and apply Chaordic design approaches. As the year drew to a close, what had been discovered was reframed into a simplified and practical approach referred to as Organic Organizational (Org²) Design. What follows is the story of the design conversations and the results.

The first session involved ten members including the author. Since most of the group had little organizational design background, Joel provided theory and context for working knowledge. In addition, the team read *The Chaordic Age* by Dee Hock. The initial session provided a whirlwind tour of the Chaordic design process. Although the Chaordic design process is a holistic approach, the team focused on the Purpose and Principles for this session. Since these two facets are foundational, the team needed agreement to proceed to the other facets. The team knew that any facet could be complete for the time but not finished due to the iterative nature of the process.

Powerful questions at each facet helped us with what the team already knew and provided access to new insights. The team was able to engage in dialogue until it arrived at a statement that worked and could guide how the organization would operate. Joel pulled the team back from becoming too locked in so that the team remained open as it worked through the rest of the facets. At each facet, the team ensured that each facet remained coherent to all other facets.

PCC Purpose

Since PCC had been in existence for several years, the team not only had their hopes but their experience of the organization. This helped the conversations for Purpose. The questions that focused the conversations were:

- What brings *meaning* to our organization?
- What do you believe our organization is *in service to?*
- What do we want to be different as a result of our work?
  - Different for myself?
  - Different for the organization?
  - Different in the world?

As a result of the discussions, the team created what they felt was a clear and simple statement of meaning and intent.[2]

> **PCC Purpose**
> PCC provides a strength-focused, whole systems participation and process to school communities to co-create desired futures

PCC Principles

Encouraged by their success in creating a Purpose statement that was both aspirational and inspirational, the team moved to Principles. Even though the team moved to another facet, the Purpose was posted for reference and coherence. The team wanted the Principles to not only guide their collective behavior but attract new members.

The questions that helped the team discover PCC's core Principles were the following:

- What principles or values would allow us to trust and give permission to enthusiastically and innovatively pursue our purpose?
- How would you answer, "This, I believe."

> **PCC Principles**
> - Focus on strengths and what brings life to the school community
> - Do not do anything about me without me
> - Engage a maximum mix of relevant stakeholders
> - Honor each other's basic rights
> - Be coherent as a whole—Work as a system: understand the connection of parts and whole. Do not sub-optimize the whole
> - Protect who and what is important to you

PCC Practices

The meeting ended with a shift in the team's understanding and commitment to PCC. The team scheduled its next session in three months. During this time, team members could inves-

[2]The above and subsequent facet statements are in their completed form. There were several iterations to get to this form but for purposes of this article, the iterations are not provided.

tigate the next facets so there would be many different proposals.

The time went by quickly, and eight continued the journey of organizational design. When the team reconvened, the previous clarity became fuzzy. Despite the ambiguity, the team continued with the main focus on Practices. The facets were becoming more tangible. The challenge was to discover the minimum amount of working agreements that would align and keep the organization coherent.

The questions that guided the Practices discussion were:

- How is power/energy and authority organized?
- Who decides where and how decisions are made?
- What agreements are needed to hold the system together as a whole?
- What are possible paths for growth and adaptation?
- Is there anything that needs to be commonly owned? How? On whose behalf?
- How do resources and value flow?

PCC Practices Grouped by Participant Type

Community of Practice (CoP) members agree to:

- Model the strength-focused whole system approach in each conversation or communication.
- Personally commit to work with schools in a way consistent with the Purposes and Principles of PCC.
- Protect and use the PCC logo in accordance with PCC policies and values.
- Exchange information generously. Actively share knowledge with the community relevant to PCC change efforts.
- Protect each others' personal intellectual property and confidentiality.
- Seek collaboration yet work with whom and how you want (regional, local). Collaborate with clear accountabilities on PCC engagements/projects to provide the

most value added services for the school community.
- Create and honor agreements freely and with commitment. Participate when and to the level you choose while providing clarity of your commitments (X by Y).
- Invite creation of new Pieces to the system.
- Create solutions and make your own decisions that reasonably represent the relevant and affected stakeholders—dominated by none.

"Lead Learners" guiding PCC projects are expected to:

- Transfer strength-focused whole system capability to school communities in which you work.
- Participate in creating a vision and operational plan for PCC bi-annually.
- Be open and welcoming to new and returning participants and ideas.
- Be fairly compensated for service and expertise.
- Be aware and abide by school policy regarding student well-being & safety.
- Maintain certification as a Lead Learner.

Center of Excellence (CoE) members operating in PCC CoE are expected to:

- Operate as servant leaders to facilitate the distribution of knowledge, authority, and resources to the maximum degree.
- Include affected Participants and equitably represent the interest of all relevant and affected parties in governance and decision making.
- Ensure no existing Participant be left in a lesser position by any new concept of organization.

PCC Participants

The next challenge was to distinguish the members or Participants of the organization. The goal was to clearly define participation level, membership eligibility, accountabilities, and benefits. Participation had to allow for growth, diversity, and movement. Movement was a key issue for PCC membership. The team wanted members to feel comfortable connecting and fully participating when they had the energy and interest. The team also understood that members were volunteers and needed the freedom in leaving and returning. The team was particularly interested in members having equitable rights and obligations. The powerful questions that guided the Participants discussion were as follows:

- Why would someone be drawn and excited to participate in our organization?
- What are the respective rights and responsibilities of participants?
- Are decision bodies small enough to work efficiently, yet large enough to represent relevant and affected parties?
- Who will participate in governance of the organization? How will members of the governance board be determined?

PCC Participant Types

Members—Community of Practice (CoP) level

- Learners
- School Community Change Agents
- Volunteers
- Resources—(Subject Matter Experts—SME)
- Presenters

Members—"Lead Learner" Level
- Mentors—Lead Learner coaches
- Context Leaders—topic specialists—e.g., Appreciative Inquiry (AI), Whole systems thinking
- Lead Learner—project leaders for a strength-focused school community change

Members—Center of Excellence (CoE) Level
- Servant Leaders
- Coordinator/administrator
- PCC project leads - Forum planning, process development, training, knowledge sharing technology, publication collaboration

PCC Processes

The Process facet is a key point of departure of the Org² Design from the Chaordic approach. For PCC, the need for more structure and simplification resulted in the desire to define processes. To fill the need for work and information flow clarity, Org² Design emerged (see Figure 36.2).

The team was interested in identifying value-creating, support, and leadership processes. Some team members worked in process driven organizations that defined the flow of work as it delivered value to the customer. Defining the work and value to the customer was a foundational item that could provide consistency and flexibility for a distributed, virtual organization. The questions that helped the team understand and define PCC processes were:

- What are our (3-5) customer value creating processes (product/service development and delivery)?
- What are our (3-5) supporting processes that enable our value creating processes?
- What are our (3-5) leadership processes that provide governance, vision, and change?
- What are our feedback/learning processes that allow us to continuously improve?
- What is the workflow, resource (esp. information), and value flow for the above processes?

PCC Pieces

The last facet was the most difficult to conceptualize. It would have been impossible without the insight to the previous five facets. The team members used Leggos®, Tinker Toys®, and various two-dimensional drawing tools to create the Pieces and how they would fit and connect to become PCC.

The team worked to provide a sense of the whole and the Pieces as interconnected and interdependent. Each of the designs strived to depict the function and participant relation-

FIGURE 36.2   PCC Processes: A High Level Map

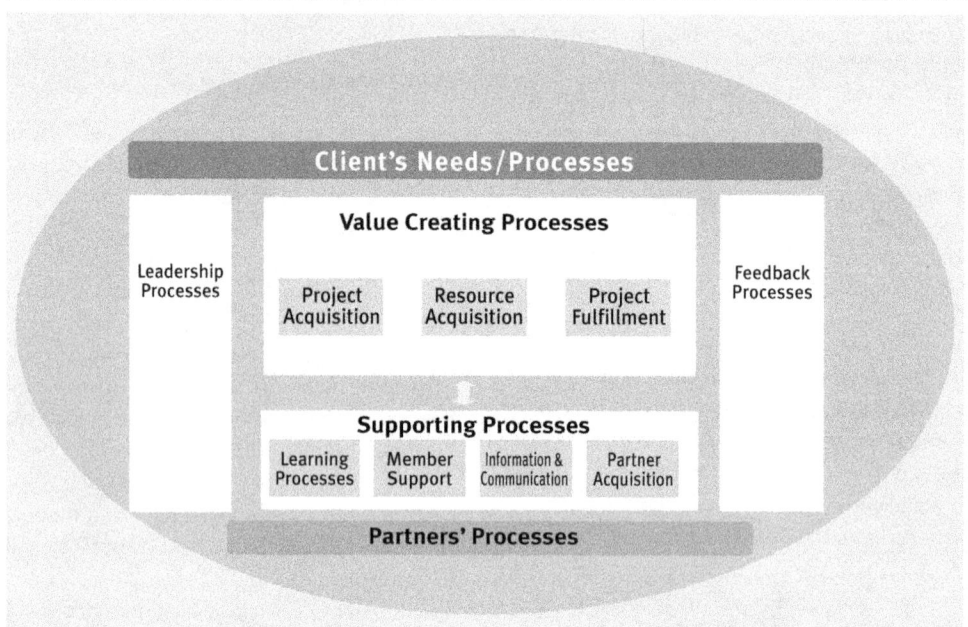

ships to support participation, diversity, novelty, innovation, adaptation, and a useful blend of competition and cooperation. The design needed to describe the location of governance, the legal shape of the organization, the nature of ownership and decision-making entities. It also needed to reflect the global and local nature of the organization. The questions that guided this facet were the following:

- How is power and authority operationalized in the unit (piece)?
- Where are decisions made at the unit/piece?
- What work and resources are located at the unit/piece?
- How is knowledge shared? Who talks to whom and when?
- How are the system/ pieces held together as a whole?
- What are the linkages and ways to stay aligned?
- How is growth and adaptation supported at the unit/piece?

- How does idea generation and innovation occur? How are the local adaptations communicated to the global and best practices deployed?
- How is risk mitigated?

The two- and three-dimensional models finally evolved into a model of the interaction of a Local/Regional Communities of Practice (CoP) with Lead Learners, and a Center of Excellence (CoE) in service to school communities. The PCC model is depicted in Figure 36.3.

The fourth session's six remaining designers iterated the facets to refine and ensure alignment. By considering and reconsidering each of the facets, the sub team improved the clarity and commitment to deliver to the purpose of PCC. The team felt the design could support local school community change agents with communities of practice, materials, and forums of knowledge exchange. These change agents could become Lead Learners to

FIGURE 36.3 PCC Model

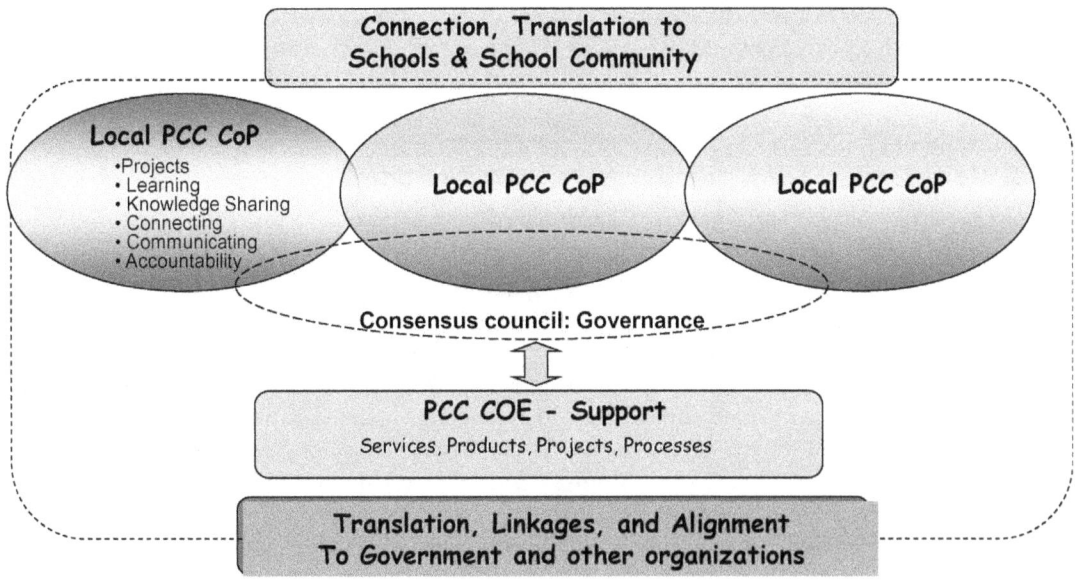

Description

Each piece needs:
- To be in service to the school and PCC community to support learning to co-create a future by bringing a context, process, and questions.

Building blocks
- School Community & stakeholders (Clients, Champions, and Cultural Guides)
- School Leadership
- Partners
- Government and Funding Agencies

PCC Roles
- Lead Learners (strength-focused whole system change process certified guides)
- Volunteers contributing time and gaining knowledge/experience
- Member – Voice in the commons but not decision makers
- Mentor/Coaches to develop Lead Learners
- Global PCC Centers of Excellence–Servant Leaders supporting CoPs and advocating with government and funding agencies

Connectors
- Conversations
- Relationships
- Agreements

Interface mechanism CoP–CoP
- Project Teams
- Members
- Sustaining Members

provide a strength-focused, whole systems approach to their school community to co-create the school community of the future.

Outcomes

The clarity from experiencing the Org² Design process has encouraged PCC members' to operate simultaneously and in a coordinated fashion to make significant progress. This has supported development of a website, training materials, articles, books, school community transformation projects, regional Communities of Practice (CoP), and a social business enterprise and 501(c)3. PCC's development is still in its early stages but is proceeding more quickly since more members are confident in their involvement. Like most social profit organizations, PCC participants are voluntary. They must feel called to the Purpose, committed to the Principles, willing to act according to the Practices, feel valued and bring value as a Participant, able to execute the Processes, and design their Piece to fit into the whole.

Beyond Social Profit

Some may feel that the Org² Design would be particularly suited to social profit organizations. It is evident that Org² Design is effective in social profit but it is also effective in For Profit organizations. The author has applied Org² Design with a global Fortune 100 company to guide the redesign of a global HR function, a large division of the company, and a smaller division that required fast-cycle innovation. The approach gained purchase because the organization demanded an approach that could support aggressive growth and innovation while providing global consistency and local responsiveness.

Org² Design workshops were conducted with the leadership of business units and functions. The workshops included knowledge leveling on the concepts, the role of leadership as organizational designers, and the iterative conversations using the powerful questions for each facet. Over a two and a half day session, the author as a consultant guided the conversations. Implementation of the design changes were accomplished within a quarter.

Conclusion

An enhancement of organizational design is called for to provide efficiency and effectiveness in a global dynamic environment as we shift to a knowledge age. Organic Organizational (Org²) Design provides just such a growth oriented, practical framework to guide organizational designers at any level of the organization (Whole or Piece). By building on solid theory and providing a practical application, organizational designers should be encouraged to deal with gaps and overlaps with a more organic approach.

References

Ashkenas, R., Ulrich, D., Jick, T., & Kerr, S. (1995). *The boundaryless organization: Breaking the chains of organizational structure.* San Francisco, CA: Jossey-Bass Publishers.

Burns, T., & Stalker, G.M. (1994). *The management of innovation.* Oxford, England: Oxford University Press.

Burton, M.B., DeScanctis, G., & Obel, B. (2006). *Organizational design: A step-by-step approach.* Cambridge, UK: Cambridge University Press.

Galbraith, J. R. (1973). *Designing complex organizations.* Reading, MA: Addison-Wesley Publishing, Co.

Galbraith, J.R. (1995). *Designing organizations: An executive briefing on strategy, structure, and process.* San Francisco, CA: Jossey-Bass.

Galbraith, J. (2007). Designing the innovating organization. Retrieved from http://www.jaygalbraith.com/resources/designing_innovating_org.pdf.

Gelinas, M., & James, R. (2007) Collaborative organizational design, Retrieved from http://www.gelinasjames.com/what.html.

Hatch, M. J., (with Cunliffe, A. L.). (2006). *Organization theory: Modern, symbolic, and postmodern perspectives* (2nd Ed.). New York, NY: Oxford University Press.

Hock, D. (2000). Birth of the chaordic age. *Executive Excellence,* 17(6), 6-7.

Miles, R., Snow, C., Mathews, J., Miles, G., & Coleman, H. (1997). Organizing in the knowledge age: Anticipating the cellular form. *Academy of Management Executive,* 11(4), 7–12.

Nadler, D., Gerstein, M., & Shaw, R., (1992). *Organizational architecture: Designs for changing organizations.* San Francisco, CA: Jossey-Bass Publishers.

Nadler, D., & Tushman, M. (1997). *Competing by design: The power of organizational architecture.* New York, NY: Oxford University Press, Inc.

Pasmore, W. A. (1988). *Designing effective organizations: The socio-technical systems perspective.* New York, NY: John Wiley & Sons, Inc.

Seiling, J.G. (1997). *The membership organization: Achieving top performance through the new workplace community.* Palo-Alto, CA: Davies-Black Publishing.

Simons, Robert. (2005). *Levers of organizational design.* Boston, MA: Harvard Business School Press.

Schein, E., (1990). Organizational culture. *American Psychologist,* 45(2), 109–119.

Waterman, R. H. Jr., Peters, T. J., & Phillips, J. R., (1980). Structure is not organization. *Business Horizons,* 23(3), 14–27.

CHAPTER 37

Participative Design

An Overview

Greg Vaughan

Things We Know to Be True

Let's be honest. There are some things we know to be true without needing proof.

- Did you ever really doubt that cigarette smoking is hazardous to your health?
- Do you doubt that talking on a cell phone while driving a car increases risk of accident?

We have a sort of collective consensus about these things. We *know* other people will agree with us. We even feel safe talking about these topics in social situations because they pose low risk of disagreement.

OK, here's another one:

- Do you really think bureaucracy is the best way to get things done?

I'll bet most of you agree that bureaucracy is a badly flawed system we grudgingly make the most of. So why, then, do organizations continue to function in ways most acknowledge to be frustratingly ineffective?

Blind Spots

We all have blind spots—areas of behavior or personality that are outside of our awareness. Organizations have their own blind spots. One

such blind spot that is the root of many problems and missed opportunities is the bureaucratic organizational design.

Organizational design is overlooked as a key to organizational breakthrough. Indeed, the design structure underlying the vast majority of companies and organizations has remained unchanged for over 200 years (Emery & Purser, 1996, p. 50). That design is the command and control hierarchy.

Often called a bureaucratic or centralized system, the command and control structure fits like a pair of bad shoes in today's uncertain social and technical environment. Most of us intuitively *know* this to be true. Management as we've known it usually means controlling the work of others, but this kind of management is rapidly becoming obsolete. The alternative is self-management.

Only Two Choices

Basically, there are two ways to structure an organization (see Figure 37.1). One is a command and control structure where responsibility for coordination and control of work occurs one level above where the work is being done. This is called Design Principle 1 (DP1), and it typifies the familiar bureaucratic organizations in which we've all worked. The other is an organizational structure where coordina-

FIGURE 37.1

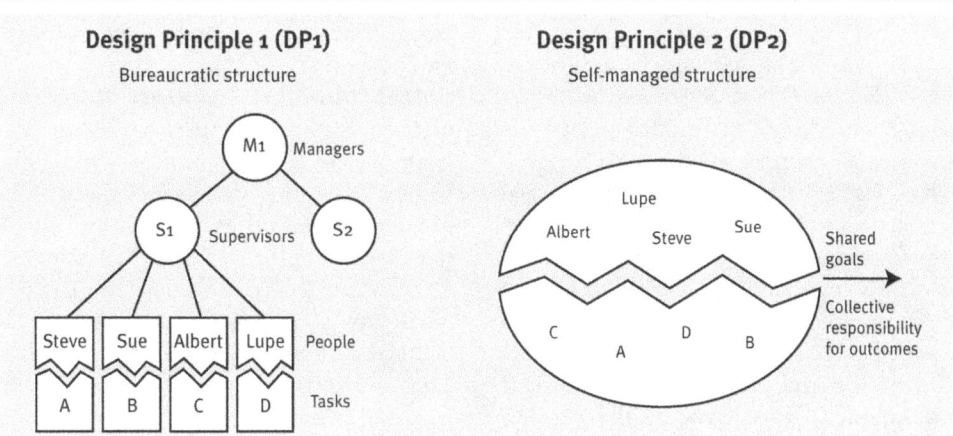

tion and control occurs by those actually doing the work. This is called Design Principle 2 (DP2) and it is the structure necessary for truly self-managing organizations (Emery & Purser, pp. 102-109).

Underlying the DP1 design are a number of mechanistic assumptions about employees. In the DP1 structure, employees are considered interchangeable and easily replaced cogs in the organizational wheel. To make this possible, concise job descriptions are established and layers of managers, supervisors, and specialists are established to coordinate and oversee the work of those below them. At an even deeper level, the underlying assumption is that employees lack the skills, knowledge, and drive to manage their own affairs. Management reveals this belief when they complain, "My employees just don't want any more responsibility."

In contrast, the DP2 design principle assumes that, given the right organizational conditions, employees are purposeful, ideal seeking, and can manage themselves. This paradigm views people as capable of contributing to a learning and planning community, collaborating to achieve a shared desirable future. In DP2 organizations, employees develop the capacity and accept the responsibility to perform multiple functions as needed by the work group to achieve its purposes.

Bye Bye Bureaucracy

Most organizations are still command and control structures (DP1). This design made sense in the industrial age, but not any more. Then, employees were viewed as easily replaceable, needing the guidance and expertise of supervisors to oversee their performance.

In today's turbulent environment, however, the DP1 structure is no longer adaptive. Managers and supervisors can't be experts in every facet of the complex workplace. Increasingly, the workforce consists of knowledge workers, who are capable of managing their own work and need to do so to maximize creativity.

Research conducted by Fred Emery and other social scientists identified a litany of problems with bureaucracy. The following are just a few they found (Cabana, 1995, p.221):

- Bureaucracy stifles creativity, learning, and enthusiasm
- The bureaucratic workplace reinforces competition rather than cooperation
- People withhold valuable information that might give another internal person or group a competitive advantage
- Those at the top rarely have an idea of what is really happening below them because sub-

ordinates distort and filter information as it travels up the hierarchy

Bureaucratic organizations create a vicious cycle. They assume employees need to be told what to do and get exactly that—employees who wait for guidance and don't take responsibility. This learned helplessness is often the catalyst for change in the first place, but improvement programs like TQM, empowerment, and re-engineering eventually bog down because they still retain centralized control and fail to alter the organization's underlying structure. "Rather than attempting to fix the bureaucratic structures and elaborate systems that have stifled entrepreneurial initiative," companies continually sidestep the primary issue rather than solve it (Ghoshal & Bartlett, p. 39).

At a personal level, it is understandable that bureaucracy retains such a tenacious hold on us. From early childhood we are socialized into command and control classrooms. The typical education experience is one based on passivity, where curriculum and learning methods are determined by teachers and school boards. From school, we move on to fill job slots where we are told what to do. Even when we attend conferences or workshops for professional development, the events are coordinated by specialists who assume what participants need to know and bring in experts to deliver it.

At the organizational level, there is tremendous fear that anything other than DP1 will lead to chaos and lack of structure. Fear is often strongest among managers and supervisors who see themselves as having the most to lose in a DP2 organizational structure. Indeed, they have worked hard within the bureaucracy to achieve status and influence, and they often circle the wagons to protect their gains. Because of this, any organizational move towards DP2 must be accompanied by extensive work with mid-level managers to help them adopt useful new roles within the organization.

What's In It for Me?

So why would an organization decide to cast aside its cherished relationship with bureau-

cracy in favor of the uncharted waters of self-management? For one thing, self-managing organizations are cheaper to run, they have lower overhead. "Staffing levels are 25 to 40 percent lower than in traditional bureaucratic organizations (Purser & Cabana, 1998, p. 29)." Fewer managers and supervisors are required in the self-managing organization because teams of multi-skilled workers absorb many of their functions.

Self-managing organizations also are more productive. A self-management structure at Southcorp yielded 60% reduction in waste, along with lower levels of rejects (Rehm, p. 151). Studies conducted by Proctor and Gamble showed productivity to be 30 to 40 percent higher in its self-managed plants (Purser & Cabana, pp. 27-29).

The self-managing organization is a more effective way to get things done. This is because both human and technical needs are taken into account in the design of the organization. Employees display higher levels of involvement, responsibility, and commitment because they have greater influence over their own work conditions. They also take more initiative and demonstrate more creativity than their counterparts in command and control organizations.

In today's constantly changing environment, survival depends on a company's capacity to respond quickly. Compared to their command and control counterparts, self-managing organizations are more flexible. They anticipate and adapt more quickly to changes in the marketplace and surrounding environment. This is because the self-managing work structure creates the necessary conditions for accelerated learning.

Been There, Done That

So, with all these compelling advantages, why isn't there a stampede to self-management? One barrier in the United States is the belief among many companies that they've already tried it. They implement programs under the guise of self-management, such as self-managed teams and employee empowerment. Unfortunately, most of these programs are just window dressing because the underlying organizational structure remains DP1. The trend in the U.S. is "to pretend you can have a self-managing group, with a supervisor who is re-labeled as a trainer, leader, or coach when in truth responsibility hasn't really been shifted to the team (Emery, F., 1995, p. 8)". Changing a supervisor's title doesn't reap the benefits of self-management unless the organizational structure is changed to DP2.

Cosmetic changes that don't address the organizational structure eventually fail, leaving both management and employees sick of terms like self-management and empowerment. Cosmetic changes that don't work also leave the organization vulnerable to grabbing the next hot management tool-of-the-month that inevitably comes along. No wonder employees groan when they hear about another new organizational initiative.

Overhaul Basics— Participative Design

Participative design (PD) is the basic building block for creating a self-managing organization. It is a method for moving from a bureaucratic model to one in which people restructure their own workplace—no design is imposed. It is unique because the responsibility for coordination and control of work moves away from supervisors to the people actually doing the work.

The vehicle for implementing the self-managing design is a one- or two-day event called the *participative design workshop* (PDW). Before any workshops are conducted, however, considerable planning and education are required.

Think and Talk Time

The transition from a DP1 to a DP2 is a profound change that requires absolute commitment from leadership and extensive education throughout the organization. It is critical that executives, managers, supervisors and team members have conceptual understanding of participative design principles. Team boundar-

ies must be negotiated within the overall vision and mission of the organization. The roles of managers and supervisors must be carefully redesigned, and support must be provided to help them make the adjustments.

Like any good initiative, the participative design process begins with an organization-wide communication and education process. This phase is more important than usual, however, because the result of the participative design process is a fundamentally new organization in terms of structure, culture and values. The outcome of this journey is heavily influenced by how clearly employees understand the design principles and concepts of self-management. Take time to make sure this happens.

Education and planning varies from organization to organization, but should always begin with senior management. Union involvement should also begin at this point where applicable. Educational workshops, presentations and discussion groups help managers understand the differences between bureaucratic and participative structures, and how their outcomes differ. One way to educate managers is to conduct an abbreviated PDW to give them a chance to experience the process directly and assess its applicability. (Purser & Cabana, pp. 209-211)

After working with management, facilitators conduct educational forums throughout the organization. Employees at all levels need time to assimilate the new concepts and learn about participative design. It is useful to distribute and discuss a Q&A booklet that addresses many of the typical concerns and questions employees will have.

The Vision Thing

Before embarking on a participative design process, the organization needs a clearly defined and compelling vision. Employees need to know where they are headed and why it is important. Ideally, the vision is established in a participatory process as well, so that widespread commitment and responsibility are achieved. An effective method for accomplishing this, also developed by Fred and Merrelyn

Emery (Emery & Purser, 1996), is called the search conference. Search conference is a participative process that enables a large group to collectively create a plan for the future that its members themselves will implement.

OK, Some Rules are Necessary

The final step before conducting PDW's is the creation of minimum critical specifications against which all designs are developed and measured. Management must spell out specific written boundaries within which teams must work. Examples might include "no increase in staff" or "maintain the same level of customer satisfaction." Minimum specifications might also include required outputs or quality levels from teams. Management must balance the need for guidance with the risk of creating too many "rules" that smother the creative process. These minimum specifications create boundaries within which teams are free to be responsible for the control and coordination of their own work.

How Many, How Long?

The PDW is a flexible process that can be adapted to fit organizational needs. Depending on the size and complexity of the organization, a PDW can last one or two days. The PDW usually consists of 20-35 people from the organization working in small groups. When a larger section of the organization is being redesigned, it is necessary to get wide participation that reflects a deep slice of the organization. The process requires one or two facilitators who have been trained in the PDW approach. Sufficient space for group movement, and plenty of flip charts for reports are needed.

Where to Start?

The participative design process usually starts at the bottom, among naturally occurring sections of the organization such as teams, work units or departments. "Change the design principle first amongst people who collectively know their section of the organization and can

readily get on with the work" (Emery, M., 1995, p.141). Once lower levels are redesigned and functioning, the higher organizational levels can be redesigned. Before starting a participative design process, it is important to have a written binding agreement for some reasonable time that the design will be DP2 rather than DP1. The agreement provides teams with the protection and freedom they need to assume responsibility for managing their own work.

The Fine Print

There are cautions to consider before embarking on the transition to a self-managed organization. Most important of these is the absolute need for understanding and commitment among top level management. Transformational change necessarily entails an increase in chaos and uncertainty in the short term, both antithetical to bureaucratic thinking and planning. Management commitment is, therefore, essential in order to support the organization through such difficult phases without jumping ship and returning to the relative safety of org-charts and job descriptions. Although employees can redesign their work processes fairly quickly, the overall transition to self-management takes years, not weeks. Because of this, senior management must sustain a long term view. *Commitment* is also necessary because the transition process will stimulate fear and resistance. Employees at all levels will understandably cling to the familiar rather than undertake a journey into unknown organizational territory. This is especially true for midlevel managers whose control functions will be absorbed by work groups. Often, mid-level managers will assume new roles, possibly becoming a group member with special skills or serving with other managers as trouble shooters and resources to work groups.

The Participative Design Workshop

First: Analyze

The PDW begins with introductions and an overview of the agenda. Top management meets with the group briefly to review organizational purpose and the minimum critical specifications.

Before the analytical work begins, the facilitator introduces the six critical human requirements for motivated work (Emery and Thorsrud, 1969) and explains how the designs of traditional work systems fail to satisfy these requirements. These six criteria (see sidebar) must be designed into the work structure for people to be fully responsible and committed to their work. The group creates a matrix that rates the extent to which their current jobs meet these six critical requirements.

The facilitator also introduces the matrix for mapping team skills. The group creates a chart that compares the essential skills required by their work function to the existence of those skills among team members. Then, groups report their findings on both matrices and will use this information during the redesign phase to diagnose where gaps exist.

Six Critical Requirements for Motivating Work

Social scientists have identified six critical requirements as the core elements for building workplaces that are psychologically satisfying and motivating (Emery & Thorsrud, 1969).

Conditions 1-3 refer to the content of the job and need to be optimal for each individual's needs and preferences. On a scoring matrix, these three work dimensions are rated from –5 (too little) to +5 (too much), with 0 (zero) being optimal.

Conditions 4-6 relate to the social climate of the workplace. People can never get too much of these things. On a scoring matrix they are scored from 0 to 10, the highest score being optimal.

1. Autonomy
People require elbow room. They need the sense that they have latitude and control over their work without someone breathing down their necks. Although some structure is necessary, people need to feel free to make decisions within that structure.

2. Learning
Learning is possible only when people can set reasonable yet challenging goals and get feedback on their performance in time to make necessary adjustments. The opportunity to learn comes from facing challenges and getting feedback on results. The currently popular "learning organization" results from individual employees being provided the necessary conditions for learning to occur.

3. Variety
The need for variety differs from person to person, but everyone needs the opportunity to vary their work in order to avoid boredom and fatigue. Variety also means allowing people to set up their own satisfying rhythm of work in which they are most productive.

4. Mutual support and respect
An atmosphere of collaboration is needed in which mutual support and respect are freely given without fear of anyone losing. A satisfying workplace results in cooperative efforts rather than competition.

5. Meaningfulness
Meaningfulness derives from the quality of work and a sense of how it fits into the purpose or bigger picture of the organization. It also relates to the sense that one's own work has worth to society. When jobs are meaningful in these ways, people feel pride and ownership of their work

6. Desirable future
People need career paths that allow for personal growth and skill development. Dead-end jobs are demotivating. Opportunities to pursue aspirations and opportunities, on the other hand, are motivating to people.

Second: Redesign

At the outset of the redesign phase, the facilitator presents the democratic design principle and explains how DP2 influences the six criteria for motivated work and how it relates to skill levels. Participants are now ready to focus on redesigning their structure.

Groups start by drawing up rough outlines of their existing work flows and structure. These charts show how decisions are currently made and how closely the current structure resembles either bureaucratic or participative designs.

Next, groups are ready to redesign their own structure to produce the best possible design for everyone. Their new designs will be measured against whether they enhance people's critical psychological requirements, build flexibility through skill redundancy, and reduce bottlenecks in the workflow system.

During a plenary session, groups present and compare their initial design options. Other groups give feedback and suggestions for improvements. The facilitator then provides a briefing on implementation practicalities and issues that must be taken into account in final designs. Based on this input, teams make additional adjustments to their designs.

Third: Implement

During this phase, groups develop a comprehensive and measurable set of goals and targets for their unit. Teams must develop their own full range of goals, addressing operational, business, human resources, and technical areas. The goals must be clear, realistic, and challenging.

Initial team goals will still require negotiation with middle management to ensure targets are consistent with and support the overall organizational vision and goals. This is a key role for middle managers in self-managing organizations.

Teams also will determine training requirements based on careful analysis of their skill matrices. In this fashion, teams develop their own training plans rather than having them imposed from above.

At this point, teams specify additional organizational arrangements that will be required to become self-managing. These might include feedback mechanisms, equipment, job rotation procedures, support needed from other groups, and staffing needs.

There's More

The PDW is just part of the ongoing redesign process. Other organizational systems must be adjusted to provide support for the new participative work structure. These changes may take considerable time to plan and implement. Communication systems have to be aligned with the new work teams to insure essential information and data is readily available to teams. This may require new data gathering and distribution systems.

Self-managed teams and groups might need additional equipment or meeting space to fill their expanded functions. In some cases people may have to be moved to new locations to work more closely with newly configured teams.

Human resources systems will need modification to fit the new organizational structure. Individual-based performance evaluation no longer fits in the team environment. New evaluation methods that hold teams accountable for outcome performance will have to be developed. Selection, orientation, and training issues will also need considerable attention. Finally, training support will be needed to help teams develop the skills and capacities to assume greater responsibilities.

Mid-level managers and supervisors will need considerable training and support to help them adapt to their changing responsibilities in the new environment. The biggest source of failure in transformational change is that managers fail in their ability to change roles and provide the freedom and support self-managed teams require (Ghoshal and Bartlett, p.62). As noted, this group often fears the loss of status, authority and job clarity. What mid-level managers may gain, however, it the freedom to support work teams in more meaningful ways and contribute to company breakthroughs by using their skills and experience in new and creative ways.

New career paths often accompany or follow the transition to self-management. In a self-managing organization economic gains must be shared equitably with those responsible for performance improvements. Self-managing teams work hard to achieve their goals, and they expect their achievements to be compensated.

Summary

Although it continues to clunk along, and many of us figure out how to make the most of it, bureaucracy is an outdated workplace model. Self-management is a more effective approach much better aligned with today's realities. Unlike cosmetic programs that espouse self-management, truly self-managed organizations must change their underlying structure to DP2. The decision to do this is far reaching.

Participative design is a process for getting to self-management. It is a unique approach that assumes the most effective organizational designs will come from those closest to the work. During the process, people redesign their own work, and do so with conscious knowledge about the two design principles, DP1 and DP2. Participative design does not change work-flow or processes. Rather, it changes the organization's underlying design structure to place greater responsibility for control and coordination in the hands of those doing the work. Such change is deep and systemic, affecting the entire organization. The PDW creates the ideal conditions for allowing people to design structures to become more self-managing. The resulting self-managing organization is more effective, productive, and flexible with employees who feel committed and responsible for achieving a shared vision.

References

Bunker, B. B, & Alban, B. T. (1997). *Large group interventions*. San Francisco, CA: Jossey-Bass Publishers.

Cabana, S. (1995, January/February). Participative design works, partially participative doesn't, *Journal for Quality and Participation* 18(1), 10–19.

Emery, F.(1995). Participative design: effective, flexible, and successful, now! *Journal for Quality and Participation* 18(1), 6–9.

Emery, F., & Thorsrud, E. (1969). Form and Content in Industrial Society. London, UK: The Tavistock Institute.

Emery, M. (1993). *Participative design for participative democracy*. Canberra, AU: Australian National University.

Emery, M., & Purser, R. E. (1996). T*he search conference: A powerful method for planning organizational change and community action*. San Francisco. CA: Jossey-Bass Publishing.

Emery, M. (1999). *Searching: The theory and practice of making cultural change*. Amsterdam, The Netherlands/Philadelphia, PA: John Benjamins Publishing.

Emery, M. (1998). Would the real participative design workshop (PDW) stand up please? Unpublished article in *Introduction to the theory and practice of open systems thinking*. Las Cruces, New Mexico State University International Institute for Resource Management.

Ghoshal, S., & Bartlett, C.,1997. *The individualized corporation: A fundamentally new approach to management*. New York, NY: HarperBusiness.

Purser, P.E., & Cabana, S (1998). *The self managing organization: How leading companies are transforming the work of teams for real impact*. New York, NY: The Free Press.

Rehm, R. (1999), *People in charge: Creating self managing workplaces*. Gloucestershire, UK: Hawthorn Publishing.

CHAPTER 38

Creating the Complex Adaptive Organization

A Primer on Complex Adaptive Systems

Dudley Tower

COMPLEX ADAPTIVE SYSTEMS (CAS) theory describes the manner in which change occurs in an increasingly dynamic and unpredictable operating environment. It also gives us considerable insight into how human systems might organize themselves in order to adapt fluidly, and even thrive, in response to continuous external change. The reason this is so important to OD practitioners is that our world is currently experiencing an escalating and irreversible trend towards increasing complexity. Old methods of understanding change and organizing human systems are inconsistent with this new reality. In the past, the world seemed a more stable place. Assumptions regarding cause and effect, prediction and control, and the desirability of semi-closed, equilibrium-seeking systems had greater merit. Today—with the rise of a global economy, increasingly interactive communications, continuous product and technology innovations, heightened competition, and rapidly changing perspectives—a new set of assumptions based on CAS theory are necessary. These new assumptions will necessarily redefine the practice of Organization Development—making "planned change" and traditional organization structures obsolete—while also providing us with a set of rules or principles that can be applied to all levels of hu-

man systems (individuals, groups, institutions, society, etc.) for the purpose of maximizing their potential in a rapidly changing world.

It is important to have a general understanding of the terms "complexity" and "complex adaptive system." Complexity arises when there are an increasing number of independent variables interacting with each other in an unpredictable manner and with accelerating frequency. Simply stated, complexity is all about interaction and relationships (Lissack & Roos, 1999). The world in which we live has become increasingly complex primarily through advances in communications technology and their effect on intensifying human interaction. These continuous advances have led to heightened interaction among an increasing number of human systems (or independent variables), which leads to even greater levels of communication, more interaction among more independent variables, and so on. Furthermore, since a majority of the world's population is only now being exposed to the most recent technology, this trend towards increasing complexity will escalate in the future.

The term "complex adaptive system" refers to an organism that is optimally suited for survival and "self-renewal" in an environment characterized by complexity. "Complex" describes the organism's ability to internally complement the level of complexity being experienced in its external environment. In other words, the levels of change and excitement internal to the CAS must be similar to that in its surrounding system arena. In order to first survive and then thrive in an environment of complexity, the system must also adapt rapidly to external change. "Adaptive" refers to the capability of an organism and its components to adjust, and become more "fit" for existence, in response to changes in the external environment. Therefore, adaptability in this case refers not only to a fluid change process, but also the system's ability to grow stronger and more "resilient" (Connor, 1998) as it changes. Finally, the word "system" is an arbitrary designation given to an interacting or interdependent set of elements that form a unified whole. The reason this is an arbitrary distinction is because most natural systems, especially human systems, form "multileveled structures" where each level displays characteristics of relative autonomy, but is also a component of several larger systems (Capra, 1982).

The Four Principles of CAS Theory

There are four simple rules or principles of CAS theory, that can be applied uniformly to the organization of all levels in a multi-leveled

human system (individuals, groups, institutions, society) in order to enhance complexity, create an emergent change process, and develop the capability for continuous self-renewal. These principles are shown in Figure 38.1.

Principle #1: Dynamic Instability

A CAS exhibits characteristics of both stability and chaos, normally operating within a range of maximum sustainable instability where there are high levels of system interaction and communication. By operating on this "edge of chaos" (Waldrop, 1992) the system is already changing continuously, and can adapt rapidly to perturbations in the external environment.

Principle #2: Emphasis on the Whole and Now

In a CAS, small changes will interact with each other and/or instabilities in the external environment, growing in intensity until the system reaches a "bifurcation point" (Prigogine & Stengers, 1984). These bifurcation points tend to actually be critical decision points in human systems, where an entity has the option of choosing a new direction from several alternatives. The resulting change will emerge (often unpredictably) based upon the current relationship of the CAS, and its chosen course of action, within the whole system.

FIGURE 38.1 Principles of CAS Theory

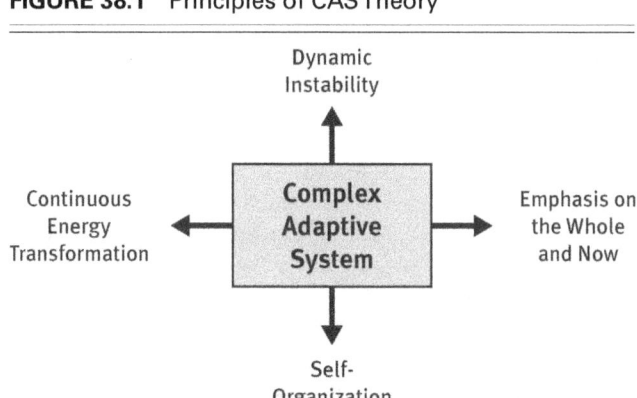

Principle #3: Self-Organization

Stuart Kauffman (1995) describes self-organization as "the root source of order" in the evolution of biological systems. A CAS is structured employing minimum rules, maximum self-direction, permeable internal and external boundaries, and with a propensity to be constantly testing the limits of these boundaries. A system structured in this manner will become fluidly changeable, and develop naturally (as positive changes are reinforced) towards greater "fitness": defined as increasing levels of coordination, autonomy, interdependence, flexibility, and integration; a continual improvement in functionality and behavior; and (with human systems) a progressively more accurate view of reality.

Principle #4: Continuous Energy Transformation

A CAS can continue to develop and co-evolve with its environment only so long as it can remain open to new energy from its environment, while also eliminating or converting internal sub-systems and processes that cause a loss of available energy. A system that can maintain a positive inflow of new energy exceeding the build-up of system "entropy" will be capable of continuous self-renewal and co-evolution with its external environment.

Human Systems Development

Human systems are unique and more complex than nonhuman systems in several ways. However, the most important difference is a human system's potential within a single life-cycle for seemingly unlimited physical, mental, emotional, social, and spiritual development. Carl Rogers (1980) believed the normal path of human development follows a "formative directional tendency . . . toward greater order, greater complexity, greater interrelatedness" (virtually the same definition as that used to describe "fitness"). This belief is reiterated in nearly every existing theory of adult human development from Erikson to Kegan. Human

development is the result of a "transformational learning process" (Mezirow, 1991), that can occur when a healthy human system is confronted with, and critically reflects on, a major inconsistency between existing mental models and actual experience. Since transformational learning is most often catalyzed by system interaction and stressful, unplanned, or rapidly changing circumstances, the process of human development becomes accelerated in a complex environment.

Under conditions of complexity, organizing to become a CAS will increase internal and external interaction, create more flexible mental structures, and enhance human development by facilitating a more fluid transformation of mental models in relationship with a dynamic environment. In addition to our previous definition, this developmental growth can be characterized as a progression from relative system stability, towards increasing flexibility and adaptability to external change, followed by progressive levels of dynamic and proactive evolutionary capability. In a complex world, the process of adult human development and that of becoming a CAS are virtually the same.

Model: The Application of CAS Theory to Human Systems

In a world characterized by escalating complexity, the purpose of organizing human systems according to CAS principles is to:

1. Match the complexity being experienced in the external environment
2. Improve system understanding and choices at critical decision (bifurcation) point,
3. Create the capability for a spontaneous and emergent change process
4. Develop the organism to increasingly greater levels of fitness,
5. Become continuously self-renewing

Human systems tend to organize themselves in a common manner, no matter which level of these multi-leveled systems we are addressing: individual, group, institution, society, etc. They usually have a choice of organizing on a continuum from rigid to flexible design. The four common functions of human systems organization are:

- **Leadership:** system responsibility, guidance, authority, and motivation
- **Planning:** method for understanding, preparing, and setting a course of action
- **Structure:** framework/design for perception, decision-making action, and interaction
- **Process:** mechanism for the accumulation, transformation, and utilization of energy necessary for implementing a plan of action and staying alive

Each of the four CAS principles becomes our dominant applications strategy in one of the four common functions of human systems organization: Leadership/ Dynamic Instability, Planning/Emphasis on the Whole and Now, Structure/Self-Organization, and Process/ Continuous Energy Transformation. Adhering

to this strategy provides a working model that can be applied uniformly to the organization of all human systems for the purpose of becoming a CAS, that will also catalyze a process of human development making the organism increasingly fit for existence. The systemic development of a human system can be envisioned as an expansion of awareness and capabilities, over time, as these qualities progress through various stages of stability, followed by levels of increasing flexibility/adaptability, eventually evolving towards a dynamic evolutionary capability: defined as an ability to both fluidly co-evolve with the external environment as well as influence "the evolution of evolutionary mechanisms and principles" (Jantsch, 1980). A human system expanding in this manner will more closely resemble an ideal CAS as its development progresses. Figure 38.2 represents our combined model.

In a world characterized by complexity, this model can be applied uniformly to the organization of all levels in a multi-leveled human system for the purpose of enhancing adaptability, development, and self-renewal.

FIGURE 38.2 Combined Model

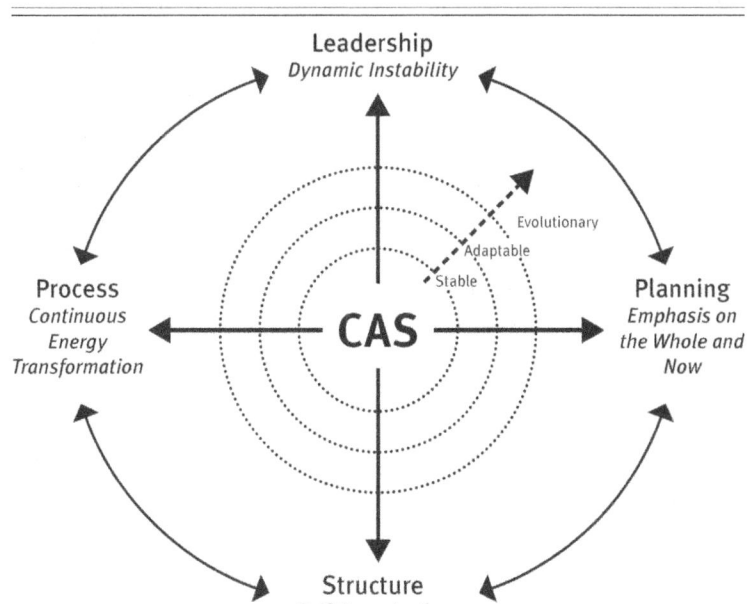

We can begin our application at any level (i.e., a group or institution), and the changes will tend to disperse both vertically and horizontally to adjacent open systems through a process of interaction and communication.

The next section will outline what I believe to be the primary strategy for each CAS principle when applying this model to a business institution, followed by a more detailed description of the applications strategy for creating a self-organizing structure.

Creating the Complex Adaptive Organization (CAO)

The appropriate application of CAS theory to a business institution involves organizing the subject system, its sub-systems, and components to become a Complex Adaptive Organization (CAO) within the larger complex system (i.e., industry, market, economy). The model must be applied systemically for optimal results—with changes being made to the leadership, planning, structure, and process functions at each level within the institution (individual employees, teams, operating groups, etc.). The resulting organization actually unlocks the collective creativity and intelligence that is constrained under a more traditional design (McMaster, 1996), allowing for the emergence of continuous innovation and organizational self-renewal. Since actually becoming a CAS is a process, and not a single act of re-organization, these changes do not have to occur all at once but should instead be prioritized, and implemented consistent with the availability of resources and in a manner that provides maximum flexibility and feedback.

The following discussion briefly addresses the single most important strategy when applying each of the Four CAS Principles to the organization of a CAO.

Leadership/Dynamic Instability

The primary task of leadership in a CAO (an individual leader, leadership team, or widely dispersed leadership function) is to motivate the system to achieve and maintain a state of maximum sustainable instability, where there is a high degree of interaction, creativity, and innovation. By keeping the organization on its collective "edge," and matching the degree of complexity in its environment, the institution will adapt rapidly to external change and develop naturally to greater levels of systemic fitness. However, to accomplish this "the social system must be disturbed in a profound and prolonged fashion" (Pascale, Millemann, & Gioja, 2000).

Jack Welch is probably best known for this strategy of keeping an organization on its collective edge. The force-ranking of employees and periodic elimination of poorest performers, combined with the requirement that operating divisions achieve a position of number one or two within their industries or be divested, are classic methods for motivating an organization to act continuously outside of its comfort zone. However, it should be noted this is only one style of keeping an organization on its edge, and Welch was trying to destabilize an overly stable company. Another institution might be experiencing too much chaos (i.e., many of the dotcoms), requiring that leadership introduce elements of more stable operations to find its edge. In nearly all cases, an organization will have some operating units, functions, and people that need a more stable work environment than others, and each of these elements must also be considered by leadership when determining an institution's sustainable edge.

Planning/Emphasis on the Whole and Now

Planning in a CAO requires a wholistic understanding of the institution in relationship with its environment, for the purpose of creating directional strategies and optimizing choices at critical decision (bifurcation) points. This methodology emphasizes: initial and emerging conditions, a "heuristic" action approach to strategy implementation, design of flexible structure and processes, and creating external relationships and processes at points of maximum system leverage. Traditional planning approaches—involving a forecast and planned action to achieve goals—are of diminishing value as we extend our planning horizon in an environment of complexity. Therefore, planning in a CAO requires some combination of traditional methods for near-term operations, while creating directional strategies subject to continuous feedback and course correction for the longer-term. This methodology will also create a deeper and more diverse understanding of the system with each spiral of action/feedback combined with the communication of differences in interpretation among employees (Stacey, Griffin, & Shaw, 2000). This knowledge can then be used to re-direct future action, optimize choices at critical decision points, and recreate all levels of the CAO.

Structure/Self-Organization

The purpose of structure in a CAO is to enhance systemic flexibility, fitness, and innovation by minimizing the use of restrictive rules, regulations, policies, procedures, and boundaries (between institutional components, and/or the CAO and its environment), while creating architecture and systems that maximize flexibility, interaction, development, and an emergent change process. We will explore a more detailed strategy for implementing a self-organizing structure in the next section.

Process/Continuous Energy Transformation

In order to first stay alive, and then co-evolve with its environment, a CAO must develop efficient processes for the accumulation and utilization of energy. The purpose of creating these processes of energy transformation is to ultimately become a "dissipative structure" (Jantsch, 1975), whereby the institution introduces within itself fluctuations and energy in the form of new ideas, perspectives, technology, actions/interactions, and other non-equilibrium flows. These sources of new energy are then utilized by the CAO to create increas-

ingly complex internal structure and processes that enhance interaction and coordination between system components. Since these new structures and processes have the potential to create even higher levels of entropy than less complex constructions, the organism must also utilize new energy to build more complex interrelationships with the external environment in order to accumulate increasingly greater future levels of energy.

Introducing new energy from the external environment—in the form of ideas, people, technology, capital, business practices, etc.—can be facilitated through multiple relationships, agreements, best practices, acquisitions/partnerships, hiring and retention practices, information/knowledge systems, and many other methods. In order to create a continuously increasing flow of new energy to the organization, these sources of energy accumulation must also be open to new energy and constantly self-renewing. Additionally, human systems have the ability to generate their own energy through qualities such as positive attitude and motivation, the use of socio-technical systems, employee and organizational development, and creative interaction. Maximizing the amount of available energy from both internal and external sources allows the CAO to implement its plan of action, build increasingly complex and efficient internal structure and processes, and create a complex network of interrelationships with the external environment. An institution that can maintain a level of new energy in excess of system entropy, and utilize this energy in the manner just described, will have the capability for continuous self-renewal, and develop an increasing ability to influence its own evolution and the evolution of its surrounding environment.

Institutionalizing Innovation Through Self-Organization

In an environment of complexity, the most fragile of all organizational positions is an existing competitive edge. Escalating change creates the need for a constant stream of new

FIGURE 38.3   Institutionalizing Innovation Through Self-Organization

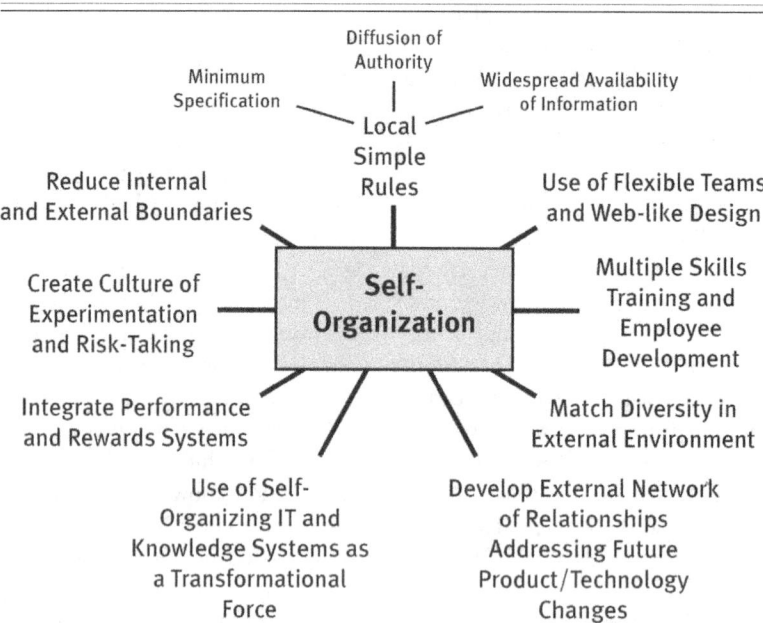

products, services, and ways of doing things. A self-organizing structure helps to institutionalize a culture of creativity, experimentation, and emergent innovation by minimizing unnecessary rules, boundaries, and other barriers to individual and organizational creativity, while maximizing systems of interaction, interrelationship, and development. Figure 38.3 outlines a set of actions for implementing a self-organizing structure.

We must keep in mind that creating a CAO and institutionalizing innovation is a systemic endeavor, requiring that equal attention be paid to the leadership, planning, and process functions of human systems organization. For instance, self-organization alone will not lead to fluid and emergent change if leadership prefers stability or attempts to control the change process. Therefore, the actions listed in this section are only a small sample of a more systemic set of actions that must be implemented in the process of becoming a CAO.

Conclusions

The importance of the model presented is that it provides a systemic framework for the application of CAS principles to all levels of human systems. It addresses the organization of these systems as a primary strategy for optimizing their own emergent change and developmental processes, in response to an increasingly dynamic external environment. It also lays the foundation for a whole new way of interpreting and practicing Organizational Development in a world growing irreversibly more complex; one that de-emphasizes traditional planned change efforts, and instead concentrates on actualizing conditions for the emergent development of an organization to increasing levels of flexibility, creativity, innovation, and overall fitness in relationship with its larger system arena.

There is some urgency to organizing your own institution as a CAO. Not only is the world changing more rapidly every day, but it is possible those organizations first implementing this methodology will have an advantage over those who delay—survival of the fittest, natural selection, etc. However, it is also possible that the higher levels of development created by the application of this model in a rapidly changing environment will ultimately generate new consciousness; one of cooperation instead of competition, sustainability instead of consumption, living in harmony with our environment instead of at odds with it, and peace instead of conflict. Ultimately, we are all on this planet together. There is only one system.

Business institutions offer the greatest point of leverage in changing this larger system. They are under the greatest pressure to adapt swiftly as market conditions or competitors evolve, and organizational leaders often have almost unilateral authority to make changes within their own organizations. Employees, work groups, and teams can be motivated to achieve greater levels of fitness by institutional leadership, leading to simultaneous change throughout all levels of a particular entity. Then, as more institutions adopt a CAS worldview and transform their existing organizations to co-evolve with the external environment, whole societies will also change and develop to greater levels of fitness. In this manner, by leveraging action taken at the institutional level, all levels of multi-leveled human systems might more rapidly achieve their evolutionary potential.

References

Capra, F. (1982). *The turning point: Science, society, and the rising culture.* Toronto, ON: Bantam.

Connor, D. R. (1998). *Leading at the edge of chaos: How to create the nimble organization.* New York, NY: John Wiley & Sons.

Harvey, D. L., & Reed, M. (1996). Social science as the study of complex systems. In L. D. Kiel & E. Elliott (Eds.), *Chaos theory in the social sciences: Foundations and applications* (pp. 295–324). Ann Arbor, MI: University of Michigan.

Jantsch, E. (1975). *Design for evolution: Self-organization and planning in the life of human systems.* New York, NY: Braziller.

Jantsch, E. (1980). *The self-organizing universe.* Oxford, UK: Pergamon.

Kauffman, S. (1995). *At home in the universe: The search for laws of self-organization and complexity.* New York, NY: Oxford University.

Lissack, M., & Roos, J. (1999). *The next common sense: Mastering corporate complexity through coherence.* London, UK: Nicholas Brealey.

McMaster, M. D. (1996). *The intelligence advantage: Organizing for complexity.* Boston, MA: Butterworth-Heinemann.

Mezirow, J. (1991). *Transformative dimensions of adult learning.* San Francisco. CA: Jossey-Bass.

Pascale, R. T., Millemann, M., & Gioja, L. (2000). *Surfing the edge of chaos: The laws of nature and the new laws of business.* New York, NY: Crown Business.

Prigogine, I., & Stengers, I. (1984). *Order out of chaos: Man's new dialogue with nature.* New York, NY: Bantam.

Rogers, C. R. (1980). *A way of being.* Boston, MA: Houghton-Mifflin.

Stacey, R. D., Griffin, D., & Shaw, P. (2000). *Complexity and management: Fad or radical challenge to systems thinking.* London, UK: Routledge.

Waldrop, M. M. (1992). *Complexity: The emerging science at the edge of order and chaos.* New York, NY: Touchstone.

CHAPTER 39

Incorporating Social Network Analysis into Traditional OD Interventions

A Case Study

Stephen K. Garcia and Edward Shin

SINCE THE Hawthorne Studies in the 1920s and 1930s, organizational researchers have recognized the importance of social interaction in the process of changing organizational behavior. This understanding has led to greater focus on the role of social relationships in organization development. According to Cross and Parker (2004), for example, social networks influence organizational outcomes by fostering collaboration, promoting knowledge sharing, and providing access to new, innovative ideas. Moreover, the changing nature of work, we suggest, has increased the importance of this perspective. As organizations design matrix structures, create virtual teams, forge alliances, and outsource functions, they are placing their faith in relationships to get work done.

In particular, informal social relationships have been identified as critical levers of organizational success. Unlike formal reporting structures or prescribed working relationships, informal social relationships are ad hoc relationships that are self-generated and self-managed by organizational members. The networks of these informal relationships within an organization often exist outside the boundaries of organizational charts, work processes,

and standard operating procedures, yet are critical to business effectiveness. Cross and Prusak write, "Increasingly, it's through these informal networks—not just through traditional organizational hierarchies—that information is found and work gets done," (2002, p. 105).

OD practitioners have only recently begun to consider informal social networks in their practice, however (Bunker, Alban, & Lewicki, 2004). According to Krackhardt and Hanson:

> Many executives invest considerable resources in restructuring their companies, drawing and redrawing organizational charts only to be disappointed by the results. That's because much of the real work of companies happens despite the formal organization. Often what needs attention is the informal organization, the networks that employees form across functions and divisions to accomplish tasks fast. These informal networks can cut through formal reporting procedures to jump start stalled initiatives and meet extraordinary deadlines. (1993, p. 111)

The lack of attention to informal social networks, we propose, creates an organizational blind spot. Fortunately, methods such as Social Network Analysis offer a way for organizations to identify, analyze, and affect this critical component of organizational life.

The purpose of this article is to introduce Social Network Analysis and to describe how the method can be integrated with other forms of OD to transform organizations. The paper begins with a brief overview of Social Network Analysis. It then describes the case of a Fortune 500 consumer healthcare company that integrated business process redesign and Social Network Analysis to increase the organization's ability to create innovative new products. Finally, the paper describes key learnings stemming from the case.

Social Network Analysis

Social Network Analysis (SNA) is a tool for identifying, analyzing, and assessing the networks of informal social relationships that exist within an organization. Some practitioners distinguish Organizational Network Analysis (ONA) from Social Network Analysis. ONA is an adapted form of SNA used specifically in business contexts. We use the term SNA in this article because the term is more widely used and because the techniques and concepts applied in this article are drawn from the SNA literature. For more information on the distinction between SNA and ONA, please see Anklam, Cross and Gulas (2005).

SNA provides an X-ray of the organization's informal communication patterns, illuminating the way in which organizational members actually work and interact with one another.

Because informal social networks are crucial to organization effectiveness but are often overlooked, the information garnered through SNA often identifies new challenges or opportunities for performance improvements. For example, SNA might show a lack of collaboration between two departments that depend on one another. Alternatively, it might identify in-

> **Examples of Social Network Analysis Questions**
>
> Typically, online or paper-and-pencil based surveys are used to collect the data needed for Social Network Analysis. The survey questions are designed to provide information on the existence of absence, as well as the quality, of the relationships in question. While typical social network questions focus on information-sharing relationships, friendship relationships, and resource-exchange relationships, the type of social relation that could be investigated is bounded only by one's imagination and the specific research question.
>
> Examples of SNA survey questions include:
>
> - Who do you communicate with on a weekly basis about New Product Development?
> - Who do you contact for career-related advice?
> - Who do you rely on for information or problem solving to do your work?
>
> For more information on social network questions or how to conduct a social network analysis, see Cross and Parker (2004).

dividuals with critical expertise whose knowledge is not being effectively tapped by the larger organization.

Figure 39.1 provides an overview of the four phases usually involved in a SNA.

Phase 1: Identify Business Objectives

The purpose of the first phase is to clearly identify the project's business objective. This typically entails meeting the project's sponsors to understand what is expected of the project. This business objective anchors the project and determines the appropriate type of SNA to be used.

Phase 2: Conduct SNA

The second phase consists of conducting the SNA. This phase entails defining the specific relationships of interest, such as information-

FIGURE 39.1

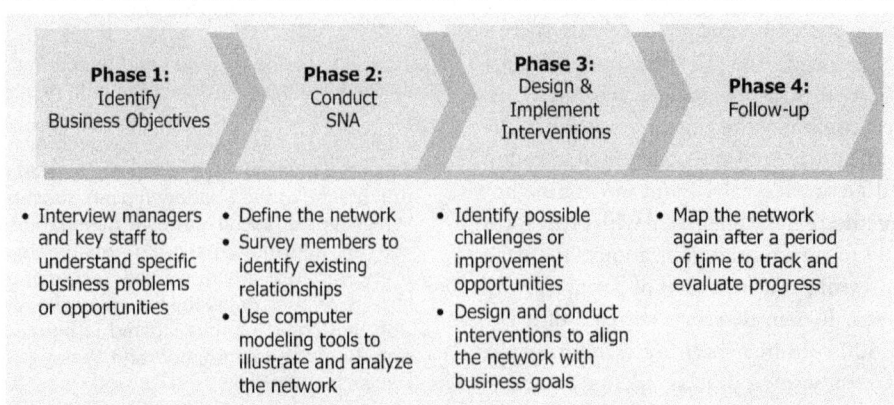

sharing or friendship, and identifying the people, teams, or departments to include in the analysis. Also included in this phase is data collection. While data can be collected in a variety of ways, including observations or examination of archival records such as email traffic, surveys are the most popular technique for collecting social network data (please see the *sidebar* for examples of SNA questions). Finally, this second phase requires the usage of computer software to analyze and illustrate the social network. During this portion of the project, SNA measures, such as density, are calculated and evaluated in the context of the organization's business objective to identify performance improvement opportunities.

Phase 3: Design & Implement Interventions

Phase Three entails sharing the SNA results with the client and working with them to design and implement the appropriate OD intervention. The specific intervention depends upon the business objective and results of the SNA but could entail individual coaching, team building, or even a large-group intervention including multiple organizational functions.

Phase 4: Follow-up

Finally in Phase Four, the network is mapped again to track progress and to make midcourse corrections. Table 39.1 provides three examples of how a SNA project might unfold given three different business objectives.

Case

In 2005, a Fortune-500 consumer healthcare products organization, Global Health Products (name changed), established a goal of increasing sales through the use of innovative product packaging. The company's consumer research indicated that packaging was growing in importance to consumers and Global Health Products wished to capitalize on this trend. Additionally, in a market cluttered with advertising, the company believed that a product's on-the-shelf packaging represented the only opportunity to communicate with 100% of potential consumers.

Despite its best efforts, Global Health Products had difficulty achieving its goal. Efforts to create innovative packaging routinely resulted in long product development delays and costly rework. In one extreme example, not only was the project delayed by over 12 months, but the company ultimately had to discard millions of dollars of manufacturing equipment and product components.

Leaders at Global Health Products believed that the root cause of the problem was a poorly-defined packaging development process. To address this issue, Global Health Prod-

TABLE 39.1

	Example 1	Example 2	Example 3
Phase 1: Identify Business Objectives	Reduce the time it takes to get newly hired R&D associates fully engaged	Improve collaboration between functional departments	Increase senior leaders' decision-making capabilities
Phase 2: Conduct SNA Define the network	Problem-solving relationships between R&D associates	Information-sharing and resource exchange relationships between departments	Problem-solving relationships amongst senior leadership team members
Conduct SNA	Web-based survey	Paper & pencil survey	Individual interviews
Analyze network data	Analysis of how connected R&D associates are to others in the network of problem-solving relationships	Analysis of the strength of relationships between departments	Identification of leaders' pattern of relationships to ensure each is accessing information from all relevant parties
Phase 3: Design and Implement Interventions	Implement mentorship program through which new hires are linked to the best-connected mentors	Cross-functional team building	Individual coaching
Phase 4: Follow up	Conduct follow up SNA to see if new hires are appropriately integrated into the network	Conduct follow up SNA to see if inter-departmental collaboration has improved	Conduct follow up SNA to see if leaders are leveraging their networks to access information and knowledge

ucts asked us to define a new process for the development of product packaging.

Initially, we believed that the project was a relatively straightforward process redesign effort in which we would interview key stakeholders, map a new packaging development process with clearly delineated roles and responsibilities, and create a set of performance-support tools to aid employees in executing the process.

As we began our stakeholder interviews, however, we became concerned. Our interviews suggested that the R&D and Manufacturing departments were not collaborating effectively. This was a significant concern because the design of effective packaging requires that the two departments work together closely. R&D needs to ensure that the packaging protects

the integrity of the product formulation while Manufacturing needs to make certain that the packaging can be produced cost effectively. Only by integrating the expertise of both departments could Global Health Products develop reliable, cost-effective and innovative packages.

As can be seen from Figure 39.2, however, the biggest themes stemming from the stakeholder interviews included misaligned missions and goals between R&D and Manufacturing; and inadequate cross-functional collaboration.

This suggested that the company's problem would not be solved simply by reengineering the packaging process.

We needed a way to improve the underlying relationships between the R&D and Manufacturing departments. Since both functions

FIGURE 39.2

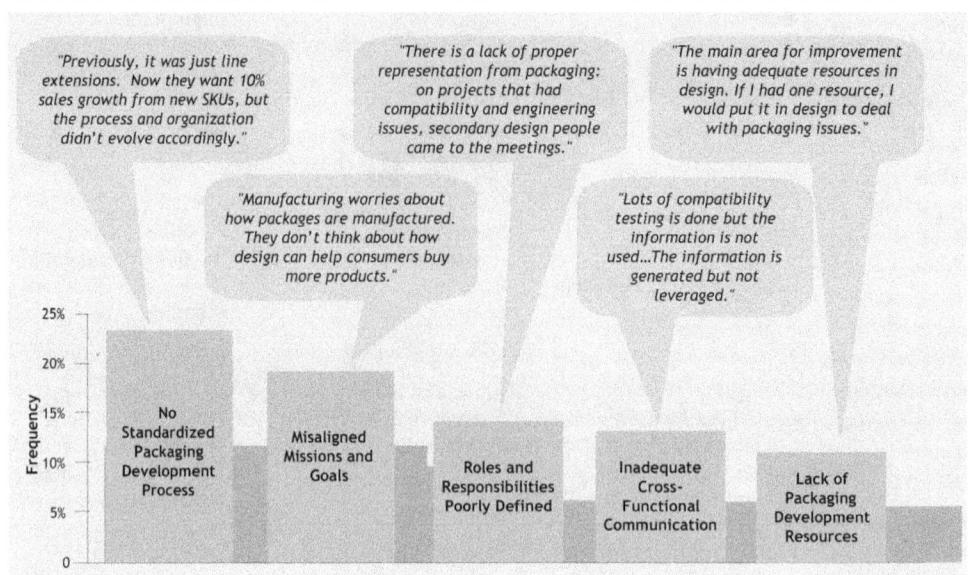

were reluctant to engage in what they regarded as "soft" team-building activities, we decided to conduct a SNA. Although SNA is a tool that can be used to improve relationships, the methodology is quantitative and appeals to those with a preference for "hard" numbers. After briefing them on the nature of SNA, our clients were more open to the suggestion that we take a closer look at the nature of their working relationships.

We began by identifying the specific type of relationships in which we were interested. In this case, it was the sharing of information related to packaging development. In SNA, identifying the appropriate network of individuals from whom to collect data is a critical step. Unlike marketing research, where data from a sample of the population can be sufficient for analysis, SNA requires data from the entire population; otherwise central members can be omitted and result in an inaccurate model of the network. We therefore surveyed all key stakeholders in the R&D and Manufacturing departments to determine who contacted whom regarding packaging development. Finally, we processed the data and used

SNA software to illustrate and analyze network characteristics.

What we found was interesting. The analysis confirmed the dramatic lack of cross-functional communication between R&D and Manufacturing. As can be seen in Figure 39.3, the only confirmed relationship between the two departments existed between Warren and Sam (names changed). Confirmed relationships are those in which one party reports that he or she communicates with a second party, and the second party confirms that the communication does take place.

This lack of cross-departmental communication helped explain the organization's inability to develop innovative packaging. Networks such as this one, which lack cross-functional communication, tend to be very efficient at completing isolated, repeatable tasks but typically struggle with collaborative work.

A second insight gleaned from the SNA was the tremendous variability in the degree to which the R&D team was contacting different members of the Manufacturing team. Recall from Figure 39.2 that one of the key interview themes was that the Manufacturing team was

FIGURE 39.3   Confirmed Cross-Functional Initial Communication Between R&D and Manufacturing

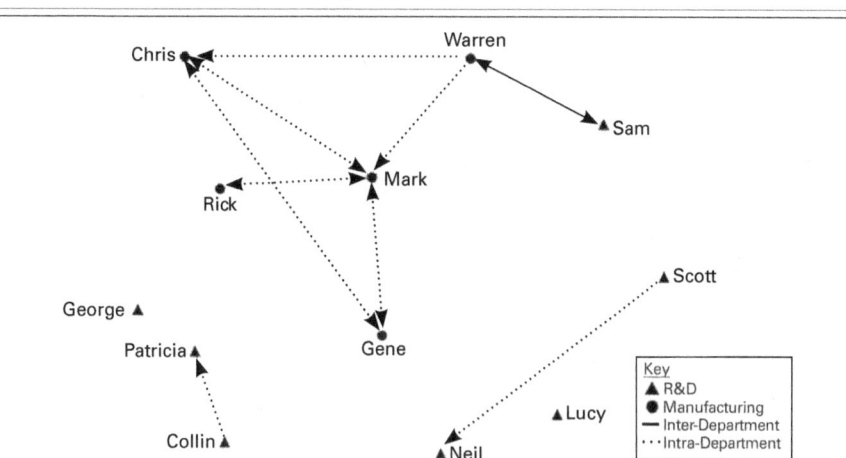

Individuals were asked to indicate who they contact for information regarding packaging development. Circles represent members of the Manufacturing department and triangles represent members of the R&D department. Dashed arrows represent confirmed intra-departmental communication, with the originator at the unmarked end and the receiver at the arrowhead. (e.g., in the network map above, Scott contacts Neil and Neil has confirmed that Scott contacts him). Solid arrows represent confirmed inter-departmental communication. Note: In the figure above, spacing between the nodes is not intended to convey information. Visual clarity was the objective for the spacing between the nodes. For more information on how network diagrams are created, see Hanneman and Riddle (2005).

under-resourced. The SNA provided an alternative hypothesis. It suggested that the issue might not be a lack of resources, but instead an uneven utilization of Manufacturing team resources. As can be seen from Figure 39.4, some members of the Manufacturing team were contacted three times as frequently as their peers.

Moreover, Gene, the most contacted member of the Manufacturing team, had been frequently identified in our stakeholder interviews as a bottleneck in the packaging development workflow. An examination of the relationships focused on Gene suggests why that may be (see Figure 39.5). Although most of the R&D team members indicated that they contacted Gene for packaging development, Gene did not confirm that these individuals sought him out. This discrepancy suggests that Gene was unaware of R&D efforts to seek his assistance (Figure 39.5). A process reengineer-

ing project on its own would have been unlikely to identify the reason for this bottleneck in the workflow.

Our SNA provided value to the project in a number of important ways. First, we used the data from our SNA to convince our clients that their failure to develop innovative packaging was caused as much by a lack of cross-functional communication as it was by an inadequate process. In addition, the social network maps had a transformative effect, helping leaders of the R&D and Manufacturing teams to visualize the ways in which their existing interaction patterns and lack of communication were undermining the organization's goal. As a result of this insight, the teams' leaders agreed to engage both the R&D and Manufacturing teams in a series of collaborative workshops to co-develop the packaging development process. Without the SNA results, it is

FIGURE 39.4   Initial Frequency of Contact by Manufacturing Team Member

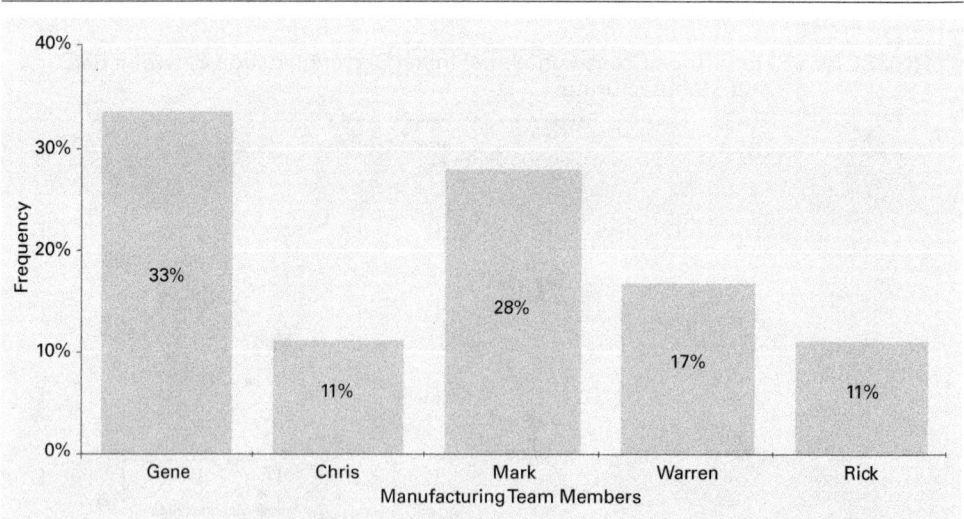

The bar chart shows the frequency by which R&D team members indicated that they contact one of the above five members of the Manufacturing department regarding packaging development. Data regarding both confirmed and unconfirmed communications were used for the above charts. We can see that the distribution is uneven since R&D team members seek Gene three times more than either Chris or Rick.

FIGURE 39.5   Initial Confirmed and Unconfirmed Ties for Gene

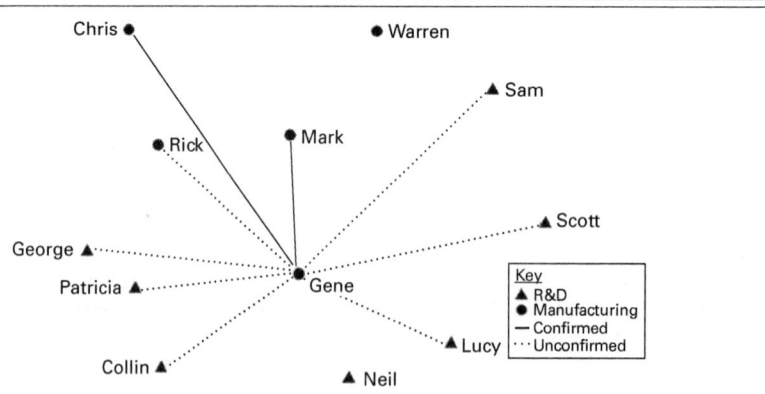

Only the communication indications directed toward Gene have been shown. The circles represent members of the Manufacturing department and the triangles represent members of the R&D department. Solid arrows indicate confirmed communication ties while dashed arrows indicate unconfirmed communication ties. The network above shows that while individuals such as Sam and Patricia indicated that they had contacted Gene regarding packaging development, Gene did not confirm that these individuals had sought him. Gene confirmed that only Chris and Mark had sought him. The contrast between the confirmed and unconfirmed communication ties illustrates Gene's unawareness of his status as a central point of contact for packaging development, exacerbating the challenges already associated with cross-functional collaboration.

uncertain that the department heads would have embarked on those collaborative efforts.

During these collaborative workshops, the members of R&D and Manufacturing interacted with one another to share information and solve the thorny issues of roles and respective responsibilities during packaging development. While the workshops produced an agreed-upon packaging development process, the biggest success was the relationship forged between the two teams. According to one VP, he was amazed at seeing the positive interaction between the R&D director and Manufacturing director when they co-presented the new packaging development process.

A second way in which the SNA contributed to the project's success was by providing a means to quantify results. At the start of the project, the R&D and Manufacturing teams were barely communicating about packaging development. A SNA map at the end of the

project's design phase showed a very different picture. Figure 39.6 shows a dramatic 22-fold increase in confirmed cross-department communication relationships compared to the initial network (Figure 39.3).

We were also able to quantitatively show how utilization of Manufacturing resources had changed after the end of the project's design phase. Figure 39.7 shows the sharp decrease in variance in the utilization of Manufacturing resources. Prior to the project, Gene in Manufacturing was contacted three times more frequently than his colleagues (see Figure 39.4). But after the project, the difference between the most frequently and least frequently utilized manufacturing resources was 1.2-fold (see Figure 39.7).

Ultimately, the SNA contributed to the overall success of the project. After piloting the new packaging development process, Global Health Products rolled-out the new process across the entire organization. An analysis of

FIGURE 39.6 Post-Project Confirmed Cross-Functional Communication Between R&D and Manufacturing

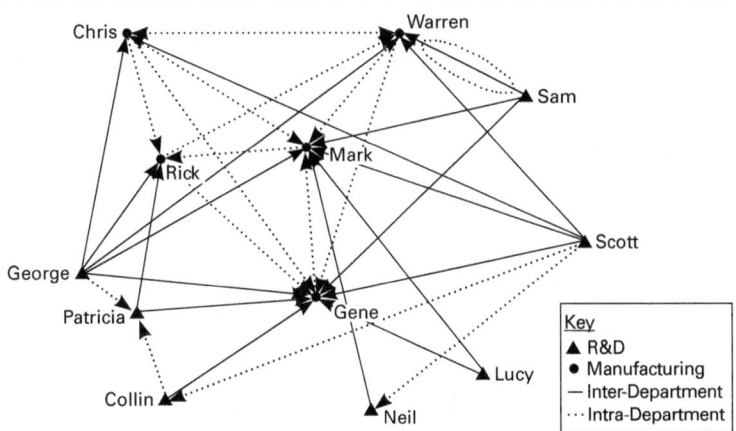

At the end of the project's design phase, individuals were asked to indicate whom they contact for information regarding packaging development. Circles represent members of the Manufacturing department and triangles represent members of the R&D department. Dashed lines represent confirmed intra-departmental communication, with the originator at the unmarked end and the receiver at the triangle end of the line. (E.g., Scott contacts Neil). Solid lines represent confirmed interdepartmental communication. The dotted oval at the top right of the figure highlights the only confirmed inter-departmental communication that had existed initially. This network map illustrates the dramatic increase in inter-departmental collaboration.

FIGURE 39.7　Post-Project Frequency of Contact by Manufacturing Team Member

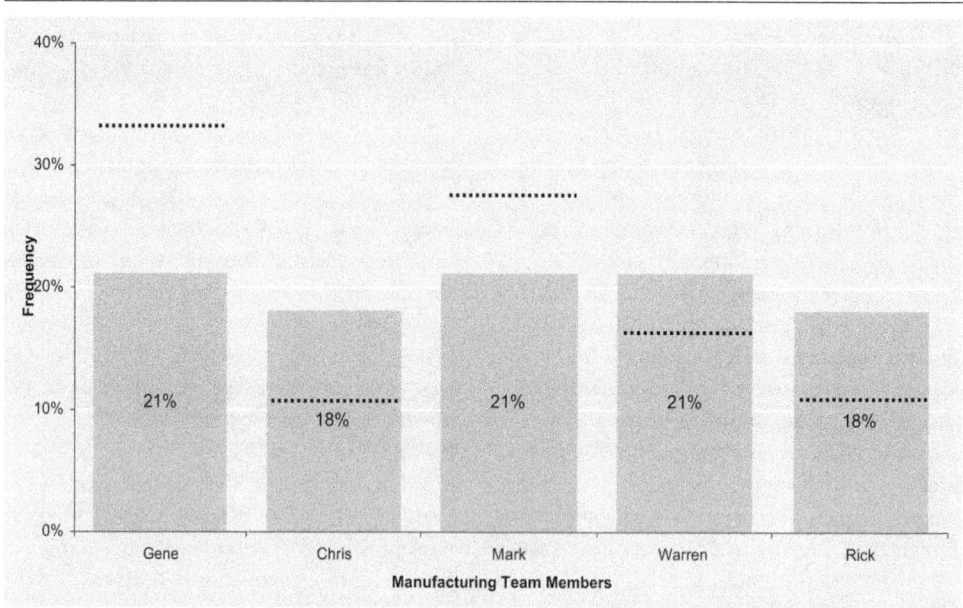

The bar chart shows the frequency by which R&D team members indicated post-project that they contact one of the above five members of the Manufacturing department regarding packaging development. The dotted line marks the pre-project frequency of contact. Post-project frequency of contact percentage values are listed on the bar charts. The bar charts reveal that utilization of Manufacturing resources became more evenly distributed post-project.

archival Project Management data on previous packaging failures indicated that the initiative would reduce new product cycle time by as much as three months.

Key Learnings

Our experience integrating SNA into our OD projects has led us to several conclusions. The first is that SNA is highly complementary with other forms of OD. In particular, SNA provides a way of quantifying organizational phenomena. OD work is often criticized as a touchy feely, "soft" discipline from which tangible, quantifiable results are difficult to obtain. While this criticism may be unwarranted, the network metrics provided by SNA allow OD researchers and practitioners to show "hard" numbers. In our project with Global Health Products, this quantification helped convince our clients to let us involve a greater

number of R&D and Manufacturing personnel in the process redesign workshops.

SNA also provides a new lens—the lens of social relationships—with which to view the organization. This perspective often provides new information, which informs our projects and improves the solutions we develop. For example, in the case of Global Health Products, had we not conducted a SNA, we may have incorrectly concluded, based on our stakeholder interviews, that the Manufacturing department was simply understaffed. Instead, we were able to show that the lack of capacity was the result of an unbalanced workload as opposed to a lack of resources.

SNA is not a silver bullet, however. Like traditional organizational surveys, SNA is one tool that can provide valuable insight to an organization. What really matters from an OD perspective is how that insight is applied to change the organization. In the case of Global Health Products, the real change took place in the interactions between R&D and Manufacturing team members during our facilitated collaborative workshops. It was during these sessions that participants shared ideas, co-developed solutions, and most importantly, built and strengthened relationships for ongoing work.

Finally, the integration of SNA into projects brings with it important ethical considerations. For example, unlike traditional survey techniques, SNA does not lend itself to respondent anonymity. For the data to be meaningful, the person analyzing the data needs to know the respondents' identities in order to record relationships between two people. While the scope of this article does not allow for a complete discussion of SNA's ethical considerations, we urge interested readers to see Borgatti and Molina (2003).

Conclusion

As described throughout this article, social relationships have taken on an increased importance in the workplace. SNA provides a means to illuminate these relationships and assess the extent to which they are helping or hurting the organization's efforts to achieve its goals. As a result, SNA is a valuable tool for the field of OD. By integrating SNA into their practice, OD practitioners can gain valuable insights and help transform their client's organization. While the case we describe focuses on integrating SNA and business process re-engineering, the interested reader need only rely on creativity to find additional SNA applications.

References

Borgatti, S. P., & Molina, J. L. (2003). Ethical and strategic issues in organizational social network analysis. *Journal of Applied Behavioral Science*, 39(3), 337–349.

Bunker, B.B, Alban, B. T., & Lewicki, R. J. (2004). Ideas in currency and OD practice: Has the well gone dry? *Journal of Applied Behavioral Science*, 40(4), 403–422.

Burke, W. W. (2002). *Organization change: Theory and practice*. Thousand Oaks, CA: Sage

Cross, R., & Parker, A. (2004). *The hidden power of social networks*. Boston, MA: Harvard Business School Publishing.

Cross, R., & Prusak, L. (2002). The people who make organizations go—Or stop. *Harvard Business Review*, 80(6), 104–112.

Hanneman, R., & Riddle, M. (2005). Introduction to Social Network Methods. Online textbook. Department of Sociology, University of California, Riverside. http://faculty.ucr.edu/~hanneman/nettext.

Krackhardt, D., & Hanson, J. (1993, July-August). Informal networks: The company behind the chart. *Harvard Business Review*, 71(4), 104–111.

For Addition Information, See Also:

Cross, R., Liedtka, J., & Weiss, L. (2005). A Practical Guide To Social Networks. *Harvard Business Review* 83(3), 124–132.

Ehrlich, K., & Carboni, I. (2005). *Inside Social Network Analysis*. IBM Technical Report 05–10.

Hanneman, R., & Riddle, M. (2005). *Introduction to Social Network Methods*. Online textbook. Department of Sociology, University of California, Riverside. http://faculty.ucr.edu/~hanneman/nettext.

Kleiner, A. (2002). Karen Stephenson's Quantum Theory of Trust. *Strategy + Business* (29), 2–14.

Laseter, T., & Cross, R. (2006). The Craft of Connection. *Strategy + Business* (43), 26–32.

CHAPTER 40

Appreciative Inquiry and Positive Organizational Scholarship

A Philosophy of Practice for Turbulent Times

David S. Bright and Mary T. Miller

IN THE FALL 2007 edition of the *OD Practitioner*, Gervase Bushe emphasized that Appreciative Inquiry (AI) is more than a focus on the positive: it is the creation of conditions that tap the generative potential of people and organizations. This article builds on this observation and suggests an approach to understanding AI that is grounded in Positive Organizational Scholarship (POS) (Cameron, Dutton, & Quinn, 2003; Bright & Cameron, 2010). The suggested model may be helpful because it illustrates the limitations and advantages of different approaches to intervention design. A POS framework also suggests important implications for the philosophy and practice of AI in these turbulent times.

To begin, two important observations are worthy of emphasis. First, as Bushe (2007) notes, an understanding of appreciative inquiry as simply "a focus on the positive" undermines its full potential to create sustainable change in organizations. A growing number of researchers have helped us understand that organizations are most vibrant and alive when they embrace the tensions of the human condition. Building extraordinary organizations is not a matter of focusing exclusively on the positive, it is a matter of understanding how

so-called "positive forces" (e.g., creativity, innovation, positive emotions, etc.) function in dynamic relationship with so-called "negative forces" (e.g., negative emotions, conflict, etc.). Healthy organizations are not characterized by an absence of negativity; rather, they generate a nurturing climate in which experiences of all colors, from positive to negative, can be harnessed to sustain and perpetuate flourishing organizational life (Bright, Powley, Fry, & Barrett, 2012).

Second, if we understand AI solely in terms of "positives," then it is easy to assume that it only has relevance to situations where "positive work" is to be accomplished. AI has been used to birth new organizations, re-energize communities, frame participatory strategic planning, resolve conflict, and so forth. However, is there a place for AI when the objectives are less glamorous? Is it possible, for example, that Appreciative Inquiry might have relevance during a downsizing, after an organizational tragedy, or as part of conflict resolution and reconciliation? Appreciative Inquiry is sufficiently expansive to nurture life-giving dynamics across the full range of human experiences, a point that is especially relevant in the current economic and social environment.

The Meaning of Appreciation in Appreciative Inquiry

Appreciative Inquiry is a philosophy and practice that puts the power of social construction to good use (Cooperrider, 1996; Cooperrider & Srivastva, 1987). Properly understood, Appreciative Inquiry creates the conditions for generativity in organizational life. As Bushe (2007) describes it:

> The most important thing social science can do is give us new ways to think about social structures and institutions that lead to new options for action. Appreciative Inquiry can be generative in a number of ways. It is the quest for new ideas, images, theories and models that liberate our collective aspirations, alter the social construction of reality and, in the process, make available decisions and actions that were not available or did not occur to us before. (p.33)

In the many typical approaches to Appreciative Inquiry, generativity is fostered through an exploration of questions such as "What gives life to an organization when it is functioning at its highest level?" To this end, a number of techniques have been developed. For instance, the prevalent 4-D model describes four phases of inquiry including Discovery, Dream, Design, and Destiny (Whitney & Trosten-Bloom, 2003). Other practitioners add a 5th "D" for "Define," emphasizing the importance of a clear and compelling theme for the inquiry (Mohr, 2001). Stavros' (2007) SOAR (Strengths, Opportunities, Aspirations, Results) model reframes the popular SWOT (Strengths, Weaknesses, Opportunities, Threats) analysis and is appropriate for situations in which strategic development is needed. These approaches all create generative dynamics in an organization, but generativity is just one part of the story.

The term "appreciation" has two important, yet fundamentally different connotations,

what can be described as *epistemological* and *operational*. The epistemological use is most common and has to do with the way we see reality. In this sense, we are "appreciative" when we perceive and understand the strengths, potential, opportunities, and richness of possibilities that surround us. Often, epistemological appreciation is associated with positive emotion and energy. From this perspective, inquiry helps people discover and understand themselves in relation to others at a higher level. Generativity is associated with epistemological appreciation when creative energies emerge in conversation and help people see new possibilities and novel ideas.

In contrast, the operational form of appreciation refers to an increase in the value of capital. Operational appreciation usually refers to the value of financial assets. In OD, we can think of it as applied to the social and human capital of an organizational system. That is, appreciation in this second meaning fosters new connections and strengthens existing relationships. It enhances human and social capital, increasing the resilience of an organization and enhancing an organization's performance capacity.

From the perspectives of these two meanings of appreciation, *Appreciative Inquiry can be defined as any inquiry that creates an appreciating effect,* and many appreciative or inquiry-based approaches (e.g. Servant Leadership [Keith, 2008], Open Space Technology [Owen, 2008]) may work because they create appreciating effects. Inquiry is a key mechanism through which people both appreciate the strengths, values, and possibilities of their organization (e.g., they become generative) and simultaneously increase in their capacity to act collectively to bring those possibilities into reality (i.e., social/human capital increases through the process).

Positive Organizational Scholarship

Positive Organizational Scholarship (POS) is a distinct approach to research that seeks to understand extraordinary human organizing (Bright & Cameron, 2010; Cameron, Dutton, & Quinn, 2003). Starting in 2001 at the University of Michigan, the concept was developed to promote scholarship that explores "positive deviance," including the processes, factors, and dynamics that makes it possible for people and organizations to function at a high level. The aspiration of POS scholars is to do this through rigorous, theoretically based research.

The POS movement has important implications for the field of OD. Scholars are helping to develop an understanding of those organizations that nurture flourishing (Fredrickson & Losada, 2005), thriving (Spreitzer, Sutcliffe, Dutton, Sonenshein & Grant, 2005), optimal functioning (Keyes, 2002), capacity building (Dutton & Glynn, 2007), and general excellence in the human condition (Cameron, 2003). Ongoing discoveries focus attention on the factors and dynamics that make organizational breakthroughs possible.

As seen in Figure 40.1, POS provides an interesting framework for understanding and exploring the unique dynamics of different types of organizing. Roughly speaking, we can think

of people and organizations as dynamically shifting between three states: the dysfunctional state, the ordinary-equilibrium state, and the extraordinary state.

As described by Bright & Cameron (2010), the extreme left end of the continuum is the dysfunctional state, a condition of negative deviance and spiraling entropy. Organizations in this extreme state are at serious risk. They may be unprofitable, ineffective, and inefficient, and may have problems with quality. A toxic atmosphere may prevail and unethical behaviors may be commonplace. An individual in this state requires hospitalization, while organizations in this state need serious, immediate intervention.

The highly desirable, right end of the continuum is the extraordinary state, or condition of positive deviance. In the extraordinary state, organizations thrive and contribute value to society; they are not merely effective, but excellent. Quality is off the charts. Interpersonally, people honor one another and organization members feel valued. Flourishing occurs at every level. Metaphorically, this state is akin to Olympic-level fitness.

FIGURE 40.1 Continuum of Organizational States and Forces Related to Change

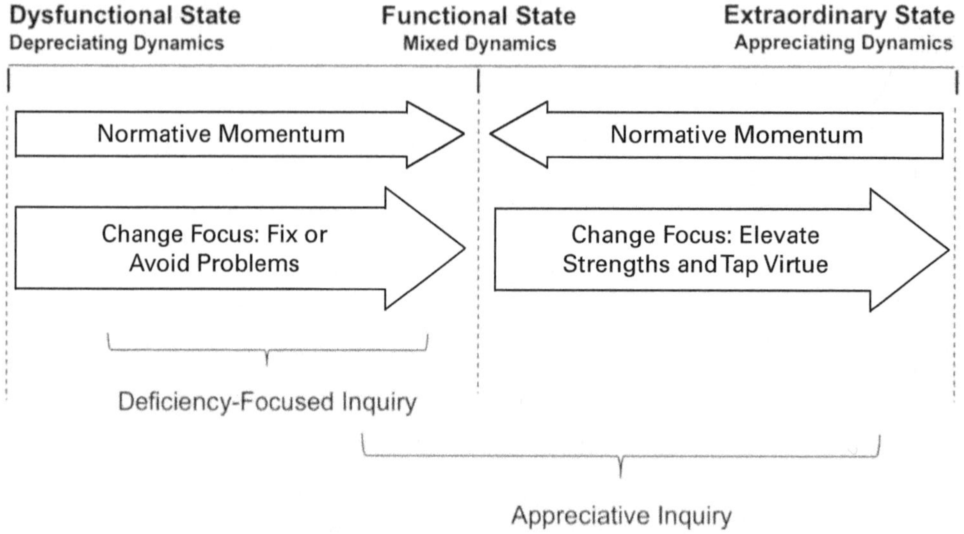

Derived from Bright (2005), Bright, Cooperrider, & Galloway (2006), and Bright & Cameron (in press).

In reality, it is rare for any organization or person to function at either extreme. To understand why, note how the arrows in Figure 40.1, entitled "normative momentum," point toward the center of the continuum. These arrows represent the direction of forces that act to reduce variance or deviance. The middle, ordinary state is a condition of equilibrium in which acceptable norms rule. Here, the preeminent concern is to uphold operating procedures and reinforce conformity and standards. Effectiveness and efficiency are defined in terms of performing in ways that perfect standards and the status quo.

By design and intent, organizations generate stability, steadiness, and predictability. It is typical for change to be accepted so long as it reinforces these perceptions, while change is resisted if these perceptions are challenged. As both people and organizations, we are conditioned to be rather ordinary because the extreme state—in either direction—is difficult to sustain.

The metaphor of physical fitness is helpful for understanding the effect of these normative pressures. At the deficiency-gap side of the continuum, most people and organizations resist being in the hospital or "on-the-ropes": there is an inherent momentum in the human condition to heal and return to the ordinary state. On the appreciating side of the continuum, the Olympic athlete has to maintain a rigorous regimen to stay in top shape. The moment this athlete slacks off, even a little, he or she will slide toward the ordinary state. Organizations operate on similar principles. When there is a perception that crisis is imminent, people often rally to embrace and support measures that lead to their collective survival. In contrast, organizations that function at a high level are susceptible to complacency and mediocrity.

This POS framework provides a meaningful way of comparing deficiency-focused versus appreciatively-focused methods of change. Specifically, when presented with the opportunity to design an intervention, the OD practitioner can ask one fundamental question: Is the change intended to *repair or fix* a dysfunctional aspect of the organization, or is the change intended to *extend or elevate* the strengths in an organization? Given a particular situation, both motivations may have merit, but the methods of accomplishing them must be fundamentally different. Reparative change *works with the normative momentum*, whereas change that is intended to elevate and extend strengths *works against the normative momentum*.

This distinction suggests that there is a place in the OD repertoire for the tools of problem solving. However, it is important to be clear about their limitations, namely that the power of problem-solving to stimulate generative change ends when the problem or crisis fades. If the intention of change is to shift taken-for-granted norms, expectations, and routines, then problem-focused techniques alone cannot summon the necessary momentum for change.

In contrast, AI is especially suited for the transformations required to extend and elevate norms—to shift fundamental assumptions about what it means to function at a higher level as an organization. As suggested in the next section, AI, properly applied, channels the instinct for problem-solving such that both abundance and deficit gaps are simultaneously resolved.

Depreciating vs. Appreciating Dynamics

As highlighted in Table 40.1, POS-related research provides a number of indicators that can be used to assess the state of organization with respect to appreciative dynamics. One way to make this determination is to examine the typical conversation in an organization (e.g., Losada & Heaphy, 2004). Where depreciating dynamics are prevalent, people are primarily interested in self-protection. They feel compelled to respond to perceived competitive threats, and advocacy is dominant in conversations. People constantly try to convince one another of their own positions, without regard for or an ability to listen to the ideas of

TABLE 40.1   A Comparison of Depreciating and Appreciating Dynamics as Demonstrated in POS Research

Depreciating (Life-Draining) Dynamic	Appreciating (Life-Enhancing) Dynamic
Organizations are a problem to be solved	Organizations are a miracle to be discovered (Cooperrider & Srivastva, 1987)
Advocacy utterances dominate the discourse	Inquiry utterances occur in equal proportion with advocacy utterances (Losada & Heaphy, 2004)
Self-oriented utterances dominate the discourse	Other-oriented utterances occur in equal proportion with self-oriented utterances (Losada & Heaphy, 2004)
Disconfirming (negative) comments occur in equal proportion with or dominate with respect to affirming (positive) comments	Affirming (positive) comments about others' utterances are at least 3 times as frequent as disconfirming (negative) comments (Losada & Heaphy, 2004)
Sense of isolation or disconnectedness with others in relational space	Sense of high-quality connectedness with others in the relational space (Dutton & Heaphy, 2003)
Fear for self-interests and/or identity discourages perspective sharing	Psychological safety encourages the sharing of any perspective (Edmondson, 1999)
Negative or suppressed emotion predominates	Positive emotions are dominant (Fredrickson, 2003)

others. They discount or disaffirm others' ideas, leaving many employees feeling like they are not valued or appreciated. As a result, they feel negatively about their work experiences, and consequently less connected and engaged.

An appreciating dynamic is characterized by conversations in which people feel highly connected and engaged. Employees are equally concerned with both their self and others' interests. People listen to one another in profound ways, and they ask questions in which issues are explored deeply and authentically. They affirm others' ideas or contributions, thus encouraging others' abilities to give voice to their perspectives. Positive affirmations in conversation are at least three times more prevalent than negative disaffirmations. The experience is dominated by positive emotions, and when negativity occurs, such moments are seen as an opportunity for learning. The hallmark characteristic of this dynamic is that people sense that their relational connections

are enriching, improving, or expanding. The appreciating dynamic leads to learning and collaboration.

The existence of an appreciating dynamic is a key condition for the success of planned change. Extraordinary organizations create a pervasive state of connectedness among members. Where interpersonal connections are strong and of high quality an organization is vibrant and full of life. When the number of connections is numerous and their configuration is extensive and expansive, an organization has a high degree of social capital. Generative capacity increases to the extent that people connect through dialogue in vibrant, healthy relational spaces.

Using AI and POS to Design a Change Initiative in Turbulent Times

Consider the following example, a real situation that the second author witnessed, to explore how AI and POS can be used to design an OD initiative at a difficult time.

The Brake Assembly Operation (BAO) of Delphi Corporation was a unionized manufacturing facility in Dayton, Ohio. The operation was originally owned by General Motors, which formed Delphi through a spinoff to create the largest automotive parts operations in the world.

Still, the domestic automotive industry had been declining for decades, and BAO had been losing money for years. At its peak, BAO employed 6,000 hourly workers and 600 salaried employees, but at the time of this case, losses in market share had required reductions to 1,200 hourly and 175 salaried employees. Delphi then suddenly declared bankruptcy, and within six months, BAO was slated to be permanently closed in two years. Though the plant closing was now inevitable, it was expected that the facility would produce high quality parts until shutdown.

Furthermore, through a negotiation between the union and corporate headquarters, a buy-out option had been offered to all union members: 84% of hourly workers have left the plant, meaning that local managers would have to hire and train a new, but temporary, work force to carry the plan to closure. Little direction or oversight on these changes has come from corporate managers, who were focused on complex, confidential negotiations with unions, customers, and creditors. Plant-level leaders were on their own to deal with the day-to-day impact of the bankruptcy and plant closing.

Thus, the challenges for the local management team were intense. How could they hire and train the 800 new employees they would need? How could they hold the management team together during this difficult time? From a POS perspective, at least three important questions should be considered:

Consideration 1*: At what point on the POS continuum is the organization right now?*

An understanding of the then-current state could be helpful in considering how much effort would be needed to build an appreciating dynamic. On one hand, the situation might have been dominated by a depreciating dynamic, characterized by a high degree of mistrust, a focus on advocacy, a perception that most members of the organization are primarily concerned with their self-protection. In this state, it would have been appropriate and necessary to create and implement techniques that will dramatically shift the tone in an appreciating direction.

On the other hand, it is possible that the organization already was a strong appreciating culture. In this circumstance the conditions for generativity would have already been present. Less time and attention would be needed on initial, condition-setting activities that reinforce or establish an appreciating dynamic.

In Delphi's Brake Assembly Operation, the situation was clearly on the depreciating side of the POS continuum. The organization had gone through a very traumatic period, and the pain was ongoing. BAO, within the larger Delphi system, had a history of conflict between labor and management, even shutting down GM production during a local strike. Managers were uncertain about how to act and lead. Employees were fearful, even skeptical about their future. The situation could easily have degenerated into a downward spiral, resulting in extreme dysfunction. It was essential to design OD activities that would help to engender an appreciative dynamic.

Consideration 2*: How can we tap, grow, or further reinforce the factors that build generativity and social capital?*

We next focus on design issues. All approaches to AI place first priority on establishing or recreating the conditions for generativity. Perhaps the most common technique for encouraging this shift is the "appreciative interview" (Whitney & Trosten-Bloom, 2003). In this technique, a critical mass of stakeholders share conversations through carefully crafted questions, designed to elicit high-point moments, to reflect on values and strengths that are important to the individuals involved, and to consider positive future possibilities. Following this paired conversation participants meet in groups, share their discoveries, and summarize convergent themes. In a larger event, group findings are reported to the rest of the organization. Invariably, this exercise produces a rich picture of best past and current experiences, organizational and individual strengths, and possibilities or opportunities for the future.

The effect of this exercise differs dramatically depending on the initial condition. For people in a dysfunctional organization, the experience is dramatically different from typical interactions in the workplace; so much so, that a high degree of positive emotionality develops (e.g. wonder, surprise, awe, etc.). Participants often describe the experience as surprising, positive, exciting, and so on.

In contrast, if the initial condition already leans in an appreciating direction, the effect is less dramatic, probably because of an existing sense of safety, a general awareness of strengths and potential, and a comfort in being generative.

In either case, once an initial degree of psychological safety is established, it is essential to respect the nature of the theme to be explored. In a dire situation, people may be hurting, they may have fears and concerns, and these aspects of reality need to be acknowledged and appreciated with an eye toward the creation of an ideal future.

In Delphi's Brake Assembly Operation, caught in a difficult and painful time, employees were experiencing a state of crisis, totally preoccupied by the question, "What does this mean for me and my family?" The personal turmoil people were going through had to be appreciated and understood. The transition team argued that managers needed to make sure to talk with and genuinely listen to employees' individual perspectives.

Thus, the first step was a very simple directive to the salaried management team: Meet with every employee one-on-one. Ask them what they are thinking and feeling. Just listen and do not talk or become defensive. Bring what you learn back to a discussion with other managers.

In this process, the transition team, consisting of one OD specialist and 12 key managers, worked hard to make it a priority to listen to employees, to let them ask questions and express their fears, to create the space for grieving, and to surface their issues, ideas, or questions. The team wanted employees to understand that the BAO leadership cared about the people as much as they cared about the organization.

At first this seemed like nonsense to managers who were used to taking action. BAO as an organization was in crisis; yet management was going to stop everything, "do nothing," and take time to listen to the people? This was a whole new way of thinking and it took commitment from senior leaders to make it happen.

What they found was surprising. Most employees opened up and shared their major concerns. For their part, managers also communicated that they wanted everyone to stay until the plant closed, and that they were willing to work collaboratively to make the transition an empowering experience for employees.

Second, a formal shutdown plan was developed only after every manager finished meeting one-on-one with all employees. They committed to be honest and open. They also committed to help employees grow professionally if they would stay until the plant closed.

Because they had a very clear picture of what was actually happening in the minds and hearts of people, they were able to create a grounded transition plan. For example, one common request from employees was to receive help in resume writing and interview skills. In response, an outplacement service was brought on site a year before plant closure. Initially, some managers were concerned that this service might encourage employees to leave early. In contrast, workers stayed because they were busy identifying potential new career interests and gaining new skills or experiences to include on their resumes. By empowering employees, management created value for every BAO stakeholder, including Delphi Corporation and GM, which continued to receive high quality parts.

Third, BAO leaders engaged in face-to-face, one-on-one sessions regularly over the course of the last two years in an ongoing learning cycle. They found that many changes emerged that required adjustment in the plan: situations shifted for an employee's family, unexpected opportunities appeared, and so forth. The transition team found that it was powerful simply to "be there to listen," to continue to ask what each person needed. They were realistic and forthright, not promising everything to everyone, but they could always genuinely listen.

Consideration 3: *How will we monitor unfolding processes to maintain and nurture an appreciating dynamic?*

This question is a commitment to ensure that an appreciating dynamic continues. Doing so requires more than a one-time event. The dualistic view of Appreciative Inquiry provides two ways to evaluate *in vivo* the effects of intervention efforts as they unfold: (1) Is the design producing a generative effect; and (2) is the intervention simultaneously developing the human and social capital that will enable the implementation of generative ideas by breaking through or transforming the normative pressure to be ordinary? If the answer to either of these is "no," then we can be certain the full potential of the process will be limited. At such moments, it may be helpful to step back, check with constituents, and engage key players in additional dialogue that explores understand emerging perspectives.

Delphi's Brake Assembly Operation incorporated this consideration into the effort to continue engaging employees face-to-face, one-on-one in a regular pattern of learning. The results were remarkable. Trust within the organization skyrocketed. People talked about their fears and their dreams, which were authentically heard and incorporated into the planning process. Managers listened to employees with genuine compassion and car-

ing. When they learned that adjustments were needed, they quickly changed course and made corrections.

Postscript

By a number of objective indicators, the Brake Assembly Operation shutdown was carried out with remarkable success. Quantifiable results included several remarkable achievements during its last two years. In terms of safety, there were no lost time accidents in the last one million hours worked. Even with a nearly new workforce, production quality continued at single-digit defects per million parts. Delivery was measured at 99.5% on-time on the shipment of over 30 million purchased and manufactured parts. Costs were reduced by $160 million and all final six-month profit targets were exceeded by 200%. This was truly world-class performance. General Motors informed Delphi that this was among their most "successful" shutdown experiences with a supplier.

But perhaps more remarkable was the reported growth in employees who completed new degree programs, achieved certifications in a diverse range of programs, developed skills and abilities that led to future accomplishments, started their own companies, reached out to others in the community who were also experiencing job loss, gained promotions inside and outside the larger Delphi corporation, and began to trust themselves and each other in new ways.

As the process unfolded, the plant manager observed, "People's lives were in turmoil, and until we focused on every individual's needs, we could not expect them to focus on the business. We had to trust that if we took care of our people, they would take care of the day-to-day business."

Positive Organizational Scholarship and Appreciative Inquiry

This chapter has illustrated how POS can be used to deepen the practice of Appreciative Inquiry, especially during turbulent times. First, POS illustrates how positives and negatives are related in organizational life. In highly functional organizations, positive, appreciating dynamics make it possible to harness the potential energy found in negative forces. Where difficult decisions have been made, people are able to talk openly and honestly about the pain they are suffering, while working pro-actively to envision a distinct, positive future. If an appreciating dynamic is strong in such circumstances, an appreciative understanding of the negative can provide substantial fuel for transformational change.

Second, POS provides a framework for understanding the movement of change in an organization. Where organizations are in a highly dysfunctional state to begin, more time is needed to nurture an appreciating dynamic, and AI-based exercises have a particularly dramatic and noticeable effect.

Finally, POS research provides an ever-deepening understanding of the nuances of functional change. Supported by the POS lens, Appreciative Inquiry can be used to frame organization interventions and initiatives in any context to create an appreciative dynamic. Indeed, nearly any inquiry-based technique can be reshaped or adapted to produce appreciating effects in organizations. The key is to always focus on nurturing an organizational state in which an appreciating dynamic is present, then foster a conversational space that maintains the appreciating dynamic. From this perspective, AI can be understood as principle-based approach to change—more philosophy than specific technique.

If the perspective proposed in this paper were more generally adopted, Appreciative Inquiry can be an especially relevant and powerful tool during the current, troubled environment. Appreciative Inquiry is always an option, even during troubled times, to create stronger, more sustainable organizations.

References

Bright, D. S. (2005). *Forgiveness and change: Begrudging, pragmatic, and transcendent responses to dis-comfiture in a unionized trucking company*. Unpublished Dissertation, Case Western Reserve University, Cleveland, Ohio.

Bright, D., & Cameron, K. (2012). Positive organizational change: What the field of POS offers to OD practitioners. In J. Stavros, W. J. Rothwell, & R. Sullivan (Eds.), *Practicing organization development: A guide for leading change* (pp, 397–410). San Francisco, CA: Pfeiffer.

Bright, D. S., Cooperrider, D. L., & Galloway, W. B. (2006). Appreciative Inquiry in the Office of Research and Development: Improving the collaborative capacity of organization. *Public Performance and Management Review,* 39(3), 285–306.

Bright, D. S., Powley, E. H., Fry, R. E., & Barrett, F. (2012). The generative potential in cynical conversations. In D. Cooperrider & D. Zandee (Eds.), *Advances in Appreciative Inquiry* (Vol. 3). Amsterdam, The Netherlands: Elsevier/JAI.

Bushe, G. (2007). Appreciative Inquiry is not (just) about the positive. *OD Practitioner, 39*(4), 33–38.

Cameron, K. S. (2003). Organizational virtuousness and performance. In K. S. Cameron, J. E. Dutton, & R. E. Quinn (Eds.), *Positive organizational scholarship: Foundations of a new discipline* (pp. 48–65). San Francisco, CA: Berrett Koehler.

Cameron, K.S., Dutton, J.E., & Quinn, R.E. (2003). Foundations of positive organizational scholarship. In K. S. Cameron, J. E. Dutton, & R. E. Quinn, (Eds.). *Positive organizational scholarship: Foundations of a new discipline* (pp. 3–13). San Francisco, CA: Berrett Koehler.

Cooperrider, D. L. (1996). The "child" as agent of inquiry. *OD Practitioner,* 28(1), 5–11.

Cooperrider, D.L., & Srivastva, S. (1987). Appreciative Inquiry in organizational life. *Research in Organizational Change and Development,* 1, 129–169.

Dutton, J. E., & Glynn, M. A. (2008). Positive organizational scholarship. In C. Cooper & J. Barling (Eds.), *Handbook of organizational behavior.* Thousand Oaks, CA: Sage.

Dutton, J.E., & Heaphy, E.D. (2003). The power of high-quality connections. In K. S. Cameron, J. E. Dutton, & R. E. Quinn, (Eds.). *Positive organizational scholarship: Foundations of a new discipline* (pp. 263–278). San Francisco, CA: Berrett Koehler.

Edmondson, A. (1999). Psychological safety and learning behavior in work teams. *Administrative Science Quarterly,* 44(2), 350–383.

Fredrickson, B.L. (2003). The value of positive emotions. *American Scientist,* 91(4), 330.

Fredrickson, B., & Losada, M. (2005). Positive affect and the complex dynamics of human flourishing. *American Psychologist,* 60(7), 678–686.

Keith, Kent M. (2008). *The case for servant leadership.* Westfield, IN: The Greenleaf Center for Servant Leadership.

Keyes, C. L. M. (2002). The mental health continuum: From languishing to flourishing in life. *Journal of Health & Social Behavior,* 43(2), 207–222.

Losada, M., & Heaphy, E. (2004). The role of positivity and connectivity in the performance of business teams. *American Behavioral Scientist,* 47(6), 740–765.

Mohr, B. J. (2001). Appreciative Inquiry: Igniting transformative action. *The Systems Thinker,* 12(1), 1–4.

Owen, H. (2008). *Open Space Technology.* San Francisco, CA: Berrett-Koehler Publishers.

Spreitzer, G., Sutcliffe, K., Dutton, J., Sonenshein, S., & Grant, A. M. (2005). A socially embedded model of thriving at work. *Organization Science,* 16(5), 537–549.

Stavros, J., & Hinrichs, G. (2007, August). SOARing to high and engaging performance: An appreciative approach to strategy. *AI Practitioner* (pp. 1–5).

Whitney, D., & Trosten-Bloom, A. (2003). *The power of Appreciative Inquiry.* San Francisco: Berrett-Koehler.

CHAPTER 41

Creating Change by Changing the Conversation

Robert J. Marshak and David Grant

If all transformation is linguistic, then we create a new future by having new conversations.
—Block, 2008, p. 36

IN RECENT YEARS interventions to "change the conversation" have become an important focus for Organization Development (OD) practice. Whether used to shift attention from problem-based to more positive orientations, change the methods or topics of inquiry and dialogue, or bring more and different voices into the room, the expectation is clear: changing the conversation leads to organizational change. The emphasis in OD practice on changing the conversation parallels and has been influenced by the *linguistic turn* in the social sciences since the 1980s wherein language, conversation, and discourse have become central concepts in understanding and indeed creating social reality.

The purpose of this article is to summarize and present a range of theory and research about language and change, where the term *discourse* is used to include conversations, written texts, stories, narratives, metaphors, slogans, and so forth. It draws upon the new field of organizational discourse studies and is intended to expand practitioners' knowledge and application of language-based premises about organizational change (see for example, Bushe & Marshak, 2009; Ford & Ford, 1995; Grant, Hardy, Oswick, & Putnam, 2004; Marshak & Grant, 2008; Shaw, 2002).

The understanding of organizational change as used in this discussion is a good place to begin. In most ways we consider organizational change to mean some alteration (something is stopped, started, modified, etc.) in the existing organizational arrangements (strategies, structures, systems, cultures, etc.) and/or processes (planning, coordination, decision- making, etc.). However, a discursive orientation frames that understanding in a more nuanced way than typical usage. For example, the assertion that something is "an existing arrangement" is itself a discursive account that positions something in a particular way and for particular purposes. Thus, in one specific organizational context "existing" might imply something is outdated and there is a need to change to something new, while in another it might imply the benefits of stability based on proven performance. Consequently organizational change involves both things and the discursive accounts of those things in contextual and recursive relationships. In essence, discourses shape how people think about things (how they "talk to themselves") and therefore how they act; and how people act and think about things shape their discourses. Changed actions can lead to changes in conversation and changed conversations can lead to changes in behavior.

Discourse and Change: An Illustration

To help illustrate the importance of thinking about the relationship of discourse and change consider the following vignette about the fictitious company Zeta. The illustration is intended to suggest the need to think about discourse and change in multi-dimensional and mutually implicated ways:

> Zeta Company's strategy and operations have been shaped by continual references to the founder's maxim to always "own and control your destiny." This led to decisions to operate independently, to own versus rent, and to use directive leadership styles. Recently, influenced by media articles and business conference presentations about out-sourcing and off-shoring, the CEO suggested that the Zeta top team consider out-sourcing as a strategy to improve financial performance. The ensuing discussions drew on discourses about the quality of rented employees, the family-centered values of the company, trends in the industry, academic debates about out-sourcing, prospects for the future, and so forth. When the Vice President of Human Resources worried aloud about the union's reaction with a major contract re-negotiation pending, the discussion polarized into a debate about out-sourcing saving costs versus costing jobs. Convergence on a clear way forward was not forthcoming and the CEO suggested having a task force study the matter carefully and come back with a proposal in three months. In later hallway conversations several of the top executives wondered if the boss had "gone

> soft" because the CEO had not made the decision and told people to implement it. Several weeks later the CEO attended a business roundtable where one of the topics was Executive Paralysis by Analysis Leads to Underperformance. Reflecting on how the out-sourcing discussion was handled, the CEO convened a meeting of the top executives to press the urgency of improving financial performance and then asked for specific proposals. When none emerged, the CEO again suggested out-sourcing as a way to enhance share-holder value and forcefully argued for its adoption. This time there was agreement to move forward, although a few of the executives lamented to each other that "the founder would never have done this," and "wait until it gets to the Divisions, they'll never support it."

Here we get a sense of the ongoing, iterative, and recursive ways that discourse impacts on change, including for example, corporate maxims, mission statements, strategy documents, hallway chatter, divisional rhetoric, on-going interpretations of corporate values, and also outside stimuli such as trade journals, media accounts, seminars, exposure to other executives in formal and informal settings, and so on.

Core Premises about Discourse and Change

The following summarizes an extensive range of the research and theory pertaining to organizational discourse and change found in scholarly journals, but with much less exposure to the practitioner community of change agents (for a more detailed discussion see Grant & Marshak, 2011)

1. **Discourse plays a central role in the construction of social reality.** We begin with the central premise found in most theories about

the relationship of language and change. Discourse does more than simply report or record information, instead it is constructive and shapes behavior by establishing, reinforcing, and also challenging the prevailing premises that guide how organizational actors interpret experience. Therefore, changing the existing dominant discourse(s) will support or lead to organizational and behavioral change. This is a central premise of social construction theory (see Gergen, 2009) and is a principle reason given for how and why changing the conversation can lead to organizational and behavioral change.

2. There are multiple levels of linked discourse that impact a change situation. The mantra to change the conversation does not speak to the level of discourse one seeks to change. However, scholarly research and theory suggest that change agents should think in terms of changing or influencing at least five levels of discourse – the intrapersonal, personal, interpersonal and group, organizational, and socio-cultural. In addition, the different levels both influence and are influenced by discourses operating at all the other levels.

- *Intrapersonal level* discourses might manifest themselves in the form of internalized stories, "tapes," and introjected beliefs that an individual tells him/herself. It also includes cognitive schema, frames, symbols, and archetypes from the unconscious that shape individual reaction and response.
- *Personal level* discourses include a consideration of the language in use by individuals, including favored concepts and topics as well as influence strategies, impression management, and rhetorical methods. For example, a number of studies have focused on the metaphors used by individuals in order to reveal their thinking and perception about organizational change (e.g., Marshak, 1993).
- *Interpersonal and group level* discourses involve conversations in many settings and

in many instances can be said to shape the social order in everyday organizational conduct. Discursive interactions at this level impact on the actions and behavior of individuals within a localized context, e.g., a department or among a specific group of actors who socially interact on a regular basis.
- *Organizational level* discourses addressing topics such as mission, strategy, values, how to succeed, and so on form the dominant thinking, organizational practices, and collective social perspectives within an organization. In order to instigate successful organization-wide change managers must develop new organizational-level discourses and communicate them through various discursive means (talk, text, email, slogans, change, campaigns, etc.) to persuade various stakeholders of the value and purpose of the change.
- *Socio-cultural level* discourses are recognized and espoused at the broader societal level and across institutional domains. They might address more or less standard ways of understanding a certain type of phenomenon within the broader context. These include phenomena such as business re-engineering, globalization, out-sourcing, sustainability, and even organizational change itself. They also include the taken for granted premises and possibilities governing an industry or organizational sector.

As mentioned earlier, the discourses at different levels do not exist independently of each other; the talk and texts within any level of discourse are linked to and informed by discourses and the talk and texts that operate from other levels. This means that it may be important to identify and address discourses pertaining to change at one level, and to also then place them in the context of the other levels of discourse. For example, it may be quite difficult for a divisional manger advocating new ways of doing things at the interpersonal and group level to institute change if the conversations and messages from higher headquarters reinforce the prevailing ways of doing things.

3. The prevailing narratives and storylines about change are constructed and conveyed through conversations. Narratives and stories are devices that focus on common themes or issues and which link a set of ideas or a series of events. As such they construct and explain the socially accepted ways of doing things and also enable and limit how people think about the world around them. Narratives and story-lines are re-created each day in the multitude of conversations occurring at all levels of an organization. Consequently to change some aspect of the organization would require changing the daily conversations that convey the prevailing narratives and story-lines that are endorsed by those presently and/or historically in power and authority.

4. Power and political processes shape the prevailing discourses concerning change. Power dynamics help to shape the prevailing discourses about a specific change and the phenomenon of organizational change itself. Organizations are considered to be political sites where particular discourses are advanced by particular organizational actors in ways that shape and influence the attitudes and behavior of other organizational members. Conversations about change related issues held among stakeholders with differing interests will involve the meanings attached to these issues being negotiated, reinforced, and privileged by those actors drawing on their various power resources. Assuming some social agreement results from these tacit discursive negotiations, a dominant narrative emerges that will influence how a change is conceived, understood, and should be implemented.

5. There are always alternative discourses of change. What any particular group believes is reality or the way things are is a social construct that is created, conveyed, and reinforced through discourse. This implies that there may be multiple social realities in any given situation. Moreover, it means that different groups or strata or silos of an organization might develop their own narratives or story-lines about a particular change issue that defines the way things are as they experience them. The extent to which any group's particular narrative comes to dominate the meaning attached to a change issue will be linked to power and political processes as previously discussed. Given these dynamics some have suggested that those leading or facilitating change use discursive practices in ways that intentionally draw out and utilize alternative discourses, for example, by using methods such as multi-level conversations, dialogue, inquiry, asking new questions, and the use of various orchestrated interactions among stakeholders. The intent being to use these discursive practices to frame new shared meanings and change mindsets that will then lead to significant and beneficial change in the organization.

6. Discourse and change continuously interact. Discourse in the form of narratives, stories, memos, official documents, conversations, email, metaphors, hallway chatter, and so on are used on an ongoing basis to maintain and further the interests of particular groups or individuals; and people continually draw on them in order to make sense of the events that continually unfold around them. Accordingly, as suggested by the earlier Zeta example, discourses at multiple levels are disseminated and consumed as a continuous, iterative and recursive process. It is also a process whereby the conversations and narratives associated with a particular discourse do not simply appear from nowhere, imbued with a particular meaning. Instead, over a period of time and through negotiation and various political processes the meanings that discourses convey, along with the agreements and mindsets that they construct, will emerge and alter the ways things are understood and enacted.

7. Change agents need to reflect on their own discourses. An appreciation of the significance of discourse in relation to change processes encourages change agents to be open to the possibility that a primary way to effect change in social systems is by changing the prevailing discourse. Changing the discourse involves changing the conversations and texts that create, sustain, and provide the enabling content and context for the way things are. This, in essence, adds discourse at multiple levels as an important target and lever for organizational change. It also suggests change agents need to be more aware and reflective about what they say and hear in relation to change than is often the case. In particular, change agents need to be sensitive to the emergence of discourses that are different from their own, and if necessary respond to or even draw upon these alternative discourses in ways that benefit the change process. Given the relationship between power and discourse, there is also an ethical need for change agents to reflect upon the power relationships between themselves and those they are seeking to influence as well as the power relationships between and among other key actors.

We have outlined a number of key considerations drawn from the scholarly discourse and change literature to help explain the importance of talk and text in shaping the thinking and behavior of key actors in organizational change. In the following section we consider the implications of this for change agents.

Implications for Change Agents

The new field of organizational discourse studies invites change agents to approach organizational change with an interpretive orientation and an understanding that language in its many manifestations is constructive and central to the establishment, maintenance, and change of what is and what could be. Some more specific implications follow and are summarized in Table 41.1.

For the change agent a discursive orientation to change means applying methods that foster attention to the ways in which discursive phenomena, at multiple levels, and in multiple ways, create and hold the current way things are. How do day-to-day conversations reinforce preferred ways of thinking established by historical, organizational, or other contexts? What are the most salient or powerful discursive phenomena one should pay attention to with respect to organizational change efforts: stories, metaphors, official documents, emails, discursive contexts, rhetorical tactics, power processes, and so on?

There are a number of strategic implications for change agents if change is a function of multi-level, discursive phenomena. First is the need to better understand how different levels of discourse influence and reinforce each other and thereby create a web of reinforcing narratives, stories, metaphors, and conversations that can make alternative discourses and change more difficult. This means that change agents may need to identify, utilize, or attempt to change the discourses at different levels (e.g., personal, group, organizational) to support a specific change effort. For example, a regional vice-president trying to put forward a new narrative about "social responsibility" may experience difficulties if the prevailing tacit or explicit discourses at corporate or local levels reinforce contrary messages, perhaps about profitability above all else. Strategically, it is also possible that changing discourses at one level may influence discourses at other levels, thereby providing change agents with alternative targets or levers depending on their resources and opportunities. One example of this would be seeking to influence corporate level discourses by changing interpersonal and group level conversations among lower level managers.

The importance of conversations to socially construct reality and frame experience versus simply convey objective information needs to be more carefully understood and cultivated by those advancing change agendas. Change agents should realize that talk is also a form of action so all conversations and communications can be used to create new premises and

TABLE 41.1 Questions for Change Agents to Consider

Premise Change	Agent Questions
Discourse plays a central role in the construction of social reality	• What discourses (narratives, stories, metaphors, etc.) are holding things the way they are? • How can discourses that are supportive of an intended change be established and maintained?
There are multiple levels of linked discourse that impact a change situation	• How might we seek to change the discourses at multiple levels to support a change effort? • Changing a discourse at one level may be easier or more important than at another so what levels should we attempt to target?
The prevailing narratives and story-lines about change are constructed and conveyed through conversations	• How can we use conversations as opportunities to construct new premises and possibilities? • How are prevailing narratives reinforced in day-to-day throughout the conversations organization and how might we change those conversations?
Power and political processes shape the prevailing discourses concerning change	• Who are the actors who will be most influential to the intended change and how can their discourses and conversations be altered to support the change? • How can we create settings where different actors and interests communicate, or where there is greater power equalization among the discussants, or where the nature of the conversation is different?
There are always alternative discourses of change	• How can we identify and use alternative discourses that may exist at multiple levels to advance and support the change? • What forms of organizational power and political processes can we use to deal with counter discourses to our change effort?
Discourse and change continuously interact	• Because there is no specific beginning, middle, or end to a change initiative how will we continuously monitor and manage our discourse to stay "on message"? • Because the discourses related to a desired change will be subject to continuous alteration how can we stay alert to new opportunities and openings to advance our initiative?
Change agents need to reflect on their own discourses	• How can we maintain a self-reflective stance about our orientations, self-talk, and biases in order to stay open to possibilities and challenges? • How might we rethink and possibly modify our discourses about change to better respond to reactions and alternative discourses?

possibilities. This also means they should pay attention to how prevailing narratives are reinforced in day-to-day conversations and messaging throughout the organization. Change agents would then seek to intentionally introduce new narratives to alter those conversations, possibly by changing the types of questions asked or introducing processes and interventions that will create new discussions among a broader set of stakeholders.

Change agents need to be more alert to the mutually constitutive nature of power and discourse. Doing so opens up the possibility of better understanding the power and political processes that shape any given change effort and then attempting to engage in directly influencing those processes. This might, for example, involve asking diagnostic questions such as who are the most influential actors regarding the intended change and how can their story-lines and conversations be altered to support the change? Change agents would also need to cultivate skills and exercise actions associated with creating settings where actors with different interests and power bases can productively communicate, or where there is greater power equalization among the discussants in order to foster the emergence of new or different possibilities. Change agents might also benefit from knowing how to identify and enlist alternative discourses to advance and support desired changes. Understanding how various forms of organizational power and political processes are used to suppress non-conforming discourses could lead to consideration of new and different change tactics. For example, exploring ways to amplify any acceptable portions of an alternative discourse as a way to bring into question one or more aspects of the dominant discourse.

Change agents also need to view the change process as ongoing, iterative, and recursive rather than as a linear journey from a current state to some future state. Consequently, change agents adopting a more discursive orientation will need to know how to join an existing conversation, shift it in new directions, and monitor and maintain new conversations over time. In other words, they will need to be mindful that there is no specific or discrete beginning, middle, or end to an organizational change initiative. In addition, because organizational discourses are open to continuous alteration, change agents should watch for emerging opportunities and openings in the prevailing discourse(s) in order to introduce new ways of thinking into the conversation. For example, changes in socio-cultural level discourses ("being green") may be used to create opportunities to introduce new possibilities or practices into more localized conversations (it might save energy if . . .).

Finally, for the change agent a self-reflective stance is critical and also sometimes difficult to sustain. Change agents may be more oriented towards promoting their own favored discourse about change than being reflective about the implicit narratives and frames that may be biasing how they approach a change situation. If we assume there are multiple social realities in organizations, this may also predispose the change agent to ignore or misinterpret important information coming from others who are guided by alternative narratives. For example, the difference between how change agents and change recipients interpret resistant behaviors can lead to self-fulfilling prophecies and self-protective stories by change agents (Ford et al., 2008). Consequently, it would enhance the effectiveness of change agents to maintain a reflective stance in order to stay open such possibilities and challenges. Otherwise change agents will always be limited by the bounds of their own dominant ways of thinking and their preferred narratives about change.

Concluding Comments

We hope this discussion demonstrates the potential contribution of a discourse based approach to understanding and managing the processes and practices of organizational change, especially those related to changing the conversation. It suggests that a number of critical constructs determine how organizational change is framed and thereby influence change processes and outcomes. Multiple levels of discourse, the construction of change-related narratives involving power and political processes, and how they are communicated and enacted through conversations are fundamentally important to the was in which people think about, describe, and make sense of change. It is also important to pay attention to latent alternative discourses that can be blocked or activated by key actors in change efforts. The recursive, iterative, and ongoing nature of discourse that leads to alterations over time is significant to understanding the nature of organizational change itself. The role of the change agent in co-creating discursive realities and the importance of their practicing a self-reflective stance is also highlighted.

Finally, we hope that our suggestion that change orientations could usefully include discourse-based premises will become part of the ongoing narratives of those who plan, manage, and facilitate organizational change.

References

Block, P. (2008). Nothing is next. *OD Practitioner,* 40(4), 35–37.

Bushe, G. R., & Marshak, R. J. (2009). Revisioning organization development: Diagnostic and dialogic premises and patterns of practice. *Journal of Applied Behavioral Science,* 45(3), 348–368.

Ford, J. D., & Ford, L. W. (1995). The role of conversations in producing intentional change in organizations. *Academy of Management Review,* 20(3), 541–570.

Ford, J. F., Ford, L. W., & D'Amelio, A. (2008). Resistance to change: The rest of the story. *Academy of Management Review,* 33 (2), 362–377.

Gergen, K. (2009) *An invitation to social construction* (2nd ed.). London, UK: Sage.

Grant, D., Hardy, C., Oswick, C., & Putnam L. (Eds.) (2004). *The Sage handbook of organizational discourse.* London, UK: Sage.

Grant, D., & Marshak, R. J. (2011). Toward a discourse-centered understanding of organizational change. *Journal of Applied Behavioral Science,* 47(2), 204–235

Marshak, R.J., & Grant, D. (2008). Organizational discourse and new OD practices. *British Journal of Management.* 18(1), 7–19.

Marshak, R. J. (1993). Managing the metaphors of change. *Organizational Dynamics,* 22(1), 44–56.

Shaw, P. (2002). *Changing conversations in organizations: A complexity approach to change.* London, UK: Routledge.

Employee Engagement

Introduction

Maya Townsend and Annie Viets

TOPICS COVERED IN THIS SECTION

- How to build organizational strength through employee involvement.
- How to foster a culture of collaboration.
- How to achieve lasting and deep change though employee involvement.

WHY EMPLOYEE ENGAGEMENT

Employee engagement makes a difference. HR Business Partners know this intuitively. So do leaders: most want employees to care about their work and actively engage with it and the organization. But now we know that employee engagement is not just something that makes intuitive sense. It also reaps financial rewards. Consider, for example:

- Operating income for organizations with high employee engagement improved 19% while it declined 33% over the same period for companies with low employee engagement (Towers Perrin, 2008).
- Development Dimensions International (DDI) estimates that "in an organization of 10,000 employees, moving a workforce from low to high engagement can have an impact of over $42 million" (Wellins, Bernthal, & Phelps, 2005).
- Earnings per share rose 28% among companies with high employee engagement but declined 11% among companies with low employee engagement (Towers Perrin, 2008).

Engagement makes a difference in the lives and productivity of employees but also in the performance of the organization as a whole. Who would not want to see their company's operating income rise 19% while competitors with low engagement were seeing their operating income decrease 33%?

Many would, but not every company understands the connection between employee engagement and organization performance. Numbers vary, but the consensus is that most companies' levels of employee engagement are low. DDI's research conducted in 2005 suggested that only 19% of employees were engaged at that time (Wellins, Bernthal, & Phelps, 2005). Blessing White (2011), suggests that 31% of employees are currently engaged and Gallup (Robison, 2010) estimates 28% are engaged. However, these numbers are still lower than most leaders would like. Clearly, there is a gap in business leaders' knowledge about the importance of engaging employees and the ability to do it well.

The challenge is compounded by confusion about what employee engagement actually is and how to use it appropriately within an enterprise. Henry Hornstein (2006), in his *OD Practitioner* article, **Empowerment as a Way to Facilitate Change,** explains:

What is empowerment? The answer is unsatisfying but comes down to "It depends . . ." It means different things to different people and is dependent on what is going on in the organization at any point in time.

Other *OD Practitioner* authors have also struggled to define employee engagement. Mastrangelo (2009) in **Will Employee Engagement be Hijacked or Reengineered** brings more clarity:

> engagement is found in employees' minds, hearts, and hands. We expect engaged employees to decide to continue working for their employer, to feel pride and motivation working for their employer, and to be willing to exert extra energy at work for their employer.

In this section, HR Business Partners will find ways to put employee engagement to practical use and engage "minds, hearts, and hands" in the important work of the organization. This section includes case studies, hard data about what works, and helpful tips and techniques for increasing employee engagement in an organization.

THE CHAPTERS IN THIS SECTION

The chapters are divided into three segments. Each covers a different topic critical to designing and implementing a successful employee engagement process or initiative:

- Working Out: Building Strength through Employee Engagement
- One Plus One Equals Four Star Performance: Engaging in Collaboration
- Lights, Camera, Action: Close-Ups of Engagement.

Working Out: Building Strength through Employee Engagement

Focusing on the employee engagement basics, this segment opens with a thoughtful chapter, **A Brief and Provocative History of Participation** (2006), by OD icon Edgar Schein. In it, he describes the history of participation in management theory and explores what it means or can mean to an organization. He delves into the complex relationship between participation and culture and offers some words of wisdom to managers and consultants seeking to realize the benefits of participation.

In **Employee Engagement and OD Strategies**, Debra Orr and Hona Mathews (2008) present the business case for employees who are committed to their organization and energized by their jobs. They suggest practical OD strategies to promote and strengthen employee participation levels.

Larry Ackerman (2010) explores the important correlations among organizational identity, employee engagement, and business performance in **The Identity Effect: How Identity-Based Management Drives Employee Engagement and Business Performance**. He clearly defines the concept of organizational identity and then goes on to present a roadmap for those seeking to understand the relevance of identity to shaping successful organizations.

In the last piece in this section, Paul Mastrangelo (2009) asks **Will Employee Engagement Be Hijacked or Reengineered?** To prevent the term from being misappropriated by organizational leaders as the term "reengineering" was in the 1990s, he recommends that the definition, purpose, and intended outcomes of employee engagement be clarified and the focus of OD interventions be on the underlying business problems that drive or undermine employee engagement.

One Plus One Equals Four Star Performance: Engaging in Collaboration

In this segment, HR business partners can find practical advice and insight into how to build employee engagement into their organizations.

In **The Power of Interactive Collaborative Designs** (2002), Jean-Pierre Beaulieu,

Emile Carriere, and Christopher Schoch explain how the utilization of interactive, collaborative design technologies such as Open Space, Future Search, Appreciative Inquiry, and The Conference Model can foster collaboration and engagement in organizations. They provide examples from four organizations where interactive collaborative designs were implemented with positive outcomes.

Nancy Southern (2006) uses her work with the managers of a city government to illustrate a process for **Creating a Culture of Collaboration in a City Government**. She asserts there are five conditions for collaboration and that, ultimately, the ideal consequence of the creation of a collaborative culture is the development of an organization-wide learning community.

Lights, Camera, Action: Close-Ups of Engagement

There are three powerful case studies in this segment. In the first, **Employee-Led Organizational Change: Theory and Practice,** Victor Woodell and Sanyani Edwards (2006) describe a case in which committed employee teams effectively design and implement a change project in partnership with, but independent of, middle and senior management. They conclude that engaged frontline employees can be highly instrumental in changing their organizations.

In **The Politics of Implementation: The Importance of Building Consensus Around Employee Performance Management**, Victor Woodell (2002) relates the story of a project that illuminates the interplay between politics and organization development. He offers lessons from the process as guides to HR Business Partners embarking on similar implementations that require employee engagement.

Managers wanted to close the plant but employees wanted to keep it open. Such are the positions held by the two sides in a fascinating case presented in **Interest-Based Problem Solving: Foundation of a Labor and Management Partnership**. Jeff Jackson and Adrienne

Easton (2006) describe how the power of interest-based decision-making was employed in engaging these two seemingly irreconcilable sides in a collaborative partnership.

FOR ADDITIONAL LEARNING

For more information about employee engagement, you may want to read the following articles.

- Frost, B. (2005). Capacity building is a verb not a noun: Developing a system for action. *OD Practitioner*, 37(4), 26-30.

  Frost provides a case study of employee engagement in a multi-organizational strategic planning effort in Tulare County, California.

- Kanter, R. M. (1981). The politicization of organizational life: Skills for critical issue management in a changing organizational environment. *OD Practitioner*, 13(3), 1–7.

  Kanter describes how to manage critical issues; learning how to position and work with critical societal and external changes.

- Lewis, S. A. (1987). Participative management: Myths vs. realities. *OD Practitioner*, 19(3), 11–14.

  Lewis discusses the misconceptions about participative management and describes the four factors necessary for its success.

- Whitney, D., & Gibbs, C. (2006) Appreciative Inquiry: Creating cultures of positive participation. *OD Practitioner*, 38(4), 46–51.

  This case study uses the appreciative inquiry technique to engage 200 people from 40 countries in an ambitious endeavor to "create a community of dedicated participants who would collaboratively generate plans needed to extend the United Religions Initiative into new parts of the world." The case contains valuable lessons on how to create engagement and collaboration across geographic and cultural differences.

References

Blessing White (2011). Employee engagement report 2011: Beyond the numbers: A practical approach for individuals, managers, and executives. Retrieved from www.blessingwhite.com/research

Borg, I., & Mastrangelo, P. M. (2008). *Employee surveys in management: Theories, tools, and practical applications.* Cambridge, MA: Hogrefe & Huber.

Hornstein, H. (2006). Empowerment as a way to facilitate change: Can process consultation help? *OD Practitioner,* 38(1) 4–9.

Lewis, S. A. (1987). Participative management: Myths vs. realities. *OD Practitioner* 19(3), 11–14.

Macey, W.H., & Schneider, B. (2008). The meaning of employee engagement. *Industrial and Organizational Psychology,* 1, 3–30.

Robison, J. (2010). Despite the downturn, employees remain engaged. *Gallup Management Journal.* Retrieved from http://gmj.gallup.com/content/125036/despite-downturn-employees-remain-engaged.aspx

Towers Perrin (2008). Closing the engagement gap: A road map for driving superior business performance. Retrieved from www.towersperrin.com

Wellins, R. S., Bernthal, P., & Phelps, M. (2005). Employee engagement: The key to realizing Competitive advantage. Retrieved from www.ddi.com

CHAPTER 42

A Brief and Provocative History of Participation

Edgar H. Schein

PARTICIPATION IS ONE of these wonderful abstractions that seems to mean something "good," yet it is very hard to define in a practical context. For many managers it means to give away some of their power to their employees, only to discover that the employees then actually want to exercise power, something that the manager had not actually bargained for or anticipated. For other managers it means telling employees what is going on, asking if there are any questions, and if none arise in 5 seconds, assuming that they have now provided their employees a chance to participate. Having had that chance they should now obey like good soldiers. For still others it is the key to higher quality work because more total involvement of the employee presumably leads to more motivation and care in getting the job done.

For many consultants it means the involvement of the client in data gathering and analysis rather than just making recommendations based on the consultant's data gathering. This is the common definition of action research and implies that the consultant as initiator chooses to involve the client in the consulting process (Reason & Bradbury, 2001). For me as a process consultant, participation means almost the opposite (Schein, 1999a). In order to be helpful, it is the consultant who must involve him- or herself in the culture of the client system in order to figure out what is going on. It is the consultant who is doing the extra "participating," not the client. As can be seen from these examples, at best "participation" is a confusing idea.

When that idea is compounded with another abstraction, i.e. *Culture*, as in the phrase *Cultures of Participation,* we are really in a conceptual morass because *culture* is itself as vague and many faceted a concept as participation. One might almost say that until it is specified exactly what behavior culture might refer to, it is an empty, useless, and confusing concept.

To make some sense of this field, I want to review my own experiences with the word *participation* and see whether that leads to any clarity as to what one might propose to managers and consultants as a viable conclusion. My experiences were sporadic and not necessarily valid indicators of what was going on in the world, but these experiences provided me with some insights on the complexity of what participation can and does mean.

Early Encounters

In the 1950s as I was starting my career at Walter Reed Army Institute of Research and at the MIT School of Industrial Management (now the Sloan School of Management), the Human Relations movement was plateauing. Being nice to subordinates was still in but waning as a viable management philosophy.

345

The role of Supervisors and Personnel Managers as champions of their employees was still an important part of their role, but scientific management, authority, and other more hierarchical concepts were resurging (Schein, 1980).

Douglas McGregor with his Theory X and Theory Y was delving deeper by noting that what managers did in how they treated people was a reflection of their deeper attitudes toward and assumptions about human nature (McGregor, 1960, 2006). If they were cynical and believed that people did not really want to work and would take advantage of their bosses whenever possible (Theory X) it would be entirely natural to install time clocks and other control devices and to give people as little participation as one could get away with.

On the other hand, if managers believed that it is human nature to want to work and that participating with others in organizations was a natural and satisfying thing to do (Theory Y), it would be entirely natural to involve subordinates and to listen to them and to delegate to them where it was appropriate. If they proved to be lazy, insubordinate or disloyal, one would, of course, institute controls. But one would not start with the assumption that all humans needed to be controlled at all times.

How one actually managed people, the degree of participation that one allowed, would depend on the specific task to be performed and one's real time experience with one's subordinates. Theory Y was a conceptual basis for what later came to be called *contingency theory* or *situational management* because the Theory Y manager would vary his or her behavior according to what the actual situation was, whereas the Theory X manager would always start with heavy controls (Hersey & Blanchard, 1977).

How much one should delegate, how much one should let subordinates participate in decision making was hotly debated in those times and some surprising stories emerged from other cultures. Several delegations of managers from the Soviet Union visited MIT and told stories of how much worker participation was valued in Soviet factories. We also learned that group decisions and consensus were often taken for granted in a plant environment and that in the Soviet Union workers who were injured or on sick leave were encouraged to work part time as they gradually got better, while in the US workers did not return to work until completely well. A middle manager from Yugoslavia who was attending our Sloan Fellows program reported to us that in his factory the employees elected their foremen.

As people began to question whether autocratic or democratic leadership style was better we also learned that the military, in being the penultimate autocratic system, was actually much higher in Theory Y managers. In working with Navy Admirals, for example, we found that they trusted their subordinates much more than our samples of industrial managers, reinforcing the idea that belief in people did not automatically mean more participation but it did mean a completely different attitude toward control.

People who read McGregor's work in the 1960's glibly assumed that Theory Y meant giving in to people, excessive amounts of participation, sometimes even labeling it "country club management," completely misunderstanding that Theory X and Theory Y referred to people's assumptions about human nature, not their management style.

The groundbreaking article on degrees of participation by Tannenbaum and Schmidt (1958) and Vroom's (1960, 1976) method of determining how much participation a leader should encourage clarified the issue and mapped the terrain by emphasizing once again the importance of the task and the situation in determining the appropriate degree of participation by subordinates. The same manager might behave autocratically on one issue and delegate the entire decision to the subordinates on another issue.

Further refinement of this issue resulted from leadership theories that talked about the *maturity* of subordinates, implying that how much participation one should encourage ought to be a function of a complex set of diagnostic decisions by the leader about the state of knowledge of the subordinates and their attitudes. The difficulty for leaders is, of course, how to determine the nature of the situation and the maturity of subordinates as the world becomes more global, complex and multicultural.

Participation in the Organization Development Domain

Practitioners of organization development (OD) split early on regarding the participation issue. One group was more humanistically oriented and favored higher degrees of participation as being intrinsically healthier for all organizational situations. Their work with clients systematically favored recommendations toward more subordinate involvement, and their coaching always favored more opening of communication channels and more listening to subordinates. For some, notably Chris Argyris, the cultural tendency in most organizations to suppress categories of information that would upset the existing order and to deny that such suppression was taking place, was the core pathology of organizational life. Only by helping people to see their *defensive routines* could one improve organizational effectiveness (Argyris & Schon, 1996). To overcome such defensive routines requires intensive involvement on the part of the client system in studying their own behavior and practicing new ways of communicating.

The other group of OD practitioners was more pragmatic and focused on the huge differences that one encountered in different organizational cultures. It became evident to me that one could not help clients if one did not understand the cultural assumptions from which they were operating and, at the same time, that one could not easily change those cultural assumptions. In fact, several client experiences taught me that one should not alter some of those cultural assumptions because they were the source of the strength of the group. Instead my model of Process Consulta-

tion (Schein, 1999a) argues for building a relationship with clients that permits the consultant to understand the culture and help the client to work with its strengths.

For example, in my work with Digital Equipment Corporation (DEC) I tried to improve group process by pointing out how rudeness and interruption interfered with communication based on my learned expertise on how good groups should work (Schein, 2003). My interventions were acknowledged but the behavior of group members never changed. I finally gave up, sat back and tried to reflect on why the group did not change. I began to try to understand their culture and discovered that the interruptions and rudeness were the direct result of the degree of passion the members felt about their new industry and potential new products. Politeness was not a high priority. But the information loss was a problem. Once I began to participate in their culture I intuitively figured out how to be helpful. I went to the flipchart and started to write down ideas as they were given. If someone was interrupted I asked him to finish his thought so that I could write it down (instead of punishing the interrupter). Before long the group was using the information on the flipcharts very constructively and giving me feedback that "Now I was really being helpful." I was now *participating in their culture* and helping them accomplish what they wanted to accomplish.

Culture is the sum total of what a group has learned in coping with its external survival problems and internal integration problems (Schein, 2004). It is to the group what personality or character is to the individual. Cultures begin when a group founder imposes his or her will on the group and only hires or retains members who fit those values. But the behavioral rules and norms do not become a culture unless that way of behaving actually works and is therefore gradually adopted by the group. Culture thus evolves over time but it cannot be created by fiat, it can only evolve through gradual learning. To advocate a certain kind of culture, e.g. a *culture of participation*, is therefore meaningless because participation is itself an abstraction and the degree to which it is a good thing varies with the situation. To argue for culture change is also unrealistic unless one is willing to engage in a long-range expensive change process (Schein, 1999b).

Should the OD field promote participation? Is the humanistic argument true that people feel better and perform better when they are involved? We all know situations where this is clearly evidenced. But my consulting experience also tells me that there are many tasks and situations where tight coordination and discipline are essential to getting the job done. In those situations it is often difficult to determine how much participation is optimal. And, finally, there is the paradox that if you empower people through participation they become powerful and harder to manage. One interpretation of why DEC failed in the 1990s is that the culture was dedicated to everyone doing the right thing and innovation, making it virtually impossible to get the discipline and cost reduction that was needed as the computer industry became more commoditized. High levels of participation had created the company, made it successful for several decades, and, in the end destroyed it (Schein, 2003).

The conclusion for leaders and managers is that they must judge each situation and be flexible in their style. The conclusion for OD consultants is, paradoxically, the same—they must be highly able to determine the realities of the situation, be able to build the kind of relationship with clients that permits those realities to surface, and be prepared to participate in the client's realities in order to be helpful.

References

Argyris, C., & Schon, D. A. (1996). *Organizational Learning II.* Reading, PA: Addison-Wesley (now Prentice-Hall).

Hersey, P., & Blanchard, K. H. (1977). *Management of organizational behavior.* Englewood Cliffs, NJ: Prentice-Hall.

McGregor, D. M. (1960). *The human side of enterprise.* New York, NY: McGraw-Hill.

McGregor, D. M. (2006). *The human side of enterprise, Annotated edition.* New York, NY: McGraw-Hill.

Reason, P., & Bradbury, H. (Eds.) (2001). *Handbook of action research.* Thousand Oaks, CA: Sage.

Schein, E. H. (1980). *Organizational psychology* (3d ed.). Englewood Cliffs, NJ: Prentice-Hall.

Schein, E. H. (1999a). *Process consultation revisited.* Reading, PA: Addison-Wesley (now Prentice-Hall).

Schein, E. H. (1999b). *The corporate culture survival guide.* San Francisco, CA: Jossey-Bass.

Schein, E. H. (2003). *DEC is dead: Long live DEC.* San Francisco, CA: Berrett-Kohler.

Tannenbaum, R. & Schmidt, H. W. (1958, March-April). How to choose a leadership pattern. *Harvard Business Review* 36(2), 95–101.

Vroom, V. H. (1960). *Some personality determinants of the effects of participation.* Englewood Cliffs, NJ: Prentice-Hall.

Vroom, V. H. (1976, Winter). Can leaders learn to lead? *Organizational Dynamics,* 4(3), 17–28.

CHAPTER 43

Employee Engagement and OD Strategies

Debra Orr and Hona Matthews

THERE'S AN INFAMOUS fairytale question that goes, "Mirror, mirror on the wall, who's the fairest of them all?" If from an organization development perspective you answered "engaged employees," then you're right on the mark and primed to understand the importance of why engaged employees are a keystone to helping move organizations forward. Take Johnson and Johnson, an internationally known healthcare pharmaceutical company where one of its teams was developing a specific drug for a critical patient population. The drug was showing a lot of promise as well as receiving positive nods from the Federal Food and Drug Administration (FDA). Using an employee engagement framework and strategy, senior management gave this group great support. As a result, team satisfaction increased as did project timelines and soon to follow, FDA approval for the drug (Catteeuw, Flynn, & Vonderhosrt, 2007).

Was this particular Johnson and Johnson success story a shot in the dark? A business fluke? Not likely. Johnson & Johnson, like hundreds of other national and international companies, are launching employee engagement initiatives because they both recognize and experience the benefits of reduced employee turnover, customer loyalty, and increased corporate profits.

Employee engagement is the amount of discretionary effort that employees put into their work. ". . . engaged workers are helping to achieve company goals by aligning their work with the strategic objectives of the firm and they are excited to do so. Full engagement means the employee's heart and mind is engaged. That is, the organization has also addressed their emotional engagement" (Buhler, 2006, p. 2).

Employee satisfaction is distinct from employee engagement. Employee satisfaction implies the meeting of traditional needs such as competitive benefits and safe working conditions, while engagement implies the active integration of the employee's attention on the business of the organization. Engagement implies direct action on the part of the employee while satisfaction becomes the responsibility of the organization to meet through the systems and processes it puts into place.

Engaged employees are more productive, more profitable and have lower turnover than employees who are not engaged with their organization. However, an engaged workforce is not easy to develop when nearly one in five employees is actively disconnected from work. To attain these higher levels of productivity and to meet customer needs, launching employee-focused strategies that encourage employee participation and involvement is essential.

Making the Case

LaBarre (2001) draws from Marcus Buckingham's Gallup Q12 survey analysis indicating that there is a definite link between people and performance. Organizations that scored in the top 25% for engaged employees have lower turnover, higher customer loyalty, higher productivity and higher profitability. LaBarre goes on to say that 26% of the working population is engaged, 55% is not engaged, and 19% is actively disengaged. In a 2003 study, consultants Lowman and Seaborn found employee engagement numbers to be even lower than that of the Q12 study where "17% of employees are highly engaged, and almost one in five is disengaged."

If senior leadership needs more data to be convinced of the need for organizational development muscle to help leverage employee engagement, then organizational decision makers need only turn their attention to the fiscal outcomes.

The Organizational Pocketbook

Many organizations implement employee engagement techniques, but the savvy ones, the successful ones, are those measuring the outcomes (Higginbottom, 2004). For example, Wheelabrator, a waste-to-energy incinerator company and subsidiary of Waste Management, implemented a program called "Workout." Developed by Leap Technologies, Workout focuses on efficiencies, cost savings, and team building. Says Gary Aguinaga, manager of business improvement for Waste Management, "It helps you address operating issues or get projects done that you really want to get done. It also gets employees engaged in the business which is something we always tried to do but never had a real formal process to achieve" (Feingold, 1998, p. 1). As an employee engagement tool, Workout resulted in big savings for Wheelabrator including a $1 million savings in year one of implementation and an anticipated savings of $2 million in year two, not to mention improvements in plant safety, efficiency and environmental records.

Lowman and Seaborn of the consulting firm, Towers and Perrin, (2003) cite an example where a hospital client experienced turnover of 30% among support services, technicians and RNs at an approximate cost of $16 million. Additionally, the hospital was forced to spend $50 million on contract labor to address staffing shortfalls caused by the high turnover and the turbulent situation. The hospital worked to make changes in staff schedules, different shift options, and paid time off for training with an anticipated ROI of $4 million. The implementation of these employee engagement strategies resulted in a turnover reduction of 7% and a savings of $3.7 million for the hospital.

Nancy Lockwood (2007) notes that "employee engagement can be measured in dollars and can yield significant savings" (p.3). She provides an example using the MolsonCoors beverage company where "engaged employees were five times less likely than non-engaged employees to have a safety incident and seven times less likely to have a lost-time safety incident. In fact, the average cost of a safety incident for an engaged employee was $63, compared with an average of $392 for a non-engaged employee" (p. 3). In 2002, MolsonCoors saved $1,721,760 in safety costs.

T & D, from the American Society for Training and Development (Employee Engagement Boosts Bottom Line, 2006) has also drilled down on the savings of employee engagement in organizations by reviewing a study by ISR, an employee research and consulting firm. The ISR study reveals a "52% gap in operating incomes between companies with highly engaged employees and companies whose employees have low-engagement scores...Other findings include a 13.2% improvement in one-year net income growth for companies with high employee engagement, and a 3.8% decline in net income during that same period for companies with low employee engagement" (p. 16).

Perhaps one of the most interesting facets of employee engagement is how simple and easy the concept is. According to the Corporate Leadership Council, employee engagement, "is the extent to which employees commit to something or someone in their organization and how hard they work and how long they stay as a result of that commitment" (p.3). Employees are seeking more than a job and a pension. They also desire meaningful jobs and development opportunities. The unsurprising bottom line is that it's in the best interest of employers to focus on the well being of employees (Harter, Schmidt, & Keyes, 2002).

Spector's (1997) work suggests that satisfied employees are more cooperative, more collegial, more punctual, and stay with an organization longer than their dissatisfied counterparts. "The emotional well-being of employees and their satisfaction with their work and workplace affect citizenship at work, turnover rates, and performance ratings (Harter, Schmidt, & Keyes, 2002, p. 3).

Why Employees Leave

With organizations competing to recruit employees, struggling to decrease turnover, and all the while raising the bar on customer service strategies, it's imperative that employers pinpoint why employees exit the organization. In *The 7 Hidden Reasons Employees Leave,* Leigh Branham (2005) notes an employee will leave an organization because:

- Expectations about the workplace or job were not met
- A poor match between skill set of the person and the job requirements
- Lack of feedback, coaching or mentoring
- Lack of promotion or advancement opportunities

- Lack of recognition or not feeling valued
- Lack of work-life balance resulting in too much stress
- Lack of confidence and trust in senior leaders of the organization

Knowing why employees leave an organization is a critical first step in developing long-term retention solutions. Branham (2005) identifies three things leaders can do to combat the above seven issues and help stem employee turnover:

- Communicate your vision clearly and vividly, develop a workable plan and possess the competence to achieve it.
- Keep your promises by following up words with actions.
- Empower the work force by giving them your trust and confidence.

Likewise, a "circle" of education and rewards leads to an engaged workforce that leads to better business results, which leads to more money for reward programs, which leads to education and rewards. Organizations wishing to create engaged employees could follow these five strategies (Lowman & Seaborn 2003):

- Reward high-performing individuals with extra development opportunities.
- Train employees on how the business works.
- Focus attention on organizational performance by creating incentives or bonuses based on metrics.
- Develop bonuses or incentives that are variable, rather than fixed .
- Communicate performance metrics results to line managers and Human Resources.

Engagement Surveys

A plethora of survey opportunities are available for companies wanting to jump in and measure employee engagement. Gallup's Q12, NBRI's employee engagement survey, Kenexa's employee engagement survey, Accord Management

Systems' Engagement 101, and HR Solutions' Sweet 16 Survey are all helping to drive the employee engagement buzz and bring into focus the idea that work and life purpose are not separate compartments in the suitcase of life. However, Gallup's Q12 survey is perhaps one of the best known employee engagement surveys.

According to Buckingham and Coffman (1999), over the past 30 years, the Gallup Organization has interviewed millions of employees. After sifting through the mountains of data, Gallup derived 12 keys questions to measure the strength of the workplace. These 12 questions measure the "core elements needed to attract, focus, and keep the most talented employees (Buckingham and Coffman, 2001, p. 28). After entering performance data from over 2,500 businesses and opinion data from 105,000 employees, Gallup's research discovered that ". . . the manager—not pay, benefits, perks, or a charismatic corporate leader—as the critical player in building a strong workplace" (Buckinghan & Coffern,1999, p. 32).

People work better when they connect their work with their overall purpose, and the importance of the front-line manager in employee retention shouldn't be surprising. If we look at employee engagement through the lens of leadership we quickly come to the question of what steps leaders can take to encourage employee engagement. Further, because leadership is an influence process—then the process that a leader chooses to exert this influence would have great relevance on the way that employee engagement might occur. A positive emotional state broadens and builds creativity, interest and cognitive potential (Frederickson, 1998; Isen, 1987; Ziv, 1976). Using positive strategies yields the most promising results. *Harvard Business Review* (Buchannan, 2004) divides the drivers of employee engagement into two major categories: Rational and Emotional. Rational drivers are those interests that are logical and direct outcomes of objective needs. In Branham's list of reasons why employees leave, rational drivers could be considered ideas like unmet expectations about the workplace or job, a poor match between skill set and the person, lack of

coaching and the job requirements and lack of advancement opportunities. Emotional drivers, identified by *Harvard Business Review* as four times more influential as rational drivers, are those issues that are subjective and speak to the individual experience, such as lack of recognition or not feeling valued, the stress resulting from an imbalance in work-life, or lost trust in senior leadership.

Employee engagement is about integrating the discretionary efforts of employees toward organizational goals. Developing positive affect in organizations would be a way to enhance that goal.

LaBarre (2001) says that middle managers are the most important person in a company. When it comes to getting productivity out of employees, research shows that

". . . the single most important determinant of individual performance is a person's relationship with his or her immediate manager. It just doesn't matter if you work for one of the '100 Best Companies,' the world's most respected brand, or the ultimate employee-focused organization. Without a robust relationship with a manager who sets clear expectations, know you, trusts you, and invests in you, you're less likely to stay and perform. (LaBarre, 2001, Attitude Adjustment #3)

The IES report by Robinson, Perryman and Hayday (2004) talks about 'building blocks' that need to be in place to raise engagement levels: "Good quality management; two-way communication; effective internal co-operation; a development focus; commitment to employee well being; and clear accessible HR policies and practices, to which managers at all levels are committed" (p. 4), and all of these are leadership driven.

Creating Engaged Employees

Given the importance of retaining employees, for fiscal, as well as productivity and humanistic reasons, developing engaged employees is more important than ever. OD is the organizational strategy that pulls these building blocks together to ignite purpose, passion and meaning in the workplace.

The Q12 provides clues as to what factors need to be in place to create engaged employees. The questions on the Q12 can be grouped according to three major categories: communication, coworkers & supervisors, and consistency.

Coworkers and supervisors are referenced in four questions in the Q12. They are:

- Question four: In the last seven days, have your received recognition or praise for doing good work?
- Question five: Does your supervisor, or someone at work, seem to care about you as a person?
- Question six: Is there someone at work who encourages your development? Question ten: Do you have a best friend at work?

The questions are about the practices of co-workers and supervisors in relationship to the individual taking the survey. The issues discussed in the questions are under the control of others in the workplace environment.

Consistency is another aspect probed in the Q12. Four questions in the Q12 ask about consistency. They are:

- Question two: Do you have the materials and equipment to do your work right?
- Question three: At work, do you have the opportunity to do what you do best every day?
- Question nine: Are your associates (fellow employees) committed to doing quality work?
- Question twelve: In the last year, have you had opportunities to learn and grow?

These questions relate to the regularity of management policies and procedures, the ability of the individual to access their own highest level of productivity, as well as the productivity of their co-workers and learning and

development. All of these items are related to the regularity of quality practices and individual growth.

Communication is the final element referenced in the Q12. Four questions in the Q12 ask about the nature and quality of communication. They are:

- Question one: Do you know what is expected of you at work?
- Question seven: At work, do your opinions seem to count?
- Question eight: Does the mission/purpose of your company make you feel your job is important?
- Question eleven: In the last six months, has someone at work talked to you about your progress?

The final group of questions relate to how purpose and feedback are enacted at work. Without an understanding of purpose, performance cannot be altered, ultimate goals cannot be understood and acted upon and feedback cannot be incorporated.

Given the construction of the concept of employee engagement, interventions and practices must center on the concepts of communication, consistency and coworkers. Table 43.1 is a synthesis of several approaches to employee engagement defined within this construct and supplemented with OD strategies that help accomplish these practices.

Communication, consistency and co-workers and supervisors are three keys to developing an engaged employee base. Communication should be frequent, two-way and allow for open dialogue. Consistent, clear expectations around performance and behavior should be fairly applied to all staff. Co-workers and supervisors should be encouraged to develop a relaxed and personable environment.

Challenges to this development include pre-existing relationship issues, lack of trust, poor patterns of communication and inconsistent policies, expectations and treatment for individuals.

TABLE 43.1 Employee Engagement Practices

	Practice	OD Strategy
COMMUNICATION	1. Connect purpose and practice, ensuring employees understand how they impact the overall goal of the organization 2. Make job requirements clear 3. Give updates when there are changes in the organization 4. Communicate directly and often, using more than one channel (written and verbal) 5. Regularly audit employee engagement levels 6. Become an organization committed to professional development, empowerment and collegial relationships	1. Develop and implement system-wide an operational and capital strategic plan—share the plan widely 2. Coach and develop managers and staff 3. Develop and facilitate All Employee Meetings/Town Hall Meetings; system-wide and departmental communication plans 4. Develop and implement system-wide and department- specific communication plans 5. Develop and implement annual Employee Engagement Surveys 6. Develop training and develop opportunities for all employee levels
CONSISTENCY	1. Develop a culture of accountability and professionalism in the organization 2. Discover the strengths of your staff and allow people to use their strengths 3. Develop an understanding of how employees view one another 4. Identify aversions to particular people 5. Hire carefully, develop routinely and retain staff meticulously 6. Maintain trust with staff—don't lose trust with "hire and fire" policy	1. Develop and implement an objective system of performance metrics. 2. Develop and implement strengths and talents assessment—train to strengths not weaknesses 3. Develop and implement 360 assessment tools to use in career management planning 4. Develop and implement diversity and conflict management training for all employee levels 5. Assess training and development needs at all employee levels—create a culture of universal learning 6. Develop and implement an on-boarding strategy that reflects the organization's commitment to its people, community, and service
CO-WORKERS & SUPERVISORS	1. Develop amiable and collegial relationships between coworkers 2. Recognize everything—birthdays, service anniversaries, goal achievements in the workplace 3. Develop respectful, productive, two-way relationships between supervisors and staff 4. Talk about and encourage staff's professional goals on a regular basis 5. Remember to say thank you and to express appreciation for good work 6. Ensure managers understand that retention of talent is a key performance metric	1. Implement quarterly employee appreciation events to celebrate employee accomplishments. 2. Develop a system-wide activities team to sponsor employee appreciation events 3. Create a culture encouraging frequent, timely and formal outcome-oriented conversations between staff and supervisors 4. Implement quarterly goals and action plans related to organizational-side goals—formally discuss outcomes. Implement a coaching or mentoring program 5. Create a "thank you" culture by sending personalized thank you cards to the employees' home 6. Develop and implement supervisory level peer and behavioral interviewing training

(Adapted from the work of Lockwood, 2007; Woodruff, 2006; Sejits & Crom, 2006; Buchannan, 2004)

On the one hand, employee engagement is research and success stories pointing toward employees embracing a "carpe diem" attitude and implementing self- driven energies and attitudes that result in positively charged employee productivity, retention, and customer loyalty. These super-charged, can-do, passionate, put-me-in coach, innovative employees know how to move an organization forward. The good news is that right this very minute engaged employees are walking corporate hallways making a difference that sometimes do and, more often don't, make business headlines. Merely tapping into these under-the-radar heroes could potentially help a company develop new strategies for realizing financial success, increased employee tenure, and customer satisfaction.

On the other hand, across today's organizations there remains a large knowledge and implementation gap when it comes to employee engagement initiatives. Multiple companies haven't flipped the switch on creating employee engagement cultures because either senior leadership isn't on board with the concept; middle management doesn't support it, as it is seen as one more thing to do on an already long to-do list; Human Resources and Organizational Development hasn't championed the cause; senior leadership defines it as too *touchy feely* and doesn't want to invest the time, money, or resources; employees don't take engagement seriously and view it as the *flavor of the month* program.

Are there corporate risks to investing in and implementing employee engagement initiatives? Absolutely, but with supporting research and existing frameworks and models in place helping to make engagement part of an organization's value proposition, the risks become less threatening and more calculated. And with that being said . . . let the engagement begin!

References

Branham, L. (2005). *The seven hidden reasons employees leave: How to recognize the subtle signs and act before it's too late.* New York, NY: AMACOM

Buchannan, L. (2004, December) The things they do for love. *Harvard Business Review,* 82(12), pp. 19–20.

Buckingham, M., & Coffman, C. (1999). *First break all the rules: What the world's greatest managers do differently.* New York, NY: Simon & Schuster.

Buhler, P. (2006) Engaging the workforce: A critical initiative for all organizations. *SuperVision.* 67(9), 18–20.

Catteew, F., Flynn, E., & Vonderhorst, J. (2007). Employee engagement: Boosting productivity in turbulent times. *Organization Development Journal,* 25(2), 151–157.

Employee engagement boosts bottom line. (2006, September). *T & D: American Society for Training and Development,* p. 16.

Fiengold, J. (1998). Team approach wins raves, cuts costs at Wheelabrator. New *Hampshire Business Review,* 20(14), 1–2.

Frederickson, B. (1998). What good are positive emotions? *Review of General Psychology,* 3, 300–319.

Harter, J., Schmidt, F., & Keyes, T. (2002). Well-being in the workplace and its relationship to business outcomes: A Review of the Gallup Studies. In C.L. Keys & J. Haidt (Eds.) *Flourishing: The positive person and the good life* (pp. 205–224). Washington, DC: American Psychological Association.

Higginbottom, K. (2004, March 11). Firms ignoring staff opinion. *People Management,* p. 7.

Isen, A. (1987). Positive affect, cognitive processes, and social behavior. In L. Berkowitz (Ed.), *Advances in experimental social psychology,* pp. 203–253. San Diego, CA: Academic Press.

LaBarre, P. (2001). Marcus Buckingham thinks your boss has an attitude problem. *Fast Company,* 49, 88.

Lockwood, N. R. (2007, March). Leveraging employee engagement for competitive advantage: HR's strategic role. *HRMagazine,* 52(3), 1–11.

Lowman, D., & Seaborn, E. (2003). Building the HR organisation of the 21st century: Five winning strategies. Towers Perrin. *ttp://www.towersperrin.com/tp/getwebcachedoc?webc=HRS/USA/2003/200309/waw_pov_2.pdf*

Robinson, D., Perryman, S., & Hayday, S. (2004). The drivers of employee engagement. Institute for Employment Studies. *IES Report 408.*

Sejits, G., & Crim, D. (2006, March/April). What engages employees most: or the ten c's of employee engagement. *Ivey Business Journal Online* 70(4), 1–5.

Silberman, M. (Ed.) (2006). *The ASTD 2006 training performances sourcebook.* Alexandria, VA: ASTD Press.

Spector, P. (1997). *Job Satisfaction: Application, assessment, cause, and consequences.* Thousand Oaks, CA: Sage.

Woodruffe, C. (2006, November). Employee engagement - the real secret of winning a crucial edge over your rivals. *Resource Magazine,* 19–22.

Ziv, A. (1976). Facilitating the effect of humor on creativity. *Journal of Educational Psychology,* 68(3), 318-322.

CHAPTER 44

The Identity Effect
How Identity-Based Management Drives Employee Engagement and Business Performance

Larry Ackerman

IN 1985, researchers Albert and Whetten provocatively declared that "the issue of identity is a profound and consequential one, and at the same time, so difficult, that it is best avoided" (p. 265). Since then, practical and academic interest in organizational identity has only continued to grow, as research has shown that identity influences many factors that account for an organization's success. For example, it has been shown that organizational identity affects strategy (Lawler & Worley, 2006; Ackerman, 2000; Gioia & Thomas, 1996); culture and image (Hatch & Schultz, 1997, 2000, 2002); mergers and acquisitions (Ackerman, 2000); individual identification with the organization (Dutton & Dukerich, 1991; Ashforth & Mael, 1989); and change management (Lawler & Worley, 2006; Ackerman, 2000).

The conversation around organizational identity seems to be gaining momentum today as companies face continuous changes through downsizing, globalization, and diversification. Taken together, these forces challenge an organization's sense of unity—who it is and what it stands for—and, by extension, the efficiency and productivity that unity implies. While there are numerous aspects to the study of organizational identity, I believe two of them are particularly salient to the question of unity and the benefits it brings: Flexible or Fixed; Multiple Identities or One.

Flexible or Fixed?

One of the persistent debates surrounding organizational identity is whether it is fixed and immutable, or flexible and subject to change as the company strives to meet new market demands. Definitions of identity that derive from the first school meet Albert and Whetten's (1985) three criteria: that identity is central, distinct, and enduring. Researchers who support this claim further believe that an organization's identity can, in fact, accommodate the need to respond to the external environment by reinterpreting how it is expressed (Lawler & Worley, 2006; Ackerman, 2000).

On the other hand, there are those who believe that organizational identity can, and must, evolve to allow a company to stay current with changing market conditions (Oliver & Burgi, 2005; Fiol, 2001; Gioia & Thomas, 1996). For these researchers, organizational identity shifts are necessary to prevent the organization from becoming too rigid in the face of change.

This article, and the research that anchors it, is based on the idea that an organization's identity is fixed, transcending time and place, while its manifestations are constantly changing. Nissan's former CEO, Carlos Ghosn, captured this view of identity when he stated that his goal was to "save the business without losing the company by preserving Nissan's identity but changing the company's strategy and operations" (Bouchikhi & Kimberly, 2003, p. 23).

Multiple Identities or One?

One of the more recent developments in the study of organizational identity is a discussion around whether an organization can have more than one identity. Balmer and Greyson (2002) suggested that there are five identities: the actual, communicated, conceived, ideal, and desired identities. These different identities reflect, respectively: the current, distinct attributes of the organization (actual); what the organization communicates about itself (communicated); the perceptions of the corporation by stakeholders (conceived); the optimum positioning for the organization (ideal); and corporate vision from the perspective of the CEO or board of directors (desired).

As implied by Albert and Whetten (1985) and for Ackerman (2000), an organization cannot have multiple identities. That would be akin to, and just as destabilizing as, a person who has multiple personality disorder.

Meeting profound and consequential issues, as Albert and Whetten described organizational identity in 1985, doesn't happen by avoiding them; it happens by confronting them in a manner that trades difficulty for discipline and mystery for method. In this article, I offer a way forward for executives and practitioners who want to better understand the dynamics of identity and how to apply them to shaping successful organizations.

Defining Identity for Strategic Advantage

Like most business terms, identity attracts different definitions, depending on one's experience. Among them all, I believe that there is only one definition that does justice to the inherent power of identity as a catalyst of change and growth.

First, let's clarify what identity is not. Identity is not a company's name and logo, even though that is a common association in the corporate world. Nor, is identity synonymous with business definition, as in, Maytag is an appliance company, IBM is a computer systems and services company. Further, identity is not the same as a company's values, as critical and influential, as they may be. The problem with all of these definitions is that none of them cuts to the heart of the matter; none explains how the organization makes a proprietary contribution in the marketplace—indeed, the world. And that is what identity is all about: *Identity is the unique combination of characteristics that reveals an organization's value-creating potential* (Ackerman, 2000).

Others, including Jim Collins, argue that, to be successful over time, companies must have an inviolable ideology, or purpose that never changes, despite the need to change strategies and cultures (Collins & Porras, 1994). And, in the world of corporate branding, there is the common belief that the promise a company makes to its customers and others, should be based on a solid foundation that isn't subject to the fickle whims of consumer tastes.

In both of these instances, the purpose of an organization (or its vision or mission) and its brand promise, are, typically products of executive consensus, corporate lore, and/or market research. By contrast, identity is the wellspring of value creation. Crack the code on it, and identity reveals purpose and defines promise. In my experience, identity is cause; purpose and all the other elements of a leadership platform, are effect.

This definition lends strategic significance to identity for three reasons: First, it acknowledges the uniqueness of every organization, calling for those qualities to be identified and applied in setting the direction of the enterprise. Second, it stresses potential; identity is about the future, not just today. And third, it implies constancy, alluding to the fact that a company's identity does not change over time, although how it is expressed can—and should—change, forever.

With this definition in mind, a useful way to understand how identity affects the success of an organization is to consider simple, everyday metaphors: What is an apple without its core? What is the solar system without the sun? Like these well-known metaphors, identity provides organizations with their centers of gravity and rudders (another useful metaphor).

Testing the Identity Hypothesis

Over the course of more than 25 years, working with some of the world's most influential organizations, I had come to believe that identity was key to understanding, and even predicting business success. But, despite the positive results numerous identity management initiatives had produced, the ability to quantify—and thus prove—the impact of identity remained elusive. Until now.

In the summer of 2009, we launched a research study—the Identity Impact Survey—to test the hypothesis, quantitatively, that identity strength influences employee engagement and, in turn, business performance. Recognizing that individual identity strength and organizational identity strength are distinctly different forces, we designed the survey to measure the impact of each, independently, as well as together. The Survey included nearly 2,000 respondents across five companies[1] which were

selected for their ability to meet the following criteria:

* Industry diversity: business-to-business and consumer
* Size: Large (>$8 billion) and small (<$100 million)
* Ownership structure: publicly-owned and privately-owned
* Geography: global and domestic

The companies participating in the study represented a range of industries including global vision care, regional health insurance and managed care, global industrial manufacturing, internet media, and institutional food services. Respondents were distributed according to the size of the company, so the larger companies contributed more respondents than the smaller ones. Employees surveyed typically included a cross-section of their company's general populations; for example, vice-presidents and directors, through plant workers and claim adjusters, as appropriate. One company chose to concentrate on their field force, alone, which controlled approximately $500 million in revenues and whose productivity was vital to the performance of the organization, overall.

The identity hypothesis was amply supported. The correlations between identity strength, employee engagement, and business performance were very high. The notion that a company's identity drives value creation was no longer just a conviction; it now appeared to be a demonstrable fact. Here are four key findings:

1. Identity strength is a leading indicator of business performance, given its significant, positive impact on employee engagement (see Figure 44.1).
2. Organizational identity strength is more influential than individual identity strength

---

[1] Why five? In recruiting organizations for the research, we promised participants, comprehensive reports on their performance. These individual assessments provided us with deeper insights into the impact of identity and added significant, additional work, separate from the public re-

port. Most important, we knew, in constructing the survey, that the right five (see segmentation criteria) would give us the foundation we needed to conduct a cogent analysis.

FIGURE 44.1   Impact of Identity Alignment Index on Employee Engagement

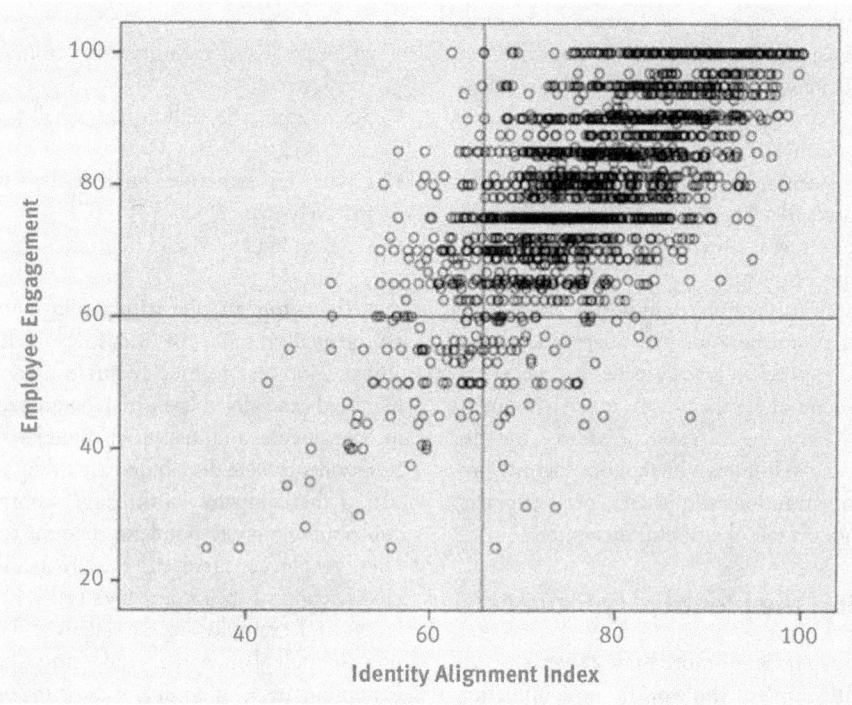

Together, organizational identity strength and individual identity strength (Identity Alignment Index) have a major impact on employee engagement (r = .686) The author's intent is to illustrate, with overlapping shadows and blurry effect, how many of the 2,000 respondents' answers showed a correlation between identity alignment and employee engagement.

in driving employee engagement and business performance. Their combined effect, however, is greater than either one alone (see Figure 44.2).

3. Increases in identity strength translate into predictable increases in revenue and other economic benefits (see Figure 44.3).

4. Although organizational identity emerges as a major performance driver, employees typically don't think that their organization actually *has* a strong identity.

The last finding may sound disturbing at first but actually presents a critical opportunity. What it suggests is that there is a significant value gap between how companies are currently performing and how they would perform, were they to close that gap by increasing their identity

strength—an entirely achievable goal. This fact is dramatized in the Identity Leadership Matrix (Figure 44.4), which shows where the five survey companies fell on this chart and what the implications are, which are called out in Figure 44.5.

The Identity Effect in Action

In order to make our research findings particularly relevant to the participants, we invited each company to describe a current challenge that the findings might help them meet. All five companies in the survey have adopted the findings as a tool for helping senior management devise strategies for bringing about desired results. Here are two cases, which illustrate how the research results are shaping the companies' thinking and actions, so far.

FIGURE 44.2 Increases in Identity Strength Drive Higher Employee Engagement

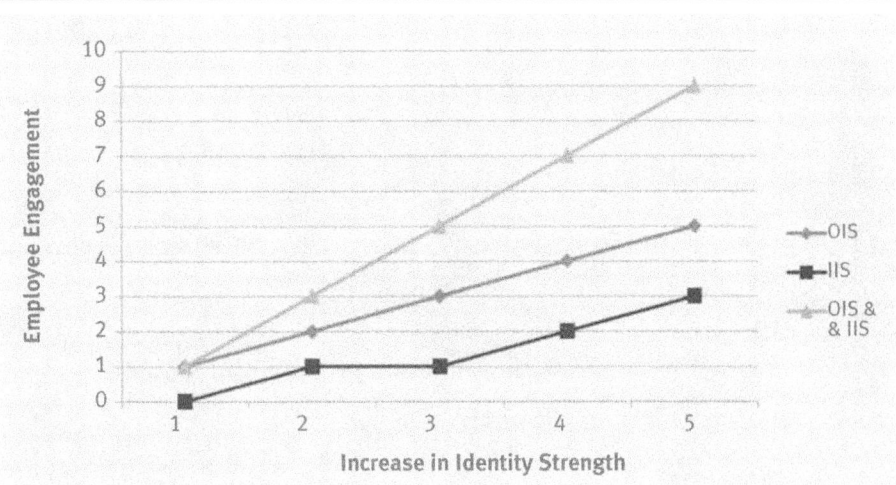

The combined effect of organizational and individual identity strength is greater than either one alone.

FIGURE 44.3 Increases in Employee Engagement Drive Revenue Up

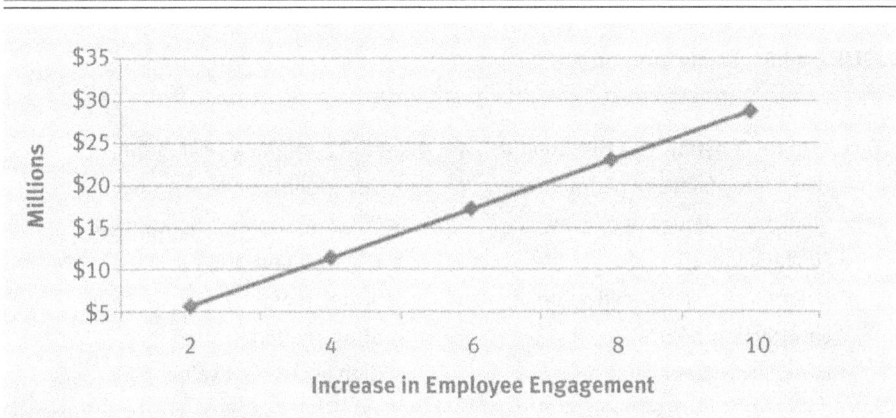

The economic benefits of identity show up in several ways, including predictable revenue increases, as engagement scores increase with identity strength.

Challenge One—Keep Success Rolling

Sometimes, it's true: Good things come in small packages. That is certainly the case for Company A, a global vision care concern, and one of the two smallest companies in the survey. Size notwithstanding, its performance on nearly all measures out-stripped all other participants. Most notably, its organizational identity strength score (OIS) was exceptional, which may, in fact, account for its success with employee engagement (Figure 44.4).

"How to keep the party going" was, in effect, the challenge offered by top management. While that challenge may seem presumptuous

FIGURE 44.4   Identity Leadership Matrix

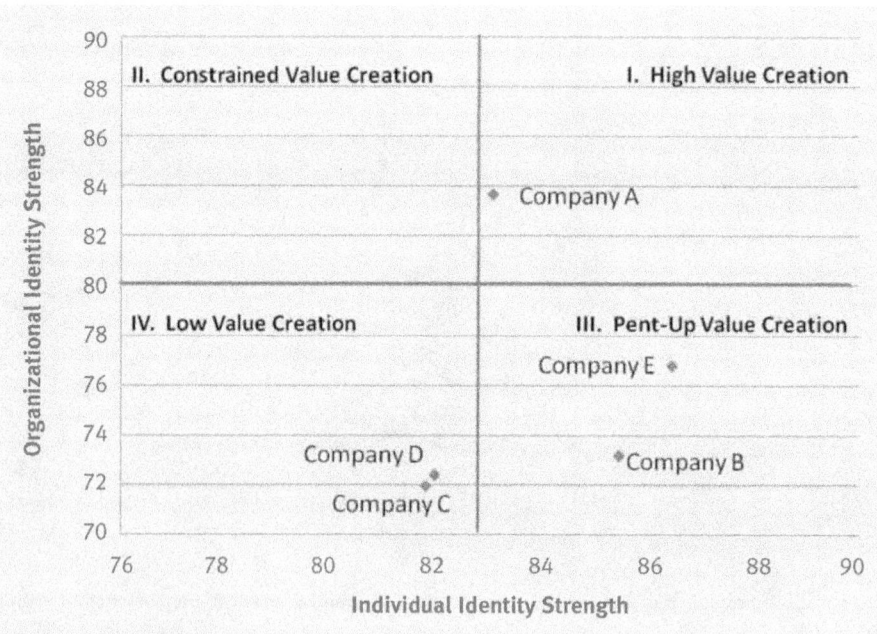

The Identity Leadership Matrix highlights significant room for improvement among all but one survey participant.

FIGURE 44.5   Likely Outcomes

Quadrant II: Constrained value creation	Quadrant I: High value creation
■ Handcuffed financial performance	■ Superior financial performance
■ Inefficient strategy deployment	■ Effective strategy deployment
■ Limited innovation	■ Efficient innovation
■ Overpromise, under-deliver on brand	■ Strong brand
■ Low-traction culture	■ Strong culture
■ Lower investment value	■ High investment value
Quadrant IV: Low value creation	**Quadrant III: Pent-up value creation**
■ Sub-par financial performance	■ Limited financial performance
■ Ineffective strategy deployment	■ Inefficient strategy deployment
■ Depleted innovation	■ Limited innovation
■ No meaningful brand	■ Brand confusion
■ Dysfunctional culture	■ Diffuse culture
■ Low investment value	■ Lower investment value

Here are the likely outcomes of falling into one quadrant or another. The various elements in these different quadrants reflect a critical combination of factors influencing leadership success.

before having taken the survey and seeing the results, the CEO was right: business performance including profitability, top-line growth and margins were all solid and had been for years. The company enjoyed a tightly-knit culture, possibly, due to its private, family-run status— owners who seemed to understand the connection between highly-engaged people and superior business results.

That's the good news; the bad news is that to simply keep on doing what has been done so far places the company at risk, putting them in a position to falter when they least expect it. It is common knowledge that when very successful companies stumble, it is because they have become wedded to the policies and processes that led to success in the first place. The idea of change gets lost in the shuffle.

If there are imperatives, then, that Company A's management can take away from this study, they need to center on being conscientious about documenting, promoting—and periodically testing—vital ideologies and practices. Specifically:

- Company A should codify the management practices, which have allowed it to get to where it is today. This initiative should not just be an executive committee action; it should involve employees at all levels, whose experience can shed detailed light on what makes the company work so effectively. Those practices should then find their way across the entire human resources value chain, from recruitment, on-boarding and training, to performance management and leadership development.
- The company should make identity-based management a deliberate part of its strategic and operational activities, including its talent management processes, since identity strength correlates significantly with its success.
- Finally, the company should institute an annual "What Should We Change?" review, in which people at all levels identify practices, large and small, that call for improvement. This form of organizational innovation will help "keep success rolling," in ways that minimize strategic and operational risk.

Challenge Two—Drive Top-Line Growth

If value creation is the sine qua non of business success, then revenue growth is one of its most vital measures. Either you are creating value in the marketplace, and growing as a result, or you are not. If you are not, you are stagnating. In the words of numerous pundits, "grow or die."

In the case of Company C, a $6 billion global industrial manufacturer, meaningful top-line growth had become an elusive goal. Nearly 100 years old, this well-known and highly-respected company had made its mark in transportation and numerous other markets that make the world go 'round. In the past several years, revenue growth had slowed, even as profitability expanded. Management understood its predicament: In order to deliver results to investors—indeed, even simply to stay healthy—the company had to spark topline growth.

Prior to taking the survey, the organization had embarked on an intensive brand development effort in which "cracking the code on its identity" was regarded as a precondition for success. The effort spanned a 12-month period, during which the company was able to articulate unique, institutional capacities, and come to a new understanding of what business it really was in—an insight that transcended the markets it served and gave the company a new way to expand customer relationships and improve its employee recruiting outcomes.

In 2009, the economic downturn took a toll on the enterprise, leading to its inability to implement critical initiatives that were central to how it planned to spur growth. This key asset—its identity-based brand—lay dormant as the company took cost-savings measures to stay profitable in the face of the financial crisis.

Still, Company C elected to be part of the identity research project. The survey, they reasoned, could offer a solid benchmark for tracking progress over time, once brand implementation resumed. The research results were disappointing. Company C discovered broad identity weakness, which was cast into sharp relief by its last place position on the Identity Leadership Matrix (Figure 44.4). Given the powerful impact identity strength has on value creation, the survey results provided revealing insight into the company's persistent lack of top-line growth, to date.

The company's low identity strength scores —organizationally and individually—point to what may be one of the most significant challenges management faces as it prepares for an economic recovery. That challenge is twofold:

- First, management must establish a clear— and clearly understood—sense of what sets the company apart as one enterprise; that is, how the organization creates proprietary value for customers and other stakeholders.
- Second, executives must enable employees at all levels to clarify and apply their own value-creating capacities to their jobs, their internal and external relationships, and their careers at the company.

While both goals are important, the first challenge is non-negotiable and, in fact, is somewhat more easily accomplished. How? By revisiting the identity and brand initiatives that were placed on hold in 2009. There is every reason to believe that, rigorously implemented, those initiatives would improve Company C's identity strength scores in material ways, along with many of the value creation outcomes identity strength affects.

Where Does Identity Strength Come From?

Beginning in the mid-1980s, I began to observe and record distinct patterns of thinking and behavior among my clients, which seemed to account for their success—or failure—over time. Over the next 20 years, these patterns revealed a set of principles, natural laws that transcended industry, size, geography, and age. I have come to call these natural laws—there are eight of them—the Laws of Identity. Without exception, so far, these laws have heavily influenced the fortunes of the organizations I have served.

Identity strength, then, flows directly from how well-aligned organizations are with these laws; more specifically, with the essential building blocks these laws imply. Here are the eight Laws of Identity, the building block each one holds, and its particular significance for leading one's company or one's self:

#1 The Law of Being—*An organization's or individual's ability to live depends first upon defining one's self as separate from all others.*

Identity building block: **Autonomy**— the degree of independence a company or individual has, which allows them to make decisions unencumbered by the actions of others.

The Law of Being implies the need for autonomy as a prerequisite to finding one's own path in the marketplace, or in life, and not being swayed or deterred by the opinions and actions of others. Without a strong sense of autonomy, leading one's company, or one's self, successfully is difficult, at best.

#2 The Law of Individuality—*An organization's or individual's natural capacities invariably fuse into a discernible identity that makes that being unique.*

Identity building block: **Differentiation** the discovery and application of a company's or individual's unique, value-creating capacities.

The Law of Individuality implies the need for differentiation—differentiation based upon one's innate capacities, not just one's strengths. While strengths clearly are important, they can be learned and do not necessarily spring naturally from who we are. Thus, they are not as powerful, or as reliable as innate capacities as the source of true differentiation.

#3 The Law of Constancy—*Identity is fixed, transcending time and place, while its manifestations are constantly changing.*

Identity building block: **Change**—a company's ability to evolve and grow, while retaining its sense of identity.

The Law of Constancy implies the need for change (corporate or individual) that is in sync with one's identity, as opposed to conventional notions of change, which imply changing everything, including identity. This law reveals a crucial paradox: The need to change from a changeless foundation, if an organization or individual is going to grow in ways that are constructive, rather than potentially destructive, which do not, in short, throw the baby out with the bathwater.

#4 The Law of Will—*Every organization and individual is compelled to create value in accordance with their identity.*

Identity building block: **Stewardship** a company's ability to steer and stay a long-term course, despite current challenges.

The Law of Will implies the need for stewardship. In the course of leading a company, or one's life, we don't always know where we are going, despite our best efforts to predict outcomes, and our resultant expectations and hopes. This lack of certainty calls for making decisions that keep us on a course we believe is the right one for creating value over time, based upon who we are, as opposed to what seems momentarily expedient. Discipline, courage, and fortitude are the leadership attributes called for by the Law of Will.

#5 The Law of Possibility—*Identity foreshadows potential.*

Identity building block: **Purpose**—a company's reason for being, beyond profit, which flows from its identity.

The Law of Possibility implies the need for purpose, as the central expression of one's identity. In articulating purpose, you are clarifying your value-creating potential organiza-tionally or individually in relation to the marketplace and/or the world-at-large.

#6 The Law of Relationship—*Organizations and individuals are inherently relational, and those relationships are only as strong as the natural alignment between the identities of the participants.*

Identity building block: **Alignment**—the extent to which a company is connected to others, where the relationship produces value beyond the transactions it calls for.

The Law of Relationship implies the need for alignment—organizationally, with all stakeholders, or individually, with all people who are at the center of how one creates proprietary value. The leadership mandate is to be discerning about the allocation of time and other resources invested in these relationships, so that the return on these investments is as high as possible for everyone involved. Being highly selective is what alignment calls for. Proper alignment is critical to shaping an elegantly efficient organization, or life.

#7 The Law of Comprehension—*An organization's or individual's various capacities are only as valuable as the perceived value of the whole of that being.*

Identity building block: **Brand**—the promise a company makes that shapes its relationship with all stakeholders, based upon its identity.

The Law of Comprehension implies the need to shape a brand as the main way companies as well as individuals present themselves to the world and are understood in return. Building an effective brand calls for making, and delivering on a promise that shapes one's relationships with all stakeholders (or other people), based upon one's identity.

#8 The Law of the Cycle—*Identity governs value, which produces wealth, which fuels identity.*

Identity building block: **Sustainability**—a company's ability to drive growth and profitability in ways that are explicitly tied to its impact on society and the legacy that produces.

The Law of the Cycle implies the need for sustainability as the prerequisite to creating enduring value and wealth in return. Organizations that invest in their own sustainability serve all stakeholders, ranging from long-term investors and generations of employees, to customers and society, which ultimately benefits from the contributions the organization makes, over time. Individuals who seek to lead themselves in ways that make their lives sustainable act in the best interests of their peers, their families, and others who stand to benefit from their unique contributions. Operating in sync with the Law of the Cycle is the key to creating a productive, durable legacy, for both companies and individuals.

How did the five survey companies perform in terms of identity strength? Figure 44.6 shows how each survey participant fared on each identity building block. Note the signifi-

cantly better performance of Company A, the global vision care company. In short, this best practice organization is in an especially good position to further improve employee engagement and business results, given its high identity strength.

Conclusion

Because they are designed to be self-sustaining, profit-making organizations have the potential to be the most powerful value-creating instruments on earth. Their collective ability to effect positive societal change, and get rewarded for it in return, is unmatched by any other form of institution. But, without embracing the core identity of the organization as a central, governing force, that value will never be realized.

If there is a secret to why identity is such a potent influence, it is because identity provides us with a unique lens through which to

FIGURE 44.6 Company Ratings for Each Identity Block

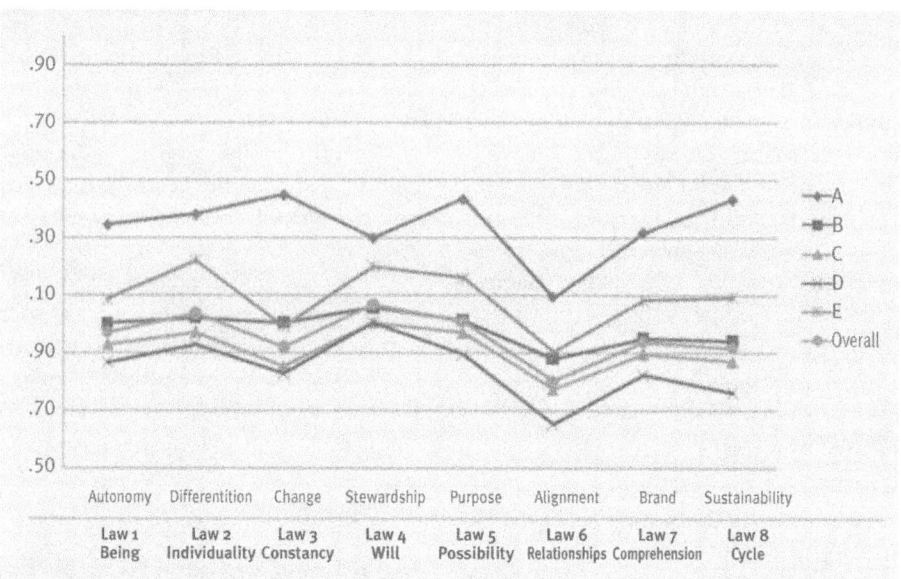

The graph above shows how each survey participant fared on each identity building block. Note the significantly better performance of Company A—in particular, their far superior capacity for change.

understand and respond to business as well as human challenges. For companies, the identity management discipline is the vital counterpoint to the discipline of economics. For individuals, identity connects us to the source of our authenticity, integrity, and natural capacities. For both, identity completes the picture we must see before we can make fully-informed choices.

Identity strength helps explain many things, including why some companies flourish while others fade. The Identity Impact Survey reveals not only many of the whys of success and failure, but also what to do about them, in order to reinforce or change management practices that have led to current outcomes. The science of identity-based management is emerging, and with it the chance for OD professionals to drive value creation in ways that benefit their organizations, the customers and investors they serve, and the employees those organizations count on.

References

Ackerman, L. D. (2000). *Identity is destiny: Leadership and the roots of value creation.* San Francisco, CA: Berrett-Koehler.

Albert, S., & Whetten, D. (1985). Organizational identity. In M. J. Hatch & M. Schultz (Eds.), *Organizational identity: A reader* (pp. 89–118). Oxford, UK: Oxford University Press.

Ashforth, B., & Mael, F. (1989). Social identity theory and the organization. *Academy of Management Review,* 14(1), 20–39.

Balmer, J. M. T., & Greyser, S. A. (2002). Managing the multiple identities of the organization. *California Management Review,* 44(3), 72–86.

Bouchikhi, H., & Kimberly, J. R. (2003). Escaping the identity trap. MIT *Sloan Management Review,* 44(3), 20–26.

Collins, J. C., & Porras, J. L. (1994). *Built to last: Successful habits of visionary companies.* New York, NY: HarperCollins.

Dutton, J. E., & Dukerich, J. M. (1991). Keeping an eye on the mirror: Image and identity in organizational adaptation. *Academy of Management Journal,* 34(3), 517–554.

Fiol, C. M. (2001). Revisiting an identity-based view of sustainable competitive advantage. *Journal of Management,* 27, 691–700.

Gioia, D. A., & Thomas, J. B. (1996). Image, identity and issue interpretation: Sense-making during strategic change in academia. *Administrative Science Quarterly,* 41(6), 370–403.

Hatch, M. J., & Schultz, M. (1997). Relations between organizational culture, identity and image. *European Journal of Marketing,* 31, 356–365.

Hatch, M. J., & Schultz, M. (2000). Scaling the tower of Babel: Relational differences between identity, image, and culture in organizations. In M. Shultz, M. J. Hatch, & M. H. Larsen (Eds.), *The expressive organization: linking identity, reputation, and the corporate brand* (pp. 9–35). Oxford, UK: Oxford University Press.

Hatch, M. J., & Schultz, M. (2002). The dynamics of organizational identity. *Human Relations,* 55(8), 989–1018.

Lawler, E. E., & Worley, C. G. (2006). *Built to change: How to achieve sustained organizational effectiveness.* San Francisco, CA: Jossey-Bass.

Oliver, D., & Burgi, P. (2005, July). Organizational identity as a strategic practice. International Critical Management Studies Conference, Cambridge, UK.

CHAPTER 45

Will Employee Engagement Be Hijacked or Reengineered?

Paul M. Mastrangelo

ON SEPTEMBER 3, 2008, Michael Hammer, the co-author of the widely acclaimed 1993 book Reengineering the Corporation, died of a brain hemorrhage (Hevesi, September 4, 2008). His book encouraged leaders to simplify how work is accomplished by redesigning processes from scratch, holding nothing sacred from the existing approach. These ideas were incredibly influential, spawning countless business process reengineering projects at Fortune 500 companies. "Reengineering" quickly became the business catchphrase of the mid 1990s, and Hammer was named by Time Magazine as one of the 25 most influential people of 1996.

Yet, if you go back and read that 1996 accolade, you find that Hammer lost control of the term that he coined. The article noted that reengineering had become synonymous with downsizing and other unintended forms of reorganization, done in the name of efficiency. Hammer was quoted as saying "It is astonishing to me the extent to which the term re-engineering has been hijacked, misappropriated and misunderstood" (Anonymous, June 17, 1996). Here we are over 12 years later, and I worry that the OD field is about to lose control of another influential idea: Is "employee engagement" about to be hijacked? Compared to the specificity that the term "reengineering" originally had, "engagement" was born at risk.

First, consider the recent scholarly review entitled "The Meaning of Employee Engagement" (Macey & Schneider, 2008). The article required 28 pages in its attempt to accomplish its purpose, noting that both academics and practitioners use ambiguous definitions of engagement. The term sometimes refers to a temporary state such as an emotion, while other times it refers to a stable trait like personality. It is sometimes defined synonymously with employees' intentions to stay with their employer, while other times it encompasses the employees' enthusiasm for their employer. Engagement also blurs the line between satisfaction with the job and satisfaction with the employer. If experts in organizational science cannot specify what employee engagement is, how can we be sure of its impact on organizational performance? What happens when organizational leaders, the consumers of our discipline, use our term and quote our research findings?

Look no further than the first page of volume one in Martha Finney's (2008) book "Building High Performance People and Organizations." Here, Jolton and Saltzman quip that engagement has become a silver bullet for organizations, promising to "make everything 'all better' by creating happy, happy workplaces" (p. 1). With executives increasingly using the term "engagement" in their discussion of business strategy (e.g., American Express CEO Ken Chenault's 2007 interview with Fortune Magazine), we in OD and strategic HRM have clearly found a seat at the big table. The concept of engagement is successfully serving as a reminder that people ultimately drive an organization's success. However, without a standard definition of engagement, we risk playing a shell game for evidence that engagement efforts are delivering high return on investment. With expectations and visibility both high, our field cannot afford to have "employee engagement" hijacked as "reengineering" was in the previous decade.

Now is the time to secure the employee engagement term and to shape the engagement conversation that we should be having with organizational leaders. To prevent a hijacking, we need to reengineer the employee engagement process by stopping our risky behaviors in favor of starting safer, more strategic behaviors. Hammer and Champy (1994) defined reengineering as "the fundamental rethinking and radical redesign of business processes to achieve dramatic improvements in critical, contemporary measures of performance" (p. 32). For our purposes here, we need to redesign employee engagement in terms of definition, benchmarking, and purpose so that we keep expectations of our interventions realistic and we deliver results. The best place to start reengineering our engagement projects is at the beginning, when we introduce the term and educate our clients about our goals. We need to be wary of the following risks:

1. In defining engagement, we often confuse the outcome with its drivers;
2. In benchmarking engagement, we often overlook basics of survey interpretation;
3. In establishing our purpose for engagement projects, we often overemphasize assessment to the detriment of producing changes.

Let's examine these three pitfalls and consider how we can lay a better foundation for our employee engagement consultative work.

Aligning our Definition of Engagement With our Measure

If you endeavored to discover what causes global warming, what would be the "outcome measure" or dependent variable for your study? Clearly, if you are interested in global warming, the measure of interest is the atmospheric temperature. Even if you also measure carbon emissions, volcano activity, deforestation, and a host of other potential "drivers" of global warming, these measures are not substitutes for temperature. When someone asks you how much warmer it is now than a century ago, you respond with a change in temperature (not molecules or trees). It is only when you are asked why that change in temperature took place that you mention those other measures. Temperature is not synonymous with the proportion of carbon dioxide or the proportion of tree coverage, even if temperature were highly correlated with both of these measures. The outcome is not the same thing as the drivers of that outcome. As clear as this seems, when we measure employee engagement, we often make the mistake of equating the outcome with the drivers.

Let's take a closer look at the concept of employee engagement. Although formal definitions abound, there is convergence around three essential components of engagement: logical commitment, emotional commitment, and discretionary effort (Macey & Schneider, 2008; Borg & Mastrangelo, 2008). In other words, engagement is found in employees' minds, hearts, and hands. We expect engaged employees to decide to continue working for their employer, to feel pride and motivation working for their employer, and to be willing to exert extra energy at work for their employer. While we could (and should) fine tune this very broad definition, if, for the sake of argument, we state that this "minds, hearts, hands" definition of engagement is the outcome, then we need to specifically ask employees about these components. As in our global warming analogy, when we ask questions related to supervision, feedback, or coworkers, we are not measuring the engagement outcome per se, but rather we are measuring what we presume to be drivers (i.e., precursors) of engagement. This is no trivial point.

In their recent description of employee engagement, Orr and Matthews (2008) frequently refer to Gallup's Q12, which is a set of 12 survey questions made popular from the book "First Break All the Rules" (Buckingham & Coffman, 1999). None of the 12 questions ask about intent to stay, or pride in the organization, or willingness to exert extra effort. Thus, using the logic that we outlined in the global warming analogy, the Q12 does not measure the outcome of engagement (assuming you subscribe to the "minds, hearts, hands" definition). In fact the Q12 was designed to measure drivers of employee retention (i.e., the "mind" component). None of this is meant to be a judgment of the Q12's value, or to suggest that the drivers measured in the Q12 are not related to engagement. Indeed, the instrument can be very valuable in understanding employee engagement. My only point is that engagement, by many definitions, is not synonymous with perceptions of supervision, feedback, coworkers, etc. Being precise in our definition of engagement is vital in preventing our term's hijacking.

When we treat outcomes as if they are synonymous with drivers, we give away a great deal of precision. Measuring drivers is helpful only if the drivers are truly causing engagement. Based on research from employee survey data from several global companies, my colleagues and I have found that engagement is driven by both "micro level" elements (personal growth, perceptions of supervisor, performance feedback) and "macro level" elements (company leadership, honest communication, belief in future company success). The ranking of these drivers from most critical to least critical, interestingly, tends to vary somewhat based on the culture of the organization. So, using a "pretested" survey of critical drivers may not provide the most efficient pathway to engagement.

To be as precise as possible with an organizational assessment, it would be better to assess both drivers and outcomes so that the relationship between the two can be tested, and a pathway to engagement can be specific to the organization. Likewise, answering the question "How many of our employees are engaged?" is made easier when you have a direct measure of engagement. Otherwise, how would executives feel when they are told engagement is X, but the data measures Y? This discrepancy might make our discipline look sloppy or, worse, deceptive. We cannot afford either label, and we have the power to avoid them both. Let us distinguish engagement from its precursors in the work we do for our clients (see Figure 45.1).

FIGURE 45.1 Two Approaches to Showing Scores on This Discretionary Effort Question, With 28% Endorsing the "Top Box" and 68% Endorsing a "Favorable" Response.

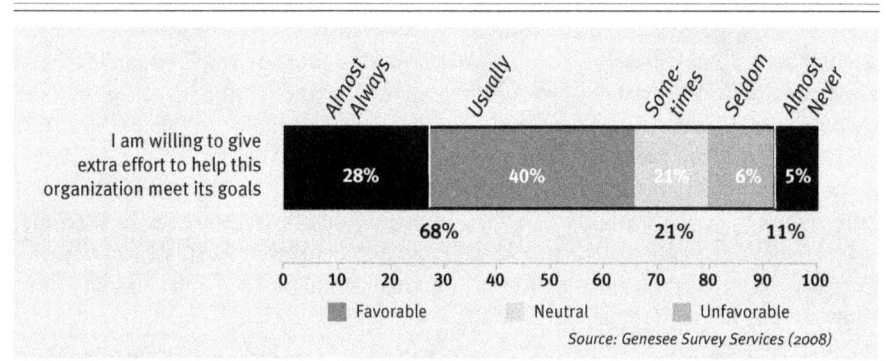

Source: Genesee Survey Services (2008)

Critically Evaluating Benchmark Statistics for Engagement

When you read that only 28% of employees are "engaged" (Esty & Gewirtz, 2008), it sounds horrible. Why aren't 100% of employees engaged? However, careful consideration of the methods used to create such benchmarks makes it clear that striving for 100% engagement is folly. At the risk of getting mired in details, let us remember that these statistics come from employee surveys that typically ask a set of related questions and allow responses on a five point scale such as "strongly agree, agree, mixed, disagree, strongly disagree" or in the example I am about to present, "almost always, usually, sometimes, seldom, almost never." Many engagement benchmarks come from the percentage of employees who endorse the "top box" response (i.e., strongly agree, almost always), ignoring those employees who give less extreme, but still favorable responses. In the graph above, you see that two thirds of employees across 14 countries regularly give extra effort to help their organization, but only 28% say they "almost always" do so. From a marketing perspective, reporting that only 28% of employees are engaged would create more interest in our consulting services than would reporting that two thirds of employees are engaged—perhaps we can be forgiven for being good salesmen and saleswomen. Organizational leaders, however, can be comforted in knowing that on average, 89% of employees report giving extra effort at work at least sometimes, and only 5% say they never give extra effort.

Of course, this survey question measures only the "hands" portion of our "minds, hearts, hands" definition of engagement, and as a result our benchmarks should be even more complex. How should we incorporate the addition of at least two more survey questions when counting the number of engaged employees? A conservative operational definition would count only the intersection of "top box" scores for the three questions: the percentage of employees responding extremely favorable on intention to stay AND pride in the company AND discretionary effort. Using that definition, a mere 4% of employees would be considered to be engaged (Genesee, 2008).

The upper limits of any engagement benchmark depend not just on the definition and the scoring algorithm, but also the consistency of responses to the questions themselves. In considering the question that asks about your likelihood to stay with your employer, your response would probably be the same today as it would be tomorrow or next week. Unless you are already frustrated by your current employer and are just waiting for an excuse to leave, you would probably report that you intend to stay where you are, and you are not likely to change your intention in a matter of days. But what if you were asked how often you were willing to work late? This question might yield different responses from day to day or even hour to hour, because your motivation to go beyond your usual effort is likely to wax and wane. For that matter, you may not be able to stay late on certain days because of personal commitments. In order to increase employee engagement as measured in part by that question, an organization would have to promote work-life imbalance, which would be a recipe for burnout (or mutiny). Upon reviewing all of these details, it is easy to see why employee engagement benchmarks are typically at 30% or lower.

What about global benchmark studies that allegedly show low employee engagement in Japan and high employee engagement in India and Latin America? Well, before you recommend major relocation efforts, once again remember that these statistics are from employee survey data. Japanese employees tend to score relatively low compared to other countries on just about all work topics measured in employee surveys. There is evidence suggesting that Japanese culture influences respondents to favor the midpoint of the five-point scale rather than provide an extreme response at either end (Johnson & Smith, 2006). There is also evidence suggesting that the Japanese have a higher standard for quality and customer service, resulting in harsher evaluations than those of employees elsewhere in the world (Mastrangelo, 2008). Both findings would explain lower survey scores for engagement or any other survey construct being measured. Likewise, much of the engagement research is based in multinational companies, which provide higher than average salaries and stability in developing nations like India, Mexico, or Brazil. Once you understand how the surveys are conducted, it is not surprising that these countries tend to rank at or near the top on global employee engagement studies. That same survey methodology also produces higher scores among managers, HR managers, sales people, and employees with less than a year of service at the company. All of these groups will have more positive perceptions of nearly every aspect of their work environment when compared to company averages. Therefore, these patterns are less indicative of "engagement" problems than they are simply "laws" of survey data (Borg & Mastrangelo, 2008). As purveyors of employee engagement benchmarks, we have a responsibility to interpret their meaning with a more critical eye.

Emphasizing Change Rather than Assessment in Our Engagement Projects

Engagement has become synonymous with surveys, and to the point where leaders who want their employees to become engaged request a survey, not a change intervention. Even some of us in the OD and HR field have come to believe that only an engagement survey creates engagement. I recall one HR manager from a unit of a Fortune 500 company who planned to improve their relatively low annual survey scores by conducting quarterly "engagement surveys." My first thought was the one liner that many of us have heard: The floggings will continue until morale improves! One reason that leaders put their faith in quarterly engagement surveys as an action plan is the erroneous belief that only the "right" set of questions are linked to business outcomes,

such as revenue, profit, and turnover. The thinking goes that without asking "engagement" questions, an OD effort cannot improve the organization's performance.

To be clear, I am calling for a more standardized approach to defining and measuring engagement, but not because all other types of survey questions are invalid. A recent comprehensive academic study (Schneider, Hanges, Smith, & Salvaggio, 2003) supported the relationship between employee opinion surveys and organizational performance, but these were questions that asked about satisfaction with pay, security, and overall job. Clearly, engagement is not the only survey metric that matters. I have seen a wide variety of survey questions correlate with revenue goals and profit. It is just as important to assess how well employees' job goals are aligned with the organization's strategic goals. Likewise, it is important to compare employees' perceptions of customer service with what their customers say about the service they receive. Not surprisingly, both of these content areas correlate with employee engagement, as favorable responses on any survey question are associated with favorable responses on nearly all other questions (with correlations usually ranging from +.20 to +.90). What we seem to be missing in our quest for the best way to measure engagement is what to do once we have the measurement.

Most post-survey actions operate under a Manager Focused model. Though rarely articulated, this model calls for continual survey measurement of engagement, with the manager of the group being held responsible for discovering and fixing whatever inhibits engagement. Because these surveys tend to be short, identifying problems and potential solutions has to come through some other medium, typically group meetings. Assuming that the members of the group feel that they can speak openly about problems and the manager has the patience and skills to collect the information, this model may help improve satisfaction. However, for this model to actually solve the business problems that the group has identified, the manager also has to have the time and resources to plan, execute, and evaluate actions until there is a resolution. Of course, if the problem is the manager, then he or she will have to be willing to process this feedback, change behaviors, and "heal" himself or herself. In short, the Manager Focused model assumes that the existing organizational structure (i.e., the system) can fix itself if it has ongoing feedback—no outside intervention is necessary. While certainly plausible, this assumption is likely to be false if (a) the manager is not able or willing to take on this role of change agent, (b) the organization does not provide enough resources and support for the manager to be a change agent, or (c) the problem is caused by factors outside the control of the manager. None of these three conditions is uncommon.

There is an opportunity and a need for OD specialists to use our knowledge of large scale organizational change to address both employee engagement and the business problems that inhibit engagement. If engagement is more than just making employees feel good, then we should do more than just look for a link between engagement and performance. We should be designing our change efforts to address what is frustrating employees and preventing them from becoming engaged. Accomplish these goals, and we improve both performance and engagement. From the very beginning our field promoted the concept that employees want to achieve and do good work. When we ask employees questions about what they see in their workplace, we find that what encourages or discourages engagement has less to do with compensation and work/life balance than it does seeing the organization's strategy and values being executed. When employees have the tools and resources that they need, when they see investment in developing skills throughout the workforce, and when they know they are delivering what their customers need from them, then they feel like they are part of something great. In other words, when employees see leaders "walking the talk" on a daily basis, their own

maximum effort is justified. For OD consultants, it is engagement that can create agreement between what leadership and employees want from a change project. Neither group wants ongoing surveys and meetings that create understanding without improvement. We can focus our clients on improvement if we change our own emphasis from "what is engagement?" to "what is engaging?"

The employees who report seeing actions that addressed the key issues from the previous survey are among the most engaged employees in a company. Therefore, our challenge as OD consultants after the survey is (a) to identify cases where the Manager Focused model of change is less likely to effectively solve business problems, and (b) to create change interventions that will solve the business problems in those cases.

Note that when we focus on changing what drives engagement, the emphasis is to solve business problems that have come to light because of the engagement survey rather than merely increasing engagement scores. The survey is deemphasized. It provided a metric that links to organizational performance, and it raised leaders' awareness of employees' perceptions and evaluations of the company—a unique and valuable perspective, but not the ultimate purpose. What matters now is putting a process in place where leaders prioritize action areas, estimate the dollar figure at stake if no action is taken, and specify which workgroups/business units can contribute to improving the situation. Guiding the leadership team through these steps will (a) focus the change initiative, (b) provide guidelines for the initiative's budget, (c) encourage input from cross-functional and cross-level stakeholders, and (d) clarify what outcome is necessary for the initiative to be deemed successful. Next, representatives of those pertinent stakeholder groups need to collaborate in order to (e) specify the business problem or problems, (f) identify root causes, (g) coordinate early actions that show a "proof of concept" change, (h) develop more in-depth actions that can provide lasting change, and (i) monitor coworkers' reactions as well as performance metrics. By showcasing this process and its milestones, the organization's leaders give employees a reason to become engaged while specifying how they expect to see return on investment. Rather than targeting engagement because of statistical evidence of ROI elsewhere, we can target ROI directly to bring about engagement.

Summary

It is great to see so much attention on engagement surveys because leaders need to hear what employees are thinking and feeling. A survey also sends messages to employees: the questions communicate what leaders consider to be important, and the focus on employees' responses demonstrates how valuable employees are to the organization. However, if organizational leaders believe that "engagement" is only a measurement process, then this concept may already be hijacked, and it will be abandoned if the measure does not change (what one of my clients called "Groundhog Day" in reference to the movie about reliving the same day over and over again). We need to progress beyond engagement's definitions, benchmarks, and correlations with performance outcomes. These are only elements of the gauge, not a process to effect engagement. When a person is driving a car and notices that the gas gauge is on Empty, what does that person want? A more accurate gas gauge? A way to break the glass and bend the needle back to Full? A statistic on how full most other drivers keep their tanks? Obviously, the gas gauge is simply an indicator that the driver needs more gas in order to reach the destination. When it comes to employee engagement, our clients want a measure and a process so they can reach their destination. Are we ready to get them there?

References

Anonymous. (1996, June 17). America's 25 most influential people. *Time Magazine, 147*(25), re- trieved from http://www.time.com/time/magazine/ article /0,9171,984696,00.html

Borg, I., & Mastrangelo, P. M. (2008). *Employee surveys in management: Theories, tools, and practical applications.* Cambridge, MA: Hogrefe & Huber.

Buckingham, M., & Coffman, C. (1999*). First break all the rules: What the world's greatest managers do differently.* New York, NY: Simon & Schuster.

Esty, K., & Gewirtz, M. (2008, June 23). Creating a culture of employee engagement. Northeast Human Resources Association website. Retrieved from http://www.boston.com/jobs/nehra/062308.shtml.

Genesee. (2008). The global employee opinion normative study: 2008. Rochester, NY.

Hammer, M., & Champy, J. A. (1993). *Reengineering the corporation: A manifesto for business revolution.* New York, NY: Harper Collins.

Hevesi, D. (2008, September 4). Michael Hammer, Business Writer, Dies at 60. Retrieved from The New York Times website: http://www.nytimes.com/ 2008/09/05/business/05hammer.html.

Johnson, S. R., & Smith, R. (2006). Taking the world's pulse: Implications of the ongoing internet based global work opinion survey. In P. M. Mastrangelo (Chair), *Patterns across global organizational surveys: Timeliness, norms, structural equation models.* Presentation at the 21st Annual Conference of the Society for Industrial and Organizational Psychology, Dallas, TX.

Jolton, J. A., & Saltzman, J. (2008). A candid look at employee engagement: Five global truths. In M. Finney (Ed.), *Building high-performance people and organizations* (pp. 1–16). Westport, CT: Praeger.

Macey, W.H., & Schneider, B. (2008). The meaning of employee engagement. Industrial and *Organizational Psychology,* 1(1), 3–30.

Mastrangelo, P. M. (2008). Designing a global employee survey process to realize engagement and alignment. In M. Finney (Ed.), *Building high-performance people and organizations* (pp. 55–79). Westport, CT: Praeger.

Orr, D., & Matthews, H. (2008). Employee engagement and OD strategies. *OD Practitioner, 40*(2), 18–23.

Schneider, B. Hanges, P. J., Smith, D. B., & Salvaggio, A. N. (2003). Which comes first: Employee attitudes or organizational financial and market performance? *Journal of Applied Psychology, 88*(5), 836–851.

CHAPTER 46

The Power of Interactive Collaborative Designs

Jean-Pierre Beaulieu, Emile J. Carrière,
and Christopher Schoch

INTERACTIVE COLLABORATIVE Designs (ICD) such as Open Space, Future Search, Appreciative Inquiry, and The Conference Model, can be more effective as a change intervention than traditional approaches, which are generally top-down, linear in nature, and tightly controlled.

Our experience has taught us that ambitious business goals can be achieved through ICD and its power to mobilize large numbers of stakeholders, provide them with a strong sense of ownership for corporate vision and strategy and obtain high levels of engagement that generate results to which management and shareholders pay attention. These include increased productivity, improved profit margins, and greater customer satisfaction. One important feature of ICD is that although its impact is immediate, it also builds the long term capabilities of organizations for continuous change and commitment to the deeper values of collaboration, community, organizational learning and democracy.

This observation is derived from hands-on experience with a variety of business clients on three continents. Unfortunately many business people and managers believe that collaborative approaches are "too soft" to be used with business organizations.

We would like to alter this impression by describing the conditions under which ICD can impact business goals and reduce time of significant organizational change from drawing board to implementation.

In spite of these powerful dynamics, managers have traditionally felt ill at ease with designs that contain few to-do lists for them, require less control, and appear less structured than the tightly bound framework of forecasting and short-term reporting to which they are accustomed. We have observed that this is generally true even if certain managers recognize the virtues of collaborative, more open approaches. They just do not believe that these approaches can deliver the goods quickly enough. Processes that appear to them as too intuitive generally raise their anxiety beyond tolerable levels.

The major difference that we have found between traditional change approaches and ICD is that the former emphasizes control of content by providing a narrowly defined framework of givens. On the other hand, the focus of Interactive Collaborative Designs is more on the process, allowing for spontaneous real time content development.

As a result of our respective backgrounds in business, we can readily understand the paradox of managers in today's difficult business environment. Managers are individually held accountable for results that can only be obtained through the active commitment of large numbers of people who, in turn, need to also behave as though they were individually accountable for those same results.

Definition

To clarify what we mean by "Interactive Collaborative Designs", we propose below eight characteristics that we think define the concept of ICD:

1. A significant number of organizational members are actively invited to contribute ideas during the reflective-elaborative stage of strategy and vision building.
2. Dialogue provides the dynamics for discussion.
3. Self-Managed Teams is the model for task performance.
4. Discussions are public, collective, and open, "working from one heart, one mind," in the words of Kathy Dannemiller (2000).
5. The nonhierarchical environment facilitates genuine emergence of new possibilities.
6. Work is done collaboratively in real time.
7. Stakeholders are involved not only in the design but also in the implementation phase of the change.
8. The strategic intent of leadership aspires to significant change in the organizational culture.

Several well-known and well-documented processes readily correspond to these characteristics. Future Search as designed by Weisbord and Janoff, The Search Conference by Fred and Miriam Emery, Whole Scale Change by Dannemiller Tyson, Open-Space by H. H. Owen, Appreciative Inquiry, by Cooperider and his colleagues at Case-Western University, and The Conference Model as designed by Axelrod. Although each of these approaches has its own features and techniques, all of them meet the characteristics enunciated earlier. No single design is universally applicable to all client needs. In our work as OD consultants, we place great importance in identifying the design or combination of designs that will meet the specific requirements of the client organization, often blending in several sub designs to meet different levels of need at different stages of the change process.

For example, Future Search and Open Space Technology can each stand on their own as powerful tools of organization transformation. However, using Future Search with a limited number of stakeholders to identify shared values, shared vision and strategic paths followed by Open Space, with substantially larger groups can be highly effective for priority selection, action planning and implementation. In so doing, more stakeholders have the opportunity to directly influence the change direction resulting in most cases with an increased commitment to the outcome.

Key Success Factors

For ICD to produce the kinds of results we have referred to, a number of conditions must come together. We have listed those we feel are most important:

Engaged and Effective Leadership

This may seem paradoxical considering our earlier critique of top-down-driven processes. The emphasis here is on direction, not on control. By direction we mean sponsorship of the change effort and providing a clear platform for change which includes the following components:

- Strategic intent—what are the premises, purpose, urgency, nature, and scope (breadth and the depth) of desired change
- Definition of key relationships linking the organization to its environment
- Assessment of the vibrant or promising initiatives within the organization that need to be leveraged through the change process

- Understanding, and support for the organizing principles of the design
- Agreement on how senior leadership will communicate on and support the change effort

Definition of the Levels of Ambition

We have found that many projects start with a lot of noise but quickly disintegrate for the lack of well-defined ambition levels and limits to the desired changes. Not only is it desirable for ultimate change parameters to be spelled out, but also to have preferred strategic paths in order to sustain change over time.

Alignment of Corporate Governance

Our concern here is to determine what changes in governance are needed so that the organization continues to be ready to adapt to further changes in the environment and modify its ambition levels and its tactics. As long as the environment is in high gear, governance structures need to facilitate alert and fast reacting responses.

The Chartering of an Empowered Design Team

Once the leadership platform has been defined and communicated we can widen the circle of change agents by creating a design team composed of opinion leaders from key parts of the organization. Sharing leadership in this way gives credibility to the change effort and demonstrates that top management is sincere in enlisting the active engagement of members of the organization.

A typical charter will define how the design team will:

- Choose a theme for the change project, a highly symbolic and powerful aspect for internal and external stakeholder groups.
- Provide guidelines for the invitation of those who will be involved in the visioning and strategy stage.

- Contribute to the definition of an outline of the large group events.
- Ensure immediate follow-up.

Real Time Interaction Among Stakeholders

A critical stage of the change process is that of bringing the community together in one or several large-scale events or forums. In such forums, all members of the organization or representatives of the different social components of the "whole system" are invited to meet in real time to collaborate the vision, the strategy, and the change tactics.

The central task before the group ranges from defining a preferred and shared future state or "vision" to action planning. The size of the group can range from twenty-five people to as many as one thousand depending on logistical constraints.

When we mentioned earlier that the community needs to be brought together, we are aware of resistance on the part of leadership with respect to the participation of particular stakeholders. For example, leaders can be unwilling to invite clients, claiming that their companies know what their customers want because they are in constant interaction with them. Our experience is that external stakeholders, particularly customers, have a deep impact on corporate vision by bringing a perspective no one else can have and by providing insights as to the evolution of their needs and the emerging dynamics of the marketplace.

We recall an example where sales and marketing members of a Design Team expressed such resistance. At a review meeting, the CEO (and prime sponsor) asked them: "What are you afraid of? Do you fear that our clients will discover that we sometimes make commitments we know we cannot respect, that we sometimes ship orders that we know are incomplete, that we sometimes ship material not meeting all quality criteria? Don't worry, he told them, our clients are already well aware of all this." As a case in point, during that company's Future Search workshop, clients said: "We appreciated so much your invitation and the opportunity you provided us to influence your and our future that we are ready to have you access our market data bank." Traditional strategic planning processes seldom get such enthusiastic support from clients. This also exemplifies the "unpredictable" nature of the forum, the unanticipated learnings and insights and unparalleled commitment, which emanate from ICD-type events.

The Need for Rigorous Follow-Up

Rigorous follow-up is critical to the success of change efforts that we have been talking about. In the case of large-scale events it is often neglected. Why? We believe that this is where Interactive Collaborative Designs become the victims of their success.

Typically, at the end of a two or three day event, the amounts of energy, enthusiasm and verbal commitment are at a level never or rarely seen in organizations. This can be misleading. Participants may tend to believe that given that level of readiness and eagerness to change, things will happen automatically. Unfortunately, although things will never be the same for those who participated in such a process, leadership, guidance and coordination of the change efforts will be needed. A large-scale event is but a preamble to action and does not replace it. As mentioned, the role of senior leaders is to ensure that commitments will be honored and that the right conditions will be nurtured to create a climate of success.

This is often a delicate part of the OD consultant's job. It is an opportunity to provide guidance at least at the initial implementation phase, and to be available to the client to guard against factors that can derail the whole process. What we bring is expertise in sustained and timely communication, in continued transparency, in good monitoring methodology and in practices that bring about the real empowerment of people at all levels.

Illustrations of Effective Application of ICD by Business Organizations

We have introduced ICD to a wide spectrum of business organizations in different sectors and in different countries. We provide below four illustrations of these applications:

Telecoms: Defining Business Strategy and Vision

A world-class Canadian telecommunications company brought together seventy-two internal and external stakeholders for a two day Future Search workshop. The task was to define a compelling vision for the organization. Up to this point the business was focused on product engineering, cost reduction, and reliance on top-down direction. They wanted to shift to a market-driven culture focused on the customer, on delivering quality, and on shared ownership.

The Search not only produced a broad consensus-based vision, it also redefined how the company needed to work with its customers and suppliers. All participants left the Search committed to bringing the vision to life through action plans that, one year later, had been carried out and incorporated into all parts of the organization, including a newly acquired European subsidiary.

Engineering: Developing Cross-Functional Teams

A large industrial multinational company embarked on a change process to achieve stronger cross-functional teamwork between all segments of its Engineering supply chain so as to get more value for each dollar spent from its Engineering budget.

One hundred and fifty stakeholders were invited to participate in a two day Open Space forum. Participants included engineers, entrepreneurs, consultants, equipment suppliers, senior leadership, project managers, union representatives, design and drafting personnel and administrative staff.

From this forum, a redefinition of the conditions for success was created, a series of solid proposals for carrying out the changes were devised, and most importantly, a positive synergy for working together to achieve a new organization work climate was achieved.

Computer Operations: Organizational Culture Change

The computer operations department of major division of a European telecom giant was faced with the challenge of being outsourced unless it could meet market standards in cost and quality.

In response to the challenge, the managing director of the department chose to involve all 80 employees in creating a new service-based culture with a commitment to better understand and meet customer needs—culture in which taking initiatives was encouraged and where working in cross functional teams would be the accepted norm.

Five three-day Future Search workshops enabled members to define a compelling preferred future. Then everyone was brought together for a one day Open Space meeting, which led to the adoption and launching of five strategic change projects that were successfully implemented within six months.

Due to its success, two years later the department won over the computer operations budget for the whole company's telecommunications business.

Credit Card Provider: Business Process Re-engineering

The director of the customer service center of France's number one private credit card provider knew that his company would have to meet the challenge of GE's global finance service business by making significant increases in the number of card holders per employee.

He was also convinced that to do so his company would need to quickly set up a much more fluid and project-based organization.

Instead of the traditional top–down approach to change, he decided to use ICD to actively involve all 1000 members of the organization. In a little more than a year, the needed change was implemented with the support and active participation of the employees who were most affected.

Enabling Factors of These Four Examples

We believe that each of the four cases benefitted from a set of unplanned fortuitous circumstances that strongly contributed to the successful use of ICD:

- The leaders were aware that somewhat radical organization changes needed to be achieved that included a change of mindset and norms governing the sharing of responsibility, information, and resources.
- There was a compelling reason to try something new; in several cases the leaders or their executive groups had experienced disappointment with earlier change efforts.
- There was awareness of urgency or of limited time to grab the opportunity.
- Leadership had sufficient confidence in themselves and the organization to experiment with a different approach.

Dealing with Resistance

When we revisit some of the points of resistance that managers experience with Interactive Collaborative Designs, many appear to be quite legitimate. These include:

- Tying up too many resources
- Difficulty in assessing the cost of opportunity of the process
- Measuring the impact of the process on business
- Monitoring and tracking progress
- Measuring and tracking individual accountability

Resistance also exists with respect to the loss of power, control and ego, all of which needs to be addressed effectively. Harrison Owen says that in our day and age, "Leaders have to let go of the control they thought they had." More easily said than done. Still, we have seen leaders really committed to ICD principles lose their composure when entering the Open Space circle where all of a sudden there is no sign of differentiation or of hierarchy. As consultants we need to provide leaders with the right amount of support and coaching to help them make the required adjustments.

Senior leaders may also be uncomfortable with the discovery that, through ICD, so much can be rapidly accomplished outside the control of hierarchy. As consultants, we can encourage leaders to air out their own resistance and provide coaching and support in dealing with their fears. An effective way to help such clients is to arrange and facilitate meetings with peers from organizations who have been in similar situations and have experienced the values and success of ICD.

Conclusion

Following fifteen years of practice in OD, our first experience with ICD in organization transformation occurred in the late eighties. Since then, our experience in Europe, Asia and North America with a dozen different clients has been that Interactive Collaborative Designs can have meaningful impact on business goals and, in the case of significant organiza-tional change, can reduce the time from drawing board to implementation. These are powerful interventions!

References

Anderson, D. , & Ackerman-Anderson, L. (2001). *Beyond change management.* San Francisco, CA: JosseyBass/Pfeiffer.

Axelrod, R. (2000). *The terms of engagement.* San Francisco, CA: Barret-Koelher.

Beaulieu, J.P., & Carrière, E.J. (2000). *Mobiliser l'organisation face à son avenir. La démarche prospective.* Boucherville, Quebec: Gaëtan Morin.

Jaffe, D. T., & Scott, C. (1999). *Getting your organization to change.* Menlo Park, CA: Crisp Publications.

Owen, H. H. (1997). *Open space technolog.* San Franciso, CA: Barret-Koelher.

Owen, H. H. (1997). *Expanding our now: the story of open space technology,* San Francisco, CA: Berrett-Koehler.

Purser, E., & Cabana, S. (2000). *The self managing organization.* New York, NY: The Free Press.

Weisbord, M., & Janoff, S. (1995). *Future search. An action guide to finding common ground in organi-sations and communities.* San Francisco, CA: Berrett-Koehler.

Dannemiller Tyson Associates (2000). *Whole scale change, unleashing the magic in organizations.* San Francisco, CA: Berrett-Koehler.

Stan, H. (Ed.). (2002). *Rewiring organizations for the networked economy, organizing, managing and leading in the information age.* San Francisco, CA: Jossey-Bass/Pfeiffer.

CHAPTER 47

Creating a Culture of Collaboration in a City Government

Nancy L. Southern

CULTURES OF COLLABORATION invite stakeholders to participate together in ways that support the organization's mission, enhance the personal development of its members, and provide a needed service to the community with a vision of creating a better world.

My work with senior and mid-level managers in a United States city government serving a diverse, rapidly growing population of over 900,000 provides a process model for creating a culture of collaboration. The city manager I worked with knew that a culture change was needed and he had already begun that process when we first met. As happens in most organizational culture changes, he had brought in new managers that were committed to collaboration, and there were many managers who had been with the organization for years who were uncertain about what the culture change would mean to them.

The focus of our initial efforts was to design an event that would have a transformative effect on the team, creating both an experience of collaboration and launching their continued cultural change efforts. We decided on an off-site, two-day retreat, the planning for which would be a collaborative effort between a steering team of volunteer senior managers and me, as facilitator.

I use an action research framework, that mirrors the participative engagement I hope to help embed in the organization's culture. Reason (2001) defines action research as a "participatory, democratic process concerned with developing practical knowing in the pursuit of worthwhile human purposes, grounded in a participatory worldview." He states that it "seeks to bring together action and reflection, theory and practice, in participation with others, in the pursuit of practical solutions to issues of pressing concern to people, and more generally the flourishing of individual persons and their communities"(p.1). As such, it serves as a way to engage with others in understanding the need for change and designing and implementing the change. Participants gain both the knowledge and the skills needed to create and sustain their own change.

Honoring an important principle of action research, I do not present myself as an expert consultant, but rather as a participant in the process, acting in the role of co-designer and facilitator. In preparation for the retreat, I asked to interview all participants to gain their perspective on the current situation and desired outcomes for the event and to personally invite them to participate in a way that could result in the transformative experience we

hoped to enable. Taking care to protect confi-
dentially, I shared the themes from these interviews with the design committee. This effort
of co-construction ensures that the organization's objectives are met and that all participants see their perspectives and objectives reflected in the design.

Not all members of the senior management team were eager to participate. Many
were skeptical that it would be one more retreat, like previous ones that ate up their time
with minimal results. The invitation I extended during the interviews uncovered limiting
beliefs and assumptions and challenged participants to consider the possibility that something different could take place. I spoke of the
importance of their participation in co-creating a new culture.

One participant told me that he had never
fully participated in previous retreats. He described his pattern of showing up at some point
during the first day, observing the process, con-
firming his belief that it would not create change,
and returning to his more important work back
at the office. If he had extra time, he might show
up for a short time toward the end of the retreat.
He described how he felt his work didn't require
the same type of collaboration, as did others who
performed more central tasks. His previous experience led him to believe that this retreat would
be the same as all the others and he was pretty
certain he wouldn't have time to attend the entire
session. I asked him to challenge his assumptions
and consider participating fully, stressing the importance of his contribution. Although he made
no commitment to do so, he showed up at the
beginning of the retreat and stayed until the end,
fully participating throughout.

The helix in Figure 47.1 displays the increasing arenas of participation from invitation to collaboration and ultimately engagement within a learning community. Once we
accept the invitation to participate in new
ways, we create the possibility to become engaged in the process. When the engagement
leads us to question assumptions, see the problems in old patterns of action, and the opportunities in new possibilities, creative energy is

FIGURE 47.1   The Collaborative Journey

The invitation to participate in co-
creating a new reality is the beginning
of the collaborative journey. The
helix displays the increasing arenas
of participation from invitation
to collaboration and ultimately
engagement within a learning
community.

set free and people become committed to the
change. If we believe in the power of intention, then commitment to change is the key to
realizing that which we want to create. In this
case, the commitment leads to collaboration
that has the potential of evolving into a learning community.

The importance of an invitation to participate cannot be underestimated. A good invitation communicates the importance of the
change effort to the organization, as well as
the larger community it serves, and addresses
the benefits to individuals. How will they develop leadership skills and capabilities through
the process? How will they increase their ability to do their jobs and accomplish their goals?

The senior management team members
were clear about their responsibility as public
servants and acknowledged the importance of
extending an invitation to collaborate to city
employees, city council members, and city
residents. Leaders of these efforts need to create time for questions and be open to hearing

perspectives that challenge their intention. They also need to create the conditions that foster collaboration.

Five Conditions for Collaboration

The primary responsibility of leaders working in participative cultures is to create the conditions that enable people to achieve the desired result. I have found that five conditions are needed to support collaboration. People need to engage in *meaningful relationships* with others and in *work that serves a greater purpose.* Cultural competence is needed to recognize the value of different perspectives and communicate effectively across cultures. The culture needs to value *shared leadership* and prepare everyone to participate as a leader. *Communicative competence embedded within dialogic communication* fosters mutual respect, and enables knowledge to be shared, assumptions to be challenged, and learning to be ever present.

The event/retreat we crafted to launch a culture of collaboration for the city government established a foundation for all of these conditions. The first step in moving people into a collaborative space is to create opportunities for them to challenge their assumptions, shift their beliefs, and create new mental models. Collaboration requires beliefs that include the following:

- I can be more successful with the help of others.
- Diversity makes us more creative and capable.
- Disagreement adds value to a conversation and results in better decisions.
- Talking about what we have learned is more valuable than talking about what we have done.
- I can speak freely and truthfully to anyone in the organization.

Unfortunately, these beliefs are rarely held in most organizations. Individual beliefs will not be changed by telling people which ones they need to hold. Beliefs are changed through experiences that challenge our assumptions and cause us see ourselves in relationship to others, our organizations, and our world, in new ways. The retreat incorporated the five conditions in the following way.

Meaningful relationships were established through a process of individuals, within groups of five or six people, sharing aspects of themselves that are not normally shared in organizational contexts. Questions such as "What influences (culture, events, people) have shaped you?" "What do you value most about yourself, your work, your life?" "What are your talents, passions, and hobbies?" and "What are your aspirations?" guide people into conversations that reveal their authentic selves and develop new appreciation for each other. Every group I have guided through this process is amazed at the depth of the conversation that emerges and the closeness they develop with their colleagues. A window is opened to appreciating the diversity of the group. Understanding and appreciating diverse perspectives is the first step toward cultural competence.

Shared purpose is established through reflective conversation about the importance of the work of the organization. Inspiration and energy abound when groups of people talk together about how they contribute to a larger purpose. It is easy for all of us to get lost in the minutia of our daily tasks and lose sight of the meaning of our work. Collaboration is fostered by continually bringing to light how others are served by the work we do together.

Shared leadership is established by thinking and talking together about shared accomplishments, challenges encountered and overcome, and what has been learned along the way. These are simple but powerful conversations that don't occur often enough in most organizations. Sharing leadership means that we recognize the strengths of others, are willing to speak openly, listen carefully, and take action together. Shared leadership requires trust, a willingness to grant authority to others, assume authority when needed, and provide the resources to enable others to act.

Communicative competence and dialogic conversation emerge quite naturally within a context that is established by good guiding questions and a process that provides everyone an opportunity to listen, reflect, and speak. The core of communicative competence is the intention for communication to reach new understanding for the purpose of informing individual and collective action. Communicative competence is based on Habermas' (1985) four principles of mutual comprehension, shared values, truthfulness, and trust (see Figure 47.2).

Dialogic communication also stems from the intention to reach new understanding through inquiry, challenging assumptions, and advocating through engagement of the four principles.

While each of the four principles needs to be present for communicative competence, each communicative event has differing qualities of principle. Managers, whose relationships are lacking in trust and mutual comprehension, might improve their communication through establishing shared values and taking risks with truth telling.

FIGURE 47.2 Communicative Competence

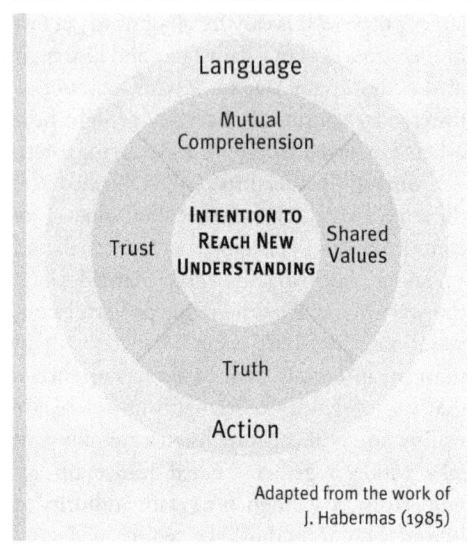

Adapted from the work of
J. Habermas (1985)

One of the processes the city managers engaged in involved courageous conversations. This process places people in groups where they most often associate and where natural tensions exist. Often these groups are comprised of individuals from operations and administration, or manufacturing and sales and marketing. Each group is asked to discuss questions such as "How do we add value?" "How can we better collaborate?" "How can we better serve our colleagues?" and "What do we need from others to enhance our effectiveness?" Once the group discussions are complete, each group is asked to speak to the other groups, responding to each of the questions.

The conversations that emerge break through many of the existing beliefs and assumptions and create new insights critical to developing collaborative mental models. People recognize how they often blame the other groups for problems that they contribute to creating and maintaining, and they realize that by changing their own patterns of action, they can change the nature of the relationship. They gain new respect for others and the contributions they make, establishing greater trust and mutual understanding. Through these conversations, they experience communicative competence and strengthen the four principles to enable future conversations to reach new understanding through dialogue.

These five conditions are necessary elements of all highly participative cultures. The work described thus far strengthened relationships and created the spirit of collaboration. Changing organizational cultures requires a greater systemic approach.

Changing Organizational Cultures

Cultural change involves change in collective and individual beliefs and assumptions, patterns of action, organizational supporting structures, and events. The model in Figure 47.3 shows how these four elements are addressed concurrently.

FIGURE 47.3   Cultural Change Pyramid

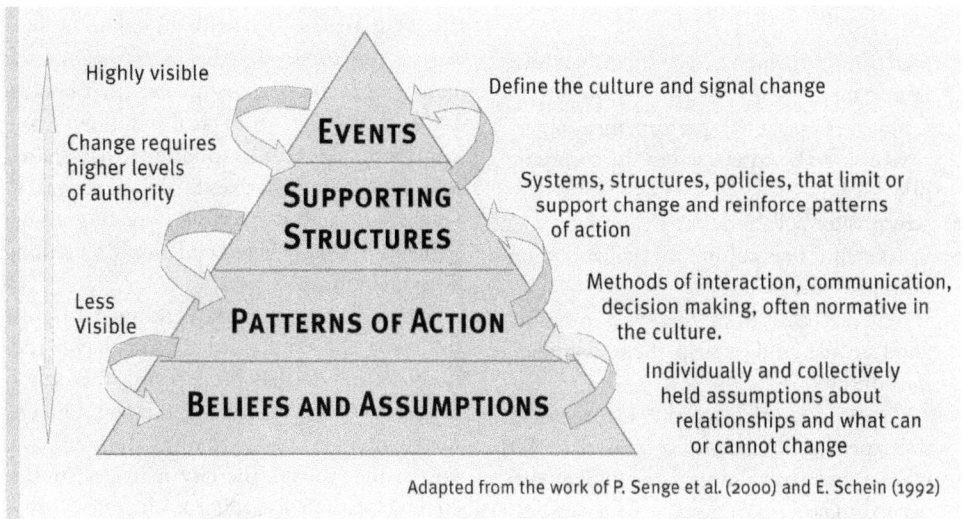

Highly visible

Change requires higher levels of authority

Less Visible

EVENTS

SUPPORTING STRUCTURES

PATTERNS OF ACTION

BELIEFS AND ASSUMPTIONS

Define the culture and signal change

Systems, structures, policies, that limit or support change and reinforce patterns of action

Methods of interaction, communication, decision making, often normative in the culture.

Individually and collectively held assumptions about relationships and what can or cannot change

Adapted from the work of P. Senge et al. (2000) and E. Schein (1992)

The pyramid shape shows how beliefs and assumptions create the foundation of a culture. Schein (1992) discusses how basic assumptions are so embedded within a culture that they are rarely recognized or discussed. Behavior based on basic assumptions is often taken for granted, as over time we become unaware of how our thinking has shaped our actions. Individual behavior based on beliefs, assumptions, values and experiences, eventually forms patterns of actions. These patterns are communicative, such as the way people contact and follow-up with each other, engage in meetings, and make decisions. These patterns are based on both the written and unwritten rules of the organization and reflect what people believe is valued and recognized or rewarded.

Supporting structures are constructed on the values and basic assumptions of the founders and senior leaders. Supporting structures include policies and procedures, performance review processes, rewards and recognition, and technology; the infrastructure of the organization that influences how people engage and take action. To support collaboration, sup-porting structures need to be aligned with the desired action and interaction, to provide the leverage to propel change. For instance, an investment in the right technology can enable collaboration outside of the limitations of time and space. Adding collaboration as a performance measure can demonstrate the importance of it and provide a structured opportunity for managers to address it, hold people accountable, and recognize success.

Events, planned or unplanned, publicly communicate what the organization believes and how it carries out its work. Like supporting structures, events create leverage for change. They provide leaders an opportunity to demonstrate their commitment to collaboration. They also provide opportunities to bring people together to envision new possibilities, experience new ways of working and create action plans for change.

During the two days the city's senior managers spent in retreat, they worked together identifying the changes needed within the organizations' culture to support collaboration among all people internally, with the city council, and with the public they served. Below are some of the points made in response to the work they needed to do.

- Staff must be helped to recognize their own importance.
- Employees' personal performance objectives need to be connected to the corporate priorities.
- Rewards for collaboration are needed.
- Roles within a culture of collaboration need to be defined.
- It remains critical to hire and promote good people, and to help them assimilate into the culture.
- We need to anticipate the management skills needed in the future and train for them, rather than simply focus on the skills needed today.
- More improvement can be made on fully engaging the whole organization and getting them all to recognize that we serve the same customers.
- The organizational structure and physical locations of our facilities can be a barrier to collaboration. We can consider how to reorganize.
- We need to start acting as if we are already working together in one building (a new city hall was being planned).
- Resources need to be brought together to deal with issues, rather than being protected in silos.

The senior managers determined that a key action was to have their direct reports engage in a similar process and then talk together about their shared vision and ways to implement it. They valued the opportunity to develop their relationships and engage in meaningful conversation and they wanted their direct reports to experience a similar process. We co-designed a one-day retreat that engaged the next level of middle managers in a similar process and brought the two groups together for a dialogue about the changes they wanted to make to foster collaboration.

Results of the Effort

The retreat provided an opportunity for the senior managers to work together in new ways. The event signaled a change in the nature of their relationship and their organizational culture. They realized how many common values and aspirations they shared and how committed each of them was to serving the public good and creating an organization that enabled collaboration among all stakeholders.

Collaborative efforts continued to grow following the event. The city held two economic summits that brought together scholars, technology leaders, real estate brokers, merchants, and representatives from arts and non-profit groups. The city manager considered the summit a significant catalytic event as it brought stakeholders into a dialogue that could support collaborative action in improving the economic future of the city. The city also collaborated with the local university to construct a new library that served the whole community.

Ultimately, the result of creating cultures of collaboration is the development of learning communities with the capacity to work together, take risks, disagree, make mistakes, learn from those mistakes, and continue the collaborative efforts. If collaboration doesn't extend into a learning community, when difficulties arise, people often revert to independent action. What does it take to keep these efforts going? When I asked the city manager to reflect on what he had learned from his efforts, he offered the following insights:

- Collaboration is built upon the professionalism of department heads and staff. The right people with the desire to work together and the knowledge that they are all serving the same constituency can accomplish great things. The city manager gives these senior managers total accountability and expects them to work together to meet the needs of the constituents.

- When people embrace collaboration they are willing to make personal sacrifices for the good of the whole. The city manager spoke about the budget process, where the city faced a $70 million shortfall. He described the organization as "breezing through it" as the managers worked together to make the cuts that were best for the city. Rather than taking the common position of protecting one's turf, he stated that the managers offered to make the necessary cuts, negotiated with one another, and committed to support each other.
- Trust the people and the process even when mistakes are made. This leader faced difficult situations where his style of management came under fire from city council members, due to mistakes made within the organization. Yet, he expressed no hesitation in continuing to pursue his vision of a collaborative culture and to trust the people whom are close to the work. He is committed to making sure the group learns from the mistakes, reviews the patterns of action that created the problems, and establishes supporting structures to avoid similar situations in the future.
- Recognize that not all people will see the value in a participative culture. Members on the city council often questioned why decisions were delegated to lower levels in the organization and why more control was not exercised. All too often, leaders who feel strongly about participative cultures have pressure to exercise more control.

Unfortunately, this leader decided to leave the city manager position earlier this year because of the challenges he faced working within a larger culture that holds different values and expectations. This work requires those of us who believe strongly in the human values of participation to work to shift beliefs and assumptions at the community, national, and global levels. That task is not an easy one, yet it is critical to realizing the ideal of cultures of participation.

Guiding Beliefs and Assumptions

My work is guided by a set of beliefs and assumptions that I have embraced through my study of organizational learning, transformative education, and hermeneutic philosophy. These assumptions guide the way I participate with others in my life and my work and I believe create the conditions for transformative learning for others and myself.

- I participate with others in co-creating the future. The fabric of this co-creation is "care" for one another and for the world.
- We are always in relationship, so the work needed is to strengthen our relationships through understanding our shared values and aspirations.
- Relationships are strengthened through our communicative competence, a way of being in the world.
- Leadership is enabled through granting authority to others and through assuming authority when granted. Granting authority graces a relationship and creates a space where we can belong and participate together.

These assumptions are more other-centered than self-centered, and, as such, enable working cross culturally. The shift to being more other-centered is important if we are to embrace our differences and care enough to create cultures where we can participate together in creating a better world. I believe the purpose of creating participative cultures is what Mary Catherine Bateson considers composing a life. We don't compose our lives alone. We co-create them through the relationships we have with others. Bateson's (2004) work speaks to the integration of people, culture, relationships, and care. She states: "More and more it has seemed to me that the idea of an individual, the idea that there is someone to be known, separate from the relationships, is simply an error . . . we create each other, bring each other into being by being part of the matrix in which the other exists." (p. 4). When we can bring all of who we are to our work, share our traditions, our joys, our struggles, and our aspirations, and come to appreciate the richness of our diversity and common purpose, we can co-create participative communities, where care and respect are weaved together to form the fabric of our organizations and our world.

References

Bateson. M. C. (2004). *Willing to learn: Passages of personal discovery.* Hanover, NH: Steerforth Press.

Habermas, J. (1985). *The theory of communicative action, vol. 1: Reason and the rationalization of society, vol. 2: Lifeworld and system: Functionalist reason.* (T. McCarthy, Trans.). Boston, MA: Beacon Press. (Original work published 1981).

Reason, P., & Bradbuy, H. (2001). *Handbook of action research: Participative inquiry and practice.* London, UK: Sage Publications.

Schein, E. (1992). *Organizational culture and leadership.* San Francisco, CA: Jossey-Bass.

Senge, P. (1990). *The fifth discipline: The art and practice of the learning organization.* New York, NY: Doubleday.

Southern, N. (2004). Creating cultures of collaboration that thrive on diversity: A transformative perspective on building collaborative capital. In M. Beyerlein & S. T. Beyerlein (Eds.), Advances in interdiscipinary studies of work teams (V. 11) (pp. 33–72). Maryland Heights, MO: Elsevier.

CHAPTER 48

Employee-Led Organizational Change
Theory and Practice
Victor Wooddell and Sanyani Edwards

IT IS A TRUISM that increased levels of employee involvement will strengthen employee commitment to change, and will increase the likelihood of achieving an organization's goals (Kiesler, 1971.) Yet little literature seems to exist on true, grass-roots or bottom-up models of organization change. Studies do abound on many related areas, including employee involvement, participatory management, and workplace democracy. Employee involvement systems typically refer to involving most or all employees in work-related decisions (Marrow, Bowers, 1967), participatory management is a management style that relies heavily on employee input (Marrow, Bowers, 1967) while workplace democracy encompasses efforts to re-structure power relations in the workplace (Greenberg, 1986).

None of these concepts corresponds very well with employee-led organization change, which we define as change projects or initiatives in which one or more front-line employees initiate, design and implement an organization change project. Obviously, in order for such projects to be successful, a partnership arrangement must be made with the organization's top executives, but in an employee-led change project, employees take the lead role. Little of the literature actually addresses the theory or practice of front-line employees undertaking responsibility for organizational change. These other models are at once too broad and conceptual, focused as they are on radical, transformative changes at the macro level. Short of transforming the entire system, might there not be practical value in addressing how employees might lead change one specific project at a time?

The purpose of this article is to identify those factors that are critical to the success of employee-driven organization change projects. Here we will present a case study that will demonstrate techniques that have allowed employee teams to successfully design and implement such projects. These techniques allow front—line employees to initiate specific changes within their organization, in partnership with, but independent from, the executive and middle-management levels. The conclusion that we reach as a result of this study is at once more practical, and yet in some ways even more radical than the mainstream literature: That ordinary employees can change an organization, even a deeply entrenched bureaucracy, if they are committed to it, and have the knowledge, skills, and support that they require.

Organizational Context

The case study presented here was one of three similar projects that involved employee-led change teams in three different public sector agencies: The public works department, the health department, and the finance department of a large American municipal government. These three teams consisted almost entirely of front-line employees or supervisors. None of the three teams directly challenged the reporting hierarchy of their department, but were given permission to temporarily work outside of it in order to develop ideas in a more creative fashion than would normally be possible in these organizations. Each of the projects developed independently under different conditions, yet they are also unified by a common set of models and practices, and by the support of one of the researchers, who acted as a consultant to the teams. Since all three teams manifested broadly similar processes and outcomes, we will examine one team as an exemplar of the other two: the Finance Department team.

The Department of Finance Team

Background and Mandate: The author first met with the Director and Deputy Director of the department in September of 2002. The two Directors wanted assistance in aligning their department with three new strategic goals. These goals were: 1) Improve the City's financial reporting process, 2) Improve the Department's responsiveness to their customers needs (i.e., other City departments), and 3) Improve the overall fiscal health of the City Government. These goals were themselves designed to facilitate an expected consolidation of the accounting function in the coming year.

The Finance Department employed somewhat less than 500 full-time employees. As is the case with nearly all city departments in the Eastern part of the US, in this finance department most front-line employees and supervisors are unionized, and also African-American. Furthermore, Finance Department employees are roughly evenly divided by gender, although males occupy most of the professional positions while females occupy most of the clerical ones. The finance department is organized in a traditional bureaucratic hierarchy, with the Director and Deputy Director at the top, Di-

visional Managers just beneath them, and one or more supervisory levels between the Division Managers and the front-line staff. The majority of the employees are physically located in a central downtown office, although between 70-80 accounting employees are placed in field locations servicing various other City departments.

The first team meeting took place in December of that year. Ten members were assigned, at least one from every division within the Finance Department. There were three managers, three supervisors, and four line staff. Six were male, four were female, one of the males and two of the female members were clerical. The team met for an average of two hours every two weeks for the duration of the project.

History of the Project

Initially, the team spent several meetings learning about change management and meeting facilitation. Real work on the project began in January of 2003. The team prioritized the Director's three strategic goals in terms of the ability of the team to make a significant contribution, thus, responsiveness to internal department customers was given the highest priority. This translated into designing and implementing organizational improvements within the Finance Department.

After receiving the Director's approval to move in this direction, the team next designed and implemented an employee survey. Since collecting data from all department employees was considered impractical due to time and other constraints, a somewhat informal sampling procedure was used, that resulted in data from over 100 employees. The survey asked employees to suggest changes and improvements that could be implemented within their division and work unit. As a result of this input, the team identified four specific projects to undertake: a) An improvement in the way data was reported on the City's standard tax bill (strategic goal 1), b) Producing a "Call Referral Directory" that would list every service the department offered with contact and other information (strategic goal 2), c) An employee recognition program for best attendance in each division (goal 2 with emphasis on internal service) and d) Mandatory Customer Service Training for all employees (also goal 2). It is worthy of note that an attempt to focus on improving responsiveness to internal customers actually produced ideas that affected external customers as well as financial reporting. The survey was completed by April of 2003.

Since it was felt that a stronger emphasis on improving internal customer service was still needed, the team undertook a mapping exercise of their department that revealed the major inter-dependencies between the divisional sub-units. This allowed the team to design a process to facilitate meetings between representatives of each of the divisions within the department to discuss improving communication and other interdependencies. The mapping process for the team was completed by June, 2003.

Another milestone for the team was designing and facilitating an off-site retreat for their department divisional managers, along with the Director and Deputy Director. The team presented their project ideas to the managers, conducted the same mapping exercise with them, and solicited the manager's support for the continuation of the projects. The off-site retreat took place in December of 2003.

A second phase of the project began in October, 2005, when the team began to look specifically at supervisor and manager performance issues. First the team identified the dimensions that were of most interest, and decided to collect data using an employee survey or assessment of leadership in the department. With the Director's enthusiastic support, the team brainstormed a list of items to include on the assessment tool, outlined an implementation plan for conducting the survey, and decided how to analyze and report the results. They approached the department's training division for assistance in collecting the data, and with their help, designed and scheduled the survey sessions. The plan was to calculate each

foreman, supervisor and manager's averages along several different dimensions of leadership, including Interpersonal Communication, Fairness, Teamwork, Relationship with Employees, Openness, Accountability, Trustworthiness, Management Competence, Advocating for the Team, Knowing and Following Procedures, Solving Problems, and Discussing Performance. Members of the team, along with the rated individual's supervisor, would meet with the rated individual and coach them regarding how to improve their performance. The intent was not to penalize the individuals for their scores, but to help them understand their strengths and weaknesses as well as to develop a better understanding regarding how to develop themselves professionally. In addition, the team intended to develop divisional averages and make these available to all employees.

Lessons Learned

One lesson is to let the employees identify their own priorities at the beginning of the project. For some of our team members, this project was the first opportunity they have had to define their own objectives and design their own project. In spite of the fact that, during the first phase of the project the team identified priorities that did not correspond exactly to the Director's initial goal ("internal customer service" had not been a strategic goal), allowing the team to address an issue that seemed more critical to them accomplished several desirable outcomes. First, it gave them the opportunity to develop new skills before addressing the more difficult objective (a series of short projects as opposed to a formal assessment and training program). In addition, the first phase of the project allowed the department to take advantage of a short term opportunity (the City was opening a new call center at this time, and new guidelines were needed). This also allowed the team to develop credibility by successfully delivering a quality outcome. Thus, they were later well-positioned to address the more difficult, and potentially more controversial, task of implementing a leadership assessment of their own supervisors and managers.

Future of the Project

Data collection is expected to be completed by August of 2006. The team anticipates that it will require two more months for the data analysis and to complete the coaching sessions. The second phase of this project should be complete by October 2006, approximately one year after it began. The team intends to have a proposal for its next project ready by the end of that year.

Techniques and Tools

Several different techniques proved to be very useful to employee teams in terms of facilitating change either within their team meetings or throughout their organization. The following is a partial list that encapsulates the experiences of all three teams.

1. *Brainstorming:* The primary tool in the beginning of the project design process was brainstorming. Whoever was acting as the meeting facilitator could simply take the next step in the project process and pose it as a question, soliciting input from the entire team (i.e.: "What should our final output look like?", "How do we get there from here?") It was very useful to share some basic principles of brainstorming until the team members became skillful at it. One particular variation, called Mad-Glad (let's list some things about working here that make us Mad, and some that make us Glad) was especially useful in helping the team identify organizational change priorities.

2. *Employee Surveys:* Once Change Teams understood that part of their purpose was to represent the line staff, they typically wanted to find some way to collect input from as many employees as possible. Usually, there hadn't been the time or the resources to conduct formal surveys or focus groups, but Team members were usually able to go back to their

own work areas and solicit feedback from their colleagues in the department.

3. *Presentations:* Commonly, concrete goals and deliverables help team members remain focused in their efforts. Since the final outcome of the project could take a year or more to reach, it was important to schedule events like presentations to the executive or the managers at regular intervals, perhaps every six months or so. Not only did this keep the organization's leadership informed and maintain their support of the project, but the need to make formal presentations periodically seemed to impose a sense of discipline on the team and kept motivation and productivity high. Sometimes, especially after completing some benchmarking research, the team members made presentations to one another, which helped keep people interested and built skills and confidence for more formal presentations. This can be important for employees that may never have had the chance to present their work to others in a professional setting before.

4. *Off-Site Retreats:* An extension of formal presentations is having the team actually organize and facilitate an off-site retreat for their organization's leadership. An off-site retreat permits a more extensive dialogue regarding organizational change and the project that is being undertaken. The Finance Team used an off-site retreat both to familiarize the management with the large number of projects that they were undertaking and to obtain the data they needed for one of their projects. Unfortunately, there were insufficient resources to permit all the employees to attend the retreats at these departments, but had this been possible, such retreats or workshops would have been an effective method of communicating the purpose and status of the change project throughout the department.

5. *"Quick Hit" Projects:* Building credibility and confidence is an important component to success in a corporate setting. Although not planned in advance, it turned out that the two Department Teams that undertook smaller-scale projects and maintained their

momentum longer, experienced fewer conflicts within the team than the one that did not limit itself to smaller-scale projects (the health department team).

6. *Benchmarking Research:* After the finance team identified the change-priorities it wished to focus on, the next logical step was to find out what other organizations had done in similar efforts. Individual team members were assigned specific areas to research, and reported their findings back to the team. This helped move the team forward, as well as helped team members to develop their presentation skills.

7. *Teambuilding Skills:* Often enough, members of change teams have little experience working on effective teams. Several sets of skills may need to be developed before they will be ready to undertake a full-scale change project.

8. *Setting Own Goals and Priorities:* The importance of this feature is difficult to overstate. The natural assumption would be that a project team that has been mandated by their senior executive to accomplish certain goals should focus exclusively on those goals—and the less time and effort spent to do so the better. Yet in two of the three Department Team cases, not only did the teams decide to propose to do something different than they were specifically mandated to do, the Directors were enthusiastic in support of this. This may partially be a consequence of the leadership styles of the Directors in question, both of whom agreed to recruit an employee Change Team at least in part because they were themselves innovative leaders with an interest in new management practices. Yet another reason, not unconnected with the first, was that the teams' proposals were evidence of a developing set of leadership skills and a sense of ownership on the part of the team members. Both Directors expressed a sense of gratification that at least one team was demonstrating the kind of enthusiasm and commitment that they were looking for from all their staff. Thus, the lesson learned was twofold: Finding the right type of executive champion is critical to support employee-led change efforts; and the executive champion must understand that one important value added by employee-led change teams is the development of leadership skills by the team members, and that such teams should not be perceived exclusively as a means to complete a specific project as quickly as possible.

9. *Representative Membership:* An important element of success to employee-led change is the credibility the team can develop with the line staff of the organization. One of the justifications for using a team dominated by front-line employees and supervisors is that they can presumably design an organizational change project in such a way that it is most likely to be accepted by front-line staff, and not resisted to the same extent as similar projects designed exclusively from the top down. Thus, it is important to take steps that will ensure this type of credibility. Recruiting members that are broadly representative of the organization, not only in terms of rank and functional areas within the organization, but also in terms of gender, race and other cultural background factors, helps ensure that credibility is developed.

10. *Push the Envelope:* In the beginning, the three Department Teams did not know how far they could go. Some of them proposed ideas that really pushed the envelope in terms of what could reasonably be accomplished with no budget and no time released from their normal duties, other than the time to meet. It is probable that no private consulting firm would agree to take these projects on under these circumstances. Strictly from the point of view of the estimated price for such projects, these teams saved their departments the several hundred thousand dollars it would have cost to contract the projects out.

In addition, by not knowing what was and wasn't possible, the employee teams had the confidence to try projects that could make a real difference within their organizations. Given the political dynamics in most corporate environments, ambitious projects receive more attention and support than modest ones do. So the lesson for future employee-led change efforts is do not be afraid to push the envelope.

11. *Time and Patience:* It is clear from the discussion above that for employee-led change projects to succeed, the major commitment from the organization is time. Executive leadership must be willing to be patient and allow the Change Team to develop their skills at a reasonable pace. Given the potential advantages of the employee-led model, the development of leadership skills, the increased likelihood of acceptance of organizational change by the front-line staff, and the cost savings as compared to contracting out services, this shouldn't be an unreasonable investment to ask from executives at many organizations. It is worthy of note, that these projects were successfully completed under three very different sets of circumstances, both blue collar and white collar environments, both centralized and disbursed locations, and taking place during a period of severe downsizing. If this model can succeed in these three organizations, there is reason to hope that it can do so in many other situations.

A Model of Employee Led Change

The following components provided the framework within which each of the three Department Teams achieved success: 1) An understanding of organizations as systems 2) The

development of Leadership Skills 3) The ability to plan, communicate and act as a team, and 4) Techniques for implementing change within the organization.

Understanding Organizations as Systems

Successful practice relies on theory as a grounding from which to develop effective plans of action (McMaster, 1995). Members of change teams must have an understanding of organizations as systems in order to intervene effectively. The key insight that will allow employees to evaluate their organization's need for change is an understanding of the importance of alignment across different components of the system. As we explained to each of the Department Change Teams, every organization consists of at least three sub-systems or components: The Executive level, the Middle Management, and the Line Staff. The Change Team itself sits in the middle of these three and acts as a bridge between them (see Figure 48.1). Various customers and stakeholders surround the system, acting as its environment.

Connections between these groups consist of formal and informal communication: the organization's Mission, its Goals, tasks and jobs, policy and procedure changes, legal mandates,

FIGURE 48.1 The Change Team as Bridge

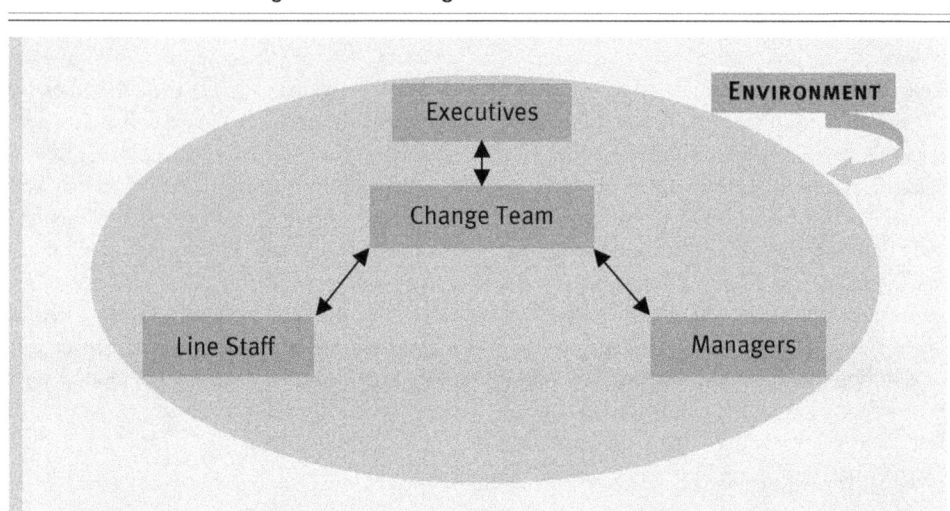

customer feedback, performance results, passive and active resistance to change, and the demands of politically powerful stakeholders.

Typically, Change Teams ally themselves with two of the three subgroups: acting as change agents on behalf of the executives, and using their executive mandate as their lever for change, they build credibility with the line staff by recruiting representative membership as well as soliciting and acting upon feedback from employees. The long-range strategic goal of an Employee-led Change Team is to identify and address misalignment between the three sub-groups and/or between these three and the external customers or stakeholders.

An intuitive way to model these kinds of problems and barriers to organization effectiveness is to emphasize the importance of misalignment or inconsistency across the organization. When the mission of the organization, the management style of its formal leaders, the procedures and policies, the reporting structure, or other components of the organization are poorly integrated, this provides opportunities for employees to propose and implement solutions.

References

Dannemiller Tyson Associates. (Eds.). (2000). *Whole-scale change: Unleashing the magic in organizations.* San Francisco, CA: Berrett-Koehler.

Danemiller Tyson Associates. (Eds.). (2000). *Whole-scale change toolkit: Tools for unleashing the magic in organizations.* San Fransisco, CA: Berrett-Koehler.

Grazier, P. B. (1989). *Before it's too late: Employee involvement... An idea whose time has come.* Chad's Ford, PA: Teambuilding, Inc.

Greenberg, E. S. (1986). *Workplace democracy: The political effects of participation.* Ithaca, NY: Cornell University Press.

Hartmann, L. C., & Bambacas, M. (2000). Organizational commitment: A multi method scale analysis and test of effects. *International Journal of Organizational Analysis, 8*(1), 89–108.

Hespe, G. (1985). Can We Legislate For Participation? *Management Decision, 23*(3), 3–15.

Kiesler, C. A. (1971). *The psychology of commitment.* New York, NY: Academic Press.

Kotter, J.P. (1995, Mar-Apr). Leading change: Why transformation efforts fail. *Havard Business Review, 73*(2), 59–67.

Landen, D.L. (1982, Aug), The future of participative management. *Productivity Brief, 16.*

Marrow, A. J., Bowers, D.G., & Seashore, S.E. (Eds.) (1967). *Management by participation: Creating a climate for personal and organizational development.* New York, NY: Harper & Row.

McMahon C. (1989). Managerial Authority. *Ethics, 100,* 33.

McMaster, M. D. (1995). *The intelligence advantage: Organizing for complexity.* Newton, MA: Butterworth-Heinemann.

Meyer, J. P., & Natalie, A. J. (1991). A Three Component Conceptualization of Organizational Commitment. *Human Resource Management Review, 1*(1), 61–89.

Meyer, J. P., Bobocel, D. R., & Natalie, A. J. (1991). Development of organizational commitment during the first year of employment: A longitudinal study of pre- and post-entry influences. *Journal of Management, 17*(4), 716–734.

O'Driscoll, M. P., & Randall, D. M. (1999). Perceived organizational support, satisfaction with rewards, and employee job involvement and organizational commitment. *Applied Psychology, 48*(2), 197–210.

Osborne, J. E.(1989, Nov). Combatting an 'Us vs. Them' Mindset—Participatory Manangement. *Supervisory Management, 34*(3), 39.

Phillips, L., & Phillips, M. (1993). Facilitated work groups: theory and practice. *Journal of the Operational Research Society, 44,* 533–549.

Senge, P. M. (1990). *The fifth discipline: The art and practice of the learning organization.* New York, NY: Doubleday.

Stacey, R. D. (1996). *Complexity and creativity in organizations.* San Fransisco, CA: Berrett-Koehler.

Varney, G. H. (1989). *Building productive teams: An action guide and resource book.* San Francisco, CA: Jossey-Bass.

Zander, A. F. (1950). Resistance to change- Its analysis and prevention. *Advanced Management, 4*(5), 9–11.

CHAPTER 49

The Politics of Implementation

The Importance of Building Consensus Around Employee Performance Management

Victor Wooddell

Introduction: Organization Development and Government

Government and the public sector generally are an important arena for organization development. Government agencies are under a considerable degree of scrutiny today as the public demands increased accountability and better quality services. Employee performance is an important component of this scrutiny. Globalization has put such increased pressure upon our public agencies and they must find a way to respond. Corporate organizations around the world are responding to the pressures of globalization by becoming more flexible and responsive – and of course governments cannot afford to do otherwise. Greater population mobility has forced local governments to find ways to keep their residents. Many cities and public agencies in the U.S. use some form of Management by Objectives, or a similar employee performance management process. As was revealed by this case study, implementing such projects can be more challenging than would first appear.

The following article describes the implementation of an employee performance management project in a large mid-western city.

The story of this project is a fascinating illustration of the intersection between politics and organization development. It began with the then current Mayor's perception that the public was demanding better services and that a performance management process would improve the situation. The ultimate goal was highly laudable: to achieve strategic alignment of goals from the top to the bottom of the City's organizational hierarchy. Yet, a significant degree of political controversy surrounded this project. A number of useful lessons have been learned from this study that will assist similar projects in other organizations:

Lessons Learned

- Seek Consensus: Partner with other major stakeholders to design a plan all can live with.
- Allow Plenty of Time: Three years is reasonable for around 18,000 employees.
- Hire Enough Internal Staff: More cost effective than externals alone.
- Pilot.
- Indirect Compensation: Make the payoff professional development rather than money.

This study will focus primarily on process issues and address concerns of interest to those who may be considering the implementation of a similar project. It is too soon to assess the impact, if any, that the project has had on employee performance, but this may be the topic of a future article.

Background to the Project

The original purpose of the project was to assure the strategic alignment of goals up and down the organizational hierarchy. Almost since the beginning of the Mayor's administration, the City was involved in a strategic planning effort which identified a Vision, Mission and "Cornerstone Goals" as well as a list of core services that were made a priority focus for all departments. The administration wanted to ensure that front-line supervisors were working with their subordinates in setting goals and demanding performance that directly contributed to the priorities that were identified in the strategic planning process. Underlying this effort was a perception that city services were not being delivered effectively. This city, over a period of decades, had been suffering from loss of both industry and population. Large sections of the city suffered from an appearance of decay, poorly functioning infrastructure and a reputation for crime. Streets, buildings, lighting and other public features had been in need of repair for many years. In addition, customer service was perceived to be poor in terms of long cycle time for processing permits and other documents and a general impression that city bureaucrats were not responsive to citizen needs. The belief of the administration was that there was a need for a more effective city workforce, and one of the Mayor's campaign

promises had been to improve city services. Therefore, a Request for Proposals was issued asking local consulting firms to submit plans for delivery of communication, training and coaching services in support of a performance management process.

Demographics of the City Workforce

The permanent employee workforce was dominated by African Americans, with a significant minority of Caucasians, and small numbers of other ethnic groups (see Table 49.1). Most city employees were male, although a majority of the clerical staff was female. The majority of employees were residents of the city itself (until recently, there had been a residency rule requiring city employees to live within city boundaries). The education level and socio-economic background of most city employees reflected that of city residents in general, which were primarily lower-middle income and from a traditional "blue-collar" background.

The executive level of the city included members of the Mayor's office staff, city Department Directors and Assistant Directors, all of whom were appointed by the Mayor and served at his discretion. This group was also primarily African American and generally from a professional "white-collar" background. Many were not residents of the city prior to their appointment.

Project Design and Timeframe

In January 2000 a design committee consisting of employees who worked in the City's human resources department was formed to solicit ideas for an employee performance eval-

TABLE 49.1 Permanent Full-Time City Employees

Male	Female	Cauc.	Black	Other	Supervisors	Non-Super.	Total Employees
65.7	35.0	22.3	74.8	3.7	22.2	77.8	18,084

Percents may not add to 100 due to rounding error.

uation process. A decision was made at an early stage not to pilot-test the project. According to a recently negotiated labor agreement, the process was to begin citywide in the first project year, and a 1% pay bonus was to be awarded to employees who "met or exceeded expectations". The performance bonus equaled 1% of base yearly salary and would have to be re-earned every year. This necessitated the use of a rating scale to be completed by the direct supervisor of the employee being rated. Supervisors were to meet with their employees three times during the year, the first to set goals and development (training) schedule, the second to monitor progress, and the third to discuss the supervisor's assessment of the employee's performance. A form was designed, based in part on forms already in use by some of the smaller unions within the city, and a four-point rating scale was adopted, which included "Exceeds Expectations", "Meets Expectations", "Needs Improvement", and "Unsatisfactory". This form was used during all three meetings.

The proposal also called for city employees to be assigned full time as "Performance Coaches". These individuals would co-facilitate the employee mass communication sessions and the training workshops until they acquired the experience to run these activities without support from the consultants. The Performance Coach training included separate workshops on basic facilitation tools and techniques, managing the specific evaluation process to be used, and training in facilitating the specific events and activities that were planned as part of the project. These included mass employee orientations, two-day supervisor's workshops, and on-site coaching services.

The next phase of implementation consisted of a series of mass meetings with front-line employees to explain the need for performance management and to help them understand the goal-setting process, how their performance would be monitored, and how the bonus would be awarded. The meetings consisted of groups of employees from the same city department or departments, and varied from half a dozen to over 500 participants at a time.

Finally, supervisor training consisted of a cascade process that began with participants from the Mayor's Office, and proceeded down the organizational hierarchy until it reached the front-line supervisor level. The training itself consisted of a two-day workshop that focused more on managing the process itself than on general concepts and models of performance management. Communication and feedback techniques were another emphasis.

Issues and Problems

Short First Year Timeframe

The following describes the start-up sequence of the project:

- The contract with the consulting firm was signed in March of 2000.
- Funding for the internal staff was identified in August, which was the start of the fiscal year.
- The first internal staff were hired that fall, and mass employee orientations began within a few months.
- Supervisor's training began in January of 2001, and the entire cascade process was completed in June.

Depending upon when a particular employee's supervisor was trained, their performance cycle began as early as February or as late as May, 2001. Since all evaluations for the first cycle had to be completed by July, according to the labor agreement, some employees had a first year cycle of only a few months. This did not allow enough time either to "work out the bugs" inherent in any new project, nor provide enough of a baseline to accurately assess many employees' performance.

Initial Scale of the Project

A decision was made in the months before implementation (see time-frame above) to extend the project citywide. This included 42 separate departments consisting of approximately 18,000 employees. Any project of sufficient complexity will have problems associated with the need to integrate with existing policies, procedures, and workplace culture. An employee performance planning and evaluation process, which is intended to change the way the employees do their work, is bound to experience problems while the organization adjusts to the changes. In this context, piloting the program within one or two departments can be a helpful way to uncover problems while the project is still small enough to make refinements relatively easily. A pilot requires fewer resources than a full-scale implementation, and if successful, provides a strong empirical argument for more resources as the project expands. As will be seen, this project suffered from a shortage of staff.

Shortage of Project Staff

Project staff consisted of 13 performance coaches, a project coordinator, a manager for the coaches, an instructional designer, and a communication publicist, plus three members belonging to the professional consulting firm, for a total of 20. The coaches were responsible for facilitating the mass employee orientation sessions, facilitating the supervisor's training, evaluating the training, collecting and processing goal and evaluation forms, writing reports, and providing on-site consulting support to city departments. Given the size and scale of the project, and the short time frame, 20 staff were very few to service almost 18,000 employees (a staff to employee ratio of 1 per 1000). During the initial implementation phase, based upon the experience of the project staff, a ratio closer to 1 per 250, or a total staff of 80, would have been more effective. As the project proceeds, the expectation is that the departments will take over the administration of employee evaluation process, greatly reducing the need for project staff, but in the initial phases more staff is recommended to implement such a large program.

Employee Compensation and Motivation

Surveys and interviews were conducted throughout the implementation phase. Comments were collected from over 400 individual employees. Preliminary results indicated that the most common responses reflected recognition of the need for performance management, even by line employees, but that more people were concerned about (and confused by) the 1% performance bonus. The concern was twofold. There was the perception that the 1% bonus was not enough money, and there was fear that City supervisors were not competent to administer performance-based compensation fairly. These two concerns were so widespread and of such a degree of intensity that they practically dominated all dialogue regarding the project.

The specific nature of the compensation offered must also be examined. Performance bonuses are a form of extrinsic motivation (Thomas, 2000) or a hygiene factor (Herzberg, 1959). Extrinsic motivators include such things as pay, bonuses, commissions, and other benefits. Basically, any reward that originates outside of the person doing the work can be considered extrinsic. Intrinsic motivation, on the other hand, includes pride, ownership of the work, and a genuine concern for the customer. It is well known that over-reliance on extrinsic reward can undermine intrinsic motivation (Deci & Ryan, 1985). In this context, it is likely that the 1% pay bonus was too small to act as an effective motivator, yet was still enough to direct employee attention toward the extrinsic nature of the reward being offered.

Labor Negotiations

Labor negotiations took longer than expected in the year before the project began resulting in reduced time to implement the project and meet the deadlines contained in the agreement. City management and the labor unions have a history of difficult negotiations going back several decades. Given the general air of mistrust that existed before the project was proposed, it was likely that labor representatives would resist implementation.

City Counsel

The City Counsel is the legislative branch of the local government and consists of publicly elected officials. They are relatively powerful in that they have final budget approval authority not only over the general city budget once a year, but also must approve all contractual agreements above $10,000 with outside third parties. Therefore, the contract with the consulting firm that was helping to design and implement the project came before the City Counsel. Extreme skepticism was expressed by many counsel members regarding the motivation of management in proposing an employee evaluation process, and although the consulting contract was approved, they did not approve a budget amendment to pay city employees to act as internal performance coaches. Consequently, current employees had to be reassigned from other duties to perform the coaching function.

It is too soon to be able to assess the impact of the performance management process on employee performance. Instead, this report will review the lessons learned in connection with process and implementation, in the hopes that this will facilitate the success of similar projects in the future.

Conclusions: Lessons Learned

1. Plan Enough Program Time:
Because of the extended nature of the negotiations and the amount of time it took to finalize an agreement, the time available to design and implement the project was greatly abbreviated. This created a more challenging project environment than might otherwise have been the case. A two to three year time-frame from the end of the design phase to full organization wide implementation is realistic and provides opportunities to refine the project design in response to feedback and initial implementation data. In this case, the lesson was to achieve agreement with all significant stakeholders on the general principle first and work out the project details later.

2. Pilot Test the Project:
For a project of this magnitude, going organization-wide in the first project year was too ambi-

tious. A more reasonable scale might have been 100-1000 employees in the first year, expanding to perhaps 4000-5000 in the second or third years. Citywide implementation should not have begun before the third year.

3. Hire Sufficient Internal Staff:
Twenty is a very small number of people to implement a project of this nature for an organization of approximately 18,000 employees. The project was indeed implemented successfully primarily as a result of the yeoman effort by the project staff. All communication and training events were conducted as planned. Nevertheless, a larger staff size is recommended, perhaps around 40-60 for a project of this scale.

4. Consider the Compensation Issue Carefully:
In this project, attaching monetary compensation directly to employee performance distracted attention away from important dialogue on performance management issues and created unnecessary controversy. Management should consider whether their strategic goals could be achieved by using other forms of compensation than a direct pay bonus. An argument can be made that creating opportunities for high performing employees to develop themselves professionally via training and promotions, as well as the intrinsic desire to do a better job, might have motivated people enough to ensure project success.

5. Seek Consensus:
The union leadership strongly objected to the plan to award a bonus based upon an evaluation of employee performance. Their perception was that the bonus plan was the first step toward replacing the current seniority-based automatic yearly pay increases with a merit pay system. Thus, the project was surrounded by controversy almost from its inception.

Efforts to address these issues with members of the City Counsel and the labor unions continue to be conducted. Union representatives have been included in the training cascade, input has been sought regarding the supervisor form, the rating scale and the process being used in order to address concerns regarding equity and fairness, supervisor bias, and some technical details. In retrospect, it would have been helpful to have included more discussion with external customers of city services including community groups and leaders who could have provided a third person perspective. Such a perspective is helpful when looking for creative ways to achieve consensus on politically sensitive issues such as those described above.

The lesson to learn is to plan on devoting time and resources to consensus building as early as possible in the project design phase. This saves time and energy later on, and helps to create a project design that more stakeholders can support, improving the chances of project success.

Democratic Management and Democracy

The most important lesson to be learned from this experience is the necessity to achieve consensus in building a common vision. As is often the case, this is most essential in organizations where it is hardest to achieve. Political organizations are unique systems in the degree to which they are open to the larger political environment. All organizations in the real world are open systems, but governments are especially vulnerable to pressures by political factions competing for influence and public support. "Reaching out" to the opposition seems to go against the grain for many of the players in the political system, yet failure to do so effectively eliminates the opportunity to develop the organization.

Particularly in the case of human resources management initiatives, consensus among stakeholders is held to be crucial to success (Beer, et al., 1984;). Beer et al. argue that ALL stakeholders SHOULD influence human resource policies. If not, "the enterprise will fail to meet the needs of these stakeholders in the long run and it will fail as an institution." In this case, input should have been sought from several major stakeholders, including those, such as labor unions and the City Counsel, who have the power to affect the success project. Yet this process has been slow and difficult, and remains an important on-going challenge.

Regarding the feasibility of implementing similar projects in other cities and agencies, there are many reasons to be optimistic. Achieving consensus around improving services to the citizens should not be a particularly hard sell in any community. So long as the design of management's initiatives is based upon accurate input from all stakeholders, promoting a common vision should be a matter of the five necessary principles that David Osbourne and Ted Gaebling outlined in *Reinventing Government:*

1. Believe deeply in government.
2. Civilized society cannot function effectively without effective government.
3. The people who work in government are not the problem, the systems in which they work are the problem.
4. Neither traditional liberalism nor traditional conservatism has much relevance to the problems our governments face today.
5. Believe deeply in equity—in equal opportunity for all Americans.

References

Beer, M., Walton, Richard E., & Spector, B. A. (1984). *Managing human assets.* New York, NY: The Free Press.

Deci, E., & Ryan, R. (1985). *Intrinsic motivation and self-determination in human behavior.* New York, NY: Plenum.

Freeman, R. E. (1984). *Strategic management: a stakeholder approach.* Boston, MA: Pitman Publishing Company.

Herzberg, F., Mauser, B., & Snyderman B. (1959). *The motivation to work.* New York, NY: John Wiley.

Osbourne, D., & Gaebler, T. (1992). *Reinventing government.* Boston, MA: Addison-Wesley.

Thomas, K. (2000). *Intrinsic motivation at work.* San Fransisco, CA: Berrett-Koehler.

CHAPTER 50

Interest-Based Problem Solving

Foundation of a Labor and Management Partnership

Jeffrey Jackson and Adrienne Eaton

IN EARLY 1998, managers representing the physician leadership of the US nonprofit healthcare giant Kaiser Permanente found themselves delivering a message no manager likes to deliver. The Optical Laboratory that produces eyeglasses for the 3,000,000 Northern California health plan members was going to be closed and over 200 jobs would be cut or, in some cases, transferred to a merged operation in Southern California.

Kaiser Permanente, the largest health maintenance organization (HMO) in the US, was in the middle of its only two years of negative financial performance in its 60year history. The plans to close the Optical Lab were part of the overall organization belt-tightening with which Kaiser responded to this performance problem. Kaiser's Optical Division, the 5th largest provider of eyeglasses in the country, had to cut costs too.

A team of Harvard and MIT senior faculty researchers characterized the situation as a "pivotal event" (Eaton, Kochan, McKersie, 2003) that had the potential to make or break a recently formed *labor-management partnership* between Kaiser Permanente and the then 26 AFL-CIO local unions representing 56,000 employees in 400 medical facilities across the country.

This article describes how internal and external consultants worked together to facilitate labor and management problem solving that resulted in a very different outcome than the one announced originally. It is written from the shared perspectives of an internal operations leader and an external research consultant, both of whom had a role for management and labor in measuring desired outcomes.

This article will explain the opposing positions initially held by labor and management and the key questions they raised that led them to search for the right process and consultants to help resolve their differences. It will then describe the problem-solving process used by the consultants, the final results, and the relevance of the case for OD practitioners and collaborative or partnering relationships in general.

Positions

Management's position was to close the lab. Their position was clear, and was based, at least in part, on an "objective" analysis and proposed solution from an external consulting firm. The analysis concluded that merging the Northern and Southern California Optical Labs would contribute $800,000 annually to

Northern California's $15–$20 million Optical Division net income. Savings could be captured by cutting labor costs and utilizing surplus plant and productivity capacity in Southern California. Management had a plan to transition some employees to other local jobs and others to Southern California. Nonetheless, some employees would lose their jobs.

Labor's position was to keep the lab open. Employees and their labor representatives were caught off-guard by management's position. They knew there were problems, but given their level of business understanding and participation in decision making, they did not think closure was imminent or necessary. Financial performance was not particularly low for the Optical Division, but it was for the broader organization.

If jobs were lost, the unions said it would be the end of the national labor-management partnership. A fragile "labor peace" would be over and the newly formed coalition of 26 partnering unions would support the lab employees, especially as all of the unions were preparing for contract negotiations.

Culture of Participation or Culture of Partnership?

The pivotal event at the Optical Lab was not only a test for the Lab's survival, it was also a test for whether the labor-management relationship could transform the organization's historic culture from one of labor participation into a culture of partnership.

Was labor going to help management implement tough decisions to save the business? Was management going to allow labor participation in decision making? These and other initial questions were quickly seen in hindsight as the wrong questions.

The bigger questions that the pivotal event at the Optical Lab helped to resolve were how a culture of participation evolves into a culture of partnership and to what extent certain forms of participation obfuscate creating a deeper partnership. Could the organizations move from labor participating in management's plan, to

labor and management creating and implementing the plan together?

Labor leaders from the Optical Lab began asking what good was participation in decision making if management could make proposals to layoff employees and ask the unions to participate in the implementation of such a decision that violated a core interest of labor and one of the core goals of the labor-management partnership, employment security. Management thought they were doing their homework in getting all the data and making a sound business proposal for the union to react to and help implement.

From the founding of Kaiser Permanente, labor had actively participated in what was essentially a counter-cultural plan of physicians and management to provide prepaid integrated healthcare to workers. Physician leadership has recently commented that Kaiser Permanente owes a debt to labor for labor's early participation in the formation of the nation's original prepaid health plan. In the 1950s, labor came to the organization's defense when Senator Joseph McCarthy attacked Kaiser Permanente as being communist and Stalinist. By the mid 1990s, this relationship and the attendant culture of labor participation had been seriously eroded by a decade of antagonistic labor-management relations. The parties, however, had begun to turn the relationship around again with the signing of a labor-management partnership agreement in 1997.

Labor-Management Partnership

For help to move beyond their diametrically opposed positions, labor and management leaders from the Optical Lab turned to a team of internal and external consultants who were jointly hired to help launch the new labor-management partnership. The new Partnership Agreement included such non-traditional goals as improving quality healthcare and making shared or joint decisions on strategic plans, capital and operations budgets and virtually everything except clinical decisions made by clinicians (Table 50.1).

TABLE 50.1 Partnership Goals

> » Improve quality of health care for KP members and the communities we serve.
> » Assist KP in achieving and maintaining market-leading competitive performance.
> » Expand KP's membership in current and new markets, including designation as a provider of choice for all labor organizations in areas we serve.
> » Make KP a better place to work.
> » Provide KP employees with maximum possible employment and income security within KP and/or the health care field.
> » Involve KP employees and their unions in decision making.
> » Consult on public policy issues; jointly advocate when appropriate.

The Partnership Agreement was grounded in a model of systems change referred to as the Partnership Equation (Schneider and Stepp, 1997) that described the relationship among partnership outcomes of performance, governance (or voice in decision making), security and rewards (Figure 50.1). The model, developed by Restructuring Associates, Inc of Washington, DC, helped the partners understand how participation in decision making in and of itself had limited value and could impede the attainment of other desired outcomes if not looked at as a whole, interrelated system.

Interest-Based Problem Solving

Before the Partnership Equation could begin to inform decision making, four critical foundational elements needed to be in place including the day-to-day use of Interest-Based Problem Solving (IBPS) for everything from high-level strategic decisions to front-line tactical decisions (Figure 50.2). Grounded in the *Getting to Yes* paradigm of Fisher and Ury (Fisher and Ury, 1981), Interest-Based Problem Solving has varied applications. It has been used by the US Federal Mediation and Conciliation Services to facilitate Mid-East peace process discussions and it is commonly used to resolve labor disputes around the world. Some have also used principles of IBPS for strategic planning and for marriage counseling.

Define the Problem

The Optical Lab partners decided to use IBPS with facilitation by the jointly hired consulting firm paired with jointly hired internal consultants. The first step in the IBPS process was to define the problem in the form of a question. At first, the question was framed as "should the Optical Lab be closed or should it stay open?". IBPS problem questions, how-

FIGURE 50.1 Partnership Equation

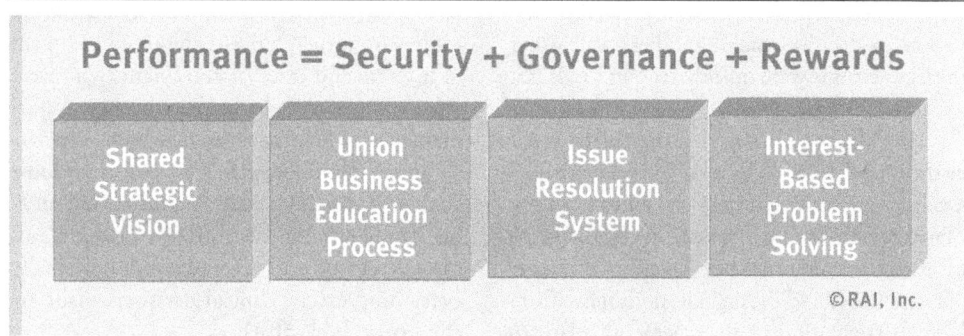

Performance = Security + Governance + Rewards

Shared Strategic Vision | Union Business Education Process | Issue Resolution System | Interest-Based Problem Solving

© RAI, Inc.

FIGURE 50.2 IBPS

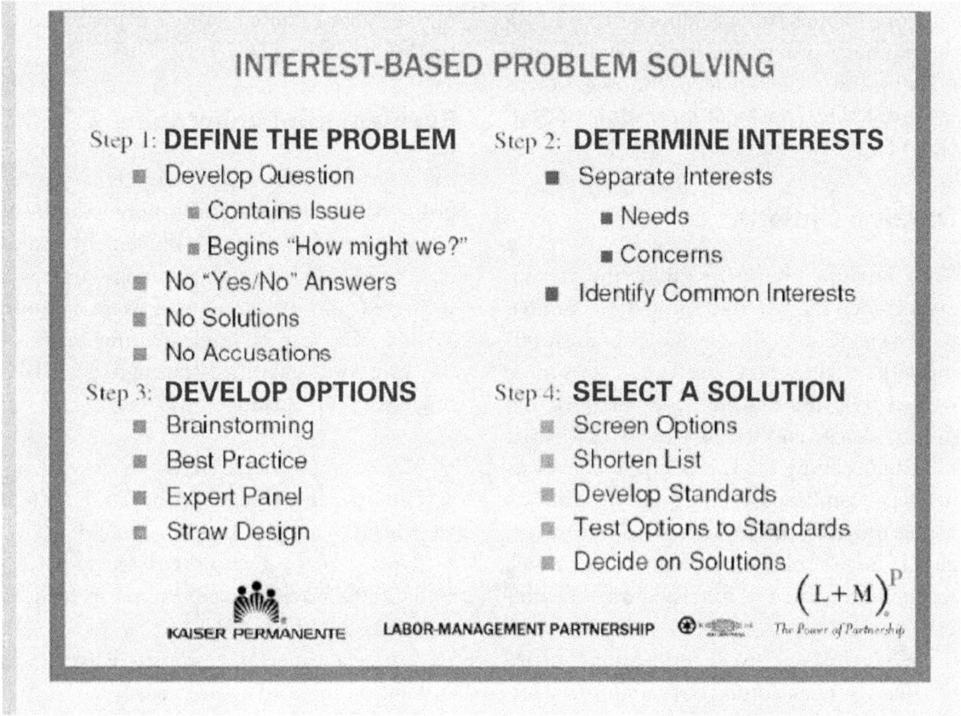

INTEREST-BASED PROBLEM SOLVING

Step 1: **DEFINE THE PROBLEM**
- Develop Question
  - Contains Issue
  - Begins "How might we?"
- No "Yes/No" Answers
- No Solutions
- No Accusations

Step 2: **DETERMINE INTERESTS**
- Separate Interests
  - Needs
  - Concerns
- Identify Common Interests

Step 3: **DEVELOP OPTIONS**
- Brainstorming
- Best Practice
- Expert Panel
- Straw Design

Step 4: **SELECT A SOLUTION**
- Screen Options
- Shorten List
- Develop Standards
- Test Options to Standards
- Decide on Solutions

$(L+M)^P$

KAISER PERMANENTE   LABOR-MANAGEMENT PARTNERSHIP   *The Power of Partnership*

ever, 1) do not answer yes/no questions, 2) begin with "how can we" or "what might we," 3) contain no solutions, 4) contain no interests, and 5) contain no accusatory or inflammatory wording (Kaiser Permanente, 1999). The consultants helped the partners to see how the question limited options to only two, and those options were actually positions. The problem question they finally agreed to was: "How can we contribute to Kaiser Permanente's turnaround by improving the performance of the Optical Division?"

Determine Interests

Once the problem question was defined, labor and management broke into caucuses to identify their own interests (that is, underlying needs or concerns that must be met as part of the solution). After caucus deliberations, the consultants helped chart-pad one interest at a time, making sure anything that sounded like a position was challenged with the question "why?", sometimes two or three times before the underlying interest was determined. Underlying interests generally answer the question, "why?" Positions generally answer the question, "what?"

The consultants made sure each interest was clear to the other group before the combined group identified common interests (those that were exactly the same). Separate and common interests would be kept in mind for later when creating criteria that would be used to narrow options in order to select an ultimate solution. Anthony Gately, the management lead for the physician group frequently said, "Almost all of our interests were the same. What was different was *how* we thought we would solve this."

Also noticeable to labor and management problem solvers was how, after identifying interests, the group dynamic changed from sitting across from each other at the meeting table, to more mixing of labor and management, demonstrating what Kolb and Williams would refer to as "appreciative shadow moves." In addition, both groups began to remind each other of, and at times defend, the other's interests reflecting "positioning shadow moves" (Kolb & Williams, 2003).

Develop Options

With interests clearly in mind, the consultants guided the group in using more familiar tools to generate options such as brainstorming, identifying best practices, consulting with experts and drafting straw designs. Significant debate and friction rose over whether to include closing the Lab (management's earlier stated position) as an option. In order to enable progress, the groups agreed to consider closure as an option of last resort, which would not be listed or discussed with the other options.

Over 250 options were identified for increasing revenues, cutting costs, improving service and improving quality. Labor and management worked long days and nights with business analysts to prepare jointly accepted cost-benefit analysis of each option so that informed decision making could take place. Employees and their labor representatives received crash courses in business understanding to facilitate informed decision making and informed implementation of any of the options.

Select a Solution

Selecting a solution first involved establishing a set of criteria by which options could be judged. At the top of the list of criteria were employment security and annual savings of $800,000. The ultimate solution adopted was to implement a combination of the prioritized options over an 18-month trial period. Some options even required additional investments.

In the process of developing and agreeing to a critical few criteria from which to select a solution, some additional options were added to the option list. One creative option that was

further developed and has been extended to the now over 86,000 partnership union employees across the country is a performance sharing incentive plan.

Evaluate Implementation

The Optical Lab did not close. Quite the opposite has happened. Within four months of selecting and beginning to implement a solution, the $800,000 original savings target was surpassed and no employees were laid-off. Within one year of implementing many of the solutions identified through the IBPS process, results included:

- Net income increased 19%.
- Gross revenues were up by $5.5 million (9.8%).
- Average sales per employee were up 6%.
- $250,000 savings were realized in reduced breakage and rework.
- Turnover time for customer delivery was reduced from 2.7 to 1.33 days.
- Overall productivity of the lab increased 8%.
- Wages increased by 3%.
- The incentive plan produced a 3% payout for employees.
- Employee satisfaction scores increased.

The Optical Lab saved far more than the $800,000 target management had set with their position to close the Lab. Labor's limited position to keep the Lab open was also surpassed; a new Northern California state-of-the-art facility was built in 2002. Revenue has increased 32% between 2000 and 2005. Net income has steadily increased along with employee satisfaction scores. The jointly developed 2006 business plan has stretch goals of a 7% revenue increase and a 15% net income increase.

The Optical Lab turnaround demonstrated the value added of a process such as IBPS in the context of an evolving culture of partnership (Figure 50.3). The learnings have enabled Kaiser Permanente and labor partners to joint-

FIGURE 50.3   Partnership Growth Since 1997

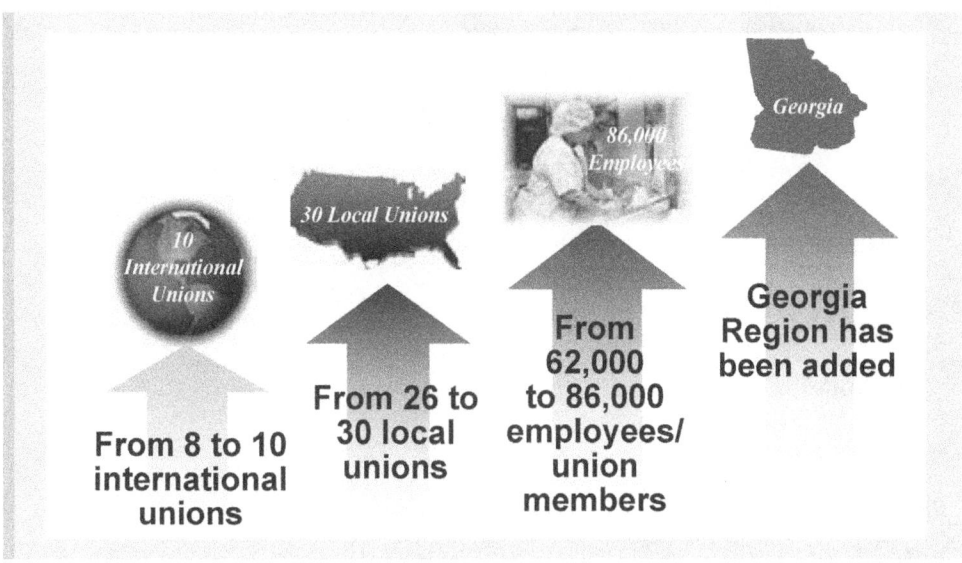

ly design and open new hospitals, identify hundreds of millions of dollars in other cost structure improvements, negotiate industry trendsetting labor contracts for the now 30 local unions simultaneously, and identify operational improvements that have resulted in better quality healthcare and health outcomes for Kaiser Permanente members (Kochan, McKersie, Eaton, Adler, Segal, & Gerhart, 2005).

Culture of Partnership

The pivotal event for Kaiser Permanente management and labor partners at the Optical Lab helped propel a culture of "participation" for labor and management into a growing culture of "partnership" (Figure 50.4). This transformation involved several shifts that have survived the test of the last seven years:

- From stating and defending positions to identifying and supporting interests.
- From participation or collaboration in implementation to partnership in the business, including planning and performance sharing.
- From participation via a set of parallel organizational structures (committees and coun-

cils) to the integration of labor into operational decision-making bodies.
- From meeting just one's own interests to anticipating and meeting the interests of the other.
- From good job security, to a 7-year tested "no layoff" policy of industry-leading income and employment security.
- From antagonism of the 80s to building on historic values of partnership.
- From a consultant-facilitated use of IBPS to a mostly unfacilitated way of doing business with IBPS.

The Optical Lab case is one of many that has led researchers at Harvard, MIT and Rutgers to conclude that the Kaiser Permanente and labor partnership is "the largest and most ambitious partnership in the US." Kaiser Permanente labor and management partners at the Optical Lab and throughout the country would and have taken offense at describing theirs as a "culture of participation." They have invested far too much over 60 years, especially in the last 10 years, to settle for defining theirs as anything short of an evolving "culture of partnership."

FIGURE 50.4   Employee Satisfaction: "KP is a Good Place to Work."

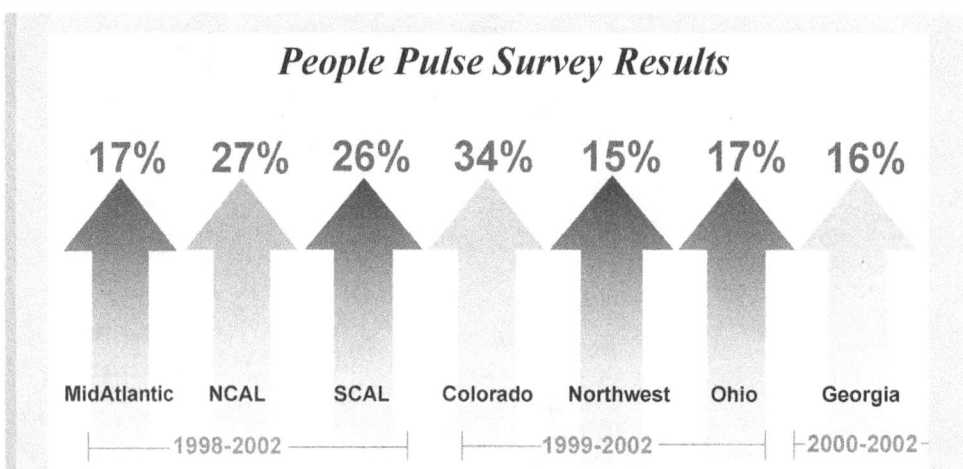

Many labor relations practitioners on both sides of the table remain skeptical about the value of Labor-Management Partnerships and interest-based techniques. This case demonstrates in concrete terms the tangible benefits for multiple stakeholders when the parties commit to a "culture of partnership." In particular, the Optical Lab represents an early example of labor and management working together to create and implement a plan that met both the interests of the organization in providing high quality service to members and the interests of employees and their representatives in maintaining high quality jobs. Further, the case demonstrates the mutually supportive roles of IBPS as a tool and partnership as a broader context for the successful use of that tool. In doing so, the case also helps OD practitioners and change leaders to stay present to some of the subtle differences of collaboration, participation and partnership.

References

Eaton, S. C., Kochan, T., & McKersie, R. B. (2003). *The Kaiser Permanente Labor Management Partnership: The first five years.* Cambridge, MA: MIT, Sloan School of Management.

Fisher, R., & Ury, W. (1981). *Getting to yes: negotiating agreement without giving in.* Boston, MA: Houghton Mifflin Company.

Kaiser Permanente & Federal Mediation and Conciliation Services. (2000). *Interest-based problem solving training manual.* Oakland, CA: Kaiser Permanente.

Kochan, T., McKersie, R., Eaton, A., Adler, P., Segal, P., & Gerhart, P. (2005). *The Kaiser Permanente Labor Management Partnership, 2002–2004.* Cambridge, MA: MIT, Sloan School of Management.

Kolb, D. M., & Williams, J. (2003). *Everyday negotiations: The hidden agendas in bargaining.* San Francisco, CA: Jossey-Bass.

Stepp, J. R., & Schneider, T (1997), A model for union-management partnerships. *Perspectives on Work,* 1(2), 54–59.

Change Management

Introduction

Maya Townsend

VOICES FROM THE FIELD

When I am at my best, my orientation is less as an expert or a recommender and more as a helper to the organization as it explores and discovers choices. Partnering with clients to develop design criteria and options fosters their ownership. I try to embrace the principle of people support what they help to create. It's less about a particular method and more about creating space to allow people to be involved.

—Chuck Mallue

TOPICS COVERED IN THIS SECTION

- How to identify the type of change needed and utilize different change methodologies.
- How to structure an active and mindful implementation effort.
- How to build organizational readiness, engage employees in actualizing the desired strategies and goals, and develop change champions.
- How to work with resistance to change.

WHY CHANGE MANAGEMENT

The pace of change is increasing and shows no signs of slowing down. The major forces of globalization, hyper-connectedness, and immediate communication have changed the marketplace significantly and permanently. We now live in a world of constant flux. Organizations initiate a change only to have six or ten more significant initiatives emerge as necessary and urgent. As a result, 81% of managers in one study report that the pace of change in their organizations has increased compared to five years before. And 69% say that their companies experienced disruptive change within the last 12 months (AMA, 2007).

HR Business Partners have the unique opportunity to lead change in organizations and the responsibility to help business leaders manage change wisely. Changes often stem directly from HR activities, such as instituting a new talent management initiative, installing performance management tracking software, or implementing a work at home policy. However, HR Business Partners' expertise is sorely needed in business-driven changes as well. These initiatives are, more often than not, disappointing. A McKinsey study reports that only 38% of change initiatives were completely or mostly successful improving performance (2006). Furthermore, 83% of CEOS reported that they expect significant organization change in the next two years, but 59% of change initiatives missed at least one objective or failed entirely (IBM, 2008). There's room for improvement and HR professionals can help make that happen by helping leaders tend to the complex, tricky issues of helping people adapt to and implement change.

The Basics: What Do We Know About How Change Occurs?

Many ideas about change are based on the work of Kurt Lewin. Often considered the father of organization development, Lewin created seminal ideas about change and how the environment affects people's and organization's ability to change. John Adams (1988) explains Lewin's approach to change:

> Kurt Lewin taught us that we first have to unfreeze a situation before we can expect any movement. This means operating in ways that will destabilize the status quo. This can be accomplished in a variety of ways including: increasing dissatisfaction, threatening adverse consequences, and (preferably) building a vision of a better way of being that people can relate to. (p. 9)

In Lewin's view, organizations move from stability through change to times of new stability. The change agent's job is to identify and reduce restraining forces that prevent people from adapting and identify and add driving forces that encourage people to alter their behavior. This work was codified in a formula popularized by Dick Beckhard, Kathie Dannemiller, and others:

$$C = (DVF) > R$$

Change is possible when the level of **D**issatisfaction with the status quo, the clarity of **V**ision, and the grasp of the **F**irst Steps to be taken can combine to be greater than the existing **R**esistance to change. (Adams, 2003, p. 24)

This formula worked for a while and still helps leaders think about the readiness of their organizations for change. However, practitioners soon learned that not all types of change are created equal. Linda Ackerman Anderson, first in 1985 and then in 2003 with Dean Anderson and Martin Marquardt, identified three major types of change: transitional, de-velopmental, and transformational. Transitional change most closely resembles the type described by Lewin in his freezing-unfreezing-refreezing model. Ackerman Anderson, Anderson, and Marquardt (2003) explain:

> Transitional change replaces what is with something entirely different. Transitional change involves the achievement of an existing state over a set period of time. It requires the dismantling of the old state and the creation of the consciously designed new state. Transitions include reorganizations, mergers, divestitures, implementation of . . . technology, or the creation of new products or services. (p. 7)

These are changes with a specific start and end date. They take the form of projects, drawing on project management expertise, and have a clear outcome that aims to improve operations, solve problems, or reduce threats to the enterprise.

Developmental change is simpler than transitional change since it focuses on improvement rather than replacement. The goal is to enhance what is rather than replace it. For example, a team may wish to improve its problem-solving capabilities. An organization may wish to reduce the time it takes to perform a specific process. Or an alliance may wish to improve communication processes. Whatever the specifics, the change is clearly defined and incremental and, thereby, usually less jarring to an organization. Ackerman Anderson, Anderson, and Marquardt (2003) write:

> In developmental change, the new state is a prescribed enhancement of the old state, rather than a radical or experimental solution requiring profound change. The degree of pain triggering developmental change is usually low, at least in comparison to the other types of change. This does not mean that developmental change is not important or challenging; it is. However, the risks associated with

it, and the number of volatile variables tied to it, are considerably less than with the other . . . types of change. (p. 6)

The third type of change, transformational change, is prevalent in organizations today. Ackerman Anderson and Anderson (2001) explain:

Transformation is unique in two critical ways. First, the future is unknown at the start of the change process and can only be created by forging ahead with the intent to discover it . . .

Secondly, the future state is so radically different than the current state that a shift of mindset is required to invent it, let alone implement and sustain it. This fact triggers enormous human and cultural impacts.

Each type of change requires that people shift—forging ahead into an unknown future, in the case of transformational change; replacing one known situation with another, in the case of transitional change; or improving the current situation, in the case of developmental change.

William Bridges (2003) explains what people experience during these processes. He differentiates the change event from the human process of understanding and accepting change. His transition model says that people go through three stages as they attempt to adjust to change. The first stage is *letting go:* releasing the hold on existing processes, services, mindsets, and/or ways of doing business. In this stage, people often experience sadness about loss, anger at the need to change, and confusion about what lies ahead. The confusion increases in the second stage, the *neutral zone,* in which people travel through a period of ambiguity before they arrive at the intended destination. While anxiety-provoking, the neutral zone can also generate creativity as people question what they thought were givens and experiment with new ways. The third stage is the *new beginning,* in which people in-

tegrate their learning from the neutral zone into their daily work, which now includes new priorities and routines. In this stage, people express excitement, optimism, and impatience to move forward. Knowing these three stages helps leaders understand the experience that they, and the people affected by the change, experience during the process and design outlets for people's feelings and opportunities for stage-appropriate learning.

Later, Bridges updated his work to address a condition prevalent in most organizations today: that of constant change. In Lewin's world, change was an event that had a beginning, middle, and end, after which the organization would achieve a new stability that would continue until the next major change process. Bridges recognized that, today, most organizations experience multiple, simultaneous changes that make stability a rare (and sometimes alarming!) experience. To cope with this environment—and the multilayered, concurrent transitions sustained by those impacted by change—he writes: "The first thing . . . need[ed] in order to handle nonstop organizational change is an overall design . . . [in which] the various changes are integrated as component elements" (2003, p. 101).

The issue of nonstop organizational change has been picked up by an emerging field called Human Systems Dynamics or organizational complexity. Proponents of this viewpoint see dynamic, continuous change as a natural an inevitable part of our world. Dudley Tower (2002) explains:

Our world is currently experiencing an escalating and irreversible trend towards increasing complexity. Old methods of understanding change and organizing human systems are inconsistent with this new reality. In the past, the world seemed a more stable place. Assumptions regarding cause and effect, prediction and control, and the desirability of semi-closed, equilibrium-seeking systems had greater merit. Today—with the rise of a global economy, increasingly interactive communications, continuous product and technology innovations, heightened competition, and rapidly changing perspectives—a new set of assumptions . . . are necessary. These new assumptions will necessarily re-define the practice of Organization Development—making "planned change" and traditional organization structures obsolete—while also providing us with a set of rules or principles that can be applied to all levels of human systems. (p. 4)

For practitioners like Tower, change is not something that can be managed. In fact, for complexity-based practitioners, the very term *change management* is an oxymoron. One can no more manage a change than one can control the weather. Instead, the role of organization leaders is to help the company adapt and navigate safely into the new world.

Complexity approaches do not make sense in all organizations. Organizations that operate in stable, predictable environments, such as a government-regulated monopolies, are insulated from complexity. Traditional change tools work well in organizations like these. In systems in which there is less stability and predictability, complexity tools are more appropriate and effective. (For more on complexity, see the chapter on Systems Thinking.)

THE CHAPTERS IN THIS SECTION

The articles in this section present the best thinking about change management that has appeared in the *OD Practitioner* over the last 40 years. The authors have led change in Fortune 50 companies, family-owned businesses, international conglomerates, nongovernmental organizations, and rural communities. They help HR Business Partners understand what they can do to foster sustainable change. The four segments are:

- Change by Any Other Name: Kinds of Change
- What Now? Understanding Change from the Change Recipient's Viewpoint
- How to Make Them Sit Up and Take Notice: The Successful Change Agent
- Special Topics

Change by Any Other Name: Kinds of Change

Linda Ackerman Anderson and Dean Anderson open the section with **Awake at the Wheel: Moving beyond Change Management to Conscious Leadership** (2001), a powerful piece about the most startling and difficult kind of organizational change: transformational change. They describe a process for transformational change leadership and the steps towards building an integrated change strategy. Importantly, they discuss the requirements for successful transformation, which HR professionals and organizational leaders will find helpful.

While Ackerman Anderson's and Anderson's work will make intuitive sense to many with a background in Western thought, Robert Marshak in **The Tao of Change Redux** (2012) posits that there are other ways of thinking about change. Marshak draws on his depth of experience in the Far East, specifically Korea, to present Confucian ways of conceptualizing and relating to change. HR practitioners leading cross-cultural change initiatives will find this article particularly meaningful and relevant.

Closing out this segment is Nicole Stragalas's **Improving Change Implementation: Practical Adaptations of Kotter's Model** (2010). Stragalas provides an orientation to common ways of approaching change and then tackles what many see as the Achilles heel of organizational change: implementation. Drawing on John Kotter's eight stages of change (2007; see Table 56.1), Stragalas details specific implementation actions that can be taken by HR leaders to successfully perform each stage.

TABLE 56.1 John Kotter's Eight Stages of Change

There are eight stages that leaders must address during the change process:

1. Establish a Sense of Urgency
2. Form a Powerful Guiding Coalition
3. Create a Vision
4. Communicate the Vision
5. Empower Others to Act on the Vision
6. Plan for and Create Short-Term Wins
7. Consolidate Improvements and Produce More Change
8. Institutionalize New Approaches (Kotter, 2007)

What Now? Understanding Change from the Change Recipient's Viewpoint

Levels of employee engagement and commitment can make or break a change effort. What Now?: Understanding Change from the Change Recipient's Viewpoint examines what HR Business Partners can do to front-load their initiatives for success by considering the change recipient to be a critical stakeholder. Michael H. Vinitsky and Adam S. Kling, in **Change from the Employees' Perspective: The Neglected Viewpoint** (2006), outline the eight questions that leaders must answer in order to maintain credibility and build employee commitment to change. Their actionable, precise questions can help HR Business Partners prepare for change themselves and coach leaders to develop coherent messages to staff about change.

Barry Dym (1997) and Thomas C. Head (2000) provide two perspectives on individual resistance to change. Dym sees resistance not as good or bad but simply a fact of life during change in **Resistance in Organizations: How to Recognize, Understand, and Manage It**. He explores the driving forces that fuel resistance to change and identifies ways to manage it.

In **Appreciative Inquiry: Debunking the Mythology Behind Resistance to Change**,

Thomas Head (2000) takes on some of the unquestioned assumptions about resistance. He challenges the ideas that HR Business Partners must "buy" employee commitment and that there will always be resistance to change. Instead of accepting these maxims, Head offers an appreciative alternative to traditional methods of viewing resistance.

A third perspective comes from Barry Dym and Harry Hutson (1997), who address the issue of organizational—as opposed to individual—resistance and readiness in **Utilizing States of Organizational Readiness**. The difference between a responsive state and an unstable state of readiness can make the difference between change success and failure. Dym and Hutson help HR Business Partners identify the dominant state in their organizations and understand how to build responsive states of readiness.

Closing out the section is Don Warrick's 2009 **Developing Organization Change Champions.** He shows how HR Business Partners can create what every organization needs: change champions. Related to, but different from change agents and change leaders, change champions are skilled at initiating, facilitating, and implementing change. They can be found at any level of the organization and, through their efforts, can help with the constant, necessary work of encouraging and reinforcing change at local levels.

How to Make Them Sit Up and Take Notice: The Successful Change Agent

How to Make Them Sit Up and Take Notice: The Successful Change Agent is the heart of this section. It represents *OD Practitioner's* best thinking on how to successfully lead change. Edgar Schein (1994), in **The Role of Leadership in the Management of Organizational Transformation and Learning**, challenges leaders to consider the degree of psychological safety in their organizations and invites them to consider the connection between psychological safety and change success. He stresses that the role of the change leader is to help employees by creating the safety they need in order to risk, learn, and innovate.

In **Change Mastery, Simplified**, Chris Hoffman (2007) presents the helpful LEFSA model that leaders can use to focus their efforts on five factors that make a difference during change implementation.

Another helpful tool comes from Larry Hirschhorn (2007) in **Backcasting: A Systematic Method for Creating a Picture of the Future and How to Get There.** He presents a clear, actionable method for identifying the change goal and creating an implementation plan.

Arthur M. Freedman addresses a methodology that has received considerable attention and popularity in recent years in **Using Action Learning for Organization Development and Change** (2011), and explores how action learning can be used in change initiatives.

Linda Ackerman Anderson and Dean Anderson (2008), in **Strategic Change Consulting: How to Leverage Your Work at the Enterprise Level,** show how leaders can create infrastructure and support for ongoing, continuous change.

Special Topics

The last segment, Special Topics, explores specific types of change initiatives led by HR business leaders and provides specific guidance on how to manage them well. Robert Barnett's **The Executive Perspective on Mergers and Acquisitions** (2005) presents research that identifies the factors that correlate with success in mergers and acquisitions.

Finally, **An Appreciative Inquiry into the Factors of Culture Continuity during Leadership Transition: A Case Study of LeadShare, Canada,** (1995) addresses succession planning, but from a totally different perspective: that of appreciative inquiry. This powerful and popular method was used successfully in a business services organization.

Mary Ann Rainey explains the process and lessons learned.

FOR ADDITIONAL LEARNING

For more information about change management, you may want to read the following articles.

- Clarke, C., McAllister, B., & Swartz, D. (1998). The journey of organizational change in EPA Region 10. *OD Practitioner*, 30(2), 18–23.

  The authors tell the story of a change in a US government agency.

- Crockett, J. (1978). No system is forever. *OD Practitioner*, 10(1), 1–11.

  Crocket deals with how to go beyond the symptoms of a problem to deal with how people behave in the organization, which can lead to more sustainable change.

- Curran, C. (2009). Taking an organization to the next level. *OD Practitioner*, 41(4), 12–17.

  Curran describes an organizational lifecycle change and transition process in an Irish nonprofit health organization.

- Heckelman, W., & Smith, R. (2004). Jump starting a corporate merger. *OD Practitioner*, 36(3), 9-13.

  Heckelman and Smith offer a case study of a merger within a large, multi-national pharmaceutical organization.

- Holder, R., & McKinnney, R. (1993). Scouting: A process for dealing with the frontiers of an uncertain world. *OD Practitioner*, 25(3), 20–25.

  Holder and McKinnery discuss the process of scouting, which helps catalyze change, create new roles, and provides information that can foster continuous improvement.

- Noer, D. (1988). Layoff survivor sickness: The issue beneath the symptoms. *OD Practitioner*, 20(2), 2–13.

Noer details the dynamics of layoff survivor sickness and its impact on individuals and organizations.

- O'Hara-Devereaux, M. (2005). The badlands: Future's tool pack. *OD Practitioner,* 37(3), 5–11.

O'Hara-Devereaux describes the traditional and creative thinking tools for thriving in a highly uncertain and unpredictable future.

- Weisbord, M. (2004). Whose resistance is this anyway? *OD Practitioner,* 36(1), 32- 36.

Weisbord recounts his experience with the University of Maryland's primary care program.

- Zolno, S. (2006). Merger mayhem leads to whole system change. *OD Practitioner,* 38(3), 26–29.

Zolno examines the merger of four mental health service providers to create a new organization.

References

Adams, J. D. (1988). Creating critical mass to support change. *OD Practitioner,* 20(2), 7–10.

Adams, J. D. (2003). Successful change: Paying attention to the intangibles. *OD Practitioner,* 35(4), 22–26.

Ackerman Anderson, L., Anderson, D., & Marquardt, M. (2003). Development, transition, or transformation. *OD Practitioner,* 28(4), 5–16.

AMA (2007). The high-performance organization. Retrieved from http://www.amanet.org/research.

Bridges, W. (2003). *Managing transitions* (2nd ed.). Cambridge, MA: Perseus Books.

IBM. (2008). Making change work. Retrieved from http://www.ibm.com.

Kotter, J. (2007). Leading change: Why transformation efforts fail. *Harvard Business Review,* 85(1).

McKinsey. (2006). Organizing for successful change management: A McKinsey global survey. Retrieved from http://www.mckinseyquarterly.com.

Quade, K., Perme, C., Eoyang, G., Barton, K., & Holladay, R. (2004). Tried and true: How the emergent theory of human systems dynamics informs the long-term success of large group events. *OD Practitioner,* 36(3) 14–18.

Tower, D. (2002). Creating the complex adaptive organization: A primer on complex adaptive systems. *OD Practitioner,* 34(3), 4–9.

Zimmerman, B., Plsek, P., & Lindberg, C. (1998). *Edgeware: Insights from complexity science for health care leaders.* Irving, TX: VHA Incorporated.

CHAPTER 51

Awake at the Wheel

Moving Beyond Change Management to Conscious Leadership

Linda Ackerman Anderson and Dean Anderson

IMAGINE DRIVING the Los Angeles free-ways at rush hour with blinders on, or shutting your eyes to the traffic altogether, determined to plow through to your destination. You couldn't possibly expect to get there safely, and would likely create havoc along the way. Not being able to see all of the signals and forces at play in your chaotic environment would make the journey impossible. How would you navigate? Maybe, if you were on a straight highway with no cars or obstacles, you might drive some distance with only minor mishaps. But driving freeways is a constantly changing experience—fast-paced, unpredictable and uncontrollable, much like leading transformational change.

In fact, leading transformation using today's change management approaches presents the same challenge. Before the birth of change management, organizational leaders defined their role as determining the destination of their change and then delegating the driving to someone else. That was all well and good when their destinations were clear and the roads were open and well marked. Eventually, when executives began to feel the sting of not being able to get their organizations to reach their pre-determined targets, they began to recognize that success required attention to things they previously had not seen, understood, or valued as important. These new insights broadened their view of what was necessary to lead change, and gave rise to the field of change management.

Change management originally reflected two breakthroughs in leaders' understanding of change. First, it became the answer to dealing with some newly recognized *human* issues, which surfaced when leaders' pronouncements were met with insurmountable resistance in the organization, and they didn't know how to overcome such formidable obstacles. In addition to helping overcome resistance, change management improved leaders' communication plans and specified training pro grams for employees, further assisting leaders to reduce their people problems.

Simultaneously, change management responded to leadership's need to improve implementation, which increased their attention to the *process of change*. By providing planning tools for implementation and applying familiar project management approaches, change management increased the likelihood of leaders actually reaching their destinations. In short, change management came into being from executives becoming more cognizant of the *human* and *process* challenges of change, and requesting help with them.

Change management's popularity is tangible evidence that executives have recognized a good deal of what had been missing from their traditional management of change. This is all progress in the right direction. However, leaders and the field of change management have not gone far enough, especially for today's "Los Angeles free way" reality of change. There are still too many change accidents occurring, and too much unnecessary road rage. There are still too many blinders impairing leaders' views of how to navigate change. It is time for leaders and consultants alike to take the blinders off, to become fully awake at the wheel and move beyond change management. Leaders and consultants both need to under-stand and embrace the next evolution in the field–change leadership.

Understanding the Requirements of Transformation

The first task of change leadership is to understand the terrain of change and how it has evolved. There are three types of change occurring in organizations, each requiring different leadership strategies. Figure 51.1 graphically portrays the three types. Change management supports two of these types—developmental

FIGURE 51.1   Three Types of Change

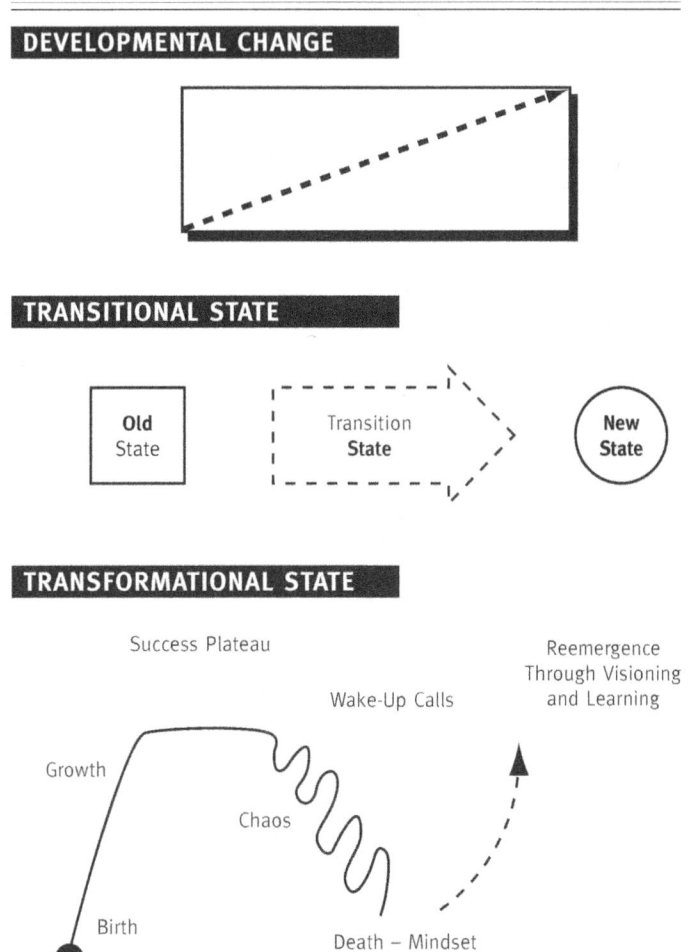

and transitional change. However, it does not suffice for today's breed of complex change —transformation.

Transformation is rampant in today's organizations. Given the number of failures, it is forcing executives and consultants to take more blinders off and expand their awareness of what is required and their skills for handling those requirements. How can executives or consultants expect to succeed in the transformational journey if their guidance systems don't allow them to see or understand the variables they face along the way?

Transformation is unique in two critical ways. First, the future is unknown at the start of the change process and can only be created by forging ahead with the intent to discover it. Without having a clear goal to manage to, leaders are forced to proceed into the unknown, dependent on broader sources of information and support to formulate a new future and put it into place. Because the future state is not clear at the beginning, the process for getting there cannot be clear either. A time-bound predetermined plan is not possible. Since the change process cannot be "managed," a new way of leading it is needed.

Secondly, the future state is so radically different than the current state that a shift of mindset is required to invent it, let alone implement and sustain it. This fact triggers enormous human and cultural impacts. Leaders and employees alike must transform their mindsets, behavior, and ways of working together. Subsequently, cultural norms must change to free up these new ways of being. People must certainly change what they do in transformation, but more importantly, they must change the way they think. The strategy for the change must focus on how to accomplish this level of personal change across the organization, leaders included.

These two attributes of transformation make both the process and the human dynamics much more complex, unpredictable and uncontrollable than in either developmental or transitional change. Change management strategies, while helpful, are insufficient for

handling these issues. Change leadership strategies that accommodate the realities of transformation are required.

Change leadership demands new executive and consulting competence in three key areas: (1) creating enterprise-wide, integrated *transformational change strategy* that attends to all of the people and process dynamics of transformational change, (2) *transforming the mindsets* of leaders and employees as required by the new marketplace and the transformation itself, and (3) designing, implementing and course correcting the transformational change *process*. We will discuss each of these change leadership arenas.

Building an Integrated Change Strategy

Building an integrated change strategy fit for transformation is the first cornerstone of change leadership. Executives clearly understand their central role in creating new *business* strategy. How ever, announcing a new business strategy alone is not enough to accomplish it. It must be executed in a way that delivers its intended business results. This requires the creation of a fitting *change strategy*. When leaders don't understand the type and scope of change their business strategy requires, they cannot create appropriate change strategy, and consistently fail to get their business results. Knowing which type of change is required is the first step in creating the right change strategy.

In developmental and transitional change, executives typically engage in very little strategic thinking about how to handle the change. Instead, they delegate it to lower level change managers, who immediately begin implementation planning using traditional project management or change management approaches. In transformation, how ever, leaders cannot hand off the creation of their transformational change strategy. Executive-level strategic thinking is a requirement. Because of the huge impacts on the business, the complex people issues and the multitude of interdependent change initiatives, the executives themselves must be involved in putting it all together. It is their responsibility to build a change strategy that:

- Correctly positions the effort within all of the organization's priorities.
- Identifies the most catalytic levers for mobilizing action toward the future state.
- Sets up appropriate participation by all stakeholders in the emergent design of the future state and its implementation.
- Clarifies comprehensive change infrastructures and leadership roles.
- Creates effective acceleration strategies and conditions.
- Sets a realistic pace for the change.

A comprehensive transformational change strategy has three equally important components: content, people and process. Most leaders attend only to content, as reflected in their primary attention to business strategy. The content of change is comprised of the new business direction and its subsequent structural, systems, product and technological changes. Until change management, executives focused solely on the content of change, which is still by far the most familiar and comfortable of the components of change strategy.

The onset of change management opened the door to the second required component of transformational change strategy—people. Change management's focus on overcoming resistance and increasing communications and training are three important features of the people component. However, these three strategies keep executive attention at the surface, exterior level—on peoples' behaviors, skills and actions. Furthermore, these strategies attempt to influence people to change from the *outside in*. They don't go far enough to do what is required in transformational change, which demands that people change their deep interiors— their mindsets and ways of being and relating. Such change must occur from the *inside out*. When people choose to change themselves from the inside out, their

changes are real and lasting, and resistance is minimal. We will discuss the changing of mindset in greater depth shortly.

The third component of change strategy is process—how the change will be carried out in a way that the organization discovers and accomplishes its business results while meeting its people and cultural requirements. Change management's attention to process focuses largely on implementation. Unfortunately, when implementation is brought in as an afterthought, it is invariably fraught with serious people problems created by neglecting the earlier phases of the change process. We will delve into leading the process of transformation later. At this point, however, let us summarize with the key point that executives must create a change strategy that is fit for the people and process requirements of transformation.

Transformation Mindset

The second cornerstone of change leadership —transforming leader and employee mindset—requires executives and consultants to attend more thoroughly to the human dynamics at play. Since most leaders need to shift their mindsets to even perceive the complex human and process dynamics of transformation, we believe that transformational efforts should begin with the leaders and directly address their mindsets.

The topic of mindset in organizations has been around for several years now, first popularized by Joel Barker's "paradigm" videos and furthered by Peter Senge's exploration of mental models (1990). Thankfully, both of these efforts brought the concept of mindset to leadership's awareness. Now, methods for actually shifting leaders' mindsets are required.

Our basic premise is that *mindset is causative*. Mindset is the primary causal factor of behavior, decisions, and most importantly, results. Leaders' mindsets about people, organizations and change determine: (1) what human, cultural and process dynamics they see and don't see in their transformations; (2) their internal reaction to those seen and unseen dynamics; and (3) their change leadership style, strategies, and results. We call the traditional leadership mindset, most prevalent today, the Industrial Mindset. This worldview contains the very blinders that prevent leaders from seeing the dynamics of transformation. In contrast, we propose the incorporation of a new leadership mindset, the Emerging Mindset, which is necessary for transformational change. A comparison of the Industrial Mindset and the Emerging Mindset is shown in Figure 51.2.

Briefly, the Industrial Mindset views all change as a predictable and controllable set of discreet events that can be managed through external force. It is a mechanistic view and neglects the power of human consciousness as a force in organizations. The worldview of the Emerging Mindset, however, understands the different types of change, and recognizes transformation as a self-organizing, continuous process that can best be facilitated through positive interaction with the human and organizational dynamics at play. The Emerging Mindset understands transformation as being primarily driven by shifts in human consciousness. Shifts of consciousness in today's businesses are reflected in the moves to e-business, globalization, customer-focused product design, and enterprise-wide software that dismantle hierarchical communications and decision-making.

Leaders operating from the Industrial Mindset have "logically" thought that: 1) transformation can occur through numerous separate initiatives and that change integration is not essential; 2) people will "obey" what leaders say is required with little communication about why change is needed; 3) resistance is a necessary evil and is best delegated to the HR department; 4) project management and change management techniques will keep the effort under control and on schedule; and 5) getting the content right is the best path to success and the only requirement of leaders.

Beyond these common misconceptions, the primary limitation of the Industrial Mindset is that it blinds leaders to the multitude of human, cultural and process dynamics that are actually occurring. Think about the profound impacts in the examples above on people, communications, relationships and culture. If leaders don't fully understand these forces, they can't possibly lead these changes.

Introducing Conscious Change Leadership

There are two different approaches to leading transformation: reactive and conscious. The reactive approach refers to leaders who see the world through the Industrial Mindset lens. Reactive leaders operate on autopilot, simply

FIGURE 51.2 Comparison of the Industrial and Emerging Mindsets

The Industrial Mindset "Reality as a Great Machine"	The Emerging Mindset "Reality as a Living System"
Separate Parts	Wholeness / Relationship
Power and Control	Co-create and Participate
Certainty / Predictability	Uncertainty / Probability
Objective / Knowable	Subjective / Mysterious
Discrete Events	Continuous Process
Entropy	Self-organization
Order into Chaos	Order out of Chaos
External Causation	Internal Causation
Scarcity	Abundance

doing what they have always done as if the transformation playing field is the same as the "running the business" playing field. They primarily pay attention to the external world, never recognizing the need to test if their habitual internal assumptions and change strategies are still effective. They simply see what they have always seen about change out in the organization, with no self-reflection. Their "Industrial" blinders and lack of introspection cause them to remain "unconscious" of the real people and process requirements of transformation, or adamant about their lack of importance or validity.

The conscious approach refers to leaders who are awake at the wheel, aware of the actual dynamics of transformation. These leaders orient to both the external and the internal worlds. Through reflecting on the content and impact of their own mindsets on leading change, they can move beyond their old "Industrial" habits and lead by the principles of the Emerging Mindset. They see the people and process dynamics at play in the organization because they look for them, knowing they are key to leading the change. These leaders intentionally strive to increase their own conscious awareness about how the organization and its people are changing, including themselves. With minds open and eyes sharp, they can effectively navigate the complex freeway of transformation.

Reactive leaders spend their time in crisis about change-related problems they didn't see coming. Change management is valuable to them because it helps manage the fallout from these self-induced problems. Conscious leaders, how-ever, proactively *lead* their organizations through these complexities successfully, thus avoiding the fallout. The key here is not just change leadership, but *Conscious Change Leadership*.

Developing Conscious Change Leaders

Conscious change leadership begins with the full realization of the power of mindset to gov-

ern perception and performance. Once leaders wake up to the central role mindset plays in their success, they more readily turn inward to investigate their own mindset.

Leaders must do this personal work either first or very early in the change process. Given the prevalence of the Industrial Mindset among executives today, this is a tough first challenge. The most common question we hear when speaking or training leaders and consultants about conscious change leadership is, "How do I get the executives to look in the mirror at themselves and see that it is how they are thinking, behaving and leading that is standing in the way of the organization's future success?" There is no pat answer to this dilemma. However, leaders wake up most readily when they see tangible evidence of how their own mindsets have effected their organizations, their change efforts, and their lives. Consultants can support them to discover the *actual impact,* both positive and negative, that their own mindsets are having on their organizations' change results.

We worked with the CEO of a utility facing deregulation. Through feedback, coaching, and participation in our leadership breakthrough program, he came to see that his mindset, controlling and paternalistic, was impeding his organization to innovate new business strategies for the deregulated environment. He also saw that his "defense" strategy was to "stay alive" as a company, rather than abundantly thrive. This was limiting his scenarios for the company's future. His personal insights were transformational for him, his change strategy, and the company.

This breakthrough work is most effective when done experientially, away from the office setting in a skillfully facilitated training environment, under well-crafted and safe conditions that enable self-reflection. Please note that the intent of this training is not personal growth for its own sake. It is *increasing change results* through personal change.

When done in the context of increasing change results, this is a powerful and necessary component of transformational change strategy. In our consulting practice, all of our clients engage in this breakthrough program at the beginning of the transformation. Once leaders have begun to change themselves, they can then model and sponsor this depth of personal work effectively across their organizations. In the case above, the CEO provided the breakthrough program for his top 1200 leaders, and sponsored a visioning conference for his top three hundred leaders, a first in their history. To model his personal changes, he opened the event by inviting everyone's creative input to shape the future of the business, no holds barred.

When leaders design their change strategy to wake up a critical mass of the organization so that it embraces the new mindset and can deal with the ongoing human and process issues, the navigation of the transformation becomes easier, faster, and more successful, as was the case with this client.

Addressing the Cultural Imperatives for Change

As mindset is to the individual, culture is to the organization. Culture is a function of people's collective mindsets. Therefore, change strategy must overtly address culture change, as driven by the needs of the new business.

The organization's existing culture must be assessed for its fit with the future state's requirements, as they are discovered. Nine times out of ten, if the organization's culture is not consciously attended to throughout the transformation, the effort will struggle or fail. One of the most powerful culture change strategies is wide-scale personal change to reinvent the mindset and cultural norms for the organization's success. This strategy, used in the utility mentioned above, requires competency in the third cornerstone of change leadership.

Understanding the Process Dynamics of Transformation

Transformational change requires leaders to shift from project management thinking to process-oriented thinking. There are several principles that define some of the key requirements of process thinking, each of which is central to conscious change leadership.

Transformational Change Cannot Be Managed

One of the flaws of change management in its application to transformation lies in its title. *Transformation cannot be managed.* This fact must be accepted and integrated by those in charge of transformation. Otherwise, if they are constantly worrying about the unknown, in fear of not having a guaranteed outcome by a certain date, or always battling the natural chaos of the process, they will never be in a position to *consciously lead* the transformation. Instead, they will always be in reaction to it.

Leaders must let go of the need to tightly control the change process, yet they still need a navigation system. We use *The Change Process Model for Leading Conscious Transformation,* shown in Figure 51.3. This process model provides a roadmap without dictating the roads to take. The roadmap helps leaders get to their destination, but they must determine the actual path they travel based on the terrain they encounter.

In this way, the change process roadmap is used as a thinking discipline. Rather than attempt to force-fit the organization's behavior into a prescribed plan and rigid timetable, the change process roadmap assists leaders to *consciously* tailor their unique change process and its pace to the ever-changing variables they face. Leaders and consultants can use the model to plan, monitor and course correct the entire change process, attending to both the organizational/technical aspects and the human and cultural components.

The Process and the Outcome Are Emergent

Even using the Change Process Model, the transformation process will have a life of its own; by necessity, both the process and the outcome will be emergent. According to Webster, emergent is defined as "arising unexpect-

FIGURE 51.3 Change Process Model for Leading Conscious Transformation

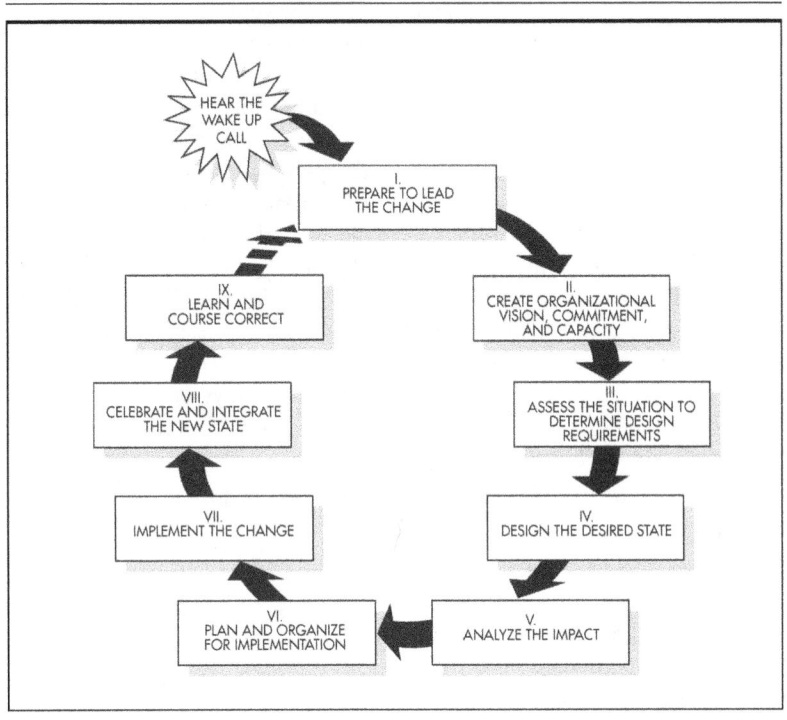

edly or evolving as a new or improved development; to become apparent or known."

The outcome is emergent because you must begin the change effort before knowing precisely where you are going. You must let go of the old trapeze before the next one is in sight. Hopefully, it will become reachable before you fall, but only if you craft a change strategy that enables that possibility. High involvement is key. Since nobody really knows what will turn out to be the best business solution early in the process, leaders must invite the intelligence of the organization to envision, create, test, and innovate until the best future becomes apparent—emerges—and can be put into place and evolved.

The process is emergent in that dynamics in the organization, marketplace and people are constantly in flux. Production or quality issues may show up; unpredicted resource demands may surface; competitors may beat you to the market with advanced technologies.

"Who would ever have guessed?" is a common comment about the transformational roller coaster. Therefore, the mindset of the conscious change leader must be "Plan as best we can, then deal with whatever shows up."

Learning and Course Correcting

A major theme of transformational change is *learn from what is happening and immediately course correct the process and the outcome.* In and of itself, this sounds obvious. However, it represents a monumental mindset and culture shift for most organizations. To really embed this principle, the change strategy must include ways to directly unravel such cultural norms as "kill the messenger of bad news," "make a mistake and you're dead," "don't rock the boat," and "prove the viability of something before taking action on it."

"Learning and course correction" is both a mindset and an operating practice. Not only must the beliefs and behavioral norms of this way of being be determined and instilled in the culture of the organization, but a system and work practices for it must also be developed. For instance, leaders must encourage feedback, new information, and two-way communication as well as make it clear where to send this information and how it will be used to influence either the outcome or the change process. In traditional organizations, leaders keep shifts in their previously communicated plans under raps. In the consciously led organization, leaders publicly invite them as contributing to the rapid discovery of the best outcome.

Creating Critical Mass Through Whole System Engagement

Transformation will only occur when a critical mass of the organization has undergone the required mindset change to perform in ways that produce the desired outcome. The fastest way to achieve critical mass, as well as wide spread commitment to the change, is through whole system involvement in the process. All stakeholders must be included in shaping the future and the process of creating it.

Large group interventions such as Future Search (Weisbord, 1995), Real Time Strategic Change (Jacobs, 1994), Visioning and Design Conferences (Axelrod, 1992), Whole-Scale Change (Dannemiller, et al, 2000) and Open Space (Owen, 1997) are excellent ways to generate collective intelligence on various aspects of the change, heighten commitment and excitement, and alter both people's mindsets and the organization's culture. These interventions are key acceleration strategies for every phase of the change process, allowing major pieces of work to be accomplished in much shorter time.

Summary

Conscious change leadership is the next generation of leading and consulting beyond change management. Becoming a conscious change leader requires you to pursue your own learning and transformation—transforming your mindset, altering your behaviors and evolving your leadership or consulting style and approaches. It means expanding your thinking about process and your repertoire for designing and facilitating the complexities of transformation. It demands taking a stand for the personal change required of leaders and the workforce. And, as you do your own individual work, you will not only benefit personally, but also become a model for everyone you seek to influence. We believe that through this conscious approach to transformation, you can create the conditions for discovering the future and ways of being that our organizations and society need to thrive.

References

Ackerman Anderson, L., & Anderson, D. (2001). *Beyond change management: Advanced strategies for today's transformational leaders.* San Francisco, CA: Jossey-Bass/Pfeiffer.

Alban, B., & Bunker, B. (1997) *Large group interventions: Engaging the whole system for rapid change.* San Francisco, CA: Jossey-Bass/Pfeiffer.

Anderson, D., & Ackerman Anderson, L. (2001) *The change leader's roadmap: How to navigate your organization's transformation.* San Francisco, CA: Jossey-Bass/Pfeiffer.

Axelrod, R. (1992) *Terms of engagement: Changing the way we change our organizations.* San Francisco, CA: Berrett-Koehler.

Dannemiller, K., James, S., & Tolchinsky, P. (2000). *Collaborating for change: Whole-scale change.* San Francisco, CA: Berrett-Koehler.

Jacobs, R. (1994). *Real time strategic change: How to involve an entire organization in fast and far-reaching change.* San Francisco, CA: Berrett-Koehler.

Owen, H. (1997). *Open space technology: A user's guide.* San Francisco, CA: Berrett-Koehler.

Senge, P. (1990) *The fifth discipline: The art and practice of the learning organization.* New York, NY: Doubleday.

Weisbord, M., & Janoff, S. (1995). *Future search: an action guide for finding common ground for action in organizations.* San Francisco, CA: Berrett-Koehler.

CHAPTER 52

The Tao of Change Redux

Robert J. Marshak

Re-Introduction

In 1993-1994, following a series of business trips to Korea and subsequent self-study of traditional Chinese philosophy, I wrote two articles suggesting that organizational change might usefully be thought of as a cyclical and continuous process rather than a linear and episodic one (Marshak, 1993b & 1994). At the time I was noticing shifts in the tempo and demands for change in the organizations I consulted with and found the Lewinian model of change still useful, but somehow limited. I was also intrigued by my Korean experiences with the possibility that the change models used in OD practice might be more culturally bound then recognized at the time. I further wished to raise the possibility that useful insights and ideas about consulting and change could come from nontraditional sources outside of North America and Europe. In the ensuing years some of the core insights revealed to me at that time through study of another culture and its founding philosophies have been recognized and expanded upon by others, for example writings about continuous versus episodic change (Weick & Quinn, 1999) and self-organizing, complex adaptive systems (Olson & Eoyang, 2001). The original article is next, followed by additional reflections in a postscript.

The Tao of Change

After more than 40 years of searching for the Promised Land of "desired end states," perhaps it is time OD as a profession started thinking about "going around in circles." This somewhat surprising conclusion came to me following a recently completed personal odyssey.

The focus of this article is on East-West assumptions about change, after previous speculation about culturally based differences in East-West learning styles (see Marshak, 1993a). The stimulus for both articles was the same: a series of training/consulting trips to South Korea during 1990-1991. Those trips came exactly 20 years after spending 47 weeks in intensive Korean language training before being stationed near the DMZ between North and South Korea. After leaving military service and Korea at the end of 1971 to resume graduate studies in OD, I thought I would never return; that my training and immersion into another language and culture had been mostly lost time.

When I eventually returned to Korea at the beginning of the 1990s, the changes were really remarkable, but none more so than my cross-cultural experiences related to change theory. I was scheduled to present a seminar on the "Strategic Management of Change," including developmental and transformational change. But just before leaving the United States, my Korean host called to tell me I was presenting on "management innovation," not "transformational change." When I inquired why, he explained: "Because there is really no word in the Korean language for transformational change the way you mean it." When I asked: "How do you say the caterpillar changed into the butterfly?" He replied: "In Korean, we say the caterpillar *becomes* the butterfly." He then went on to say that many of the Korean words/concepts associated with "transformational change" also carried negative connotations of violent revolution, loss of social order, dissolution, and the like. That telephone conversation, combined with later experiences discussing change and change concepts with Korean managers and trainers, convinced me I needed more than a good English-Korean dictionary to really understand the differences in how change can be viewed on each side of the Pacific Ocean.

Change: The Perspectives from East and West

The clues to my questions regarding change somehow were located in the cultural roots of Korea and East Asia. Because Korea, like most of East Asia, is a post-Confucian society, my curiosity led me to the great Chinese sage, Confucius (K'ung Fu-Tzu, 551-479 BCE) and Confucian/Neo-Confucian philosophy. Along the way I learned, among other things, that the *I Ching* (*Book of Changes*, circa 1143 BCE) is one of the five classics of Confucian philosophy and that, by attribution and legend, Confucius himself wrote the first philosophical commentaries that are incorporated as part of the text. I also learned much more about *yin* and *yang*, and the five forces of wood, fire, earth, metal, and water as primary concepts in Neo-Confucian philosophy. Most important, I discovered an entirely different world view about the universe and about change. Furthermore, the more I began to understand the Confucian world view, the more clearly I came to understand, through contrast, my own world view based primarily in Judeo-Christian, Greco-Roman, and European Enlightenment (e.g., Descartes and Newton) beliefs, assumptions, and concepts.

My intention now is to provide a glimpse of these two views of change as I have come to understand them, and my thoughts about some of the potential implications for OD

theory and practice. A more in-depth discussion and analysis of these two models is available elsewhere (Marshak, 1993b).

Change: The OD Perspective

The primary model of change underlying most OD theory and practice is Kurt Lewin's three-stage change process of unfreezing, movement, and refreezing (Lewin, 1947). This model is in the tradition of the Western, scientific world view that presumes linear time, progressive evolution, free will, and the preeminence of rationality (see, for example, Tarnas, 1991). This world view also contains an inherent dualism, including the belief that human beings exist independent of a mostly static phenomenal world that they plan, manage, and otherwise act on. In terms of conceptualizing a change effort, this world view and change model imply a managed process to move from a current state to a more desired future state through the use of planned interventions to overcome resistance, get movement, and thereby alter the status quo. This is shown in Figure 52.1.

The assumptions inherent in this approach/model include beliefs that change is:

1. Linear. One moves from one state to another state in a forward direction.
2. Progressive. One moves from a less to a more desired state.
3. Destination oriented. One moves toward a specific goal or end state.
4. Based on creating disequilibrium. In order to get movement from the current state, one must alter the equilibrium of the status quo.
5. Planned and managed by people who exist separate from and act on things to achieve their goals. One learns the principles and practices about how to master and/or facilitate the forces in the world in order to achieve preferred outcomes.
6. Unusual, because everything is normally in a quasi-stationary or static state. Unless something is done proactively, things will tend to stay the same. After all, according

FIGURE 52.1 The OD Model of Change

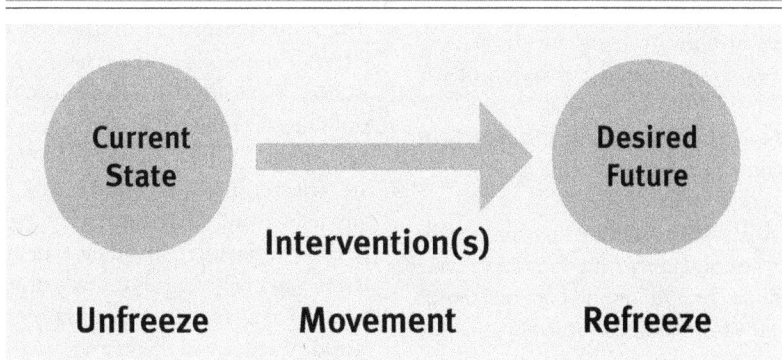

to Newton's First Law of Motion, a body at rest stays at rest unless force is applied.

This way of thinking about change is so much a part of OD theory and practice, and the cultural milieu from which it was created, that I never thought twice about these underlying assumptions until I discovered a world view based on a different set of assumptions.

Change: The Confucian Perspective

Underlying both Confucian and Taoist philosophy is an alternative world view that pre-sumes the inherent oneness, or interdependence, of everything and everyone in the universe. All are governed by the universal principles of the Way (the *Tao*), including the principle of continual cyclical alternation between the polarities inherent in everything (*yin* and *yang*). In terms of change, this world view is represented by the images of the *T'ai Chi* (the union of *yin* and *yang*) and the *Wu Hsing* (the ordered cyclical relationship among the five forces of the universe represented by wood, fire, earth, metal, and water). These are shown in Figure 52.2.

In brief, everyone and everything in the universe is part of on-going processes of cyclical change. Therefore people, who are interde-

FIGURE 52.2 The *T'ai Chi* and *Wu Hsing*

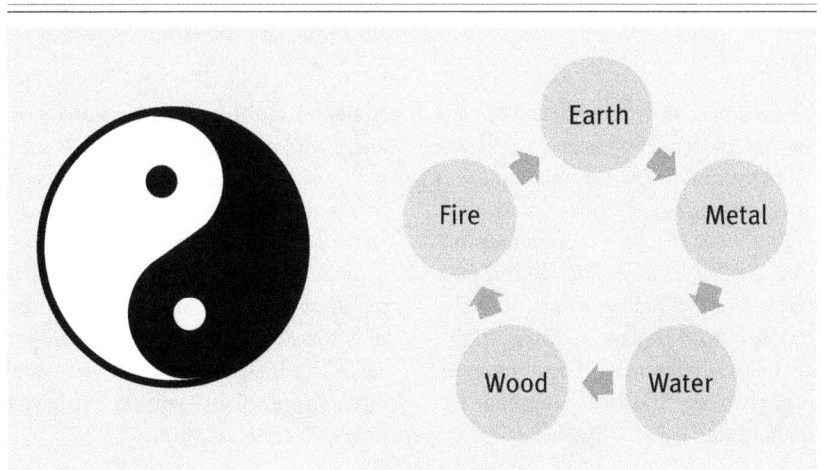

pendent with everything else, must observe and align themselves with the on-going cyclical changes in order to maintain the natural harmony, equilibrium, and perfection of the universe.

The assumptions inherent in this approach/model include beliefs that change is:

1. Cyclical. There is a constant ebb and flow to the universe and everything in it is cyclical.
2. Processional. Everything and everyone moves constantly from one condition/form/state to the next condition/form/state in an orderly sequence through a cycle.
3. Journey oriented. Because there is continual cyclical change, there can be no end state, per se. What matters is how well one conducts the journey, i.e., follows the Way.
4. Based on restoring/maintaining equilibrium. Everything is naturally in harmony and perfect. Therefore, one acts only when and how needed to restore balance and equilibrium.
5. Observed and followed by people who are one with everything, and must act correctly to maintain harmony in the universe. One must constantly strive to be in harmony with the Way, the natural order of the universe.
6. Usual, because everything is normally in a continually changing dynamic state. The continual process of everything in the universe is change. The Yin-Yang Law of Opposites says everything contains its own negation, so nothing stays the same forever.

This dynamic, interdependent, cyclical world view has formed Chinese and East Asian ways of thinking and acting for millennia. It is also the foundation for such practices as traditional Chinese medicine (e.g., acupuncture), martial arts (e.g., *T'ai Chi Chuan*), and geomancy (*Feng Shui*). Needless to say, in a dynamic, cyclical world, day becomes night, honor becomes shame, loss becomes gain, death becomes birth, and the "caterpillar becomes the butterfly"—naturally.

Reflections

The more I began to understand these two views of the world and of change, the more I realized not only the cross-cultural implications but the inherent limitations of the "pure" OD model. While I know OD practitioners are eclectic, inventive, and rarely bound by any model, still I had previously known of no alternative paradigm to guide dramatically different ways of acting and intervening. Besides, a model of change that specifically addressed a world of continual change seemed intriguing after dealing with the paradox of how to unfreeze and refreeze "permanent white water" (Vaill, 1989). When I then began to consider the implications of each model of change, several meta-themes emerged. These seemed to follow logically from the assumptions underlying each model and help to contrast the two differing world views.

Implications: The OD Change Model

I believe the assumptions underlying the Lewinian model of change are likely to lead to several tendencies in the theory and practice of Organization Development. These include the following orientations:

Focusing on the Future. Emphasis is placed on the desired future state where the problems of the past and present will be resolved and/or transformed. This tends to produce a future bias wherein most of the attention and activities focus on creating a compelling image of the future and forgetting or getting away from the past and present.

(Clients) Holding on to a Satisfactory Present. Paradoxically, because one is supposed to move (change) only when there is a clearly better alternative, clients may want to hold on to the present state, particularly if it is satisfactory and/or better than all known options. After all, why should anyone want to move to a downsized, pressurized, highly competitive future? This is especially true when—as this view of change implies—you do not have to move unless "forced" to do so.

Focusing on Overcoming Resistance. In order to change, resistance to movement (inertia) must be overcome, usually by altering the field of forces. Holding on to the present tends to be viewed (by change agents) as resistance. The intervention approach, as a result, focuses on ways to overcome the resistant forces/persons. This, in essence, ends up casting the change effort as a win-lose conflict between the forces of movement and the forces of inertia.

Thinking in Terms of Either/Or. A tendency toward dichotomous either/or thinking is created and reinforced by several dynamics. By far the most important is the inherent dualism embedded in the change model and most Western thinking since at least Descartes. In dualism, entities are considered to be not only different but separate and independent of each other as well. For example, one may choose the current state or a future state, but not both. Finally, in an either/or dualistic world, when the future is presumed to be better and therefore good, the present must be unsatisfactory and therefore bad. Thus, in a blink of the eye a change effort can become a drama between the forces of good seeking to establish a more progressive, preferred future and the forces of evil seeking to maintain the flawed current state.

Planning and Managing. Because change (movement) results when something is acted on, it is possible to choose what to change and how to change it. To insure you get what you want, it is appropriate and necessary to plan and manage your actions. Planning and managing movement toward the desired future state also presumes both dualism and causality. A separate, independent entity (change agent) acts on/with (intervenes) another separate, independent entity (client system) and thereby causes (facilitates) movement (change).

Thinking Analytically. Good analysis is needed in order to anticipate, plan, manage, and/or deal correctly with the myriad factors and forces that must be considered in order to successfully move to the desired future state. Analytic thinking, i.e., the separation of a whole into parts, is the preferred way to plan and manage because entities are conceived to be separate and independent and to act on each other causally. Remember even Lewin equated planned change with social engineering (Lewin, 1951, p. 172).

Intervening Based on Reason and Logic. Intervention choices are supposed to be made on the basis of reason and logic, i.e., rationally. Interventions should be data (fact) and theory (premises) based, using reasoned logic to infer conclusions about appropriate actions. Emotional and unconscious forces may be addressed, as long as they are surfaced, named, and then worked (in a rational manner). Interventions based on emotionality, spirituality, intuition, instinct, and/or feelings are suspect, because such factors are presumed to detract from "pure" reason and logic. It is no accident that action research is the name given to the core methodology of OD. Action research involves, in essence, an iterative, systematic, participatory process, using data-based reason and logic, to address and resolve systemic issues.

Measuring Progress. Because the implicit theme of most change efforts is to move toward a more desired future state, ways to measure "progress" become integral to the change process. Progress can be measured in many dimensions, the more the better. These include distance traveled (milestones and gaps), speed and time (how fast and how long), increases in things (e.g., more money, markets, productivity, quality, effectiveness, satisfaction, etc.), and decreases in things (e.g., less cost, time, defects, problems, turnover, etc.). Inability to measure "progress" on at least one dimension becomes, therefore, a valid reason to question whether or not a change is needed, possible, or has occurred.

These tendencies, if left to their own excesses, can conspire to create scenarios wherein change efforts become win-lose struggles between the forces of progress and the forces of stagnation. The forces of progress will try to use superior planning, management, analysis, and reason to overcome the resistance and defenses of the forces of stagnation who seek to hold on to the current flawed conditions by being emotional, irrational, or demanding concrete, measurable proof before they will even consider movement.

Implications: the Cyclical Change Model

In contrast, the Confucian cyclical change model generates an alternative set of tendencies. These will be described and contrasted with aspects of the OD change model to help highlight salient differences. The cyclical change model is likely to lead to the following orientations:

Focusing on the Past-Present-Future. In a cyclical change model becoming and transformation are continual processes. To understand the present requires understanding the past from which it emerged and the future it is becoming. The future in turn will soon become the present and then the past. As a result, diagnosis and intervention must focus on the entire past-present-future cycle, rather than being primarily concerned with getting to the future. Origins and legacies, the pattern(s) and procession of change, and knowing where one is in a cycle of becoming and transformation are all as important as focusing on the future.

Letting Go and Aligning With the Emerging Future. In a cyclical-processional model of change, every condition/form/state is presumed to be both a beginning and an ending. Furthermore, no condition/form/state is considered to be better than another. They are just different, and all are needed to maintain the balance, harmony, and equilibrium necessary to keep things moving in a dynamic universe. As a result, the dominant orientation is less on "holding on" to a desired (end) state, and more toward "letting go" in order to "join up" (align) with a newly emerging state. In short, how to maintain balance and equilibrium

while aligning with a newly emerging situation becomes the principal concern.

Focusing on the Relationships Needed to Maintain Balance and Harmony. Attention is focused on balance and harmony as necessary requirements to maintain the dynamic equilibrium of continuous, cyclical change. One does not "overcome resistance" so much as one looks to "release blockages" or "re-balance relationships" in order to maintain harmony and equilibrium among the constantly changing aspects of a system. In addition, the win-lose dynamics that often emerge from an "overcome resistance" orientation are replaced by the recognition that "coordination-collaboration" is essential for maintaining balance in a constantly changing universe.

Thinking in Terms of Both/And. Recognition of the need for continual coordination-collaboration helps contribute to syncretic both/and thinking. More important, however, is the concept of monism ("all is one") that is inherent to the cyclical change model and most East Asian traditional philosophies. In a monistic universe there may be different aspects/manifestations, but all are interdependent and essentially one. This is most strongly represented by the polarity of *yin* and *yang* wherein each creates and is created by the other, and both are aspects of the *T'ai Chi*, the Great Ultimate. Consequently, in a monistic universe one cannot "win out over" or negate another without negating oneself. Thus, for example, the orientation is not past vs. present vs. future, but rather the relative balance and emphasis of each. How much of our history and traditions will be part of our future, given where we are (in an on-going cycle)? What new traditions do we wish to create in the future so they will become part of our on-going legacies? What if our thinking and acting were guided by simultaneous consideration of our past, present and anticipated future? From this view, a change process is a continual dance among polarities where attention to balance, harmony, grace, and natural movement becomes the focus.

Self-Renewing Through Release and Augmentation. In a dynamic cyclical model of change, attention is focused on maintaining balance and harmony during the inherent changes so that the appropriate next condition/ form/state in the cycle will be fully and properly realized. As a result, efforts related to release and augmentation (letting go and adding on) become critical. Also, because the universe is monistic and therefore interconnected and interdependent, no thing/person acts on another thing/person. All action and change is self-generated. The concept of causality is replaced by self-renewal or self-cultivation. In short, when interdependent aspects (clients and consultants) act to maintain on-going balance and harmony in a system (release and augmentation interventions) there will be natural self-renewal (change). For a related discussion, see Land and Jarman (1992).

Thinking Holistically. A cycle is a circle, and circles are inherently holistic. All is part of, or contained within, the circle. One is immediately and constantly conscious of the whole and the parts. This differs from a linear orientation where the tendency is to focus on one end (aspect) or the other (aspect). When everything is interdependent and self-creating, the ability to maintain proper balance and harmony throughout the continual change processes is essential. This calls for holistic thinking, seeing the patterns and relationships as well as the parts. This means more than just seeing the forest and the trees; it also means seeing the natural ecosystem that is the forest and the interrelationships and balance among all aspects of the forest throughout the seasons and years. Consequently, diagnosis and intervention must constantly stress a holistic, systemic orientation. Emphasis is on linkages and putting more things together. After all, in a monistic universe to see and deal with anything apart from the rest is to misread reality.

Intervening Based on Artistry and Composition. Because everything is self-evolving, holistic, and must be in balance and harmony for optimal conditions to prevail, interventions are based more on artistry and composition than on pure reason and logic. In essence, the logic of artistic composition, rather than the logic of scientific research, guides actions (see Hall and Ames, 1987). Factors, forces, values, thoughts, feelings, moods, etc., are all constituent elements that, in combination, compose any system and/or intervention. Thus the resulting total aesthetic, or "beauty," of a system becomes the legitimate objective for any intervention. This logic/approach is aided by the traditional Chinese concept that mental activities are located in the heart. The Chinese word *hsin* means the "heart-mind," i.e., thoughts and feelings are inseparable. This, of course, contrasts with the complete separation, and presumed opposition, of the mind (thoughts/reason) and the heart (feelings/emotions) postulated by Descartes and embedded in the scientific thinking of the West. To coin a new phrase: *action composition* is an iterative, participatory methodology, based on artistic sensibilities, used to compose and recompose situations and systems to reflect harmony and balance in thoughts, feelings, and actions.

Being Values Centered. When change is self-generating, continual, and cyclical, the primary consideration is how to maintain balance, harmony, and equilibrium. In Confucianism, this was done by following the Way (the *Tao*) and adhering to the five constant virtues of benevolence or human-heartedness (*Jen*); righteousness or duty (*Yi*); propriety or following correct principles (*Li*); good faith or living up to one's word (*Hsin*); and wisdom or using knowledge to benefit the world (*Chih*). One might thereby become an exemplary person (*Chün Tzu*) or a sage (*Sheng Jen*) who could serve as a model for others to emulate. Consequently, respect ("face"), not fame or fortune, was most important (see Munro, 1969; Hall & Ames, 1987).

Thus, how well one adheres to values or principles (e.g., is "centered" in virtue) replaces linear progress as the primary consideration.

In OD, this would mean clarity about and adherence to a set of core values that should be exhibited constantly throughout any change process. This might include, for example, core values related to humanism, democratic processes, equality, respect, dignity, and so forth (for a more detailed discussion of OD values see Gellerman, Frankel, & Ladenson, 1990). In a cyclical process, being centered is paramount. Remember, a wheel does not roll very far if the hub is misaligned.

These tendencies, in combination, are likely to lead to change processes and interventions intended to help maintain harmony and balance while fully realizing the current condition/form/state, and also being prepared and able to let go and align with another condition/form/state as it begins to emerge. This is accomplished from an aesthetic, values centered, both/and, past-present-future, holistic orientation.

Commentary

The discussion so far has been primarily devoted to a presentation and analysis of the two different change models (see Table 52.1 for a summary of the meta-themes). Next, some of the "so whats" that are implied or raised by the presentation will be highlighted and briefly discussed.

OD is Culturally Based. Much or all of OD is based in the cultural tradition of the Western

European Enlightenment, i.e., the "modern era" in the West. Consequently any organizational change beliefs, assumptions, theories, practices, etc., that exist outside that cultural matrix are likely to seem strange, illogical, nonscientific, and/or mystical. This includes both premodern and postmodern (e.g., the "new sciences") assumptions and theories.

OD is Culturally Biased. Over the years a wide range of theorists and practitioners have wondered whether or not some, or all, OD values are culturally biased (see, for example, Jaeger, 1986). What is suggested here is that the fundamental model of change underlying OD is culturally based and therefore inherently biased toward that culture. This does not necessarily mean OD cannot be successfully applied outside its originating culture; it does mean that a lack of awareness and appreciation for the underlying assumptions and values of OD and the host culture could be a recipe for failure.

Different Fundamental Models of Change Reveal Different Options and Approaches. Most or all OD practitioners face the same "chronic" issues in their work, e.g., getting people to focus on the future, dealing with resistance, measuring success, to name a few. We also are alert to any new and/or different interventions for addressing these issues. What we may not be doing, however, is searching for different paradigms of change that would sug-

TABLE 52.1 Two Views of Change

OD/Western	Cyclical/Confucian
• Focus on the Future	• Attend to the Past–Present–Future
• Assume Satisfied People Hold On	• Assume Wise People Let Go and Realign
• Overcome Resistance	• Maintain Balance and Harmony
• Think in Terms of Either/Or	• Thinks in Terms of Both/And
• Plan and Manage Change	• Cultivate System Self-Renewal
• Think Analytically	• Think Holistically
• Use Reason and Logic	• Use Artistry and Composition
• Measure Progress	• Be Values Centered

gest fundamentally different ways to think about, and therefore deal with, change and change issues. It may not be time to "start going around in circles," but it is certainly time to explore options in addition to "un-freezing-movement-refreezing."

Raising Questions about the Fundamental Model of Change Underlying OD Will Feel Threatening and/or Disorienting. Much like change work that raises questions about an organization's deep culture, looking critically at some of OD's most basic assumptions will feel threatening and/or disorienting to some or many in the profession. Nevertheless, this is the avenue that offers the greatest potential for innovation in the field.

OD, as a Profession, Must Attend to its Own Renewal. We, like the systems we serve, are at a turning point (Capra, 1982; Katz & Marshak, 1993). This is amply documented by the ODN's Future Search process, the themes and topics of recent ODN conferences, and our own experiences as practitioners. Therefore, in the spirit of this article, following are some brief Confucian cyclical change perspectives to consider.

- Focus on our past-present-future. We should honor our origins and legacies, consider what we are becoming, and help shape and be shaped by the future. We should continually conceive of the profession as "in process." Debates pitting our past against our future against our present are ultimately a waste of energy and should be avoided.
- Let go and align ourselves with the emerging future. We cannot afford to delude ourselves into believing we can hang on to our past practices and orthodoxies. Nothing stays the same forever. We should discern what will be needed to be successful in the emerging future, and then create, continue, and/or align with the required theories, methods, and techniques.
- Focus on the relationships needed to maintain balance and harmony. As conditions

and contexts change, we should continually balance and rebalance the profession's range of theories, technologies, and work foci. This also includes addressing the relationships needed to maintain harmony and balance among the different aspects and components of OD, the members of the practitioner community, our relationships with client systems, and our own supporting systems such as the OD Network.
- Think in terms of both/and. It would be helpful if we could use a both/and orientation to explore innovative and established ideas and practices together. Too much of our professional energy seems, at times, to get caught up in discussions about whose approach/idea is "right" or "wrong." We need innovation, and the essence of creativity has always been to bring together what had previously been disjoined.
- Think holistically. It would also be helpful to expand our horizons and use more holistic thinking about who we are, what we do, and where and how we fit in the scheme of things. This also includes incorporating more holistic approaches and methodologies into our work, and working more interdependently with a wider range of others.
- Intervene based on artistry and composition. In working to compose our emerging future, we must be mindful of our heads and hearts and use artistry as well as rationality in our efforts. Practitioners and clients are attracted to OD not only for what it can do as a tool, but by the moods, feelings, emotions, and sensibilities it helps engender. In short, we should be guided by our heart-minds as we compose and re-compose the heart-mind of the profession. OD in the future must continue to be both efficacious and emotionally evocative.
- Be values centered. We should continually, and especially now, reexamine and rededicate ourselves and the profession to a set of values. This not only centers and unites us as a profession, but also forms us as a professional community worthy of emulation.

- Seek self-renewal through release and augmentation. We should trust that renewal will emerge naturally as we follow the above precepts and thereby release what is no longer needed, while adding or augmenting that which becomes essential.

The individual items discussed above may not necessarily seem new or different. In some ways, what may be most different is their interrelationship as a whole, as well as what is not included. What I can unequivocally assert, however, is that before I studied the Confucian cyclical change model (1) I would not have conceived of the situation facing OD in the same way; (2) my list of proposed remedies would have been different; and (3) my overall "sense" or gestalt of this moment in the life of the OD profession would have been quite different.

Endings and Beginnings

This discussion has chronicled some of my wanderings and discoveries over the past 20 years and marks both endings and beginnings. I am reminded that the journey of the hero is also cyclical: an outward search followed by a return home, transformed (Campbell, 1968). I returned to Korea after 20 years, bringing my knowledge and experience related to organizations and change. I returned from Korea and my subsequent research with new insights about organizations and change. From the vantage point of the present I looked to the ancient past to discover new ideas to address the future. Endings and beginnings and endings. Cycles of cycles; one journey ends, another now begins.

Postscript

Looking back at the ideas and experiences that led to this article triggered a number of reflections I would like to share.

First, is the importance of an "anthropological mind" in all aspects of OD work. By that I mean developing the orientation and skills to be able to discern or develop hypotheses about the deep assumptions that may be underlying action in a particular social setting. Working through the ideas that led to this article convinced me that there are underlying assumptions to everything we do and provided me with some insights into how to observe, reflect upon, and test cultural assumptions, especially based on what is said and written. This orientation has become a core part of my practice and leads me to believe that some training in cultural anthropology might usefully be included in the education and training of OD consultants.

Second, I am reminded of how the context of OD has shifted and remained the same over the past decades. At the time I wrote this article OD was reacting to questions about its continued efficacy. The question "Is OD dead?" had been asked as early as 1989 and the field was in one of its periods of doubt and self-reflection. At the same time calls for ways to help organizations deal with on-going change and "permanent white water" were increasing; and all in an increasingly cross-cultural and global context. Recently, however, when I re-read the article for this publication just after the OD Network Conference in Baltimore in 2011, I was struck by how many of my comments about the state of organization development and the OD Network in the early 1990s seemed once again true in the early 2010s. I had thought before I re-read it that that part of the article would surely prove dated. Of course if things really are cyclical this should not be a big surprise.

Third, I would like to remind today's readers about the original intent behind the article. For me it was an opportunity to raise questions about the then dominant assumptions shaping OD ways of thinking about change in order to encourage new assumptions and new possibilities, rather than trying to advance a specific, alternative model as somehow "superior." In other words, it was a way through contrast to highlight potentially unexamined and limiting aspects of OD. Of course that also reflected my dominant way of knowing and learning, which is to note differences more so than similarities (Marshak, 2009). Interestingly, over the years I have made many trips to the post-Confucian countries of Japan, Korea, China, Hong Kong, and Singapore where I found my hosts were mainly interested in learning the latest Western models of change (Marshak, 2004). So instead of my insights about *yin-yang* and five forces change dynamics being called upon, what instead proved most helpful was what I had learned from my readings in Chinese and Confucian philosophy about some of the core cultural dimensions shaping the social order and etiquette in all of those countries. These include, for example, hierarchy as a central aspect of the natural way of all things, the five fundamental relationships, the primacy of family, and the importance of harmony in all matters. It is also worth noting that after officially repudiating Confucianism about 100 years ago there is now a revival of Confucian philosophy in China and throughout the region. For those who might aspire to work in the East Asian region, I would encourage learning the basic ideas of the Confucian social order. I found that knowledge helped me to be more culturally literate throughout East Asia.

Finally, I'd like to thank the *OD Practitioner* for once again recognizing my work and also to acknowledge and thank my Korean host for the trips, experiences, and discussions that led me to study Confucianism and write this article, my longtime colleague Dr. Jeong, Jae-Chang. —*RJM, 2011*

References

Campbell, J. (1968). *The hero with a thousand faces* (2nd ed.). Princeton, NJ: Princeton University Press.

Capra, F. (1982). *The turning point.* New York, NY: Simon & Schuster.

Gellerman, W., Frankel, M. S., & Landenson, R. F. (1990). *Values and ethics in organization and human systems development.* San Francisco, CA: Jossey-Bass.

Hall, D. L., & Ames, R. T. (1987). *Thinking through Confucius.* Albany, NY: State University of New York Press.

Jaeger, A. M. (1986). Organization development and national culture: Where's the fit? *Academy of Management Review*, 11(1), 178–190.

Katz, J. H., & Marshak, R. J. (1993). Innovation: Reinventing our profession. In S. Zilber (Ed.), *Celebrating the spirit of renewal: Proceedings of the 1993 National OD Network Conference* (pp. 303–307). Portland, OR: National OD Network.

Land, G., & Jarman, B. (1992). *Breakpoint and beyond.* New York, NY: Harper Collins.

Lewin, K. (1947). Frontiers in group dynamics. *Human Relations*, 1(1), 5-41.

Lewin, K. (1951). *Field Theory in social science.* New York, NY: Harper & Row.

Marshak, R. J. (1993a). Training and consulting in Korea. *OD Practitioner*, 25(2), 16–21.

Marshak, R. J. (1993b). Lewin meets Confucius: A re-view of the OD model of change. *Journal of Applied Behavioral Science*, 29(4), 393–415.

Marshak, R. J. (2004). Organization development and post-Confucian societies. In P. F. Sorenson, P. F., Head, C. T., Yaeger, T., & Cooperrider, D. (Eds.) (2004). *Global and international organization development* (4th ed.). Champaign, IL: Stipes Publishing, pp. 295–311.

Marshak, R. J. (2009). *Organizational change: Views from the edge.* Bethel, ME: The Lewin Center.

Munro, D. J. (1969). *The concept of man in early China.* Stanford, CA: Stanford University Press.

Olson, E. E., & Eoyang, G. H. (2001). *Facilitating organization change.* San Francisco, CA: Jossey-Bass/ Pfeiffer.

Tarnas, R. (1991). *The passion of the western mind.* New York, NY: Harmony Books.

Vaill, P. B. (1989). *Managing as a performing art.* San Francisco, CA: Jossey-Bass Publishers.

Weick, K. E., & Quinn, R. E. (1999). Organizational change and development. *Annual Review of Psychology*, 50: 361–386.

CHAPTER 53

Improving Change Implementation

Practical Adaptations of Kotter's Model

Nicole Stragalas

Introduction

While it is common for corporate management training programs to provide examples of change *process* models, discussion of change *implementation* models is infrequent. Given the high percentage of failed change management efforts, it is essential for corporations to direct more attention to the specifics of change execution. Managers would also benefit from the review of broad-scale organization approaches, rather than primarily focusing on process models at the individual level, where the emphasis is on employee reaction rather than practical execution of specific steps. One comprehensive implementation model, developed by John Kotter, offers clear guidance for large-scale change management efforts. While the Kotter framework is more closely related to organizational behavior, in that it targets macro-level organizational theory, it is also appropriate as an organizational development tool, providing a three-dimensional linkage between individuals, groups, and the organization.

Although Kotter's work has been validated through significant research and is a staple component in graduate management programs, the seemingly limited use of the model to guide many corporate change initiatives suggests there are gaps in translation. A cursory examination of recent research into successful change management interventions may provide information that would expand and clarify Kotter's implementation model. By matching specific recommendations from recent research with each stage in Kotter's design, specific themes emerge. These themes, grouped by stakeholder—leadership, employees, organization—reveal valuable insights, enhancing the usefulness of this model for corporations seeking to improve the odds for positive, lasting organizational change.

Change Process Models in Corporate Training Programs

A significant number of transformation models have been introduced and analyzed within the field of organizational development. In corporations, however, three change models are most commonly reviewed in leadership development programs. Two, by William Bridges and Edgar Schein, are process models that can be applied at an organizational level, but are typically discussed at the individual or team level. The third, by Kotter, is more appropriately classified as a change implementation model. Certain elements are common in all three approaches.

Bridges proposed there are three significant stages in managing transitions. He defined these stages as "Ending, Losing, Letting Go; Neutral Zone; and New Beginning" (Bridges, 2003, p. 5). Individuals begin a change process with a certain sense of loss and feelings of discomfort, move through a period of "psychological realignments and repatternings" (p. 5), and come through the transition with a "new identity . . . new energy . . . and new sense of purpose that make the change begin to work" (p. 5). Two areas developed by Bridges, but often left out of management training, are (1) the four rules for the New Beginning to take hold and (2) actions to deal with continuous and simultaneous change. The core actions for reinforcing new beginnings include: consistency in messages (p. 69); strategically selected quick successes that increase morale (p. 71); applications of symbolism linking the past and present (p. 71); and celebration of achieved goals (p. 72). Bridges also advocated the development of activities that would ensure companies were primed for ongoing transformations. Some of these processes have been identified as repeated clarifications of purpose (p. 107), modeling of trustworthiness (e.g., listening carefully, asking for feedback, following through on statements) (p. 109), and providing pressure valves for the expression of frustrations related to the past (old baggage) (p. 111). Another important continuous change preparation action is "selling problems, not solutions" (p. 111); this framing helps managers avoid the pitfall of "selling each change piecemeal" (p. 111). Overall, Bridges outlines implementation considerations in his model, but the information is limited in scope and does not offer concrete steps for execution. Further, in leadership training, managers typically only learn about the three stages and are not provided an opportunity to analyze the other facets inherent in Bridges' work.

Edgar Schein, basing his model on the original design of Lewin (Schein, 2004), also described three stages in a change process: Unfreezing/disconfirmation; Cognitive Restructuring; and Refreezing (Schein). Using a more traditional psychological approach, Schein discusses his analysis in terms of disequilibrium, leading to emotions of anxiety and guilt, which results in a cognitive restructuring to reestablish equilibrium in the new context. In the Unfreezing stage, Schein posits ". . . Some sense of threat, crisis, or dissatisfaction must be present before enough motivation is present to start the process of unlearning and relearning" (2004, p. 32 4). To achieve change, a sufficient environment of psychological safety must be created to support problem-solving and learning without loss of identity (Schein, 2004). For psychological safety to exist, while sustaining sufficient anxiety to motivate an individual to participate in the organizational change process, two conditions must be met: (1) "Survival anxiety . . . must be greater than learning anxiety" and (2) "Learning anxiety must be reduced, rather than increasing survival anxiety" (p. 331). To that end, specific conditions for psychological safety, such as presenting a compelling positive vision, involving the employee learner, and providing positive management role models, must be established in the Refreezing phase (Schein).

Key aspects of Schein's change process model are reflected in Kotter's implementation model. It can be argued that individual employee requirements, necessary for adaptation to occur, are addressed through the eight stages defined by Kotter (refer to Table 53.1). Organizational implementation must address the needs of the individual employees; additional research into follower behavior and antecedents to employee acceptance of change helps define the action steps necessary for effective implementation. Further, Schein's model, with its emphasis on arguably negative emotional states such as anxiety, guilt, and survival anxiety, presents a contextual framework that may subtly undermine change efforts. A more positive "world view" is instrumental in defining employee engagement strategies, which in turn provides the proper antecedents for employee receptiveness and adaptability to change in the organization.

TABLE 53.1 Comparison of Change Process and Implementation Models

William Bridges	Edgar Schein (Lewin)	John Kotter
Three stages: Ending. Losing, Letting Go Neutral Zone New Beginning (Bridges, 2003)	Three stages: Unfreezing/Disconfirmation Cognitive Restructuring Refreezing (Schein, 2004)	Eight Stages: • Establish Sense of Urgency • Form a Powerful Guiding Coalition • Create a Vision • Communicate the Vision • Empower Others to Act on the Vision • Plan for and Create Short-Term Wins • Consolidate Improvements and Produce More Change • Institutionalize New Approaches (Kotter, 2007)
Four rules for the New Beginning: • Be consistent • Ensure quick successes • Symbolize the new identity • Celebrate the success	Three sub-processes in Unfreezing: • Sufficient "disconfirming data" to create discomfort/imbalance • Data connected to important goals/ ideals, causing "anxiety and guilt" • Psychological safety exists in sufficient form to enable problem-solving and learning without loss of identity (p. 320)	Key conditions for success: • All stages are necessary (no shortcuts) • At least 75% of managers must believe "the status quo is more dangerous than the unknown" • Coalitions, in larger companies, need to be 20-50 people • Communication must be multi-channeled and continuous • Thousands of people must be willing to help with "short-term sacrifices" • Need to allow for broader job latitude • Need rewards/performance appraisal to match new vision • Managers must be positive, visible role models • Proactive explanations made showing connections between new approaches and improved performance
On Simultaneous Change: "The first thing . . . need[ed] in order to handle nonstop organizational change is an overall design . . . [where] . . . the various changes are integrated as component elements." (p. 101)	On Unfreezing: ". . . Some sense of threat, crisis, or dissatisfaction must be present before enough motivation is present to start the process of unlearning and relearning." (p. 324)	
When "no larger strategy exists" (for a rapidly developing change situation), the organization must proactively define the "underly-ing common purpose" (costs, new competitor, need for agility, etc.) (p. 101)	On Refreezing (conditions for transformative change): • "Survival anxiety or guilt must be greater than learning anxiety" • "Learning anxiety must be reduced rather than increasing survival anxiety" (p. 331)	On Urgency: "Well over 50% of companies... fail in this first phase... Executives underesti-mate how hard it can be to drive people out of their comfort zones. [Some] become paralyzed by the downside possibilities... [which] often comes from having too many managers and not enough leaders. Management's mandate is to minimize risk and to keep the current system operating. Change, by definition, requires creating a new system, which in turn always demands leadership" (p. 3).
Actions to deal with "non-stop" change include: • Make transition to "change as the norm" • Clarify purpose • Rebuild trust • Unload "old baggage" • Sell problems, not solutions (cannot sell each change "piecemeal") (p. 106)	Creating Psychological Safety includes 8 conditions, such as: • A compelling positive vision • Involvement of learner • Positive role models • Reward and discipline system consistent with new model (p. 332-333) Based model on work of Lewin, with modifications	

Change Implementation Model: Kotter

In the third model, Kotter defines eight stages in change adaptation and organizational transformation: "(1) establish a sense of urgency; (2) form a powerful guiding coalition; (3) create a vision; (4) communicate the vision; (5) empower others to act on the vision; (6) plan for and create short-term wins; (7) consolidate improvements and produce more change; (8) institutionalize new approaches" (Kotter, 2007, p. 4). He further provides broad action steps within each stage, based on his extensive primary research with more than 100 companies (2007). These action steps are delineated in Table 53.2.

Kotter identifies specific conditions essential for successful transformations. It is important to review the salient factors he identified, as the other later research results expand and inform Kotter's analysis. For example, in stage 1, "Create urgency," at least "75% of managers must believe the status quo is more dangerous than the unknown" (Kotter, 2007, p. 4). This observation links back to Schein's process theory: "there must be sufficient disconfirming data to create discomfort/imbalance" (2004, p. 320). Managers must also be positive, visible role models, offering proactive explanations to illustrate the connection between new approaches and improved organizational performance (stages 2 and 4) (Kotter, 2007). Attention should be paid to providing employees more latitude in their job tasks, encouraging risk-taking and innovative thinking (Kotter). The reward and performance appraisal systems must be realigned to directly support the vision and actions associated with the changes (stages 6 and 7) (Kotter).

Expanding and Refining Kotter's Action Steps

In analyzing Kotter's model from an organizational practitioner's perspective, the stages and action steps are clear, but broad. A business seeking to implement a strategic change initiative based on this original information could become frustrated with the gaps in explanation; the model is designed to provide a framework and starting points, rather than offer a step-by-step action plan. A meaningful consultation would need to incorporate further research and guidance based on those findings. To begin developing an updated and synthesized construct, it is beneficial to select studies offering cross-functional perspectives. Accordingly, the research review included two articles by corporate organizational development practitioners, three articles examining change management from the employee (follower) perspective, including one theoretical model, another two studies from the leader perspective, and finally, the presentation of a general theoretical model. The relevant findings are summarized in Table 53.2.

The research analysis yields information and insights that significantly enhance the original action steps and observations presented by Kotter. In Table 53.2, the relevant activities drawn from each research study are matched to the appropriate stage from Kotter's model. As some actions would be important in more than one stage, these specific findings are listed in *each* applicable element. To emphasize that the goal is the identification of detailed implementation steps, the matched findings are presented as directives (action items).

Current evaluations of successful change management determinants suggest there is a wealth of empirical support for the central eight-stage framework, and recommendations from individual studies provide contextual dimension and practical activities that an organizational development practitioner could use in creating a comprehensive strategic change management intervention. One area not addressed in Kotter's model or in the literature review was the factor of continuous or simultaneous change. To counter this potential limitation, Bridges' recommended actions for "dealing with non-stop change" (2003, p. 106) are incorporated into the enhanced implementation steps for stage 8 (refer to Table 53.2). Clearly, not all change interventions are at

TABLE 53.2   Implementation Steps, Drawn from Research, As Associated with Kotter's 8 Stages

Kotter's Eight Stages	Implementation Steps from Outside Research to Support Stages
(Kotter, 2007, p. 1 table, all)	(Brower et al., 2007, p. 67–80), (Cowley, 2007, p. 25–30), (Choi, 2006, p. 24–43), (Hoover, 2008, p. 37–44), (Leybourne, 2006, p. 73–95), (Parish et al., 2008, p. 32–52), (Soltani, 2005, p. 1009–21), (Van Dam et al., 2008, p. 313–334)
Establish a sense of Urgency Actions: • Analyze environment for potential crises and opportunities • Convince 75% of managers status quo is more dangerous than the unknown	• Communicate specifics regarding expected results, time tables, and employee change (Cowley) • Build understanding before commitment (Brower) • Break down, through language, old models—nullify information no longer relevant or functional (Brower) • Promote, through language, disengagement from outdated commitments (Brower) • Confront "brutal facts" (Brower quoting Collins, p. 70) • Establish intellectual and emotional actualization (Hoover)
Form a powerful guiding coalition Actions: • Assemble group with commitment and power to lead effort • Encourage them to work as team outside hierarchy	• Signal involvement (senior leaders), including change advocacy through informal channels and deployment of resources through formal processes (Cowley) • Build a "linked arm" coalition (senior leaders) (Cowley)
Create a vision Actions: • Create a vision that guides transformation • Develop strategies for turning vision to reality	• Motivate followers through empathy, envisioning, and empowerment, including establishment of high standards for performance and creative strategies for goals (Choi) • Emphasize what data is now relevant, affirm the mission, inspire energy towards that (Brower) • Establish intellectual and emotional actualization (Hoover)
Communicate the vision Actions: • Communication is multi-channeled and continuous • Coalition managers model the new behaviors/actions	• Communicate expected results in advance (Cowley) • Signal involvement (senior leaders), including change advocacy through informal channels and deployment of resources through formal processes (Cowley) • Establish behavioral and perceptual actualization (Hoover)
Empower others to act on the vision Actions: • Change or eliminate processes and factors impeding transformation • Encourage risk-taking, innovation, and action	• Signal involvement (senior leaders), including change advocacy through informal channels and deployment of resources through formal processes (Cowley) • Communicate specifics regarding expected results, time tables, and employee changes (Cowley) • Recognize followers may respond to charismatic leader because of sense of trust and self-efficacy (Choi) • Allow and officially sanction improvisation, which can provide new ways of completing tasks when resources are in limited supply (time, materials, staffing) (Leybourne)

(continued)

TABLE 53.2   Continued

Kotter's Eight Stages	Implementation Steps from Outside Research to Support Stages
	• Build high-quality leader-member exchange relationships through increased sharing of information, mutual trust, and encouragement of employee participation (change process quality). When there are high-quality LMX relationships, employees are receptive to change (Van Dam et al.)
Plan for and create short-term wins • Define and proactively promote visible improvement successes • Recognize and reward employees	• Ensure senior manager signals are communicated in order to create sustained employee accountability (commitment to see the projects/changes through) (Cowley) • Allow and sanction improvisations which can provide new ways of completing tasks when involved resources are in limited supply (time, materials, staffing) (Leybourne)
Consolidate improvements and produce more change • Build on credibility from early successes to advance more implementation plans (e.g., removing barriers, getting additional resources, etc.) • Promote/hire individuals who support and can enact the vision/ implementation plans • Energize the process with additional targets	• Establish and sustain key antecedents to affective commitment to change (employee engagement): positive employee-manager relationships, job motivation, and role autonomy (Parish) • Build and sustain positive leader-member exchange relationships through increased sharing of information, mutual trust, and encouraged employee participation (change process quality). (Van Dam et al.)
Institutionalize new approaches • Proactively explain connections between new approaches and transformation successes • Create succession plans that identify individuals who can carry the vision forward in the long-term	• Balance use between formal and informal channels necessary for sustainable accountability (Cowley) • Control management mobility to manifest benefits of organizational learning, ensure consistency in leader style and prioritization, and ensure manager accountability for long-term outcomes (Soltani) • Clarify purpose, unload "old baggage" (past frustrations with change processes), and sell problems, not solutions (Bridges)

the organizational level, and many change initiatives are taking place in concurrent time frames. A well-defined implementation plan must address this reality in many business environments.

While the linking of enhanced action steps with Kotter's stages offers practical value in change management implementation design (as reviewed in Table 53.2), it can be difficult to gain perspective on over-arching themes represented in the literature. In relation to the

organizational development professional's role, while the change process may move through progressive stages, the actual action steps must be managed in groups, with subprocesses addressed simultaneously. For example, leadership skills, behaviors, and actions are important in stage 1, but equally significant in the other seven stages. An organizational development professional would recommend projects that address leadership characteristics across all stages, developing training or coaching interventions that (a) improve language choice (Brower, 2007), (b) bring awareness to employee antecedents impacting receptiveness to change (Van Dam et al., 2008), and (c) provide practical action steps for communicating expected change results and measurements from the beginning (Cowley, 2007). Essential enhancements to the Kotter framework, as drawn from the research review, will thus be discussed through the lens of stakeholder groups. The three identified stakeholders are leadership (senior, middle, and front-line managers); employees (followers); and the organization (system).

Enhanced Action Steps: Leadership

An important insight for leadership (see Figure 53.1 for summary) is the acknowledgment managers have the most impact in generating change management success. From communicating the vision, modeling new behaviors, and signaling support for change, to rewarding employees for innovation and improvisation, to building employee engagement—managers carry the keys to unlock the benefits of transformational change. Organizational development professionals should devote considerable energy to the design of corporate-wide development tools and measures that proactively develop core change management competencies.

These skill sets and behaviors include:

1. Communicating specifics regarding expected change process results, including how performance will be measured, what resources will be committed, and projected employee changes (Cowley, 2007).
2. Using "building up" and "breaking down" language (Brower et al., 2007, p. 69) to

FIGURE 53.1   Recommended Enhanced Action Steps to Kotter Model, Grouped by Stakeholder

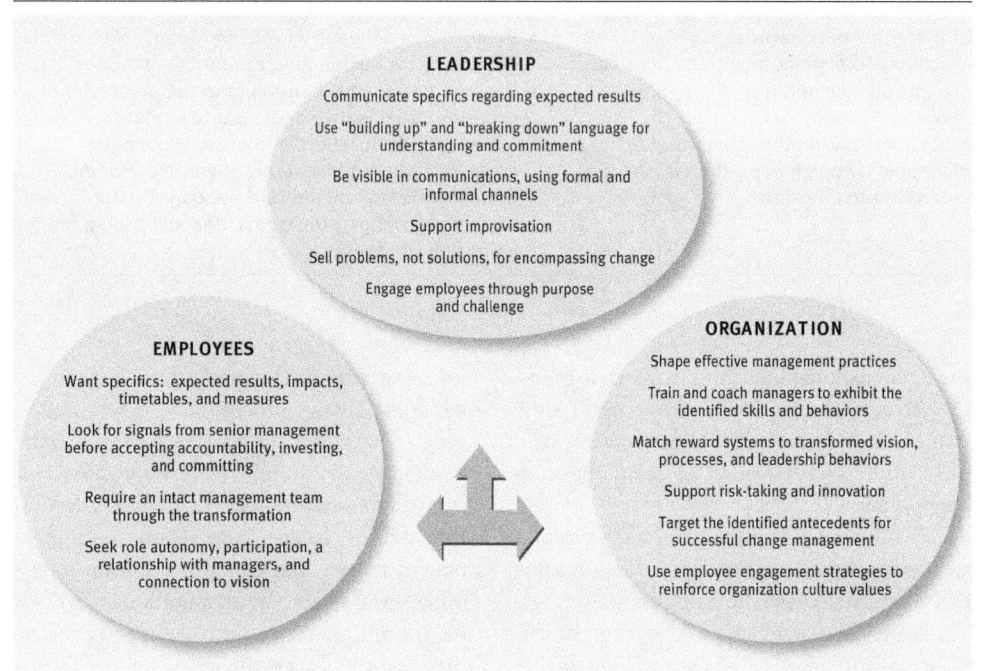

generate understanding and commitment, where establishing understanding is the first priority. *Breaking down* language means negating information no longer relevant or functional, then promoting disengagement from outdated commitments (Brower et al.). *Building up* language includes emphasizing information directly relevant to the new vision, then "affirm[ing] the [company's] mission and inspir[ing] commitment to it" (2007, p. 69).

3. Developing high-quality "leader member exchange relationships" (Van Dam et al., 2008, p. 315) to increase employee receptivity to change. High-quality relationships exist when the leader communicates relevant information frequently, follows through on actions to build trust, and empowers employees to participate in decisions, especially those relating to the change process (Van dam et al.).

4. Supporting innovation and improvisation. Improvisation can lead to positive results, where team responses are faster, processes are improved experientially during the change process, and employees feel empowered in the change implementation (Leybourne, 2006). Managers must signal support for creative approaches and sanction activities that do not necessarily fall within normal formal channels and processes (Leybourne).

Enhanced Action Steps: Employees

The proposed action steps for employees substantively mirror the action steps for leadership. Many of the leader recommendations were based on the evaluation of motivating followers. Charismatic leaders affect organizational outcomes through envisioning, empathy, and empowerment (Choi, 2006). They meet followers' needs for achievement, affiliation, and referential power through such actions as demonstrating innovative strategies to reach goals, setting high standards for employ-

ee and organizational performance, establishing trust and emotional bonds, and modeling behaviors others wish to imitate (Choi). Cowley's research at Eli Lilly supports Choi's components, indicating employees look to senior management for signals the change process is accepted. These signals include visible support for the initiative, action in coordination with a senior management coalition, and the use of informal and formal organization channels to initiate the allocation of resources for the change initiative (Cowley, 2007). When employees register these signals, they will commit to the process and take accountability (assuming the envisioning, empathy, and empowerment activities have been successful).

These recommendations are all linked to employee engagement. Employee engagement is the level of employee commitment to the work and to the organization, which is linked to motivation, satisfaction, and direction of energy. One specific employee engagement model, Gallup Q12, identifies twelve elements, or questions, that identify and measure levels of employee engagement (actively engaged, somewhat engaged, actively disengaged) (Asplund, 2007). Organizations pursuing change implementation success can take action to increase organizational levels of employee engagement, using the Gallup Q12 action process or another design. Many of the factors identified in Kotter's model and through the research review, collectively viewed as antecedents to effective change management for leadership and employees, can be positively influenced through proactive employee engagement design and implementation.

Enhanced Action Steps: Organization

At the organization level, the analysis leads to summary conclusions used to develop company-wide interventions. The organizational development professional, in examining the action steps related to Leadership and Employee stakeholder groups, can build a comprehensive list of targets for organizational development; these goals, if successfully achieved, set up the company for success in many change implementation processes, not simply for a specific strategic change initiative. This point is significant when considering the current business environment, where change processes are occurring continuously and simultaneously.

The systemic intervention goals on the organizational development professional's agenda might include: (1) Employee engagement program with corresponding management action planning; (2) Re-tooled reward and recognition programs matching change management priorities, expected goals, and associated measures: and (3) Management training and coaching targeting communication messages, communication language, high-quality leader-member exchange relationships, job design and worker autonomy, appropriate application of new reward/recognition systems, and team activities designed to promote innovation and improvisation.

It is important for organizations to recognize that managers across the organization are at different levels of development. Successful change management, particularly in continuous changing organizations, hinges on systemic improvements in management and leadership execution. Since some change initiatives are taking place at business unit or departmental levels, it is difficult to target management skills and behavior on a "case by case" basis—this strategy is inefficient and generally ineffective. Concerted management development programs, focused on key change implementation skill sets, will help ensure that change efforts are successful and organizational performance in projects unrelated to change will also be enhanced.

Conclusion

Dynamic business conditions lead to rapid corporate change on several levels. Typically, organizations have trained managers in change pro-

cess models rather than change implementation frameworks. Given the track record for failed change interventions, there is an opportunity for organizational development professionals to provide effective guidance through the application of a comprehensive change implementation model, Kotter's eight-stage process. Recent research supports Kotter's design and provides insights into more detailed action steps that can ensure appropriate and relevant application of the outlined process. Organizational development professionals can use this information to design concurrent development interventions for leadership, employee, and organization (system) stakeholders. A proactive approach to change management can potentially improve implementation and increase the percentage of successful change initiatives—saving organizations money, sustaining employee engagement and retention, and ensuring business competitive advantage.

References

Asplund, J., Fleming, J., & Harter, J. (2007). Return on investment in engaging employees. *The Gallup Management Journal Online*, pp. 1–2. Retrieved from http://gmj.gallup.com.

Bridges, W. (2003). *Managing Transitions* (2nd Ed.). Cambridge, MA, Perseus Books.

Brower, H., Fiol, C.M., & Emrich, C. (2007). The language of leaders. *Journal of Leadership Studies,* 1(3), 67–80.

Choi, J. (2006). A motivational theory of charismatic leadership: Envisioning, empathy, and empowerment. *Journal of Leadership and Organizational Studies,* 13(1), 24–43.

Cowley, B. (2007). Why change succeeds: An organization self-assessment. *Organization Development Journal,* 25(1), 25–30.

Hoover, J.D. (2008). Cognitive mapping and diagnostic aspects of organizational change. *Organization Development Journal,* 26(1), 37–44.

Kotter, J. (2007). Leading change: Why transformation efforts fail. *Harvard Business Review,* 1-10. Retrieved from http://www.hbr.org.

Leybourne, S. (2006). Managing improvisation within change management: Lessons from UK financial services. *The Services Industries Journal,* 26(1), 73–95.

Parish, J., Cadwallader, S., & Busch, P. (2008). Want to, need to, ought to: Employee commitment to organizational change. *Journal of Organizational Change Management,* 21(1), 32–52.

Schein, E. (2004). *Organizational culture and leadership* (3rd Ed.). San Francisco, CA, Jossey-Bass.

Soltani, E., Lai, P., & Gharneh, N.S. (2005). Breaking through barriers to TQM effectiveness: Lack of commitment of upper-level management. *Total Quality Management,* 16(8-9), 1009–1021.

Van Dam, K., & Oreg, S. (2008). Daily work contexts and resistance to organisational change: The role of leader–member exchange, development climate, and change process. *Applied Psychology: An International Review,* 57(2), 313–334.

Yacovone, L. (2007). Organizational design for a supply chain transformation: Best practice at Johnson and Johnson Health Care Systems, Inc. *Organization Development Journal,* 25(3), 103–109.

CHAPTER 54

Change from the Employees' Perspective

The Neglected Viewpoint

Michael H. Vinitsky and Adam S. Kling

IMAGINE THAT YOU, an organization development practitioner, are having a conversation with an employee of an organization whose CEO has just communicated the roll out of a new performance management system. The components of the system include goal setting, ongoing performance feedback, and coaching. During the presentation, the CEO described how the new system would help increase employee motivation, competence, and productivity—all of which are needed to support the company's growth strategy of new product development and movement into vertical markets. As a first step, he asked employees to meet with their supervisors to discuss and agree on performance goals within the next month. This would enable the system to be in place for the beginning of the next fiscal year. At the end of the communication, the CEO asked everyone to support this new system, so it will be more effective than the two year old system it is replacing, and said he is counting on everyone to do their part.

When you question the employee about his thoughts on the new system, he mentions being faced with deciding whether or not he will do what has been asked of him. At first glance, this appears to be a relatively straightforward decision to make. Will he discuss and agree on his goals with his supervisor? Will he

support the new system? He also tells you that the more he thinks about it, the more he finds himself asking several questions. They include:

- Is there really a need for us to change to ensure the success of the company's growth strategy?
- Is another new performance management system an appropriate way to support the company's growth strategy?
- Do I believe the new performance management system will be implemented successfully, so it achieves its intended results?
- Do I trust the people who are sponsoring and leading the implementation of this new system?
- Do I know exactly what I am being asked to do to contribute to the success of the new system?
- Do I have the knowledge and skills necessary for me to succeed?
- Is it worthwhile for me to do what I am being asked to do?
- Do my coworkers support this new system?

Why are the answers to these questions so important? They are important because they will influence and affect an employee's readiness for change. Readiness to change is a state of mind reflecting a willingness or receptiveness to changing the way one thinks. It is a cognitive state comprising the beliefs, attitudes and intentions toward a change effort (Armenakis & Bedian, 1999). "Yes" answers to these questions indicate that an employee will more likely be willing and able to start, stop, increase, decrease and continue specific behaviors that will be needed in the future to support the success of the new system and the desired business results. Uncertain answers such as "maybe", "I don't know" or negative responses, indicate that an employee will be less likely to make the needed behavioral changes for the initiative to succeed.

Upon further reflection, the employee realizes that his answers to these questions will change over the course of the implementation process (Kling, 2004; Vinitsky & Ayars, 2000). Subsequent communication and conversations may lead to changes in his conclusions about the initiative. Depending on what he sees or hears, or the results produced at critical milestones, answers to the questions may vary. Thus, the amount of energy and effort he puts forward to continue the new behaviors are likely to fluctuate in a way that has an impact on the success of the new system.

The Eight Questions of Change

This article first describes the factors that influence employees' readiness to change, and then explores how internal or external consultants can influence change readiness to contribute to the success of a change initiative. Organizational change researchers (Armenakis & Harris, 2002; Cummings & Worley, 2004) suggest several key components to create readiness for change. They include discrepancy, appropriateness, trust, self-efficacy, and personal valence. These components are typically described from the change agent's perspective. We have taken these five components, added three more (probability of success, change awareness, and coworker support), based upon our experience with many organizational change initiatives, and discuss them from the change target or employees' perspec-

tive. We focus on how employees' answers to questions related to these components influence their readiness for change.

Discrepancy — Is There Really a Need for Change?

Creating a sense of urgency, or readiness to change involves attempting to influence beliefs, attitudes and behavior, by sensitizing people in the organization to internal and external pressures for change, revealing discrepancies between current and future states, and communicating positive expectations for change (Cummings & Worley, 2004).

This information creates a gap between a current state of affairs and some desired future state and energizes people. This energy can be used defensively to deny or explain away the gap or can be used productively for the change.

This gap can be viewed as either a problem or opportunity. A *problem* exists when the current level of performance is not acceptable and must be improved in the future. This requires a sense of urgency on the part of employees. An *opportunity* exists when the current level of performance is acceptable, but someone believes people could or should do something different to improve their performance. This creates a sense of positive energy and enthusiasm. Asking employees to identify what is working in their organization, then encouraging them to do more of what works can create energy and a desire to enhance their performance. Without a sense of urgency and/or positive energy and enthusiasm, employees will maintain the status quo, because they do not perceive a reason to change their current behavior. How employees view the change (i.e., problem or opportunity) will influence how they react when change leaders are creating a sense of urgency. For example, if employees in the company mentioned above do not believe they need to make any changes to ensure the success of the new growth strategy, then employees will put little or no energy towards the new performance management system.

Appropriateness — Will This Solution Solve the Problem?

Employees will evaluate a solution (i.e., change) to determine how appropriate it is for achieving the desired results. They may agree, disagree or be unsure if the project sponsor and change leaders have selected the right course of action. Armenakis and Bedian's model suggests that creating a vision for a change initiative is a way of communicating the appropriateness for reducing the discrepancy. Continuing with the performance management example, employees may or may not view the new system as an appropriate way to increase motivation, competence, and productivity to support the success of the new business strategy. If it is viewed as an appropriate solution, employees will be more likely to support it than if they are unsure, don't understand, or don't agree with the rationale for the system.

Probability of Success — Will the Change Be Implemented Successfully?

People continually estimate the probability of success of the change initiative. Based on a number of factors, including experience with past change initiatives and personal characteristics such as optimism and pessimism, people will predict the probability of success. Employees will make an initial prediction as well as several subsequent ones throughout the duration of a change initiative. Peoples' estimation of the probability of success may increase, remain constant, or decrease based on signs of progress at any of several milestones along the way (Vinitsky & Ayars, 2000). If a critical milestone is missed (e.g., an employee's manager does not follow through and schedule a goal setting conversation according to the announced timeline), a once optimistic supporter of the initiative may change her view to reflect a lower estimated probability of success. That may lead to putting forth less energy and effort to make the initiative a success.

People will not support a change initiative unless they see compelling evidence within 6–18 months that the change program is producing expected results.

Experience with failed change initiatives may negatively affect what employees pay attention to when change leaders communicate about the current initiative. Instead of listening for how this initiative could be a success, people may have already decided the current initiative will not work. This conclusion will lead them to minimize, ignore, or tune out the possibility of success for the initiative. They may look for flaws and what might go wrong, not for constructive purposes, but rather to prove they are right. Experiences with past initiatives may lead to skepticism rather than cynicism. Instead of attempting to prove this initiative won't work, the skeptic listens for examples and experience that may lead to learning from past failures. In this case, past experience can be used to support the initiative and increase the estimated probability of success. Listening "for" the success of an initiative is quite different from listening "to" another person talk and looking for reasons "why this one won't work."

Trust — Do I Trust the Leaders Who Are Supporting This Change?

During times of change and uncertainty, employees look to formal and informal leaders to help them decide how to react. If they conclude that organizational leaders believe in the change and trust within the organization is high, then the change will be responded to in a positive light (Rousseau & Tijoriwala, 1999).

Organization trust is comprised of supervisory trust and trust in management. Supervisory trust refers to the relationship one has with one's own supervisor, while trust in management focuses on upper management. Supervisory trust depends on a combination of ability, benevolence, and integrity. Ability refers to the skills and competencies of the supervisor. Benevolence is the extent to which an employee perceives the supervisor to have his or her best interests at heart. Integrity is the perception that the supervisor lives by a set of principles that the employee accepts. When supervisory trust is high, people are more likely to accept direction and respond to requests (Tyler & Degoey, 1996). Trust in management depends upon employees' perceptions of organizational policies and procedures (Tan & Tan, 2000).

When employees perceive that organization policies and procedures are fair, and that upper management behaves in a consistent and ethical way, they are more likely to accept the reasons and legitimacy for change (Rousseau & Tijoriwala, 1999). For example, if employees believe there is a hidden agenda motivating the replacement of the two year old performance management system, then their trust will be diminished and they will be less likely to accept the reasons for change.

Change Awareness— Do I Know What I Am Supposed to Do Differently?

People are often not clear about what they are being asked or told to do to support a change initiative. At the conclusion of a change communication meeting you may hear people asking "What is he or she asking me to do?" or "Am I supposed to be doing something different?" A call to action may be quite general and vague or not exist at all. Or it may provide direction without a timeline for completion. Without a firm directive or request to take action by a specific time, people will have difficulty in gauging how best to respond.

Ford and Ford (1995) proposed that there are four different types of committed conversations that can be used in the effective implementation of change. These are initiative, understanding, performance, and closure conversations. An initiative conversation is the call or proposal that creates an opening for change. Conversations for understanding help employees comprehend what's behind the initiative conversation and determine what will or could change.

These conversations produce two important by-products. The first is the measures and observable conditions for the change to be declared successful. The second by-product is some degree of involvement, participation, and support on the part of those engaged in the change. Conversations for performance include a combination of requests and promises spoken to produce a specific action or result. These are intended to make things happen by having people begin to take action towards the desired future. By increasing the frequency of conversations for performance, the velocity with which changes are implemented can be increased. Finally, conversations for closure serve to bring about an end to an event or happening. Closure allows the past to remain in the past and allows for new possibilities to be created for the future.

A combination of conversations for understanding and performance will focus employees' attention and energy on the specific behaviors needed to make a change initiative successful. In the example above, the CEO asked employees to meet with their supervisors to discuss and set goals within the next month. This directive provides employees with information about next steps. Additional communications and directions will need to be provided in the near future so employees can respond to the CEO's request to support the new system.

Self-Efficacy—Do I Have The Knowledge and Skills Necessary for Me to Succeed?

Self-efficacy is defined as an individual's judgment of his or her ability to perform certain tasks. Collective efficacy is a group's judgment of its ability to perform. Both individual and group efficacy have been shown to relate to the amount of effort and persistence people are willing to put forth to reach specific outcomes (Bandura, 1982).

During stressful times, such as organizational change, people with low self-efficacy will judge themselves as incapable of coping with environmental demands, and will tend to dwell on personal deficiencies and magnify the severity and difficulty of the task at hand (Beck, 1976). Self-doubt and worry elevate arousal, which in turn creates stress and impairs performance by creating a focus on lack of effectiveness (Bandura, 1982).

During times of change, focus is diverted away from how to be successful and doubt may consume the person. In contrast, high self-efficacy individuals will focus attention to the demands of the situation and increase the effort to succeed. In the performance management example, offering skill development workshops on goal setting, providing effective feedback and coaching could build the confidence and competence of employees so they have the skills needed to make the new system a success.

Personal Valence— Is It Worthwhile for Me to Change? (WIFM)

Personal valence is the process where employees evaluate the significance of the proposed change for their own wellbeing (Armenakis & Harris, 2002). They may consider the tangible and intangible gains and losses for themselves. If consequences of the change are believed to be negative, employees will likely be unreceptive to the change. If the change is viewed as potentially positive, employees will be more receptive and willing to embrace the initiative. Employees will increase their commitment to the change effort when they conclude that the change will benefit them (Kling, 2004).

When employees see these benefits, they will seek out ways to make the change a success. For example, supervisors could increase employees' receptivity to the new performance system by discussing benefits specific to each person during their goal setting conversation.

Coworker Support—Do My Coworkers Support the Change?

The network of conversations among people at work will influence an initial decision about

change and how much energy and effort is put forth to maintain the change over the long run. When coworkers, who are trusted and respected, are supportive of the initiative, they reflect that in their conversations with others. When they are indifferent or against the initiative, that too is conveyed by what and how they speak about it. A network of positive conversations will focus people's attention and energy on moving forward to achieve the desired outcome. A network of negative conversations, filled with skepticism and cynicism, can prevent action needed for forward movement and success.

Over time, it may be difficult for people to resist being enrolled into either the positive or negative conversations about the initiative. Producing and managing change involves shifting a network of conversations by intentionally bringing into existence new (i.e., pro-change) conversations while completing and removing current (status-quo) conversations (Ford, 1995). For example, if all members of a work team speak positively with one another about the value of their goal setting conversation and the personal benefits of the new performance system they will have started a network of conversations to enable its success.

Building a Network of Conversations for the Initiative

As an internal or external consultant, you are aware of the questions people who are faced with change are asking. You can make a valuable contribution to the success of a change initiative. You can take an active role in building and sustaining a network of conversations in the organization, and create positive attitudes and beliefs about the change effort.

What can you do with people who are asked to change?

1. Make them aware of the eight change-related questions.
   - Share your knowledge of the types of issues and concerns people being asked to

change are dealing with and how the eight questions are relevant to those issues and concerns.

2. Ask them to reflect on their current answers to these questions.
   - Suggest they share their answers to the eight questions for the current initiative with you. Then, ask them what their answers are based on, and if they are willing to talk with selected others to gain additional information.
3. Help them identify sponsors and leaders of the change initiative with whom they could talk to gain information needed to answer "yes" to the questions.

What can you do with the change leaders?

1. Make them aware of the eight change-related questions.
   - Share your knowledge of the critical role of people's attitudes and beliefs toward the change initiative for its success, and how answers to the eight questions reflect those attitudes and beliefs.
2. Ask them to identify several people in the organization who are key to the initiative's success.
   - Suggest that they include both key stakeholders and informal opinion leaders at different levels and areas of the organization.
3. Encourage change leaders to initiate conversations with these people to assess their answers to the eight questions.
4. Then, based on the answers, focus the conversation on what is needed to increase the number of "yes" answers.

Building the ripple effect

1. Ask people in both of the above groups to encourage the people they talk with to have similar conversations with several others in the organization.
2. Ask them to assess their answers and then provide information. Or, suggest who they can talk with to obtain what is needed to answer "yes" to these questions.
3. Make people aware of the impact their conversations have on the overall success of the change effort.
   - Let them know their conversations, positive and negative, can have the effect of enrolling others into attitudes and beliefs that will support or prevent successful change.

Coaching others to create effective change conversations

A coaching session would include the following five components:

1. Setting the stage and clarifying the purpose of the conversation.
   - Recognizing or creating an opening to have a conversation about the person's attitudes and beliefs about the change initiative.
2. Active listening and asking open-ended questions to encourage reflection, inquiry and shared understanding.
   - These will help surface a person's answers to the eight change-related questions.
3. Generating alternative courses of action that would lead to different answers to the change-related questions.
   - These might include identifying whom to talk with, nature of the information needed and what the person would need to see, hear, or the results that would lead the person to modify answers to the questions.
4. Making requests that lead to action and results—how to gain agreement on who will do what, by when.
5. Assessing the effectiveness of the conversation.
   - Summarizing the impact of the conversation on the person's attitudes and beliefs about the change initiative.

Conclusion

Because your goal is to build and sustain a network of conversations across the organization to support the initiative, you will have an ongoing role throughout the initiative. You will need to encourage people to conduct conversations about the eight questions in both the planning and implementation phases of the initiative. Conversations in the planning phase will contribute to a successful launch. Conversations during the implementation phase will be needed to sustain or regain sufficient energy, focus, and action. You will find opportunities for change-related conversations every day. They include project, staff, and regularly scheduled communication meetings. And, don't forget hallway conversations, those candid comments and opinions before and after formal meetings when employees share their "true" feelings. Your ongoing efforts to help build and sustain a network of positive conversations about the change initiative will go a long way toward creating the conditions for success.

References

Armenakis, A. A., & Bedian, A. G. (1999). Organizational change: A review of theory and research in the 1990s. *Journal of Management,* 25(3), 293–315.

Armenakis, A. A., & Harris, S. G. (2002). Crafting a change message to create transformational readiness. *Journal of Organizational Change,* 15(2), 169–183.

Bandura, A. (1982). Self-efficacy mechanism in human agency. *American Psychologist,* 37, 122–147.

Beck, A. T. (1976). *Cognitive therapy and the emotional disorders.* New York: International Universities Press.

Cummings, T. G., & Worley, C. G. (2004). *Organization development and change* (8th ed.). Cincinnati, OH: South-Western College Publishing.

Ford, J. D., & Ford, L. W. (1995). The role of conversations in producing intentional change. *The Academy of Management Review,* 20, 541–70.

Kling, A. (2004). Commitment to organizational change: Assessing the effects of identifying benefits to change and its relationship with organizational trust. Unpublished doctoral dissertation, Alliant International University–Los Angeles.

Rousseau, D. M., & Tijoriwala, S. A. (1999). What's a good reason to change? Motivated reasoning and social accounts in promoting organizational change. *Journal of Applied Psychology,* 84(4), 514–528.

Tan, H. H., & Tan, C. S. F. (2000). Toward the differentiation of trust in supervisor and trust in organization. *Genetic, Social, and General Psychology Monographs,* 126(2), 241–260.

Tyler, T. R., & Degoey, P. (1996). Trust in organizational authorities: The influence of motive attributions on willingness to accept decisions. In R. Kramer & T. Tyler (Eds.), *Trust in organizations. Frontiers in theory and research* (pp. 331–356). Thousand Oaks, CA: Sage.

Vinitsky, M. H., & Ayars, P. J. (2000). *Mastering momentum: A practical and powerful approach for successful change.* Toronto, ON: Momentum Organization Consultants.

CHAPTER 55

Resistance in Organizations

How to Recognize, Understand, and Respond to It

Barry Dym

CHANGE AND RESISTANCE go together, hand in glove. Each is natural, pervasive, and universal. Resistance is neither avoidable nor bad. It is a fact of organizational life. As such, it must be managed, not avoided.

Resistance is feedback and feedback is information. Poorly managed resistance, like poorly managed information about productivity and markets, can be costly. Well-managed resistance permits you to execute projects and implement change efforts with a minimum of difficulty. We have all heard the old "saw": "If only my employees would follow my instructions, management would not be so difficult." Of course, developing effective partnerships with employees is the work of management. So it is with feedback. Managing the feedback contained in resistance is critical to effective work partnerships.

Like all living systems, organizations thrive when they balance the need for stability and change. To manage it effectively, resistance must be understood as a system's effort to regain the equilibrium that has been disrupted by change. From this perspective, resistance is feedback about those disruptions and the troubles they create for people. Thus, if you look carefully enough, you'll see that the feedback derived from resistance points out how the relationships required to implement change are poorly aligned with each other, and with the goals of your change project.

Managing resistance means using the information it provides to realign relationships in the service of achieving goals. The purpose of this paper is to teach leaders and managers how to understand, recognize, diffuse, and manage resistance through the formation of partnerships working towards common goals.

The Many Faces of Resistant Relationships

Try to fundamentally change a person or an organization and you encounter resistance. "It can't be done," people say. Or "It shouldn't be done." Alternatively, they agree to the desirability and feasibility of changing, and then fail to do so, perhaps growing inexplicably lethargic, incompetent, or busy. Resistance does not always surface immediately. At first, projects may roll along exactly as planned, but, sooner or later, no matter how careful the plan, threats to established ways of thinking and behaving, or to the structures and groups to which people belong, call forth resistance and obstruct the straight paths of progress.

Resistance wears many, many faces. They include outright refusal, denial, skepticism, lethargy, incompetence, pessimism, and helplessness. At times, people resist by questioning the competence, credentials, or motives of their leaders, or by behind the scenes lobbying. At others, they become secretive, entering a bunker-like mode until the siege of change passes.

We can divide these many forms into four main types. Some forms are direct and intentional, as when a worker says, "I won't do it that way because . . . ," and provides a cogent reason for the refusal. Some faces are direct and unconscious, as when workers oppose a change even though they are unsure of their own motives. Still others are indirect and conscious. This is true about manipulation and back room lobbying, while slowing down on the job. Finally, resistance may be both indirect and unconscious. Here I'm thinking about the genuine lethargy, incompetence, and pessimism that overtake some of us when we don't believe in what we're doing but can't explain why.

Resistance as Feedback

Let's examine some of the faces of resistance to see how they provide feedback about the alignment of working relationships.

1. Denial

Denial may be the most common and the most frustrating form of resistance. Presented with the need to change, colleagues and employees say, in effect, there is no problem, or there is no problem serious enough to get exercised about. Worse, still, they mock, as inexperienced, reactive, unskilled, or moved by hidden motive, those who push for change.

It is hard to read the meaning of denial. People deny problems when they actually don't see them and when they do but are afraid to tackle problems. People deny problems posed by others for many reasons. These include: competitive feelings, discomfort with the authority of others, and loyalty to a third party who doesn't want the problem-poser to succeed. Denial tends to be a passive form of

resistance, whose precise meaning often remains hidden from both sides.

When denial is met with denial, when, for instance, a manager claims is wrong or stupid for an employee to deny the need for change, this tends to amplify the problem, setting managers and employees or colleagues against each other in a struggle over phantoms. By the time this kind of struggle transpires a few times, it begins to take on a chronic quality in which virtually any proposal for change meets resistance.

2. Lack of Motivation

If not denial, then a lack of motivation is the most common form of resistance. Instead of directly opposing change, people don't work hard on its behalf. The subsequent failure of the project confirms their belief that the program never should have been started in the first place.

Why, managers ask, do people lack motivation? Do they not see the value in successfully completing a project? Perhaps they feel underpaid or undervalued. Perhaps there is no career path that rewards hard work. Do they not like or trust their managers? There are, in fact, innumerable reasons why workers are not motivated. When many lack motivation, not just one individual, however, it is unreasonable to characterize them as lazy, stupid or obstinate.

The problematic relationship highlighted by an unmotivated work force may not be with a particular manager or colleague. Rather, the problem may be with upper management or with unexamined company policy. The problem may be caused by a union. Often enough, workers, wanting to respond to challenges or to improve their lot, are discouraged by unions —or placed in a dispiriting double bind by the conflicting demands and values of management and unions. The main point, then, is that comprehending the meaning presented by unmotivated people may be difficult to come by, but nonetheless understanding it is the starting point for infusing motivation back into individual colleagues or whole work forces.

3. Incompetence

Incompetence comes from and creates similar troublesome patterns. When people fear or resist change, they often do so indirectly and largely unconsciously by not working up to even their own standards. Incompetence may be intentional—an indirect form of anger and opposition. More often, it derives from anxiety about the nature of work: will it lead in dangerous directions like pay cuts and layoffs? Will I be seen as incompetent if I try something new? This kind of anxiety interferes with one's capacity to learn and to operate smoothly. Perfectly intelligent people, for example, freeze, when presented with unfamiliar tasks and new learning assignments.

4. Skepticism

People are often, reasonably, skeptical about the value or direction of change projects—could layoffs, for instance, be in the wind?—and about the ability of both leaders and colleagues to bring them off, Then, too, managers are often skeptical about employee reservations, assuming petty self-interest, ignorance, or fear of trying something new. Sometimes managers are skeptical about projects, don't confront their superiors, and project their own skepticism onto the team they manage, That is, they deny their own skepticism but see it in others. Often skepticism concerns the attitude or the inadequate resources that the larger organization brings to a change process but is directed at the nearest representative of the organization— their manager or their close colleagues.

The point I am making is that skepticism is no single thing and certainly not a quality that exists only within employees who resist. It is generally embedded in organizational relationships. Take, for example, a history of union-management conflict and mistrust, or the reaction to the too-frequent introduction of the latest and greatest management ideas.

Managers are also skeptical about projects to which they are assigned and this, too, creates problems. When reluctant to implement a program or change one's way of working, managers may attribute their reluctance to others. Managers, for instance, convince themselves that they would introduce the new program they dislike, except that their employees would resist. Sometimes these types of attributions— called "projections" in psychology—are conscious and manipulative. Sometimes they are unconscious. They almost invariably lead to an oppositional relationship.

A habit of skepticism may build up between individuals and between managers and their teams. Team skepticism breeds skepticism in managers and their ability to get the job done; managerial skepticism about the skills and attitudes of employees almost invariably brings out the worst in them, thus producing a self-fulfilling prophesy. After a while, these attitudes may grow habitual. A rigid reciprocity develops. Skepticism in one immediately brings out skepticism in the other.

Skepticism often begins a familiar, escalating sequence of behaviors between colleagues and between managers and employees. Here is how it goes. Employee skepticism is met with explanation and encouragement. This exchange may take place several times, with growing discouragement and disbelief. With time, management explanation yields to argument, then diatribes and, eventually, to threats—generally in response to increasingly indirect forms of employee opposition. Alternatively, the escalating sequence emerges into open conflict.

5. Questioning the Competence, Credentials, Skills, or Motivation of the Change Leaders

This is a particular and common form of skepticism, directed at leaders. Those who resist say, for example, that their leader is "wet behind the ears," that she has never run a company this big, this complex, and this technical. Consultants leading change projects are dismissed for their ignorance of a particular business, for their lack of commitment, and for their greed. They are carpetbaggers who do not care.

In fact, most of these challenges have at least a partial basis in truth; and, within themselves, most managers and consultants share these same anxieties. If they are too nervous and ashamed to admit their own fears and limitations, these managers may respond defensively or angrily. It is not uncommon, for example, to punish or banish vocal challengers: In the name of maturity, managers may simply dismiss the challenge, all the while guarding their uncomfortable secret agreement.

The troubled relationship that builds around this form of resistance tends to go underground and to be expressed indirectly. Challenge and response may begin openly on both sides, but employees fear retribution and managers fear discovery. As a result, effective collaboration built on candid conversation disappears.

6. Pessimism

Pessimism may represent an ingrained and extreme form of skepticism. It is directed towards at least three targets: self, projects, and organizations. The upshot of each is a depressed attitude and decreased productivity.

To counteract pessimism, managers frequently find themselves explaining the importance of a project until they are blue in the face. Then they might try reassurance and motivational speeches. When these tactics fail to motivate employees—and when the manager's own deadlines are threatened—they may try to bully. If they have the power, they may fire whoever cannot get with the program. In general, "complementary" relationships—those that polarize the way two parties respond to each other—tend to build up around pessimism.

To state the obvious, collective employee pessimism is neither character—alogical nor biochemical in its origin. It grows up around organizational failures, frequent worker layoffs,

stagnant wages, constant criticism, or management pessimism that is, in response to legitimate problems. By treating the symptoms—some people's pessimism—instead of problems in the broader system, we help to create a frustrating and futile battle with no winners.

7. Impatience With the Change

As change proceeds, it is often undermined by people's impatience. They say that a project has taken too long or it should have worked already; and the absence of rapid success is said to indicate that the change is not a good one. Then the impatient people fight the change.

This is one side of the problem. Often those driving change do not provide clear timelines, perhaps because they cannot. Spurred by unrealistic hopes of their own or pressure from superiors, they pressure co-workers and employees, who, at first, believe in the schedule, then grow impatient. Change leaders may, themselves, grow impatient with the pace of change and fear that projects will not come to fruition; but, for fear of disheartening others, they keep their impatience to themselves. Then, when others complain, they may continue to say nothing. What could be a mutual expression of anxious impatience, instead, becomes a struggle between colleagues or, more frequently, between managers and employees.

This kind of struggle also grows chronic. With each new project, employees tend to express their impatience quicker. Managers reassure less and are quicker to express their frustration with their impatient workers. It is this chronicity that demonstrates so dramatically how resistance is a relationship problem.

Causes of Resistance

In the previous section, we learned to see resistance as feedback on misfiring relationships. This section will describe some of the causes of resistance. Understanding the cause is essential to building strategies to respond effectively, that is to repair the relationships that show themselves as resistance.

1. Preserving What Is Presently Valued

Resistance frequently represents an effort to preserve those values, traditions, techniques, and organizational structures that those who resist deem valuable and preferable to the new ideas, methods, and programs that are being introduced. Without addressing these potential losses, resistance is likely to persist. Respect for what is being lost or preservation of some aspects of a stable environment while changing others tends to mollify this kind of resistance. If, for example, there were a way to introduce a new work method while preserving certain traditional ways of approaching the work situation, one might reduce resistance.

2. Feeling Out of Control

In their natural state, systems maintain an equilibrium between change and stability. To survive, they adapt to changes in their internal and external environments. For example, organizations adapt to new personnel and new technologies, to changing market conditions, government regulations, and labor supply. Even as they change, however, systems must retain their essential character. In this effort, resistance is stability's trusted lieutenant.

Periods of stability and change oscillate throughout the life of organizations. At times, the capacity for change will have to overcome the lethargy and opposition that builds during stable times. The adaptability represented by an initial change, however, can be followed by a period that seems out of control. When feeling out of control, people dig in their heels and resist change. At such times, organizations must try to slow the change process so people will feel secure enough to adapt. Too rapid change can distort an organization's normal ways of doing business and push it outside its core competencies. Well-paced change provides people the opportunity to perform well, and this diffuses resistance.

3. Threats to Dignity, Respect, and Autonomy

At times, resistance represents an effort to maintain the dignity and autonomy of those who resist. People, for example, often experience the demand to change as a statement that they are not good enough as they are, and resist being judged, misunderstood and pushed around. People have ideas of their own when it comes to improving organizations and implementing projects. Sometimes they experience the introduction of other people's ideas as an imposition, and experience the imposition as disrespectful or coercive. Often people feel they are doing the best they can "under the circumstances," that their capacity to improve has been constrained, and believe that the circumstances (the organizational structure; managerial attitudes or lack of skill; the compensation system], not them, should be changed. And, often enough, those who resist change are at least partially correct.

Current management theory emphasizes empowering workers, spreading decision-making, and gaining "buy in" for projects before acting on them. All of these are excellent strategies to head off resistance before it gets started. But resistance often grows even with the best initial planning. When it does, it is important to return to these basic themes of dignity, respect, and autonomy, asking how people feel these vital aspects of their identity have been violated.

4. Genuine Misunderstandings

Misunderstandings often stimulate what looks like resistance, and failures to correct misunderstandings compound the problem. A manager, for instance, proposes a particular approach to product development. Believing they are following the managers instructions, his design team proceeds in a somewhat different manner. Observing this, the manager can interpret the divergence in many ways: as a misunderstanding, as non compliance, as defiance, as ineptitude. If he proceeds on any but the first, he will compound the difficulty. If, for instance, he assumes non compliance and berates the team, he is likely to encourage a control struggle. If he treats the misunderstanding as defiance, he might fire or relocate team members, building resentment that will later show itself as resistance. If he treats the misunderstanding as ineptitude and lowers his expectations for the team, he may create a self-fulfilling prophesy and contribute to the team's poor performance.

In each of the last three instances, a poor reading of the initial misunderstanding aggravated the problem and led to a new type of resistance. This is bad enough, but often the problem will not stop there. Poor management of control struggles, resentment, or temporarily poor performance can harden resistance. In this case, I hope it is clear that resistance is not an accurate description of what is happening. A dysfunctional relationship has emerged between manager and employees. With each step, the initial problem recedes further from view, the problem worsens, and chances of resolving the misunderstanding grow more distant.

5. Genuine Conflict of Interest

People resist change when they disagree with its direction or when they feel endangered by it. The problem may be as simple as a difference of opinion about a technique used at work. But the conflict may be more dramatic. People are often asked to participate in projects, for instance, that may threaten their jobs, in the worst case, or the roles that have made them feel useful. They may be asked to take on jobs whose risk seems well beyond the pay and recognition it yields. Even such apparently simple and advantageous changes as learning a new technology may threaten the workers who fear where this may lead or who, for family reasons, prefer a stable work life to new opportunities. In other words, many changes present at least an apparent conflict of interest between managers and their employees. Simi-

larly, projects may promote the ambitions of one colleague and do little for another. When the first pushes, even slightly, the other may balk. If the different degree of investment is not acknowledged, balking may turn into opposition, and a vicious circle of pushing and resistance may develop.

There are many conflicts that are usually dormant but are hard to avoid and sometimes lead to powerful resistance. I am thinking, for example, of value conflicts between individuals and between individuals and organizations. Equally common, are the conflicting demands of work and family, work and religious observance, work and community.

6. Struggles Over Power and Change

From yet another perspective, resistance can be described simply as a control struggle between those who want to change and those who don't, or between those who want to change others and the others who don't wish to be changed. What sustains resistance is pushing from the change agent after resistance has shown itself. The more one pushes, the more the other resists. This creates a vicious circle.

When change agents consistently push their point of view, it brings out a one-sided response in those who resist. In general, most people who resist change do so ambivalently. In other words, they see both reasons for change and reasons not to change. They experience the ambivalence as an internal debate. When a person external to this debate, powerfully and relentlessly, takes up one side of the argument, it has a preemptive impact: the person who has been pushed can let go of one side of the debate—it already has a champion and argue more vociferously for the side that resists change. This is perhaps the central dynamic of what might be called *chronic resistance,* a pattern of resistance that becomes a general response to the introduction of virtually all change projects, during which people's own recognition of problems and their own motivation to change is nullified and lies dormant.

It goes without saying, that people struggling for control do not perceive themselves as sharing a common goal. From this perspective, intervention seeks to alleviate, resolve, or divert the control struggle by trying to clarify shared goals or to develop them anew.

7. Treating Opposition as Noncompliance

Resistance builds when those driving change fail to see it as a two way street, an interaction. More often than not, managers treat resistance as noncompliance. In this formulation, resistance resides inside those who oppose change, and those who insist on change take little or no responsibility for the problem. They fail to reflect on how they have prepared others for change, how sensible or threatening the change is, how autocratic or inarticulate they might have been, or how pessimistic they might have been under the surface. If only the resistors would get a better attitude, they believe, all would be well.

When resistance is treated as noncompliance, resistors feel demeaned, coerced, or misunderstood. There is a natural, undignified hierarchy built into the idea of non compliance. It says, "I know better than you. I even understand your (resistant) actions better than you do." Conceived this way, resistance implies there is something wrong with those who resist. In turn, resistors will resist this judgment long after the correctness of the change is explained and even agreed to. Framing resistance as non compliance demeans those who think they oppose change for good reasons. It appears self righteous—especially when the change agent's frustration with resistance is accompanied by anger and bullying and articulated as blame.

Treating resistance as noncompliance leads almost invariably to control struggles. When employees do not believe their job is jeopardized, the struggle may open, showing itself as direct opposition or skepticism. When employees feel threatened, the control struggle will go underground, showing itself only as lethargy, incompetence, or a lack of motivation.

8. Illegitimate Authority

Authority is often assumed, not earned. And it is often thought to be a one-way relationship. Yet mutuality and reciprocal responsiveness are inherent in any successful authority relationship. When this reciprocity breaks down, when those asked to follow do not believe that the person in authority is sufficiently responsive to their needs, their meanings or their dignity, the relationship begins to break down. Then, no matter how clear a leader's explanation of goals and expectations, people will not follow wholeheartedly. They will resist. Often enough in such cases, their resistance will directly challenge the manager's credentials or his capacity to lead. But, just as often, if employees are afraid, they will "act out" their resistance in some of the indirect ways I have described.

9. Problems in the Larger Organizational Context

Often resistance encountered in a particular domain—individual, team, or business unit—can only be explained and managed by intervening in the larger system in which the encounter is located.

This is a complex issue to understand, but let me offer two brief illustrations to shed some light on this dilemma.

- *How conflict among leaders leads to resistance among managers and employees*

You are a national sales director. You ask your district and regional sales managers to take a firm hand in promoting a new marketing campaign but they seem unable or unwilling to mobilize the representatives from their districts. You patiently explain the importance of the campaign, as do your managers. Still the representatives seem unmotivated. You and your managers grow insistent. Still nothing. After careful inquiry, however, you discover that the Human Resource Department has let it be known that representatives need not accept "bullying" by managers, whose excesses should be reported as harassment. It turns out that the Vice President of Human Resources and the Vice President of Sales don't agree on management technique. Until they resolve their differences, each manager will be faced with what looks like simple, passive resistance from sales representatives.

- *How conflict with one's boss leads to resistance in one's employees*

You are a mid-level manager in the claims processing division of an insurance company. Your boss proposes a work redesign project that, by training everyone as generalists, dramatically reduces "hand offs," for example from a Blue Cross to a Medicare specialist and from there to many others. You don't agree with this reorganization but have discovered that it is futile to argue with your boss. So you say nothing and, with great ambivalence, begin to implement the work redesign. Your team, having grown comfortable in their specialized roles, doesn't particularly like the change either and, in addition, they sense your attitude. As a result, they proceed in an extremely lackadaisical manner. You report their behavior to your boss, who pressures you to succeed. You, in turn, pressure your team, which seems increasingly resistant to you. At least you and your boss can agree on that, and that agreement on the team's resistance is important to your standing in the company. In effect, you agree to the location of the resistance, which might as accurately be located in you or in your relation to your boss—or in the interaction of you, your boss and your team.

Qualities of Resistance

These are only some of the causes of resistance. For anyone charged with leading a real-world change project, they are probably too much to digest all at once. So let me try to simplify my description by naming the three qualities of

resistance that seem to stand out from all the rest.

1. Direct and Active vs. Indirect and Passive

Current management theory encourages direct, challenging, 360 degree feedback. Without it, leaders are said to grow isolated. Ideas and information are lost. Organizations stagnate. The same theory applies to the management of resistance. The meanings of denial, lethargy, incompetence, and helplessness are difficult and time consuming to tease out. The more direct and active the resistance (feedback), the more readily it can be understood and handled—either through instruction or negotiation.

2. Flexibility vs. Rigidity

When first expressed, resistance is generally still flexible; the problem is still generally resolvable through open conversation. However, consistent misreading of resistance and efforts to override it by management often lead to rigidity. The more they insist on a point of view, for instance, the more others resist. The more employees resist, the more managers insist. The longer this kind of interaction persists, the more the relationship grows polarized and the more the differences grow immovable.

The opposite is also true. Were managers to change their own behavior—by acknowledging that they had explained poorly, for example, or that they had not listened well to another's objections—then resistance would likely diminish or disappear. If employees got together and decided to give their manager, whose job was threatened by their poor performance, a break, his attitude and behavior might change. When polarized, each side blames the other, but the more useful focus of attention is the relationship.

3. Situational vs. Chronic Resistance

When resistance emerges because of a particular situation, it is still easy to intervene. But resistance can become chronic. Whenever some managers propose a project or a change, for example regardless of the content of the change —their employees respond skeptically. This chronicity rarely emerges during first or second encounters but builds, incrementally, over time. Employees come to expect certain (to them) unacceptable instructions and react automatically. Managers have comparable negative expectations and present their instructions with the expectations in mind. Once this chronic situation emerges, no one can win unless the relationship pattern is identified and changed.

Resistance is out of control when it loses contact with its original cause. It might have arisen through distrust in leadership but, by the time it is seriously addressed, looks like a difference of opinion around a marketing strategy. It might begin as a series of misunderstandings, grow into a chronic control struggle, and transform itself into a pessimistic, lethargic work force, following the firing of a popular worker. Resistance is out of control in these situations because it is so hard to effectively address the causes. In such cases, it is often necessary to trace the origin of the difficulty before you can break the hold of the resistant relationship.

Responding to Resistance: Developing and Repairing Partnerships

I believe that many of the principles of good management have been implicitly stated in my reconception of resistance and need primarily to be formalized. Here is a practical, five step approach to the management of resistance.

Step 1: Anticipate Resistance

Assume that no matter how well planned, well prepared and articulated the change project, no matter how logical and well-conceived, there will likely be resistance, if not at first, then later. Even successful implementation leads indirectly to resistance, When people change they get nervous. They reach a point when they are too far from their traditional way of doing business but not yet secure in the new way. At such times, often close to the completion of a project, they sometimes dig in their heels. So don't be surprised by resistance.

Regularly scan the horizon in the manner of a sailor guarding against an unpredictable sea. Look for the many faces of resistance described above. Name it aloud. Check out with colleagues that your observations are accurate.

Step 2: Explore the Problems for Which Resistance Provides Feedback

Actively explore the meaning of the resistance. Do not try to determine the meaning by yourself, in the quiet of your mind. Instead, ask others:

- Ask those who appear to be resisting what their idea about the problem is. Ask them why the change initiative is not working out. Ask what you may be doing to cause the problem. Ask questions about larger organizational goals and trends, like downsizing.
- Ask those who seem compliant.
- Particularly ask those who are in between. In any group, there are "bridge" people, those who see both sides of a question. They often provide the most complete information. Later, as allies, they may help reconcile differences of opinion.
- Ask colleagues who have a different perspective than you do.
- Ask your boss.

As you inquire, keep in mind some of the causes of resistance that were explored above. In that vein, ask:

- What conflicts of interest does it emerge from?
- What misunderstandings?
- What violations of legitimate authority?
- Which partnerships are misfiring? Those with colleagues? Those with your employees? Your Boss? The organizational culture?

- Are you drawing the circle of inquiry large enough? Sometimes, for example, the conflicting demands of work and family or work and community create resistance.
- Is the resistance active and direct—what you see is what you get—or passive and disguised, requiring you to explore further?

The better you become at exploring and articulating the reasons for resistance, the less others will persist with passive, indirect forms. The more those in conflict come to a shared idea of the meaning of resistance, the better chance they have to resolve the difficulties. In fact, the very act of mutual inquiry is the first, major step towards building a partnership capable of solving the problems that led to the resistance in the first place.

Step 3: Join and Validate the Resistance, Thus Empowering Those Who Resist

In order to change a system, you must join it. Joining means to share sufficiently the values and culture of another. This makes others feel safe. If you appear safe, you can come close; and it is close we must come in order to influence another person or group.

Respectful inquiry into the meaning of resistance begins to bring us close. People are reassured when we really want to understand their experience. This process is very different than the rhetorical questioning commonly used in the face of resistance. Rhetorical questions make a point. They speak at people, not with them, Respectful questions aim to learn. They side-step hierarchy. They say, in effect, we are in this together, both learners. Respect, or what some call "appreciative inquiry," is a craft that takes time to learn. But, at its core, it can be characterized by simple prompts and questions that do not have hidden agendas. Here are a few:

- "Say more?"
- "What do you mean?"
- "Could you elaborate on that point?"

- "What would that mean for our common enterprise?"
- "Is there something I can do to improve the situation?"

Not only do these questions aim to understand those who resist, they also invite resistors to understand you. So often, resistance arises because people simply react to instructions—a holdover from childhood, no doubt. They react because they feel powerless in the face of another person's, and particularly a boss's, instructions. They react because the reaction, itself, momentarily a least feels like it equalizes power. In the long run, reacting is ineffectual for everyone. When we invite others to question us, we invite them to take some of the initiate in solving our problem. In taking initiative, people feel empowered. When empowered, they are much more likely to join in partnership to solve problems. Joining does not mean jettisoning hierarchy. A manager can and should maintain his or her basic role and the essential purpose behind a change initiative. The purpose of the inquiry is to ask how we have gone wrong; and how can we accomplish our task together.

Validating resistance does not mean affirming its many indirect and passive forms. We do not mean to encourage lethargy, denial, or incompetence. But we do want to say that beneath the manifest resistance there is important information about how and how not to mobilize people behind a project. By affirming the hidden or deeper meanings, we accomplish two things: we let people feel understood; we encourage them to be direct the next time, so that we can enter productive conversation quicker.

Here's the paradox: to overcoming resistance, we must join it. In other words, managers must acknowledge that they are part of the resistance—not a distant but an integral part. They must own it: by empathizing with the part played by others; by seeing their own part; by understanding that their role and ours are intertwined, interdependent.

Step 4: Form a Partnership to Solve the Problem Addressed by the Resistance

When your efforts to join the resistance are sufficiently authentic, a partnership is formed with those who resist. In Step 3, the partnership turns inward, towards understanding the difficulties within the work teams. This effort to achieve a common understanding of the problem pointed out by resistance is sometimes enough to break the problem's hold; and the work team get on with its business of completing the temporarily aborted project. In Step 4, you agree to join together in seeking a solution to those difficulties that don't fall away with understanding and require new action.

Step 5: Problem Solving

The craft of resolving all conflicts of interest, power, legitimacy, and mistrust is beyond the scope of this paper, but let me offer a few, brief suggestions.

When the problem is misunderstanding:

When the problem is misunderstanding, begin simply; go back to basics:

- Clarify the project. its goals and strategies;
- Clarify the misunderstanding;
- See if a common understanding is easily reached.

If this simple method does not succeed, it may be because feelings are still intense and trust still low. In this case, try the same process with a facilitator present. If this process does not succeed, it is likely that misunderstanding is a cover for deeper problems, like a basic conflict of interest or a mistrust of authority.

When the problem is a conflict of interest:

Genuine conflicts of interest rarely resolve with understanding alone. When, for example, reorganization threatens jobs, many will enter the reorganization process reluctantly. Con-flicts of interest must be carefully negotiated—by colleagues or by managers and employees, themselves, if they basically trust each other. Otherwise, seek the help of a professional negotiator or facilitator.

When the problem is a breakdown of the authority relationship:

If negotiations fail to produce compromise solutions, you can assume one of two things: that the mistrust is strong on both sides, such that neither trusts the other to live up to his or her side of the compromise; that the dysfunctional partnership is so chronic, that they cannot even imagine solutions. In this case, you should reorganize the work group, joining different managers and employees. Or, if the work team is so valuable and immovable, engage the services of a very skillful interpersonal facilitator.

Summary

In this paper, I have described some of the many faces of resistance and proposed that they are best understood as feedback about the poor alignment of relationships. I have described how reactions like denial, skepticism, and a lack of motivation develop from a number of causes, such as misunderstandings, conflicts of interest, power struggles, and threats to dignity and autonomy, and how these experiences are compounded when change agents and those who resist do not take the time to understand one another.

Finally, I have proposed a five-step approach to resolving the relational difficulties which rest at the core of resistance, It has been my experience, and that of others who have applied this method, that an honest use of these five steps does untie many of the tangled threads that bind up organizational change processes, Surely, these steps, alone, are not the sword that slices the "Gordian Knot." But, when used with patience and compassion, they can be the lubricant that loosens the knots of resistance and, if they do, they are well worth trying.

CHAPTER 56

Appreciative Inquiry

Debunking the Mythology Behind Resistance to Change

Thomas C. Head

APPRECIATIVE INQUIRY, as a method for introducing and facilitating organizational change, has proven itself a successful and robust methodology. In many ways Appreciative Inquiry might be considered Organization Development's aspirin. It works for almost everyone and for almost any problem, but no one knows exactly why. One possible explanation, explored here, is that Appreciative Inquiry is successful because it almost entirely eliminates resistance to change.

Briefly, Appreciative Inquiry is a process for diagnosing an organization's need for change, but one that focuses on the positive elements of the organization. Appreciative Inquiry requires organizational members to identify those "peak" times when everything operated perfectly. Next, the participants establish what factors were behind these peak experiences. Finally, it is an easy step (at least conceptually) to establish interventions that will make the peak experience factors the norm, rather than the exception.

Appreciative Inquiry appears, and actually is, quite simple (again, at least conceptually). Without a doubt simplicity is one key to its remarkable success. Just as important for its success is how the Appreciative Inquiry process assists change agents in managing resistance to change. This assistance is two dimen-

sional. First, Appreciative Inquiry debunks the mythology surrounding change resistance. Second, Appreciative Inquiry removes, or at least reduces, many of the underlying causes of resistance to change.

Appreciative Inquiry and the Myths of Resistance to Change

Everyone recognizes the significant role employee resistance plays in the change process. However, for some reason this recognition has not led to equally significant research efforts, and therefore to understanding. Few Organization Development books devote more than a few pages to managing resistance. Its importance, coupled with the lack of knowledge, has led to many myths surrounding resistance to change. Designing and implementing interventions based upon these myths at best might lead to minor inconveniences, but at worst will surely derail the entire change program. Appreciative Inquiry, by its nature, permits the change agent to see the truth behind the myths.

Myth 1: Resistance Is Always "Bad"

Psychologists often say that fear typically is not harmful to an individual. In fact fear can lead to some positive outcomes. Fear often builds character and, more importantly, stops an individual from performing stupid and dangerous acts. While fear might contribute to change resistance, resistance and fear are not the same constructs. However, what is true for fear is also true for resistance to change.

Most consultants, and clients, perceive resistance to change as an evil dragon that must be vanquished before attaining the goal. There is no question that managing resistance to change is essential for a project's success, but the same is true of all aspects of the change process. Resistance to change is not "bad," nor is it "good"; it simply "is," and if managed correctly will prevent an organization from doing something "stupid." Resistance can serve as a signal that there ·is disagreement about how to proceed, and that the organization should "look before it "leaps."

Resistance to change may also significantly improve an intervention's quality if managed correctly. Change resistance does not develop from nothing—there are concrete reasons behind employees' resistance. Identifying these reasons provides a wealth of information for improving an intervention and its implementation. If there are aspects of the change which are not understood by the employees clearly additional information is required. But why do the people require information? Was the change not originally described with sufficient information quantity and quality? Was the description believed? Was there an explanation at all? The change agent must seek, rather than avoid, the answers to these questions. Granted, the answers may point out previous shortcomings, but they will also provide clear directions for smoother implementation. Resisting change also develops from concerns about the intervention's details. These concerns, from individuals with an intimate knowledge of the current situation, need to be examined instead of dismissed. If the concerns are unfounded providing more information is all that is needed. If the concerns are valid incorporating them, through collaboration, into the inter-

vention's design shall only improve the intervention's quality.

To properly manage this particular myth requires creating an environment where resistance to change is not perceived as an "evil" by those designing and implementing the change. The environment must encourage all members to honestly and openly contribute input (both facts and opinions). Appreciative Inquiry is an excellent methodology for creating such a positive change environment. Because people offer their comments from a position of what is "right," "good," and "desirable" in the organization, instead of "wrong," "bad," "ineffective," no one is reluctant to contribute. Of equal importance, when focusing on the positive, is that no one seeks to attach blame. Putting it succinctly, no employee has ever been executed for being the bearer of good news—and the employees are comfortable in this role.

Myth 2: There Will Always Be Resistance to Change

As with many myths, there is some truth behind the belief that no matter what is being attempted the change agent will meet with resistance. Walk into a crowded room and offer everyone twenty-five dollars with no "catches." Inevitably many will ask questions, other will be suspicious, and a few will refuse to take the money (author's note this is all supposition, I've never actually tried this experiment, but have always wanted to).

The moral of the experiment is that no matter how attractive the change some employees will be suspicious enough that they put up some resistance. One must remember, however, that most people took the money, just as most employees will embrace the change after their questions have been answered.

The danger in this myth lies not with will there be resistance, rather with how significant is the resistance. If the change agent and client assume that the inevitable resistance will be significant (as they often do) they will integrate this assumption into the intervention's design and communication. In essence, by anticipating significant resistance, the change agent establishes a self-fulfilling prophesy. Employees perceiving this negative assumption buried within the communications will naturally seek to establish the "truth." After all, if everything is as the management say, why do they think the employees will be reluctant to accept the change?

It is safe to assume that no matter how attractive the change some resistance is to be expected. The change agent must find a way to ascertain where resistance will arise, its roots, and its severity, all without planting, or reinforcing, the idea in the employees' heads. Appreciative Inquiry provides an excellent method for accomplishing these tasks. First, as will be discussed later in detail, Appreciative Inquiry naturally eliminates many of the standard reason behind change resistance. Appreciative Inquiry operates under the assumption that resistance actually will not occur, for who would resist Therefore, if any self fulfilling prophesy develops, it will be to inhibit, instead of facilitate, resistance to change. Appreciative Inquiry could actually push the organization too far. The extreme positive environment arising from the technique might convince employees that their concerns are groundless or absurd, thus robbing the change agent from valuable diagnostic information.

Myth 3: With Resistance, It's All or Nothing

Change is all or nothing. Change is win-lose. Change is war. This is often how managers view resistance to change. The employees are either "for us or against us." Change resistance typically does not occur as either black or white, rather there are numerous shades of gray.

Most employees are reasonable, sane, and somewhat rational. When faced with an understandable need for change, and an intervention that makes sense, people will accept the process. Refer back to the fictional experiment. When offered money with no "catches"

it is normal to expect people with questions—either spoken or unspoken. Either way once the questions are reasonably answered, most individuals will accept the offer. Granted, their acceptance will range from wild enthusiasm to moderate suspicion, but they will take the money.

When confronted with change, it is natural that employees will have questions. These questions are not meant as signs of hostile resistance. The employees are simply gathering information with which to form an opinion. The way a manager, or change agent, responds will significantly impact subsequent opinions. So, how do many managers react to employee questions? First, they might feel challenged or threatened, in which case their response might be, "I think it is a good idea, and that's why we're going to do it." Managers might also be surprised, or baffled, by the questions and respond by simply repeating themselves assuming they simply weren't heard correctly the first time. Finally, the managers could fail to understand the significance of the question, or simply be unprepared to answer, and respond with all the clarity of a politician running for office. In all of these cases the result is the same: the employees' questions remain unanswered and the subsequent frustration can easily lead to resistance escalation.

Managers and change agents need to perceive questions as simply employees seeking information. There are no deep hidden meanings that threaten success. Employees need answers to their questions, both those asked and unasked.

Appreciative Inquiry's positive approach to introducing change creates an environment where data and ideas are freely exchanged in order to discover all the possibilities instead of the problems. Information answers the questions, often before they are verbalized, and therefore resistance is minimized. If anything, the probing created by the tentative resistance to change will enrich the discussion surrounding the intervention thereby leading to creative dialogues, and therefore a much improved version of the proposed change process.

Myth 4: Resistance to Change Is a Group Level Construct

An interesting phenomenon often occurs sometime early in the change implementation process. Managers, when thinking of change, switch from first person singular to third person plural.

Managers begin with "I think this project is a good idea" but end with They (employees) will fight it." This perspective may lead managers to a set of faulty decisions, for they are working under a false assumption. Managers believe that resistance to change is a group level construct when it actually occurs at the individual level. Resistance to change, like motivation and satisfaction, takes place in the human mind, and therefore managing it must also take place within (and not between) the employee.

Groups cannot be resistant to change. Granted, every single group member might resist the change, but each individual will resist it for his/her own personal reasons. If each individual has his/her own reason for resistance, group level solutions will always prove inadequate. In using a group level approach to managing resistance the best a change agent can hope for is to placate a majority (you can't please all the people all the time). The worst case is that no one will be satisfied by the perceived halfhearted attempt or alienated by the attempt ("Don't 'they' get it?"; "Didn't 'they' listen to me?").

Resistance occurs within the individual, and therefore any attempt to bring the resistance out in the open and work with it must also be focused within the individual. What is needed is a technique where each person's concerns and ideas are included into the planning process. Appreciative Inquiry, again, is an excellent method to accomplish this task. Just as everyone's reasons for resistance will be unique, everyone's peak experience (or at least the reasons for identifying that peak experience) will be unique. Appreciative Inquiry encourages everyone to contribute their own peak experiences, and the reasons behind them. Conse-

quently, all employees are heard and (more importantly) understood, thereby permitting the maximum integration of individual ideas into the final solution. Resistance to change becomes a tool for improving the intervention rather than an obstacle to overcome

Myth 5: You Must "Buy" the Employees' Commitment

It is often said that immediately upon hearing the organization is going to change three questions pop into all employees' minds. These three questions, in order, are: (1) Why? (2) How will this affect me? and (3) What is in it for me? Managers, having experienced many changes themselves, are well aware (even if it is at the subconscious level) that each subordinate is thinking these questions. Herein lays the root of the myth that if you want employees to commit themselves to the change you will have to "buy" it through pay raises or similar concessions, and this purchase will be expensive.

Obviously, this myth is pure Theory X, which is interesting in itself because almost all contemporary interventions utilize Theory Y for a base. Gary YukI (1983), in his classic work on power, points out typically one cannot "buy" (reward power) commitment. The most likely outcome with reward power is simple compliance—employees will go along with the change, but without real motivation. Another possible outcome from attempting to "buy" employee acceptance is increased resistance to the change. First, offering incentives to accept changes can easily appear as bribery. Most employees do not like to think they can be "bought," particularly at the level many managers offer. Once again, managers also run the risk of creating a self-fulfilling prophesy. If the change is so desirable, why must management buy labor's commitment? For example, one hospital offered its nurses a five-cents-an hour pay increase for accepting a major change in scheduling policy. The nurses' response was anger, suspicion, and open resistance. The nurses, who quite possibly would have agreed to the change with no additional compensation, were insulted that management felt they could "buy" loyalty for an additional two dollars a week. The nurses also engaged in heavy speculation about "what was really going to happen." The hospital abandoned the change.

When discussing any organizational change, managers must be prepared to supply the answers for the three questions (Why? How will it affect me? What's in it for me?). If management and change agents do not have the answers, possibly they have not thought the change out in sufficient detail. Either the leaders need to slow down and develop the answers, or they need a process for employees to quickly obtain their own answers. This myth about buying commitment obviously comes from the final question. The question is not, by definition, based on greed—it is a natural result of the motivation process. Management is asking employees to change behaviors and improve the organization, effort-to-performance in expectancy theory terms, and they want to know that the performance is linked to outcomes, and that the outcomes are desirable. Management also forgets that often the strongest outcomes are intrinsic (pride, growth opportunities, achievement, enjoyment) rather than extrinsic (pay, benefits).

Appreciative Inquiry overcomes both managerial shortcomings. Employees immediately answer their own questions. By emphasizing the desire to recreate the peak experiences the "why" is obvious the organization wants to get to where everything works at the optimum level. Employees, knowing what the peak experience involved, also know how it affected them. Finally, the reward lies in the simple fact that if successful, the change will lead to dramatic increases in employee satisfaction and morale.

Appreciative Inquiry and the Reasons Behind Resistance to Change

Head, Sorensen, Preston, and Yaeger (2000) first presented the idea that Appreciative Inquiry's success is due primarily to the fact that it naturally removes most of the major reasons why employees resist change. Without doubt, there are reasons for employee resistance to change not covered here, and it is probable that Appreciative Inquiry does not address all the reasons, but it is clear that the technique does significantly remove many of the major sources of resistance.

One of the primary driving forces behind employee resistance is the uncertainty and ambiguity that change creates; in other words, the fear of the unknown. Using Appreciative Inquiry's process working through the employees' past peak experiences, there is no unknown.

The employees are actually the source of all information, and this data is used to recreate, and possibly improve upon, what has already been experienced.

Often, resistance to change is simply based upon the fact that employees like the old system. They are comfortable with what, and how, they operate, and have been for many years. Even people who don't like everything about the old ways must have some things they find enjoyable or else they would have left. The employee likes what he/she has now and might even acknowledge the possibility of enjoying the new system even more. At the same time there is an equal probability of disliking the new order. Many people are risk takers, but few are willing to gamble on something as important as job satisfaction. Appreciative Inquiry begins the change process with what employees like most about the existing system, making the peak experiences the norm. There is no risk involved in the change because the employee is certain she/he will like the new system. Many will not even perceive the change as a new system, rather it is simply recapturing the best of the current system and removing any difficulties.

Another primary reason behind resistance is that change often causes the employee to question her /his self-image, forcing the question "Can I do the new task?" Those of us who grew up before the personal computer era witnessed the significant panic and subsequent resistance that ensued among clerical staff as these mysterious boxes out of science fiction were placed on every secretary's desk. Because Appreciative Inquiry builds upon what the employee has experienced there is no self doubt. The employee is certain they can do "it" because they have already successfully done "it." In fact, because the new system most likely will focus upon those elements which employees feel are their strong points, they will view themselves as more competent for the new system than they were in the old.

Often in change efforts employees resist because they feel imposed upon. Labor does all the work in implementing the change, management gets all the credit, and only the organization's stockholders reap the benefits. Appreciative Inquiry clearly provides a personal "gain" for all employees. Each individual sees how their efforts will be rewarded through increases in job satisfaction and an "ideal" working environment.

Most diagnostic approaches create an environment of blame. When a consultant begins the change process by listing all the organization's problems, no matter how positive she/he tries to be, everyone in the process will seek either to establish who's responsible, or to avoid taking responsibility. This negativity can even carryon into the change process. People will be reluctant to take responsibility for activities to avoid the blame if the change fails. Groups will fall into the paralysis by analysis trap for the same reason. Consequently, the change is doomed to failure. However, when the consultant uses Appreciative Inquiry, becoming the focus of attribution is a source of pride. Few, except for modesty, would be reluctant to admit their role in establishing a peak experience. Individuals and groups are excited to assume responsibility in creating a system they know will not fail.

A final source for resistance to change is simply that the employees view the intervention as just another fad. A common question, often verbalized, is "Why adopt anything new

when management is only going to forget it in a .couple of weeks anyway?" Most changes are, by definition, revolutionary in nature. Interventions are planned and deliberate attempts at throwing out the old and taking on the new. It is also a fact of life that most interventions never succeed in establishing the new order. Management and labor lose interest, either because the results are too slow in coming or because they were not as significant as hoped for. Either way the organization quickly shops around for the next sure-fire solution. Employees quickly realize that it is easier to resist any change rather than bounce around from one new process to another. Appreciative Inquiry is not a "revolutionary" change process. The goal is simply to take the current system to its greatest known potential. There will be few, if any, artificially high expectations, and implementation should be comparatively rapid. The changes Appreciative Inquiry brings are logical and fit into the current organizational paradigm.

Conclusion

Beckhard and Harris (1987) suggest a formula that predicts the degree of resistance an intervention will encounter. The equation focuses on three primary factors: level of dissatisfaction with the status quo, desirability of proposed change, and the practicality of the change. Another variable, the cost of changing, is also included into the equation. Beckhard's equation lends further support to the belief that Appreciative Inquiry works, at least in part, because it permits the change agent to easily manage resistance to change.

Establishing employees' peak experiences as the organizational norm should make the change highly desirable for most, if not all, employees. Because the process is recreating what has already been accomplished few will doubt its practicality. Finally, no matter how dissatisfied, or satisfied, people are with the status quo they should all see that the change process will simply emphasize what is currently the system's best while eliminating what is worst. Therefore, according to Beckhard's model, the only real threat for developing significant resistance lies with the intervention's cost.

Cost will always be a concern, especially when dealing with managerial resistance to change. However, assuming that a cost-effective intervention is possible, Appreciative Inquiry will remove the base causes for resisting change. The technique also naturally debunks the common held myths surrounding resistance to change. Appreciative Inquiry provides the consultant with a process for facilitating change that properly manages change resistance. Overcoming the resistance barrier does not guarantee a successful change, but clearly it is a major part of the battle.

Appreciative Inquiry is a highly useful tool for Organization Development change agents. For many, this knowledge is enough. But think of how much more useful the technique would be if we understood how and why it worked. To answer these questions will require significant research effort. Such research projects must begin with speculation. The belief that Appreciative Inquiry is successful because it naturally reduces resistance to change is speculation (based on logic). Orga-nization Development, as a field, must take the next step and empirically test this, and other, dimensions of Appreciative Inquiry.

References

Beckhard, R., & Harris, R. (1987). *Organizational transitions: Managing complex change* (2nd ed.). Reading, MA: Addison Wesley

Cooperrider, D., Sorensen, P., Whitney, D., & Yaeger, T. (2000). *Appreciative Inquiry.* Champaign, IL: Stipes Publishing.

Head, T., Sorensen, P., Yaeger, T., & Preston, J. (2000). Is Appreciative Inquiry OD's philosopher's stone? In D. Cooperrider, P. Sorensen, D. Whitney, & T. Yaeger (Eds.), *Appreciative Inquiry.* Champaign, IL: Stipes Publishing.

Moomaugh, R, & Associates (1995). *Re-Engineering: Why it so often fails.* Valley Center, CA: Organizational Universe Systems.

Packard, T. (1995). TQM and organizational change and development. In B.Gummer, & P. Mc-Callon (Eds.), *Total Quality Management in the social services: Theory and practice.* Albany, NY: Rockefeller College Press.

Yukl, G., & Taber, T. (1983). The Effective Use of Managerial Power, *Personnel*, 60(2).

CHAPTER 57

Utilizing States of Organizational Readiness

Barry Dym and Harry Hutson

A LOT OF US like to think that good planning and solid management are the keys to successful change. However, the course of most change efforts frequently belies this orderly expectation.

Those of us who are experienced change agents—whether managers or consultants—certainly, at one time or another, have been confounded and frustrated by the inconsistent outcomes of careful planning.

It seems that some interventions work effortlessly—a little advice, a simple instruction, or some just-in-time training is all that is required. Even for complex and difficult problems. On the other hand, many of our best efforts, ones which combine our most brilliant, time-consuming analyses and shrewdest planning, fall flat, meeting unexpected and crippling resistance. What makes the difference?

Is it luck? Maybe. But you cannot count on luck. Is it the quality of the people involved in the change project? That would be convenient. But we have often succeeded and failed with the same people, in what seems like similar circumstances. Is it our delivery? Maybe. But even compelling and charismatic leaders meet resistance a good percentage of the time.

Or, is successful change more a function of timing than any of us have heretofore acknowledged? Is organizational change dependent on, perhaps even governed by, *organizational readiness?*

Some Interesting Answers

Seeking answers to this conundrum, we investigated successful interventions by asking participants "What made the difference?" "What helped you change?" Their answers ranged from the confusing to the insulting. For example, they said, "We just did it" or "We tried hard". Or they cited relatively minor suggestions and off-handed comments which they had taken for wisdom. They described being influenced by experiences outside the work situation; perhaps influenced by a book they had read, a lesson learned at home, or something a friend had said. So, while we as leaders and consultants had been working steadily and systematically to help facilitate change, credit was given by our interviewee to what seemed to us like peripheral, almost random events. How should we interpret this?

After much thought, the logic beneath these explanations seems unavoidable: people and organizations change—rapidly, strongly and thoroughly—but only when they're ready to change.

Consequently, it now appears to us that, in all organizations, there are deep currents of readiness. Like underground rives, these currents, once tapped, can serve as powerful catalysts for change. While this statement may appear mysterious, it does in fact, reflect two of the most basic premises of science and systems theory. First, physicists know that systems far from equilibrium, systems outside their normal constraints, are vulnerable to change, vulnerable to the impact even random experience, much in the way that an avalanche can be triggered by a loud noise. Second, during periods of disequilibrium, there are many potential paths of growth and development that emerge—what biologists call "bundles of opportunity." Like new sprouts in the spring time, these bundles are quietly waiting to be watered and fertilized. By supporting these pre-existing bundles of opportunity, we can fuel and guide changes.

Moreover, we now think that readiness takes many forms. Sometimes, for instance, people and organizations are in so much pain—a manager has failed miserably while trying to carry out his last three assignments, or a corporation has not been profitable for years – that they believe they must change. Sometimes systems are so out of kilter, so uncertain, so disorganized, they can't help but change in their efforts to regain their balance. Sometimes people are so open, so curious, so receptive to outside input that they see every new idea or program as pointing to the path of successful action. The variety here may be endless, but the fact is straightforward—organizations change when they are ready.

Our purpose in this article is to introduce a way to categorize these patterns of readiness —we call them "states of readiness"—and describe intervention styles that match these states of readiness and consequently enhance an organization's potential for change.

The Pitfalls of Ignoring Readiness for Change

The pitfalls for ignoring the readiness factor are legion. In fact, they are well documented. Without identifying readiness in others, we encounter resistance, denial and a failure of change strategies to get securely off the ground. When people are ill-prepared, they deny that there is a problem or that it must be addressed, instead resisting change in an unending vari-

ety of direct and indirect ways. Only sometimes will these people refuse outright to try a new program. More often, their resistance is passive, appearing (in individuals and teams) as lethargy, pessimism, fear, incompetence or rigidity and (in organizations) as cumbersome bureaucracy.

Many managers plan and implement change efforts with hardly a thought to the readiness of their employees. Others think about readiness, but in ways that do not facilitate change. For instance, they all too often equate the need for change, as they perceive it with readiness for change, as experienced by others. Many mangers and consultants think about readiness but lack the patience to look for it. They forget that their own past successes either rode the back of fear and instability that occurs when an organization has lost market share during a brief window of responsiveness among employees, or occurred after they discovered strong employee initiatives that they could support.

Managers and consultants often assume that persuasion and reason will always win the day. Consulting teams enter corporations, perform exhaustive analyses, produce voluminous and excellent recommendations for change, and then expect that these recommendations will be followed. How could organizations, one's which invest immense amounts of money and time for these recommendations, do otherwise? Yet, when all is said and done, the success rate for change programs introduced this is scandalously low.

Other managers may insist that change depends on motivated work forces, citing singular methods of motivation like inspired leadership, the development of visions, or broadly participatory decision-making processes. Yet, as we all know, inspired leadership is often hard to find and the other motivational techniques frequently fail.

Some managers try to create a permanent state of readiness for change. The latest such effort is the "learning organization," which suggests that we can build a state of constant readiness by creating a culture build on open dialogue and constantly challenged assumptions. Yet, as we are re-discovering, people naturally seek stability in the way they structure their lives and in the way they think. Without the spur of readiness due to challenging or threatening circumstances, the desire for stability seems to always overtake the desire to change and learn. Even learning can become a stable ideology, blinding us to the need for alternative approaches to readiness.

The Need for New Theory

The idea of readiness is as old as time. Traditional teachers, for example, often waited years before they thought their students were ready to receive their wisdom, offering it instead at just that moment when their students either let go of conventional expectations or grew so confused and disheartened that they were eager for any anchor in an angry sea.

Nowadays, the importance of intervening when the time is right is pivotal in theories of change across many disciplines. The education theorist, Eleanor Duckworth (1975) emphasized identifying and capitalizing on "teachable moments." Organizational change theorists recognize the importance of readiness, chiefly Michael Beer (1990), Richard Beckhard (1987), Robert Schaffer (1988), Warner Burke (1994) and Ronald Heifitz (1994).

Building on the insights of these authors, as well as our own, we are proposing a new conception of readiness, one that can both predict and help change. Our theory is intended to provide change agents a much broader range of sites for introducing change, and, to complement these sites, a wide array of interventions that match well with the state of readiness found in each.

Readiness is derived from the Greek work, *arariskein,* which means "fitting," "joining," or "being arranged for use." So it is that certain kinds of interventions fit best in particular organizational climates at particular times. A system can be entered at any point, for that is the nature of the interconnections and interactions that we know as systems. But there must be a fit at the point of intervention. This is the nub of it: the alignment of interactions. Fit is the key variable in determining success; we call this arrangement readiness.

Three States of Readiness

Our research shows that readiness exists in three different "states". Each requires its own specific kind of interventions.

The three states are (1) *Forays* that are changes in progress that either have not come to fruition or are not yet sufficiently recognized to exert a strong influence on the whole organization; (2) *Responsive States* of *Readiness,* such as curiosity, receptiveness and determination, which are best served by information, advice, and guidance; and (3) *Unstable States* of *Readiness,* like confusion, anxiety, and crisis, which need to be reframed as integral aspects of the change process, and then cultivated as seed-beds of creative thought.

This three-fold categorization gives options. It helps us identify whether or not clients are ready and, if so, how. It allows us to design interventions with their states of readiness in mind. Then, if the intervention targeted to one form of readiness shows signs of failure, we can look elsewhere to intervene. This transforms the development of change strategies from guesswork into an empirical process.

Forays

No matter how rigidly or bureaucratically organized a system is, or may appear, there always are changes afoot, people who are trying to improve things. Their efforts are what we call forays.

We, as change agents, must learn to see these forays for what they are: as tentative, incomplete moves that people and organization make to improve their situation. Their efforts literally are forays from one way of thinking about things into another way. As they catalyze our move from one condition to another, forays represent a potential for transformational experience.

Individually, forays look like this: You resolve not to react defensively to a colleague or boss whom you find pushy, and succeed for a few days. You wake feeling optimistic about a project that has been plaguing you and work effectively that day. But the next day, your optimism is gone. Without even trying, you find yourself being more assertive than usual, but you cannot maintain it in the face of your boss's withering stare.

Organizationally, forays look like this: amidst an entire division that slugs its way through the work day in a bored, lethargic fashion, there is a small group that pushes to see how much it can do and new ways to do it better and faster. In an organization slowed by departmental boundaries, there are managers who regularly and knowingly cross those boundaries and de facto work in an interdisciplinary climate. Sluggish groups, for example, have moments of creative energy. Groups that scapegoat one person have moments when compassion for the same person runs high. Managers find that they can motivate certain work groups for a while but never for long.

Creative strategies and new work processes that build strength but then get ignored or voted down are forays. Successful projects and teams whose modus operandi spread automatically to the general culture of the corporation are forays. If we can learn to see forays and then begin to help them grow, to use the momentum of peoples own energies, then we have hold of the most powerful change agent possible.

In most organizations, there are forays everywhere. The only issue is spotting them. So here are a few more examples: the executive team of an operating division decides to transform its manufacturing plants into "high performing work systems" using a comprehensive model advanced by an outside consulting group. Yet in each plant in the division, there is something special—and incomplete—going on, something worth preserving and building on. In one factory the safety program is leading the way for the whole company, in another, there is a team-based-manufacturing cell

making great gains in cycle-time reduction, in a third, there is an employee/management team hammering out a set of plant-wide operating principles. These are forays. Each is at risk if left out of the loop of the general culture or by passed in the new change program. Yet each provides an opportunity for leveraging change, if only they are encouraged.

We think there are at least five ways of capturing and encouraging a foray.

1. Acknowledge the Foray
Simply noticing a foray is the first step. Simple statements like the following often are sufficient:

- The collaboration among department heads has been very encouraging, lately.
- You seem more assertive lately.
- We've been talking about teams for years —it's nice to see we've actually begun acting like teams.
- Safety is a priority for the corporation, and this plant is making real progress.

It's important to keep noting the changes, whenever they arise. These verbal frames add life and validity to the foray.

2. Highlight the Foray's Direction
Once noticed, you should return to the foray often, spotlighting its progress:

- If the collaboration among department heads continues, I can imagine them forming a solid executive committee.
- Your recent assertiveness seems to have put you in position to take on more important projects.
- Now that the teams are so effective, I'd like to place more responsibility in their hands.
- Other plants now have something to learn from the improved safety record here.

3. Engage the foray
You can provide resources and support for a new foray. For instance, you can determine what results are being achieved by innovative

people and reward them, create a metric for results that can work across the board, or build improvement targets and monitor them regularly and publicly.

Often, forays require new responses from the change agent. Take a CEO who has been trying unsuccessfully to get her Executive Committee to become more decisive while they keep deferring to her judgment. When, in fact, they make a strong decision, even one she does not entirely agree with, she could choose to support their decision.

4. Assume the Foray Is Here to Stay
As forays gain strength, you can treat them as though they are the rule, not the exception. This encourages them to be so. In Alcoholics Anonymous, for example, they say that you often talk the talk before you walk the walk. This means that you must act as though an attempt to change yourself were already accomplished, thereby giving yourself the courage and momentum to change for real. In organizational settings, a comparable approach would look like this:

• Even though economic value analysis has just begun to influence the way work is conducted, it represents the company's future, and so we lend ourselves to its demands.
• The CEO gives full reign to his Executive Committee, and lets the rest of his company know, before they have developed in all aspects of their collaborative leadership.
• We respond to assertiveness in a coworker and largely ignore times when it is missing.

5. Support the Foray Until It Can Stand on Its Own
Few forays flower with one-time support. They may have to be engaged many times. While persistence can be a pain in the neck to people who are not ready, persistence in support of forays is much appreciated.

We may not always succeed in identifying and supporting forays. Or, our support during stable times may prove inadequate. We therefore may have to wait for unstable times, when patterns of thought and behavior loosen, to push forays into lasting change.

Responsive States of Readiness

Responsive states include curiosity, receptiveness, urgency, and determination. Managers and consultants frequently assume Responsive States because they are the easiest to manage, especially through information, planning, advice, and guidance.

While there states are familiar enough, we would like to review the four variations we have noticed and suggest interventions specific to each.

1. *Curiosity.* Organizational leaders and consultants often wonder what is out there, what kind of technologies, marketing strategies, and improvement methods they have not paid attention to. There's a general itch that keeps some managers wondering if they have a problem, or if a problem is just over the horizon. "What's happening in the market over the next few years, and what should be our response?" Hence the emphasis on constant change and the need to be alert to both the competition and to anything that will provide a competitive edge. To scratch the itch, managers may decide to find out; they bring in a consultant to talk to them or they go to a conference.
   Preferred Intervention Style: Offer information and don't push. Suggest alternatives and expand the field of vision. Diverge, do not converge. Future scenario planning can be ideal for this state of readiness. If you try to sell or persuade, however, or move to action steps, you are moving too fast and will probably alienate potentially open minded workers and clients, or you may enter an early control struggle that will doom even the best of projects.
2. *Receptivity.* When receptive, people are opening minded. They are looking for, and are not yet locked into, a solution. They are prepared to hear proposals for change. This

comes in the form of a request. They have identified a problem but do not yet have a solution, and are asking to be told what can be done. "We know we have a problem finding enough talented managers to provide needed bench strength. What are our choices?

Preferred Intervention Style: Narrow the field of change strategies. Present a few strategies to the organization, and a few clear recommendations about how to choose among them. Pros and cons are welcome, as well as preferences backed by experience. This is not the time to brainstorm possibilities, nor is it the time to create Gant charts showing the critical path toward a solution. Trials may be welcome, however, or pilot projects where not everyone needs to get involved.

3. *Urgency.* When there is urgency, there frequently is a strong, perceived need to do something and a strong perceived need for help. Time is of the essence. "Are we too late?" "Can we fix what is clearly broken?" "Is there a shortcut to the usual solutions?" Urgency is often experienced during a sudden downturn in business or a missed deadline for a product launch, deliverables, accountabilities, and due dates.

Preferred Intervention Style: Make *alternative* clear, decisive suggestions. Recommend solutions to the perceived problem. "I've got the answer and know what to do," is the most helpful response to urgency. At this stage, multiple suggestions preferred by curious and receptive people will only frustrate. Converge, don't diverge.

4. *Determination.* When determined, people have identified a problem and want to solve it. Even if they don't yet know the solution, they know a specific solution is required and are anxious to act. Or people know both the problem and the solution and want help in implementation. When events are dramatic and their consequences are well understood, the determination to get on with things closes down the psy-

chological space available for alternative solutions.

Preferred Intervention Style: Provide technical assistance. This could be informational or process oriented. The call is for "all hands on deck" and the assumption is that "everyone's on board." Suggestions about other approaches may be considered disrespectful, diversionary, and even disloyal. This is the moment for project plans and a clear orientation towards deliverables, accountabilities and due dates

There is a limit to these Responsive States that is important to note. People and organizations in Responsive States are not threatened. This means that they do not anticipate radical change, either in the form of a dramatic restructuring or in the form of a paradigm shift in the way business is conceived. Transformational experiences derive either from considerable instability or from small powerful new forces in an organization's life that, with support, have the capacity to pull the organization into entirely new ways of conceiving and performing work. Thus, the intervention strategies offered above are not quite appropriate for radical change situations.

Unstable States

Physical scientists have demonstrated that systems in disequilibrium are vulnerable to change. This observation is equally true for people and organizations. Individuals, groups and organizations, whose "lives" are disrupted, find themselves confused and anxious, sometimes feeling helpless and ready for relief. When confusion stretches our ability to cope with even ordinary matters, we reach out for almost any way to get oriented—even if what we find is new and unfamiliar. We become alert for people who can help us. We pay attention to thoughts, strategies and feelings that had been buried and forgotten during stable times. Or, we take risks and behave in uncharacteristic ways, as when crisis brings out the best in some individuals and organizations. Unstable states provide the soil in which forays grow.

Where, you may ask, do Unstable States come from? And, do they come frequently enough for impatient planners to make use of in designing interventions?

The answer is yes, they do. Frequent leadership changes, reorganizations and challenges from the marketplace, all periodically throw people into states of confusion, anxiety, panic and crisis.

Like Responsive States, Unstable States range from mild to very intense. So far, we have identified three Unstable States: (1) confusion; (2) anxiety; and (3) panic. The appropriateness of the intervention is based as much on the intensity as on the particular character of the state.

1. *Confusion.* We become confused and disoriented at work more often than we let on. No wonder. When change is dizzying, we do our best to keep our balance. It has been said of today's world, "if you are not confused, you don't know what's going on!" We might sense something is off but have no clear description of just what. And, if we do, there may be too many potential solutions and no way to choose. We might not know what to do. Or, we might feel that something is wrong but have no clear description of the problem. There may be too many solutions and it seems impossible to choose from among them. There might also be an absence of leadership. While leaders, themselves, may find it confusing that employees do not follow, they should find it confusing that the leadership style that worked previously does not work now.

Preferred Intervention Style: Name and affirm the confusion. Frame it as a source of potential energy and creativity. Instead of rapidly resolving the confusion to mollify the anxiety, sustain or amplify it. Get people together and give them permission to wonder out loud what is going on.

While clarity is absent or random, potentially creative thoughts emerge—forays that can be noted and supported. Or curiosity and urgency may emerge—a Responsive State calling for direct responses.

2. *Anxiety.* Anxiety combines confusion with worry. Organizational problems are personalized and we take them home. Problems remain somewhat vague, unfocused. The nature of anxiety is that it lacks a clear object. Anxiety draws people inward, away from colleagues, realistic evaluation, and collaboration.

Preferred Intervention Style: To get anywhere in an anxious climate, we must name —not ignore or deny—the anxiety. Otherwise, people will be preoccupied, unable to concentrate on and commit to thinking, planning and problem solving. It helps to draw out both the individual and the collective elements of the anxiety—what people fear for themselves and for the organization—in order to see the connection, i.e., "If we don't get this product to market on time, the company will be in trouble and I'll be fired."

Once anxieties are recognized and vented, people can get down to the productive work that has evaded them for a long time. One of the best ways to initiate this kind of process is for the leader to model it, that is, to express his own anxieties, without adding facile explanations for how he resolved them. His efforts to resolve his own anxieties should come after others have vented theirs, and as part of a collective process of coming to terms.

During times of high anxiety, it is also important to provide structure. First, a structure that acknowledges the anxiety, like a peer support group or a facilitated project group. And second, a structure that encourages creative management efforts that breaks the rules of business as usual. Third, it's often helpful to provide an organizational structure to work towards clear definition of the problem and potential solution.

3. *Panic.* There are times in organizational life when people panic, become fearful and frenetic, grow irrational, and lose their capacity for practical problem solving. Panic can be contagious. It can begin with one or two people, with one team or unit, and spread to others like a grass fire on the prairie. All this while leaders, if they haven't initiated the panic or been contaminated themselves, look on helplessly.

Preferred Intervention: This is a time for leadership to step forward and normalize the process. For example, they might suggest that during any creative enterprise—say a product launch, a new venture, or the introduction of a new technology—people, before clearly conceptualizing and experiencing what is new, feel like swimmers out to sea. They are fearful, and may panic. The Challenge is to remain calm, to share thoughts, both practical and impractical, that can become the seeds of creative solutions.

Besides normalizing and stating the potential in such moments, it is essential to contain the panic. You can call an all-day meeting, saying "We'll stay until we come to a solution." Time is also important since people panic when they think time is running out. Strong leadership is required from someone who is not in a panic, someone who has perspective, someone who watched groups and organizations enter and leave such crises several times before, and come out better for it. Thus organizations can become transformed, because the extreme disorganization created by panic loosens all patterns and opens the door to radical new patterns of experience

Readiness in the System

Readiness is neither a personal nor organizational character trait. A person can be ready to change in one situation or with one particular person and not with others. Context determines readiness as much as the particular quality of determination, urgency, openness or vulnerability one brings to the context. If two people are joined in their urgency, for instance, they are more likely to move than if one is urgent for change while the other is bored.

We have to be prepared to meet the readiness of others when and where it emerges. There's no point in asking advice from someone who is prepared only for resistance. There is not much value in others taking chances, to leave familiar shores, if we are made nervous by risk, instability, heated discussion, or intimacy. We have to engage and encourage the potential to change inherent in the readiness of others.

When people are ready to change, they must also have the resources to change. Someone may listen, yet lack intelligence or creativity. A colleague may learn to consider opinions in a respectful manner but may never become intuitive or deeply empathic about feelings. Behavioral changes—listening, cooperating—may not be enough. And peoples' limitations extend far beyond their character. Conditions matter too; difficulties at home affect performance at work.

Before committing to a course of change, then, it is vital to figure out what can be realistically expected of the people and systems one intends to change.

Creating Readiness

While we generally can find at least one of these three states of readiness, this is not always the case. Yet, even in these situations, an opportunity remains: the patterns that hold a system in place and make it resistant to change can be disrupted. By disrupting ingrained patterns, we can generate a state of readiness.

For example, we may disrupt patterns of thinking. Chris Argyris (1996) does this by challenging assumptions. Dialogue groups frustrate easy, rational modes of thought, push participants, first towards confusion (Unstable States), and then towards more creative modes of thinking (forays). A similar experience occasionally takes place with particularly compelling speakers or inspiring leaders, who first connect with their audiences through shared ideas and experiences and, once the audience is rapt, lead them to entirely unexpected conclusions.

Similarly, we may disrupt the behavioral field. By asking a group of employees to rotate through each other's roles, we frequently confuse them (Unstable States) as much as we broaden their appreciation of each other's activities, and the confusion sets the stage for creative thinking about roles and collaboration. When we restructure teams, divisions, and work processes, old patterns of behavior and cognition are similarly disrupted.

And we may change the way people feel about their work. When, for example, a leader says to a complacent group that the competition is nipping at their heels, that the company is already losing business, and that jobs are at stake, he may create Unstable States and a seed bed for forays may result.

A Decision Sequence

As the three states of readiness suggest, there are many roads to change (see Table 57.1). But this array of options can also be bewildering. Consequently, we have developed a thought sequence to help decide how to begin and then, if necessary, move from one type of readiness to another. The order is based on two principles: (1) moving from the least to the most intrusive, and (2) emphasizing change that is native to the system we intend to change.

First, identify and support forays. Forays are the most natural to the people and systems we're trying to change, so they offer the best chance of long term success. If, for some reason, you cannot find forays to support or your support doesn't bring about substantial change, turn to Responsive States.

Second, address Responsive States. The interventions here are straight forward and simple: generally providing information and guidance. Because people are curious or receptive, you have been invited to intervene and there is little to lose. Worse comes to worst, you will be ineffective. Do not push. Pushing will create resentment and control struggles. Instead, if your approach to a Responsive State fails, look for forays.

Third, sustain Unstable States. Remember, you do not have to create crises. The natural ups and downs of organizational life create natural experiences of instability and confusion.

Fourth, disrupt patterns of thought, behavior, and feelings that inhibit change. The purpose of such disruption is not to force change —you cannot make people think the right thing—but to open gaps in patterns that permit people to learn and grow.

TABLE 57.1 Readiness and Rigidity: Choices for Change

| Forays | Readiness | | Results |
	Responsive (R States)	Unstable (U States)	
• Note	Curiosity? • Offer Information	Confusion and Disorientation? • Acknowledge and Affirm Situation	• Disrupt Patterns of Thinking
• Highlight	Receptivity? • Make Recommendations	Anxiety? • Name it and Provide Structure	• Disrupt Patterns of Behavior
• Engage	Urgency? • Insist on a Solution		
• Support	Determination? • Provide Technical Support	Panic and Crisis? • Normalize and Seed New Ideas	• Look for Forays

Conclusion

Changing organizational systems always requires changing the people who work in them. These are generally people with whom we have a relationship. Generally, leaders, managers, and even consultants who have worked for a long time with organizations become integral parts of the patterns of thought and action that inhibit change At such times, the most important thing they can do to create states of readiness is to change their own relationship to the organization or to the problem they are trying to fix.

To take a simple example, suppose that a manager exhorts her staff to work harder but they do not. Upon closer examination, she discovers a pattern where the harder she pushes, the more they resist; the more they resist, the harder she pushes. This is a pattern that needs breaking and the easiest way to break it is to change her behavior.

Imagine, for instance, that she waits until a moment when she is expected to push but she does not. At first, the team is bemused, a little confused, but as she continues not to push, they grow disoriented—entering an Unstable State of Readiness—and call for help. Their rare initiative in this instance is a foray, and she can identify, highlight, and support it through acknowledgment and praise. If she persists in this way, she will alter the course of her employees' behavior.

In this chapter, we have taken on a practical and immensely important issue—readiness for change. We have described how to navigate around the shoals of lethargy, resistance, denial and other obstacles to change, how to identify the times and places in both individuals and organizational systems when change is most likely to take place, and perhaps, most significantly, how to design interventions that match well with specific states of readiness.

References

Argyris, C., & Schon, D. A. (1996). *Organizational learning II, theory, method and practice.* Reading, MA: Addison Wesley.

Beckhard, R., & Harris, R.T., (1987). *Organizational transitions: Managing complex change.* Reading, MA: Addison, Wesley.

Beer, M, Eisenstat, R., & Spector, B. (1990). *The critical path to corporate renewal.* Boston, MA: Harvard Business School Press.

Burke, W.W., (1994). *Organization development: A process of learning and changing.* Reading, MA: Addison-Wesley.

Duckworth, E. (1987). *The having of wonderful ideas and other essays on teaching and learning.* New York, NY: Teachers College Press.

Dym, B. (1995). *Readiness and change in couple therapy.* New York, NY: Basic Books.

Heifetz, R.A. (1994). *Leadership without easy answers.* Cambridge, MA: The Belknap Press of Harvard University Press.

Schaffer, R.H. (1988). *The breakthrough strategy: Using short- term successes to build high performance organization.* New York, NY: Harper Business.

CHAPTER 58

Developing Organization Change Champions

A High Payoff Investment!

Don Warrick

WHAT IF ORGANIZATIONS actually knew how to manage change? In today's environment of dynamic, unpredictable change and increased competition, the amount of change taking place in organizations can be overwhelming. In efforts to be competitive in a global marketplace, organizations are changing their missions, strategies, goals, cultures, processes, systems, practices, technologies, who owns them and who they own, and in some cases, even their core values. They are flattening their organizations, downsizing, restructuring, redefining roles of people from top to bottom, and struggling to keep up with constantly changing technology. The reality is that how organizations manage change has become a significant factor in their success or failure and their competitive advantage or disadvantage.

The problem is that studies tracking various types of organization changes indicate that 70% or more of significant organization changes either fail to achieve the desired results, fail altogether, or make things worse (Burke, 2008; Doyle, 1992; Miller, 2002; Senge, 1999).

Imagine the impact of a 70% or more failure rate at implementing change. Consider the disillusionment, frustration, chaos, waste of time and human and capital resources, the loss of trust and confidence in leaders, the damage to morale, and the growing resistance to change and skepticism towards each new announcement of change. The costs of change mismanagement to organizations and the people in them can be considerable!

The Potential Payoffs of Skillfully Managed Change

On the other hand, consider the competitive advantage that could be gained and the confidence in leaders and the organization's ability to make needed changes that would also be gained if the organization became skilled at managing change and could achieve a 70% or more success rate. Resistance to change would be minimal and change could be accomplished much faster with success being the norm. In other words, investing in developing skills in managing change is a high payoff investment for organizations of all types and sizes and should be a high priority for any organization that is committed to thriving or even surviving in rapidly changing times.

Why So Few Changes Succeed

The primary reason so few change efforts succeed is a lack of understanding of how to successfully manage change, particularly by top management, but also by management at all levels and others involved in change efforts. The people initiating change may be visionary leaders, excellent managers, or star employees. However, they may have little knowledge of how to manage change which requires excellent instincts about change or training in how to champion and manage change. It is the equivalent of expecting a person to intuitively know how to play tennis or the piano with no training when both require a high degree of skills to do well. With change, even the right changes implemented the wrong way are likely to fail.

A Possible Solution: The Need for Organization Change Champions

An alternative for addressing this important issue of change mismanagement and for significantly improving the success rate of organizational changes is to develop change champions throughout the organization, and especially at the top, who can effectively champion important organizational changes. A change champion can be defined as a person at any level of the organization who is skilled at initiating, facilitating, and implementing change. Change champions are to be distinguished from change agents who are trained specialist in organization development and change. Every organization large or small needs to have or have access to one or more change agents. Change agents can provide many valuable services to organizations and are definitely needed for helping manage large scale or complex changes. They can also be helpful in training change champions. However, what is being proposed here is developing change champions at all levels of the organization, encouraging them to champion needed changes, involving them in various change efforts when needed, and making them available to help others involved in making changes. This simple approach would require minimal time from the regular jobs of change champions and would significantly improve an organization's success at making and managing changes.

Change champions have always existed in organizations and have been responsible for most of the significant changes that succeed (Beatty and Gordon, 1991, Maidique, 1980, Schon, 1963). While there may not have been a formal name to describe this important role or training to prepare people for this role, the fact is that change is rarely accomplished without someone championing it. The term as used in this article would certainly include people who by nature are skilled at championing change but in particular refers to people in organizations who have been trained to champion change.

All executives and managers should be trained in this role because of their involvement in initiating most of an organization's changes. Imagine the impact on an organization if only the CEO was trained to champion change. Then consider the impact if all senior leaders were trained to be change champions. Or, if you want to grasp more of what is possible, consider training leaders at all levels to be change champions. However, this article is about going even a step further and in addition to training leaders at all levels, training key employees throughout the organization to be change champions.

Understanding The Role of Change Champions

Drawing from various research studies on people who are skilled at championing changes (for example see Kanter, 1983, Chakrabarti, 1987, and Leavitt, 1987), and over 30 years of experience in observing and working with people who excel at championing change, I have identified three major roles played by change champions: (1) Initiating; (2) Facilitating; and (3) Implementing. These roles are shown in Table 58.1 and explained below.

Initiating

The first step in learning to be a change champion is to develop a change mindset. Those with a change mindset are always looking for

TABLE 58.1 The Role of Change Champions

	Change Champion A person at any level of an organization who is skilled at initiating, facilitating, and implementing change
ROLE	**SKILLS**
Initiating	• Developing a change mindset • Providing visionary leadership • Being well informed about the issues, opportunities, and how to get things done • Involving key stakeholders and building commitment
Facilitating	• Working with people • Working with teams • Networking and getting the right people together
Implementing	• Planning and managing the change process • Making things happen • Keeping people focused and motivated • Developing feedback mechanisms to evaluate and monitor progress • Persevering until the change succeeds

new and better ways of doing things and for opportunities to launch new programs or ideas or to inspire, motivate, or encourage others to do likewise. They are reasonably savvy about what can and cannot be changed, whom to involve and gain support from, how to get things done, and they are not easily deterred by obstacles.

Providing visionary leadership is perhaps the most important skill of all in championing change. Skilled leaders provide vision (a clear understanding of the purpose and advantages of the change), direction (simplifying and clarifying goals, milestones, and what needs to be done), and inspiration (inspiring and engaging people in the change process). It is important also for change champions to be well informed about the issues, the opportunities, and how to get things done. Credibility plays a major role in being able to initiate change so it is important that change champions are well informed and are treating the real issues rather than symptoms, that they have a clear vision

of what is possible, and that they know how to get things done. Finally in initiating change it is important to involve key stakeholders and build commitment to changes. Key stakeholders are people who are in the best position to influence or contribute to the success of the desired change. The involvement of key stakeholders is critical to designing and implementing successful changes and the need to build and rebuild buy in and commitment to change is something for which change champions must be constantly aware.

Facilitating

Another valuable role change champions can play is facilitating a variety of activities in the change process either for changes they are involved in or for others. Much of facilitating involves working with people so change champions should be trained in a variety of people skills. For example, they can be trained in listening skills, coaching skills, and skills in leveling, confronting, and conflict resolution. Frankly, a genuine concern for others and practicing the golden rule of treating others the way you want to be treated will take care of most people skills.

Change champions particularly need to develop skills in working with teams. This could include learning to facilitate a variety of activities such as building change teams into high performance teams, guiding brainstorming, problem solving, planning, and conflict resolution meetings, and helping teams design and implement successful changes. Facilitating also requires skills in networking and getting the right people together. Networking and building relationships with key people makes it possible to pave the way for change. In addition change champions need to learn the value of bringing the appropriate people together to gather information, plan, address issues, and accomplish tasks. Thinking strategically about who to involve and how is important in keeping the interest high.

Implementing

With skillful implementation, the success rate for change efforts improves significantly! At the heart of successfully implementing change is developing skills in planning and managing the change process. Much has been written about the change process. Change has been described by many labels such as evolutionary, incremental, discontinuous, transactional, and transformational and numerous authors go into great depth about the complexities and messiness of change (for example see Burke, 2008, Cawsey and Deszca, 2007, Palmer, Dunford, and Akin, 2009). However, for the change champion, the clearest models for understanding, designing, and managing the change process are the three stage models that began with Lewin and evolved through other authors. Table 58.2 shows examples of three stage models.

Some have criticized the three stage process as being linear and not representative of

TABLE 58.2   Three Stage Change Model

MODEL	STAGES IN THE CHANGE PROCESS		
Lewin (1947)	Unfreezing	Moving	Refreezing
Beckhard & Harris (1977)	Present State	Transition State	Future State
Kanter (1983)	Departures From Tradition And Crisis	Strategic Decisions And Prime Movers	Action Vehicles And Institutionalization
Tichy & Devanna (1986)	Awakening	Mobilizing	Reinforcing
Nadler & Tushman (1989)	Energizing	Envisioning	Enabling
Warrick (2005)	Preparing for Change	Implementing Change	Sustaining Change

how change works but the three stages are intended to be dynamic, interactive, and overlapping (see for example Schein, 1987). It is recommended that an organization adopt an existing change model or develop one tailored to the organization so that all change champions can be trained to understand, plan, and manage changes based on the model.

Once a change model is chosen or developed, changes can be conceptualized and designed around the model. Table 58.3 provides an example of a *Change Planning Form* based on a three stage model that can be used by change champions to design and manage change. It should be understood that like all plans a change plan may go through many revisions during the change process. However, it should provide a clear focus on what needs to be done to achieve successful change.

Several other skills are important in implementing change. Change champions need to be skilled at making things happen. This typically involves demonstrating tangible progress and results, making sure commitments are kept and goals achieved, and overcoming obstacles and barriers to change. It is also important for change champions to keep people focused and motivated. Recognizing that most people involved in change are already over-committed and have probably experienced change efforts as simply meaning more work with less resources, it is important for change champions to make the incentive for change greater than the incentive to stay the same and to be diligent in keeping people focused and motivated.

Two additional skills are important in implementing change. It is very important for

TABLE 58.3   Change Planning Form

PRESENT SITUATION AND REASONS FOR CHANGING

DESIRED CHANGE AND WHO WOULD BE THE BEST PERSON TO CHAMPION THE CHANGE

CHANGE GOALS
What goals or outcomes would you ideally like to accomplish with the changes?

REALITY CHECK
What forces would be working for and against the desired change?
    Forces Working For Change *(Advocates, Compelling Reasons To Change, Timing, Etc.)*
    Forces Working Against Change *(Opponents, Reasons For Resistance, Obstacles, Etc.)*

STAGE I - PREPARING FOR CHANGE
What needs to be done to prepare the organization for change such as building support and buy in, assessing reality, educating and training people, planning, etc.?

STAGE II - IMPLEMENTING CHANGE
What needs to be done to successfully lead and manage the implementation of the desired change and to build in feedback mechanisms to monitor progress and make adjustments?

STAGE III - SUSTAINING CHANGE
What needs to be done to ensure that the changes last and are working successfully and to assure that the organization is aligned to value the changes and to learn from the change process and share the information?

change champions to develop feedback mechanisms for evaluating and monitoring the change process. Feedback mechanisms could include soliciting feedback from key people, particularly those most affected by the change, and using questionnaires, interviews, and focus groups to gather information. Without feedback mechanisms changes can get derailed with those involved in making the changes being the last to know. Feedback mechanisms make it possible to know how changes are being received and to make needed adjustments.

Finally, change champions need to remain strong and persevere until the change succeeds. Being a change champion is not an easy role to play. The role is exceptionally important to the organization and can be very rewarding. However, it can also be filled with obstacles, frustrations, and setbacks. Organizations that have the foresight and wisdom to develop change champions need to support, encourage, and value change champions for their efforts in helping the organization succeed.

Guidelines for Training, Developing, and Utilizing Change Champions

How change champions are trained, developed, and utilized will determine the success of a change champion program and the payoffs to the organization. Here are some guidelines for developing a program.

1. Name the program to fit what the culture is most likely to accept. The term change champion may or may not be readily accepted. In fact, in some cases it may be best to do the program on an informal basis without formally designating people as change champions but keeping track of who has been trained so they can be called on when needed.

2. Tailor the program to the unique needs and culture of the organization. Some programs may be endorsed enthusiastically by top management and fit the existing culture. Oth-

ers may need to be implemented on a smaller scale and more slowly because management is reluctant to embrace the concept fully and the culture will need to change to realize the full potential of the program.

3. Develop a set of tools (e.g., questionnaires, interview questions), methods (e.g., an agreed-upon approach to developing teams and facilitating groups), and strategies (particularly important is an agreed-upon change process) that can be readily learned and utilized by change champions. This can be done prior to training by involving potential change champions in working with an expert on developing tools, methods, and strategies that are tailored to the unique needs and culture of the organization.

4. Select high-impact people to become change champions. It is usually best to begin with a small group, prove the worth of the concept, and then begin developing change champions throughout the organization. The first group should include leaders or people who would be naturals for the role such as human resource professionals and people who have already earned a reputation as being champions of change. Ideally, one or more top-level managers should also be trained so top-level commitment will be evident. Some screening requirements and a selection committee may be needed.

5. Use an action training model. Train change champions on specific roles, tools, methods, and change models using a practice-partner-coach learning model. For example, following training each change champion could identify a project in which to practice skills, work with another champion on the project, and rely on an experienced coach for guidance.

The action-oriented approach to training results in a fast learning curve for participants. Using this approach, I have found that change champions can be trained in-depth with two days of formal training, several practice assignments with another champion and/or coach directly or indirectly involved, and a 1/2-day follow-up session where participants can share experiences, learn from one another, and modify the tools, methods, and strategies. More streamlined training can be used depending on the goals of the organization. For example, managers can be trained in the fundamentals of championing change in a one day session.

6. **Build on the strengths of change champions.** The change champions will learn and grow at different rates and develop different strengths. One may excel at initiating change, another at facilitating, and another at implementing. An awareness of these strengths among the change champions can result in better match-ups on projects.

7. **Create a learning community for change champions.** A stimulating learning community can be created by using imaginative ways for change champions to keep up to-date, share information and experiences, and continue to learn and grow. For example, assignments can be made for keeping up-to-date on books, journals, CDs, and current practices. Periodic meetings can be held to share what has been learned. Short workshops can also be organized for change champions to share new tools, methods, or strategies. Another alternative is to start a Change Newsletter where information, ideas, and what has been learned from change efforts can be shared.

8. **Value and reward change champions for their contributions.** One of the risks of becoming a change champion is that the organization will continue to value and reward champions solely for their regular job duties, which they continue to perform. If this additional role is not recognized, valued, and rewarded, it will be difficult to persuade anyone to continue in the role even though it is occasional. Conversely, if a high value is placed on the role, the number of change champions will

continue to increase, which should produce substantial benefits to the organization.

9. **Keep the change champion program flexible and relevant.** As is the case with any program, the program can develop a life of its own, become a bureaucratic or time-consuming activity trap, and render the cure worse than the disease. Continuously look for ways to improve and simplify the program and increase its contribution. The program needs to be flexible enough to adapt to changing conditions and even downsize or move on to better alternatives. Entry into and exit from the program should be smooth and flexible, with no stigma attached to opting out.

Conclusions

Unprecedented and non-stop change will be the norm for organizations now and in the future. Unfortunately, few of the changes will be successful. This fact has significant implications for organizations. Failed changes can be costly, demoralize employees, reduce competitiveness, and start an organization on the road to mediocrity or obsolescence. The problem exists because few people responsible for change understand how to manage change. Developing champions who understand how to initiate, facilitate, and implement needed change is an alternative that offers considerable potential for addressing this important issue. What does your organization plan to do about managing the tidal wave of change it will face in the future? Organizations must find a viable solution to this problem if they are to remain competitive.

References

Beatty, C., & Gordon, J.R.M. (1991, Spring). Preaching the gospel: The evangelists of new technology. *California Management Review, 33(2)*, 73–94.

Beckard, R., & Harris, R. (1977). *Organization transitions: Managing complex change.* Reading, MA: Addison-Wesley.

Burke, W. W. (2008). *Organization change: Theory and practice.* Thousand Oaks, CA: Sage Publications.

Cawsey, T., & Deszca, G. (2007). *Toolkit for organizational change.* Thousand Oaks, CA: Sage Publications.

Chakrabarti, A. K. (1974). The role of champion in product innovation. *California Management Review,* 17(2), 58–62.

Doyle, K. (1992). Who's killing total quality? *Incentive,* 166(8), 12–19.

Kanter, R. M. (1983). *The change masters.* New York: Simon & Schuster.

Kanter, R. M., Stein, B. A., & Jick, T. D. (1992). *The challenge of organizational change: How companies experience it and leaders guide it.* New York, NY: Free Press.

Leavitt, H. J. (1986). *Corporate pathfinders: Building vision and values into organizations.* Homewood, IL: Dow Jones-Irwin.

Lewin, K. (1951). *Field theory in social science.* New York, NY: Harper and Row.

Maidique, M. A. (1980). Entrepreneurs, champions, and technological innovation. *Sloan Management Review,* 21(2), 59–76.

Miller, D. (2002). Successful change leaders: what makes them? What do they do that is different? *Journal of Change Management,* 2(4), 359–368.

Nadler, D., & Tushman, M. (1989). Organizational framebending: Principles for managing reorientation. *Academy of Management Executive,* 3(3), 194–202.

Palmer, I., Dunford, R., & Akin, G. (2009). *Managing organizational change.* New York, NY: McGraw-Hill/Irwin.

Schein, E. (1987). *Process consultation: Vol. 2. Its role in organization development.* Reading, MA: Addison-Wesley.

Schon, D. A. (1963). Champions for radical new inventions. *Harvard Business Review,* 41(2), 77–86.

Senge, P. (1999). *The dance of change.* New York, NY: Currency Doubleday.

Tichy, N., & Devanna, M. (1986). *The transformational leader.* New York, NY: John Wiley and Sons.

Warrick, D.D. (2005). Launch: Assessment and action planning. In W. J. Rothwell, & R, Sullivan (Eds.), *Practicing organization development,* (pp. 271–312). San Francisco, CA: John Wiley & Sons.

CHAPTER 59

The Role of Leadership in the Management of Organizational Transformation and Learning

Edgar H. Schein

LEADERSHIP NOWADAYS bears a heavy burden. Leaders must create visions, must know how to articulate them, and must be able to implement them (Bennis, 1989). They must create learning organizations (Senge, 1990). They must create, embed, evolve, and change culture (Schein, 1992). They must be charismatic (Conger, 1989). They must be servants rather than masters (Greenleaf, 1977). And in all of this they must be authentic, credible, wise, and decisive (Kouzes, 1993; Kotter, 1990).

I would like to add another set of "musts" to this list, but to be a bit more specific than many of the prescriptions offered nowadays. We are in an era where organizations are under tremendous pressure to transform themselves, yet we have lots of evidence that this process of unlearning the old and learning the new is not going very smoothly. Reengineering and quality efforts are often not successful. Downsizing is causing massive pain and loss of morale. Innovations such as Saturn are gradually undermined. And the creation of "learning organizations" is painfully slow. And so, my question is this: What can formal leaders, those empowered by current hierarchies, do to improve this situation? My answer is that leaders should use their power to make learners feel psychologi-

cally safe instead of threatened. Change models have put far too much emphasis on the disconfirming aspects of unfreezing and not nearly enough on the creation of psychological safety for the change targets. And it is the formally appointed leaders who are in a unique position to provide such psychological safety, yet they often see their role to be that of disconfirmer or threatener.

Having identified how leaders can facilitate learning, I will point to the constraints that operate in western managerial culture and to the role that the OD function can play in dealing with those constraints.

Learning Anxiety and Survival Anxiety

I have previously argued that generative learning of the sort that is required for organizations to genuinely transform themselves involves the balancing of two kinds of anxiety (Schein, 1993). Learning Anxiety is the fear and tension that accompanies the learning of something new. New learning, especially when it involves unlearning something, produces anxiety because adaptive learning in individuals, groups, and organizations tends toward stability. We seek to institutionalize those things that work. We seek predictability and meaning. We seek novelty only when most of our situation is pretty well stabilized and under control. Instability or unpredictability or meaninglessness are uncomfortable because we do not know what is ahead. The unpredictable is potentially threatening. We also know from our own past experience that when we have to unlearn something in order to learn something new there will be a period of incompetence and loss of identity that is painful. Only if I have a high level of motivation will I subject myself to the trauma of giving up my incorrect golf or tennis swing in order to learn a better one. Learning anxiety is the ultimate basis for resistance to change and it is entirely normal.

But learning anxiety is not the only anxiety in the picture. We all recognize from various kinds of disconfirming cues that we have to learn some new things; that our present routines and habits of perceiving, thinking, and feeling are not producing enough of the kinds of results we expect and hope for. If things are going well, we will continue in our adaptive mode, but if we discover that our expectations, hopes, and dreams are not being met, we experience what we can call *survival anxiety,* or guilt. If, as many predict, the economic, political, technological, and sociocultural global environment will become more turbulent and unpredictable, then new predicaments will emerge and the solutions we have developed will become increasingly inadequate. We will discover that if we do not change and learn how to learn, things will go badly—we will experience more survival anxiety and guilt.

The dilemma of generative learning, then, is how to manage the psychological situation of being damned if we do and damned if we do not, of having one kind of anxiety if we decide to become learners and another kind of anxiety if we decide to risk staying put. For generative learning to begin, we can state the general proposition that survival anxiety must be greater than learning anxiety. Somehow we must reach a point where the fear or guilt as-

sociated with not learning is greater than the fear associated with entering the unknown, the unpredictable and the state of temporary incompetence.

On the personal level, this is the state that precipitates our going to a therapist or counselor, or to a tennis or golf camp to take some more lessons, or to a human relations workshop to get some insight and feedback. On the organizational level, this is the state that precipitates reorganizations, the calling in of consultants, reengineering or downsizing efforts, the firing of CEOs and the various other activities that we have observed in organizations that feel they are in deep trouble and in need of learning something new. What these situations have in common is that survival anxiety or guilt is greater than the anxiety associated with learning something new. As we think about this from the perspective of leaders, especially those who are personally motivated to produce learning and change in their organizations, the question is how do they make sure that survival anxiety is greater than learning anxiety? Logically there are two ways of accomplishing this goal. The method I observe most often is that the manager escalates survival anxiety by making change non-negotiable, by threatening, by shaming and by various other devices. This is often the method of choice because it is entirely within the manager's control. We can threaten the learner in various ways or provide such strong incentives for learning that the prospect of losing what the incentives offer serves to escalate survival anxiety and guilt. For example, my boss might make me feel that if I don't learn to use the electronic mail system and conduct my meetings with the latest groupware I will not get promoted in this organization. At that point, logic would dictate that I begin to learn something new and overcome my resistance to the computer. That is what the boss hopes for.

Unfortunately, we don't always do what logic dictates. Our learning anxiety may be so high that we may become defensive, misperceive the situation, deny reality, rationalize, become hostile and attribute incorrect motives to the managers. Or, if forced into a change program, we may learn only superficially, eventually fail, and then wonder what happened, or worse, blame others for our failure. Especially in relation to the introduction of sophisticated information technology tools, consultants frequently complain that the clients do not learn the tools to a sufficient level of competence to gain the productivity increases that are promised and possible. The problem here is not that we have been bad to have done this. None of us can tolerate very high levels of learning anxiety, so we need to develop psychological defenses that reduce the survival anxiety.

Change oriented managers often give up in frustration at this point and retreat to the rationalization that it is "human nature" to resist change. In that frustration they overlook a second way to achieve the state of having survival anxiety be greater than learning anxiety, namely, to reduce learning anxiety.

We can concentrate on making the learner feel more comfortable about the process of learning, about trying out new things, about entering the perpetual unknown, about being temporarily incompetent. In fact, if the world is already as unpredictable as most pundits allege, most of us already have enough survival anxiety just from the daily disconfirmation we experience. Most of us already know at some deeper level that our old habits are no longer adequate coping strategies. From the trivial problems of not knowing how to program our VCRs to the complex problems of not knowing how to organize ourselves for more productive output, we already have plenty of survival anxiety and guilt. What we need from our leaders is help in coping with our learning anxiety.

Creating Psychological Safety to Reduce Learning Anxiety

How then do leaders, as change agents, reduce learning anxiety? How can they make learning, even perpetual learning, a safe and desirable process? There are eight overlapping and related mechanisms or processes that produce psychological safety. They are cumulative and, in principle, should all be created simultaneously.

1. Provide a Positive Vision of the Future. Instead of threatening learners with scenarios of disaster if they do not learn, leaders can provide them a vision of a better future that makes it worthwhile to put in some effort, run some risks, and tolerate some pain. Developing a positive vision for ourselves, the group we belong to, and the organization we work for can become very important in facilitating learning. Sometimes leaders actually provide such visions but often it is the learners themselves that create it if leadership is supportive, and such involvement reduces resistance to change.

2. Involve the Learners in the Process. Involvement of the learners can be anything from giving them a voice in setting the ultimate targets to giving them some voice in determining how the day-to-day learning process itself will be managed. Often the targets are non-negotiable and hence simply have to be imposed by the leader. But the learner can still get involved in deciding how the learning process will be implemented. Such involvement is crucial to the reduction of learning anxiety because much of that anxiety has to do with perceptions of what it will be like to actually try to learn something new, i.e., fear of what others will think, fear of making a fool of oneself, fear that one will be "slower" than the others, etc.

The point is that the manager leading a change effort should not second guess these fears and try to fix them a priori, but, rather, involve the learners in a process where they can design the learning situation to reduce some of those fears. For example, in learning how to manage a computer, some learners might have a strong preference for individual cubicles rather than an open room with many terminals, and it would be more cost effective to provide them, rather than to risk partial learning in an open environment that left the learners too self-conscious.

3. Create a Climate of Support and Encouragement. Leaders have to reassure learners that learning something new will not cause a loss of identity or a loss to their overall sense of competence. Learners will not embark on a path that they perceive to be destructive to their sense of self-worth. Friendly and supportive encouragement from the leader in the role of manager and/or teacher/coach is essential to creating this kind of climate. Ridicule, impatience, putting down early attempts at learning, and any other negative behavior will immediately exacerbate all the learning anxiety.

4. Provide a Practice Field, a Safe Learning Environment. One of the most common mistakes organizations make is to try to create a generative learning situation on the job. While it is true that adaptive learning can be managed effectively on the job, it is absolutely impossible for people to re-examine their basic assumptions and to try new ways of perceiving, thinking and feeling while trying to be productive in terms of the old assumptions, habits and routines. As Senge has noted, leaders have to provide a practice field where it is OK to take time out, to make mistakes and to take the time to analyze and learn from them. One of the main reasons why we do not learn from our mistakes is that we immediately go on to the next action and fail to reflect on why the mistake occurred, what it meant subjectively, and how our behavior might be changed. Organizations that take time away from work to do postmortems of their major actions, that review major decisions, and that conduct post-hoc analyses of their operations are much more likely to facilitate generative learning.

Providing practice fields means giving people: (1) some time off to learn; (2) a place where they can play around, experiment, and practice; and (3) the necessary resources and facilities to practice new ways of behaving. It is in the practice field where coaches, consultants, teachers and fellow learners have their biggest impact because in the safety of practice we can listen and begin to hear alternatives that we may have never before had the mental freedom to entertain. It is in the practice field where learners can be taught some of the necessary tools of learning so that they can continue learning on their own. For example, they

can be taught to take some time after each major action or decision to reflect on why they did what they did and what consequences it had. One of the most destructive scenarios many organizations are caught in is trying to create generative learning while pressing for productivity, downsizing and in other ways reducing both the time and the resources needed for learning.

5. Provide a Clear Direction and First Steps. In order to get the learning process started, leaders must provide some direction and show people what the first steps might be. Often the source of learning anxiety is that the learner simply does not know where to start or how to go about it. Giving the learner some direction—a "yellow brick road"—and a little guidance on how to get started can be crucial in reducing learning anxiety. I remember vividly my embarrassment some years ago when I wanted to learn how to use a word processor and, in the company of several colleagues, could not find the "On" button which had cleverly been put at the back of the terminal "to keep people from accidentally hitting it with their knees."

6. Create a Group Setting for Learning. There is a good deal of evidence that when we are anxious we seek out others, primarily to share our anxiety and to get some sense of not being all alone in a difficult situation. Starting the learning process in groups is, therefore, an important principle. If I see that I am not alone in being anxious, temporarily incompetent, and slow in catching on, it makes it easier to keep going. In a way this is paradoxical because learners also do not want to make fools of themselves in front of others, so a group process only works if it is combined with learner involvement and a climate of support.

There is also a growing body of research done by the Institute for Research on Learning that suggests that some kinds of learning can only be done in groups because one needs the practical insights and support of peer group members to acquire the particular concepts, skills and know-how. For example, kids who cannot learn math in the classroom learn it very fast as members of gangs involved in the financial aspects of dealing drugs. The more complex the new learning, the more likely it is that the learning has to be supported ultimately by peer group members who have gotten the concept and can pass it on at the practical level. In other words, the best teacher is likely to be a peer group member who is slightly more advanced in the learning process than the learner. Leaders must be aware of this and facilitate such group/peer learning rather than focusing primarily on themselves as teachers.

7. Provide Role Models and Coaching Help. When complex new concepts or skills are involved in the generative learning effort, it is essential to be able to learn through psychologically identifying with someone who already has mastered the new way of thinking and acting. Coaches must not only be able to guide the new way of thinking and behaving looks and feels. Here again we have a paradoxical situation in that the role model must be sufficiently far along to be able to demonstrate the new, yet not so far along that the learner cannot identify with him or her. From this point of view, the best coaches are usually recent learners who can still remember what the problems of learning were all about. Using the computer as an example once again, I can learn far more from a colleague who has recently mastered a program than from a virtuoso hacker who is likely to be impatient with my level of incompetence. But the leader often has to be the coach in the early stages to demonstrate the direction of learning that is desired, i.e., he/she must "walk the talk."

Another essential element of good coaching is to provide useful feedback during practice periods. It is especially important to reward even the smallest steps in the direction of learning, lest the learner gets discouraged and assumes, often correctly, that the coach doesn't care anyway. The evidence is overwhelming that rewarding correct steps is far more effective than punishing mistakes. In either case, the main guiding principle should be to be helpful by which I mean "do that which will most help the learner to learn, allowing for individual and situational differences." Where one learner may need hand-holding another

may need to be left alone to work things out; where one situation may call for demonstrations of how to do something differently, another may call for the learners to figure out a new method for themselves.

8. Create Norms and Incentives that Encourage Embracing of Errors. Eighth, and most important of all, leaders must provide a climate in which making mistakes or errors is viewed as being in the interests of learning, so that, as Don Michael has so eloquently noted, we come to embrace errors rather than avoid them because they enable us to learn (Michael, 1985). Though these conditions might be difficult and expensive to implement, they are not mysterious. We do know how to get a learning process started. What we know much less about is how to keep learning processes going. And that gets us to the issue of cultural constraints, particularly some of the western cultural assumptions of managerial effectiveness.

Cultural Inhibitors: Assumptions about Managerial Effectiveness

The dilemma of creating conditions for effective organizational transformation is that the very leaders who have to create the conditions outlined above are burdened by their own history and the myths they have probably bought into in arriving at their leadership position. What are these myths and assumptions?

1. The Myth of Male Dominance. Human history has left us with a legacy of patriarchy and hierarchy, and a myth of male dominance and superiority based on the male as the warrior and protector. One can think of this as almost a state of "arrested development" in the sense that we have very limited models of how humans can and should relate to each other in organizational settings. The traditional hierarchical model is virtually the only one we have and to arrive at a position of formal leadership requires one to be willing "to climb the ladder."

2. The Importance of Being in Control. One consequence of this set of historically based cultural assumptions is that managers (who are mostly male) start with a self-image of having to be completely in control, decisive, certain, and dominant. Neither the leader, nor the follower wants the leader to be uncertain, to admit to not knowing or not being in control, to embrace error rather than to defensively deny it.

In reality, of course, leaders know that they do not know all the answers, but few are psychologically strong enough to be able to admit this and to share power with others in their organization. And, since the subordinates also demand of the leader a public sense of certainty, they reinforce the façade that leaders adopt. Yet, if organizational learning is to occur, leaders themselves must become learners and in that process begin to acknowledge their own vulnerability and uncertainty.

3. The Force of Rugged Individualism. In the US we have the additional cultural force of the "rugged individualism" that makes the lone problem-solver the hero. The dependent cooperative team player is not typically a hero. Competition between organizational members is viewed as desirable, as a way to identify talent—"the cream will rise to the top," while teamwork is viewed as a practical necessity. If teamwork were more natural, "team building" would not be the popular topic it is in the field of organization development. Individual competition is perceived to be the natural state, while the search for community is viewed as a sign of weakness. Groups as problem solvers are viewed with suspicion and the notion of group accountability or group rewards is almost totally rejected as unworkable and unsound. Individual accountability is management's sacred cow.

4. The Divine Rights of Being a Manager. Another myth that has grown up in managerial circles might be identified as the myth of the divine rights of managers (Schein, 1989). I have often heard senior managers defend secrecy around the financial condition of their company on the grounds that employees "have no right" to that information. Management is viewed as having certain prerogatives and obligations that are intrinsic and that are,

in a sense, the reward for having worked oneself up into management.

5. Leaders are More Expert, Skilled, and Wise than Their Followers. A closely related myth is that leaders, by virtue of their successful climb to the top, are more expert, skilled, and wise than their subordinates. As the late Karl Deutsch, the eminent MIT political scientist, once put it, "power is the ability not to have to learn anything." The relatively young and egalitarian social structure of the U.S. emphasizes achievement over formal status, and so we have, as yet, no clear class structure that provides people position power in society. Hence, they have to rely on earned power as represented by organizational position, title, and visible status symbols such as cars, fancy homes, and other material symbols. Given this situation, it is not surprising that once one has been promoted into a managerial position one wants to use one's authority, to act like a boss. Otherwise, what was the point?

The competition-based work hierarchy ultimately becomes the main source of security and status, and therefore, higher level managers can be expected to act in a more decisive and controlling manner to express that status. In other words, power that is earned or achieved through individual competition corrupts all the more in a society that does not have an aristocracy or class structure as an alternate source of status.

6. The Separation of Self from Work. Another barrier to creating safe learning environments is the fact that work roles and tasks are very compartmentalized in the US. These roles are separated from family and self-development concerns, and they are supposed to be treated in an unemotional and objective manner. This separation makes it very hard to examine the pros and cons of organizational practices that put more emphasis on relationships and feelings. Even to talk about anxiety in the work context is taboo.

Within the work context, we have the further problem that task issues are always given priority over relationship issues. We build relationships only if they are pragmatically necessary, but we automatically pay attention to the demands of a task even if that forces us to sacrifice relationships. Our task-focus is typically viewed as the strength of western management. Latin and Asian preoccupations with building relationships are viewed as time wasters and irrelevant.

7. Management is only about the "Hard Things." A major set of cultural constraints to learning is the myth that management can be sorted into "hard" and "soft" things. Our public images of management, the depiction of management in textbooks and other literature, the implicit model of management held by many teachers of business, all proliferate the notion that management deals with hard things such as data, money, bottom lines, payoffs, production, competition, structure. And it is even better if these hard things can be quantified.

Everyone pays lip service to the notion that people and relationships are important, but basically our society's assumptions are that the real work of managers is with quantitative data, money, and bottom lines. People are de facto treated as nothing more than another resource that can be manipulated like any other resource. In this model, people and their feelings are not the primary focus of management. If we have any doubts about the reality of this myth, consider how many performance appraisal and potential systems in our organizations prefer to reduce both performance and potential to numbers rather than dealing with qualitative descriptions of performance and leadership potential.

This bias shows up most clearly in graduate schools of business where the popularity of quantitative courses in finance, marketing, and production, is much greater than the qualitative courses in leadership, group dynamics, or communication. If one examines the implicit assumptions about people held by professors of economics and finance, one will find that, in their theories, people are assumed to be machine-like, rational actors, not humans with feelings. Though they will argue that this model is a necessary convenience for theoriz-

ing, teaching from such a model, nevertheless, sends a strong message to all business students that people are just another resource, not a prime factor of concern to management.

8. Management is Short-Term Oriented. Associated with the myth that management is only about hard things, is the myth that management is basically a short-time horizon occupation. Driven by reporting systems, managers learn early on to pay close attention to the progress of their financial numbers than to the progress of the morale or development of their employees. To create an environment for learning is a long-range task, and few managers feel they have the luxury to plan for people and learning processes.

What all of this adds up to is that it is one thing to specify what leaders should do to create the conditions for learning that is generative and perpetual, but it is quite another thing to get there, given some of the strong cultural inhibitors that are acting on leaders and followers all the time. The first and most necessary step, however, is a frank appraisal of reality. If we understand our cultural biases, we can either set out to overcome them (which is a slow process), or, even better, figure out how to harness them toward more effective learning.

Ultimately, an organization's culture cannot be judged except in relation to some goal it is trying to accomplish. If learning is our goal, then we must figure out how to become effective learners with the culture we have. Because even if we decided that some elements of our culture were dysfunctional, it is not likely that we could quickly produce culture change. Such change is itself a long and slow process. How then do we proceed?

Proactive Pragmatism

I believe that one mechanism by which culture change occurs is to re-prioritize some of the shared assumptions that conflict with other shared assumptions. For example, I believe that the U.S. is a very proactive, pragmatic, task-driven culture and that such pro-active pragmatism will eventually force leaders to pay more attention to people, to teamwork, to relationship building and dialogue. As we discover that competition and rugged individualism fail in solving important problems, leaders will experiment with other forms of organizing and coordinating. Initially, they may do it only because it is pragmatic. But gradually they will discover the power of teamwork in getting certain tasks done better and the learning that comes from the experience. As mentioned earlier, groups are anxiety reducers and, in the end, we will do more things together because the levels of both learning anxiety and survival anxiety will be higher than ever. So, if I allow myself a bit of optimism I think our proactive pragmatism will eventually force leaders into creating the conditions for the learning identified above.

The Role of Organization Development

Implicit in the above argument is a message for the organization development field and its practitioners. If OD focuses on collaboration, teamwork, and relationship building as its prime ideology and value system, it is taking a counter-cultural position and, thereby, putting itself into a power struggle with the existing managerial culture.

If, on the other hand, the ultimate purpose of OD is to be helpful to organizations and to managers in accomplishing their mission, then we must sympathize with the leadership dilemma, understand the cultural assumptions by which most managers have been socialized, and help them to see that collaboration, teamwork, and relationship building are pragmatic necessities for certain kinds of tasks, not ideologies to be bought into willy nilly.

For example, I find that team building is often touted as a general solution to organizational problems, even in situations where the task interdependence is so low that there is no need for teamwork. In this kind of situation, the OD practitioner can help leaders analyze

more precisely, the tasks to be accomplished and determine where there are true interdependencies that require collaboration and teamwork (Schein, 1995). As long as we are in a task driven, pragmatic culture, OD must help organizations to think more clearly about tasks, and let managers learn for themselves the need for groups, teams, collaboration and relationship building.

All too often we get irritated with our clients instead of truly understanding the cultural assumptions that drive them. We can spell out, as I have done above, what the leader must do to transform organizations, but we cannot impose this as a prescription. We can only hope that if our own pragmatism and cleverness are sufficient, leaders will catch on to what they must do and will seek our help in getting there.

References

Bennis, W. (1989). *On becoming a leader.* Reading, MA: Addison-Wesley.

Conger, J. A. (1989). *The charismatic leader.* San Francisco, CA: Jossey-Bass.

Greenleaf, R. K. (1977). *Servant leadership.* New York, NY: Paulist Press.

Kotter, J. P. (1990). *A force for change.* New York, NY: The Free Press.

Kouzes, J. M. (1993). *Credibility.* San Francisco, CA: Jossey-Bass.

Michael, D.N. (1985). *On learning to plan and planning to learn.* San Francisco, CA: Jossey-Bass.

Schein, E. H. (1992). *Organizational culture and leadership* (2nd ed.). San Francisco, CA: Jossey-Bass.

Schein, E. H. (1989). Reassessing the 'divine rights' of managers. *Sloan Management Review, 30*(3), 63–68.

Schein, E. H. (1993). How can organizations learn faster? *Sloan Management Review, 34*(2), 85–92.

Schein, E. H. (1995). *Career survival strategic job/role planning.* San Diego, CA: Pfeiffer.

Senge, P. M. (1990). *The fifth discipline.* New York, NY: Doubleday Currency.

CHAPTER 60

Change Mastery, Simplified

Chris Hoffman

Introduction: The Need

Try an experiment. Take a deep breath and look at your watch to see how long you can hold your breath. For most people it's somewhere between 45 and 90 seconds; few can hold their breath longer than a couple of minutes.

As I tell my management students when they start gasping for air, this is how long you can survive without change.

Mysteriously, we can't live without change. Because we human beings want to understand life, we have been trying to understand change for a long time. The oldest book on the planet (about 3,000 years old) is the Chinese *Book of Changes* (*I Ching*). Facilitating change is also at the heart of organization development work. So we have professional reasons for wanting to master the mysteries of change.

In the early days of the OD field, we were taught that to bring about change in a social system we needed to do three things: "unfreeze" the system, "make the change", and then "refreeze" the system in its new configuration (Lewin, 1951). As the field matured, we realized that this model was a bit too simplistic, that nothing is really ever "frozen" but that in fact we live in a world of "permanent white water" (Vaill, 1989). Our current understanding of change is fairly sophisticated, with models, theories, and techniques both for coping with change as an individual (Kubler-Ross, 1969; Bridges, 1980), and for leading change

in organizations and other large social systems (Kotter, 1995, 1996).

As internal organizational development consultants in a Fortune 500 electric and gas utility, my colleagues and I faced the challenge of taking this sophisticated understanding of change and translating it into something that could be remembered and readily used by managers and supervisors. Working mangers realize that they need to know something about change, but they want a practical level of understanding, not an academic level. I tried to find a way to make this complex material simpler . . . accurate, yet memorable and useful.

Change Mastery, Simplified

I came up with a couple of basic assumptions and five key factors that a manager should keep in mind when leading or managing a change. What is new in the model is not the content but the conceptual structure: most of what we know about organizational change can be collapsed into the five factors: Linkages, Energy, Focus, Skills, and Anchor. I learned from one of my clients in Minnesota that the initial letters of these five factors can be arranged to spell the name of a traditional Norwegian potato pancake. A good model needs a good mnemonic acronym, so the LEFSA model it became.

In the remainder of this article, I'd like to describe the basic assumptions, discuss the five factors, and show how they relate to organizational change and the change aspects of project management. The sidebar gives a set of practical questions for anyone who is managing, leading, or even just contemplating a change.

Basic Assumptions and LEFSA

We take as a given that change is happening all the time, that life is change. It may not always be as turbulent as white water. Sometimes it is the slow steady drip of water that, as the *Tao Te*

LEFSA—USEFUL QUESTIONS FOR THE CHANGE LEADER

Linkages—Strength in Numbers
- Is there a powerful guiding coalition?
- Are relationships built & maintained among the informal leaders?
- Are relationships built & maintained with key customers and other stakeholders?
- Is there a critical mass?
- Are we communicating frequently, simply, & consistently?
- Are relationships built & maintained among people with key skills & resources?
- Are key conflicts being resolved?
- Are we expressing empathy for the emotional reactions to change?

Energy—Motivation to Get There
- Is there a clear and *compelling* vision of the future state/goal?
- Are people able to see themselves in this vision, and the benefit to them?
- Does the majority share a sense of urgency?
- Is there clear discrepancy between what is and what could be?
- Is intrinsic motivation being supported?
- Is extrinsic motivation being supported?
- Is there a first step and a clear path of steps?
- Are we building energy and credibility through early wins?
- Are we amplifying the positive (evens, wins, stories)?
- Are we dampening the negative (removing obstacles, responding to rumors, redirecting inappropriate behavior)?
- Are we expressing empathy for the emotional reactions to change?
- Are we seeing "resistance" as useful feedback?

Focus—Where Are We Headed?
- What is the most effective leverage point for influencing the system?
- Is there a *clear* and compelling vision of the future state/goal?
- Is there a coherent & relevant metaphor?
- Is the leader modeling the changes?/Is there a positive role model?
- If relevant, is there opportunity for hands-on experience, at least with a prototype?
- Are the boundaries/scope/"container" of the change clearly defined?
- Have we defined measures of success: what success will look like?
- Have we limited ourselves to the minimum specifications?
- Are we allowing the system to self-organize, without micro-managing?

Skills—Skills to Do It
- Do people have the needed skills?
- Are we making the new way easy to learn?
- Are we providing training and time to practice?

Anchor—Woven Into the Fabric of the System
- Is positive behavior being recognized/reinforced?
- Have we considered the systems structures, power dynamics, traditions. or habitual ways of thinking that could interfere with (or support) this change?
- Have to made needed structural changes?
- Are we recruiting, hiring, promoting, and training in a way that supports the change?
- Are we developing symbols and lore . . . our new story of "who we are"?

Ching reminds us, can wear away the hardest stone. Slowly or swiftly life is always flowing, never frozen.

Since change is happening all the time, we have choices in two areas: (1) How to respond to it, whether more or less effectively; and (2) How we work to shape it. This article addresses how we work to shape change.

Ideally, in shaping change the change leader has considered the ethical and sustainability aspects of the change. We would like to take this as a given, but we also try to clarify it in the contracting phase of a consulting engagement. Will the change bring about a preponderance of good? Will it meet the needs of the present without compromising the ability of future generations to meet their own needs? At best, is it healing and restorative?

One way to think of shaping change is to think of a musical instrument . . . a pipe organ for example. Energy goes into all the pipes of the organ in the form of moving air. The notes that come out depend on the shape of the pipe that is activated. Long fat pipes give low notes; short skinny pipes give high notes. Each pipe resonates at a certain note because it is shaped to reinforce or amplify that note and cancel out all others. A slide trombone can play many different notes because the musician can make the resonating "pipe" shorter or longer, depending on what's needed.

Similarly, in shaping a change in an organizational system, you need a certain amount of energy and you need to set up opportunities that reinforce or amplify the output you want and dampen other behaviors. The effect of reinforcement is partly what makes Appreciative Inquiry so effective as a change approach. It reinforces, amplifies and helps focus the positive energy that is already in the system (Whitney & Trosten-Bloom, 2003). Energy and Focus are two of the five key factors to keep in mind when shaping change. Here is the full list:

Linkages
Energy
Focus
Skills
Anchor

Linkages—Strength in Numbers

The Linkages factor highlights John Kotter's conclusion that change efforts tend to fail unless there is a powerful guiding coalition (Kotter, 1995, 1996). We also know from Art Kleiner's work (2003) that in every social system there is a core group whose blessing can make a project and whose blessing withheld can break a project, regardless of the rational arguments for or against the project. The guiding coalition or core group is not necessarily limited to the executives of the system. What is needed are linkages among combinations of people collectively representing position power, expertise, credibility, and leadership relevant to the scope of the change. When this group is enrolled in the change, the change is much more likely to occur.

Other linkages are helpful too. The more productive linkages there are in the system, the more likely the system is to self-organize around a solution to the challenges of change (Olson & Eoyand, 2001). Examples of productive linkages include linking people with relevant key skills or resources. Effective change efforts use good communication and networking strategies to build linkages and develop a critical mass moving toward the change.

The Linkages factor also directs attention to the power that informal leaders or *sociometric stars* hold in an organization (Moreno 1934, 1953, 1960; Hoffman, et al, 1992). In any group of people, readiness or predisposition for a given change varies along a continuum, from early adopters to laggards (Rogers, 1962). We know from studies of social learning that people tend to be more influenced by those who are more like them than by those who are less like them (Bandura, 1977). When the informal leaders are enrolled in a change, regardless of where they stand along the change continuum, linkages between the informal leaders and those nearby on the change continuum help build the critical mass needed for change. The linkages among people on the change readiness continuum are like couplings on a train. Without adequate linkages, the engine of change may go merrily ahead while leaving the rest of the train standing at the station (see Figure 60.1).

Energy—Motivation to Get There

Just as an organ won't make music unless there is air moving through the pipes, an organization won't change unless there is some motivation to make the move. Extrinsic motivation —rewards (money, for example) or punishments —can make a difference in the short run, but over the long haul intrinsic motivation is more sustainable (Thomas, 2000). Intrinsic motivation means that a person is energized by the work itself. A related form of motivation, *identified* motivation, means that the person is energized to do something because the activity supports the person's self-identity, as for example doing a good job because it supports a self identity as a professional. Intrinsic and identified levels of motivation are the deeper and more enduring levels. They tend to yield

discretionary effort—going the extra mile— beyond simple compliance with expectations.

In shaping a change, motivation also comes from developing a clear and compelling vision of the desired future state, a vision in which people can see clear benefits to themselves. Depicting a clear discrepancy between what is and what could be also helps. As Kotter (1995; 1996) points out, change efforts tend to fail if the majority don't share a sense of urgency. Presenting data about where the relevant markets, regulators, and competitors are headed can foster this sense of urgency. Kotter suggests that at least 75% of a company's management should be honestly convinced that business-as-usual is totally unacceptable.

A major common misconception about motivation for change is that people resist change. People do *not* resist change if they desire the change and see some advantages in accepting the change, and if the emotional costs or losses associated with the change are not too

FIGURE 60.1   The Change Management "Field" and The Project Management Cycle

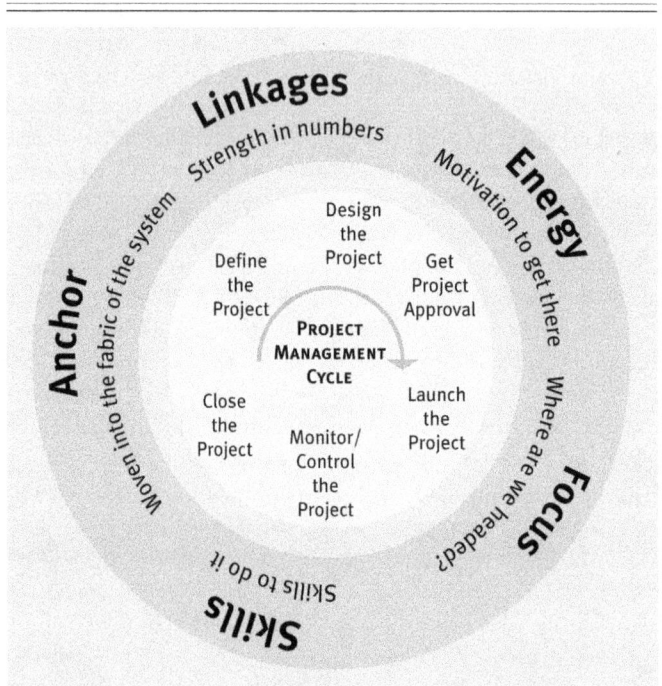

high. Consider changes such as these: Would you resist accepting a 15% raise? Would a teenager resist getting a driver's license? Would you resist marrying the person you love? In deciding to make a change people resolve an internal decisional cost/benefit balance (Miller & Rollnick, 2002). People *do* resist change if the perceived benefits are too low and/or the perceived costs are too high. People also tend to resist change if they feel coerced. This tendency has been well documented by psychologists as "psychological reactance".

Focus — Where Are We Headed?

Every effective change effort needs a clear and compelling vision of the desired future state. Frequently this is where change efforts begin. Unfortunately this is where change efforts also often end, if the Energy and Linkages factors have been neglected or come as an afterthought. Generally the first three factors should be considered as a cluster, followed by the last two factors, Skills and Anchor.

The vision for the change is most effectively communicated when the leader is modeling the change or there is a visible role model or there is opportunity for hands-on experience, at least with a prototype. The boundaries or scope or *container* of the change should be clearly defined. (Think again of a musical instrument and the resonating *container* of the sound.) We have choices about where we focus our attention. A primary role of change leader is to direct the focus and shape the container.

Though the boundaries should be clearly defined, the details of the change should not be micro-managed. Human systems will tend to self-organize, given enough energy and minimum critical specifications. In fact, too much detailed management can bog down a change. A huge portion of the population has changed its behavior to conduct business over the internet in recent years without any top-down management of the overall process (though distributed instances of the transition have been closely managed). The internet itself provided the Linkages. The benefits demonstrated by the early adopters provided the Fo-

cus for others to emulate and served to Energize people. As computer interfaces became simpler the Skills needed became easier to acquire. Now this way of doing business seems Anchored in our culture.

A clear and compelling Focus also helps build Energy. We know that it takes energy to change. When people focus on problems they tend to get depressed and lose energy. Focusing on the positive future state energizes people for change. Furthermore we tend to move towards what we focus on. When we focus on the obstacles in our path we spend time and energy dealing with those obstacles, rather than on getting where we want to go. This does not mean that we should ignore or minimize the problems with the present state. It simply suggests that the ratio of where we devote our attention (Present & Past/Forward) should be weighted toward Forward. A good rule of thumb is 20% Present & Past focus/ 80% Forward focus (Oakley & Krug, 1991).

One other key Focus question is: "What is the most efficient leverage point for influencing the system?" In a classic article several years ago Donella Meadows (1997) described nine key points in terms of increasing leverage, ranging from parameters like subsidies, taxes, and standards (relatively low leverage) to the mindset or paradigm out of which the goals, rules, and feedback structure of a system arise (high leverage). As a simple example, changing the tax structure could alter consumer behavior to some extent, but changing a belief system about what is important in life could change consumer behavior much more radically. Those who would shape change need to consider the relevant level of intervention.

Skills — Skills to Do It

An organization may be trying to introduce a new customer service support system. Though it may be clear to everyone that the new system has many benefits, and though the customer service agents may be motivated to use the system because it will make their lives easier; the system change will fail unless the agents are trained on the system and have time to practice. Similarly, a widely desired change requiring new interpersonal behaviors, such as improved communication skills, will fail unless the participants are trained and have time to practice. When people feel competent at a task, it tends to support their intrinsic motivation (Thomas, 2000), which helps build Energy for change.

Change that has not been sought out tends to produce anxiety. How that anxiety is handled will determine the degree of success or failure of the change. Change begins with a *disconfirmation*: some fact or event that shows that things are not going as well as they could or should be. The *disconfirmation* produces anxiety related to survival or guilt, either: (1) "I will not survive in some sense unless I change"; or (2) "I will not achieve my own goals and aspirations unless I change"; or some combination of (1) and (2) (Schein, 1999).

Regardless of the type of anxiety produced by the disconfirmation, the need to change itself produces another kind of anxiety: "I may not be able to learn and master the new (changed) behavior required." This is called "learning anxiety."

The anxiety produced by the disconfirmation (and therefore the disconfirmation itself) must be big enough to get people's attention. And it must be bigger than the learning anxiety. This tips the decisional balance so the costs of changing (overcoming the learning anxiety) are less than the costs of living with the survival/guilt anxiety.

The most effective way to tip the decisional balance in the direction of change is *not* to increase the survival/guilt anxiety, but instead to *decrease* the learning anxiety. Increasing the survival/guilt anxiety at some point immobilizes people and makes them incapable of change (or even of productive work). Making it easy to learn the new behaviors is the smart and effective approach.

Anchor—Woven Into the Fabric of the System

A common error of change leaders is declaring victory too soon. The push to celebrate victory

too soon can come from an unconscious collusion between the change advocates and the change opponents. The advocates want to believe that they have succeeded. The opponents are eager to find any way to call a halt to the whole process. A victory celebration serves both (Kotter, 1995, 1996).

A change can to some extent be imposed by fiat, but it will not endure beyond the tenure of the leader unless it becomes woven into the fabric of the system. Leaders need to recognize and reward the new behaviors and also to recruit and hire in a way that ensures the next generation of leaders embodies the change. Policies, procedures, and systems structures such as information systems and physical layout may need to be redesigned to facilitate the new behaviors. The easier it is to pursue the new way, the less "resistance" there will be.

Probably most important, new symbols and lore—new stories about "who we are"—will embed the changes into the culture. For example, when new apprentices are hired, they listen for the stories to find out what their new work environment is like. If they hear legends about journeymen "being macho, brave, and taking risks to save time on a job," the apprentices will tend to develop into unsafe journeymen. If the apprentices hear the story about "Bob who took risks, was badly burned and nearly died, and how everyone has been scrupulous about safe practices ever since," they will tend to develop into safe journeymen.

Practical Application

These five LEFSA factors are like five pulses that a change leader should keep his or her fingers on when working on a change. Although different factors are naturally salient at different phases of a project (Focus nearer the beginning, for example, and Anchor nearer the end), they all pertain throughout a project or change initiative (See Figure 60.1).

As a consultant I have found the LEFSA model helpful in keeping my clients focused on the key steps to take throughout a change effort. I use the worksheet shown in Figure 60.2

FIGURE 60.2 LEFSA Factor Consulting Worksheet

[With examples of client entries in *italics*]

FACTOR	COMPLETED	A C T I O N S CURRENT	POTENTIAL
Linkages Strength in numbers	*Joint problem-solving— maintenance and operations* *Assess key linkages (Sociometric analysis)*	*Leader holds meetings with yard shift personnel*	*Build linkages with "sociometric stars"* *Other…*
Energy Motivation to get there		*Hold meeting to celebrate successes to date*	*Fair and accurate informal feedback* *Other…*
Focus Where are we headed	*Develop list of desired attributes of ideal plant from our point of view* *Mgt. team* *Supervisors group* *Safety* *Other?*		*Continue developing attribute lists throughout the organization* *Next quarterly leadership forum will discuss desired direction for this year*
Skills Skills to do it		*Communication skill-building classes to be scheduled*	*Assess: What other skills are needed? (conflict resolution, etc.)* *Other…*
Anchor Woven into the fabric of the system	*Reflection of positive stories (embodying the attributes of a healthy organization) back to the organization*	*Celebration planned to recognize fewest injuries ever in the history of the plant. Distribute recognition jackets*	*Continue reflection of positive stories (embodying the attributes of a healthy organization) back to the organization* *Other…*

to track the completed, current, and potential actions in each of the five areas. LEFSA has been a component of helping a management team as they guided a large electric power plant to its best safety record in 30 years. I'm currently using LEFSA in consulting on the corporation's drive toward environmental leadership.

Conclusion

Just as breathing is an ongoing process throughout life, change, too, is a process not an event. The recent work on the transtheoretical model of behavior change (Prochaska & Velicer, 1997; DiClimente & Velasquez, 2002) describes five steps, from never having thought about a change through taking action and then maintaining the changed behavior. Especially today, with so much productive change so urgently needed, it's important to be patient, and not to be disappointed when sudden leaps don't happen. The change lights come on with a dimmer knob, not an on/off switch.

Acknowledgments

Thanks to Claudia Bruber, Diane Hill, Julie Theobald and Eric Zakovich for useful questions and feedback, and to Terry Coss for introducing me to lefsa. Many recipes for lefsa (also spelled: lefse) are available on the internet.

References

Bandura, A. (1977). *Social learning theory.* New York, NY: General Learning Press.

Bridges, W. (1980). *Transitions: Making sense of life's changes.* New York, NY: Perseus Publishing.

DiClimente C., & Velasquez M. (2002). Motivational interviewing and the stages of change. In W. R. Miller & S. Rollnick (Eds.). *Motivational interviewing: Preparing people for change* (pp 201–216). New York, NY: The Guilford Press.

Hoffman, C., Wilcox, L., Gomez, E., & Hollander, C. (1992). Sociometric applications in a corporate environment. *Journal of Group Psychotherapy, Psychodrama & Sociometry,* 45(1), 3–16.

Kleiner, A. (2003). *Who really matters: The core group theory of power, privilege, and success.* New York, NY: Doubleday.

Kotter, J. (1995, March-April). Leading change: Why transformation efforts fail. *Harvard Business Review,* 73(2), 59–67.

Kotter, J. (1996). *Leading change.* Boston, MA: Harvard Business School Press.

Kubler-Ross, E. (1969). *On death and dying.* New York, NY: Macmillan.

Lewin, K. (1951). *Field theory in social science.* New York, NY: Harper and Row.

Meadows, D. (1997, Winter). Places to intervene in a system. *Whole Earth.*

Miller, W. R., & Rollnick, S. (2002). *Motivational interviewing: Preparing people for change.* New York, NY: The Guilford Press.

Moreno, J. L. (1934, Revised edition 1953). *Who shall survive?* Beacon, NY: Beacon House.

Moreno, J. L. (1960). *The sociometry reader.* Glencoe, IL: The Free Press.

Oakley, E., & Krug, D. (1991). *Enlightened leadership.* Denver, CO: StoneTree Publishing.

Olson, E. E., & Eoyang, G. H. (2001). *Facilitating organization change.* San Francisco, CA: Jossey-Bass/Pfeiffer.

Prochaska, J. O., & Velicer, W.F. (1997). The transtheoretical model of health behavior change. *American Journal of Health Promotion,* 12, 38–48.

Rogers, E. M. (1962). *Diffusion of innovation.* New York, NY: Free Press.

Schein, E. H. (1999). *The corporate culture survival guide: Sense and nonsense about culture change.* San Francisco, CA: Jossey-Bass.

Thomas, K. W. (2000). *Intrinsic motivation at work: Building energy & commitment.* San Francisco, CA: Berrett-Koehler.

Vaill, P. B. (1989). *Managing as a performing art.* San Francisco, CA: Jossey-Bass.

Whitney, D., & Trosten-Bloom, A. (2003). *The power of appreciative inquiry: A practical guide to positive change.* San Francisco, CA: Berrett-Koehler.

CHAPTER 61

Backcasting

A Systematic Method for Creating a Picture of the Future and How to Get There

Larry Hirschhorn

A CHALLENGE WE FACE in envisioning a goal is the difficulty of imagining the conditions that have to be true in the future if our goal is to be achieved. If we posit a goal, say, "our revenues are 50% higher," it is apparent that many other conditions must also be true, e.g., "our work force is bigger," or, "our product appeals to customers who have never before purchased this kind of product." But how can we envision fully the texture of such a future state? What are the conditions that need to be in place in order for us to have accomplished our goal?

This is not a theoretical question, since without a relatively complete picture of the future state, we will not be able to map out an implementation plan for achieving our goal. For example, if we believe that revenues can grow 50% *only* if we attract customers who have never before purchased the kind of product we sell, then our conception of the actions we have to take now to achieve our goal must include steps for attracting new customers to our product category. Our understanding of our desired future state and our plan for getting there are inextricably intertwined.

Goldratt's Methodology: The Thinking Process

How can we identify the network of future conditions surrounding a goal? When we do so, how do we use this knowledge to implement a change within an organization?

To answer these questions we draw directly on, while also modifying, the rich and creative methodology developed by Eli Goldratt and his colleagues, called "the thinking process" (Goldratt, 1994). They developed a four-step thinking process for identifying how to improve a situation or setting. In the first step organization actors link identified symptoms to a root cause, in the second, they describes how an intervention, by overturning the root cause, can transform the symptoms into desired conditions, in the third, they specify the prerequisites that must be in place to implement the intervention, and in the fourth, they delineate the tactics to put these prerequisites into place.

For example, confronting the problem of low productivity, organization members would in the first step list the symptoms of low productivity, for example, poor morale, work hoarding, turnover, conflict, an incentive scheme which punishes collaboration. Then using Goldratt's thinking process, they would connect these symptoms together in a causal thread. The resulting diagram, called a "current reality tree" looks something like Figure 61.1.

While the tree, as shown here, looks like a standard "problem map," it is distinguished from the latter by the rigorous cause and effect reasoning used to build it ("If A and B then C").

FIGURE 61.1

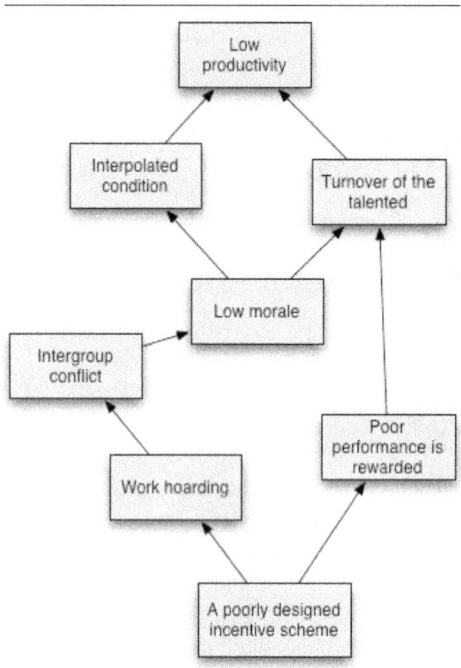

This reasoning may lead to the inference that other conditions not named in the initial catalogue of symptoms must also exist (we call them here "interpolated conditions) if the set of symptoms are to be part of a single underlying reality. The diagram when complete points to one symptom or interpolated condition, not caused by any other symptom, which becomes, in this case the "root cause." We have confidence in our identification of the root cause because our thinking has been rigorous. The central philosophical premise of this method is that there is one underlying reality that gives rise to the identified symptoms and therefore they are all connected causally.

In the full Goldratt method we would as a second step specify a condition that is the opposite of the root cause, for example, "we have an incentive scheme that rewards good performance and stimulates collaboration." We then create a "future reality tree," which by applying the same logic of cause and effect leads to conditions that are the opposite of

each of our symptoms, e.g., "good performance is rewarded," or, "work is shared appropriately." Confident that we have a picture of how to eliminate our symptoms we then ask what *pre-requisites* we have to put in place, to insure that our incentive scheme is an effective one. The result is a third tree, called the "pre-requisite tree."

The Backcasting Approach

As rich as this method is, it is also time consuming and difficult. Many clients are reluctant to engage with it. We developed our backcasting method to overcome their resistance to this way of thinking. Our method short-circuits the first two steps and substitutes an interviewing process for the client's work of rigorously thinking in cause and effect terms. Instead of beginning with symptoms, we posit a goal, e.g., "we have a suitable incentive scheme" and then employ our structured interviewing process to help an organizational actor identify rigorously the pre-requisites. We call this interviewing method and the tree of prerequisites it helps us produce, "backcasting."

Our approach consists of four steps.

- Specifying the goal.
- Interviewing the organizational actor(s).
- Creating a draft backcast and its corresponding accomplishments map.
- Developing a project plan based on the backcast.

Let us describe each step

Specifying the Goal

Ask the organizational actor or client to specify a desired end state, for example, "Our incentive scheme rewards collaboration." The only rule in specifying the end state is that it *not* be stated as an action, e.g., "we replace our incentive scheme with one that rewards collaboration," since the latter describes a process for reaching our goal, rather than the goal itself. The goal can be stated in somewhat general terms, because the interviewing process itself will elicit the specific meaning or import of the goal to the organizational actor(s). If we ask for too much specificity in defining the goal we are in essence anticipating the backcasting work itself.

Interviewing the Organizational Actors

Interview the actor(s) using an iterative process based on the following two questions

1. What obstacles would you have to overcome to achieve this result?
2. What accomplishments represent the overcoming of these obstacles?
   a. What obstacles you would have to have overcome to achieve these accomplishments?
   b. What accomplishments represent the overcoming of these obstacles? Etc.

The following is an example of such an interview protocol conducted with a nurse manager.

Interviewer: Let's take as the goal; "Nursing turnover is reduced to a minimum." What are some obstacles?

Client: People don't feel comfortable working outside of their specialty areas. It would be good to have them spend most of their time in their specialty areas.

Interviewer: What are obstacles to achieving that?

Client: We don't have a staffing model that supports staying in your specialty areas.

Interviewer: If you had the staffing model what would be the obstacle to that?

Client: We can't build the teams we need on evening and weekends.

Interviewer: If you had the staffing model what would be the obstacles to building the teams?

Client: Right now we have people with seniority in the operating room on days. The newest people are doing the weekends and evenings, which is stressful for them.

Interviewer: How could you overcome this problem?

Client: We should look at a dedicated pool of senior nurses for the evenings and weekends and pay a premium rate. A lot of interest has been piqued in that. They could proctor the new nurses who work nights.

Interviewer: Are there obstacles to paying a premium?

Client: I also have to pay the OR tech a premium, but one way to do this is to offer more school benefits. I think the culture would support this. People should get paid for their inconvenience.

Interviewer: Is there another obstacle to getting the dedicated pool?

(continued)

Client: Maybe too many experienced nurses will want to shift to evenings and weekends. You have to protect the day shifts. We should try to attract some ex-employees back who already know our systems. They will like the premium pay. We could also increase the number of senior people on call.

Interviewer: Are there any other obstacles to reducing turnover?
(Client turns to issues of proctoring and educational support for new nurses).

FIGURE 61.2

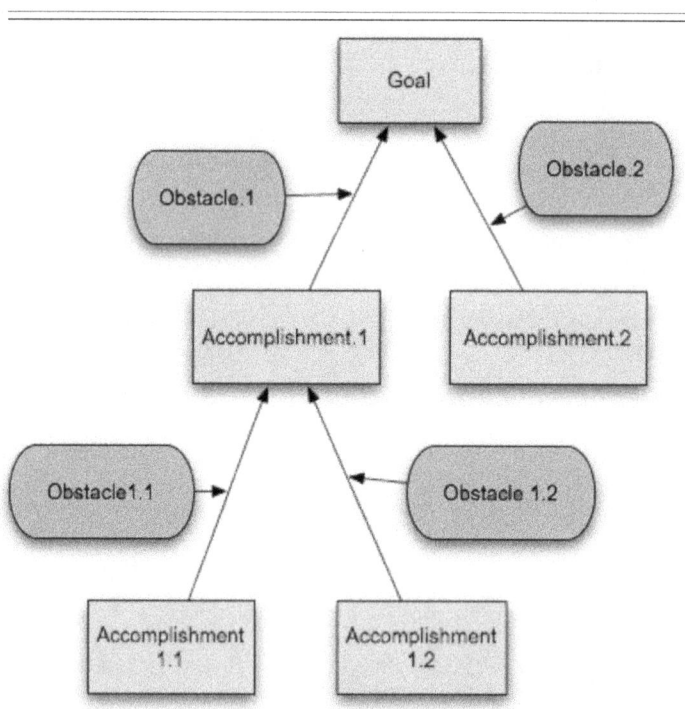

The interview in effect, replicates Figure 61.2 where the goal and the accomplishments are shaded in green rectangles, the obstacles in red "squashed" rectangles. The map is read in the following way. Looking at Accomplishment 1 it says, "If we want to achieve *Accomplishment 1* we will have to overcome *Obstacles 1.1 and 1.2.* Achieving *Accomplishment 1.1* is a way to overcome *Obstacle 1.1,* and achieving *Accomplishment 1.2* is a way to overcome *Obstacle 1.2.* While the map is read "downwards," the arrows point upwards to indicate that an accomplishment at a level below, e.g., *Accomplishment 1.1,*

is a precondition for achieving an accomplishment a level above, e.g., *Accomplishment 1.*

The Interview

One important question is how to conduct the interview? There is a tension between a "vertical" and "horizontal" approach. In the horizontal approach we would ask the client or actors to first list all the high level obstacles, to then list all the accompanying accomplishments, then to list all their obstacles to these accomplishments, etc. Alternatively we could follow one line of causation all the way down to the "bottom" of the backcast tree much as the protocol above reads. Our own experience is that people more naturally follow the second path. Once they start with one obstacle they are comfortable working their way down through the resulting cascade of accomplishments and obstacles. This means that the interviewer has to periodically pull the client "back to the top" to start on a second obstacles.

We have found that it takes practice to master this kind of interviewing protocol. The challenge is to enable the organizational actor to follow his or her own lines of thought, while periodically asserting the logical structure of the protocol. This sometimes means allowing the actor to think horizontally as well as vertically, while keeping track of the implicit logic. It helps to have two interviewers present one to facilitate the conversation and one to take notes and keep track of where the actor is in his or her thinking

As the above protocol suggests, the structure off the interview helps people access their implicit theory of the causal structure of the setting in which they work. For example, the nurse manager believes that seniority interferes with good staffing practices on the evening shift, because nurses on the evening shift, who are less experienced, work out of their specialty areas. Novice nurses experience this as stressful and as a result some fraction of them leave. If more senior nurses worked on the night shift, novice nurses, if still required to work out of their specialty areas, could get good informal supervision from the senior nurses. Our philosophical premise is that organizational actors have an intuitive understanding of the causal structure of the environments they are in, and that the interviewing protocol helps them *access and verbalize* this intuition.

The Challenge of Verbalizing Accomplishments

What happens if this intuition fails them? What if they get stuck, that is, they cannot en-

vision an accomplishment that represents the overcoming of an obstacle they have just named? In this case the interviewer simply reframes the obstacle as an accomplishment and follow the logic down the tree. So for example, if the organizational actor says, "the obstacle to more sales is that our service quality is low," and then cannot think of any avenues for increasing service quality, the interviewer then posits the accomplishment, "our service quality is high," and then asks the ask the interviewee to list obstacles to *this* accomplishment. In naming these obstacles the interviewee then begins to describe what has to change to insure high quality. For example, one obstacle might be, "we don't really understand what our customers will pay for." An accomplishment might then be, "customers regularly give us feedback on the quality of our service." So now we have at least one accomplishment that contributes to overcoming the obstacle of low service quality. The capacity to envision an obstacle is the first step to envisioning a solution. Or, to reference a more general methodological point, *the problem stated correctly, is simply another way of describing the solution.*

Creating a draft backcast

The interviewer then analyzes the text of the interview, and maps it onto structure shown in Figure 61.2. Let us return to our interval protocol with the nursing manager. We posited there the goal that, "nursing turnover is at a minimum." Using the interview protocol, we then create the following backcast (see Figure 61.3).

This map is read in the following way, "If we want to achieve the goal 'nursing turnover is reduced to a minimum,' then we have to overcome the obstacle that 'newer nurses work out of their specialty areas on the night shift.'" To overcome that obstacle we need "a dedicated pool of senior nurses who work on the night shift." However, senior nurses have no incentive to move to nights. Therefore we must, "offer senior nurses premium pay at nights." But if we do this we might "raid the day shift." So, "we should also have incentives to attract

FIGURE 61.3

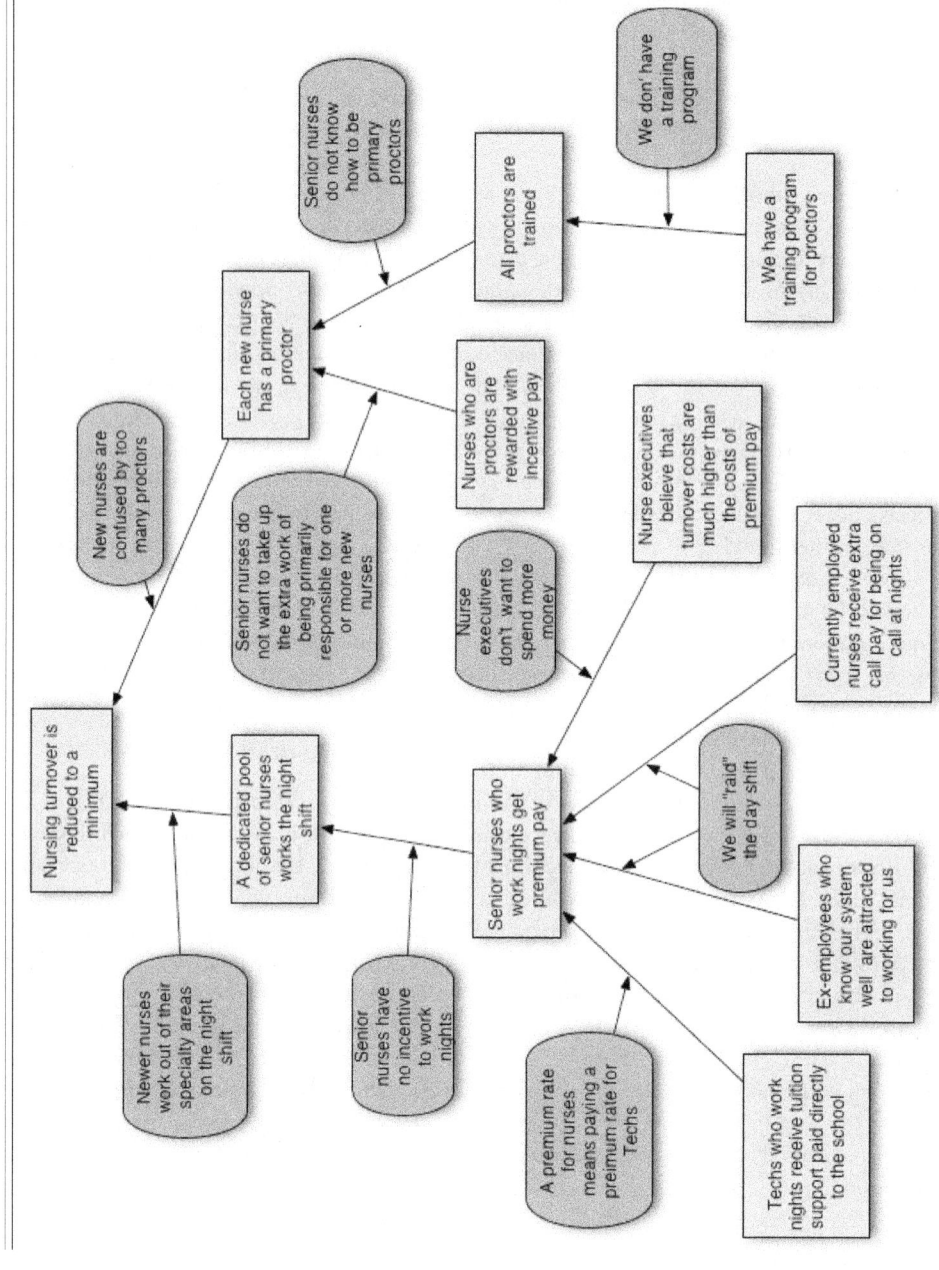

day-senior nurses to be on call for nights, and we should attract ex-employees back to work for us." This backcast also shows the beginning of the second branch related to the mentoring of new nurses, a theme which first appears at the end of our protocol.

One question is how exhaustive in its logic must the map be? For example, the backcast assumes that it is more difficult to cover each area of surgery with nurses trained for that area, for example neurosurgery, on evenings and weekends. In the interview protocol this is a taken-for-granted assumption, it is a "fact of life" which any insider knows. The interviewer can of course ask for clarification about this, if the rationale for the taken-for-granted assumption is unclear. But the rule of thumb in building the backcast is to include as much detail about the underlying logic that

helps the client scrutinize and then revise the backcast tree, and that serves as a good enough communication vehicle among all of the organizational actors.

The Accomplishments Map

As was noted in the introduction, to create an implementation plan we need to develop a textured picture of a future state that includes among many other conditions our original goal. To do this we create an *accomplishments map* by eliminating all the obstacles (see Figure 61.4).

We built our backcast by asking what accomplishments must be in place to overcome each obstacle. This means in turn that each accomplishment must logically be a part of the future in which our goal is achieved. Taken to-

FIGURE 61.4

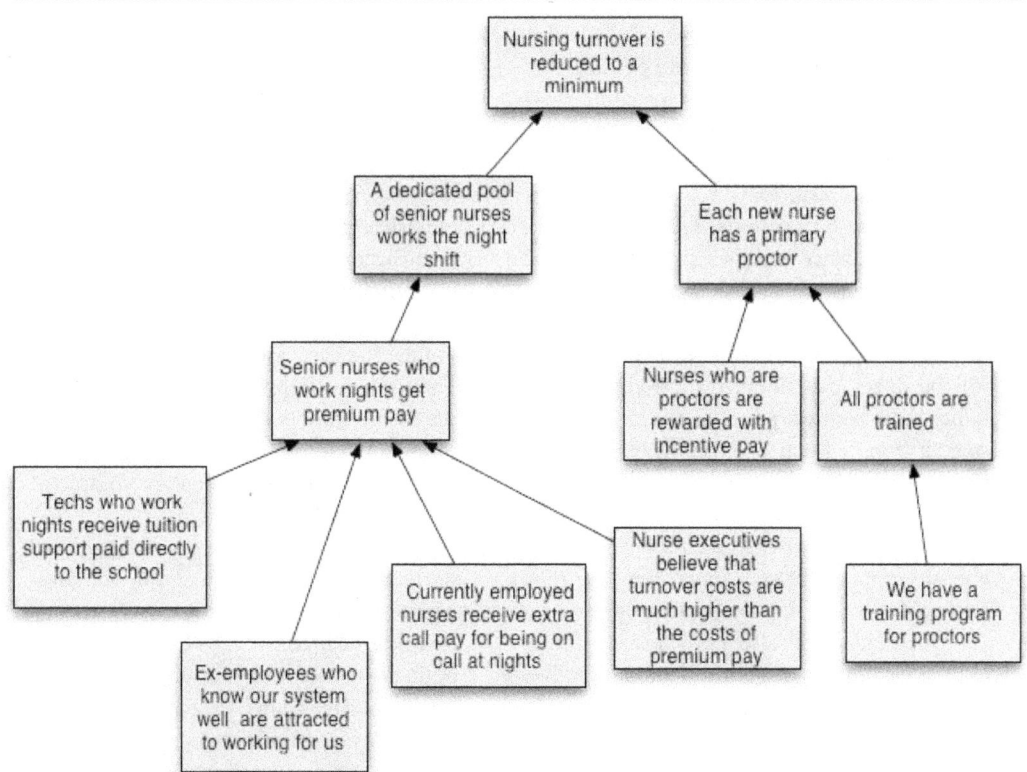

gether, we now have a richer picture of the future state we want to achieve. It entails at least ten different conditions. If we had not worked through this logical process we could never have intuited that our future state must include at least these conditions. This method of describing a future state is more exacting than simply asking people to imagine how the future might look. The latter is based on brainstorming, a process that offers no assurance that the picture of the future will be complete or even coherent. The backcast method provides a much higher level of assurance that such criteria will be met.

Logical Time Versus Historical Time

The reader can now see why it is important to phrase each accomplishment as a condition in the present tense, rather than as an action. If instead of using the phrasing, "techs who work nights receive tuition support paid directly to the school," we write instead, "we increase rewards to techs who work nights by giving them tuition benefits," we would be describing an action *that is on the way* to accomplishing our objective rather than the accomplishment itself. We would have shifted from logical time to historical time. The thinking process we use in the interview is based on the logic of precedence, what must precede what, *logically speaking,* rather than in actual time. In this sense the backcast is just like a forecast that states how the future will look, e.g., "it will be a hot day tomorrow (Wednesday)," rather than how we get to a hot day. ("The cold air front will move out to the ocean pulling a warm air front in behind it"). The only difference we add is that, to keep us focused on conditions rather than actions, we phrase everything in the present tense, e.g., "In the future, Wednesday, the temperature is hot."

The reader will also note that we have used what Goldratt calls the "logic of sufficiency" rather than then "logic of necessity." Every obstacle we name is sufficient to prevent an accomplishment, but it is not neces-

sary to prevent it, since there may be other still un-verbalized obstacles that could also prevent the accomplishment. In other words, our method does not guarantee that we have an exhaustive list of obstacles for each accomplishment. Instead, we arrive at a "good enough" set of obstacles by asking organizational actors to scrutinize the tree and add obstacles that they believe are important in moving from the present to the desired future. We use an iterative process to get to good enough set of obstacles.

Creating an Action Plan: Interpreting Logical Precedence

We can use the accomplishments map to create a project plan. The project plan is the picture of how we get from the present to the future. Consider the diagram below (see Figure 61.5). We eliminate references to "on-call" nurses and to "giving techs tuition benefits" to simplify our diagram.

The above action plan has five distinct features.

1. The action steps, in the "cut" rectangles are all verb phrases. We are now in the realm of action.
2. We display the action steps horizontally to indicate decisions taken over time.
3. Each accomplishment is associated with one or more action steps. When the action plan is complete the action steps "surround" the backcast.
4. These actions steps are not descriptions of the future state but how we get to the future state. For example, once the task force designing the training program completes its work, it will disband.
5. The sequence of steps is determined partly by the logic of precedence but also by considering the amount of lead-time we will need to complete each action step. For example, we begin discussions with human resources even before we have completed the design of the training program because we know it will take some time to get their agreement.

FIGURE 61.5

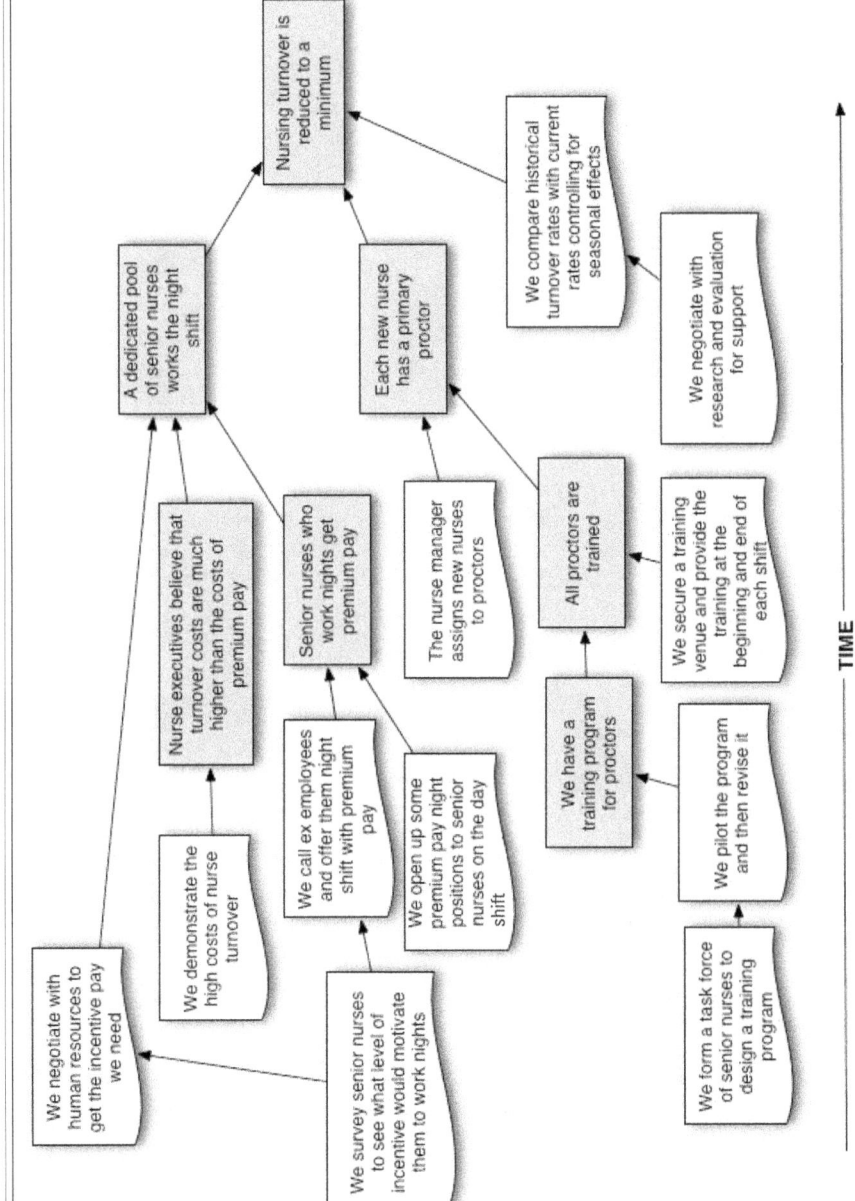

Nursing turnover is reduced to a minimum

A dedicated pool of senior nurses works the night shift

Each new nurse has a primary proctor

We compare historical turnover rates with current rates controlling for seasonal effects

We negotiate with research and evaluation for support

Nurse executives believe that turnover costs are much higher than the costs of premium pay

Senior nurses who work nights get premium pay

The nurse manager assigns new nurses to proctors

All proctors are trained

We secure a training venue and provide the training at the beginning and end of each shift

We negotiate with human resources to get the incentive pay we need

We demonstrate the high costs of nurse turnover

We call ex employees and offer them night shift with premium pay

We open up some premium pay night positions to senior nurses on the day shift

We have a training program for proctors

We pilot the program and then revise it

We survey senior nurses to see what level of incentive would motivate them to work nights

We form a task force of senior nurses to design a training program

TIME

The action plan demonstrates an important link between logical time and historical time, which guides the development of a project plan. The accomplishment "nurse executives believe that turnover costs are much higher than the costs of premium pay" logically precedes "a dedicated pool of senior nurses works the night shift." This means that while I can start working on the latter by starting my discussions with human resources, I can't get my pool of dedicated nurses until I have demonstrated that the costs of nurse turnover are high. Lead-time, can trump logical precedence in terms of when I begin an action step, but logical precedence determines when I reach my goal.

Creating a History of the Future

An added benefit of an action plan is that it provides the outline for writing a "history of the future" by enabling us to combine historical time and logical time together in a believable story of how we reach our goal. Our practice is to write the story as if it were an interview that takes place in the future with one or more of the organizational actors. The interview can be described as having been published in the organization's newsletter. So for example it might begin in the following way.

Reporter: I understand that you were able to significantly reduce nursing turnover Our readers would be very interested in knowing how you did this.

Nurse manager: Well we knew that the problem was with our newer nurses. They were being thrown into the night shift, and because we did not have as much coverage of all the specialties we wanted at nights, they were sometimes working outside their specialty without much supervision. It was too stressful for them and some left.

Reporter: How did you address this specific issue?

Nurse manager: We knew that we needed more senior nurses working nights to provide the newer nurses with more supervision.

Reporter: I would think it would be hard to get the senior nurse to shift to nights. Working days is one perk of seniority.

Nurse Manager: Well it was. But we did a survey of the senior nurses on days focusing on those we knew had no young children at home. We asked them what increment in pay it would take for them to switch to nights. It was not trivial, but when we ran the numbers we could see that we would still be saving money if turnover fell.

Reporter: How did you justify paying them more then standard premium, and didn't this mean that everyone on night got a boost in pay?

Nurse manager: We worked with human resources on this. We realized that we could justify this pay if the senior nurses were proctors for the new nurses while on the night shift. This is what we wanted to do anyway. HR was accommodating once they saw that the job description was changing.

Reporter: Was it hard getting the nurse executives to sign off on this extra pay?

Nurse Manager: Well we had already calculated our cost of turnover and we could show to our executives that there was a good chance that the extra cost of turnover would outweigh significantly the extra cost associated with our proposal for the night shift. Of course we could not prove this for sure, but the executives were willing to take a risk, since high turnover of new nurses was such an obvious waste of money. We invest so much training in them.

Reporter: So once you got there buy-in it was a go?

Nurse Managers: Well not exactly. We had to promise the clinical director of nursing that we would put in place a good evaluation plan to see if in fact turnover really fell. This took some time to develop and held up our implementing the program. In retrospect I wished we had started this earlier.

Reporter: But when it was done you went ahead?

Nurse Managers: Yes, except that......

We have found that the texture of the backcast and the action plan provides an excellent level of realistic detail to write readily, a plausible interview. Moreover, because the interview is framed as the telling of a story of success, when circulated to the project team it is motivating. People begin to see how they can get from the present to the future by facing and overcoming all the serious obstacles in their way.

Summary

A goal describes how we want our part of the world to look in the future. But a goal does not stand alone. It is part of a network of conditions all of which also have to be true in the future if we are to realize our goal. It is difficult for people to imagine this network of conditions simply by brainstorming or playfully imagining the future, because this network depends on the causal structure of obstacles that stand in our way of accomplishing the goal. Backcasting helps us reveal this causal structure and gives us a relatively complete and coherent picture of the network of conditions we need to achieve if we are to overcome these obstacles. In addition, the backcast guides us in building a detailed action plan that combines our accomplishments and the steps to achieve them. The action plan helps us create a vivid and realistic "history of the future," which as a story of success can be very motivating.

References

Goldratt, E. (1994) *It's not luck.* Great Barrington, MA; The North River Press.

CHAPTER 62

Using Action Learning for Organization Development and Change

Arthur M. Freedman

THIS ARTICLE conveys some practical information about the application of a powerful "tool"—Action Learning (AL) theory, method, and skills—for organization development and change (OD&C) practitioners. AL is not new. Neither is it is widely known or understood by most OD&C practitioners. Therefore, I intend to demonstrate how AL theory, methods, and skills can enhance current change management efforts—particularly those in which technical expert consultants partner with OD&C practitioners.

In this article, I define AL and AL Team Coach (ALTC). I also offer a definition of the discipline and practice of OD&C. Moreover, I compare and contrast these disciplines with management consulting (MC), and present a case study of OD&C consultation that incorporated ALTC. I conclude with some observations about how AL contributes to organizational learning.

Sources of the Felt Need for Organizational Change

Intentional organizational changes are initiated in a number of different ways. In one instance, the impetus is supplied by stakeholders' expressions of dissatisfaction with the status quo. Dissatisfaction may be globally expressed by dropping revenues, decreased profit margins, dissatisfied customers, low levels of employee satisfaction, or turnover.

Specific points for organizational change may be identified in a variety of ways—surveys, focus groups, audits, or changing regulatory requirements. The change effort may focus on such problems as repairing or replacing something that does not work as efficiently as required; capitalizing on new, emerging opportunities; or managing persistent dilemmas.

Generally, these are problems discontinuous with organizations' past experiences. In dealing with such unprecedented problems, organizations find themselves in unknown territory, i.e., their existing problem solving tools/methods are not effective. Organizations discover they must buy or develop new approaches and skills to cope with unfamiliar problems.

While it may be easy to identify *what* should be changed, it is less clear and more complex to determine *how* to set realistic goals and develop implementation plans while enlisting stakeholder commitment to executing those plans. AL provides the theory, methodology, and skills that augment the practice of OD&C.

AL and ALT Coach

According to Marquardt, Leonard, Freedman, and Hill (2009), AL involves analysis and action and also learning. This triad optimizes the power and benefits of AL.

A Problem (the Gap Between the Current and Desired State). AL focuses on critical problems whose solution is highly important to an individual, a team, or an organization. AL is most appropriate where the problem is complex, the desired outcome is vague, and the solution is uncertain or unknown. In addition, the problem should be complicated enough to provide learning opportunities, knowledge building, and the development of specialized skills.

Action Learning Team. The ALT consists of four to eight people with diverse backgrounds and work experiences. Diversity enables team members to perceive the problem from various perspectives and to offer innovative viewpoints. Teams may consist of volunteers or appointees who come from various departments or hierarchical levels. They may include individuals from other organizations or professions. They may involve suppliers as well as customers or other stakeholders. One or more team members may also be problem presenters. Some team members may serve as observers.

The process emphasizes insightful inquiry and reflective listening. AL requires team members to reflect and respond to questions. By crafting great questions, AL taps into the collective wisdom of team members and relevant stakeholders.

Questions are asked to clarify the exact nature of the problem, to identify possible solutions, and to determine implementation in a manner acceptable to senior management. The reflective inquiry process builds team cohesiveness, promotes systems thinking, introduces innovative strategies, and generates individual and team learning.

Taking action. The problem may be presented by team members or by an executive who serves as a sponsor. A senior executive may serve as champion for an AL project that is composed of several teams. An executive management team generally decides whether or not any team's recommendations will be enacted.

Sponsors or champions must grant ALTs sufficient authority to take action both between ALT sessions and on recommendations when approved. Reflecting on the action taken and its results provides the best source for learning and organizational change.

A commitment to learning. Solving an organizational problem provides immediate short-term benefits to the system. The greater, long-term, multiplier benefits occur when team learning is shared and applied strategically throughout the organization.

AL emphasizes the learning and development of individuals, the team, and the organization. The smarter the team becomes, the quicker and better the quality of its problem solving, decision making, and action taking.

ALT Coach

While team members focus on solving problems, the ALT coach is devoted to enabling the team to learn. The coach identifies learning opportunities that enable the team to reflect on and improve its participative problem solving, conflict management, decision making, goal setting, action planning, and strategy creating capacities.

Lacking a coach, teams tend to focus their time and energies solely on solving the problem and neglect the more important individual, team, and organizational learning. Through inquiry, the coach enables team members to reflect on all aspects of communications relevant to the problem.

AL Process

The AL process must start with one or more critical organizational problems. ALTs are mobilized and deployed to analyze and develop solutions for the problems. Team members are recruited, selected, and provided with an orientation to AL.

A coach is provided to each ALT. The ALT presents solutions to the executive management team (EMT) for approval by a specific date established in advance by the EMT.

AL is applied in extraordinarily flexible configurations. The configuration largely depends upon the amount of time that the EMT makes available for creating solutions. The complexity and scope of the problem(s) are also factors; very complex problems require more time, commitment, and support.

Problems with a limited scope and moderate to low complexity may require only a little time for the ALT to complete its work. An unexpected crisis also may require a limited or massed time schedule. Crises or predictable surprises (Bazerman & Watkins, 2008) often occur during the implementation of large complex transformational changes. A Special Action Learning Team (SALT) can be quickly mobilized to deal with such crises (Marquardt et al., 2009).

Typically, AL requires a four to six month period (a spaced configuration). ALTs meet every two weeks for three to four hours with their coach. At the outset, the team sponsor presents and explains the significance of the problem. Through a process of inquiry and reflection, the ALT clarifies and reaches agreement on the problem and the goal, identifying also the stakeholders involved in the problem.

Team members—acting as emissaries (Freedman, 2000)—interview and collect information from stakeholders between sessions, and transmit the information to the ALT. The new information may modify the Team's initial understanding of the problem. New information from stakeholders also helps team members to identify which proffered solutions are likely to be viable.

Once the ALT believes it has sufficient information, the Team begins to develop provisional strategies, solutions, and recommendations. Teams will typically present their ideas

to all involved stakeholders for input and feedback. Additionally, a Team may also conduct a pilot test of their solution to assess its effectiveness before presenting it to the EMT (see Figure 62.1).

OD&C

The aim is to affect meaningful OD&C—"the systemwide application and transfer of behavioral science knowledge to the planned development, improvement, and reinforcement of the strategies, structures, and processes that lead to organization effectiveness" (Cummings & Worley, 2009, p. 1).

Most transformational organizational changes address the root source of executive dissatisfaction with prevailing conditions, e.g., operational deficiencies or inefficiencies. Notwithstanding, organizational changes are best planned and implemented when each of five vital signs is operative (Freedman & Jules, unpublished): (1) dissatisfaction is high; (2) there is a clear and compelling vision of a desired future state; (3) at least the first few steps of an action plan is accepted by all significant involved parties or stakeholders; (4) executive leadership is totally and publicly committed to support the change initiative; and (5) there are meaningful incentives for planners, implementers, and stakeholders to accept and contribute to the change. The ultimate value of any change must be perceived to be greater than the financial, opportunity, and psychological costs incurred by undertaking the organizational change.

The desired future state can be compared with the current state of affairs to clarify what might be eliminated, preserved, or added. The gap between the current and future states can be Force Field Analyzed to determine: (a) why it is important to achieve the desired state, and (b) why it is difficult to achieve the desired state. Action steps leading to the achievement of the desired state can be derived from this Force Field Analysis and will comprise a workable implementation plan. In the final analysis, the most interesting, complex, important,

FIGURE 62.1 The Action Learning Process

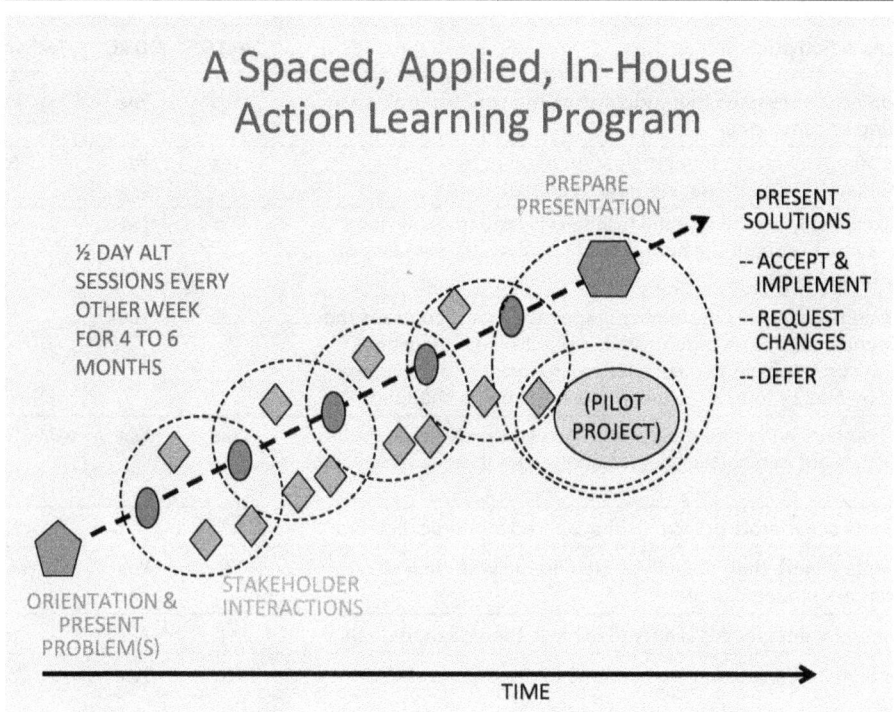

A Spaced, Applied, In-House Action Learning Program

PREPARE PRESENTATION

PRESENT SOLUTIONS

½ DAY ALT SESSIONS EVERY OTHER WEEK FOR 4 TO 6 MONTHS

-- ACCEPT & IMPLEMENT

-- REQUEST CHANGES

-- DEFER

(PILOT PROJECT)

STAKEHOLDER INTERACTIONS

ORIENTATION & PRESENT PROBLEM(S)

TIME

and neglected (or taken for granted) part of major organizational change is the implementation phase (Freedman, 1997).

Most transformational change projects are conceived and planned by executives working with *techspert* Management Consultants (MCs)—e.g., financial, engineering, or legal technical experts (Freedman & Zackrison, 2001).

While techspert-driven management consulting is essential, it is insufficient by itself. Techsperts tend to limit their attention to that part of an organizational system in which they specialize. They tend to ignore those parts and people who are not directly involved in their efforts. Yet their efforts affect other parts and people, and those parts and people often affect the techsperts' efforts. Techsperts tend to ignore the systemic context in which they operate. The results often include unanticipated cost increases and missed schedules that are usually caused by predictable discontent

and resistance by stakeholders whose legitimate interests in the change effort are ignored. Most OD&C practitioners do not make such errors.

Few of these techspert-driven change initiatives involve OD&C practitioners or ALTCs —until they run into unexpected difficulties. This is a powerful argument for creating multidisciplinary consulting teams composed of techspert MCs, OD&C practitioners, and ALT Coaches. Each is prepared to deliver different but complementary services (see Table 62.1).

The OD&C consultation process consists of 10 interconnected phases:

1. pre-entry, entry, contact, and negotiating a consulting agreement;
2. data collection from all relevant stakeholders;
3. organizing and preparing data for feedback;
4. top-down or bottom-up data feedback to and analysis by clients;

TABLE 62.1   A Comparison of Practices of ALT Coaches, OD&C Practitioners, and MC Techsperts

Functions & Activities	ALTC	OD&C	TechspertMC
Utilize an action research methodology as the core technology in consulting engagements	Yes	Yes	Yes
Utilize optimal involvement/participation of all parties (stakeholders) as an integral element of consultations	Yes	Yes	No
Focus exclusively on the specific technology, structure, system, or process that brought the attention of client system leaders on the need for change	No	No	Yes
Utilize a comprehensive systemic perspective that recognizes the interdependencies of an organizational psycho-socio-techno-structural system, including correlative organizational functions affected by and, in turn, affecting whatever is being changed	Yes	Yes	No
Enable planners and implementers to achieve the desired results by helping them to create strategies and tactics to achieve specific goals	Yes	Yes	No
Help clients collaborate in establishing shared strategic direction	Yes/No	Yes	No
Help clients ensure their objectives are aligned with their organization's strategic goals	Yes	Yes	Yes/No
Recommend strategies for clients to achieve their desired goals	No	No	Yes
Get involved in the substantive contents of the organizational problems	No	No	Yes
Help clients effectively plan and take action in pursuit of desired results, goals, or objectives	Yes	Yes	No
Explicitly help clients identify, reflect on, and develop leadership competencies	Yes	No	No
Explicitly help clients identify, reflect on, and develop team problem solving, conflict management, and decision-making skills	Yes	No	No
Explicitly help clients identify, reflect on, and develop under-standing and skills for dealing with systemic organizational dynamics (including organizational politics)	Yes	Yes/No	No
Explicitly help clients to develop communications skills	Yes	Yes	No
Plan and take action in pursuit of desired results, goals, or objectives	No	No	Yes
Assist clients to explicitly learn how they do what they do effectively and how they can improve their effectiveness	Yes	Yes	No
Utilize inquiry and reflection to enhance self-reflective awareness	Yes	Yes/No	No
Help clients recognize and manage how assumptions, beliefs, and values influence (e.g., distort and limit) perceptions of the world and, as a result, how to think, feel, and act	Yes	Yes/No	No
Help clients recognize what they do not know and increasingly accept and utilize other diverse perspectives in collaboratively defining, analyzing, and dealing with complex organizational problems	Yes	Yes/No	No

(continued)

TABLE 62.1 Continued

Functions & Activities	ALTC	OD&C	TechspertMC
Work with teams to help them understand complex organizational problems by creating an indigenous or local theory that explains the dynamics and cause-and-effect relationships operative in the situation	Yes	No	No
When clients feel blocked, introduce a conceptual model to explain the situation	No	Yes	Yes/No
When clients feel blocked, introduce a pre-established method or process that guides team members to a desirable and practical outcome	No	Yes	Yes/No
When clients feel blocked, help team members create their own viable models and methods	Yes	Yes/No	No
Help clients explore possible and probable consequential risks and potential implications	Yes	Yes	Yes/No
Help clients evaluate progress and results of planned change initiative	Yes/No	Yes/No	No
Explicitly strive to transfer theory, methods, and skills to members and leaders or client organizations in working oneself out of a job and enabling clients to become self-reliant and independent of consultants	Yes	Yes	No

5. creating implementation plans;
6. executing the implementation plan;
7. monitoring and evaluating progress achieved;
8. identifying and dealing with emerging predictable surprises;
9. ending or recycling to the next highest priority problem;
10. maintaining a functional feedback loop.

These phases unfold in a cyclical, iterative fashion, often jumping ahead and/ or falling back from one phase to another. Most techspert MCs follow a similar path, but the distinguishing characteristics of the OD&C application are its highly participative and non-authoritarian qualities.

OD&C practitioners serve as guides performing the tasks and responsibilities required by each phase. In large organizational change projects, OD&C practitioners consult with EMTs and project management teams. ALT Coaches augment OD&C and MC functions by intervening when a change effort encounters ambiguous, unprecedented problems, and predictable surprises—i.e., discontinuous problems for which an effective solution does not already exist.

Changes in the Environment Create the Need for Organizational Change

Leaders in organizations in all sectors realize they are often confronted with increasingly rapid, multiple, and radical changes to which their organizations must quickly and effectively adapt if they are to survive, if not profit. The external environmental variables include a wide range of sudden and extreme fluctuations wrought by new technology, geopolitical uncertainty, extreme weather, and other catastrophic, adverse events.

Such changes can precipitate unpredicted organizational disasters. Nonetheless, changes create both threats and opportunities corresponding to an organization's internal strengths and weaknesses. Most organizations have developed their strengths from continuous, incremental improvements of their strategies and operations under variable but fairly predictable environmental conditions.

Still, unprecedented, discontinuous environmental changes usually map to organizational vulnerabilities. For one thing, organizations tend to react to disasters after they have occurred. They are not likely to consider predictable surprises (Bazerman & Watkins, 2008). Their first preventive strategic option is to conduct a risk analysis to identify what could go wrong. The organization may choose to incur the projected costs of attempting to prevent or minimize risks, as well as to determine and prepare to take immediate corrective action once a disaster occurs.

Their alternative strategy is to gamble that the likelihood of disaster is not probable. If the event fails to materialize, the organization saves considerable time, energy, and money. However, if it does occur, recovery costs will probably greatly exceed the costs of prevention or preparation.

To prepare themselves to adapt to rapid environmental changes, organizations must change themselves both to protect against threats and to exploit newly emerging opportunities. Such organizational changes are not likely to fit easily with an organization's values and practices. However, if organizational leaders recognize that they lack the knowledge and skills needed to cope with the predictable surprises, they may seek external expertise. To acknowledge they need assistance requires considerable courage on the part of otherwise competent organizational leaders (Schein, 2009).

To determine what to change, organizations usually seek the services of various MC firms who are techsperts in some relevant specialized discipline. These techsperts (Freedman & Zackrison, 2001) have generally learned that planning and implementing organizational change require much more than just the creation and installation of some innovative process (Freedman, 1997). Accordingly, many consulting firms market a support service such as change management. Change management (CM) specialists have adopted and integrated many strategies and processes from OD&C with project management and the practice of various technical disciplines. However, the effectiveness of CM tools varies considerably (Pfeffer & Sutton, 2006).

A Case Study of Organizational Change Using AL

The CEO of a Large Gas & Electric Utility (LGEU) initiated a corporate-wide transformation with the intent of converting the utility's culture from an impersonal technocracy to a humanistic, high-involvement, participatory culture (Freedman & Stinson, 2004). Based on the results of an extensive employee and customer attitude/ opinion survey, LGEU's Executive Management Team (EMT) identified a number of operational areas requiring rapid and effective change. The issues affected large segments of the company and were trans-organizational, i.e., not specific to a single department or function.

The survey indicated that employees did not feel recognized or rewarded for their loyalty, dedication, and commitment. Furthermore, the survey revealed that the customer service department often ignored persistent complaints by residential, commercial, industrial, and governmental customers. At best, they were referred from one specialist to another to get partial answers to their concerns.

The EMT decided to create 14 Natural Action Teams (NATs) comprised of members drawn from different professions, departments, and levels. Each team was assigned a different problem and had its own OD&C consultant.

As the CEO's coach and EMT consultant, I served as an advisor to a respected middle manager who the EMT had selected to coordinate a team of OD&C practitioners. He and I screened the OD&C practitioners and assigned them to consult with one or more NATs. We asked each team in turn to study and develop recommendations to ameliorate one of 14 identified problem situations. We created a multi-team AL project, including sponsors and champions.

The OD&C practitioners focused on helping NAT members learn from their unfolding experiences. The OD&C practitioners refrained from involving themselves in the contents of the NATs' problems. Rather, they helped NAT members reflect on:

- What they were learning about themselves as individuals;
- How teams can improve their effectiveness in solving problems;
- How to develop useful interactions among interdependent subsystems;
- How to utilize organizational cultural dynamics; and
- How to improve and sustain mutually satisfying interactions between the organization and its external stakeholders.

However, from time to time, NATs required specific information that related to the problems they were trying to solve, e.g., what information technology was available that would enable a single customer relations specialist to access all information about the services a specific customer has been receiving. So, occasionally, each team identified and sought additional assistance from one or more techspert consultants—not as problem solvers or team leaders but as informational resources. When they completed their work, each NAT presented their recommendations to the EMT.

The results of this systemic intervention included: enhanced pride and self-esteem among NAT members; EMT recognition of NAT members' talents and capacities to participate in solving complex organizational problems; enhanced appreciation for the value of a high involvement, high participation culture; and diminished dependency on techspert opinions on organizational issues.

AL Projects Sustain Learning Organizations

AL is a small team process that enables team members to solve real problems in real time while also enhancing team members' capacity

to learn about themselves, participative problem solving and decision-making, intergroup dynamics, and organizations as dynamic systems. As team members better understand AL theory and acquire proficiency in the use of its methods of inquiry and reflection, they invariably apply their acquired abilities beyond the ALT.

At first, team members use their developing competencies between ALT meetings as they engage persons and groups that have an interest in the problem being analyzed. As they gain mastery of these competencies, team members tend to take risks and experiment with applying AL in fulfilling routine work responsibilities. As team members and their work associates recognize the efficacy of these new skills, they begin to support one another as they apply AL theory and methods to appropriate organizational problems.

To achieve optimal results, the involved parties learn to apply AL only to urgent organizational problems where their senior managers are dissatisfied with the current state, the goal is ambiguous and/or the solution is uncertain. They also discover that where the goal is clear and specific, and the solution is well known and established, the AL process is counterproductive. Instead, they find that an existing, techspert-based solution is usually best under such circumstances.

Diffusion of Innovations

Using AL as a means of creating and sustaining a learning organization is a vital innovation. Senge references Rogers (1964) who believed that diffusion of innovations occurs through a five-step process that flows through a series of communication channels over a period of time among the members of an organization or major subsystem. This process includes:

- Knowledge (awareness)
- Persuasion (interest)
- Decision (evaluation)
- Implementation (trial)
- Confirmation (adoption)

The rate of adoption is the relative speed with which some percent of organizational members adopt the innovation. The percent of adopters may vary but the result is reaching critical mass, which occurs when enough individuals have adopted the innovation to assure that its acceptance and utilization is self-sustaining.

There are two principals who can facilitate the diffusion process. First, Opinion Leaders are influential in spreading positive (or negative) information about an innovation. They are most influential during the decision or evaluation stage of the innovation-decision process and on late adopters. Second, Champions need to support an innovation and clear away obstacles or break through opposition that may be provoked by introducing the innovation.

Rogers (1964) defines five intrinsic characteristics of innovations that influence an individual's adopt-or-reject decision. The characteristics include the relative advantage of an innovation over the existing legacy technology or process; the compatibility of the innovation with an individual's preferred ways of working; the complexity of using an innovation; trialability or how easily an innovator may experiment without risk with the innovation; and observability or how visible the results of the use of the innovation is to others and whether this evokes positive or negative reactions.

Rogers (1964) also describes various adopter categories. These help to manage expectations about the extent and the speed with which innovative AL and organizational learning may be diffused and adopted. The categories are: innovators, early adopters, early majority individuals, late majority individuals, and laggards. The adoption of an innovation tends to follow an S-curve over time.

Both OD&C practitioners and ALTCs must pay close attention to the extent to which a viable, explicit strategy and plan is developed to disseminate organizational learnings generated through their efforts.

Of considerable concern is the extent to which a learning organization can capture learnings in a systematic manner, archive the learnings, and create a mechanism through which learnings may be retrieved and applied at a later date when they are both relevant and appropriate.

It is conceivable that someone will soon create a vehicle similar to Wikipedia that allows users to enter learnings about any given topic or issue that are acquired and captured.

Conclusion

AL augments and works well with OD&C, supplements the work of techspert management and change management specialists, and enhances efforts to create and sustain organizational learning.

References

Argyris, C., & Schön, D. (1978). *Organizational learning.* Reading, MA: Addison-Wesley.

Argyris, C., Putnam, R., & Smith, D.M. (1985). *Action science: Concepts, methods and skills for research and intervention.* San Francisco, CA: Jossey-Bass.

Bazerman, M. H., & Watkins, M. D. (2008). *Predictable surprises: The disasters you should have seen coming, and how to prevent them.* Boston, MA: Harvard Business School Publishing.

Cummings, T.G., & Worley, C.G. (2009). *Organization development and change, 9th edition.* Mason, OH: Thomson/South-Western.

Csikszentmihalyi, M. (1990). *Flow: The psychology of optimal experience.* New York, NY: Harper & Row.

Freedman, A.M. (1995). The consultant's sense of urgency: Steady-state vs. frontline combat OD. In J. W. Pfeiffer (Ed.), *The 1995 Annual: Volume 2, Consulting* (pp. 213–219). San Francisco, CA: Pfeiffer & Co.

Freedman, A.M. (1997). The undiscussable sides of implementing transformational change. *Consulting Psychology Journal,* 49(1), 51–76.

Freedman, A.M. (2000). Multigroup representation: Representative teams and teams of representatives. *Consulting Psychology Journal,* 52(1), 63–81.

Freedman, A.M., & Zackrison, R.E. (2001). *Finding your way in the consulting jungle.* San Francisco, CA: Jossey-Bass.

Freedman, A.M., & Stinson, G.H. (2004). Herding cats: Lessons learned from managing and coordinating organization development consultants. *Consulting Psychology Journal,* 56(1), 44–57.

Freedman, A.M. (2006). Action research: Origins and applications for ODC practitioners. In B.B. Jones & M.B. Brazzel (Eds.), *The NTL handbook of organization development and change.* San Francisco, CA: Pfeiffer.

Freedman, A.M. (2006, October 19). Organizational diagnosis: The swamp model (a psycho-socio-technical systems model). Philadelphia, PA: Center for Organizational Studies, College of Arts and Sciences, University of Pennsylvania.

Freedman, A.M., & Jules, C. (unpublished). Vital signs: Assessing readiness for/and managing change. Washington, DC: Freedman, Leonard & Marquardt Consultancy.

Gladwell, M. (2000). *The tipping point: How little things can make a big difference.* Boston, MA: Little, Brown & Company.

Marquardt, M.J., Leonard, H.S., Freedman, A.M., & Hill, C.C. (2009). *Action Learning for developing leaders and organizations: Principles, strategies, and cases.* Washington, DC: American Psychological Association.

Marshak, R.J. (2009). *Organizational change: Views from the edge.* Bethel, ME: The Lewin Center.

Pfeffer, J., & Sutton, R.I. (2006). *Hard facts, dangerous half-truths & total nonsense.* Boston, MA: Harvard Business School Press.

Schein, E.H. (2009). *Helping: How to offer, give, and receive help.* San Francisco, CA: Berrett-Koehler.

Senge, P. (1990). *The fifth discipline: The art & practice of the learning organization.* New York, NY: Doubleday/Currency.

Senge, P., Kleiner, A., Roberts, C., Ross, R., & Smith, B. (1994). *The fifth discipline fieldbook: Strategies and tools for building a learning organization.* New York, NY: Doubleday/Currency.

Senge, P., Kleiner, A., Roberts, C., Ross, R., Roth, G., & Smith, B. (1999). *The dance of change: The challenges of sustaining momentum in learning organizations.* New York, NY: Doubleday/Currency.

CHAPTER 63

Strategic Change Consulting

How to Leverage Your Work
at the Enterprise Level

Linda Ackerman Anderson and Dean Anderson

ACROSS BOTH PRIVATE and public sectors, executives are unleashing increasing amounts of change—change that is growing in magnitude, complexity, and urgency. Unfortunately, most of these efforts are failing to deliver on their promise. They never fully realize the proposed ROI, or worse, they create internal conflict, overwhelm, and chaos. Though none of these consequences are intended, the way leaders are, or are not, setting up these changes is the cause.

Many executives face a dire situation regarding change. Change is essential to their organization's success, yet as the imperative for change increases, so does the cost of failure. The lost ROI from change is not from choosing the wrong direction, but rather from how the change is executed, on both individual initiatives and across the totality of change. Because today's most important change efforts are often enterprise-wide, they are much more difficult to design and implement successfully.

The more change efforts an organization launches at one time, the greater the risk of failure. The less coordination and integration leaders set up across change efforts, the greater the waste and overwhelm. And, the less leaders place conscious attention on the organization's *entire* change agenda, the more the negative impact on results, productivity, customer service, and employee morale. Simply put, the complexity and urgency for change has outpaced most organizations' skill at leading and implementing it.

This condition needs executive recognition and action. Consider that every effective organization has predictable financial management requirements. Leaders establish essential mechanisms to track and handle the financial requirements to support the business. Every organization has predictable human resource planning and management needs. Leaders have established comprehensive human resources policies and practices. The same is true for having a capable IT infrastructure and appropriate supply chain processes. Finance, HR, IT and supply chain requirements are recognized as core to a business' success, and all are supported and led with concrete strategies and practices.

Now, apply this thinking to the leadership of change. If change is so prevalent and equally essential to business success, why are organizations not putting in place the infrastructure, resources, and capability to lead change effectively at the enterprise-level? The need is the same, but the recognition and appropriate response has not yet manifested. *It needs to.*

Strategic Change Consulting

This is where change consultants can make a real difference at the system level—through the creation of a strategic change consulting function. Ideally, this function serves both the change agenda for the entire enterprise, as well as providing direct change strategy consulting to major initiatives within the overall agenda. It ensures that the organization has the change leadership capability it needs while enabling success in its priority change efforts.

To lead an organization's enterprise change agenda effectively, the organization requires standards for change strategy, infrastructure, and common practices. Attention is required for governance, scope, timing, resourcing, and capacity for all critical changes. Leadership, resources, and continuous improvement must support these standards. They create the conditions for successful execution of all of the changes going on in the organization. Getting each of these conditions recognized by senior leadership—and implementing them across the organization—is the responsibility of the strategic change consulting function.

How do you get all this going in your organization? There are four key strategies. The first is to raise executive awareness about the need for greater change leadership and change support. This need must be driven by actual business results. Typically, you can raise awareness by assessing the organization's track record in leading change, and the level of risk it faces if it does not proactively improve its record. This historical data produces the *executive wake-up call* necessary to set the stage for the next three strategies.

Next is to identify the strategy and work required to *strengthen the organization's capability and infrastructure*— to improve its leadership and ROI from change. The third is to carry out these plans and build *change leadership capability* through training and embedding a common, best practice change process methodology to consistently guide all change efforts in real time. The fourth is to *support*

actual change efforts—as they are scoped, designed, and implemented. This work is performed at the change strategy level rather than the tactical level, ensuring that changes are set up for success from the beginning. This article discusses each of these focus areas and how you can step into these shoes to leverage your value to your organization and clients.

Focus 1: Generating the Executive Call to Action to Build Change Leadership for the Enterprise

How do you get your executives attention regarding the need for enterprise-wide change leadership? Our practice is to use assessments to generate relevant and enlightening data about the state of change leadership in the organization. You can gather two different types of information about the strength of change leadership. The first focuses on the leaders' actual track record in leading change successfully—what they do well and what they repeatedly fail at. Then tie the weaknesses to the risk that the organization faces if it fails at producing its ROI from change.

This first type of assessment can be accomplished via a change history audit of some kind. There are numerous data points to consider when assessing how well change efforts have been led, as well as many ways to generate this information. Which factors do you need to evaluate to reveal the organization's real track record with change? Consider what the leaders have consistently done well, as well as the specific dynamics or patterns that have caused change efforts to fail. Table 63.1 offers specific factors to consider.

You can undertake this type of audit through an accelerated online survey, such as *ChangeCheck*™ which is an online survey that can be used as a rapid change history audit. It is one of several change audits available that can be used with a Change Leader Assessment. You can also reveal this data through focus groups of key stakeholders knowledgeable about the organization's change history. Online surveys are often faster and produce valid

TABLE 63.1 Factors to Consider from Past Change Efforts

How effective have the sponsors of change efforts been on their ability to set their changes up for success from the beginning and see them through to completion?
Have the change leaders accurately scoped and resourced the efforts?
Are the timetables for the completion of the changes realistic and humanly possible?
Have they created space and time aside from the normal workload to achieve them?
Have change efforts competed with each other for attention and resources?
Is there too much change going on at once, and none of it succeeding?
How many different change models are being used, and do they compete?
What services and capabilities does the organization have internally that support change efforts, and how effectively are these used?
Has change raised or threatened employee morale and performance? What is missing that is necessary—change strategy, a common change model, change infrastructure, support services, skills, tools, practices, knowledge, metrics?

data in graph form which can quickly point to the areas where leaders need more attention. The reporting of this data is key to your generating the wake-up call for executives to realize that their change efforts are at risk of failure, and the organization is in need of greater change capability and infrastructure.

The second type of data to generate is the current reality of how much significant change is underway within the overall organization, your *Enterprise-Wide Change Agenda*. Identify the size and magnitude of all change work going on in the organization—changes that reach across the entire system, focus on major business lines, or those within key functions. All of the change work going on can then be compared with the organization's true capacity to accomplish it while operations continue.

Executives need to understand that all change runs simultaneously—and in competition with ongoing operations. A typical assumption among the "C"-Suite is that change somehow just occurs on top of operating priorities. Inevitably, you will reveal that the leaders have unleashed too much change in the organization -which has not been supported with adequate leadership, time, methodology, and capacity. When inadequate time and resources have been allocated for change, opera-

tions typically take precedence, and the changes flounder.

This mismatch of resources has created a very serious capacity issue in organizations today, so much so that this is the *Number One* issue revealed across all of the change audits we have performed! It is also the leading cause of failure at change. This fact surfaces the need for executives to manage their enterprise-wide change agendas more realistically, and the need to set up adequate infrastructure and monitoring mechanisms that ensure greater success. It is critical that the strategic change consultant can support the organization to "get real" about change— and its leadership.

Most leaders do not know what is on their change agenda. They may be able to name several strategic initiatives, but they are hard-pressed to understand what else is underway in various segments of the business—or at different levels of the organization. In one healthcare system, the executives attempted this exercise and discovered 220 change initiatives underway in the organization! This was not only a wake-up call, it was a blaring siren. Understanding that these changes were occurring, while providing patients top quality care, they reassessed their priorities, and the next year brought their change agenda down to 58 initiatives. They discovered that this number of initiatives was also too much of a stretch, and the next year cut it down to 32.

All of the change efforts on an organization's change agenda have cumulative and direct effects on the organization's stamina and performance. Once you have mapped the entire change agenda, and once executives acknowledge how much change is going on, they can make more intelligent decisions about how to set change up strategically to succeed. One of their greatest risk factors is imposing too much work—change, along with operations—over too long a period of time, which the workforce cannot humanly take on and succeed at. This issue needs strategic attention.

Generating your change agenda is not a one-time event. The agenda is never a static thing. Business strategy will evolve and in turn, pull for different change efforts. Operations will cause adjustments. Workforce capacity may be stretched too thin and require the executives to further adjust their change expectations. These adjustments cause the need for flexibility in the change agenda. Oversight of the change agenda and its requirements for success are key functions for the strategic change consultant.

The change agenda sets up the very important conversation about what infrastructure and resources are required to serve it over time. As a strategic change consultant, your goal is to move the executive discussion to what is required to provide the resources and support needed for greater success. This leads directly to Focus 2.

Focus 2: Identifying Requirements to Strengthen the Organization's Change Capability and Infrastructure

All of the data generated in Focus 1 is input to this task. Here is where you work with your senior executives to identify their priority needs for building the organization's change capability. You will need them to agree to establish a standard change process and infrastructure to support all of the changes under-

way and planned. Your task here is to clarify the most important areas, and secure executive sponsorship to proceed with planning and resourcing this work.

Take heed! Sponsorship is not just 'blessing you to go off and train others'. Sponsorship entails what the senior leaders also need to do—themselves—to ensure that (1) the enterprise change agenda is sound and realistic, and (2) they understand and use the change infrastructure and practices they will be sponsoring.

In the healthcare system previously mentioned, the leaders agreed to spend a total of three days learning, discussing, and tailoring an entire change strategy, infrastructure, and methodology adequate to their change agenda. These discussions led them to cut the magnitude of their expectations. They realized that leading major change required more than announcing new practices, more than delegating to project teams, and more than checking the boxes that research and pilots had occurred. They needed to engage their organizations and themselves as change leaders to truly complete the process of change to produce real results.

What makes up an organization's change infrastructure? Consider the elements in Table 63.2.

Designing the organization's change infrastructure is an essential task in setting up the organization to succeed at change. You might get the blessing to take on all of this work, or just some of it. What are your priorities? From the list in Table 63.2, focus your attention on templates for case for change, change strategy, and a common change process methodology that drives the rest of what is needed in the course of executing your change efforts.

Focus 3: Building Change Capability and a Common Change Methodology

Once you have a well-supported mandate, this part is easy—scoping, sequencing, and pacing the development work through good planning, engaging the right experts, selecting the right change process methodology replete with

TABLE 63.2   Change Infrastructure Elements

Standard practices for producing a case for change
Standard templates for developing an integrated change strategy
Common expectations for how to govern large change efforts, including change leadership roles, charters, decision-making protocols, and cross-project integration strategies; how to proactively interface with ongoing operations
Knowledge of all of the organization's resources that can be applied at the right place and time to support the design and execution of change projects, such as project management, OD, change management, quality improvement, Lean practices, Six Sigma, and so on
A common change process methodology that can be applied to all change efforts to ensure continuity and cross-initiative integration from start to finish
Standard conditions for success and change metrics
Standards for change communication plans and stakeholder engagement plans
Expectations and requirements to ensure a robust course correction process
Expectations and requirements to ensure a multiple project integration strategy and process
Change leadership competencies—skills, knowledge, behaviors, and mindsets
Cultural expectations for the masterful leadership of change
Roster of best change practices and tools for use across all efforts
Electronic support mechanisms, such as intranet sites, project software, and communication protocols

best practice templates, and determining your rollout and training strategy. It will be necessary to design your strategy to match the readiness and capacity of the organization, especially the change consultants and project leaders who will be directly involved from the start.

There are a range of start-up strategies to consider. Some organizations choose a "soft launch" involving just a few select projects on which to apply and demonstrate value and success. Others decide to invest in deep training of their in-house change consultants who then consult 'just-in-time' on live projects. And, some organizations have rolled out their methodology across the system. If you select this strategy, be prepared to address how you will map your new methodology onto change efforts that may have been initiated using different change models.

Consider the elements in Table 63.3 in your rollout plan.

Focus 4: Using the Common Change Methodology to Drive Results on Live Change Efforts

Embedded in the previous suggestions is the idea to teach the model while working on live change efforts. You can also consult directly to change initiatives using your change methodology without conspicuously teaching it. The work of this focus area is critical to demonstrating value from having a common change process, and to ensure that it is used to support the organization's real change work. Internal change consultants may work on projects on their own, or in teams, to deepen their "bench-strength" in using the methodology over time.

Clients or project leaders may request consulting on live change efforts in two ways —as additional support to the detailed work of the change team, or as a strategic coach on change strategy and process design. The first is

TABLE 63.3 Elements of a Rollout Plan

An engagement strategy to gather the best contributors from both inside your organization and external experts to design your best practice templates and tools
Training for specific audiences to develop the change leadership mindset, knowledge, skills, and behaviors; and to learn how to use your chosen templates and tools
Offering change strategy coaching to ensure optimal application of your methodology to live projects
Project Team trainings and working sessions that enable change teams to learn while doing . . . and make real progress on their change strategies and plans in the sessions
Establish a community of practice to ensure ongoing learning and the identification of best change practices
Ongoing periodic "learning clinics" with intact teams or across teams

what we call *pairs-of-hands* and does not usually involve much strategy. Our recommendation is for the latter, which is specifically the work of the strategic change consultant. This role involves staying in the high level observation and advisory role, and less so on doing detailed change work. See Table 63.4 for the responsibilities of the strategic change consultant on a focused change initiative.

Some OD consultants already offer some of these services; others work in different ways that contribute to them, but do not completely fulfill them, or are not known for providing these services. Consider how you are positioned

TABLE 63.4 Responsibilities of the Strategic Change Consultant

Building the case for change, scope, and desired outcomes for the project
Developing change strategy, or facilitating the leaders to do so
Designing high level change process plans to accomplish major pieces of work
Coaching change sponsors on their change leadership abilities, mindsets and behaviors, also how to model the personal changes required from their efforts
Facilitating the identification and creation of conditions for success
Starting up the change leadership team and setting them up for success with a comprehensive charter, roles, and governance
Observing executive and change leadership team meetings to ensure understanding and alignment, and to minimize political dynamics, confusion, and poor follow through
Designing and consulting to the multiple project integration strategy
Inputting to various decisions and assessing implications on pacing, capacity, culture, emotional reactions and resistance, leadership credibility, or change plans
Inputting to the stakeholder engagement and change communications strategy
Inputting to the course correction process and helping to facilitate essential course corrections
Providing high level change education
Ensuring full organizational alignment in the design and execution of the change effort

in your organization and the services you offer. Consider how to rebrand yourself and reeducate your organization about the value that these services can provide the organization.

Benefits of the Strategic Change Consulting Function

All executives want change to happen faster with less financial and human cost. Establishing a strategic change consulting function that attends to the enterprise-level of change capability supports these results. At the whole-system level, this function is tasked to ensure that each new change fits within the organization's entire change agenda. It reduces duplication of effort, ensures that the outputs from one project flow seamlessly as timely inputs to others, and stops the competition across projects. The strategic change consulting function also strives to increase people's understanding of the big picture of change and how all change efforts work collectively to implement the organization's business strategy. This alignment speeds up change dramatically and increases stakeholder buy-in.

In terms of establishing a common change methodology and best change practices, this role can: (1) develop consistent change skills and competencies across your leadership ranks, (2) enable a better exchange of work products across change initiatives, (3) provide a consistent change process model so staff can seamlessly move from project to project, (4) integrate projects with their requisite inputs and outputs, and (5) gather, document, and teach best change practices.

The strategic change consulting function can also become the owner of the organization's common change methodology, tools, and best practices; disseminating them throughout the organization. With focused commitment to a common change methodology, the executives and line change leaders can develop far greater understanding and skills in change. Through this work, let them be known as great change leaders.

At the change project level, the benefits of the strategic change consultant's role can be summarized as ensuring that each critical change effort is set up for success; has a realistic strategy, plan, and timetable; and can be accomplished in a way that the workforce is able and willing to achieve the ROI needed for business success. With each project's success, the value of this role is fortified, and the organization is ever-more change ready and able. This role, in whole or in part, is a smart investment in ensuring the organization can actually achieve the results and create the value it needs from change over the long term.

CHAPTER 64

The Executive Perspective on Mergers and Acquisitions

Robert C. Barnett

MERGERS AND ACQUISITIONS (M&As) have been referred to as the ultimate change management challenge because of the complex and often stressful dynamics involved in integrating one company with another. To be successful, companies need to find suitable candidates for merger or acquisition that meet specific strategic, financial, legal, and operational criteria. In addition, most companies recognize the need to pay attention to the softer side of M&A activities, including determining whether HR and management practices are compatible, how employees can be retained and motivated, and whether there is a "fit" between the cultures of the merging firms. Even in situations where there is a good business rationale for the integration of two firms, cultural differences and poor people practices can be significant factors leading to merger failure.

Evidence on M&A success provides little reason to be optimistic. The conventional wisdom is ripe with 'best practices' for making mergers successful: focus on synergies, move quickly, conduct thorough due diligence and detailed planning, don't lose sight of your customers, communicate, and pay attention to cultural issues. (DeCamara and Renjen, 2004). However, most studies of M&A integration report that up to 60-75% of M&A efforts fail—usually measured by changes in stock price post-merger, return to shareholders, or profitability metrics (for example, see Mergers & Acquisitions, 2005; Business Week, October 14, 2002; or The McKinsey Quarterly, 2001).

Other research confirms what managers, HR professionals, and OD consultants have recognized for some time: declining productivity is generally associated with employee stress and anxiety during a merger or acquisition; and, that cultural and human resource issues are of critical importance to merger success—and are at least equal to financial factors in making a deal work (The Conference Board, 2001). This trend is alarmingly clear in the results of a recent national study of employee opinion and satisfaction (Gantz-Wiley Research, 2004). That is, employees in organizations that are acquired or merged with other organizations report lower overall satisfaction, lower trust in management, and a diminished sense of job security compared to employees in acquiring firms or employees in organizations not involved in M&A activities.

Organization leaders understand the implications: higher employee morale and stronger employee commitment lead to increased levels of quality and productivity which, in turn, lead to increased customer satisfaction and retention and, as a result, stronger organizational performance (Heskett, et al, 1994).

The opposite trend predicts nothing but trouble. In stressful change situations when clarity, courage, and engagement are most needed, managers and employees tend to become less flexible, less adaptable, less autonomous, less self-managing, more rigid, and more defensive (Cameron & Whetten, 1987).

This magnifies the need to find and practice the most effective ways to address employee concerns, reduce anxiety, and increase employee commitment and morale in complicated change situations. To address these challenges, consultants, psychologists, and OD practitioners recommend a number of change management practices that are particularly relevant to M&A activities. These include the necessity for strong leadership, clear communication, employee involvement, and team approaches to planning and implementing change. But most of the evidence for the success of these practices in M&A efforts is anecdotal—and more is understood about what makes mergers *fail* than what makes them successful. We wanted to study this problem by collecting the opinions of key organization leaders to learn what they believed led to *success* in complicated (i.e., merger and acquisition) situations.

Our Approach

Our approach was straightforward. Based on a review of the literature, we identified a number of commonly recommended change practices that were particularly relevant to M&A situations. A questionnaire was designed that asked organization leaders to rate how important any of these management and people practices were in helping gain the cooperation and commitment of employees in a *successful* merger or acquisition in which they had been involved. "Success" referred to cultural or integration success—helping employees overcome concerns and apprehensions about the change process, and make a full commitment to the new organization.

Our intention was to collect as many opinions from senior organization leaders as possible. We limited our subject pool to line executives with titles of vice president (or above). We identified approximately 125 executives experienced in M&A activities and invited them to complete the questionnaire in the Spring of 2004. Sixty-two (57%) returned completed questionnaires. Those who responded represent M&A experience in approximately 30 organizations across a variety of businesses and industries. In some cases, we sent and received several responses from executives in the same organization. However, given the number of responses we received, and the breadth of organizations in which these executives were involved, we were confident the results would be meaningful and relevant for other change leaders. (A list of the companies represented in the study is provided at the end of this chapter.)

We did, however, want to make sure that our respondents' opinions were valid—that is, that they reflected the experiences of change leaders who had been *highly involved* in M&A integration processes that were *successful*, and that had been implemented over a *period of time*. In fact, 87% reported that their opinions were based on an M&A experience they judged to be successful, largely successful, or extremely successful. Only one respondent categorized his M&A experience as *"minimally"* successful. Similarly, 9 of 10 indicated that they were involved, highly involved, or extremely involved in leading the M&A integration process. The average amount of time they reported for achieving integration was slightly over three years.

The Results—An Overview

The results are clear. According to our respondents, some practices have a much greater impact than others on the success of a merger or acquisition. We found that six categories of change practices were critical, and that four others were rated significantly lower in terms of their perceived effect on employee morale, commitment, and cooperation.

The most important change practices that respondents believe to be important to the success of a merger or acquisition effort include (in rank order based on the analysis of respondent ratings):

1. **Clarifying Strategy and Direction.** Ensuring the business rationale is clear and widely understood, developing and communicating the vision for the new organization, and helping employees see and understand the benefits of the merger or acquisition.
2. **Involvement Strategies.** Meaningfully involving employees in decisions and plans that affect them in the change efforts and initiatives beginning to end, including involving key organization leaders, and making appropriate use of transition teams and cross-company task forces.
3. **Communication Strategies.** Extensive, candid communication about the status and progress of change, including repeated opportunities for employees to hear directly from change leaders and decisionmakers.
4. **Staffing Practices.** Making special efforts to retain key employees, staffing the new organization intelligently, and treating those whose jobs may be eliminated in a fair and equitable manner.
5. **Structure/Process Decisions.** Ensuring alignment among key structural elements, systems, and processes through decision-making groups empowered with authority to act with speed and urgency.
6. **Culture Interventions.** Analyzing and re-analyzing culture "fit", and establishing and reinforcing (new) organizational values that reflect the behaviors that are desired in the new organization.

The practices found to be statistically less important and impactful to integration success included:

1. **Management Training.** Preparing managers to understand, communicate about, and lead change.
2. **Feedback and Accountability.** Collecting employee feedback to ensure that management "walks the talk", including use of employee opinion surveys, focus groups, and 360 feedback processes to keep the integration effort on track.
3. **Employee Training.** Preparing employees to deal with change, "culture clash" or other anticipated difficulties.
4. **Special Employee Support.** Special efforts to assist employees who may be especially vulnerable to stress or other symptoms or "merger uncertainty", e.g., financial counseling, career counseling, stress management, etc.

A closer look suggests that the most important types of change practices are those that meaningfully involve employees most directly in the business of changing the organization. The lower-rated practices are "one-offs". That is, they generally represent efforts to prepare people for things that *might* happen or provide information that management may or may not use, rather than ways that most directly involve people in the change or integration process itself.

Digging Deeper— Which Change Practices Matter When?

Successfully implementing the integration of a merger or acquisition takes time. 80% of our survey responses indicated that integration activities spanned two years or longer. One particular aspect unique to M&A activity is that the change and integration process typically involves three distinct phases (Marks and Mirvis, 1998).

- **Planning Phase**—Searching for and selecting a suitable merger or acquisition candidate. Activities include clarifying strategy, performing financial analyses, establishing a business case, conducting due diligence processes, and developing preliminary integration plans.
- **Legal Combination Phase**—Completing financial and other negotiations, formally closing the transaction, announcing the

combination publicly, and planning for implementing the integration process.

- **Execution Phase**—Implementing the merger plan, and addressing unforeseen problems related to combining two firms. Activities include clarifying roles and responsibilities, retaining staff, maintaining employee morale, and developing employee commitment to the new organization.

By analyzing responses that reflected specific change practices within a change category, we were able to see not only *what* our change leaders were endorsing as important and useful, but also *when* they felt it was important to implement that particular practice. Intuitively, there are certain things change leaders need to do throughout a complicated change process. For example, few could argue that "communication" should be limited to only one phase or another in the M&A process. But knowing what to emphasize when and how to focus or adapt communication efforts at different points in the integration process is a different question.

Table 64.1 was developed to help change leaders with this challenge. Within each of the critical change categories, specific change practices that are particularly relevant to merger and acquisition integration success are shown, along with when (i.e., in what phase of the process) it is most important to implement that practice.

The specific change practices included received clear support from the change leaders who participated in the study. They represent the top 34 (of 54 total) items in the questionnaire. Not one specific change practice from the 4 lower-rated change categories was included in these top-rated items.

The table can be used as both a blueprint for planning integration activities, as well as a diagnostic tool for understanding stalled integration. As the table and its specific change practices suggest, clarifying direction, involving people, and focusing on communication are particularly important in the planning and legal combination phases. Change practices

that relate to staffing and retaining employees, developing an effective organization structure and aligned systems and processes, and shaping the culture of the new organization are more important in the execution phase. For those who have already initiated a merger or acquisition process, using the list of practices as a checklist to evaluate progress and plans can help pinpoint why problems might have emerged, or help change leaders pay attention to important activities they may not yet have planned for.

Where and How OD Can Help?

Traditionally, executives look to legal and financial experts for help in M&A efforts. However, OD practitioners are particularly well suited to help change leaders design and implement the change practices endorsed by the executives in our study. They are trained in evaluating opportunities for designing, and implementing interventions that improve organizational health and the well-being of the organization's employees. They are attuned to the organization's culture, and the organizational dynamics that reflect the interplay among the elements of the organization's strategy, structure, processes, and systems. Cummings and Worley (2001) have proposed a number of ways OD practitioners can or should be involved in M&A efforts.

Peoples' Concerns Make a Difference

In their book, *Joining Forces,* Marks and Mirvis (1998) make a compelling point: people matter! They argue that people have legitimate questions and concerns at each stage of a merger or acquisition. Paying attention to their concerns is a change leader's critical responsibility, and is one of, if not the key ingredient for achieving integration success. They describe people's concerns as they relate to feelings of insecurity (e.g., *What will happen to me?*), uncertainty (e.g., *Who's in control?*), and finally to the process of adapting to the new

TABLE 64.1 Change Practices That Lead To Successful M&A Integration

	Planning	Legal Combination	Execution
Clarifying Strategy & Direction	• Clarifying the strategic intent and investment criteria. • Conducting a thorough due diligence processes.	• Developing a vision for the new company. • Restating the business case for the combination. • Establishing critical success factors for the new organization's performance. • Helping employees see the benefits—or answer the question "What's In It for Me?"	
Involvement Strategies	• Involving key people in planning the transition. • Planning for transition teams that will identify synergies and design change efforts.	• Assembling cross-company task forces to study integration problems. • Using cross-company task forces to make recommendations about the design of the combined organization. • Appointing key leaders as transition managers or task force members. • Appointing the transition team to provide oversight and coordination throughout the integration phase.	• Providing teambuilding activities for developing effective post-combination teams.
Communication Strategies	• Developing a communications strategy that manages the "rumor mill" effectively.	• Implementing a comprehensive communications program for all employees to keep them informed of integration progress. • Conducting communications sessions by senior leadership to deepen understanding and build commitment to the new organization. • Developing and communicating a powerful message to employees to generate enthusiasm for the combination.	• Implementing a communications program to keep employees informed of implementation progress and successes. • Conducting communications sessions or "town meetings" by senior leadership to build acceptance of the new organization.

(continued)

TABLE 64.1 Continued

	Planning	Legal Combination	Execution
Staffing Practices	• Designing a plan or making special efforts to retain desired talent (e.g., stay bonuses).	• Developing a comprehensive staffing plan for the combined organization.	• Designing a lay-off policy (if necessary) that is fair. • Administering a lay-off policy consistently. • Providing outplacement services, severance packages, job-location assistance, or other services to support displaced workers.
Structure/Process Decisions		• Clarifying and implementing an effective transition structure.	• Implementing a resource allocation process to fund priorities to move the combined business forward. • Developing good decision mechanisms for aligning policies and practices. • Developing good decisions mechanisms for aligning or re-structuring teams or departments. • Developing a structure or a way by which plans and decisions can move forward with appropriate speed and urgency.
Culture Interventions	• Formally analyzing the culture of the candidate firm to assess culture "fit".	• Establishing organizational values and principles to guide behavior and decisionmaking.	• Continuously analyzing the cultural differences of the two organizations to improve culture "fit". • Mapping out and implementing culture integration activities. • Identifying shared values that characterize the desired culture of the new organization.

organization (e.g., *How do I succeed here?*). Change leaders that address these questions—by implementing the practices described above—are those who will likely have the greatest success.

To test this notion, we included a final question in our study. We wanted to understand how change leaders viewed the importance and impact of good management and people practices relative to other factors such as financial or competitive issues in achieving success in integrating a merger or acquisition. Our results clearly support Marks and Mirvis' position. Over 90 percent of the respondents indicated that effective change management and good "people practices" were as, or more important in determining integration success as financial, economic, or other competitive issues.

As one telecommunications industry executive stated:

> During integration, it's important to remember why you made the acquisition to start with—and to treat people in a manner that retains value for you—since in all cases they involve a significant human component. Only 1 of 1000 are acquisitions of technology or a patent. All others involve key relationships and know-how.

Some may want to argue with this executive's statistics, but the point is clear: people matter, their concerns are important, and the full value of a merger or acquisition can only be realized by paying attention to them.

Conclusions

Our study is not representative of all M&A activity. It focuses specifically on the change practices that work in *successful* mergers and acquisitions. Moreover, we surveyed change leaders—not the 'recipients' of change. From their perspective, perhaps employees would rank or value many of the change practices differently. Nonetheless, we think the data in our study support several obvious but useful conclusions:

- Compelling business reasons need to drive merger and acquisition efforts.
- People's concerns matter—addressing them is as important as other factors in M&A activity.
- Meaningful involvement in the execution of the change has the most impact on gaining employee cooperation and commitment to the change.
- Continually clarifying the direction; and extensive, candid, and ongoing communication is critical.
- Treating people fairly, and designing systems and processes that can flex with the needs of the organization during the integration are important.
- OD practitioners have a clear role in guiding and supporting change processes and change

Companies of Respondents Represented in the Study

Adayana	Ecolab	Pentair
ADC Telecommunications	GMAC	Polaris
Allianz Life	Great River Energy	Polo Ralph Lauren
Assurant	Highland Banks	Sunoco
Blue Cross Blue Shield	Honeywell	Tennant
Bremer Banks	ING	Thrivent Financial
Cargill	International Multifoods	Upsher Smith
CenterPoint Energy	Lifetouch	US Bank
Deutschebank	Medtronic	Verizon Wireless
Community First Banks	Novartis Pharma	Xcel Energy

leaders in M&A activities. They are particularly capable and expert in supporting the change practices that enhance employee involvement, morale, and commitment.

References

Association for Corporate Growth. (2005, February). 2004 M&A profile, 29.

Bekier, M. M., Bogardus, A. J., & Oldham, T. (2001). Why mergers fail. *The McKinsey Quarterly,* 4, 6–10

Business Week. (2002, October 14). Mergers: Why most big deals don't pay off. 3803, 60–67.

Cameron, K. S., Whetton, D. A., & Kim, M. U. (1987). Organizational dysfunctions of decline. *Academy of Management Journal,* 30, 126–138.

Cummings, T.G., & Worley, C.G. (2001). *Organization development and chang3* (7th ed.). Cincinnati, OH: South-Western College Publishing.

DeCamara, D., & Renjen, P. (2004). The secrets of successful mergers: dispatches from the front lines. *Journal of Business Strategy,* 25(3), 10–15.

Han, A.L. (2005). A strong year underway, M&A rises to $599 billion. *The Investment Dealer's Digest,* April 18, 1.

Heskett, J. L., Jones, T.O., Loveman, G. W., Sasser, W. E., & Schlesinger, L. A. (1994, March-April). Putting the service-profit chain to work. *Harvard Business Review,* 7(2), 164–174.

Marks, M. L., & Mirvis, P. H. (1998). *Joining forces.* San Francisco, CA: Jossey Bass.

Schein, L. (2001). *Managing culture in mergers and acquisitions.* The Conference Board.

Wiley, J., (2004). *Work Trends.* Minneapolis, MN: Gantz-Wiley Research Consulting Group.

Wall, S.J. (2005, March 1). Looking beyond the obvious in merger integration. *Mergers & Acquisitions.*

CHAPTER 65

An Appreciative Inquiry Into the Factors of Culture Continuity During Leadership Transition

A Case Study of LeadShare, Canada

Mary Ann Rainey

LEADSHARE (LS), a partnership of nearly 350 accountants and management consultants in Canada, embodies a unique blend of tradition and innovation which has proved successful, often placing it at the forefront of change. LeadShare's inception dates back to the mid-nineteenth century, close to the time Canada became a country Within the past 25 years, LeadShare has expanded its spectrum of client services and reshaped itself for double digit growth, currently ranking among the top accounting firms in Canada.

Human Resources is a critical function at LeadShare. The firm values human capital and recognizes the need to hire the right people to produce and deliver quality products and services. Today, individuals recruited by LS have far more complex qualifications because competition for competent people is intense. The need for professional development is just as urgent.

More than ever, LS people have to be futurists. The firm must be capable of looking ahead, discerning what is on the horizon, and preparing for it. The goals LS has for itself are the same as those of its clients: do the best today and anticipate and be poised to do even better tomorrow. As a partnership of shared management, preparation for tomorrow is a collective effort.

Roundtable

In anticipation of transitions in two key executive positions within the span of three years, the organization set in place a succession plan to ensure minimum disruption and to prepare for leadership entering the next millennium.

LeadShare launched the "Roundtable" initiative; Roundtable to suggest leadership without hierarchy, shared resources, and cross functional networks. The objective of Roundtable is to enlighten the next generation of leaders about the firm's history and tradition and their ingredients of success. A desired outcome for Roundtable participants is to develop a group of agents of culture who sustain the firm's traditions, practices, and behaviors while multiplying the factors of success.

Using current values, assumptions, and motivations as stepping stones to new ones requires knowledge of what the current ones are. Unfortunately, cultural assumptions are usually taken for granted and therefore difficult to see (Schein, 1985). LeadShare realizes that it must find ways to articulate the im-

543

plicit aspects of its culture if it expects to grow in new directions. A move in that direction is to provide a venue for partners to talk about their experiences and views about what is different, special, and valuable about -the firm. Freud (1921) spoke of five principle conditions for raising collective life to a higher order: 1) some degree of continuity; (2) some definite idea; (3) interaction among the group; (4) traditions, customs, and habits; and (5) definite structure. These principles serve as a useful preamble to the methodology that guided Roundtable. That methodology is Appreciative Inquiry

Appreciative Inquiry

Appreciation is a *selective perceptual process* which apprehends "what is" rather than "what is not." It represents a capacity to be selectively attentive to the lasting, essential, or enlivening qualities of a living human system. Appreciative management, as a process of valuing, consists of a rigorous ability to disassociate all seeming imperfections from that which has fundamental value (Cooperrider, 1988, p. 4).

According to the theory's creators, David Cooperrider and Suresh Srivastva, in its most basic meaning, Appreciative Inquiry is a form of organizational study that selectively seeks to locate, highlight, and illuminate the "life-giving" forces of a firm's existence (1987).

There are two essential questions behind any appreciative study:

1. What makes organizing possible; and
2. What are the possibilities of newer and more effective forms of organizing?

Four basic principles guide Appreciative Inquiry:

1. Exploring the life-giving forces of the firm should be *appreciative* in nature. The appreciative approach looks for what "works"; those peak aspects that serve to activate partners' energies and competencies.

2. Exploring the life-giving forces of the firm should be *applicable*. It should lead to knowledge that can be validated and used productively.

3. Exploring the life-giving forces of the firm should be *provocative*. Appreciative knowledge is, by nature, suggestive of what might be. Looking at the best of "what is" kindles the thought of "what might be"; it also challenges the firm to become the best of "what is possible."

4. Exploring the life-giving forces of the firm should be *collaborative*. It should foster healthy dialogue about the way things were, the way things are, and the way things can be.

Several dimensions of the AI process contribute to its uniqueness as a tool for succession planning (see Table 65.1). Foremost is the shift from the traditional "great man" approach to succession to one that emphasizes collectivity and collaboration. Harlow Cohen argues that managerial high performance is a function of collective effort (Cohen, 1986). Cohen believes that managerial work is characterized by 1) high dependence on others; 2) continuous ongoing activities with no defined beginning or end; and 3) a preponderance of time spent in face-to-face interaction. Collaboration is defined in terms of consciousness, choice, caring, and commitment. Collaboration operates within a relational system characterized as a just system based on fairness, mutuality and responsibility (Appley & Winder, 1977).

The primary objective of AI in the Roundtable program is to assist LeadShare in envisioning a collectively desired future, and then collaboratively carrying forth that vision in ways which successfully translate intention into reality and belief, and then into practice.

The Roundtable was a component in a major organization development intervention that spanned two decades at LeadShare. Roundtable itself was a multiyear intervention with core activities occurring during a six-month

TABLE 65.1 Comparison of Traditional Approaches to Succession and AI

	Conventional	Appreciative Inquiry
Unit of Analysis	Primacy of Individual	Primacy of Group
Type of Analysis	Problem and Organization Diagnosis	Embraces a Solution
Source of Vision	New Leader, the "Messiah"	Three Generations of Current Leaders
Pre-Succession	Psychological Trauma	Valuing, Visioning, Dialogue
Succession	Disruption	Creating Vision
Post Succession	Alienation	Culture Continuity

TABLE 65.2 Roundtable/AI Design

May	• Data collected to identity affirmative topics to be explored • Affirmative topics identified • Affirmative topics discussed with Management Committee and modified
June	• Questionnaire developed
June/July	• Roundtable participants conduct interviews
July	• Interview data summarized
August	• Roundtable participants and staff receive samples of data from interviews

September	• Roundtable participants and staff receive summarized version of interview data
	• Roundtable session focused on:
	  1. Reaffirming the affirmative topic choices and creating a common base of data for all participants
	  2. Stating provocative propositions about the life-giving properties in the firm
	  3. Consensus validation of propositions using force-field analysis and debate
	  4. Identifying the next steps by experimenting with provocative propositions

October	• Administration of Consensus Validation Survey at Annual Partners' Meeting

period (see Table 65.2). Work included development of the AI interview protocol, data collection, and thematic analysis of data, data feedback, and identification of future direction.

Collection of Data

Over 700 pages of data were collected throughout an 18-month period using common social science methods that included:

1. Interviews. The 40 partners who were selected to participate in Roundtable conducted open-ended formal interviews with the entire population of partners in the firm. Each interview lasted about two hours and covered questions about their experience in the firm and six topic areas: (1) partnership; (2) determination to be winners; (3) diversity; (4) Consensus decision making; (5) possibilities/positive thinking; and (6) conditions for people to excel. The topics and interview questionnaire were created by external consultants in collaboration with members of the organization's Management Committee. Roundtable participants were instructed by video on how to conduct an Appreciative Inquiry.

2. Historical Documents. Reports, articles, speeches, newsletters, unpublished papers, and memoranda were reviewed and content analyzed.

3. Observations. Office visits, committee meetings, and retreats were attended that provided a firsthand experiential basis for understanding the culture of the firm.

4. Survey. In a second phase of the research, a survey was conducted at the Annual Meeting of the partners to provide convergent validity to the interview data. Developed by the 40 Roundtable participants, the survey summarized the six topic areas based on the "7 S framework" (Peters & Waterman, 1984). The partners gave two ratings on a 7-point Likert scale: (1) the extent to which they felt the survey statement represented an important "ideal" to continue to be pursued by the firm, and (2) the extent to which the survey statement was reflected in practice.

Analysis of Data

For purposes of reliability and objectivity, the raw data was analyzed by two independent researchers in addition to the author. Word counts and interpretations were consistent among the three. The qualitative data and results from the survey provided a set of descriptive themes. From these themes emerged a preliminary description of a set of characteristics around the concept of "culture continuity."

The following are the major themes of our analysis:

1. **The Feeling of Unity**. This refers to general solidarity Unity that is exemplified through shared decision making, partner support, working and playing together, the annual meeting, other meetings and anniversary celebrations.

2. **Respected, Responsible, Inspirational Leadership**. Partners focused on "success generating success" and confidence in the courageous and responsible leadership of the firm. Service to the client is not sacrificed through the commitment to success, growth, and profitability. Automatic committee rotations increase understanding and appreciation of various factors in the firm

and provide continuity. Communication and participation before action and major changes build consensus and strengthen the feeling of "partnership." Deliberation guards against hasty decision making and the potential loss of things absolutely critical to the success of the firm.

3. **Justice and Equality**. The consensus building process, the "one partner, one vote" decision making structure, the development and partnership system. The financial and remuneration structure, the commitment to diversity and autonomy, and the partner exit counseling program breed an environment based on fairness, choice, appreciation, openness, and care.

4. **People Development and Professional Competence**. Constant learning and the development of partners are priorities. Partners should not only be competent in their respective skill areas, but they must also have the ability to attract and retain top quality people and instill in them personal pride.

Major Themes with Selected Data

The following are the major theme areas with selected representative data. These examples are provided to build some sense of clarity around the thematic framework.

1. **The Feeling of Unity**
   - LeadShare does a very good job of making all the offices feel that they are a part of the whole. There is an ongoing feeling of unity among the partners, most likely from day-to-day experience. The partnership seems to work well. When you come away from the annual partners' meetings, you walk with a spring in your step.
   - Different specialties are encouraged to combine forces. Also, there is the "one firm" attitude, which fosters cooperation. Different groups are combined with a unified top management team and national profit sharing, which allows the success to be shared.

- The managing partner's monthly memos are very important. It is clearly evident that he puts a lot of thought and time into them and through them the feeling of one firm is created. The feeling that we as a firm and as individual partners are very valuable, i.e., the feeling of "wholeness" comes through.

2. **Respected, Responsible, Inspirational Leadership**
   - The leadership does not dictate. It sacrifices quick decisions for gathering a majority view. This is the way it should be.
   - Through the whole process of choosing our leaders, we provide for continuity within the firm for building consensus.
   - Communication is the key word. It's letting partners know what the issues are prior to final decisions and obtaining feedback and input from them. Obviously, where partnership is so large, it may be difficult to do this on all issues, but we have found it beneficial at annual partners' meetings to have break-out groups where partners are able to have input on things of national concern.
   - No matter how small your office is or how far away you may be from the center of Canada, you still have very good feeling that you are making a contribution. Someone is listening to what you are saying. Your input counts.

3. **Justice and Equality**
   - At LeadShare, it is equality: it is one pot, one partner, one vote.
   - There is a great sense of pride among partners that LeadShare, against heavy odds, turned a challenging region into a success story. The managing partner spared no expense for translations and set an example by learning French.
   - I have been involved in two or three instances where we have counseled partners out—it's a difficult process; and without a doubt, the firm has been fair with these, maybe more than anyone else would have been.

- We started out being autonomous, and organized into a national firm later. Our roots through the merged units are to be autonomous, so we centralized. The main thrust was to keep the autonomy of the local offices.
- Merger issues with [a particular firm] where certain outstanding merger issues were settled through cooperation in a manner that was most fair.
- When the firm lost a lawsuit, the manner in which the partners rallied around the individual partner involved was quite impressive.

4. **People Development and Professional Competence**
   - In recognition that we are in a knowledge business, our leaders direct and the partners accept responsibility for significant self development—including personal, professional and people management skills.
   - We feel that management of continuity is prepared well in advance so that when a change does occur, it is not disruptive. The confidence is in younger partners. There are efforts to develop the management potential of younger partners.
   - The Roundtable. It is an interesting process in worrying about continuity from one leadership to the next. This process involves a number of perspectives from different partners as well as getting in touch with our strengths so that we do not move too quickly to change things that are absolutely critical to our success.

The Factors of Culture Continuity

The following are eleven propositions that emerged when the thematic framework was taken to a higher level.

1. Commitment to the concepts of "partnership" through communication, consensus building, "one partner, one vote," face-to-face interaction, partner development and evaluation, profit sharing, and confidenti-

ality of unit allocation, all which supports a feeling of fairness and trust.

2. The firm continues to provide high quality, personalized, prompt, and diversified services as well as offering clients the best value for their money

3. The vision of the firm is communicated through everyday behavior and performance.

4. The concept of shared ownership demands that each partner be responsible for the future of the firm.

5. The concept of leadership goes beyond professional services and management processes—it includes the ability to inspire and nurture talent and innovation.

6. People at all levels are developing professional and client service skills. These skills include technical competence in their respective disciplines and a knowledge of current technology

7. The firm attracts, recruits, and retains the best people across disciplines to develop as professionals.

8. The partnership attracts, develops, and retains people who are intelligent, hard working, energetic, possess good interpersonal skills, and have the courage to change barriers into opportunities.

9. The firm aggressively pursues specialty mergers, acquisitions of service firms and hires recognized experts to expand the diversity of services, skills and people, all to expand the firm's base.

10. The basic strategy for obtaining profitable growth in both the domestic and international environments is through harnessing positive and innovative thinking and using the most current technological and communications capabilities available.

11. Each partner is responsible for leaving a legacy in terms of building firm assets, which includes people, clients, and services.

Conclusion

To the extent that organizations want to maintain internal effectiveness and external adapt-

ability, they need to know what their fundamental values are so they can build a template by which to juxtapose people. Appreciative Inquiry is one technique that can highlight values and help build consensus around what is important to individuals in a firm. AI can help an organization know where it is and where it wants to go, by defining criteria and identifying people who can get them where they need to go.

Appreciative Inquiry highlights the values individuals stand for and allows for rearticulation and reprioritization of those values. In this context, it is a process in pattern enhancement. Values are not simply rearticulated through AI, they are rearticulated more profoundly. Appreciative Inquiry is designed to elicit the ideals of the organization and to give substance to those ideas through a concrete interactive process. It also is designed to make sure people see the connections between their values and the system's.

Beyond this, we found that Appreciative Inquiry builds culture. By tapping both common ground and shared values, AI mobilizes the maximum amount of commitment and increases members' confidence in what it is doing. It helps individuals clarify what it is they want to do and promote solidarity that represents a key source of rejuvenation as hard work depletes people's energies.

We also found that Appreciative Inquiry permits adaptation to the environment. In a professional organization, where the likelihood is high that new employees will bring with them the latest techniques, expertise, and knowledge necessary for keeping pace with emerging environmental demands, AI is likely to lead to the cementing of values that are indeed adaptive. If recruitment and development is from good schools and brings individuals with good sensors, and the system allows for learning and adaptation, then sharing values will be a growth process for the organization.

On the other hand, in those organizations displaying low recruitment and turnover, AI may prompt inbreeding and reinforce values that are behind the times, and therefore, threatening to organizational survival. Organizational culture may be very satisfactory for its members but not very adaptive to its environment. Consequently, Appreciative Inquiry could reinforce old, outdated systems values, thereby cementing blindness to the environment.

When AI is used as a succession technique, there is always the threat of demotivating persons not identified as fast trackers. There also is the very legitimate question of: *Are those who are identified as leaders of the future really managers or are they heretics?* To the extent that the system reflects the ideals of the membership, the organization may be down the path of its greatest ignorance. Other approaches to the succession process that introduced actors who backed the prevailing values may represent better guards or protection against this drawback.

Finally, it's clear that Appreciative Inquiry provides many contributions to collective and collaborative efforts and may be most ideal in those settings. It also appears that Appreciative Inquiry may be better suited to environments where fundamental changes have a low probability of occurrence because as much effort is required to maintain specialized cultures as is required to create them. Who should know that better than the partners of LeadShare, Canada.

References

Appley, D.G., & Winder, A.E. (1997). An evolving definition of collaboration and some implications for the world of work. *Journal of Applied Behavioral Science,* 13(3), 297–291.

Cohen, H. (1986). The social construction of managerial high performance. Unpublished Ph.D. dissertation; Case Western Reserve University; Cleveland, OH.

Cooperrider, D. (1988). Appreciative Inquiry: Toward a methodology for understanding and enhancing organizational innovation. Unpublished Ph.D. dissertation; Case Western Reserve University; Cleveland, OH.

Cooperrider, D. L., & Srivastva, S. (1987). Appreciative Inquiry in organizational life. In W. Pasmore, & R. Woodman (Eds.), *Research in organization change and development* (Vol. 1, pp. 129–169). Greenwich, CT: JAI Press, as reproduced on the Appreciative Inquiry Commons: http://ai.cwru.edu.

Freud, S. (1922). *Group psychology and the analysis of the ego.* London, England: Hogarth Press. Complete works, v.18.

Peters, T., & Waterman, R. (1984). In search of excellence. New York, NY: Warner Books.

Schein, E. (1985). *Organizational culture and leadership.* San Francisco, CA: Jossey-Bass.

Globalization, Cross-Cultural Interaction, and Virtual Working Arrangements

Introduction

Annie Viets and Cathy Royal

TOPICS COVERED IN THIS SECTION

1. How to work with the diverse employees in global organizations.
2. How to respect national cultures and norms yet abide by globally applicable values and ethics.
3. How to become culturally competent, manage across both virtual and physical borders, and sustain the performance and engagement of multi-ethnic, multifaceted employees.
4. How to be open to the contributions of local experts and understand the influences of race, gender, and age in business relationships particularly in developing nations.
5. How to effectively collaborate in global organizations and take advantage of virtual working arrangements.

GLOBAL ORGANIZATIONS IN TRANSITION

There is no question organizations today are globalizing at a frenetic rate. The purely domestic enterprise is rapidly becoming a curiosity of the past. To be successful, even so-called "local" businesses must look beyond their own geographic areas for customers, clients, employees, information, materials, and other resources. The emerging challenge for most is in understanding the changes this widening sphere of influence will have on their organizations and the way their activities are conducted.

Never has the need for Human Resource management and Organization Development collaboration and integration been more imperative. The importance of knowledge sharing and management; information technology and security; and cultural integration between nations will be part of this new collaboration.

A 2010 study by the Economist Intelligence Unit titled Global Firms in 2020: The Next Decade of Change for Organizations and Workers addressed some of the organizational and workforce issues that will face organizations over the next several years. Its findings indicated companies are, not surprisingly, predicted to become larger, more global, and spread over ever larger geographic areas but each will have its own unifying culture.

Within organizations, information flow and cross-border collaboration will improve in reaction to and anticipation of more complex management challenges. Decentralization of decision-making will enable local operations to quickly pursue opportunities while leaving centralized corporate offices the tasks of creating and maintaining a single brand experience, establishing global standards and processes, and defining culture and values. Companies will be flatter with project work and matrix structures, where employees will be called upon to form and reform into teams rather than occupy one well-defined role. It will become increasingly common for employees to be defined by skills rather than job titles.

The workforce, according to the study, will be far more diverse than it is today, coming from a wide range of backgrounds and countries. Expatriates will be sent for only short term overseas assignments as organizations will choose local hires for geographically dispersed operations to utilize their familiarity with local customs, customers, and employees. There will be a scramble to fill the ranks of retiring Boomers by promoting young, internationally savvy managers into strategic decision-making roles at a younger age and with less experience than the previous generation of managers. Contingent, contract-workers who are content experts will make up an increasingly larger percentage of the workforce. In time, their numbers may overtake those of permanent hires. Some roles will be automated or outsourced and more employees will work flexible hours or remotely.

The cultural divide between core and contingent employees will need to be bridged if organizations are to maintain morale and boost collaboration. To maintain a common brand experience for both customers and employees, employees worldwide will be required to operate within certain common frameworks. Corporate cultures will need to make explicit the globally applicable values and ethics with which organizations will function. To embed these common principles, organizations will need to orient and integrate new employees quickly while instilling a sense of community and unified purpose over wide geographic areas.

Greater diversity of employees will mean organizations are obliged to work harder to realize the inherent synergies in differences. Employees will be seeking support in acquiring a better appreciation and acceptance of their co-workers. Systems to enhance inclusiveness and participation will, of necessity, become commonplace. And, organizations will seek to acquire a more sophisticated understanding of what is important and motivating to this modern workforce.

A new breed of global managers will require careful career planning to maximize their worth to their organizations. They will need to quickly learn how to make judicious strategic decisions, manage across borders virtually and physically, and sustain the performance of multi-ethnic, multifaceted employees. They will need to learn to manage in a fluid and changing environment where project teams define employees' roles rather than titles and hierarchies.

Flatter organizations will require more systemic means of managing collaboration and accountability, more intra and intergroup cooperation and new ways of communicating both laterally and horizontally. Heightened competition will also necessitate increased collaboration across borders and seamless communication to spur innovation and idea-sharing.

The profound effects of these trends on organizations over the next decade will be myriad and provide important and urgent work for professionals competent in the Human Resources and Organization Development disciplines and capable of being both tactical and strategic business partners with organizational management.

THE CHAPTERS IN THIS SECTION

In this section are a series of articles and cases written by international OD professionals that explore issues and questions faced by organizations seeking to operate successfully in the global environment. The articles highlight the challenges and complexities of organizational integration, collaboration, and communication in global enterprises. The five broad topic areas are:

- Creating Global Glue and Alignment
- Leadership
- Consultant Role
- Community and Sustainability
- Communication in Global Enterprises

Creating Global Glue and Alignment

Annie Viets (2011), in **Global Glue and the Case of Fonterra**, describes how a New Zealand based cooperative that grew quickly to become a major player in the global dairy products industry reinvented itself as a globally cohesive and relevant organization greater than each of its operating units.

Therese Yaeger and Peter Sorensen (2011), in **Organization Development's Role When Going Global,** present an excellent example of the complexities of expanding a US based company to other countries. With the help of Narneen Razi, Dalitso Sulamoyo, and Katherine Shroeder, they provide insights into best practices for meeting the challenges of working in India, Sub-Saharan Africa, and Asia.

In another case study by Yaeger and Sorensen (2006), **Implementing a Global Corporate Strategy: The Role of OD,** two important issues involved in working globally are addressed: (1) partnering in the development and implementation of strategy, and (2) implementing global strategy. The authors and three experts weigh in on the involvement of OD in implementing a new CEO's mandate for a common vision, culture, and way of working among offices in 20 different countries.

In **Socio-Economic Approach to Management,** John Conbrere and Alla Heorhiadi (2011) describe a tradition of organization development that has evolved in France called the Socio-Economic Approach to Management (SEAM). This movement shares many of the beliefs and practices of traditional OD but incorporates some distinct practices and a core belief that "organizations do not exist only to make money, they exist to serve society in general and all the employees in particular."

Amanda Trosten-Bloom, David Cooperrider, Nadya Zhexembayeva, and Diana Whitney (2003), in **Business as an Agent of World Benefit: A Worldwide Action Research Project Using AI,** tell the story of a multi-company project's vision, challenges, and areas of immediate learning and impact. Their message that doing good for the world builds good businesses heralds a future where OD is an integral and essential tool for world development.

Leadership

Maya Hu-Chan (2008), in **Leadership Connectivity: Building Global Partnerships,** focuses on the key elements of global leadership and highlights some of the trends in changing global organizations. She provides an interesting analysis of Asian managers and descriptions of cultural behavior often displayed by managers in Asian societies while stressing the importance of developing coaching skills.

Presenting the results of a global study of managers in 40 countries on what needs to change in the face of globalization, Patricia Shafer (2008), in **Global Leadership: A Virgin Landscape for OD Practitioners in the Vanguard,** concludes there is a strong emerging need for new management skills. These new skills characterize hybrid leaders who are multidimensional professionals equipped with transformational, transnational, and transcultural competencies.

Consultant Role

When Western practitioners are asked to work internationally it is important they understand the unconscious assumptions and attitudes that could impact performance in other cultures. Therese Yaeger (2002), in **The Core Values of OD Revisited: A Compass for Global and International OD,** presents the results of a study of the values that inform effective global OD consulting particularly in addressing resistance to change.

Using Hofstede's (1980) four dimensions of national culture, Anne Litwin (2007), in **OD: Dancing in the Global Context,** compares how OD change interventions could be conducted in seven different countries. She shows how differences in these dimensions can predict which interventions will be effective and emphasizes that successful international consultants are sensitive to cultural context while always remembering to ground their work in values.

Community and Sustainability

How can HR professionals work with cultural dynamics that place a high emphasis on the work of the group and the community? John Schere and Kakuta Ole Ole Maimai Hamisis (2008), in **Organization as Community: What We have to Learn from the Maasai about OD,** showcase several principles of a Kenyan tribe's group dynamics that organizations could find useful in creating high performing teams.

Mambo Mupepi, Ram Tenkasi, Peter Sorensen, and Sylvia Mupepi (2007), in **Creating High Impact Organizations in the SADC: Adapting OD Methods and Practices,** highlight some of the values shared by the countries that make up the Southern Africa Development Community (SADC). They review some of the literature pertaining to change management and current OD practice and make suggestions for how these core OD concepts might be used to unleash innovation and facilitate change in organizations in the SADC region.

Virtual Collaboration in Global Enterprises

Steve Gens and Deb Torchia (2011), in **Addressing the Global Virtual Competency Gap,** identify a core set of interdependent competencies that are important for successfully working together in a virtual global environment.

Finally, in **OD 2.0: Shifting from Disruptive to Innovative Technology**, Kathleen Iverson and George Vukotich (2009), present how to use web-based technologies for team-building, product development, knowledge sharing, and relationship building.

FOR ADDITIONAL LEARNING

For more information about globalization you may want to read the following articles.

- Coghlin, D. (2002). Inter-organizational OD through Action Learning. *OD Practitioner,* 34(1), 9–13.

  Coghlin describes how interorganizational networks, in which members of distinct organizations form learning sets to explore change issues of common interest, are in-creasingly being utilized as a vehicle for organizational change and learning.

- Head, T. (2002). Organization development and the People's Republic of China: An interesting partnership. *OD Practitioner,* 34(1), 45–48.

  Head discusses how to adapt practices and assumptions to the Chinese culture so Organization Development can be useful in The People's Republic of China.

- Lippert , K., Rivo, R., Banwell, E., & Stepakoff, S. (2007). Human relations training in post-war Sierra Leone. *OD Practitioner,* 39(2), 24–29.

  The authors describe their experiences providing T-group focused human relations training to the Witnesses and Victims Section of the Special Court for Sierra Leone.

- Rodriguez, R. (2002). Organization development in Barbados: Overcoming an exploitation mindset. *OD Practitioner,* 34(1), 37–43.

  Rodriguez tells the story of an OD intervention that took place in the Caribbean country of Barbados. The intervention involved a manufacturing facility set up in the country by a large, U.S. based printing company. He discusses the cross cultural issues that surfaced during the intervention and how a group of OD practitioners was able to help with the improvement turnaround of the Barbados facility.

- Sharkey, L., & Sorensen, P. (2002). Survey feedback: An alternative to a classic intervention experience in the U.S., Japan, and India. *OD Practitioner,* 34(1), 32–35.

  Sharkey and Sorensen deal with one of the oldest and mainstream OD interventions —survey feedback. The first section of the article reviews the history and nature of survey feedback and activities at Benedictine University that sharply depart from traditional survey feedback. The second section briefly reviews the topic of international and Global OD, and the question of application of OD across diverse national cultures. The third section deals with recent findings and applications using work with the revised survey feedback model in the U.S., Japan, and India.

- Tobin, R. I. (2002). The six traps of global organization development and how to avoid them. *OD Practitioner*, 34(1), 3–8.

Tobin presents the six traps and the required set of unique personal and professional skills for global organization development—hypersensitivity to others, ability to bring diverse groups of people together, courage and risk taking, negotiation and mediation skills, deep cultural knowledge, and strength in mobilizing networks of community resources.

- Zaldivar, S. (2008). International development through OD: My experience in Afghanistan. *OD Practitioner*, 40(1), 4–9.

Zaldivar describes her experience with what organization development can provide for work in such an ancient culture as Afghanistan. OD informed how she entered a complex system, as well as how she identified and negotiated with stakeholders. She also came away with a deeper appreciation of the power of presence and awareness over a problem fixing orientation, which is especially critical in a traditional culture.

Reference

Economist Intelligence Unit. (2010). *The next decade of change for organizations and workers*. London, UK: The Economist.

CHAPTER 66

Global Glue and
the Case of Fonterra

Annie Viets

Introduction

Globalization is here to stay and organizations that can make it work for them are the ones that will survive and thrive. *Global Firms in 2020: The Next Decade of Change for Organisations and Workers*, a study conducted by the Economist Intelligence Unit (2010), predicted organizations able to operate seamlessly across borders, in different cultures, and with workforces that are extremely diverse will be the enterprises of the future. These firms will also be larger, more global, and spread over ever larger geographic areas.

The executives polled for the study predicted the workforce will be far more diverse than it is today, coming from a wide range of backgrounds and countries. First country nationals will become the employees of choice with long term expatriate assignments becoming rarer and rarer. Young, internationally savvy managers will be quickly promoted to replace retiring Baby Boomers. Contingent workers will be more common. Flexible and remote working arrangements will increase.

The effects of these trends on organizations over the next decade will be myriad and provide important and urgent work for professionals competent in the Human Resources and Organization Development disciplines and capable of being Business Partners.

Specifically, according to the study's participants, core and contingent employees will need to learn to work harmoniously. Great diversity among employees will also compel organizations to work harder to realize synergies and promote acceptance and appreciation while acquiring a more sophisticated understanding of what is important and motivating to this modern workforce. Employees worldwide will need to operate within certain common frameworks, and corporate cultures will become increasingly instrumental in instilling the firm's globally applicable values and ethics over wide geographic areas.

A new breed of global managers will need to learn how to manage across borders, and sustain the performance of multiethnic, multifaceted employees, the study predicted. They will need to learn to manage in a fluid and changing environment where project teams define employees' roles rather than titles and hierarchies. Flatter organizations will require more systemic means of managing collaboration and accountability and heightened competition will necessitate more, faster, and increasingly innovative teamwork across borders.

How will these sizeable global organizations avoid becoming lumbering giants and operate efficiently and synergistically over their vast geographic domains? They will need to apply "global glue," a set of shared values and a common corporate culture. In fact, Noel Tichy (1983) actually defined organizational culture as shared values. In a review of studies related to values in international business practice, Sandra Williams (2011) concluded one of the characteristics of organizations able to successfully adapt to different cultures and anticipate change in an uncertain global environment was shared core values. She stated, "Shared core values can transform a random group of individuals into a coherent and committed team, creating a synergy of community" (p. 323).

During a critical study of twelve large multinational corporations headquartered throughout the world, Rosabeth Moss Kanter (2006) uncovered similar characteristics of successful global companies. She found that at the core of each firm's effective global reach was a "strong guidance system" consisting of standardized systems and shared values. Values that were nurtured in "hearts and minds," she found, constituted the "key ingredient in the most vibrant and successful of today's internationals" (p. 45). They enable employees in widely dispersed locations to "communicate and collaborate efficiently even despite great differences in backgrounds and cultural traditions, because they have a strong sense of business purpose and company identity" (p. 45). Patrick Lencioni (2002) took this concept a step further by insisting if values are "going to really take hold in your organization, your core values need to be integrated into every employee-related process... employees should be constantly reminded that core values form the basis for every decision the company makes" (p. 117).

The subjects in the Economist Intelligence Unit study (2010), according to the authors, appeared to corroborate the observations and assertions of Kantor, Williams, and Lencioni by collectively predicting that: "Defining a company's culture and promoting it globally is another way companies will create a sense of community . . . When the core principles of an organization are understood by employees they develop a common sense of

purpose and belonging" (p. 9). "It is this unified culture," they foresee, "that will define successful global companies" (p. 5).

In this exciting and changing environment, OD and Human Resources professionals will increasingly be called upon to work as Business Partners with organizational leadership to critically examine and help transform organizational cultures while defining and refining global core values. They will also be major contributors to the design and delivery of corporate-wide programs to embed the shared values and common culture that make up an organizations' global glue.

Fonterra

One organization has already begun to spread its global glue. The leaders of Fonterrahttp://www.fonterra.com (*www.fonterra.com*), a New Zealand cooperative that grew rapidly to become a major player in the global dairy products industry, recognized early in the organization's process of globalizing that global glue was needed. Its subsequent successful initiative to reinvent a globally cohesive and relevant organization that was infinitely greater than each of its operating units illustrated the strength of the concept of shared values discussed in the Economist study (2010) and noted by Kantor (2006) and Williams (2011). By incorporating the OD principles of Appreciative Inquiry storytelling, the leadership, human resources, and corporate marketing worked together to embark on a wide ranging, cross-cultural change initiative to bring a unified culture to the firm's widely dispersed global operations.

At first glance, storytelling might not seem to be a vehicle of choice for a large multinational attempting to unite and reinvigorate its global organization. However, storytelling, particularly from the Appreciative Inquiry perspective of "listening together to moments when the organization was 'alive' and the future becomes visible through ideals interwoven with actual experiences" (Cooperrider & Whitney, 1999, p. 14), can be a pivotal transformational tool. Filmmaker, Peter Gruber (2007), described storytelling as "one of the most powerful tools for achieving astonishing results" (p. 55). For leaders, he claimed, "storytelling is action-oriented—a force for turning dreams into goals and then into results" (p. 55). Nancy McGaw and Lisa Fabish (2006), writing on the results of an Aspen Institute/Booz Allen Hamilton survey of global executives, advise organizations to overcome challenges and gain a competitive edge by encouraging "employees to share stories about how they have used a corporate value . . ." and to "invite employees at all levels and across all functions to talk about what these values mean to them" (p. 3).

According to Kenneth Gergen (Krattenmaker, 2001), current president of the Taos Institute, peoples' behavior in organizations is shaped by the way they talk about their behavior, and "if we could construct a world in which something is possible, we can talk about that in such a way that we might be able to achieve it together. Suddenly, you create a tremendous positive energy" (p. 3). It follows that "Good news stories are used to craft possibility propositions that bridge the best of 'what is' with collective aspiration of 'what might be'" (Cooperrider & Whitney, 1999, p. 15).

Appreciative, values-focused storytelling, therefore, became the technique of choice for Fonterra. The cooperative was in its eighth year since inception and had matured to the point where management recognized it was an appropriate time to revisit its core vision and values to ensure they resonated with the organization's diverse employee base and refreshed organizational strategy. According to Joanne Fair, HR Director for the Cooperative's Global Ingredients and Foodservice business unit, the organization's leadership was faced with an issue not uncommon in organizations that grow globally from strong local roots: "The question we asked ourselves was, 'How can we celebrate our New Zealand heritage while recognizing our new global identity and do both under the umbrella of one, cohesive entity?'"

With operations and activities on six continents, research and development centers in New Zealand, Australia, the US and the Netherlands, 16,000 employees, and a product line-up of 900 different dairy ingredients that were supplied to food companies and pediatric applications around the world, this need to engage employees around a common vision and values presented a formidable challenge.

While the organization had always had a vision and a set of robust values, they tended to be very formal, and didn't always translate well to other languages. "We did not," Joanne said, "articulate our strategy and values in a globally relevant way. We wanted to provide our managers throughout the world with a lens through which to set priorities, make the right decisions, and have the tough conversations." Without this, it was felt, strategic business units might drift and lose a sense of common purpose and goals.

What ensued was a creative and insightful top-down and bottom-up collaboration based on "keeping it personal" and storytelling among senior management, corporate marketing, and human resources to design, roll-out, and continuously promote a global identity for the dairy giant.

The process of achieving this began with 300 appreciative inquiry interviews with employees from all levels in the organizations and from all geographic locations as well as with a number of stakeholders: farmers, members of the shareholders' council, board directors, and customers. This information, together with the research from a study of corporate brand essences, a study of the New Zealand psyche, and a review of Fonterra's history was then processed by board directors, members of the shareholders' council, the executive council, and a group of "future thinkers" comprised of twelve managers and executives from across the organization.

One of the most interesting cultural exercises during this phase involved teasing out the meaning of the organization's deeply entrenched Kiwi values in a way that made sense to international employees. For instance, one value articulated as "Kia Kaha" (literally "forever strong") in Maori, or "Stand Tall," evoked the strength of the tall, strong stands of kauri trees native to New Zealand's North Island. It was a concept deeply resonant with New Zealanders but of limited relevance to employees living in other countries. It was therefore enveloped into "Make it Happen," the fourth of four core values, as "Aim high; deliver exceptional results" and, "Step up; take accountability." Another Kiwi value important to retain was "Fair Play," a rugby expression familiar to almost everyone in a country that loves its rugby. It became "Treat others as I would expect to be treated," a supporting concept for the second value, "Do What's Right." The other two values that emerged were "Co-operative Spirit," and "Challenge Boundaries," both of which could be easily understood across cultures.

During the Design phase of Appreciative Inquiry, the rich lode of data resulting from the interviews and studies was distilled into *This is Fonterra*, the organization's story that consisted of its vision, its corporate strategy and its values. According to Joanne, it laid out "who we are, why we exist, where we come from, how we will conduct our business and what our fundamental reason for being is, over and above profit and financial gain. The corporate strategy provided a clear focus on what needed to be done commercially and organizationally to achieve the vision with a reinvigorated set of values that were to be our guiding principles and moral compass."

The most exhilarating phase of the project, the Destiny phase or rollout, came next. How do you communicate something this huge and fundamental to a company that is widely dispersed and yet keep it personal, relevant, and impactful? The phrasing of this step, the "Bring it to Life" phase, was therefore very deliberate.

This is Fonterra was launched at the organization's annual global congress attended by its 200 top leaders. Toolkits were distributed to assist them to roll out the initiative in their own operations in their own countries within thirty days. Leaders were encouraged to overlay the Fonterra story with their own stories that they had developed at the congress. Each roll-out was culture-specific. For instance, in Australia and New Zealand, managers tended to take traditional approaches with leadership workshops. The Brands Asia division, on the other hand, involved its entire workforce in a "big-bang" celebration. In Joanne's division, she, the Managing Director and the Commercial Director "kept it personal" by visiting all its regional offices and engaging employees in six countries over a six-week period.

Sad stories abound about organization change initiatives that are rolled out with much fanfare only to fizzle when put to the test so the Fonterra change leaders were wary. When *This is Fonterra* was presented to the organization, they were ready to begin the process of consolidation by embedding its story, vision, strategy, and values into everything about the organization. The look, feel, and tone of its brand and communications about the brand were aligned with the story's opening statement, "We are Fonterra—we are of the land." It was used as a lever to develop leadership capability and engage employees. It became a driver for performance through its clear and consistent communication of vision and strategy and by focusing the organization on consistent behavioral competencies. Human Resources immediately incorporated the concepts in *This is Fonterra* into people processes and systems from hire to exit. Values became an integral part of the interview for every candidate. Everyone's performance was measured not only on the "what" but also on the "how." Leaders, in particular, were held accountable for being able to point to specific actions he/she had taken to live and exemplify the values.

It was also finessed by each and every strategic business unit in every country into language and concepts that resonated with the stories of local employees. Leaders were encouraged to put *This is Fonterra* to the test using it as a framework for making decisions, solving problems, and coaching teams and to report back on what worked and what did not. It was an effort that involved every employee in every operation throughout the world.

Two years after the launch, Human Resources and Marketing continue to partner to drive awareness and connection to the vision and values throughout the organization. This is done in a non-corporate way, reflecting the tone and essence of *This is Fonterra*. "The values are living and breathing in the organization," remarked Joanne. "They have become a part of our language, how we think about ourselves and how we conduct our business." This is not a small claim for a global, culturally diverse organization. Fonterra has demonstrated that even with a large, diverse operation, you can create the "global glue" to keep it personal and engage employees at a meaningful level.

Appreciative Inquiry storytelling and process appeared to enable this global enterprise to reach and inspire employees at every level in every part of its organization throughout the world. The coalition of leadership, human resources, and marketing introduced a movement and embedded the "glue" of values and culture that will continue to serve and develop the organization and its employees as they incorporate what Cooperrider and Whitney (1999) have called the "poetic principle." As such, "an organization's 'story' is constantly being rewritten by everyone in the organization and everyone who interacts with it. The organization, like a poem, is constantly being interpreted and reinterpreted" (Watkins & Mohr, 2001, in Krattenmaker, 2001, p. 3).

As more organizations expand internationally and communication and information technologies change the way we organize and interact to conduct business, the importance of a common culture and values to unite dispersed and diverse operations will only grow. Global glue, as an organization development concept, will have applicability far into the future.

References

Cooperrider, D.L., & Whitney, D. (1999). *Appreciative Inquiry*. San Francisco, CA: Brett-Koehler Communications, Inc.

Economist Intelligence Unit. (2010). *Global firms in 2020: The next decade of change for organisations and workers*. Retrieved from www.energizers.eu/GlobalFirmsHRM2020.pdf*www.energizers.eu/* www.energizers.eu/GlobalFirmsHRM2020.pdf *GlobalFirmsHRM2020.pdf.*

Guber, P. (2007, December). The four truths of the storyteller. *Harvard Business Review*, 85(12), 52–59.

Kantor, R. M. (2008, January). Transforming giants. *Harvard Business Review*, 86(12), 43–52.

Krattenmaker, T. (2001, October). Change through Appreciative Inquiry. *Harvard Management Communication Letter*, 3-4.

Lencioni, P. (2002, July). Make your values mean something. *Harvard Business Review*, 80(7), 113–117.

McGaw, N., & Fabish, L. (2006, January). Put your values to work. *Harvard Management Update*, 3–4.

Tichy, N. (1983). *Managing strategic change: Technical, political, and cultural dynamics*. New York, NY: Wiley Publishing.

Watkins, J.M., & Mohr, B.J. (2001). Appreciative Inquiry: Change at the speed of imagination. In T. Krattenmaker (2001, October). Change through Appreciative Inquiry. *Harvard Management Communication Letter*, 3–4.

Williams, S. L. (2011, July 15). Engaging values in international business practice. *Business Horizons*, (54), 315–324.

CHAPTER 67

Organization Development's Role when Going Global

Therese F. Yaeger and Peter F. Sorensen

PHARMA is a successful pharmaceutical company operating, until now, solely in the United States. As a result of their successful hard-line sales history, the environment at Pharma has been described as "entrepreneurial." Pharma's corporate culture has always been aggressive, competitive, and power-oriented, which has contributed to its success.

However, being U.S.-centric must now change, and Marcus, the new CEO at Pharma, has charged the organization to become global by next year. Marcus has identified three global regions—India, Asia, and Africa—to begin Pharma's global efforts.

You are the U.S. OD consultant reporting directly to Marcus. Marcus wants to involve you in the overseas future growth development for Pharma. He has told you, "Failure is not an option. We might be a great US pharmaceutical corporation, but as CEO, I insist that we become global, and make it happen now. The announcement of our new global efforts will be in the press next week."

As the OD consultant you have expertise in Global OD, with limited exposure to regions in Africa, India, and Asia. You understand Pharma's past culture, but you are also aware that in these different national cultures start-ups do not succeed as quickly and aggressively as the U.S. Pharma culture. In fact, with your global knowledge, you know of instances where start-up efforts failed because US manage-ment teams were unaware of the context in which they were operating.

You understand the no-fail approach that Marcus has taken. But you also wonder what will be needed to support all the future efforts. Perhaps with the right people and the right knowledge this global effort might just work. But you realize that this effort is bigger and broader than OD.

Right now, more questions than answers exist. Some of these questions include:

- How might OD be of strategic relevance in helping Pharma?
- Does Pharma understand the economic, political, and legal issues that must be addressed?
- Does everyone understand the societal and national cultural values?
- How will the role of OD be perceived?
- What specific OD strategies would you incorporate with on-ground Pharma management?
- Finally, how would you measure success on this global undertaking?

We have asked three consultants with global expertise to help unpack all the answers and questions for this huge corporate global project: Nazneen Razi with HR and OD knowledge operating globally, particularly India; Dalitso Sulamoyo, with first-hand change experience in Africa (particularly Malawi); and Katherine Shroeder with expert OD knowledge and experience working in Japan.

Nazneen Razi

The challenge of doing business globally cannot be underestimated, particularly in a country like India, one of the most culturally, socially, and politically complex countries in the world. The initiative to take Pharma across U.S. borders provides tremendous opportunity for an OD consultant who can leverage both local OD talent and healthcare experts to assess the current situation and develop an outcome-based strategy for success.

According to a recent IMS report (2010), the pharmaceutical industry in India is a $10 billion business and among the top four emerging markets, forecasting double digit growth over the next five years. If Pharma wishes to enter the Indian market, the role of OD will be critical in assessing and addressing the following:

- Market strategy
- Launch readiness
- Acquisition of key talent
- Cultural and societal forces
- Legal and regulatory environment
- Competitive landscape

The pharmaceutical industry in India is extremely fragmented. Large retail drug chain stores like Walgreens or CVS do not exist, rather pharmaceutical retail outlets are operated by local small business owners who are well known by the communities around them, including medical practitioners and hospital staff. If Marcus wants a plan that is guaranteed to succeed, several key decisions will have to be made, guided by good research and advice. Various scenarios can be contemplated with varying outcomes. For example, should Pharma sell its own U.S.-manufactured products in India, or leverage the low cost, highly intelligent pharmaceutical local labor market to do the R&D work, and then market products to

India and potentially to other markets; should Pharma penetrate one geographic market one product at a time, or proliferate rapidly?

To optimize the decision-making process, the following five-step process should be proposed to Marcus for implementation this year to ensure a successful launch next year, using OD interventions that are conducive to large scale initiatives:

1. Quarter One—**Select High Powered Teams:** A strategic sourcing strategy should be deployed to engage a group of skilled local OD and business consultants who are also market and industry experts. A global leader, either an expatriate from within the firm or a qualified local hire, should be appointed to lead the strategic effort. Using the right assessment tools to select and develop a strong leader, who has the cultural sensitivity to lead teams in a very diverse setting, is critical to this initiative.

2. Quarter Two—**Conduct Rigorous Research:** The OD and business teams should focus their energy to collect data on the technical aspects of the industry as well as around the societal, economic, and regulatory aspects of doing business in India. Marketing and legal experts should review the competitive and legal landscape of the business, while cultural OD experts should examine the behavioral norms that define consumer habits and employee needs.

3. Quarter Three—**Apply Research to Inform Key Decisions:** Once this data is collected, the teams should bring key stakeholders together, including health-care practitioners, pharmacists, doctors, chemists, and others to develop a powerful global strategy. Scenario planning should be used to create a variety of possible future scenarios in deciding which direction Pharma should be headed using the data to support its trajectory.

4. Quarter Four—**Define Strategy and Criteria for Brilliant Execution:** In Weisbordian fashion (1987), the team should gather the en-

tire system in the room, using an "all-purpose view finder" to understand the market, economic, and government forces at work in this business. During this session, strategy, structure, design, and other organizational constructs can begin to form and get vetted.

5. 2012—Launch and Measure for Global Success: The launch should be a collaborative effort by Marketing, HR, and the business teams. Appropriate financial and non-financial metrics and measurements should be developed to keep plans on track.

The OD function should continue to monitor progress on an ongoing basis to ensure that both top line and bottom line objectives are being achieved and teams are engaged and productive for continued success.

Dalitso S. Sulamoyo

Marcus should be commended for his vision to expand Pharma's operations globally. He should also be commended for engaging the services and expertise of an OD consultant to aid in the facilitation of this expansion to Africa, India, and Asia in general. There are indeed many questions that need to be considered and answered with regard to the role that OD should play with this expansion particularly on the continent of Africa south of the Sahara. My OD approach to this proposed growth and expansion onto the continent of Africa would involve a two-pronged approach designed to address the critical questions.

The first order of business would be the identification of local African OD practitioners that would partner with me in the specific African countries that Pharma intends to set up its operations. The partnership with these local African OD practitioners would first serve the purpose of gaining and building trust with the local workforce and operations. Relationships are very important in any African setting, especially if they involve any cross-cultural work. It is important to recognize local African talent in an age where Afri-

ca is going through a rebirth that some have described as the African Renaissance. Global operations have tended to focus more on bringing expatriates with less recognition of existing talent on the continent of Africa. A partnership that is built on cross-cultural OD would be beneficial to its implementation in this new venture by Pharma. Secondly, since many of the OD applications and techniques are western developed, it is critical that these local OD practitioners serve as the cultural translators and indigenizing agents for their acceptance and success. Indigenization in this instance would be the convergence of these OD techniques and approach with local African culture. Thirdly, the local OD practitioners would assist in the identification of successful indigenous applications such as the utilization of African metaphors and proverbs to facilitate change and convey OD practices to the local setting. Fourthly, the local African OD practitioners would assist in designing appropriate surveys to assess and understand the political, economic, social, environmental, technological, and legal issues that need to be considered as part of Pharma's strategy in establishing its operations. It is critical to utilize the local OD practitioners so as to ensure that the questions that might be in a survey are appropriate.

The second order of business would be to educate Pharma about African culture, particularly the collectivist culture of Ubuntu whose principles are common in sub-Saharan Africa. Pharma's corporate culture which has been described as aggressive, competitive, and power oriented has contributed to its success. However, those cultural factors are in many respects the antithesis to the prevalent African culture found in sub-Saharan Africa. Ubuntu represents a powerful philosophy and cultural approach whereby African's view their existence through others in their society. The approach for Pharma would be to utilize Ubuntu and its principles as the cultural integrator for strategic OD. The western world as exemplified by Pharma, emphasizes efficiency while the five principles of Ubuntu emphasize effectiveness in relationships. I would propose the convergence of these two approaches to productivity to design an indigenized approach for Pharma. These five principles should provide Pharma with a different approach to competitiveness as follows:

Importance of Relationships with others— Relationships are very important in an African culture. Africans view relationships as being reciprocal. The whole notion of people viewing themselves through others or the existence of empathy is an important dimension in African relationships. Pharma should consider this as it establishes its operations in Africa because people are intrinsically motivated to contribute more when they are valued members of the work place. Solidarity and social harmony are also important components of African culture when viewing relationships. In an Ubuntu culture, Pharma would have sustainable and competitive advantages due to the strong loyalty Africans have to group goals. Pharma could utilize this cultural component to foster group synergy when developing new ideas and products.

Shared Decision Making—Participatory decision making will be important in gaining commitment to Pharma's goals and the effectiveness of its operations in the long run. Africans like to reach decisions by consensus where dissenters are recognized so as to foster harmony. This would be a different approach for Pharma where perhaps decisions are primarily top-down. Creating and fostering harmony builds a strong sense of commitment in an African setting.

Time—An observation that is generally shared by those who visit Africa for the first time is the difference in the perception of time between westerners and Africans. In Ubuntu, time is recognized as not being a finite commodity, but a healer if enough time is allowed for important decisions to be made. Western perception is that Africans are not punctual and treat time carelessly, while Africans' per-

ception of time as a healer could offer Pharma a competitive advantage. If more time is taken on thinking things through, then all aspects are considered and decisions are rational as opposed to rushed. It would offer Pharma a competitive advantage in the sense that the best decisions for the corporation can be made. Africans also value and respect older workers because they bring experience and wisdom to the workplace. This would be a competitive advantage for Pharma if some of the organization's leadership consists of older workers. There is great respect for the elderly which would result in a more cohesive work setting for Pharma.

Belief Systems—Africans subscribe to belief systems that are based on both organized religion from the East and the West and traditional African spiritual beliefs. These belief systems are in most respects part of the African psyche. To respect them would be to allow the best in people to come out for the betterment of the workplace.

Loyalty—Africans in an Ubuntu culture place their personal interests secondary to the collective, tribe, or the workplace. There is an African saying that states "the river that forgets its source will soon dry up." If the Ubuntu or components of African culture that have been discussed here were considered as part of Pharma's OD approach in Africa, then Pharma can expect to have loyalty and commitment from its workforce which are very valuable dimensions in the long term.

In generalized terms, African's view their place of work as their second home. Ubuntu would help to facilitate the human touch and family driven environment in the workplace. This does not mean that Pharma should completely negate its competitiveness. What this means is that Pharma can maintain its competitiveness while being culturally appropriate in an African setting. Then the Pharma OD approach will be more successful at the organizational and group levels.

Katherine Schroeder

While "going global" is attractive for many industries in this day and age, particularly pharmaceutical organizations, it is imperative that top executives undertaking such a venture are grounded in the reality of what it truly takes to complete such a task. The first step, of course, is a clear commitment from top leadership not only to globalize, but to devote the resources that it takes to be successful. While Marcus's decision is clear, I would recommend several probing conversations with him and his senior leadership team to ensure that they have a solid understanding of the organizational resources—time, energy, and money—that are required for success. You can present various case studies of other U.S.-based pharmaceutical companies who have made the attempt to go global, highlighting key elements for success and pointing out the many quagmires Pharma may face. It is critical that you erode any false sense of confidence Marcus has about how simple and straightforward this will be. Globalizing requires developing the best laid plans, but remaining open to the unknown factors, which will most certainly be encountered on the path.

After grounding Marcus and the senior leadership team with a less rosy and more realistic perspective of what it takes to globalize, I would focus on negotiating a realistic timeframe for the globalization process. There is no magic wand to wave that "makes you global" by next year just because the CEO proclaims it should be so. Part of your job as the OD Consultant is to ensure development of a realistic timeline. Of course planning the trajectory of this organizational change depends primarily on the methodology Pharma will follow to globalize. Make sure that Marcus hires a Business Development Resource with solid pharmaceutical experience who can do the business analysis to recommend the best way to expand globally. A strategic alliance or acquisition may prove to be more effective than a straight expansion of the Pharma organization into these markets.

To ensure that the legal, political, and market perspectives have been assessed, you should ensure that the Business Development Resource does a thorough assessment of the markets in Asia, India, and Africa to ensure that these truly are the best options for expansion of Pharma's footprint. While it is unlikely that Marcus came up with these areas by throwing darts at a world map, you need more data to ensure that targeted expansions fit with your overall strategic plan and that the markets can support your entry. Also, choosing one entry point for 2012 is worthy of serious consideration and would narrow your scope, increasing your possibilities for success.

If Marcus and the Senior Leadership Team do decide to expand into Asia, your work shifts into not just ensuring effective execution of the business strategy, but providing the context for effective cross-cultural relationship building that will be imperative to Pharma's success. Help the senior leadership team begin with the position that you do not know enough to make assumptions about what it takes to create a successful partnership. Humility in this regard will serve you better than false confidence.

As you target your territory in Asia, expand your "cultural due diligence" to the specific country you have targeted. You may want to find a resource that can provide you and the senior leadership team with key cultural guideposts to avoid major stumbles out of the blocks. For instance, the Japanese approach to partnership requires an extended period of due diligence not just to do fact finding and data analysis, but to build a strong working relationship. What may appear as secondary "socializing" to the U.S. executive is an essential part of business in Japan. In fact, key conversations that may make or break a partnership occur over drinks and dinner in the evening.

A global expansion such as the one Pharma is considering is complex on many levels. This broad focus makes your OD role even more critical. Your job is to not only draw attention to key OD perspectives, but ensure that key areas of the business are coming together to make sound decisions. In the end, your most important work is to probe and ask the questions that will keep Marcus and his senior leadership team focused on the reality of what it takes to succeed as Pharma begins the journey to globalization.

Yaeger and Sorensen Respond

Applause for these three exceptional OD contributors who have three very different approaches to assist Marcus at Pharma! Nazneen, Dalitso, and Kathy illustrate how different OD can look when delivering OD support in three different cultural regions—India, Africa, and Asia. But even beyond the three different regional perspectives, these three respondents have provided different approaches specific to assisting Marcus at Pharma. Each respondent begins their discussion by emphasizing the complexities of working in a global environment. Nazneen integrates business and OD strategy, and builds on and uses some of the best in OD work (i.e., high-powered teams, data collection, and measurement).

Dalitso does an exceptional job of integrating his understanding of the African culture with Western OD. He reminds us of the need to identify local African OD practitioners to partner with, and to understand the collectivistic culture and Ubuntu principles when working in Africa.

The cautions of going global cannot be emphasized more, as Kathy Schroeder reminds us of the importance of a realistic strategic plan. The macro business issues of "cultural due diligence" and continuing to evaluate whether all of the business components are coming together make good business sense. Often, as consultants we have exceptional OD knowledge to assist the client, but we are naïve at the larger global business plan that OD must contribute to.

References

IMS Health. (2010, March 16). IMS announces 17 countries now rank as high-growth "Pharmerging" markets; Forecast to contribute nearly half of industry growth by 2013 [Press release].

Weisbord, M. R. (1987). *Productive workplaces.* San Francisco, CA: Jossey Bass. Vol. 43 No. 1

CHAPTER 68

Implementing a Global Corporate Strategy

The Role of Organization Development

Therese F. Yaeger and Peter F. Sorensen

THIS CASE deals with two of the most important issues that face the field of Organization Development: 1) OD as a partner in the development and implementation of strategy, and 2) the implementation of strategy on a global basis. In other words, OD as a partner with management in dealing effectively with critical issues of survival and growth. These are not new issues. Over the last ten years a number of prominent contributors to the field have argued that Organization Development must become a strategic partner in order to survive. We believe that in increasing numbers OD executives and practitioners have, in fact, become partners in strategy.

This case is real, but rather than a single organization case, it is a composite of experiences of several organizations that are dealing with strategic global initiatives. As a composite, it represents generic issues faced by global organizations.

We have asked three expert panelists to comment on the case.

Two panelists represent a team from Abbott, the largest Chicago-based global organization and one of the largest health care companies in the world. Abbott has an exceptional history of performance, and was one of the organizations featured in the best seller *From Good to Great*. The panelists are **Philip Ander-**

son, director of Change Management/Business Transformation at Manpower North America, and **Ghazala Ovaice**, manager of Strategic OD at Abbott. Both are experienced OD practitioners, but with different educational backgrounds—Phillip has a PhD in OD, while Ghazala has a background in Human Resources/HRD. We asked both to comment on the case expecting that their educational backgrounds would contribute different perspectives to the case commentary.

The third expert panelist is **Jennifer Smith,** a Benedictine University student in the masters OD program and Corporate Manager of Training & Development for Molex Incorporated, another Chicago-based global organization with an exceptional performance record.

Case

You are an experienced OD practitioner with responsibility for the implementation of organizational change projects within your corporation. Although you are the Director of OD you have a limited number of OD personnel working with you. Your strategy has been to elevate the role of OD in your corporation and, on the U.S. side, that has been fairly successful. In fact, executive management has asked you to play a role in domestic strategy and future vision, and to develop a global strategy representing the work developed at corporate headquarters.

Your company is 100 years old with a reputation for high quality manufacturing products. Thirty years ago the company began international activities; now the organization has manufacturing and sales operations in 20 different countries including the U.S., Scandinavia, Central Europe, Africa, and Asia, including recent activity in China and South America. Each of the regions has its own sales, marketing and production functions and has operated on a decentralized, fairly autonomous basis. The organization has been successful in each of its regional operations with only minor difficulties that were successfully handled.

Generally, the immediate past administration was relatively passive, resting on a history of success, and leading to a tradition of strong, highly decentralized regional operations. This has created a situation where there is some discontinuity in the perceptions of the mission of the organization, and agreement as to its future. The strong decentralization has had the advantage of building robust regional managers with the ability to adapt operations to regional cultures and political and economic environments.

The one consistent core value across all regions is the commitment, tradition, and dedication to high quality products. Also, there is a strong commitment on the part of employees to each of the regional operations, but not necessarily to the corporation or the U.S. home office

The organization recently experienced a change in top management with a new CEO. The previous administration was fairly passive in their acceptance of OD, although not resistant. As they had not been terribly encouraging, the OD function had to be highly innovative in developing support among line managers. Now the new administration is more receptive to OD initiatives and also is more aggressive in shaping the future of the organization. The CEO has a desire to create greater identity and continuity of operations, consistent with the U.S. corporate culture and vision.

It is your job as the Director of OD to develop and implement this executive vision. What is your strategy and recommendation to your OD Director who has successfully become a partner in developing domestic strategy and change, and as a consequence, is faced with this global challenge?

Jennifer Smith

I would first look at how the domestic organization viewed my role in assisting with the implementation of strategy and future vision. I attribute the success I have experienced thus far to the knowledge I have gained in understanding the business itself. By engaging with individuals throughout various levels of the organization I have been able to understand the pressure points critical to the business and align the work I do with the key critical business indicators identified by management. When I approach a situation, I view it not only from the human aspect, but also from a business aspect, to determine how potential solutions align with the business model. My intention is to show value to the organization in a language the executive level speaks, increasing revenues and profits or decreasing costs. This strategy can be labeled: Engagement, Understanding and Language.

The strategy to implement a consistent identity and provide continuity throughout worldwide operations would be similar: Engagement, Understanding and Language. This might be challenged by various cultures, and perhaps is a role not as recognized across the world. One recommendation I would make to the Director of OD is to not only understand the business as a whole, but to concentrate on understanding the business practices that have been in place in each region that have made them successful. Prior to implementing a corporate strategy, it is crucial to understand how it will fit within each region's current business model.

The Director of Organization Development could suggest that evaluation research be initiated with data compiled, and feedback reported to the executive level management team. This would give the OD Director the opportunity to engage and learn practices in the other regions with senior management. It will be important for the feedback to be given using business language. This would be sensitive research, as any time thoughts of structure change are suspected, individuals tend to become protective of their territory. Patience will be critical in order to gain credibility and respect in other regions. It will be the Director of Organization Development's role to help facilitate the breakthrough of these barriers and communicate the message to improve the whole organization in order to attain accurate feedback.

A second recommendation is to engage the employees in the formulation of the strategy. The Director of OD can orchestrate a worldwide survey and focus group project to gather input on globalization. This will give the employees a sense of belonging and identify pressure points throughout the worldwide organization. The message the Director of OD needs to communicate to this team is that if the employees feel a part of the strategy, the implementation will be more successful. Data gathering, synthesis and feedback presented to executives in a company-specific manner demonstrates the value OD can play in the organization.

A third recommendation for the Director of Organization Development is to help the executives see the effect of aligning the organization strategy in order to achieve long-term high performance. This can be accomplished by identifying critical gaps that occur when strategy is not clearly planned or executed and the impact that has on both short and long term business goals.

Philip Anderson

This is a classic dichotomy in our field—OD needs to become more strategic, yet rarely is the OD function sufficiently resourced to allow them to make significant strategic investments.

However, there are a myriad of strategic OD interventions going on in all successful organizations—that is what makes them successful. In some cases, it is not the exclusive domain of OD practitioners. Most OD activities are designed and executed by organizational leaders. Successful organizations are inevitably led by people who have good OD skills. Often those skills are indistinguishable from their overt leadership style. After all, our field embraces the same values that constitute good leadership behavior, i.e. participative management, equal opportunity, autonomy, fair rewards, and cooperation. In the end, OD is simply 'just in time' leadership.

Our job is to support leadership, not take ownership of it or claim exclusive rights to the field. To do so is the antithesis of what we claim to value. So, rather than asking how OD can become more strategic, the real question is how OD practitioners can become strategic partners.

With that said, let's turn our attention to our OD Director. There are a number of things she can do to be seen as a strategic partner, most of which must be done through influence rather than direct authority—a competency that is often underrated by internal practitioners.

First, she should look for strategic alliances. OD is not the exclusive domain of OD practitioners, nor is it only a leadership style. Marketing, Human Resources (HR), Training and Communications professionals are deeply vested in OD practices. She can use these alliances to build a robust internal practice.

For instance, most companies are financially driven. It is usually a financial crisis that spawns significant organization change. Market analysis is the vehicle by which the organization assesses future financial stability. It is the primary function that keeps the company attuned to changes in their external environment—the very essence of strategic management. The OD Director can help by assuring the internal climate is congruent with the external environmental changes. Research shows that there is a correlation between customer and employee satisfaction. Knowledge like this can be the foundation for a culture assessment that would provide leaders with compelling data that can be translated into a corporate strategic plan for OD.

However, a corporate plan is not enough. If the OD Director is to be successful, she must somehow connect with the business leaders. One avenue could be the Human Resources function. The organization depicted in the case has a divisional structure. In a divisionally structured corporation, the corporate function (in this case where OD sits) is responsible for prescribing in what business (products, services, etc.) the company should be involved. The Business Units or Divisions are responsible for producing those products or services. In this type of structure, the OD Director will rarely have the opportunity to work with business leaders—she will be relegated to working with staff functions because she is too far away from the business. However, HR professionals are often matrixed. In addition to corporate guidance, they have direction from the business and they understand its culture and leaders. By developing a partnership, she can gain access to the business and identify issues with which leaders are struggling. If OD professionals want to become strategic partners, we must gain access to leaders and help them solve their problems, not problems we perceive them to have.

Ghazala Ovaice

My response to this case will focus primarily on the assessment and joint diagnosis stages. Specifically, the political and cross-cultural implications of building a global strategy for operations will be discussed from the perspective of the Director laying the foundation for managing this change.

While the Director of OD has domestic success in partnering with business leaders, the Director will need to make political connections globally. Her first line of action should be around understanding the expectations of the CEO and his staff regarding creating a vision of global operations. Second, the Director needs to have a champion in the Senior Vice President of Human Resources as well as the Senior Vice President of Operations, both who were privy to, and benefited from, domestic partnerships with this Director on local organization development initiatives. These key individuals will serve as "plants" in building a coalition for OD support (i.e., they have reaped the benefits of previous partnerships with OD). The hard reality of internal consulting (and consequently internal politics—especially in a large organization) is that once OD has had a successful client intervention, they have built trust with that client. Third, the Director must understand the needs and expectations of the various stakeholders globally.

The Director must also realize that she or he is working on two levels:

1. building a global vision for operations, and
2. building a global partnership for OD. The latter will be a consequence of successfully achieving the first.

Through clarifying expectations, building a need for change, working with the client to create a desired end state, and understanding the needs of the various stakeholders globally, the Director is laying the foundation for the change process (i.e., a new global strategy for operations).

Through the act of garnering sponsorship and setting expectations, the Director will also need to assess the readiness for change. Is a global strategy for operations (GOS) prudent for the organization? Is the organization ready for a global strategy? What are the benefits and threats of having a GOS? What are the various stakeholders likely to gain or lose with a global strategy? What are the cross-cultural implications of a GOS? How will a global strategy translate literally and figuratively across cultures in the various international regional offices?

During an assessment with the CEO, his staff, and key global stakeholders, such questions must be flushed out to jointly determine if a Global Organization Strategy is the right strategy for this organization. More importantly, going through this process will allow the key stakeholders to assess their own readiness for change (both individually as well as for the organizations they represent) as well as garner support and commitment for this process. These discussions tend to be cathartic in nature because often times this is the first opportunity key stakeholders have to sit at the same table discussing options, opportunities, threats, history, and expectations together.

One caveat to note at this point is that the key stakeholders and champions should drive these discussions of problem diagnosis, creating expectations, and envisioning a desired end state. The OD Director's personal bias should not be present. Moreover, the Director should simply serve as a process consultant. While this viewpoint seems obvious to most OD professionals, in the heat of the moment even the best of OD professionals must hold themselves back from interjecting their opinions or preferences. The OD Director's domestic success with her key internal clients rested on the fact that the domestic operations strategy was rightly perceived by the organization as being driven by the CEO and not an HR or OD professional. The OD and HR Directors domestically took on the mantra that, "my job is to make my leader look good—consequently the employee populations shouldn't even know who I am." Therefore the owner of the GOS should be the Global Vice President of Operations with sponsorship from the CEO and his executive staff.

Once the expectations have been set, the current situation assessed, and the problem jointly diagnosed, the OD Director can work with the CEO, his executive team, and global stakeholders to align expectations regarding a GOS with the overall strategy of the organization. In other words, now that the decision has been made for a global strategy, and the readiness for this change assessed, how will this strategy align with the organization's global business strategy? What are the implications domestically and internationally for design and implementation around structure, people, processes and culture (both organization cul-

ture and the various regional cultures affected by this new strategy)? Ensuring alignment among stakeholders, across structures, and between cultures will allow for commitment, ownership, and execution of the proposed strategy.

Included in this strategic alignment is the need for a robust communication plan. Ideally, the Global Communications Director will be involved from the initial sponsorship discussion to ensure consistency of message, alignment with other global initiatives, and timely communication among and between employees.

Once these key elements of sponsorship, readiness for change, strategic alignment and strategic partnerships are in place, the key stakeholders can build a strategy. The reality is that these are not linear processes and that many of these steps and discussions will happen simultaneously and may be revised and revisited. Yet, starting with these key elements will lay the foundation for successful strategy building especially given the global nature of this intervention.

Therese Yaeger and Peter Sorensen Comment

Each of our panel experts focuses on both different and common aspects of the case. Each draws on their own unique experiences and history in the field. Jennifer, our first expert, with extensive international training experience, stresses the importance of understanding the business, key critical business indicators, and the language of the executives.

She also stresses the importance of understanding the complexities introduced by national cultural differences, the fit of the business model with each region, building credibility, and patience. In addition, her comments include the role of providing data, building inclusion, and working as a partner with management, and understanding the role of strategy for short and long-term performance.

Our second expert, Philip, immediately identifies the dichotomy of having significant responsibility and limited resources. He makes the point that OD extends beyond OD as a specific function and is a set of skills and actions that characterize effective leadership. His sensitivity to working with limited resources is probably a result of many years of experience as a Director of OD. His comments include influence through demonstrated competence, compensating for limited resources through building alliances, including marketing and particularly Human Resources. As a Corporate Director of OD he reflects an understanding of the potential in working with the HR function that frequently has a longer history and is embedded in the business units and/or divisions. Building alliances is one of the key functions in working with limited resources.

Our third expert, Ghazala, focuses on the need to clarify expectations, and again the need to build alliances and support. Her comments also add the critical factor of building trust.

CHAPTER 69

Socio-Economic Approach to Management

A Successful Systemic Approach to Organizational Change

John Conbere and Alla Heorhiadi

IN THE UNITED STATES organizational change and development work has a rich history, including the influence of Kurt Lewin, Rensis Likert, Douglas MacGregor, Warren Bennis, the socio-technical tradition of Tavistock, and more recently, work in large scale change, appreciative inquiry and chaos/complexity. In France, a different tradition has evolved, the Socio-Economic Approach to Management (SEAM). This movement, based in the Socio-Economic Institute of Firms and Organizations Research (ISEOR), began in 1973. SEAM shares many of the beliefs and practices of American OD, but adds some premises and practices that make this approach quite distinct.

While courses on SEAM are taught at two business schools, Central Michigan University and New Mexico State, the SEAM approach is not widely known in the United States. There have been some articles and books (Boje & Gomez, 2008; Boje & Roslie, 2003; Buono & Savall, 2007) mentioning SEAM but they mostly describe how to do SEAM and are not specifically focused on the value system that underlies this approach. The purpose of this article is to introduce the reader to the SEAM approach, pointing out its values, along with similarities to and differences from traditional OD consulting.

In a way, the SEAM approach seems simple. None of the steps is surprising for an American OD practitioner, and some of its management tools share common grounds with the OD tool-kits. A socioeconomic intervention "can be considered a 'machine for negotiating' innovative solutions, with the underlying goal of reducing the dysfunctions experienced by the enterprise" (Savall, 2007, p. 3). Innovative solutions are data driven and these data have accumulated over 35 years of experimenting into a solid database, which is part of why the SEAM intervention has been effective repeatedly. The difference comes from the deeper goals of the intervention, systemic aspect of the consulting team, and the researcher-intervener role of each consultant.

SEAM offers a methodical, tested way to assess the hidden costs in an organization. Identifying such costs is not a practice one often finds in other management consulting, although there is the OD consultants' intuitive belief that the hidden costs are very real. Without the SEAM measurement, however, the hidden costs remain hidden, and can be easily shrugged off by managers as *soft*.

SEAM is based on a set of values and a belief system about management that is different from traditional management premises. Traditional management features a fragmented analysis of organizations that is based on financial data without sufficient attention to the persons involved. SEAM, the socioeconomic approach, factors both people and finances into analysis. The result is an intervention that works with the whole organizational system. A core belief of SEAM consultants is that organizations do not exist only to make money, they exist to serve society in general and all the employees in particular. Therefore SEAM rejects the idea that employees are human capital, a term that degrades employees into non-human commodities. Once an employee is a commodity, there is no moral issue in firing the employee. Instead, SEAM's values insist that the cause of employees' poor productivity begins with the way the employees are managed. This is akin to the belief of W. E. Deming and others, who believed that poor production begins with poor management. The result of the SEAM approach is the development of trust and security among employees, which are prerequisites to full productivity.

Before describing the process, we should offer definitions of the terms that for us are almost a business card of SEAM. The first term is *actors*, the term that SEAM practitioners use to talk about all employees in organization. In sociology, the term actors is used to describe all members of an organization. The purpose of this deliberately non-hierarchical term for owners, leaders, and employees is to reinforce the idea that all actors have significant impact on the organizational effectiveness.

The second term is *hidden costs and performance*. According to Savall and Zardet (2008), "A cost is said to be hidden when it does not explicitly appear on the company information system, such as the budget, financial accounting, and cost accounting, or in the usual ledgers and logbooks" (p. xx-xxi). Hidden costs include "absenteeism, industrial injuries and occupational diseases, staff turn-

FIGURE 69.1   The Elements of SEAM

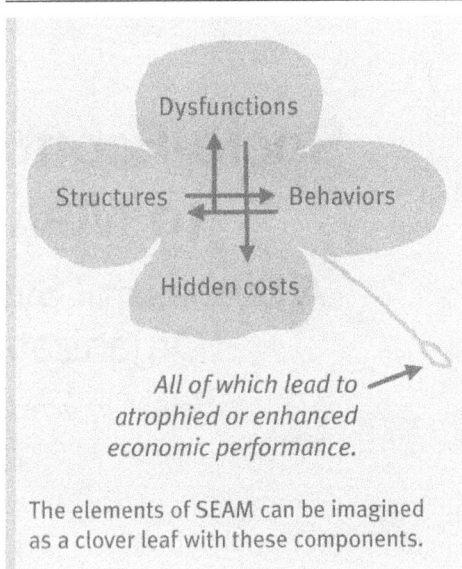

The elements of SEAM can be imagined as a clover leaf with these components.

over, non-quality, and direct productivity gaps" (Savall, Zardet, & Bonnet, 2008, p. 149). Hidden performance issues lead to poor productivity and thus to hidden costs (see Figure 69.1).

The SEAM Process

The process is referred to as Intervention-Research and is a more transformative process than traditional action research. Before the intervention, SEAM consultants meet with the organization's leader, educating the leader about SEAM. When the leader decides to use the SEAM process, one or more SEAM consultants enter an organization, gather data from participants, synthesize the data, and feed the synthesized data back to the participants. The next important step is to work with the participants to assist them to identify the necessary changes and ways to implement these changes. The last step is to assess the effectiveness of the change process.

Essentially SEAM is a deliberate process which includes a very specific approach, using data from over 35 years of research to shape an intervention that will involve actors from throughout the organization to uncover hidden costs and potential and make changes that will increase the organizational effectiveness. The SEAM design first involves top leadership to get their support and understanding, and then cascades the change work through the organization as needed. The outcome is an intervention that flows two ways: (a) top-down, when leaders begin and support the change work; and (b) bottom-up when all actors are engaged in identifying and reducing hidden costs and performance issues. This is the French blend of top down and participative OD. The intervention begins with the commitment of top management and modeling of new practices, and then moves on to extend the intervention to the rest of the organization in a highly participative manner. The assumption behind this is that the actors have the knowledge and ability to do the changes necessary to improve the climate and effectiveness of the organization.

SEAM emphasizes the importance of the buy-in of the leaders of the organization, for which purpose the CEO and other top managers are invited for a seminar to understand the basic premises of SEAM concepts. The second step is a diagnosis, in which consultants interview all top level actors (the leadership team) for 1 to 2 hours each. Themes are identified, illustrated by field-note quotes, with a thorough analysis of root causes of the hidden dysfunctions. The ISEOR database consisting of 3,450 categories of dysfunctions is there to help guide the analysis. This use of the database is the application of a generic contingency principle (see below for definition) to the specific organization.

The analyzed data are fed back to the top management team in the "mirror effect." The first part of the mirror effect is the detailed feeding back of what the consultants heard. Typically, there are at least 50 to 100 "chunks" of severe types of hidden costs that are found. The leadership team sees data indicating the extent to which the organization is not reaching its potential. The response typically is a mix of shock and recognition. Shock happens

due to the overwhelming data presented in the sheer volume of information about organizational dysfunction and hidden costs. Using Lewin's language, the mirror effect helps thoroughly "unfreeze" the top management team, shocking them into action. The outcome is agreement about the need to invest time and effort into organizational change.

Typically the leaders sensed some of the hidden costs and missed potential, but had no idea of the magnitude. The overall result of the mirror effect is threefold. The first is the leaders agree to work on projects within their scope to begin to reduce hidden costs. The second is the leaders become supportive of the vertical interventions—moving the analysis and correction of hidden costs down through the organization. The third result may be less obvious. The leaders have begun a process of change, which will include changing their beliefs about the nature and role of management. Whether or not they realize it, the leadership team has embarked on a journey in which a combination of participative and directive management will shape the organizational culture, changing the roles of all organizational actors. In the language of Chris Argyris, the SEAM intervention works to shift the organizational beliefs from Model 1 theory-in use to Model 2 theory-in-use (Argyris & Schön, 1978).

A few weeks later, the mirror effect continues with the expert opinion of the consultants. Note that this is not "expert consulting" as described by Schein (1990), in which the consultant gives the solution to the organizational problem. Rather it is the consultants using their experience and 35 years of ISEOR research to help identify the root causes of the dysfunctions. Thus, the discussion is about what seems to be invisible, such as taboos and unstated ideas. The skill of the consultants in identifying the root causes, and presenting them in a manner that actors can hear without feeling blamed, is part of the core skill set of SEAM consultants. What tends to happen in the mirror effect is that actors are not surprised by the dysfunctions themselves. What they are surprised at is the magnitude of the dysfunctions and the resulting hidden costs.

The diagnosis stages are the most labor intensive, and the diagnostic preparation often takes the majority of the consultants' intervention time. Following the diagnostic in the top management group, the participants begin to identify and work on projects that will convert hidden costs. Consultants facilitate these projects. At the same time, diagnosis begins in other groups, lower on the hierarchy of the organization. This is the *horivert process* (in French, pronounced "ori-vair"): working with the leadership team is the *horiz*ontal phase, and then cascading down the hierarchical flow chart and working with a number of other teams or groups are the *verti*cal phases.

As the intervention progresses, the horivert process shapes the next steps. The leadership group starts on one or more projects. The leadership group chooses the project(s), which is the mark of their taking ownership of the need for change in their level of operation. At the same time, detailed SEAM analysis begins within one or more vertical silos. In each silo, the process cascades down the organization in the same order: diagnosis, mirror effect involving the actors in that part of the organization, and one or more projects developed by these same actors, with the goal of reducing hidden costs. The vertical diagnosis records in detail the extent to which hidden costs and underperformance are present in that part of the organization.

The tools used in the vertical diagnosis are the result of the experience, documented through the ISEOR database, of the most prevalent failings that lead to hidden costs in organizations. For instance, there are five indicators of hidden costs: absenteeism, occupational injuries and diseases, staff turnover, non-quality, and direct productivity gaps. These data are gathered and analyzed to assess the extent to which they are present. In the SEAM intervention, for the first time, the organization receives detailed feedback based, on solid data, on the extent of the specific

losses that accrue from hidden costs and poor performance.

The change in leaders' attitude to how they lead may become important here. Another important task is getting employees to believe that the change process is done fairly and that the change work that employees undertake will be rewarded and not punished. Employees need to believe that their environment will improve if the intervention succeeds. Too often during organizational change work, employees' experience is that their participation in interventions does not lead to real long-term change, or even may be punished in some manner. The task of the leadership group and the consultant(s) is to create a realistic hope in employees that participating will really make a difference.

The diagnosis in the vertical level proceeds by gathering data and assessing the extent to which the six financial consequences of dysfunctions are present: excess salary, overtime, overconsumption, non-production, and risks. (Excess salary means additional expenses when higher salaried actors are paid for the work that is assigned to lower paid actors.) The vertical work groups then explore the extent to which the six dysfunctions are present: working conditions, work organization, communication-coordination-cooperation, time management, integrated training, and strategic implementation. The specificity of the diagnosis, which looks for six financial consequences and six dysfunctions, is no accident. These issues have been identified through more than 1,200 interventions that are recorded in the ISEOR database. As with the mirror effect, consultants feed the results of the analysis back to the employees.

The next step is to reduce the dysfunctions and thus the hidden costs. Six management tools drive the change:

1. The internal/external strategic action plan is a 3–5 year plan that allows all actors to know the direction of the change work and their roles therein.

2. The priority Action Plan is a half-yearly plan that allows the organization to identify the new valued added tasks to be implemented.

3. The competency grid is used to assess the skill level of each employee, to make sure people are trained and can gain efficiency in their new activities. This process is not used to fire people, but to find the areas in which employees can be more effective, and as result, satisfied.

4. The time management tool helps assess how well actors use their time.

5. The strategic piloting logbook is a tool for measuring "the results in terms of the value created through management changes" (Savall, Zardet, & Bonnet, 2008, p. 6).

6. The periodically negotiable activity contract is used "to negotiate additional effort required to implement the new activities" (Savall, Zardet, & Bonnet, 2008, p. 109).

Henri Savall sees the SEAM interventions as based in the three major principles: generic contingency, cognitive interactivity, and contradictory inter-subjectivity. *Generic contingency* is the principle that allows for the uniqueness of each organization, and "postulates the existence of invariants that constitute generic invariants" (Savall, 2010, p. 2). In other words, there are commonalities among organizations that allow researchers to predict what is likely to be present in each organization.

Cognitive interactivity pertains to knowledge creation and can be enhanced through interaction between actors and the SEAM consultants. Through successive feedback loops, the sharing of knowledge leads to added value for the organization. The principle of *contradictory inter-subjectivity* refers to the fact that actors perceive truth differently, and they all are right, according to their beliefs and perceptions. Contradictory inter-subjectivity draws on the ontological belief that in human societies, truth is socially constructed, and therefore is not an objective and unchanging fact. This belief allows consultants to accept different views without having to prove who is right or wrong.

In essence, the SEAM approach is aimed to help actors realize that there is potential to convert hidden costs into something productive that will benefit the actors and the organization, and to help the actors in each of the parts of the organization to design and implement projects to convert hidden costs into added value. That may sound like what many OD consultants claim to do, but there are some differences worth noting.

What Is Different About SEAM?

In one sense, the SEAM intervention is classic OD. The intervention is based on the assumptions that different people may see truth differently, and that all participants need to be involved in order for the change work to be successful. In another sense, the research of 35 years has made clear that there are typical patterns that cross all organizations. For instance, in looking for dysfunctions in an organization, the SEAM process identified five types of indicators of dysfunction: absenteeism, occupational injuries and diseases, staff turnover, non-quality, and direct productivity gaps. For each of these, qualitative and quantitative evaluations are used to identify the estimated hidden costs. Here is where SEAM is very different from traditional management approach, because the cost of the five dysfunctions is not included in the financial balance sheets of the organization, or in the loss/ profit accounting of the budget. Hidden costs and hidden performance issues should be part of every financial report, but they are not. As a result, organizations make decisions based on less-thancomplete data and without leaders taking into account critical factors that shape the financial bottom line.

Assessing hidden costs and performances allows an intervener to demonstrate return on investment. Without assessing hidden costs and performances, an intervener cannot effectively address ROI. Hidden costs and loss in value by underperformance are high. The amount tends to differ by type of activity, so the hidden costs range from town councils, with hidden costs of €8,000 per capita per year (35% of payroll), to electronics manufacturers with hidden costs of €46,000 per capita per year (220% of payroll) (Savall, 2003).

Hidden cost and poor performance come from organizational dysfunctions, which are the result of a failure to align properly structures and actors' behaviors. These dysfunctions are the result of management's failure to listen carefully to customers and employees, and so that the problems that are occurring in the field are not addressed. In the US and British management approach to change, more emphasis is put on changing behavior, and in traditional French approach, more emphasis is put on changing structures. SEAM emphasizes the need to include both behavior and structure in its intervention.

When traditional management reaches a financial crisis (which is often the result of management's actions), the response often is to cut costs by *down-sizing* employees to achieve a short-term gain. In the long term, employees are hurt, and the capacity of the organization is hurt, a result that is neither ethical nor fiscally wise. SEAM consultants resist the idea of laying off employees, because firing people is poor business practice and poor ethical practice. Not only is morale trashed, but when the organizational economy recovers, the organization needs the people who were fired in order to be fully productive. Rehiring and training slows any returns to productivity. Further, it is ethically wrong to fire employees when management has caused the problem. Ironically, most of the current management training focuses mostly on profit and bottom line, and not on people, which is contradictory to the universal ethical command to treat all employees with love and dignity. By focusing on people, management can develop new income through reducing hidden costs and performance.

SEAM's core belief is that there is significant untapped potential in each organization,

and a better approach than downsizing is to uncover this potential. The SEAM approach is ethical, in that it treats employees as valuable persons rather than as human capital. The SEAM approach is also economically effective, in that it taps into unused potential so that employees are retained and profits increase. To demonstrate the economic effectiveness, a mid-sized company may recoup its investment of €300,000 in the SEAM intervention within a year, and sometimes within three months. (€300,000 is an average fee for a SEAM intervention in a mid-sized organization in France.)

The other difference is that SEAM works as a system that engages in changing organizations systemically. Often when an external consultant intervenes in an organization, it is one or a small group of consultants working to change the organizational system. There is a somewhat lonely sense of a small body working to bring about systems change. SEAM itself is a system that engages other organizational systems. The database is shared memory that carries the results of 1,200 interventions; it is a systems memory, a knowledge base that is used to shape the slowly evolving SEAM interventions. Consultants also share their experience, during and after interventions. The fortunate ones live near Lyon, and meet monthly to discuss their work. Others gather annually to share their experiences. Each intervention has the collective input of the larger team of consultants and the trends indicated by the database. Often consultants seem to be individuals or small groups who try to change a larger organizational system. With SEAM, the SEAM system of the consultant team and the database works to change the organizational system.

Finally, SEAM consultants are both interveners and researchers. This intervener-researcher function is similar to the scholar practitioner role of American OD consultants, discussed so often at conferences. The task of SEAM consultants is two-fold: to help the organization, and to collect data for the SEAM database. The database is used to assess the short- and long-term impact of SEAM interventions, and to discover the trends of the problems in industries. The intervention aims at leading the actors in the organization to examine the hidden costs and collectively find new ways of operating that will improve individual and collective performance so that hidden costs are reduced.

Conclusion

SEAM offers an approach to OD that is consistent with the core values of OD, as described in the OD Network Principles of Practice (http://www.odnetwork.org/ aboutod/principles.php), particularly the respect for and valuing of the person that is too often missing from organizational change efforts. ISEOR's use of intervener-researchers has allowed them to establish a database of over 1,200 interventions as a base for the evolution of SEAM management tools and practices. The collection of economic data, in which the hidden costs of organizational dysfunctions are documented and used as a basis for decision-making about change is a unique and powerful aspect of the SEAM approach. This approach should capture the imagination of any consultant who is interested in demonstrating the ROI of organizational change and having a long-lasting impact for their consulting effort.

References

Argyris, C., & Schön, D. (1978). *Organizational learning: A theory of action perspective.* Reading, MA: Addison Wesley.

Boje, D., & Gomez, C. (2008). A study of socio-economic interventions of trans-organization storytelling among New Mexico arts organizations. *RSDG-Management Sciences-Ciencias de Gestión, 65,* 199–220.

Boje, D., & Roslie, G. A. (2003). Comparison of socio-economic and other transorganizational development methods. *Journal of Organizational Change Management, 16*(1), 10–20.

Buono A., & Savall H. (Eds.) (2007). *Socio-Economic interventions in organizations.* Charlotte, NC: Information Age Publishing.

Savall, H. (2003). An updated presentation of the socio-economic management model. *Journal of Organizational Change Management, 16*(1), 33–48.

Savall, H. (2007). ISEOR's socio-economic method. In A. Buono, & H. Savall (Eds.), *Socio-economic interventions in organizations* (pp. 1–31). Charlotte, NC: Information Age Publishing.

Savall, H. (2010). *Work and people: An economic evaluation of job-enrichment.* Charlotte, NC: Information Age Publishing. (First published in 1974.)

Savall, H., & Zardet, V. (2008). Mastering hidden costs and socio-economic performance. Charlotte, NC: Information Age Publishing. (First published in 1987.)

Savall, H., Zardet, V., & Bonnet, M. (2008). Releasing the untapped potential of enterprises through socio-economic management. Geneva: International Labour Office, and Ecully, France: ISEOR. (First published in 1974.)

Schein, E. H. (1990). A general philosophy of helping: Process consultation. *Sloan Management Review, 31*(3), 57–64.

CHAPTER 70

Business as Agent of World Benefit

A Worldwide Action Research Project Using Appreciative Inquiry

David L. Cooperrider, Nadya Zhexembayeva,

Amanda Trosten-Bloom, and Diana Whitney

The Call

While major headlines decry fraudulent CEO's, environmental damage, and corporate scandals, a remarkable revolution is emerging all over the world in the relationship between business and society. Business—considered by some to be the nemesis of human and ecological wealth and well-being—has become one of the most capacity-filled institutions on the planet. Obviously such capacity is being used for both good and ill. But how do we elevate and expand the positive organization development opportunities of the former, and do so in ways that are rigorous, relevant, and value creating for business and society leadership? What does it look like, for example, when business is a force for peace and security in high conflict zones? Where are the models—especially the how to's—of business as a force for the eradication of extreme poverty? And where and how are businesses turning some of our largest global issues into business opportunities for eco-innovation and industry leading performance? While the times are unstable and difficult, businesses around the globe are turning to the call to express their distinctive

strengths and systemically take up the universal responsibility to build a better world that is sustainable, inclusive, and just. And this trend is not temporary or isolated. It is our shared distinctive moment in history, where the task is increasingly clear: to achieve the massive transition from the unsustainable present to a sustainable economy and ecology of organizations, societies, and cultures.

Business as Agent of World Benefit (BAWB) is a worldwide action-research project that uses Appreciative Inquiry (AI) to discover organizational innovations at the intersection of business and society that create mutual value. The project's goal is to identify business innovations that, if further developed and applied, could vitally transform creative capitalism itself so that businesses can excel, people can thrive, and nature can flourish.

Conceived in 2001, BAWB does not impose a superficial sense of hope on a troubled time. Instead, it singles out and creates dialogue related to the one arena that we believe has potential like no other: the relationship between business and society. Catalyzed by Case Western Reserve University's Weatherhead School of Management and a growing network of world-class partners, BAWB offers up new ways for people to share stories of exceptional business and social practices, connect and conference with one another, experience each other's talents, and articulate across cultures a 21st century vision of business as an agent of world benefit.

On the tenth anniversary of the project, we now invite you to trace the project's original vision, challenges, and some areas of learning and impact. We transmit stories that have surfaced—of companies like Green Mountain Coffee Roasters, Reebok, and Nutrimental Foods—that herald a future in which organization development and world development are seamlessly one.

From our beginnings, we in the field of organization development have known that organizations and the larger world are integrally connected. We have done our work within human systems in part to contribute to global social good and a better life on the planet. Now, we put forth an even bolder hypothesis. The future of OD involves consideration of much wider societal horizons and new, exciting languages of change: sustainable enterprise, natural capitalism, eco-industrial clusters, social entrepreneurship, embedded sustainability, conscious evolution, and the discovery and design of positive institutions.

Why Appreciative Inquiry?

Appreciative Inquiry (AI) is a strength-based process of inquiry that searches for everything that "gives life" to organizations, communities, and larger human systems when they are most alive, effective, and healthy in their interconnected ecology of relationships. Created at Case Western Reserve University in the 1980s by David Cooperrider and Suresh Srivastva with colleagues, AI has emerged as both a practical approach for leading change and a key research approach in the positive organizational scholarship movement (Cooperrider & Srivastva, 1987; Cameron & Spreitzer, 2011). AI is founded on the assumption that inquiry-and-change is a simultaneous moment: inqui-

ry into and conversation about strengths, successes, moments of flourishing, values, hopes and dreams triggers life-giving change; and human systems move in the direction of what we most persistently, actively, and authentically ask questions about (Cooperrider & Whitney, 1999).

So, why is Appreciative Inquiry the "right" approach for a project of this nature and scope? AI is uniquely suited to the BAWB project for three reasons. First, it is based on a non-deficit model of change called the establishment-and-eclipse theory of positive change (Cooperrider & Godwin, 2012). Unlike so many deficit-based approaches, which leave us devoid of images to describe what we want, AI immediately reveals grounded stories and data points of possibility that are anchored in the direct experience of inquiry participants. These vivid utopias—accounts of the world that help us see our valued future in the texture of the ideal actual—serve to build a storehouse of relational resources such as trust and new language of possibility. They also generate positive emotions such as hope, inspiration, and joy. And ultimately, they plant seeds for the kind of design thinking that builds collaborative capacity for the joint creation of the future.

Second, more than almost any other approach to change, AI can work at a scale of wholeness moving from micro strengths to macro. Through a process known as mass-mobilized inquiry (Whitney & Trosten-Bloom, 2003, pp. 36-38), it can engage hundred, thousands, or even millions of people in system-changing conversations—over a period of weeks, months, or even years. Similarly, through a process known as the Appreciative Inquiry Summit, it can involve hundreds or thousands of people in multiple-day meetings, during which participants discover the best of what is, dream what might be, then design and deliver the preferred future (Ludema, Whitney, Mohr, & Griffin, 2003). Together, these two whole-system technologies address the question of overwhelming scale that is involved in the BAWB project. By combining mass-mobilized inquiry with in-person and virtual AI Summits, we can potentially engage millions of people in the process of re-conceiving and advancing the role of business as a positive institution that not only connects our highest human strengths, but also serves to refract and magnify our highest human strengths outward into our world.

The Initiative

BAWB is a vehicle for people and organizations across societies and cultures to collaborate in a new kind of world dialogue. Organized as a series of one-on-one interviews, discussion groups, classroom conversations, virtual summits, publications, and international conferences, it is dedicated to discovering, appreciating, and mobilizing the best in business with a task of creating prosperous, inspired, and sustainable societies that work for all. Is it possible, for example, that radical productivity increases can happen at the same time that businesses not only conserve—but proactively help enrich—the environment? Can we discover and develop ways of running businesses and making investments that are socially and environmentally responsive and commercially successful? Might we determine what inspires and motivates people to change, and what supports change at three levels—from that of key global systems, to the organization, and to the level of individual consciousness?

BAWB grew out of conversations at Case Western's Weatherhead School of Management, immediately following the collapse of the World Trade towers on September 11, 2001. As a result, an innovative experiment in Appreciative Inquiry as the second-generation action research approach was launched. The initiative invited the world to participate in creation of a new, cross-cultural vision of business as an agent of world benefit. People everywhere could participate by downloading the appreciative interview guide, contextualizing it, and then doing interviews with business innovators in their home region. Within months, hundreds of stories poured in from London to

Tokyo, and from Brazil to Rwanda's most remote villages.

The original concept paper says BAWB's aspiration is: "to tap into the positive potential of Appreciative Inquiry as a way of mobilizing millions of face-to-face interviews with business leaders, visionaries, students, and scholars, and to link these to the original potential of the internet as a medium that inspires creativity, collaboration, and worldwide education" (Cooperrider, 2003).

To realize this aspiration and experiment with a worldwide call to inquiry, a five-month pilot took place in early 2002. Volunteers from around the globe again downloaded interview guides, conducted interviews with "positive change leaders," and submitted interview summary reports to a website. Recognizing that leadership is a multifaceted phenomenon, five categories of potential interviewees were identified:

Senior Executives: Leaders at the top levels in business organizations (e.g., Presidents, CEOs, COOs, and Chairpersons) who wish to share their highest hopes for the future of the world and newest examples and practices of "business as an agent of world benefit."

Change Agents: Leaders of every level in business organizations, who operate from a new vision and practice of how real change occurs in the world and are committed to harnessing the very best elements of business in service of the whole.

Idea Leaders: Organizational scholars, futurists, and visionary critics of business (from the grassroots) whose transformational ideas have the potential to disrupt assumptions of the status quo, elevate our sense of what's possible, and raise new options for better living.

Social Entrepreneurs: Dedicated innovators, networkers, and/or collaborating business partners from the not-for-profit or community sector, who believe the same inventiveness used historically to create great wealth can be applied to world issues and change agendas.

Wisdom Companions: Children, wise elders, respected spiritual teachers and others who care about a positive future for our planet, and who can elevate the dialogue and bring practices for accessing our best human strengths, meaningful commitments, and purposes.

During the pilot period, more than 200 interviews were conducted and reported. Within a couple of years over 2000 interview stories were submitted and culled for their meaning by Ron Fry and doctoral student colleagues from the Department of Organizational Behavior at Case Western Reserve University. There were stories of: factories being designed to give back more clean energy to the world than they use; micro-enterprise and BOP strategy models eradicating poverty through profitability; corporations realizing radical increases in resource productivity through lessons from natural capitalism; smart companies using leadership in corporate citizenship to open new markets, create regenerative value, and build competitive advantage. Likewise there were models of striking design: green homes and buildings; healthier food; hundred-dollar laptops; plug-in hybrids; sustainable packaging; living systems (e.g., mushrooms) capable of cleaning toxic sludge; algae ponds designed to produce biodiesel; the breakthrough combination of fuel-cell technology with bio-digesters focused on bringing electricity to billions; historic introductions with the concept of "millennium development villages" capable of putting an end to extreme poverty; and, of course, huge shifts in venture capital investments into clean technology, including solar, wind, smart grids, and plug-in automobiles.

The pilot was enthusiastically received at the Spirit in Business conference in New York, NY (April 2002), and was awarded a Provost Opportunity Grant from Case Western Reserve University to seed a full-scale project, led now by the newly christened Fowler Center for Sustainable Value at the Weatherhead School of Management. In the span of few short years the tiny initiative grew to become one of the most productive interdisciplinary projects in the history of the Weatherhead School and a truly global center of excellence. In scholarly terms, one can celebrate the initiative's book publications, dissertations, and articles, including *Positive Design and Appreciative Construction: From Sustainable Development to Sustainable Value* (Thachenkery, Cooperrider, & Avital, 2010), *Embedded Sustainability: The Next Big Competitive Advantage* (Laszlo & Zhexembayeva, 2011), *Sustainable Value: How the World's Leading Companies are Doing Well by Doing Good* (Laszlo, 2008), and *Handbook of Transformative Cooperation* (Piderit, Fry, & Cooperrider, 2007). In terms of educational impact, BAWB created the MBA Institute for Sustainable Value (singled out by Forbes Magazine as one of the ten most innovative courses in the MBA world), along with the new Masters in Positive Organization Development (MPOD), and a series of executive education programs helping companies ask the important questions: "How can we use the lens of sustainable value creation to spark innovation in new products and operations, open new markets, ignite customer passion and loyalty, energize an entire workforce, accelerate learning, build greener supply chains, reduce risks?" Dozens of companies—including Alcoa, Parker Hannifin, Sherwin Williams, Forest City Enterprises, Dealer Tire, Go Jo, the Federal Reserve, Cleveland Clinic, Eaton Corporation, and Fairmount Minerals—served as early thought-partners and collaborators. And in 2004, UN Secretary General Kofi Annan called upon the BAWB initiative to design and lead a global Appreciative Inquiry summit with 1,000 CEOs from Hewlett-Packard to Coca-Cola and from Novartis to Tata Industries "to unite the strengths of markets with the social and global issues of our day." Today, the UN Global Compact is made up of more than 8,000 corporations, and the Weatherhead School of Management—because of BAWB and its distinctive strength in Appreciative Inquiry and applied sustainability—has been named the Secretariat of the North American Network of the UN Global Compact.

The Initial Findings

The Business as Agent of World Benefit dialogue is a dynamic and emergent project in continuous motion. A powerful action research initiative, it integrates theory and practice, providing ongoing opportunities for social change that leads to discovery, learning, and invention.

The first year of the project yielded rich, inspiring insight and experience. As visionary thinkers like Peter Drucker, and top executives of Abbott Laboratories, Wal-Mart, and Shorebank opened their doors to this conversation, we have learned that people are hungry to talk about and consider this crucial topic. When volunteers in Argentina, Sweden, Nepal, and Kazakhstan have taken interview questions and recrafted protocols to make them relevant for their socio-political situations (with minimum training in Appreciative Inquiry), we have discovered that cross-cultural conversation is possible.

Powerful, urgent, and pertinent examples of "golden innovations" and future visions of business acting as an agent of world benefit have already emerged in the first wave of interviews. At the same time, the cross-cultural nature of the initiative has already begun to create a new vocabulary of what's possible. (For example, during an interview with an executive from Sweden, we learned that the Swedish word for business is "naringsliv"—translating literally into "the nourishment of life.") All of these factors, combined, reinforce our belief in the crucial importance of this project.

The stories, insights, ideas, and themes surfaced during the pilot phase—too numerous and complex to report—are summarized in the preliminary report prepared for the April 2002 Spirit in Business Conference. Three of the themes or clusters that were surfaced during that analysis are particularly relevant to the field of Organizational Development.

Doing Good Builds Good Businesses

One particularly provocative and puzzling theme continuously emerged throughout the interviews: doing good for the world at large builds good business. It suggests that organization development work is both fostered and accelerated when organizations' stakeholders share a clear, compelling picture of their larger role in society. Rather than focusing people's attention within, we must help organizations to turn their gaze to the world around them. In so doing, changes never before contemplated become real and possible. Green Mountain Coffee Roasters (GMCR) is a colorful example of this proposition.

GMCR is a fast growing company, internationally renowned for its sustainable business practices. Featured in many top media outlets—including Forbes Magazine, Business Ethics Magazine, and PBS—the company's story powerfully testifies to the relationship between overall financial success and doing good in the world. Bob Stiller, CEO and Forbes 2000 Entrepreneur of the Year, says:

> At Green Mountain Coffee Roasters, our improvement programs, seeking efficiencies in production and administration, had little energy and minimal success until we started looking beyond ourselves. When we turned our attention outward, seeking to use our capacities to work on global environmental projects and Fair Trade initiatives with the coffee growers in many poor regions of the world, our people made breakthrough changes internally.
>
> Let me be absolutely and unapologetically clear on one point: profitability is our goal. But our profitability soared and our efficiencies improved when we turned our attention to being of benefit to society and building a sustainable ecology "out there." In its cover story featuring Green Mountain, Forbes Magazine talked about this apparent paradox. It seems like a paradox—but it is not, because "out there" is really "in here." When people feel good about themselves via doing good, it reverberates.
>
> I am an entrepreneur. And this kind of entrepreneurship—being of benefit

to each other and building a better world while making extraordinary profits—is something that is not describable in traditional business school terms. If I had not experienced its power personally, I might never have believed it. It is inspiring, powerful, and fun. It feels like a revolution. It is a thrill.

Every Global and Social Issue Is a Business Opportunity

Another consistent proposition that emerged from the initial BAWB conversations is that every social and global challenge of our day can be turned into a business opportunity. This challenging theme appeared most prominently in the interview with Peter Drucker, a thinker often referred to as "the father of management thought." He was convinced that any and every social, political, and environmental issue of our time can be turned into a successful business opportunity, with the right combination of social entrepreneurship, knowledge, and pragmatism. This conviction was echoed in the stories of both Sager Family Travel Foundation and Roadshow and Reebok Corporation.

Sager Family Travel Foundation and Roadshow is a brainchild of Bobby Sager, a successful American businessman. The Foundation's work is built upon the "eyeball to eyeball" philosophy, which calls the Sagers to play active, hand-on parts in each initiative. Sager projects range from youth leadership, skill development, and education to micro-enterprise and peace and reconciliation programs. They are focused on creating long-term, deep impact and positive change in some of the world's most troubled communities.

One of the most innovative initiatives of Sager Foundation, organized in the spirit of social entrepreneurship, is a reconciliation effort in Rwanda; a country that suffers intense poverty, overshadowed by the residue of the recent violent conflicts between the Hutu and Tutsi. Here's how Bobby Sager describes the project:

We decided to set up cooperative groups of women. In so doing, the wives of the people who were murdered in the genocide went into business with and partnership with the wives of these 150,000 people that are in prison, accused of participating in the genocide.

The basic idea is this. If you want really powerful results, use business as a device for substantive reconciliation, not simply as a way to alleviate poverty. Although they're not by any means mutually exclusive, you get both at the same time by bringing together groups that are 50% Hutu and 50% Tutsi. Let these women pursue their dreams together, and bring their extended families into the process. Now that's the way to get to substantive reconciliation.

Another great case of a merger between social and business innovations comes from Reebok Corporation. Here is a story of Reebok's three-phase plan to eliminate the use of child labor in the manufacture of soccer balls, as related by Marilyn Tam of the US Foundation:

The shapes stitched together to make soccer balls are so small, that children's hands had been traditionally well suited for the task. However, the children were working 14–16 hours per day.

Reebok realized that many companies were buying from these suppliers, so one company's refusal to buy because of working conditions would have hardly any effect. They also saw that if the children were taken off of the sewing lines to go to school, there were no schools for them to attend; and children would simply move on to the next labor opportunity—making and carrying bricks.

So, we designed a three-year, multi-layer program. First we trained the parents to do the work. Second, we got parents to agree to let the kids go to school—if there was a school. And third, we created a school and trained teachers.

It took three years for Reebok to get this whole project done. But now, we have soccer balls for the United States, made by adults making a regular livelihood, with kids going to school.

"Wealth" is Well-Being

A third and proposition extracted from our initial pool of appreciative action research is that "wealth" is more than just financial gain. True to the word's Middle English roots, wealth is "wellbeing" for the whole: people, profits, and planet. In keeping with this proposition, wealth is best calculated using "triple bottom line" measures of profit, people, and planet. The story of Pavilion Technologies' Austin People's Community Clinic vividly illustrates said wealth.

People's Clinic is a healthcare facility for the working poor and uninsured. One of Pavilion's major business enterprises, it was projecting repeating shortfalls over a period of months. Rather than cutting Clinic services to address the shortfall, Pavilion sponsored an annual community event to raise money. In the face of a declining economy, the economic impact of 9-11, and many who challenged the idea, the People4People event exceeded increasing goals for two consecutive years, with similar projections for the third. Multiple large donors were significantly influenced by the spirit of community camaraderie and philanthropy, and a single donor pledged $1MM to directly support the ongoing and expanding efforts of the project.

By redefining wealth as well-being, we raise questions about the relationship of meaning, purpose, and values to a business' overall success. We also bring more people—more voices —into conversations about how this wealth can and should be generated. By fostering more inclusive conversations, we deepen and enrich people's experience of their work, and enhance businesses' overall capacity for sustained success. This, in turn, creates more wealth that extends across business, to society at large.

Invitation and Potentials for the Field of OD

From its inception, the field of Organization Development has committed itself to lead or-

ganizations in directions that are well suited both to the people who populate them, and to the world as a whole. For years now, our OD methodologies have increasingly reflected that commitment, engaging larger and larger stakeholder groups in conversations of greater and greater collective significance.

The Business as Agent of World Benefit inquiry breaks new ground, however, by demonstrating that whole-system inquiry and action research can be done at a global scale. Even in its pilot period, it has confirmed that thousands—even millions—of people can be engaged in re-envisioning and recreating business as we know it and that global development and organization development are integrally interconnected. In short, it tells us that, as OD practitioners, we can and should be fully explicit about the outward implications of the work we do. We should be more conscious about building a world that is sustainable. And we should remember that we are not just working to create better organizations: we're working to create organizations that in turn create a better world.

In his BAWB interviews, Peter Drucker reinforced this position when he said:

> What you are talking about—even the words Business as an Agent of World Benefit—will be difficult for many to understand, because too often we talk as if there is business on the one hand and good work on the other ... and never the twain shall meet. But this is not empirically, or even theoretically true, in the real world. Why? Because we are all connected. No organ can survive the body that it serves; and the business enterprise is an organ of society and community. There is no such thing as a healthy business without a healthy society, and no such thing as a healthy society without healthy business. Defining what this means for the new century, and developing competence and know-how in this area, is one of the most important tasks of our time.
>
> So may it be.

References

Cameron, K., & Spreitzer, G. (Eds.). (2011). *Oxford handbook of positive organizational scholarship*. New York, NY: Oxford University Press.

Cooperrider, D., & Godwin, L. (2011). Positive organization development: Innovation inspired change in a new economy and ecology of strengths. In K. Cameron & G. Spreitzer (Eds.). *Oxford Handbook of positive organizational scholarship*. New York, NY: Oxford University Press.

Cooperrider, D. L. (2003). *Current commentary on AI and positive change: Peter Drucker's advice for us on the new AI project*. Published on the AI Commons: http://appreciativeinquiry.cwru.edu/intro/comment.cfm.

Cooperrider, D. L., & Dutton, J. (Eds.) (1999). *Organization dimensions of global change: No limits to cooperation*. Newbury Park, CA: Sage Publications.

Cooperrider, D. L., & Srivastva, S. (1987). Appreciative Inquiry in organizational life. In W. Pasmore & R. Woodman (Eds.), *Research in organization change and development* (Vol. 1, pp. 129–169). Greenwich, CT: JAI Press, as reproduced on the Appreciative Inquiry Commons: http://ai.cwru.edu.

Cooperrider, D. L., & Whitney, D. (2005). *Appreciative Inquiry: A positive revolution in change*. San Francisco, CA: Berrett-Koehler.

Kanter, R. M. (2002, June). How to fire up your employees without cash and prizes. *Business* 2.0, 3(6), 134–135.

Ludema., J., Whitney, D., Mohr, B., & Griffin, T. (2003). *The Appreciative Inquiry summit*. San Francisco, CA: Berrett-Koehler.

Whitney, D., & Trosten-Bloom, A. (2003 and 2010). *The power of Appreciative Inquiry: A practical guide to positive change* (1st and 2nd editions). San Francisco, CA: Berrett-Koehler.

BAWB interview guides, featured profiles and articles, and a searchable data base of stories and innovations are available on the web at: www.worldinquiry.org.

CHAPTER 71

Leadership Connectivity

Building Global Partnerships

Maya Hu-Chan

Leaders of the Future and Globalization

In *Global Leadership: The Next Generation,* we interviewed 200 high-potential leaders from 120 companies around the world. Based on this information we determined 15 dimensions of leadership for the effective global leader of the future and developed a list of 100 success factors, ranked by importance, for leaders past, present and future. Interestingly, for leaders of the future, globalization ranked number 2 in importance on the list; for current leaders, it ranked 71st, and for leaders of the past, 77th.

For OD practitioners, who build for the future as they serve as catalysts for change in organizational systems, this shift is significant, and not only in Fortune 500 companies. Emerging leaders have put globalization center stage. In my work as an international management consultant, executive coach, speaker and leadership development educator, I have found that facing the challenges of globalization requires focused intervention in the areas of global leadership, executive coaching and cross-cultural business skills.

In this article, I will first provide some context on how globalization has changed the rules of the game as far as operating within an organizational context. Then I will offer a two-fold analysis of factors critical for the success-ful global practitioner: (1) the leader as coach, and (2) the power of diverse partnerships.

A global organization standardizes and integrates its operations worldwide, requiring leaders to align themselves with supply chains which may appear seamless in a strategic plan but which in reality involve real people with diverse cultural backgrounds and communication styles. The new organizational prototype demands new individual skills to meet this complexity; it presents planning and communication challenges requiring new tools in response.

A foundational element for any global leader is the need to look at the big picture while at the same time consult with key stakeholders at every level, working to align the overarching goals with local objectives. One of my recent clients, a Thai Vice President with a high technology multinational, faced exactly this dynamic. As his coach, and since coaching is a very individualized development tool, I helped him to approach this duality with cultural sensitivity and awareness, using the appropriate communication approach to get the message across. My approach modeled how he himself needs to deal with his supervisees.

In working with this VP, I applied the two critical skills that any global coach must use: listening and probing. A coach needs to listen actively and effectively to fully understand the situation and the coachee's needs, asking the right questions to guide the coachee to solve problems. The coach must keep practicing these skills and continue to encourage, support and hold people accountable.

With consistent coaching, the Thai executive could set up his own sequence of communication with staff globally. Since his outreach spanned not only hierarchy but continents, his strategy would have to meet the complexity of the landscape. He began his first management initiative by interviewing his supervisor, and then his boss's supervisor, clarifying short and long-term goals, and asking "what's our mission?" and "what's our strategy?" From there he consulted with his team, planned a two-day retreat, and followed up with regular virtual staff meetings spanning Asia, the United States and Latin America. The result has been overwhelmingly positive, clarifying the group's direction, being specific about what is accomplished, and ultimately defining the overall impact of actions.

Leader as Coach

In working with leaders, teams and large groups, then, the OD practitioner must demonstrate this awareness of the dual forces of global and local, and the many organizational levels in between. To develop coaching skills, the global leader must focus on helping others develop solutions, rather than giving them the answers or telling them what to do. She must get feedback from the people she is coaching to see how they are doing, and, working with her own coach, develop specific coaching strategies for the individual employees she is coaching. Ongoing practice may be strengthened through supplemental training. The global leader builds organically.

Creating a Developmental Virtual Workspace

To lay the groundwork for coaching and communication at all levels, the practitioner creates an environment inclusive enough to span borders, cultures and personalities. The most important element for a leader is being able to surround himself with diverse people and create a setting in which others can excel on their own terms. In terms of being a leader, this means having the discernment to create a developmental virtual workspace, taking into account both short and long-term staff working in multiple modalities and time zones.

To be effective coaching people across cultures in this setting, leaders must understand both the effect of cultural differences on communication and recognize that at the person-to-person level, people are pretty much the same. Our ability to connect is based on fundamental respect for differences, and a sort of curiosity about others rather than standard multi-cultural concepts (for example, that Asians are all reserved or that North Americans are generally extroverts). This seeming contradiction is fundamental: the world is complex, people are complex, but ultimately connecting involves simple authenticity and genuine interest in others. Yoshio Ishizaka, former president of Toyota US and now a senior advisor to the board of Toyota Motor Corporation, lays forth eight rules which emphasize leadership elements which include "an open mind . . . a student for life . . . respect others . . . building the entire team . . . knows how to have fun." He also stresses the importance of building a strong, healthy family and spending time with one's spouse and children.

Supporting Basic Human Communication

My own work draws from Marshall Goldsmith, a leading authority on executive coaching, who brings a refreshing directness and honesty as part of his global brand. He suggests that there are simple tools that tap basic universal processes. For example, he offers a Six-Question Process for executives to coach their direct reports: Where are we going? Where are you going? What is going well? What are key suggestions for improvement? How can I help? What suggestions do you have for me?

As the leader moves into the arena of coaching, it is important to understand the difference between coaching and mentoring. Coaching involves empowering others to bring about change in their own lives. Mentoring includes a modeling and sharing of knowledge as mentor/protégé.

Empowering Employees Through Development

With the appropriate listening skills, respect for the individual and curiosity regarding the situation in place for the employee ("coachee"), growth can begin. A primary role is to empower employees through development. Development comes in many sizes and shapes. Our research uncovered 15 dimensions of leadership, including, Developing People, Achieving Personal Mastery, Appreciating Diversity and Building a Shared Vision.

In the organization of the 21st century, leadership is about sharing and imparting knowledge. In my coaching work we encourage leaders to use the G.R.O.W. model to coach their employees.

Goal—What do you want to achieve? Identify specific goals.

Realities—What are the coachee's and key stakeholders' perceptions of what is going on?

Options—What can you do to close the gaps between your goal and realities? Explore possibilities.

Will—How much does the leader want to change?

The classic predicament for new "global" leaders is to find themselves quickly overwhelmed by trying to take personal responsibility for others through a series of one-to-one interventions. That series of meetings becomes quickly unsustainable. The more savvy strategic approach is to find creative ways to either coach groups of people or to coach individuals who will in turn relay the coaching message to their respective teams within the organizational system.

Recently I coached a senior Chinese executive at a Global Fortune 100 company. She was particularly innovative in her method and successful with her coaching strategy. As a global leader, she managed a large group that spanned multiple organizational levels. "I've been busy managing a global business unit with a large team of young and inexperienced employees. It's difficult for me to spend time one-on-one with all of my direct reports to provide coaching and mentoring," she said. "After brainstorming with my coach, I came up with an idea that really worked."

Her team of nine direct reports had varying learning styles and levels of experience. She needed to develop her people and grow the capacity of her team quickly and strategically in order to meet the challenging demands of the business. Fortunately, the group was energetic and willing to learn. The leader began by dividing her direct reports into learning groups. She appointed the most senior direct report to act as a coach (as well as herself) to work with the learning groups, then had the groups focus on learning one critical business topic every two weeks through research and discussion. She and the other "coach" attended the learning group meetings regularly, participated in the discussion, and offered insights. To add to the stretch assignment, the learning group meetings were conducted in English to help participants improve their language skills. For native Chinese speakers, this was not easy!

The experiment proved successful, initiating a period of ongoing learning and creating stronger bonding within the team. The leader fostered a positive learning environment for her employees to acquire new knowledge about the industry, their customers, and market trends on their own. They learned faster from teaching each other, and became more comfortable and confident in speaking English. The result was a win-win situation: everyone was coached, and it didn't take up a lot of her time!

Consultant World: Local, Virtual, Constantly Changing

As evidenced earlier in the case of the Thai high-tech executive, the leader of the future maximizes interaction at every level. He must face one of the most significant shifts in the international workforce in recent years: the move from "free agent nation" to "free agent world." Even the longer-term direct reports are, in a sense, consultants in their own right, in that they must quickly adapt to change and define work in terms of projects. We now live in a project-based world. Projects/consultancies may be defined in any area of labor and for any type of engagement. A global leader must come to terms with this reality and set the parameters for clear definition of objectives and norms for communication with consultants under his supervision; for example, she must:

- Always reach a clear understanding of the project from the beginning.
- Experiment with optimal time zone connections.
- State that she would like progress reports at agreed-upon intervals.
- Come to know the work and learning styles of those who work with her.
- Treat her consultants with respect and dignity
- Be sensitive to and respectful of others' culture values

An increasingly common way of working is in virtual teams. As a coach I help leaders to build the skills necessary to make virtual meetings work, using for example, methods like these from the *Interglobe Quarterly Newsletter:*

- Have a face-to-face kick-off meeting.
- Use videoconferences instead of teleconferences.
- Establish regular meetings and "share the pain" when time zones need to be bridged.
- Send as much information in advance of virtual meetings.
- Create a team website or virtual team space.
- Post holiday and vacation schedules on the team website or virtual workspace.

Leveraging Diversity

One recent coaching client exemplified how bridging diverse perspectives can be critical to the functioning of a work team. This particular executive, an Indian Malaysian national, had a personality which was an amalgam of characteristics which in Western circles might appear vague and contradictory. On the one hand he would never give an assertion such as "this is what we need to do" to his supervisor and peers. With his own team of mostly younger American employees, however, his tone often became overbearing and dictatorial, following the traditional Asian role of the sometimes benevolent but more often critical "father."

In the same way that an inwardly proud Asian parent may belittle or berate his own family to demonstrate humility and discipline, so this executive criticized his supervisees when approached with criticism by an external contact. Not only was his team not culturally receptive to this traditional form of paternal attack, but they carried a particular Generation Y defiance, responding with "I'm outta here" rather than bowing to the cane.

To help this leader salvage his role, I worked with him to (1) understand generational in addition to cultural differences; (2) see that he must find a way to motivate his team so that people can perform better and don't feel beat up; and (3) learn to think of himself as a team leader and not a parent. At the same time, I coached this executive to develop a more direct and transparent communication style when working with his American and European supervisor and peers.

The Power of Diverse Partnerships

The leader of the future must treat coworkers as partners, not competitors, unite individuals within the organization as teams, reduce negativity and build alliances with other organizations. To be successful, the leader just taking off must rely on individuals who are particularly equipped to connect others. A recent article in the *Wall Street Journal* refers to "boundary spanners," or "people who, as a result of their personality, skills or work history, have lots of connections to useful people outside the team." It is the boundary spanners who serve to connect important global processes.

As to the specific skills and actions which boundary spanners employ, they include the capacity to build internal and external networks, identify internal key stakeholders beyond their own functions, proactively reach out to them to build closer relationships, participate in global projects that give them opportunities to get to know key stakeholders, identify external organizations to build external networks, and maintain long-term relationships (i.e., alumni, colleagues, customers).

Partnership-building thrives particularly well in organizations where lateral movement is fluid. In the era of globalization, many organizations are establishing structures which facilitate boundary-spanning interaction.

Working Effectively by Flattening the Organizational Structure (*The Matrix Organization*)

Accenture provides an example of effective process integration built on horizontal leadership structures. Although it has more than 129,000 employees and over $15 billion in revenues, Accenture has "neither an operational headquarters facility nor any formal branch facilities." Teams group, disband, re-group and meet virtually. Working within a "matrix" organization—flat, with multiple reporting lines and shifting projects—is becoming more the norm than the exception.

In a matrix organization, the leader must influence without authority. Influence requires networks and affiliations of many types. In the new world of the matrix organizations the leader faces challenges such as dealing with ambiguity, moving quickly to make decisions without the data necessary for a consensus, and reaching beyond the limitations imposed by geography and time differences.

An example of success in managing without extensive vertical authority comes from a current coaching client—a global executive of one of the world's largest multinationals. To grow the market share of his key products, he

followed two tracks: (1) thinking horizontally, finding new ways to leverage internally, connecting clients to drive innovation and growth among the vendors; and (2) building collaborative and cross-boundary influence.

"After going to my coach, I went back to work and convened several brainstorming sessions with key stakeholders," he said. "I took the time to contact each person, telling them why their input would be critical and how each stakeholder would benefit from this collaborative effort. By the time the group came together, they were primed, and we quickly developed an action plan."

Gaining Influence Without Formal Authority Through Relationships and Multi-Leveled Networks

This global executive learned that by staying in touch with individuals and groups, he was able to organically gather needed knowledge and talent to build his plan and grow the business. More importantly, he knew that by staying connected over time, he would constantly have access to the knowledge and support needed to run a profitable business.

Networking, like globalization itself, is hardly new. In his article "You Say Guanxi, I Say Schmoozing," Frederick Balfour notes that the Chinese phrase *"guanxi"*, which literally means "connections," is a concept that "goes back thousands of years and is based on loyalty, accountability, and obligation—the notion that if someone does you a favor, you will be expected to repay it one day." The new part, however, is that guanxi of the East is meeting networking of the West in new business contexts all over the globe, from fashionable executive MBA programs to corporate gatherings. Relationship is everything.

In the world of Organization Development, relationships within systems have been foundational working theory. Using the OD base as the launch point for change, the successful organization learns to creatively incorporate connections as part of its modus operandi.

W.L Gore & Associates, for example, organizes regular global meetings to bring its Human Resources staff together from 20 different countries. They also have global IT, finance, legal, and supply chain meetings to bring people together for networking, strategic planning and professional development. Since everybody is an "associate," there is continual associative movement. Terri Kelly, the woman at the helm, is referred to by *Fast Company* magazine as "the un-CEO," likely because she brings this connecting value to the work of the company.

Putting It All Together

In some ways, the work of equipping global leaders is that of creating more "un-CEOs." New leaders are those who are adept at building partnerships, both one-to-one and one-to-many, as a matter of habit. They emphasize the horizontal through many modern modalities —such as peer coaching, for example, helping project stakeholders to help each other, creating a chain reaction to maximizing the full pool of talent within reach.

In my work with multinational corporations my global clients have often pointed out that 'building partnerships' is one of the most important competencies for global leaders of the future. Leaders have to successfully build trusting and long-term strategic relationships, internally and externally, and leverage those relationships, in order to get the job done. To do this, they must first acknowledge differences, then leverage them. The aforementioned Thai executive serves as an example of a leader learning to build relationships by first acknowledging differences in both culture and generational perception, then beginning to create solid relationships on the team.

Adding together the themes of this article, coaching and partnerships, you'll find that the leader of the future will be constantly adapting to "emergency" conditions by quickly connecting business and people. As such, he is much like a pilot flying a plane during turbulence: up one minute, adjust the metrics, down the next minute, instruct the co-pilot, up the next minute, call-in to the airports in the area to have all options open. Ultimately the plane, like any successful project, will have to land. Then comes the next flight.

Summary

In this article we have taken a quick tour through the new arenas of global leadership, exploring the emergence of trends which have their roots in the ancient realities of globalization: specifically, the leader as coach and the power of diverse partnerships. As Toyota's Yoshio Ishizaka would remind us, the global leader is not a theoretical construct but a human being. Global leadership is about maximizing a very human ability to connect, form partnerships and create a context for learning and innovation.

Global leaders must be curious about other cultures and enjoy the challenges of communicating in a competitive business environment whose pace is faster every day. In coaching, management consulting and the wider field of Organization Development, our common mission is to bring about positive change in new ways, serving as global partners with leaders of the future.

References

Balfour, F. (2007, November 8). You say guanxi, I say shmoozing. *BusinessWeek,* 1–2.

Ball, D. A., McCulloch, W.H., Jr., Geringer, J.M, Minor, M.S., & McNett , J.M. (2008). *International business: the challenge of global competition* (11th ed). New York, NY: McGraw Hill Irwin, Chapter 1 PowerPoint Slide 6.

Deutschman, A. (2005). The un-CEO. *Fast Company,* 98, 96.

(2005). Global virtual teams. *Interglobe Quarterly Newsflash.* 1(2).

Goldsmith, M., Hu-Chan, M., Greenberg, C.L., & Robertson, A. (2003). *Global leadership: the next generation.* New York, NY: FT Prentice Hall.

Goldsmith, M. (2002, winter). The six-question process: helping executives become better coaches. *Insights.*

Gratton, L. (2007). Working together . . . when apart. *The Journal Report, WSJ*, R1.

Fine, A. G.R.O.W. Model: Insideout development. Retrieved from http://www.insideoutdev.com/site/history_grow_model/

Hymowitz, C. (2006). Have advice, will travel. *The Wall Street Journal*, as cited in the text *International business: the challenge of global competition* (11th ed.) New York, NY: McGraw Hill Irwin, 396.

Ishizaka, Y. (1999). Eight rules for developing global leaders. International Consortium for Executive Development Research Remarks.

CHAPTER 72

Global Leadership

A Virgin Landscape for OD Practitioners in the Vanguard

Patricia Shafer

IT'S A RARE TREAT as an OD practitioner to have an opportunity to be in the vanguard, isn't it? Often, practitioners find themselves asked to adapt to and adopt trends and tools fueled by media attention. Much of the language of OD has been absorbed into organizations—a good phenomenon but also one that makes some important and useful concepts seem "been there, done that" and trite. Bookshelves and file cabinets are brimming—some would say choking—with texts, popular books, and articles on leadership, change management and effective communications. Certain assessment tools, once viewed as cutting edge, can feel like standard fare and old news at times. Coaching, executive coaching and life coaching are sometimes almost too familiar with 60,000 people in the U.S. identifying themselves as professionals in these realms.

Yet, to borrow an old phrase, "every once in a blue moon" something shifts in the organizational landscape. Forces converge and a heretofore unknown and unmet need begins to come into view.

Personally, I became convinced that I was witnessing such a phenomenon during a two-year period that I was completing a global research initiative called "The Whole World at Work: Managers Around the World Tell Us What Still Needs to Change in Organizations"

(Compel Ltd.). The undertaking was designed to detect global patterns in manager views about the "ideal" organization of the future, what works in change, and effective leadership qualities (see Table 72.1). By the time I was done, I had interviewed or completed focus group work with managers in 40 countries. But during the process, I began to detect an emerging organizational development need exemplified by the following excerpt:

> We will open 64 hotels in China. We are having an issue coming up with an international management profile . . . Where do you get personnel, and what do you train them to do? [The company is] insisting that European and Asian managers [come] to Washington, D.C., and we're going through training together . . . It's important because our company is going to change, and our customers are going to change.

The interviewee was and still is a vice president and general manager for an international hotel and hospitality company based in the U.S. As a subsequent conversation and follow-up underline, and as a number of other interviews and environmental signals confirm, this business leader is not alone in his chal-

TABLE 72.1 Emerging Convergence (E-vergence) Summary Framework

E-vergence Level	The Ideal	The Barriers	The Implications
	What did people tell us about their yearnings/longings/aspirations?	What did people tell us about what gets in the way? What are the paradoxes and tensions people are experiencing?	What can be done to overcome the barriers to achieve the ideal?
Ideal Organization	Balance shifts from pronounced task focus to more on people – valuing, aligning, collaborating, connecting, listening	Focus on short-term results, pressure to perform, over-emphasis on process and technology, no time, no balance	Action Inquiry – reflection/dialogue on identified aspects of the ideal organization, structure, systems, processes, policies
Managing Change	Successful change is characterized by alignment of teams, engaging people, communications, integrating cultures	Stuck in cycle of doing versus being, "change by checklist," constant and ubiquitous change, misaligned cultures and political interest	Action Inquiry – reflection/dialogue on experiential change learning, integrating cultures and teams, elements of sustainable change
Effective Leadership	Hybrid/blending of West/East/other, masculine/feminine, integrated groups, levels – no one way is best, learn from each other to capitalize – succeed	"Lip service" paid to diversity, sense of disempowerment, lack of appropriate training/people development	Action Inquiry – reflection/dialogue on trans-national & transformational competence, development of continuous learning and global outlooks

lenge. Executives and managers increasingly face a complex organizational dilemma in this era of accelerating globalization. "Tell me, please" more than one manager will say, "what I can do to help this organization think and act more globally!"

My own experience indicates that executives and managers across industries and hierarchies are being challenged to craft more global strategies, policies and practices, and there's evidence to boot. The average size in square feet of a Wal-Mart store in China is now bigger than the U.S. average; new and surprising mergers are occurring across borders on all continents; and organizations in general face growing demands for better coordination of globally dispersed operations. Companies are relocating facilities closer to lower-cost resources essential to production. Even small and mid-size companies are compelled to think of themselves as *multinationals*

and adopt new habits for global success. Driven by competition and survival instincts, managers are forced to consider cost, logistics and human resources on a global scale.

All of this represents a fundamentally different kind of globalization than we have known in the past. Expansion is not just geographic, involving test entries into new markets or finding long-distance and low-cost suppliers. A new level of organizational connection and complexity has developed from wider, faster and more virtual flows of goods, services, knowledge, project travel, and influence. Moreover, several surveys point to an executive perception that there is a scarcity of managers qualified to work effectively on a multinational scale, and that in turn has become a constraint on future competitiveness. These leadership shortages are viewed as a damper on organizations' abilities to meet future global business risks.

Emerging Managerial Mandate

Consequently, consulting with and coaching managers on topics related to achieving global competencies and competitiveness is one of today's pressing organization development challenges, raising a host of previously unanticipated issues and questions for OD practitioners:

- How do I help organizations define and design more global structures, systems and strategies?
- How do I work with my clients to think across and interact with fast-changing, far-flung organizations?
- How do I do so in ways that are specific to the organization's unique needs and circumstances?
- How do I deal with the big, hairy challenge of developing leaders with a global mindset for the 21st century—those that Schon Beechler and Mansour Javidan (2007) define as: "a new and different breed of global leaders who can make decisions and take actions that facilitate the development of the complex network of internal and external connections with individuals, teams, and organizations with many different political, social, and cultural systems."

The big missing factor is that the organizations comprised of evolved leader clients with whom OD practitioners can partner on these opportunities mostly do not yet exist. I often refer to the people who comprise this leadership approach as "The *New* Hybrid Leaders," and describe them as multi-dimensional individuals who are equipped with "transformational," "transnational," and "trans-cultural competencies." The New Hybrid Leaders would consistently behave and be recognized as global citizens, eager to:

- Integrate, respond to, and lead diverse groups;
- Demonstrate situational flexibility in management style;
- Be effective in a variety of geographic, cultural and dual-gender settings.

No Roadmap or Best Practices

The fields of organization development and human resources also haven't kept pace. A ready set of principles and approaches to which practitioners can refer for learning and support is lacking. Even though the term "global" was first applied to executives and jobs in the early 1980s, organizations, professional practitioners and academic researchers have mostly continued to think domestically. There remains a near negligible percentage of organizational and human resource management articles published in leading management journals and devoted to international topics.

Conferences and workshops around the world generally focus on transferring North American approaches to management, leadership, and change, as opposed to integrating views into more globally relevant approaches. Few meaningful case studies exist on effective global management approaches, and the literature reads like a catalogue of proposed leadership traits. In a phrase, the notion of developing global organization and leadership skills is in its nascent stage.

On a personal note, I'm regularly struck by the degree to which we remain insular and localized in our thinking about organizational needs. At this year's annual Society for Human Resource Management Global Conference and Exhibition, I led a discussion on developing global leaders and was initially pleased with interest and participation. Only in retrospect did I recognize the obvious. Attendance at the conference was disproportionately American, but three-quarters of my discussion participants were Austrian, Polish, Indian, and French. This global conference for HR professionals, the attendees eager for information on leadership development with a global outlook, hailed from outside the U.S. Similarly, I recently noticed that the 2009 program for the largest annual HR summit in Asia, with anticipated attendance of more than 3,000 Asian professionals, features a roster of keynote speakers almost entirely from the U.S. and U.K. Strung together with other similar events, a pattern emerges. In a time when global diversity is an inherent driver, ethnocentricity is still ingrained in the way we think about and guide organizations.

Barriers to Overcome

Moreover, as confirmed by "The Whole World at Work" interviews that I referenced earlier, there exist several habitual barriers that generally get in the way of organizations moving beyond a focus on how we do it around here, and how we do it in this country—so to speak. These are organizational attitudes and behaviors that get in the way of development—are intrinsically present in what we often think of as a U.S. management style—and are being broadly exported and emulated outside North America. The barriers can be categorized as:

• Policies and practices perceived as not valuing people
• Over-reliance on technology and process for change
• Emphasizing only cost and performance measures
• Under-investing in training and development
• Dragging on diversity
• Re-structuring without reasoning

These taken together get in the way of envisioning, developing and implementing new approaches more consistent with likely organizational futures.

Need for OD Reflection

However, this stark reality can be viewed as good news of a sort. The disconnect between the need for integrated, multinational outlooks contrasted with a paucity of supporting tools and available resources represents an exciting opportunity for OD practitioners. The landscape is wide open for forward-looking practitioners proposing and experimenting with new consulting and coaching frameworks in companies increasingly curious, even hungry, for ways to help their people "go global."

For the willing, OD practitioners have blossoming opportunities to influence organizational structures, systems and strategies for multinational and multidimensional effectiveness. New organizational puzzles are yet to be resolved, pieced together from answers to questions such as:

• Will the profile of tomorrow's successful leaders differ greatly from today's?
• How important will the qualities of *global mindset* be to manager success?
• On what criteria should organizations select members into and facilitate multinational, multicultural teams?
• What should be the OD practitioner's role in re-shaping training and development?
• What self-development and experiences do OD practitioners require in this global environment?

As globalization has evolved from corporate buzzword to basic economic reality, more organizations seek to competently operate in the international arena, but many organizations do not know how to identify and develop people for such complex responsibilities. As examples, organizers of annual state Human Resources conferences in Illinois, California and a tristate area of the Northeast added globally-focused topics to workshops for the first time in 2007. Value-adding practitioners will be those who offer thoughtful views on how many "global leaders" must an organization have; which managers should develop a worldwide outlook while others stick to their proverbial knitting; and which global leadership development interventions offer the best return on investment (ROI).

A Place to Begin

OD practitioners are in unique positions to launch dialogues on these issues and to contemplate ways to groom silhouettes of The

New Hybrid Leaders through leadership development programs that acknowledge global realities and influences.

Where do OD practitioners begin when there is no vetted formula, scorecard, checklist or best practices? Moreover, how do they begin when they are under pressure to prove that management education options actually achieve change, and organizations are shifting away from long-term investments in education toward development that is short, intensive, flexibly delivered, and consistent with corporate objectives. Just as important, how does OD partner with HR practitioners and executive and manager stakeholders at a client site?

First and foremost, it's essential to consider a range of parameters that can affect global organization and leadership development efficacy:

- Is the organization in question *experienced* or *inexperienced* on the global scene?
- When an organization has an established multinational history, how has it gone about preparing (or not preparing) managers to work in different cultures and contexts?
- Where should interventions take place and with whom? For instance, are the managers of interest a multicultural group all seated within the corporate headquarters? Or, will the work be done within a specialized function, like IT? Or, is the need greatest with sales and marketing professionals who are becoming familiar with new markets? At what organizational level are the executives/managers—C-level? Mid-level? Supervisors?
- What is the nationality or nationalities of the managers?
- What is the purpose of the development experience, and what time and financial resources exist to support the effort?

Many practitioners are surprised to hear that depending on circumstance, the range of options—even in this embryonic field of global organizational development—can be quite broad (and untested). Accepting and communicating that there is no full-proof one-day seminar, executive education program, or international degree is a sound and honest start. Therein, the art vs. the science of OD must take hold, with practitioners casting themselves as catalysts for exploration in three arenas: (1) prompting executives and managers to re-conceptualize their world in reference to the big, wide world; (2) exposing managers to development experiences that alter ingrained mental models and habits; and (3) facilitating conversations to re-think organizational designs in light of global realities. These best play out in thoughtfully-designed dialogue sessions that:

- Explore divergent ideas across geographies, functions, levels and cultures
- Embrace convergent ideas and build shared organizational understanding
- Address barriers to effective global operations
- Take into consideration which managers are equipped with a so-called "global mindset"—a key component of global leadership because cognitive abilities (mindsets) influence how managers shape strategy, thus determining behavior and outcomes.

Consistent with this last point above, 360-degree assessments naturally become part of the organization and leadership feedback mix. A single 360-degree global assessment tool hasn't yet been broadly used and validated, but it is possible to combine elements of several tools that help individuals and teams talk about the extent to which they do or don't exhibit global mindset and an effective global leadership style. Working with colleagues and collaborators, I've moved toward several rating instruments, including: the Global Executive Leadership Inventory (GELI), complemented with a Whole Work™ work culture survey, further complemented by customized interviews. GELI was developed by Manfred F.R. Kets de Vries from investigations of the daily actions and behaviors of effective global leaders. Whole Work™ tools were inspired by research involving interviews with managers, consultants and coaches working in multinational companies on five continents. I supplement tools like these with narrative interviews designed with the organization in mind.

With assessment results in hand, OD practitioners can conduct exercises and simulations that help managers redefine paradigms from which they make decisions. One experience might involve working with a group to envision how to best choose members of an imaginary global team. Participants could receive information on a company's business environment, strategies, and current leadership profiles; be provided with information on effective global leadership traits; and then, together, build the "best global team."

Similarly, a cross-cultural consultant with whom I'm collaborating told me about a leadership development workshop that he conducted for a multinational company with operations in Asia. The company was a U.S.-China joint-venture, and the workshop took place in Beijing. As he recounts, participating America managers spent 45 minutes openly discussing their beliefs about leadership while the Chinese team members waited patiently. When the Chinese had their turn, they began to energetically discuss four different interpretations of "leadership" from their perspectives. Ten minutes after the non-English discussion began, the Americans asked if they could go outside until their counterparts were done. What an eye-opener it was for them when the facilitator pointed out how little room and tolerance they had for waiting to listen to the outcome of an alternative exploration of leadership concepts.

Whatever the methods, an overarching goal is always to help managers recognize beliefs and habits that help or hinder success on a global scale. That includes the degree to which individuals and their organizations appreciate diversity, adapt, think flexibly, and integrate previously unimagined and more expansive ideas and solutions. For OD practitioners, this entails determining processes and practices to facilitate individuals, groups, and organizations to achieve organization goals across diverse cultural and institutional systems.

Sharing Continuous Learning

Last but not least, and this gets to the heart and spirit of a member organization such as the Organization Development Network (ODN), the broadly defined arenas of global organization development and global leadership development offer opportunities for OD practitioners to begin documenting and sharing experiences for the purpose of continuous learning. In mostly uncharted territory, the programs and services that companies will ask OD practitioners to provide become a de facto learning laboratory on the role and efficacy of interventions on development of global mindsets and behaviors, as well as the interplay of organizational and individual factors on interventions. There is knowledge to be gained and shared.

For instance, I recently co-designed a development framework for use with a multinational company in the early stages of establishing a global leadership development discipline. As envisioned, participants will be distributed across several groups experiencing distinct development interventions. These groups are identified through a sample of managers in headquarters and overseas sub-units identified as "high-potential" within the organization, and accounting for characteristics of age, nationality, geography, functional specialization, and job level. The groups will participate in either a customized one-day diversity immersion experience intended to enhance global mindset; a three-day intensive program incorporating an overview of global leadership concepts and case study- and simulation-based dialogues; or a combination of the programs. For additional insight, there will be a comparison of the impact of the interventions with an "expatriate readiness" program already in place at the client. To measure changes, all participants will complete assessments of global leadership skills and global mindset before the interventions and at a specified point in time after.

In the Vanguard

This "global newness" to organization and leadership development presents a rare high-stakes, high impact opportunity for OD practitioners and their counterpart HR professionals to be in the vanguard. OD and HR remain the *go to* sources for people policies, procedures, principles and practices. They are often management's eyes and ears for monitoring reactions and responses to strategic global decisions. Taking responsibility for developing organizations and managers with multidimensional, multinational outlooks is just one step removed.

The challenge is to work through current ambiguities about how best to do this. In fact, I often say that global organization development is less about a checklist and more about pursuing what Andrew H. Van de Ven, et. al, called "Cycling the Innovation Journey" (see Figure 72.1)—an organizational process of exploring divergent ideas and exploiting convergent views about which ideas to implement.

FIGURE 72.1   Cycling the Innovation Journey

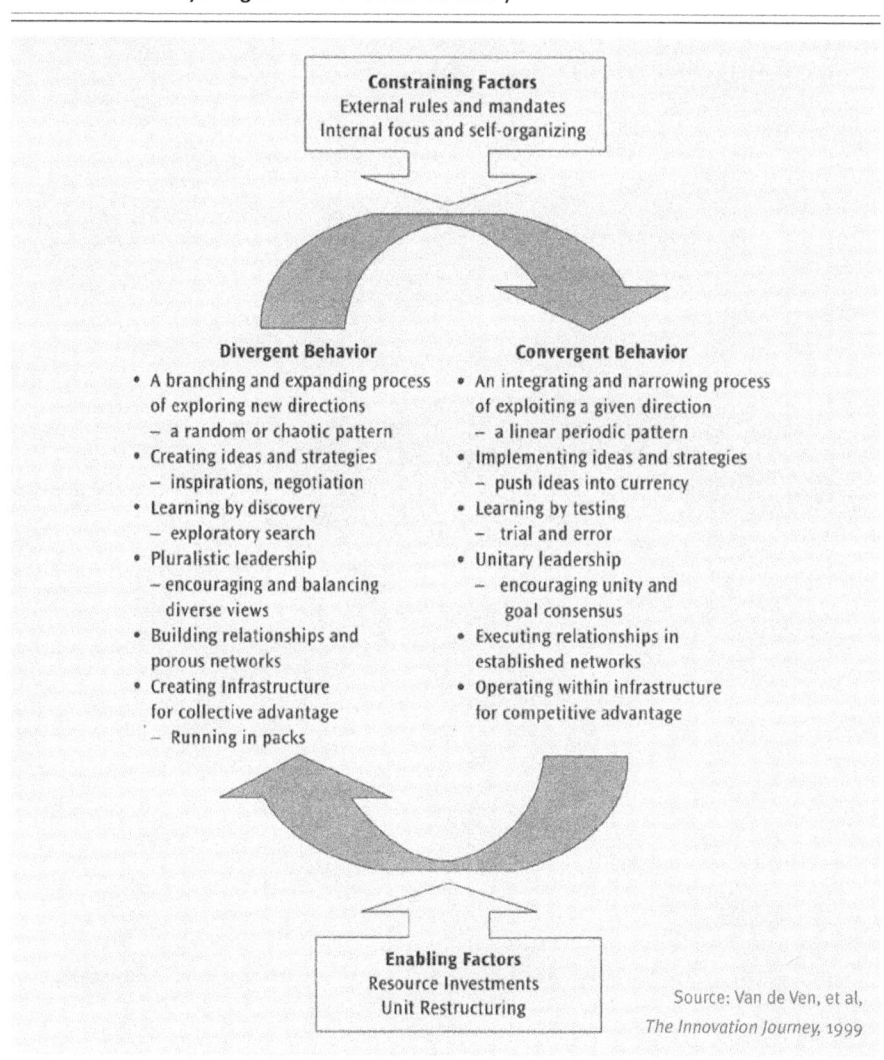

Constraining Factors
External rules and mandates
Internal focus and self-organizing

Divergent Behavior
- A branching and expanding process of exploring new directions
  - a random or chaotic pattern
- Creating ideas and strategies
  - inspirations, negotiation
- Learning by discovery
  - exploratory search
- Pluralistic leadership
  - encouraging and balancing diverse views
- Building relationships and porous networks
- Creating Infrastructure for collective advantage
  - Running in packs

Convergent Behavior
- An integrating and narrowing process of exploiting a given direction
  - a linear periodic pattern
- Implementing ideas and strategies
  - push ideas into currency
- Learning by testing
  - trial and error
- Unitary leadership
  - encouraging unity and goal consensus
- Executing relationships in established networks
- Operating within infrastructure for competitive advantage

Enabling Factors
Resource Investments
Unit Restructuring

Source: Van de Ven, et al,
The Innovation Journey, 1999

For one company, the vision might start with executive team alignment on what the global landscape will look like and who will be our leaders, continued with a proactive recruiting plan for high-potentials across multiple countries. For still another, a robust and culturally sensitive 360-profile of key managers with ongoing feedback might be appropriate. For another, perhaps the hiring of an anthropologist for a cross-creating forums and experiences in which cultural learning journey would be useful. organizations take time to ask tough but The approaches might be vastly different neces-

sary questions: How global are we and highly customized, but would all going to be? And how must we change to have one thing in common. They involve get there?

References

Beechler, S., & Javidan, M. (2007). Leading with a global mindset. In M. Javidan, R. Steers, & A. Hitt (Eds.), *The global mindset* (pp. 131–169). Bingley, UK: Emerald Group Publishing.

Van de Ven, A. (1999). *The innovation journey.* New York, NY: Oxford University Press.

CHAPTER 73

The Core Value of OD Revisited

A Compass for Global and International Organization Development

Therese F. Yaeger

OUR WORLD IS DIFFERENT now as a result of the events of September 11, 2001. A new understanding that one's values and personal beliefs are not necessarily the same values and beliefs that members of different cultures adhere to has been realized. For this reason, what becomes of OD, as it was founded as a value-laden, primarily American, approach to change? Further, what are these values and do they apply universally? More important for this *OD Practitioner* issue dedicated to Global OD, for a prospective view of OD in the global arena, are present OD values being maintained, or are these values being replaced with other more current principles? Based on interviews with Global OD consultants, this study may provide the direction, or compass, for the global OD consulting.

Globalization is changing the markets and environments in which organizations operate. New governments, new leadership, new markets, new countries and new technology are emerging and creating a new global economy (Cummings & Worley, 2000) that presents unique opportunities and challenges for business and management. Increasing rates and scope of change have forged tremendous opportunities for international consulting work, particularly for OD consultants, who can play significant roles in creating the futures of corporations, governments, communities, and non-profit organizations (Dannemiller & Jacobs, 1994). Recent opportunities range from process work for the Peace Corps and teambuilding work in the new Soviet Republic to assisting community members in overcoming gender issues in South Africa. Given such opportunities, OD consulting should become an expanding force in international business.

However, to this point, it appears that perhaps more questions than answers can be provided. What is it about the effective global OD consultant that is distinctive from a "home-country" OD consultant? How is global OD occurring amidst all the cross-cultural complexities and divergence among people worldwide? Finally, as the business world goes global, how optimistic can the global OD consultant be for the future of this field?

Global OD Consulting: Fit Or Mis-Fit?

The applicability and effectiveness of OD in countries and cultures outside of the United States have been a recent subject of debate. Because OD was developed predominantly by American and Western European practitioners,

605

its practices and methods are heavily influenced by the values and assumptions of industrialized cultures. Thus, the traditional approaches to planned change may promote management practices that conflict with the values and assumptions of other societies (Cummings & Worley, 2000, p. 554). With particular reference to Americans, Boyacigiller and Adler state, "Americans have developed theories without being sufficiently aware of non-U.S. contexts, models, research, and values", suggesting that OD practices must be more sensitive in an international context (1991). The Dutch industrial psychologist, Geert Hofstede, who conducted landmark research on differences in culture-based values, found more divergence than convergence regarding international consulting work. He states that "not only will cultural diversity remain with us, but it even looks as though the differences within countries is [sic] increasing" (1997, p. 238).

A second basis for this research involves the concern of shifting OD values raised by many practitioners. From its beginning, OD practitioners have promoted a set of humanistic and democratic values, which have played a crucial role in OD (Cummings & Worley, 2000). According to OD experts Warren Bennis and Edgar Schein, these values include democracy, a matter of choice, and most important, a spirit of inquiry that includes checking the validity of one's assumptions, and experimentalism (1965).

Concern exists that these original values remain part of the OD canon of values, as eleven years ago, Margulies and Raia (1990) emphasized: "Values may be more important today than they were in the era of the 1950's and 1960's ..." They underscored their concern for OD values claiming, "We are concerned that in the service of being relevant, a plea heard from both theoreticians and practitioners, that the field has succumbed to the imperative of organizational efficiency and effectiveness, perhaps at any cost" (pp. 29–30).

Church and Burke (1995) and Church, Burke, and VanEynde (1994) support the concerns of Margulies and Raia. They note that OD values have shifted away from the traditional,

humanistic concerns under which the field was founded to a stronger concern for business effectiveness outcomes and contemporary, systemic, business-related issues (1995, p. 11).

These two sets of factors, the compatibility of OD values worldwide, and the possibility of divergence of cross-cultural issues in consulting, combine for OD consultants to experience higher than usual apprehension when undertaking global OD work. The immediate challenge is that of global managers and consultants; they must operate on a number of different premises at any one time (Trompenaars, 1993). Even though all human beings may be more alike than different, it is the differences that can exacerbate the problem, impede an intervention, and mitigate effectiveness (Wigglesworth, 1995).

Much of the success of an OD intervention can be measured through the OD consultant. Warner Burke (1982) insists, "The primary instrument in OD work is the consultant-practitioner" (p. 358). One way to examine the OD consultant's role and function is to consider the degree of personal use of oneself as an instrument of facilitation, feedback, and change . . . the OD consultant should be a finely tuned instrument" (p. 350).

In an effort to investigate successful global OD consulting through consultants' recounting of high point stories and complexities of global OD consulting, the investigative process was guided by basic research questions, namely, 'What are the contributing factors to successful global OD consulting? What role, if any, do OD values play in global OD work?'

The Study

To understand the values of today's Global OD consultants, fourteen interviews with Global OD practitioners were undertaken. While no formal definition of the global OD consultant exists, for purposes of this research, the construct of a global OD consultant is:

> a practitioner who has worked outside
> of his or her native country, has used

OD techniques in his or her work, has encountered different cultures during OD practice in those countries, and is able to reflect on at least three stories (learnings) from these experiences.

To obtain data from a broad variety of global consultants, a conscious effort was undertaken to research global OD consultants from various fields of OD work, both internal and external, in both the for-profit and not-for-profit sectors, with a balance between male and female, and US versus non-American consultants (see Table 73.1).

To aid the research process, throughout the entire investigation, this study was guided by broad research questions such as, "What drives the global OD consultant? What role, if any, do OD values play in global work?"

The Findings

In response to the interview questions, it appears that one contributing factor of successful global OD consulting is advocating two different but necessary types of OD values. Both the humanistic values and the values surrounding the business concerns of OD con-

TABLE 73.1 Demographic of Global OD Consultants Interviewed (n=4)

Birth Place	Age Range
US = 11	40–50 = 7
Non US = 3	50–60 = 5
	60–up = 2

Gender	Education
Male = 8	Undergraduate = 2
Female = 6	Masters = 6
	Ph.D. = 6

Number of Years Consulting	Type of Organization
10–20 years = 7	For profit = 9
20–30 years = 3	Not-for-profit = 3
30 up years = 4	Both = 2

sulting are contributing elements for creating and driving successful global OD work.

1. The Humanistic Values of OD are at the forefront of successful Global OD Consulting. Interviewees' demographics, countries where their OD work occurred and learnings gained from each interviewed consultant were documented. Other findings from this data (interventions used, motivations, reasons for entering global work, etc.) are beyond the scope of this article and will be investigated in future publications.

From this data, it was determined that critical values of the global OD consultant appear to be the humanistic values as modeled by predecessors and founders of the OD field, such as Kurt Lewin and Douglas McGregor. The spirit of inquiry, as proposed by Kurt Lewin in the 1940s, consisted of two elements: the hypothetical spirit that allowed for inquiry and innovative-ness, and the experimentalism component that allows for testing the validity of assumptions and error. These two components are supported alongside four other components as a result of these qualitative and quantitative findings, those elements of community, collegiality, democracy and authenticity. It appears this spirit of inquiry value is strengthened, not weakened, in global consulting, making global OD work not only possible but promising for even more global OD consulting (see Table 73.2).

These humanistic, often traditional, OD values can facilitate the possibility of more effective global OD consulting as the impact of humanistic values appears to transcends cross-cultural boundaries and allows for innovative and democratic OD concepts to support an intercultural change process. Interview data confirmed that the fundamental values of OD, democracy, authenticity, and experimentalism, are alive and well, and necessary for working cross-culturally in complex environments.

2. Findings from both interview and survey data indicated that the global OD consultant is still focused on the business concern of global organization development efforts.

TABLE 73.2 Humanistic OD Values

Humanistic Value	Interview Terms
Innovation	Discovering cause and effect, learning, discovery, new discovery from interrelationships. Innovative learning, intellectually growing through experiences.
Community	Community effort creates change, spirit of human concern, rewards from group work, spirit of excitement, growth from community experience, spirit from realization, OD opens communication.
Authenticity	Exercising humility, humbling experience from small contribution, authenticity through genuine interests, elements of surprise, openness toward others.
Democracy	Democracy with trust, raising collaboration, democracy through overcoming ethnocentrism, democracy through equality, willing to work together.
Experimentalism	Experimenting for new opportunities, groundwork to check validity, all voices crate democratic process, feedback for validity, decisions through valid information, creating legitimacy through inquiry.
Collegialship	Candidness, listening, good listener, wanting betterment, comfort with humor, genuine, collegiality.

For the global OD consultant, the concern for business effectiveness is not stronger than the humanistic value of OD; it is a *both/and,* not an *either/or* situation. Contrary to Church and Burke's 1995 U.S. findings, in the global OD consulting arena, it appears that the Global OD consultant advocates both sets of OD values.

For this study there were varying degrees of this business concern as differences in these business values existed between the two phases of this study. Although the concern for business effectiveness value did surface in the interview findings, it appears that business effectiveness was a more important value in global OD consulting in later survey findings.

In secondary survey data collection, to support this business effectiveness concern, responses indicated that the first eight highest ranked value statements of the *Today* column were all business concerns which included enhancing productivity (M = 3.83), focusing on profitability/bottom line results (M = 3.75), increasing effectiveness and efficiency (M = 3.73), enhancing competitive advantage (M = 3.62), and promoting quality of products and services (M = 3.42).

However, in the *Ideal* (or future) side of responses, it appeared that business concerns did not appear until the fifth-ranked enhancing productivity response (M = 4.46). In the survey responses, the first eight highest ranking responses involved business concerns, which indicated that the global OD consultants see the business effectiveness side of OD as important, or more important, than the humanistic values listed. Closely following these top eight business values, the humanistic values of collaboration, community, participation and democracy followed. These findings strongly support the findings of Church and Burke's 1995 results of 416 US consultants who found OD values of both humanistic concern and business effectiveness remain at the forefront of OD work.

Quoting Church and Burke who noted the similar results:

Basically, it can be concluded that the humanistic roots of the field are still present among practitioners in their work. The relative emphasis of these values may have changed, however, to focus more on business outcomes in an effort to achieve quantifiable results and prove one's worth. (1995, p. 39)

Church and Burke also remind us that these findings do not indicate that the traditional values of OD have not been lost, and that in the global OD arena, these values should be seen not as different but as similar and necessary elements of success in OD work globally. More importantly, that both humanistic and business results had stronger scores on the *Ideal* responses indicates that the future of OD appears promising.

3. Global OD practitioners have the acute ability to encounter and overcome cross-culture complexities while accomplishing successful global OD work. Findings involving cross-cultural complexities acknowledged the presence of challenges in global OD consulting. Stories of language difficulties, religious differences, ethical misunderstandings, and gender issues surfaced throughout the interviews. More interesting, however, is that these successful consultants, through their acute ability, were able to acknowledge and overcome the complexities.

Cross-cultural complexities are the elements of international and global consulting that business consultants often fear, and for this reason, often avoid international consulting work. Simply stated, we are reminded by Nancy Adler that consultants need to recognize cross-cultural differences and learn to use them to their advantage rather than ignore them or allow them to cause problems (1991). Similarly, with regard to cross-cultural consulting, this research indicated that to be proactive and address cultural nuances might be the best approach to overcoming these complexities and creating change in the world outside of our home country.

In the interview process, the global OD consultants shared their levels of comfort with such cultural complexities. Such statement as:

- My comfort zone is in the gray areas, entering new cultures.

- My biggest challenges were not overseas — those feel good . . . that for me is when I really get the chills.

- When you talk about traveling into those nations, that is going into my comfort zone.

These type of statements indicate a willingness to encounter and work amidst complex issues. This element of awareness mirrors what Adler suggests: the issue of not ignoring, but instead, acknowledging and appreciating so as to overcoming cross-cultural complexities in OD work. On a similar vein, one can now address concern regarding divergence in cross-cultural OD work.

4. Consistent with Hofstede's statement regarding divergence, it appears that while divergence continues within cross-cultural consulting, that convergence in the future may be the preferred future state for the global OD consultant. Research surrounding the present OD and cross-cultural literature underscores a need for this convergence-divergence research. According to Hofstede, "Research about the development of cultural values has shown repeatedly that there is very little evidence of international convergence over time except an increase of individualism for countries that have become richer. For the next few hundred years countries will remain culturally very diverse" (1997, p. 238).

Contrary to Hofstede's belief it appeared from these findings that geographic boundaries are becoming less important in OD consulting work, indicating convergence of cross-cultural concepts for the global OD consultants.

Perhaps these Phase One findings complement the convergence side of this debate, and spark ideas for the future of global OD consulting. Hickson and Pugh support the concept of convergence stating, "As enterprises move more and more towards operating internationally, they are producing a convergence in management functioning which could mean that, in due course, there will be a common global 'management culture'" (1995).

However, a secondary quantitative portion of this research indicated a higher awareness of divergence among global OD consultants at an even higher level than the interview findings. Factors contributing to these two separate findings could be attributed to: (a) the method by which data was collected in the two phases; (b) the ability to share positive stories about individuals and successful projects, thereby seeing the global consultants as "like me"; and (c) the ability to be anonymous in survey responses.

5. Global OD consultants are optimistic about the future of global OD consulting. Finally, consistent with US respondents, when asked: *"To what extent are you optimistic about the future of OD as a field,"* these global consultants were *optimistic or extremely optimistic* about the future of the OD field. It is this element of global OD work that can propel the future of successful OD outcomes. Beyond power and financial desires, these global OD consultants have the ability to do what OD is defined to do: improve organizations through people, because these individuals have a sense of optimism to create a promising future for OD.

The findings of this study supported the concept that global OD consultants possess a powerful set of values that allow for successful Global OD work. These consultants are bellwethers, leaders for the future of OD work. Their attraction to this work is a result of their strong OD values base, similar to that of Lewin who accepted the unknown, not as a mystery, but as a frontier against which all scientists must strive to push back if they are to achieve a better understanding of the social world about which science still knows so little (Marrow, 1969). The aim of the global OD consultant, like Lewin, is to discover the determining conditions of human events and human success. Through these elements, the OD consultant can achieve success globally.

U.S. CENTERED

This study was based on responses from fourteen interviewees and numerous anonymous survey responses of global OD practitioners. However, two limitations of this study should be addressed; namely the issue of language and the issue of non-US respondents. The survey and interviews were created in the English language. This limitation may have inhibited some responses to the study. All survey work and interviews were based and written in the English language. Further research by this author will attempt to have translation of the survey for consultants of languages other than English.

Further, responses from global OD consultants did indicate that only one-third of the sampled group were from outside of the US. Recommendations to create more effective means to locate a larger non-US audience have been suggested.

Conclusion

This study represents a first step toward identifying necessary values for effective global OD work. The investigation of these values was accomplished through interviews and survey data from global OD consultants, who are the primary instruments in an OD effort. The OD consultant must forge and maintain fundamental values for the consulting relationship to endure the challenges brought by the humanistic resistance to change. OD values are key to nourishing the innovative and inquiring spirit, and thereby contributing to successful OD interventions through successful relationships.

Powerful and promising findings lie ahead for the OD field with the unfolding knowledge gleaned from these global practitioners. In addition, while our world has moved rapidly toward global business, the potentially pervasive effect of OD has yet to be truly tapped. The dramatic possibilities for OD consultants who desire new knowledge of international and global work at present remain unrealized. The significance of this research will be both practical and relevant as it connects previous OD theory to practical future applications in global management and consulting work.

References

Adler, N. J. (1991). *International dimensions of organization behavior* (2nd Ed.). Boston, MA: PWS-Kent Publishing.

Boyacigiller, N., & Adler, N. (1991) The parochial dinosaur: Organization science in a global context. *Academy of Management Review,* 16(2), 262–290.

Burke, W. W. (1982). *Organization development: Principles and practices.* Boston, MA: Scott, Foresman and Company.

Burrell, G., & Morgan, G. (1984). *Sociological paradigms and organizational analysis.* Portsmouth, NH: Heinemann.

Church, A. H., & Burke, W. W. (1995). Practitioner attitudes about the field of Organization development. In W. A. Pas-more & R. W. Woodman (Eds.), *Research in organizational change and development,* (Vol. 8, pp. 1–46). Greenwich, CT: JAI Press.

Church, A. H., Burke, W. W., & Van Eynde, D. F. (1994). Values, motives and interventions of organization development practitioners. *Group & Organization Management,* 19 (1), 5–50.

Cummings, T., & Worley, C. (2000). *Organization development and change* (7th ed.). Cincinnati, OH: South Western College Publishing.

Dannemiller, K., & Jacobs, R. (1995). *Practicing organization development: A Guide for Consultants.* San Francisco, CA: Jossey-Bass.

Hickson, D., & Pugh, D. (1995). *Management Worldwide: The impact of societal culture on organizations around the globe.* New York, NY: Penguin Books.

Hofstede, G. (1980). *Culture's consequences.* London, UK: Sage.

Hofstede, G. (1997). *Culture and organizations: Software of the mind.* New York, NY: McGraw-Hill.

Margulies, N., & Raia, A. (1990). The significance of core values on the theory and practice of organization development. In F. Massarik (Ed.), *Advances in Organization Development* (Vol. 1, pp. 27–41). Norwood, NJ: Ablex.

Marrow, A. J. (1969). *The practical theorist.* New York, NY: Basic Books.

Trompenaars, F. (1993). *Riding the waves of culture.* London, UK: The Economist Press.

CHAPTER 74

OD: Dancing in the Global Context

Anne H. Litwin

THE PURPOSE of this article is to challenge those of us who are Western OD consultants to increase our understanding of global cultural differences. We need to recognize that OD is a discipline rooted in Western values. As OD practitioners, we need to learn to dance with the differences between our Western values and the values in different global cultures in order to bring OD to the global marketplace. It is not always easy to know when or whether to alter the steps we have learned for the dance of OD. In what global contexts will participative interventions not be effective? In which contexts will the needs of individuals vs. the needs of organizations not be appropriate to discuss? In what contexts will transparency not be acceptable or expected? These values of participation, individuality, and transparency are central to Western-based OD (Fagenson-Elan, Ensher et al., 2004, p. 461), but sometimes antithetical to the values of other cultures. Where are we willing, as individual OD practitioners, to learn new steps in our OD approach in order to be effective? In this article I will share an existing framework on national cultural differences that has been very helpful to me, and I will share experiences from my practice as examples of how this model can help OD practitioners dance with global cultures.

According to Fagenson-Eland and Ensher, OD is now practiced in every region of the world as the global expansion of many organizations has generated complex and rapid growth. Issues of global cultural differences are not new to the OD field; OD has had its roots in diversity and globalization for more than 25 years. Given the complexity and rapid growth brought about by globalization, it has become even more important for us to examine our assumptions, frameworks, and biases.

Swimming in Confusion

As an Organization Development consultant who has worked in many different organizational and country cultures, I have always known that I need to adjust my way of working to be effective in different cultures. Anyone who has worked in a new organizational culture knows that feeling of swimming in confusion about how to make meaning of the reactions and interactions around you. This challenge intensifies in global companies where the intersection of local cultures and company cultures creates added complexity for the consultant. A recent study by Fagenson-Eland, et al. provides a useful framework for understanding how practitioners can avoid some of this confusion and find a starting place for designing OD interventions in different national cultures. This study compares OD change interventions in 7 different countries using Hofstede's (1980) framework on dimensions of national cultural differences. It shows how differences in national cultures can predict which interventions will be effective.

Hofstede first developed his framework when his research of IBM employees in 40 different countries showed how differences in national cultures affect management practices. He and his son have continued to expand this research (Hofstede 1991; 2001; Hofstede & Hofstede 2005) and other researchers have replicated and expanded the work and found support for Hofstede's dimensions of national culture.[1] The four key dimensions of culture originally identified by Hofstede and replicated in other studies—power distance, uncertainty avoidance, individualism/collectivism, masculinity/femininity—were found by Fagenson-Elan et al., (2004) to be good predictors of the usage of different OD interventions in different national cultures. A fifth dimension of culture, long-term/ short- term orientation, has been added by Hofstede and Bond (1988) and is included in this analysis. I will describe each dimension, the findings from the research on differences in use of OD interventions, as well as examples from my own practice about how these differences manifest.

Power Distance and OD Interventions

Hofstede (1980, 1991; Hofstede & Hofstede 2005) defined the Power Distance dimension as the extent to which individuals who are less powerful members of institutions and organizations within a country expect and accept that power is distributed unequally. Some nations with high Power Distance are the Philippines, Russia, Venezuela, the People's Republic of China, India, and Malaysia. Examples of those with low Power Distance are New Zealand, the United States, Britain, and Costa Rica.

Fagenson-Elan et al.(2004) note that OD interventions, such as team building, may be appropriate in both high and low Power Distance countries, but the approach to each must be quite different to be effective. When doing team building in China, a high power distance

culture, I found that I needed to acknowledge to the workers of low status that asking for their participation was a change. I then needed to ask these workers to express their opinions first, before hearing from people in positions of higher power, and wait patiently (sometimes for a long time). The workers would wait to see if it was really all right to give their opinions, and would eventually give them, first with caution, and then with enthusiasm.

Power distance is often a significant factor in virtual teams when Western managers want and need team members in different parts of the globe to contribute to decisions from their regional perspectives and experiences, but hear little or nothing from these employees. One thing that is going on in these situations is that in High Power Distance cultures, employees have deeply held beliefs that the boss *should* have the answers and that it is not appropriate for them to give their opinions. Employees in these cultures may even feel it is deeply disrespectful to give their opinions. Getting higher participation from these team members requires a Western boss to understand this dynamic, acknowledge it, explain why she needs their input, and be patient while reassuring them that she will not feel disrespected. This change can be highly satisfying for all involved and essential for global teamwork, but can represent a significant change.

Bringing together teams of both low and high power cultures is now a constant challenge both inside the U.S. and outside. One way that I have found to help teams build a bridge across these differences is to have them identify, in culture-similar groups, their most important values regarding work and relationships. They present their most important values to each other, and develop team norms that incorporate as many of these values as possible. For example, a team with Thai, Chinese, European, and American members was able to incorporate the value of humility into the following ground rule:

> We value humility, therefore, even though we may think our idea is the best, we

encourage other people to share their ideas and we are open to understand and incorporate them.

This team was able to develop ground rules based on the values of respect, humility, freedom, loyalty, trust, integrity, friendship, honesty, gratefulness, and honor. In the process, they came to understand a great deal about their commonalities, as well as find creative ways to name and bridge their differences which enabled them to become a high performing team.

Uncertainty Avoidance and OD Interventions

This dimension of difference in national cultures was described by Hofstede (1980) as the extent to which organizational members do not tolerate unpredictability and ambiguity. Fagenson-Elan et al. (2004) found that in countries high in Uncertainty Avoidance, such as Russia, France, and Japan, there is less likelihood that OD efforts that require long periods of ambiguity, such as culture change efforts, will be implemented. The researchers note that high Uncertainty Avoidance countries, as in high Power Distance countries, hierarchy is respected and decision-making is expected to be top-down. Risk-taking behavior is discouraged and having clear and stable rules is important (p. 437).

It is not that culture change interventions aren't possible in both high Power Distance and high Uncertainty Avoidance cultures. Culture change interventions can be successful, but must be approached with the recognition that resistance to change may be subtle but even more deeply entrenched than in other types of cultures. One colleague[2] recently related an experience of being tasked by his U.S.-based company to impose a new set of procedures developed by the U.S. corporate office on an offshore manufacturing facility. This colleague knew from past experience that the leaders of the offshore site would pretend to agree to the change, but would not implement them because of, among other factors, their aversion to change and the risk they would perceive to be associated with deviating from proven ways of doing things. Instead of telling the offshore group, "you have to do this because corporate says so", this colleague gave the site a choice and supported them in exploring the benefits of the new process in their own way. In their own time, they agreed to the changes and implemented them. By respecting the values of this high Uncertainty Avoidance culture, he found a strategy that was successful in bringing about change.

Individualism/Collectivism and OD Interventions

Hofstede (1980, Hofstede & Hofstede 2005) described this dimension of national culture as the extent to which people believe they should be primarily responsible for themselves as opposed to the collective. Countries with high Individualism cultures, such as the U.S. and Britain, look to OD for interventions that will promote personal initiative, such as executive coaching and the development of performance appraisal and reward systems to promote individual productivity (Fagenson-Eland et al., 2004). There has been an explosion of executive coaching services in these countries in recent years,[3] and this trend is likely to continue.

Countries with high Collectivism cultures value allegiance to one's own group or family rather than individual achievement. I had a chance to learn the hard way that a direct focus on career development is not very effective in high Collectivism culture, unless put in the context of the family or group, when I was hired to be an executive coach to a Thai man who was identified for the "fast track" by the American company for which he worked. After some initial relationship building with him, I began our coaching work the way I usually do by asking about his career goals. I hit an unfamiliar brick wall when he would not discuss his career goals with me, and realized I needed to suspend my cultural assumptions. When I explored his cultural and religious beliefs, he explained that he felt it would be disrespectful to his family to selfishly focus on career goals for himself. When I asked him what he thought his family would like, he was able to say that he thought his family would be proud if he was acknowledged by his company for his talents. By learning to dance with his cultural context, I was able to help him identify some ways to ensure that his talents were noticed in a U.S. company. He felt comfortable with this approach, as long as the focus was on having his talents acknowledged for his family's sake, and not for pursuing individual gain and material success.

Hofstede and Hofstede (2005) note that most of the world's cultures are collectivist, and individualist cultures are the exception (p. 79). In collectivist cultures, motivating and developing employees is best done in groups with a team-based focus and rewards, unlike in individualist cultures where individual coaching may be the intervention of choice. Interventions such as team building should also be approached differently in collectivist and individualist cultures. An example of a collectivist approach was a team building project that I conducted in Tanzania for the Catholic Church for groups of Western and Tanzanian nuns who were not working well together because of their cultural differences. The team building approach that I used was sub-group based. I did not ask individuals to express any opinions, other than to report out the work of their small groups as a representative. Grounding the work in their oral tradition, the African nuns developed dances and songs to describe their values and goals for serving their communities, and the Western nuns did the same. Then they talked about what they had learned about each other. Mixed groups of African and Western nuns then developed dances and songs and other representations of shared visions about how they would work together in the future. Strong relationship bonds and shared visions were developed that greatly improved their collaborations after the workshops. In an Individualist culture, as in low

Power Distance cultures, I would ask individuals to speak for themselves during team building, using individualist group work techniques such as round robins and straw polling. This is one example of the dance for practitioners where modification of OD practices that reflect the culture can make the difference in whether or not the intervention is successful.

Masculinity/Femininity and OD Interventions

The fourth dimension of national difference identified by Hofstede and Hofstede (2005) is the Masculinity/ Femininity dimension. They explain that, "a society is called *masculine* when emotional gender roles are clearly distinct. Men are supposed to be tough and women are supposed to be tender. A society is called *feminine* when emotional gender roles overlap: both men and women are supposed to be modest, tender, and concerned with quality of life" (p. 120). This was the only one of the four original dimensions where Hofstede (1991) found a systematic difference in the answers between women and men (p. 82). While he agrees that gender is socially constructed, he notes that, "the effects of both nationality and gender cultures on our mental programming is largely unconscious . . . (and) we learn their consequences so early that we never knew anything else, and we are usually unaware of other possibilities" (p. 85).

Hofstede and Hofstede (2005) note that cultures high on Masculinity value overall achievement, rapid advancement, and high earnings. Work is central in these cultures and people live to work. Fagenson-Elan, et al., (2004) found that coaching and career development are OD interventions that work well in both high Masculinity and high Femininity cultures, but the focus is different. In high Femininity cultures, people work to live, rather than living to work. Masculinity/Femininity cultures differ in their values around achievement versus work/life balance. People in Femininity cultures believe they can have successful careers and have a life. Examples of high Masculinity cultures are Italy, Japan, the United States, and Mexico. Sweden, Norway, and Thailand are examples of high Femininity cultures.

With the entry of large numbers of women into the workforce and into the ranks of management in the U.S. over the last 30 years, pressure has mounted to change organizational cultures in the U.S., which are traditionally high Masculinity cultures, to reflect higher Femininity values. OD consultants have been involved with major culture change interventions to help make organizations more inclusive of these, and other minority values. Various structural interventions have been introduced that reflect Femininity values, according to Hofstede's definition. Work/Life balance programs that allow for flexible work hours, job sharing, and family leave programs have been created, but have not been fully embraced.

I frequently hear a lament from women clients in Masculinity cultures about the lack of work-life balance in their organizations. I have had women clients from the US, Mexico, Columbia, and India complain bitterly about wanting both a career and a family, but being forced to choose one or the other by the policies and practices of their organizations. By contrast, these problems don't exist for my women clients in Sweden and Thailand. In a recent leadership workshop with young women MBA's in India, a medium-high Masculinity culture, I found myself challenged when the women pleaded with me for answers about how to have both careers and families when they were expected to work 60 hour weeks. I know that these values are deeply entrenched in Masculinity cultures, and that change will not occur from individual solutions. I encouraged these young women to join together in their organizations to create enough voice and presence to raise issues and propose solutions to create more family-friendly work environments. I also strongly encouraged them to support the advancement of women leaders who could leverage their positions to bring about change for other women.

These changes, like all culture change efforts, require systemic analysis, long term vision, and persistence (Litwin & O'Brien Hallstein 2007). Western OD practitioners can also help give voice to these issues where they have not been considered. As a Western woman, I always listen for all of the minority voices in an organization, including the women, and try to represent them to the parent company. I also know that because I am an American woman, I am often dismissed as "one of those American feminists" who are seen as "creating problems" when I report on the complaints of female employees. Nonetheless, I feel it is important to use my position as an external consultant to amplify the subordinated voices.

Long-Term/Short-Term Orientation and OD Interventions

The fifth dimension of national culture, identified by Hofstede and Bond (1988), is Long-Term versus Short-Term Orientation. Hofstede and Hofstede (2005) explain that the Long-Term Orientation (LTO), "stands for the fostering of virtues oriented toward future rewards—in particular, perseverance and thrift" (p. 210). Some other characteristics of LTO cultures are that work and family life are not separated, personal connections in business are essential, long term gains are the focus, the good of the whole is important (p. 225). The Short-Term Orientation (STO) is defined by Hofstede and Hofstede (2005) as, "the fostering of virtues related to the past and present" (p. 210). Some characteristics of STO cultures are that work and family life are separate, personal loyalties vary with business needs, short-term profits are the focus. The six strongest LTO cultures are identified by Hofstede as China, Hong Kong, Taiwan, Japan, Vietnam, and Korea (South). Brazil and India follow close behind. European countries fall in the mid range, and the U.S., Britain, and other Anglo countries score on the short-term side.

LTO cultures are ideally suited for culture change efforts because these interventions require patience and long periods of ambiguity. I remember a Chinese colleague explaining to me about the silliness of the U.S. position on Taiwan, relative to the view of the situation from China. He explained to me that there was only one China, and that Taiwan would eventually return to the fold. His exact statement stays with me as an example of LTO thinking. He said, "it may take another 100 years for Taiwan to return, but in the context of our 5000 year history, 100 years is nothing. We can wait." By contrast, I refer back to the culture change effort that I described as underway in the U.S. around the Masculinity/Femininity dimension. Because the U.S. is a STO culture, the persistence is lacking that is required for sustainable culture change.

Other Findings on OD Interventions

Of course, there are examples of OD interventions that do not fit neatly into Hofstede's five dimensions. Yang (2002) notes that currently popular OD interventions such as 360 Feedback, or multi-rater feedback, is not used in countries such as Taiwan, where "saving face" is valued more highly than receiving feedback to correct performance. Burke (2002) also found that conflict resolution, as practiced in the U.S. with direct confrontation, does not translate to Japan, where third-party go-betweens are used to resolve conflicts. Chin (1997) reports on the effectiveness of using Appreciative Inquiry in Asian countries, such as China and Japan where, again, "saving face" is very important.

The study authors (Fagenson-Eland, Ensher et al., 2004) also found that interventions such as team building, which reflect the values of a high Masculinity culture, were not highly utilized in countries such as South Africa, Ireland, and New Zealand where protracted internal conflicts have existed between specific groups. Even though the study authors predicted that team building would be commonly used in these three countries with high Masculinity cultures, the entrenched conflicts made

the use of team building unsafe, pointing out why the political context must be considered in designing interventions (p. 459).

The Role of Values for the OD Practitioner and the Client in the Global Context

As can be seen from the discussion of Hofstede's (1980; Hofstede & Hofstede 2005) dimensions of culture and the application of OD interventions, it is values and the way they are held that define culture, and differences in values that determine when and what type of OD intervention is or is not appropriate. In addition, the field of OD itself is values-based, and originated in the West. OD practitioners must continue to ask the question noted by Fagenson-Elan et al. (2004) as posed by Harzing and Hofstede, ". . . how much do OD values reflect U.S. values . . . and how transcultural are they"? (p. 461) What is the dance we must do around values to leverage OD's strengths in the global context and help develop healthy and thriving organizations? As we have seen, people in high Power Distance cultures expect leaders to know what's best and do not expect openness or transparency, and people in high Uncertainty Avoidance cultures do not feel comfortable with confrontation and tension. Collectivist cultures focus on the needs of families and groups, not on the needs or rights of individuals. Cultural values need to be respected and acknowledged if OD is to add value in these cultures.

A strength of OD has always been that it is values-based. As practitioners we must be sensitive to the cultural context we are working in while grounding our work in values that can guide us to make honorable and ethical decisions that help create healthy organizations. As in any dance, there are many possible configurations of dancers. In this case, the partners are the OD practitioner and the national or organizational client cultures. You may each have learned different rhythms regarding values that have taught you different steps. It can be very helpful to partner with an in-country colleague who can be a cultural guide and can show you the steps and interpret the rhythms of the culture you are in. We must also each figure out how far we are willing to go in changing our own dance in order to be effective.

While there are many factors to consider, frameworks can provide a useful starting point for cultural sensitivity in determining appropriate use of OD interventions in a global context. Key things to keep in mind are:

- Most of the world's cultures are Collectivist, not Individualist as in the U.S.
- Each practitioner needs to start with understanding of her own cultural beliefs and how they differ from those of other cultures
- Inquire constantly about what things mean. Don't assume you understand what is going on when working in other cultures.
- Partner with an in-country colleague who can be a cultural guide.

OD continues to have a great deal to offer in the global context, and Western OD consultants can contribute to the global marketplace. The art, however, is in the dance.

References

Burke, W. W. (2002). *Organization change: Theory and practice.* Thousand Oaks, CA, Sage.

Chin, A. L. (1997). Internationalizing OD: Cross-cultural experiences of NTL members. Alexandria, VA: NTL Institute of Applied Behavioral Science Monograph.

Fagenson-Eland, E., E. A. Ensher, et al. (2004). Organization development and change interventions: A seven-nation comparison. *The Journal of Applied Behavioral Science,* 40(4): 432–464.

Hofstede, G. (1980). Motivation leadership and organization: Do American theories apply abroad? *Organization Dynamics,* 9(1), 42–63.

Hofstede, G. (1991). *Culture and organizations: Software of the mind.* New York, NY: McGraw-Hill.

Hofstede, G. (2001). *Cultures consequences.* Thousand Oaks, CA, Sage.

Hofstede, G., & M. H. Bond (1988). The Confucius connection: From cultural roots to economic growth. *Organizational Dynamics,* 16(4), 4–21.

Hofstede, G., & Hofstede, G. J. (2005). *Cultures and organization: Software of the mind* (2nd Ed.). New York, NY: McGraw-Hill.

Litwin, A. H., & O'Brien, H. (2007). Shadows and silences: How women's positioning and unspoken friendship rules in organizational settings cultivate difficulties among some women at work. *Women's Studies in Communication,* 30(1), 111–142.

Yang, T. (2002). *Interdependent self, power distance, face saving concerns for others and their relationships with attitudes toward upward appraisal in Taiwan.* New York, NY: Columbia University.

End Notes

1. Hofstede and Hofstede (2005) are careful to note that, "strictly speaking, the concept of a common culture applies to societies, not to nations," which are historically recent creations. (p. 19) Yet they also note that "nation" is often the only feasible criterion for the purposes of classifying and comparing. They caution that we maintain awareness of the differences that can exist within a national boundary. For example, India contains groups speaking fourteen major and three hundred minor languages as well as multiple religious and ethnic groups. Generalizations are, obviously, difficult to make, but have some utility at the same time if mindfully done.

2. Personal communication with David Green.

3. Based on membership in the two largest professional coaching organizations, International Coaching Federation and Coachville, the number of executive coaches globally was well over 50,000 in 2005.

CHAPTER 75

Organization as Community

What We Have to Learn from the Maasai About OD

John J. Scherer, with Kakuta Ole Ole Maimai Hamisi

The Challenge: Our Built-In Western OD Biases

As the history of our field unfolded, most of our OD ancestors were white males from America and Western Europe. They were extraordinary men like Frederick Taylor, Kurt Lewin, Wilfred Bion, Ken Benne, Warren Bennis, Ed Schein, Herb Shepard, Dick Beckhard, Ron Lippitt, and others. All white. All men.

Many of our well-known and mostly linear organization change and leadership models developed by these pioneers *do* work in non-Western, non-white male cultures, *but many do not*. What an effective organization looks like in our world is, in many respects, nothing like what an effective organization looks like in other worlds. As Jared Diamond proved in *Guns, Germs and Steel* (1997), we in the West cannot simply write off the way people in less-developed cultures do things. These less-developed people, in fact, have much to teach us.

For example: you want to learn something about how to maintain an effective and sustainable organization? Take a look at ancient cultures that have been surviving, even thriving, for centuries, often in the face of life-threatening challenges. Puts those things that cause a slight dip in market share into perspective.

In recent years, I have come to learn about effective, sustainable organizations, about lead-

ership—and about life—from my experiences with the Maasai of Merrueshi, Kenya, where my friend and brother, Kakuta Hamisi, resides most of every year.

The Basic Concept: Western Managers Meet Maasai Wisdom

Several years ago, after meeting Kakuta, he and I decided to invite a small group of clients, colleagues and friends to travel to his community of Merrueshi, Kenya, for a unique experience. Working with Crooked Trails, a Seattle-based eco-tourism company with a solid reputation and a strong connection to Kakuta, we planned the ten-day trip. The concept was that during the day we would work side-by-side with the Maasai in constructing a building to house faculty for the school Kakuta was creating for his people in the middle of the bush. In the evenings, we would gather with Kakuta and reflect on what we were learning.

What we learned changed lives and enriched or shifted several of my sacred principles of organization development.

One example: During one of our early morning walks into the surrounding Savannah, Kakuta picked up a slim stalk of a plant and asked one of our group to break it—which they did easily. Then he gathered a bunch of the same size stalks in his hand and asked us to break them. Even with great effort, we could not break the group of stalks. *"One is weak. Three or four are strong,"* he said. *"This is how we teach our children the power of community."*

You rarely see a Maasai man or woman standing alone. They are always in twos or threes. Building a hut, for example, is the entire community's responsibility, where each villager steps forward to help (like the Amish communities in America). Even the Maasai children in school sit beside a friend on a bench built for two. It reminded me of one of my mentors, Herb Shepard's favorite sayings: "Never send *one* when *two* will do."

As we learned more about how the Maasai have survived for centuries in harsh, forbidding conditions with such grace and joy, it became apparent that they have a secret. That secret also explains how some of the familiar aspects of our Western world and its organizations, like jealousy, greed, ego-driven competitiveness, sarcasm, criticism, self-centeredness and fear of failure, simply don't exist for them. It is that same secret that allows them to solve problems and keep the difference between the Haves and the Have-Nots (e.g. who has the most cattle, or goats, or pots, or tea cups) from being a divisive thing. Those differences are present, but Maasai people rarely navigate off those distinctions.

Their Secret: Profound Respect for the Community

It would not be unusual for a Western organization member, especially a leader, to operate with inner programming along the lines of:

What will be the impact of what I am about to do on my career?

Among the Maasai, that would be highly unlikely. They would be much more likely to ask themselves:

What will be the impact of what I am about to do on my community?

Community survival comes before anyone's interest in self-preservation.

Even at the personal level, the individual Maasai man or woman—or child for that matter—would think long and hard about doing something that would threaten the well-being of the community. The preservation of the community comes first, last, and always. That might help explain why they have little crime, or theft, or rape, or other community violence. My colleagues and I left valuable equipment in our open hut all day and never had a thought about not finding it when we came back. Why? Because stealing would cause potential harm to the fabric of their community and is therefore ruled out.

The Individual and the Organization

It seems as if the Maasai get their identity from belonging to their group. They live in the *we* much more than the *me*.

Among the Maasai it is hard to spot what we would call possessiveness, as in, *'That's mine!'* Even when I traded my binoculars to one of the warriors, he held them lightly, as if it were his to take care of on behalf of the entire community, rather than his to possess. The binoculars might hang on Kwenya's belt for a while, then be used by Kobole, then Loolpapit, but they belong to whomever need them. Just as our own Native Americans/First Nations people did not consider land a thing to be owned, the Maasai seem to hold things as belonging in some way to the community first, and then to them personally—to hold on behalf of who might require it at some future point.

They act as if they are stewards of what is in their world. I am sure they see things they would like to have access to, or use, but that impulse doesn't override their respect for the community and what might happen if they became self-centered.

My OD colleague, Lynnea Brinkerhoff, on one of the trips to Merrueshi, reminded me that one significant difference with the Maasai (as is true with other indigenous peoples) is that *a sentence worse than death for them would be to be ostracized from the group.* They know they will never be separated from one another—unless they do something that puts the group at serious risk.

Leadership: A Functional Model

Suffering for almost a year from a terrible cattle-killing and life-threatening drought, they continually offered us tea made from their precious goat's milk. In the Western world, one might expect a constricting of generosity and a more self-concerned stance in the face of such scarcity. And conflict over who had what. But not here. The things that precede conflict in our culture, usually driven by a scarcity fear of some kind—like loss of status, control or resources—simple aren't an issue among the Maasai.

One example: when Kakuta is not in his Kenyan community (he commutes back and forth from Seattle, where he has a base of operations), other Warriors step up to lead and make decisions. The power structure shifts to adjust to his absence. After two or three months, when he comes back to the community, you might expect his fellow warriors to feel a little put out: *"Oh, here comes Mister Big Shot, bringing in all the people and showing them everything he knows. While he was gone in America, I/we've been here, taking care of everything. Who does he think he is?!"* On the contrary. Each morning, when we would go out on our little morning walk before breakfast (sometimes 4–5 miles!), the other warriors joyfully stepped aside and allowed their respected brother, Kakuta, to take the lead. The flowing back and forth of leadership appeared seamless and without rancor.

The Maasai Conflict Process: *Do You Want Peace?*

But let's say two people do have a conflict that they have not been able to resolve. *This in itself would be rare.* The elders would go to Person A and say, *"Do you want peace?"* Then to Person B: *"Do you want peace?"* Kakuta tells us, "There is only one right answer to that question! If either person says 'No' they will be gently but firmly escorted out of the community." Nothing, certainly no personal agenda, is more important to the Maasai than maintaining the community.

So, let's say they both say "Yes." At that point they are put in a hut (think of something about the size of one of your bedrooms) with 4–5 of their best friends with instructions to "work it out." Person A then gets to tell his or her version of the story, taking as long as it takes, with no interruptions. Then Person B tells his or her version, again with no interruptions.

At that point the friends start to speak among themselves, saying what they heard each of them say (Paraphrasing or Mirroring in our lingo), and working toward a kind of consensus as to what happened. What they are working toward is an agreement as to who will be the one to *yield.* It's not about who was *wrong,* but who must *yield,* a marvelous distinction! The friends make their decision known to the two people. Let's say Person A is told he or she must yield. Person A can appeal to the Elder(s) waiting outside if they choose. But as Kakuta explains it, the Elders almost always support the decision of their friends or send them back into the hut for more conversation.

When Person A agrees to yield, they have to give Person B one of his or her goats as a sign of their reconciliation. Now there are three kinds of goats in the herd, two special and one not-so-special: 1) Milking Goats (they have names), 2) Breeding Goats (they have names) and 3) Meat Goats, which will be eaten—and do not have names. Person A must give Person B one of their goats with a name. (This is the origin, by the way, of the expression, 'He got your goat.')

Thereafter several things happen: First, no one brings the issue up again. It is a done deal. Finished. Second, every time the two people encounter each other, they greet each other using the name of the goat: "Hey, how is Susie?" thus reinforcing the reconciliation—for themselves and the community. Finally, their respected place in the community is *completely* restored. There is no such thing as guilt-tripping in the Maasai world, no put-down laughter, no sarcasm or ridicule, no holding on to an issue.

Management, Leadership, and Two Types of Time

One afternoon I traded my wristwatch, binoculars, a Swiss Army knife, and some Kenyan dollars, for a Maasai spear and a shield. Even though I knew it was for a good cause, letting go of my favorite Triathalon Watch was a little hard. The warrior must have intuited this, because after some coaching me on how to hold these ancient weapons, he reached down to the blanket where all his family's items were, and handed me a beautiful beaded bracelet.

As he put it on my wrist, he said, with Kakuta translating, *"John, this is a Maasai wristwatch! Now you will always know what time it is!"*

As an Eagle Scout with some wilderness and military experience under my belt, I immediately started thinking about how he's probably next going to show me how to stand a toothpick or small twig on the little blue dial and use the shadow made by the sun to tell the time. But his "instructions" not only surprised me, they *rattled* me. . . . Pointing to the bracelet, the Warrior smiled and said, *"Look, John . . . It's time to be doing exactly what we are doing right now!"*

I can't tell you how powerfully that struck me. Suddenly, I deeply understood something about Time that I had known intellectually for many years, starting with my study of ancient languages like Latin, Greek and Hebrew. About how we walk around with two kinds of time in our consciousness: Chronos (clock time) and Kairos (natural time). The technological Western world is based on—you could even say *addicted to*—Chronos (clock time). "It is 4:00 PM, therefore we must _____." The less technological cultures use mostly Kairos (natural time). "What does this moment require

from us now?" The ancient ones—before the invention of clocks—were moved through their lives by natural phenomena: Seasons, weather, the circadian rhythms, temperature, rain, and such. The well-known biblical passage from Ecclesiastes, made popular in the song, "Turn, Turn, Turn" by the Birds, is a perfect example of Kairos or natural time:

To everything there is a season and a time for every purpose under heaven—
A time to be born and a time to die,
A time to plant and a time to uproot,
A time to kill and a time to heal,
A time to pull down and a time to build up,
A time to weep and a time to laugh. . . .

Chronos (clock) time comes from the *outside in*. What is the clock or the calendar telling me?

Kairos (natural) time comes from the *inside out*. What does this moment "need" or suggest or require or demand. Here we don't look outside at a clock or calendar to determine what to do, but inside the moment, inside ourselves, inside the situation, to *learn* or *figure out* what to do.

Management and Leadership: Chronos and Kairos?

Standing there with my new Maasai friend, another thought struck me: Perhaps management is attending to Chronos things, and leadership is attending to Kairos things. . .

Interestingly, I never saw a Massai running (except children), never saw anyone looking anxious or late. Once, when a Maasai woman working beside me on the construction project accidentally dropped a large batch of small stones she had been meticulously picking off the floor, she simply smiled and started picking them all up again. You or I might easily have given out a spontaneous expletive and felt *something*—incompetent, stupid, clumsy? But she was working with Maasai time, making whatever it is that happens just that: what was happening.

As we were packing to leave on the last day in the community (a sad day for us all), I overheard Kakuta saying to some of the Warriors and the drivers of our Land Rovers, "OK, guys, let's get going! The airplanes in Nairobi do not run on Maasai time!" For everything there is a season— even for clock time in a Maasai village. . .

What a great lesson for us. As people responsible for managing other people and results—or even just making it through our day, we need to know how to master the clock (Chronos). That's management. AND, there are moments when we need to know how to look deeply into the situation in front of us and ask another question: *What does this moment tell us we need to be doing?* That's the essence of leadership.

Possible Lessons for Us as OD Consultants

- What would our client organizations be like if we framed everything we did with them in the larger context of
- *pulling together for the long-term wellbeing of the community?* How could such an organizational culture be created and reinforced?
- What if all the organization's stakeholders were held as crucial elements in that community: customers, leaders, managers, employees, vendors, even competitors?
- What if the organization's culture reinforced people holding what they had—status, perks, power, position, budgets, programs —*lightly* as if they were taking care of them on behalf of the entire organization or community?
- What if there was no word for orphan or outcast in our client organizations? How would people be let go (perhaps with great respect)?
- What if our clients and we saw that everyone in the organization—*because* of their uniqueness, not in spite of it—had a contribution to make?
- What if we cared so much about community that we would not rest until our clients and we found a way to connect each person to that community, and empowered them to make their contribution?

It's a long way from Merrueshi, Kenya, to where you and I live and practice OD. These images may seem quaint, naïve, Utopian, even ridiculous to home, yet I find myself drawn to them, wanting to reach for them in my OD practice—and in my own life, believing that the reaching is itself a form of having them.

CHAPTER 76

Creating High Impact Organizations in the SADC

Adapting OD Methods and Practices

Mambo G. Mupepi, Ram V. Tenkasi, Peter F. Sorensen,

and Sylvia C. Mupepi

THIS ARTICLE discusses the opportunities for organization development (OD) that exist in the Southern African Development Community (SADC). The premise of our discussion is that American management concepts of OD provide applicable incentives and means to change international organizations, and these applications can be localized. Organizations operating in Africa face a myriad of socio-economic problems that can lead to resistance to change; OD methods and technology are especially applicable because they enable organizations to recreate themselves within their context and grow. OD is flexible, offering African organizations greater sustainability in varied environments.

The article contains four discussions. In the first, we give an overview of the socio-economic background of the countries that make up the SADC and highlight some of the values these countries share. In the second, we review some of the literature pertaining to change management and current OD practice. In the third, we look at some current issues faced by organizations in the SADC region and make suggestions for how OD ontology may be used to unleash innovation and facilitate change. Finally, in the fourth section, Sum-

mary and Suggestions, we discuss research and issues.

The Socio-Economic Background of the SADC

The SADC is a new organization having been created in the late 1980s as a forum to develop effective trade and political dialogues among the member states. South Africa and Namibia are latecomers to the organization and the business has expanded amidst many economic problems some of which can be addressed by deploying organization methods that advance efficiency. We seek to answer the following questions:

1. What are some of the factors that must be considered when deciding what OD concepts apply in the SADC, and
2. Given those tools, how might they be applied?

Scholarship and practice in the OD field can be adapted and used in the context of local knowledge and practice, in particular within such socio-economic environments as the SADC. OD has been described by many practitioners such as Warren Bennis (1966); French and Bell (1999); among others. Bennis views OD as a complex strategy intended to change the beliefs, attitudes, values, and structure of organizations so that they can better adapt to new technologies, markets, and challenges. French and Bell (1999) emphasize that effectiveness in organization arises when there is a planned change effort which must emanate from the top going to all systems in the organizational structure. They assert OD is a continual process that focuses on the organization's culture, activities and structures deploying a total systems perspective. Organizations in the SADC need to embrace change as they move from a colonial, apartheid and state-controlled economic past to a democratic future in which free markets advance innovation and progress.

The Composition of the Community

The SADC is made up of 12 independent southern African countries: Angola, Botswana, The Democratic Peoples' Republic of Congo, Malawi, Mozambique, Namibia, South Africa, Swaziland, Tanzania, Zambia, Zimbabwe, and the Indian Ocean islands of Mauritius and Seychelles. All these countries share a legacy of colonialism. Each was a colony of Belgium, England, Germany, or Portugal. Colonialism began with the Dutch in the 16th century followed by the Portuguese, the English, and the Germans—all disrupting the cultural equilibrium by their introduction of western civilization. Present boundaries separating these countries, villages, kingdoms, and cultures were designed and effected at the Berlin Conference held in 1888 (Weinstein, 2001).

Lewin (1951), treating the organization like a living organism, argues that the organization must take cognizance of its environment for survival. The Community of Practice (COP) can co-construct and craft organizational capabilities in relation to the environment in which it operates. Etienne Wenger's (1998) breakthrough research in group dy-

namics concluded that COPs are a group of people who share the same pursuits and often meet regularly to share their passion. Wenger acknowledges that because of their ability to discuss and learn work-related issues, COP's can affect performance. The COP can create an organizational culture that will find the most effective means of installing desired core values into the hearts and minds of each member of the organization. It will be in a position to create and disseminate explicit knowledge about what the organization does. A competitive advantage can be developed in this manner as well. The aim of OD is to make organizations effective at their businesses by improving the understanding of the relationship between the cultural environment, the organization, technology, and the economy.

A number of OD concepts can enable the SADC to effectively address the developmental needs of the region, position itself to meet the challenges of the dynamic, ever-changing complex globalization process, and take advantage of the opportunities presented by globalization.

OD Ontology Applied

In *Leadership Lessons from Emperor Shaka Zulu the Great,* Madi (2001) highlights management principles that were fostered by the military leader Emperor Shaka Zulu (1787-1828), such as getting to know and understand the problem, collectively constructing a sense of mission, leading the change from the front and building a fanatical team. This historical context fits well with Action Research. Organizations that get to know their customers well serve them better.

Spiritual Leadership

Another military leader in the region at the time of British occupation was Mbuya Nehanda, a woman whose spiritual leadership spanned the entire region of Zimbabwe, Mozambique, and parts of Namibia, Botswana, and South Africa (Mutswairo, 1978). Mutswairo argues that Nehanda's abilities to lead, mobilize, and sensitize the people concerning the culture, values, and property of the African people led to the First Chimurenga War (1890-1898), in which she was the Commander in Chief. He states that those beliefs and practices are still resilient in local cultures throughout the region (1978:13). Other scholars such as Bhebe and Ranger (1991) argue that the influences and recruitment methodology of Mbuya Nehanda were adopted in the Second Chimurenga War (1966-1980), leading to victory and creation of the modern state of Zimbabwe. Mutswairo (1978) and Mudenge (1986) discuss the importance of African traditional practices and how leadership such as that provided by Nehanda and Mapondera used the drive derived from African values and traditions to defend themselves against invaders. Culture and values are critical factors in OD practices. The way a people learn is important. Successful change can happen when learning has taken place. Narratives play a pivotal role in African organization learning. African narratives define the spiritual, health, and work practices, and virtually all aspects of daily life. Knowledge of these histories, beliefs, and practices enables management to fine tune performance in an organization.

Socio-Economic Background

The socio-economic background of this region is critical to the understanding of any measures to introduce change. Although the practice of apartheid was only in South Africa, discrimination, however, was practiced throughout the SADC states prior to self-rule. While, apartheid has been dismantled, Mbeki (2005) argues that discrimination is still embedded in organizations throughout Southern Africa, organizations in which the colonialists had a majority stake.

In the same report, President Mbeki states that employment in the formal non-agricultural business sector increased in the second quarter of 2005 creating 131,000 new jobs, an increase of 1.9% of the estimated number of employees in that sector, with many of these new jobs requiring fairly sophisticated skills. Capacity building will entail technology–knowledge transfer in all sectors, particularly mining and manufacturing. Although there is no more overt discrimination in the region to prevent anyone from learning new skills or pursuing higher education and training, the question of resources arises. In addition, the labor market is growing faster than the combined economies can create new jobs. Furthermore, in some states such as Zimbabwe, the issue of land redistribution has caused many farmers, who normally employ the majority of rural populations, to leave the country. This turbulent socio-economic context provides significant opportunities for productive OD intervention.

Democracy: Improving Health and Quality of Life

Political freedom in African countries is easily swayed by external forces such as financial or food aid, International Monetary Fund borrowing conditions, and the influence of the old colonial masters in other aspects of the economy. Hoogeveen (2005) believes that democracy—not the mechanics of elections, but the quality of life and freedom supposedly characteristic of democracy—is also of concern in many member states, especially in Zimbabwe. OD methods and technologies, because of its capacity to increase productivity and efficiency, can help address some of the causes of poverty and disease facing the region. Therefore OD is important as a means to address long-term growth, prosperity and quality of life.

Democracy and Equal Opportunity

Aspirations to and practices of democracy exist in these sovereign states, and the end of apartheid has empowered millions of blacks and other previously marginalized races such as Indians and Coloreds (mixed races). All types of businesses are now open to a new breed of entrepreneurs whose education, training, and learning needs vary from basic business plans to sophisticated business strategies. Tapping successfully the region's entrepreneurial renaissance may bring long-term rewards for all the countries involved. Of course, facilitating these second-order changes has been lucrative for OD practitioners, particularly those connected to international accounting firms, multinational corporations, and aid organizations operating in the region. As organizations improve productivity with the help of OD, the field also expands when such organizations grow.

A Focus on Competency Development

Training and development to enable those that were underserved to do their jobs effectively takes precedence. This initiative is crucial in the transformation of any economy. With the many theories that range from social constructivism to learning mental models, there are no other professionals better equipped to deal with this transformation other than OD practitioners. In occupations such as education, health and mining, the region, particularly in Zambia and Zimbabwe, is faced with increasing numbers of capable people leaving to seek greener pastures elsewhere. Such relocation shows little confidence in local organizations, and the result is a brain drain and a loss of invaluable human capital. Central governments need to develop incentives to stop such a migration very quickly. Lawlessness and lack of investment returns and incentives to keep skilled workers are obstacles to the practice of OD. It will be imperative for organizations to work with local institutions and OD experts to devise plans for building and diffusing explicit organizational opportunities.

Literature of Change Management OD Practices

Current literature provides the context for the adaptation and application of OD methods and techniques in the SADC. Measurement of the distribution of knowledge, expertise, and practices of an organization is the starting imperative for effective management design, and it involves effective evaluation technology and methods. There are many OD methods and technologies that can be adapted to improve productivity, and make better organizations.

Socially Constructed Competency Model (SCCM) A Strategy for Developing Capabilities

This method of change management is based on the premise that collective intentionality expressed through one voice of the Community of Practice (COP) enables the co-construction of organizational reality. The SCCM method was developed at Benedictine University. Mupepi et al (2005) suggest that the communities within the organization construct, create, and legislate what constitutes expertise, fitting and relevant technology, practices and behavior, and they are the only group of people who can validate an organization's reality. They suggest that the social context in which an organization operates has an important bearing on how teams and communities of practice will succeed in their goals. Knowledge and practices index the situation in which they arise and are used. The SCCM makes it possible to collectively identify explicit knowledge, skills, and the technology necessary for organizations to accomplish specific goals. The SCCM can be deployed to assess organizational culture and the results used to realign the people to the mission. While OD offers many methods and choices of interventions that can make organizations efficient, the SCCM offers an added advantage of enabling the development of hopes and dreams for the future focusing on organizational strengths and capabilities. Each SADC state might have different and varied natural resources. For example, Angola has more crude oil and diamonds than any other state, while South Africa has a bit of everything including mineral and manufacturing resources. The situation in which each organization finds itself will ultimately determine the capabilities necessary for its success.

Relevant Cutting-Edge Change Methods

Identifying the Prevalent Culture

Schein (1992) states that culture is a phenomenon that surrounds us all and it is important to understand it before devising any change initiatives. He argues that having this knowledge helps us understand how culture is created, embedded, developed, manipulated, managed, and changed. It also helps us to understand leadership, management and the organization.

Assessments and Measurements of Organizational Culture

Capacity building in developing countries implies that local people should be empowered to create and implement their own policies best suited to their own conditions. But before a subject community is empowered to do something, managers need to identify the performance gaps to enable a complete competency plan.

Dimensions of Culture

Hofstede & Hofstede (2005) identify five dimensions of culture as Power Distance, Individualism vs. Collectivism, Masculinity vs. Femininity, Uncertainty avoidance and Long vs. Short Term Orientation. They argue that in most countries there is a power distance between those who have the power and those that do not have it. This distance can be assessed and a high score suggests that there is an expectation that some individuals wield larger amounts of power than others. A low score reflects the view that all people should have equal rights. Countries with high power distance ratings are often characterized by a high rate of political violence. Some countries such as Zimbabwe have shown more political violence at each general election meeting. Others,

like South Africa, have accepted equal rights and there is less political violence than before.

While OD practitioners may chose to concentrate on the assignment at hand, such unfair practices may "put spanners in the works" of change efforts. There are many OD methods of introducing and managing change. Assessing each situation separately enables the OD practitioner to select the best intervention method.

Other Relevant Techniques

Process Consultation (PC)

An understanding of what the organization does is crucial to the implementation of successful change programs. Schein argues that PC will help to identify the cultural make-up of the organization. Once the variables are identified, it will be easier to assess the extent and distribution of knowledge, attitudes and practices, and to reframe the organization using the identified strengths and weaknesses. Process consultation compels the practitioner to incorporate the technical information in the system to make meaningful changes. It is a way of getting deeper into the reality of the desired change. Schein (1987:4) asserts that working in the present reality and understanding the ebb and flow of the new knowledge as it shifts from one operation to another within the structure will bring better perspectives of how change should be articulated.

Appreciative Inquiry (AI)

One of the most effective and well-established ways through which knowing communities can facilitate change is by using AI, a dynamic change management method originally developed by David Cooperrider and colleagues at Case Western Reserve University. Since then, the method has been perfected by many other scholars/practitioners, including Peter Sorensen of Benedictine University, Illinois, U.S. (Mupepi, 2005:14). The method focuses on those aspects of an organization that are functioning at their optimum. AI philosophy of positive psychology enables the community to share a concern about current and future potential performance. The positive past enables the organization to co-construct a better future.

Future Opportunities for OD Application

Competency Development

The dismantling of segregation policies has led some of the proponents of apartheid to leave the region, and forced governments to promote ill-prepared indigenous candidates. Organizations may need competency development strategies to maintain high quality products and services and to continue exporting to the Anglo-American markets where quality is much more important than price.

Given the arguments drawn from the social construction philosophy, there are opportunities for and the need to conduct research on culture, productivity, diversity, work ethics, learning and group dynamics in different settings as these will differ from those of the West. But, these are all critical if indigenous talent is to be successful.

Some Barriers to Change Management

Illiteracy remains the biggest hurdle to introducing and sustaining change, especially in rural populations. Communicating in written languages is a major challenge. OD may not have solutions for all problems, but many interventions available may enable a community to identify and appreciate the problems and issues that are important, and be able to find solutions using the lenses of the community of practice. Emulating the traditional ways of learning and training, effective communications about what matters to the community can be facilitated through narratives of hope and success. The illiteracy in the Zambezi Valley of Zimbabwe is one of the many challenges faced by all types of organizations. The importance of phonics in reading, group interactions,

and the sharing of information cannot be overestimated. This approach will certainly be the way forward given that attitudes and practice form the basis of adult learning. Barnett & Storey contend that illiteracy rates are high and governments are giving directives for black advancement as well as offering citizens opportunities for continuing education and training where workforce reading and writing, and health and safety education take precedence over other learning programs. There is a clear need for workforce education and training. Literacy in these communities varies from 40-45% to 85-90%.

Innovation and Enabling Legislation

The rule of law is important for any form of organization to take place. Organizations need a safe environment to do business and one of the perquisites for innovation to take place is free market systems where individuals may take calculated risks in the development of new ideas and methods. Organizational innovation involves the creation or alteration of business structures, practices, and models, and may therefore include process, marketing and business model innovation. This may require organizations to be more transparent and accountable to the stakeholders, something that is lacking in the region at present.

The Skills Development Act in South Africa and Manpower Development Act in Zimbabwe are examples of strategies aimed at encouraging investment in education, training, and raising funds for apprenticeship and supervisory education The opportunities that arise as a result of equity and employment legislation are team building programs, performance management interventions, organization assessments, and human awareness. In addition, management training has been made compulsory by other legislation such as the Health Safety and Manpower Development Acts making employers responsible for nondiscriminatory human resources development at all levels for all races.

Summary and Suggestions

Democracy's introduction has called for organizations to be more accountable, transparent, and self-reliant. The most important challenge for the SADC organizations is to develop democratic and transparent organizations that embrace the dreams of the people and to remain accountable to the electorate. Fighting corruption and maintaining transparency in all aspects of organizational life appear to be challenges faced by leadership in the region. Indeed these are critical obstacles to change. African scholars argue that it is not only lack of transparency, but crises such as those happening in the Congo Basin of the DRC, Rwanda, and Burundi and in Zimbabwe that have a negative effect on the continent as a whole. These problems discourage international investment. Democratic processes, ethics, and governance are topics that can partially be addressed in the field through leadership and supervisory development programs. The SADC offers a unique opportunity for understanding the African concept of social construction encompassing continuous learning and improvement through strategies developed by the COP. The result is that OD can offer appropriate advice based on a variety of theories, including grounded theory that is appropriate within the society of the SADC.

Future Research

Action Research through AI

Cross-cultural research that can be facilitated by the use of AI may enlighten practitioners as they continue to work with diversified communities locally and globally. Cultural research through the medium of AI enables practitioners to identify some of the reasons why people in organizations may resist change. AI is one of OD's interventions that has been used successfully around the globe. AI can be used to assess what the organization knows, what it needs to know, and what it wants to accomplish, as well as charting the way to satisfy those needs.

Productivity and Motivation

Research could seek to answer the following questions: Do people from Malawi work harder and better than those from Zambia? Is there a difference between what motivates these two communities? If there is, what is the difference? Why is development in rural areas slow at best or non-existent at worst, given that the vast majority of people reside in these very same rural areas?

Problems and Issues Encountered in Integrating People of Different Cultures

The convergence of different cultures means that different problems will arise as groups are combined. It becomes necessary to find different forms of governance to develop new boundaries as new authorities, languages, and customs emerge. These become an obstacle to change. The opportunities for research are immense. One way to facilitate the introduction of cutting-edge change management approaches would be to contact authorities from each individual organization or each country's embassy and seek permission to conduct organization development research.

References

Bennis, W. G. (1966). *Changing organizations.* New York; McGraw-Hill.

Bhebe, N., & Ranger, T.O. (1991). *The soldiers in the Zimbabwe's liberation war.* Harare, ZM: Heinemann.

Blake, R.R., & Mouton, J.S. (1964). *The managerial grid.* Houston, TX: The Gulf Publishing Co.

Boland, R. J., & Tenkasi, R. V. (2001). Communication & coordination in distributed cognition. In G. Olson, T. Malone, & J. B. Smith (Eds.), *Coordination theory.* New York, NY: Lawrence Erlbaum & Associates, Inc.

Brown, J. S., & Duguid, P. (1991) Organizational learning and communities-of-practice: Toward a unified view of working, learning and innovation. *Organization Science,* 2(1), 40–57.

French, L. W., & Bell, C. H. (1999). *Organization development: Behavioral science interventions for or-*

ganization improvement. 6th Edition. Upper Saddle River, NJ: Prentice-Hall.

Hofstede, G. H., & Gert, J. H. (2005). *Cultures and organizations software of the mind.* New York, NY: McGraw-Hill.

Hoogeveen, J. G. (2005). Measuring welfare for small but vulnerable groups: Poverty and disability in Uganda. *Journal of African Economics,* 14(3), 503–531.

Lewin, K. (1951). Field theory in social science. New York, NY: Harper & Collins.

Library Congress Information. (2001). Keys to the kingdoms: New illustrated guides to the Library's African Middle Eastern collections available. *Library Bulletin,* 60(10), 233.

Madi, P. M. (2001). Leadership lessons from Emperor Shaka Zulu the Great. *The Academy of Management Executive,* 13(3), 141–142.

Mbeki, T. (2005). Re-defining political engagement. *ANC Today,* 5(24). Available from http://www.anc .org.za/ancdocs/ anctoday/2005/text/at48.txt

Mudenge, S. I. G. (1986). *Christian education at the Mmutapa court. A Portuguese strategy to influence events in the Empire of Munhumutapa.* Harare, ZM: Zimbabwe Publishing House.

Mupepi, M. G., Tenkasi, R. V., & Sorensen, P. F. Jr. (2005). *Building effective entrepreneurs into sustainable organization.* Proceeding of the Eastern Academy of Management, Cape Town Business School, South Africa.

Mutswairo, S. M. (1978). *Mapondera, soldier of Zimbabwe.* Washington, DC: Three Continents Press.

Schein, E. H. (1992). *Organizational culture and leadership.* San Francisco, CA: Jossey-Bass.

Schein, E. H. (1987). *Process consultation revisited: Building the helping relationship.* Boston, MA: Addison-Wesley.

Tenkasi, R. V. (2002). Some contextual antecedents of cognitive oversimplification processes in R&D environments. In H. Tsoukas & N. Mylonopoulos (Eds.). *Proceedings of the Third European Conference. Athens Laboratory for Business Administration,* Athens, Greece, pp. 35–48.

Weinstein, J. (2001). Scramble for Africa; Lessons of a continental war. *Peace Research Abstract* 38(5), 603–751.

Wenger, E. (1998). *Communities of practice: Learning as a social system.* Available from www.infed.org/ biblio/ communities_of_practice.htm

CHAPTER 77

Addressing the Global Virtual Competency Gap

Steve Gens and Deb Torchia

Introduction

Globalization and organization virtualization are driving the exponential growth of global virtual work environments faster than most organizations can develop the competencies required to effectively manage the increased operational complexity. Having the competency to effectively manage global virtual complexity typically has not been viewed as a strategic lever to increase performance; however this is changing as organizations continue to struggle with facilitating cultural differences, effective virtual teaming, and establishing productive collaboration methods with external partners. Overcoming these obstacles requires a more focused strategic approach that proactively develops and applies relevant cultural and virtual skills across the organization in a way that integrates those skills into the day-to-day execution of work. Organizations that do not take this strategic approach often struggle with execution of their global business and operational plans, significantly reducing the likelihood that predicted business results are achieved.

Attaining Global Virtual Competency

Through our client work and continuous research, we have identified a core set of interde-pendent competencies (see Figure 77.1) that are required for people to successfully work together productively in this new and permanent global virtual environment. This competency framework can be applied at an organization, group or individual level, and can be used as a diagnostic tool, an educational aid, or as a development roadmap. The framework enables an organization to strategically focus on the specific levers to pull (green boxes) that will improve overall organization performance and business results. Initially it focuses on developing individual and interpersonal competencies to form the foundation for highly effective leadership, cultural competence, and appropriate technology use.

Individual awareness is a key underpinning of global virtual competency as the more conscious we are of our own and others' personal style and preferences, the more we are able to adjust our interactions with them to ensure more positive and productive outcomes. Increasing emotional intelligence and actively using self-awareness to appropriately adjust one's style to the situation at hand is a crucial first step toward developing global collaboration skills.

Being culturally competent means much more than just being aware of national and organizational differences, it means having the skills and ability to facilitate the co-existence of cultural differences to proactively manage the

FIGURE 77.1 Gens and Torchia Global Virtual Competency Model

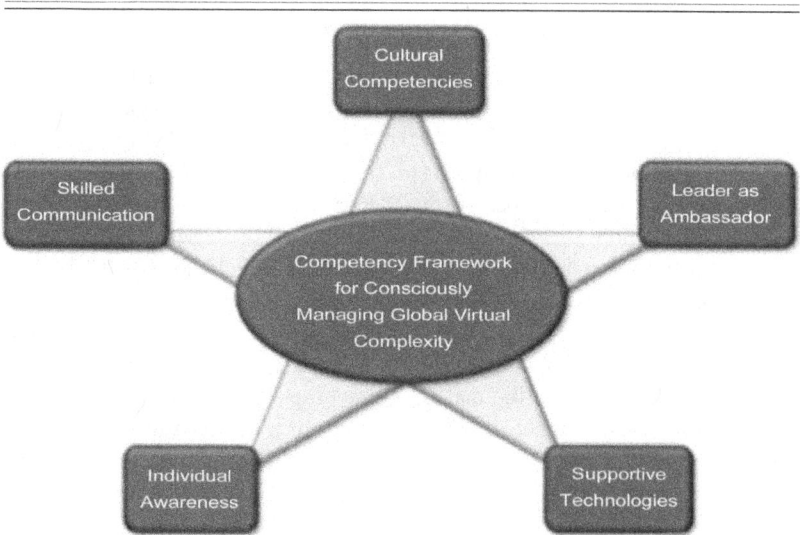

inevitable dilemmas global or virtual teams create. For example, there are many resources available to gain knowledge of individual countries' customs and protocols, however leading or facilitating teams that are comprised of multiple cultures, requires having the competence to establish collaborative group processes that work for all involved. Team dynamics are magnified in these environments so it is important to establish productive processes for new team formation, goal alignment, communication, decision-making, negotiation, and conflict resolution, just to name a few.

Having high individual awareness and cultural competence alone will not serve team members and leaders well if they are unable to communicate effectively with their colleagues. Skillful communication in global or virtual environments is all about taking the time to provide proper context, build shared meaning, and ensure that group members understand each other's contexts. Skillful communicators also balance advocacy with inquiry knowing that more creative and insightful realizations occur when people combine multiple perspectives. This requires the ability to communicate clearly - taking care to make evident the mean-

ing or lack of meaning - to ensure everyone is talking about the same thing whether in a tele-conference, video-conference, web-conference, or e-mail correspondence where visual cues are absent or minimized.

Effective leadership in global virtual teams requires an "ambassadorial" style and approach. These leaders are liaisons to group members and are highly competent in "bridging" geographic, cultural, and generational boundaries. This new leadership style fosters trusting, productive relationships among group members and supports the development of high performing teams. These leaders provide guidance around intentions and larger goals helping the group to form a collective identity that is recognized by others and aligned to the goals of the organization. They demonstrate cross-cultural resourcefulness and agility by respecting different value sets, encouraging other viewpoints, and leveraging cultural diversity to enhance innovation and outcomes.

The ever-changing technology landscape gives organizations many options to support working virtually and globally. The right application of technology is often dependent upon the business situation and cultural makeup of a team. It is important to consider team dynamics, cultural preferences, and the project stage (beginning, middle, or end). This will guide technology choices of voice-only, web collaboration spaces, video-conference, point-to-point video (e.g., Skype), or some type of combination. For example, a team comprised of French, Korean and U.S. members with established working relationships could most likely conduct a new project kickoff session over the phone or by web-session. Although the French and Koreans are more relationship based than their U.S. counterparts, their already established working relationship makes this technology a viable choice for their situation. Alternatively, if the same group did not have an established relationship, a technology choice of multi-point video conference would be appropriate since "social presence" or the degree to which the technology facilitates a "personal connection" would be a high priority.

Conclusion

The rapid pace of change driven by globalization and working virtually is forcing organizations to develop strategies to quickly build a critical mass of global virtual skills and capabilities. This requires a consulting-based approach that leverages both Organization Development (OD) methodologies and leading management practices to build lasting global virtual competence. The application of transformational change methodologies and a combination of appropriate business tools, processes, and training support increases adoption and raises commitment levels to ensure a successful outcome. This combined approach enables organization members to translate awareness and knowledge into positive actions that will enable them to proactively manage day-to-day complexity and attain desired behavioral changes. This gives OD practitioners the opportunity to be a strategic partner with the business.

CHAPTER 78

OD 2.0

Shifting from Disruptive to Innovative Technology

Kathleen Iverson and George Vukotich

PRIOR TO THE INTERNET, the last technological innovation that had a significant effect on the way people sat and talked together was the table (Shirkey, 2003). The web has transformed the way we communicate, learn, and work, and in the very near future, it will transform the way we practice organization development. In their second annual survey of Web 2.0 use in business, McKinsey reported a 25% increase in application adoption in just one year (Bughin, Manyika, & Miller, 2008). Their use of these technologies is also expanding from the sales and marketing arena to employee engagement. Organizations are using Web 2.0 tools to recruit, onboard, and develop their workers.

Web 2.0 technologies including blogs, wikis, social networking sites, and virtual worlds are more personalized and interactive than first generation web applications (Web sites and e-mail) and offer opportunities for proactive participation, sharing, connectivity, and collaboration, the very underpinnings of OD practice.

As leaders in planned change, we can have significant influence over how organizations reinvent themselves in terms of performance and culture as they form a virtual identity. Practitioners must be comfortable enough with new technologies to support their use as communication tools, virtual work environments, and community building (Feyerherm & Worley, 2008). While Cyber OD presents new opportunities for consultants to increase organizational effectiveness using virtual technology, this expanding frontier requires the development of new methodologies to address the unique challenges it brings (Speake, 2008).

As many organizations implement internal social networking applications (Bersnen, 2008), they will be looking for guidance in how they might best utilize these technologies to facilitate change and improve organizational functions. They are looking for opportunities to implement widespread, global change quickly and efficiently. With greater emphasis on cost reduction, Web 2.0 technologies offer the opportunity to expand communication and interaction anytime, anywhere, allowing practitioners to reach members virtually. Team-building, product development, knowledge sharing, and relationship building, are just few of the processes that can be enhanced by Web 2.0 technologies (Bersin, 2008). Consultants are often asked to bypass the diagnosis and assessment stages (Feyerman & Worley, 2008), but corporate blogs, wikis, nings, and other virtual sources of communication can offer rich data that can provide a valuable source of information about an organization and its members' beliefs and practices. By combining evidence based research and practical application we will explore this emerging field, developing a framework of OD 2.0 implementation

From Disruption to Innovation

In its infancy, Web 2.0 was viewed as another distracting element; a toy for college students and Gen Y workers that took them away from the important aspects of school and work. Nearly anyone with an Internet connection can be a web developer, creating wikis, blogs, virtual identities, even live a second life in a virtual world. The architecture of participation created by Web 2.0 moved the "average Joe" from the passenger's seat to the driver's seat of web knowledge creation. Over time, we learned from early mistakes and found ways to channel the capabilities of Web 2.0 technology to facilitate learning, innovation, and relationship building.

Web 2.0 tools allow employees at Dell, Starbucks and IBM to connect with each other to share ideas and information and form communities. IBM also uses social networking to capture expertise throughout the organization and 3M uses it for the sharing of ideas and research information among experts (Bersin, 2008). IBM's internal social networking site, the "Beehive," enables employees to create social networks and collaborate with fellow employees across the globe. Gensler, Honeywell, and Nestlé are using both external (You Tube) and internal streaming video to communicate culture, teamwork, and share best practices.

Web 2.0 has gone beyond blogs, wikis, and video to include a virtual world known as Second Life where conferences, learning and social networking events are hosted by hundreds of organizations as diverse as Harvard University, IBM, and Cisco. Participants create avatars and communicate with words and gestures. IBM is deeply involved in Second Life, using it as a medium to reach customers and connect staff. They are one of the first corporate users of Second Life to develop an enterprise system that allows its users to not only meet publicly, but to also move behind their

corporate firewall to hold private sessions. Their IBM Academy holds multi-day virtual conferences that include many of the same components of a traditional conference including poster sessions, break out sessions, interactive training and discussion.

Another Second Life success story involves Margaret Regan, a diversity consultant who has created an island for her FutureWork Institute where she hosts diversity workshops and networking sessions. Participants can experience diversity first hand by inhabiting an avatar that differs from their own age, race or gender.

Table 78.1 contains a list of Web 2.0 applications and their potential uses in OD practice. Although this list is not exhaustive, it is good starting point for those who want to learn the talk or delve deeper into the various technologies. When working with clients who are currently utilizing Web 2.0 technologies, consultants must treat the technology as they would any other organizational practice, first assessing its contribution to organization function and then considering how it might best be utilized to support the change initiative.

Although interest in Web 2.0 value is building, and our chronicle of best practices grows, to truly understand the foundational issues of this phenomenon, we must move beyond examples to theory. As we move from disruption to innovation, we must find a theoretical landscape with which we can examine the benefits of Web 2.0 applications.

Theoretical Context

Social networking theory provides a rich context to examine Web 2.0 practices. Social networks are the formal or informal connections among people. Originated in the field of sociology, social network analysis has recently become more popular as Web 2.0 has evolved. Social networks are ties of goodwill, mutual support, shared language, shared norms, trust, and a sense of mutual obligation that add richness and value to our lives. The people in the networks are called nodes and their relationships are ties. Perhaps the most fascinating

TABLE 78.1 Web 2.0 Tools Mapped to OD Practice

Web 2.0 Tool	OD Practice	
Blog: User-generated website where entries are made in journal style and displayed in a reverse chronological order. Blogger: www.blogger.com Typepad: www.typepad.com	· Knowledge management · Sensing and assessment · Data collection · Culture building · Communication	· Project collaboration · Visioning · Building trust · Organization Alignment
Wiki: a website that allows the visitors themselves to easily add, remove, and otherwise edit and change available content, typically without the need for registration. Wikipedia: www.wikipedia.org PBWiki www.pbwicki.com Wetpaint www.wetpaint.com	· Communication · Project management · Knowledge building	· Collaboration · Consensus building · Visioning
Folksonomy: Collaboratively create and manage tags to annotate and categorize content. Metadata is generated not only by experts but also by creators and consumers of the content. Delicious: www.delicious.com Furl: www.furl.net	· Knowledge management · Consensus building	· Project management · Mentoring
Social Networking: Websites that focus on community, encourage interaction, discussion, debate, offer public member profiles and user-generated content LinkedIn www.linkedin.com Facebook www.facebook.com Ning www.ning.com	· Relationship building · Mentoring · Teambuilding	· Building trust · Onboarding
Twitter: Communication tool that lets users publish updates under 140 words to answer the question "What are you doing?" via tweets. published on their website, IM, browser, or mobile phone Twitter www.twitter.com	· Project management · Communication · Performance management · Assessment	· Feedback · Networking · Relationship building
Video Sharing: Users can upload, view, and share video clips You Tube: www.youtube.com Meat Team: www.meatteam.tv	· Communication · Teambuilding · Group process · Knowledge management	· Culture building · Visioning · Storytelling
RSS Feeds: Allows you to stay current with all your favorite news, blogs and feeds--in one place Bloglines www.bloglines.com Google Rdr www.google.com/reader	· Communication	· Knowledge management
Slide sharing: Share your powerpoint presentations publicly or privately, search thousands of presentations or join groups Slideshare www.slideshare.net	· Project management · Knowledge management	· Best practices
Virtual Worlds: Build a 3D virtual world and explore, meet other residents, socialize, participate in individual and group activities, and create and trade property and services with one another, or travel throughout the world. Second Life www.secondlife.com Vivaty www.vivaty.com	· Meetings · Conferences · Team building · Group process	· Culture building · Training · Networking · Onboarding

findings regarding social networks are the theories of weak ties and structural holes. When we move outside our typical landscape of relationships we receive greater benefit from the non-redundant information these "weak ties" provide (Granovetter, 1973). We further benefit from ties that span "structural holes" or the gaps in networks because they support the importing and exporting of new information and ideas between groups (Burt, 2000). Technology can support the formation of weak ties by connecting members across groups through blogs and internal social networks. Structural holes can be spanned virtually when members of different organizations connect in public blogs, social networks, or virtual worlds.

Social capital is defined operationally as the resources embedded in social networks that are accessed and used by individuals (Nin, 2002, p. 25), or the product of rich networks. Social capital has been linked to a variety of positive outcomes such as better public health, lower crime rates, and more efficient financial markets (Adler & Kwon, 2002). Participation in social networks allow us to draw on resources from other members of the network and to benefit from connections with multiple social contexts by sharing information, job opportunities, relationships, and organizing of special interest groups (Paxton, 1999). Executives who were educated to use networks to build social capital were significantly more likely to get top performance reviews, be promoted, and be retained by their company (Burt & Ronchi, 2007). As OD practitioners, we can not only facilitate the development of rich social networks among our clients, but also amongst ourselves. By connecting professionally via Linked In, developing our own blogs, creating and building wikis and nings, we not only connect with colleagues but can share our knowledge and promote our field.

Web 2.0 technology provides unlimited opportunity to span structural holes and create ties, both weak and strong, with internal and external constituents around the globe. No longer limited to the physical water cooler to form relationships and share knowledge, workers can now interact virtually with members anytime anywhere. Those who telecommute are no longer invisible, but can create a strong virtual identity that makes them a highly visible and valuable organizational member. Knowledge sharing in the Web 2.0 organization will become viral, spreading from person to person, spanning organizational lines and geographic barriers.

Although research and theory on social networks and social capital in virtual environments is in its infancy, a few studies had prom-

ising results. College students who participate in an online social network site demonstrate a robust connection between usage and indicators of social capital (Steinfield & Lampe, 2007). In the context of learning environments, Web 2.0 applications are excellent vehicles for experiential learning activities such as case studies due to their collaborative nature (Huang & Behara, 2007) and may support lifelong learning by connecting people in borderless collaborative environments (Klamm et al., 2007). Safran, Helic, & Gutl (2007) emphasized the potential of Web 2.0 to uphold critical and analytical thinking, facilitate intuitive and associational thinking, support analogical thinking through easily accessing to rich information and interacting with diverse opinions.

To respond quickly and nimbly to rapid change due to technological innovation and economic downturn and recovery, organizations must be able to generate, analyze, support, and communicate new ideas and practices beyond the borders of time and space. They must be able to foster collaborative thinking and action at every level of the organization. Web 2.0 technologies, though not an end all answer to every organizational challenge, can provide an additional arena for collaborative knowledge sharing, idea generation, and dissemination.

As Web 2.0 applications move from the disruptive to innovative, there are still drawbacks that must be addressed. Concerns about privacy, transparency, and a decline in face-to-face communication are of immediate concern as we expand virtual communication networks. In the following section we will explore the drawbacks of Web. 2.0 adoption.

The Dark Side of Web 2.0

There are several risks involved in implementing Web 2.0 practices. First, and perhaps foremost of concern is the need for privacy. We may erroneously assume that because we are communicating virtually, that we are invisible, but in reality, the privacy of individuals who use public social networks is limited. Many companies are using information posted by their members in online social networks (OSN) to make employment decisions (Genova, 2009). Although the legality of this practice is under debate, it is becoming common practice for organizations to scan OSNs when making decisions about hiring or promotion. In addition to concern about member privacy, organizations are also concerned about maintaining control of proprietary information, fearing that corporate secrets will fall into the hands of competitors, or that the organization image might be damaged by inappropriate comments. Next, as firms outsource more OD processing to third party vendors, extra care must be taken to protect the identities of those that provide information. Questions also come into play regarding who actually owns the data that

is provided and for how long it will be stored in various databases.

To control for these potential risks, best-practice organizations develop a clear policy statement about appropriate use and behavior of Web 2.0 tools. For example, IBM has developed a clear policy on social computing (www.ibm.com/blogs/zz/en/ guidelines.html) and found that group norms have controlled potentially negative communication.

Figure 78.1 contains a diagram that assesses both the transparency (public domain) and involvement (creative opportunity) of various applications. Some activities like listening to podcasts, viewing webinars, contributing to folksonomy, and managing RSS feeds are neither particularly transparent nor do they involve a lot of creative contribution on the part of their users. On the other hand, participa-

FIGURE 78.1 Web 2.0 Applications and Levels of Transparency and Creator Involvements

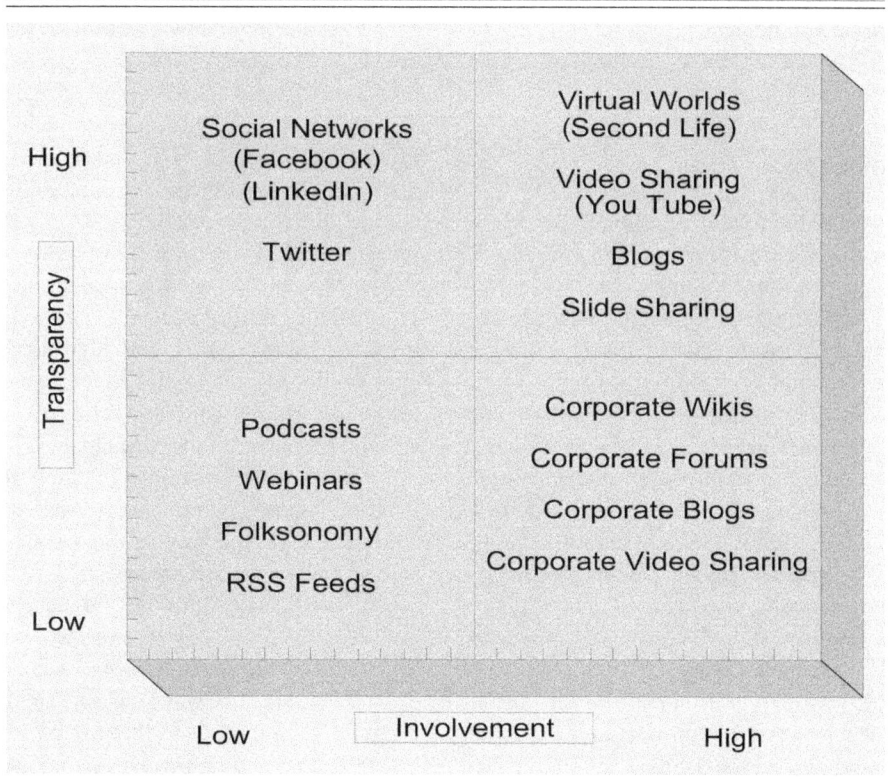

tion in applications such as Second Life, blogs, producing You Tube videos, and slide development can be highly transparent and also highly involving. Organizations can reduce the transparency of some of these applications by adopting an enterprise Web 2.0 system that limits public access.

Not only are social networks changing the way we do business, they are also changing the way we communicate and connect with others. As we spend more time communicating virtually, we have less time to connect in our physical worlds. As electronic media use increases, time spent in face-to-face social interaction decreases (Sigman, 2009) and this lack of social connection can affect our emotional and physical well-being. Although other researchers present a positive view of socialization and internet use (Shapira, Barak, & Gal, 2007), we must be cautiously optimistic about virtual communication, ensuring that we do not lose track of our first life by spending too much time in Second Life.

Next we will examine a framework for initiation and implementation of OD 2.0 applications with a focus on both potential benefits and limitations.

Initiation

The initiation of Web 2.0 technologies due to its open and participatory nature readily lends itself to an action research process. The "felt need" that triggers organizational change initiatives is evident in the widespread use of the social networking applications in our society. As we look for ways to bridge the gaps of time and space, we turn to social networks to create connections that would otherwise be impossible. It is only a matter of time until these new venues for communication permeate organizational practice. Web 2.0 is also *pull technology* by nature. People who are excited by it use it, and get others excited, creating the opportunity for emergent change.

As we initiate Web 2.0 practices in organizations, we might submit them to the spiral of steps and the circle of planning, action, and fact finding that defines action research (Burns,

2006, p. 140). For example, we might look carefully at how group communication changes when it takes place in a blog as opposed to a face-to-face meeting, noting the benefits and deficiencies of each mode. Participants become co-researchers engaged in cogenerative dialogue as they ask questions to guide their understanding (Elden & Levin, 1991). Questions that guide action research such as "was it ethical, democratic, collaborative?" and "did it solve practice problems or did it help us to better understand what will not solve our problems?" will provide insight and guidance as we explore and learn about these technologies.

Implementation

If action research indicates a need for a broad or full scale adoption of Web 2.0 practices, then a framework for implementation can provide structure to the process (see Strategy, Policy, Process, and Application in Figure 78.2).

First, focus on developing a strategy and vision for the adoption of Web 2.0 technologies. Consider how it will contribute to the overall organizational vision and mission. Information gathered from action research during the initiation stage can provide rich data to guide this process. This information will drive the features, function, specifications and benefits of the technology that you choose to provide a unified mission and overarching goals as you move forward with the implementation. You might use a scenario planning approach to "test" the feasibility of various strategies. You may also develop a business case for the implementation, further communicating the value added components of the technology.

Next, it's time to consider the application. First and foremost, consider ease of use. Those who are active in public social networks, blogs, and virtual worlds are accustomed to platforms that are highly intuitive and user friendly. Internal delivery systems must mimic the simplicity of Facebook, Blogger, and Wikipedia if they are to be widely accepted and utilized. Consider tools that will comply with the current infrastructure and that can be customized to fit your need.

FIGURE 78.2   Web 2.0 Implementation Framework

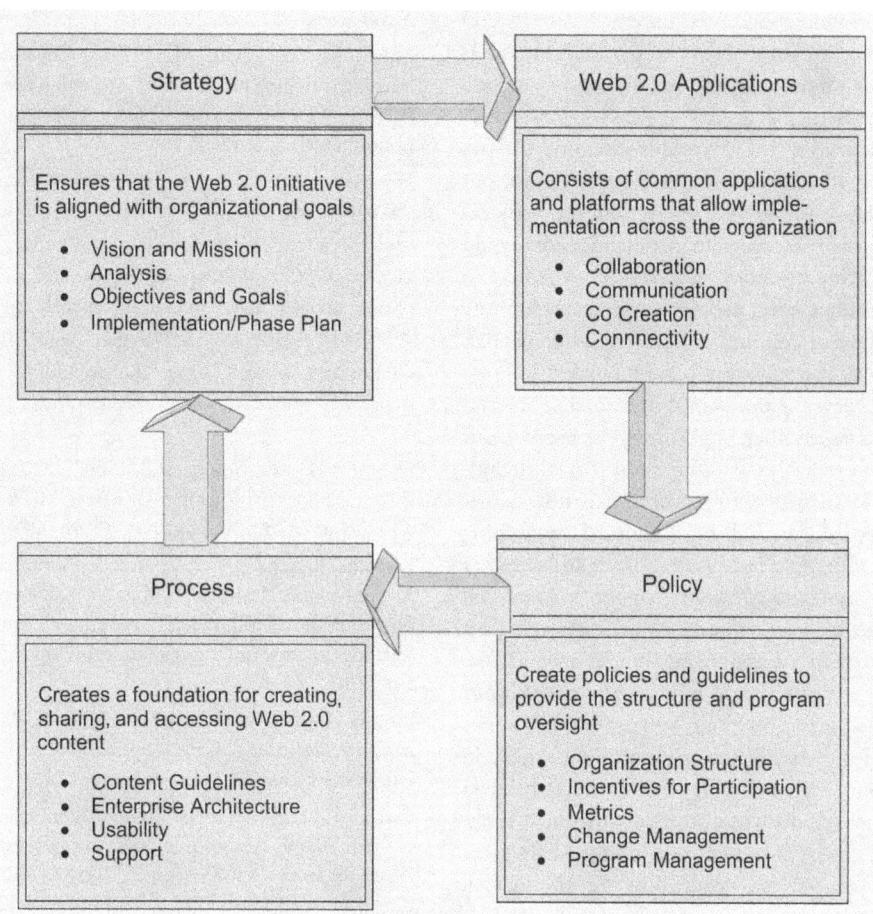

When you consider the policies that will guide the implementation and management of the Web 2.0 system, first think of how you will garner buy-in from top management and organization members. An infrastructure must be in place to shepherd the system and incentives must be available to encourage participation. Just because you build it, don't assume they will use it. Empty blogs, wikis, and virtual worlds will become wastelands without the active involvement of members. If collaboration and collective participation were part of your initiation process, then active involvement should follow.

Finally, think about process or how the system will operate. Consider whether you will adopt a complete enterprise system or will have some opportunity for public connection outside the organization. Also, think about how much freedom members will have to create their own content and use the tools to create special interest groups. Also consider how information will be tagged and catalogued so that future users will have quick and easy access to knowledge creation.

As we initiate and implement new social networking technologies, we must continue the planning, action, and fact finding process. Just as we can't understand an organization without trying to change it, we can't understand technology without continuous improvement.

Conclusion

As technology becomes more pervasive in OD practice, we must always keep in mind that it is nothing more than another tool and that good OD whether delivered in face-to-face conferences or in a virtual world is still good OD no matter the delivery system. Yet we cannot put our heads in the sand and ignore the Web 2.0 revolution no more than our ancestors could ignore the invention of electricity. It is here to stay and its effect on the way we communicate will be dramatic and pervasive. As professionals who are committed to continuous learning, we must view the new world of virtual social networks as another opportunity to expand our area of expertise. If you are not part of the online social network explosion, it is time to get on board (see Table 78.1); start by joining LinkedIn; get a Facebook account and see what your teenagers (or your neighbor's teenagers) are up to; visit some blogs or start your own blog; create an avatar and wander around Second Life; add to a Wiki or create one of your own; at least check out Twitter; and of course, You Tube. As you become more comfortable in our new virtual world, consider ways that you might enhance your practice with these tools. Start slowly, document your results, share them with others, and contribute to the overall knowledge base of this exciting new frontier.

References

Adler, P., & Kwon, S. (2002). Social capital: Prospects for a new concept. *Academy of Management Review, 27*(1), 17–40.

Bersin, J. (2008). Social networking and corporate learning. *Certification Magazine, 10*(10), 14.

Bughin, J. Manyika, J., & Miller, A. (2008) Building the Web 2.0 Enterprise: McKinsey global survey results. Retrieved from http://www.mckinseyquarterly.com/building_the_web_20_enterprise_mckinsey_global_survey_2174

Burns, B. (2006). Kurt Lewin and the planned approach to change. In J.V. Gallos, & E.H. Schein (Eds.) *Organization development : A Jossey-Bass reader,* San Francisco, CA: Jossey-Bass.

Burt, Ronald S., & Ronchi, D. (2007). Teaching executives to see social capital: A field experiment. *Social Science Research, 36,* 1156–1183.

Elden, M., & Levin, M. (1991). Cogenerative learning: Bringing participation into action research. In W. F. Whyte (Ed.), *Participatory Action Research.* London, UK: Sage Publications.

Feyerherm, A., & Worley, C. (2008). Forward to the past: Reclaiming OD's influence in the world. OD *Practitioner* 40(4), 2–8.

Genova, G. (2009). No place to play: Current employee privacy rights in social networking sites. *Business Communication Quarterly,* 72(1) 97–101.

Granovetter, M. S. (1973). The strength of weak ties. *The American Journal of Sociology,* 78(6), 1360–1380.

Huang, C.D., & Behara, R.S. (2007). Outcome-driven experiential learning with Web 2.0. *Journal of Information Systems Education,* 18(3), 329–36.

Klamma, R., Chatti, M.A., Duval, E. Hummel, H., Hvannberg, E. H., Kravcik, M., Law, E., Naeve, A., & Scott, P. (2007). Social software for lifelong learning. *Journal of Educational Technology and Society,* 10(3), 72–83.

Lin, N. (2002). *Social capital: A theory of social structure and action.* Cambridge, UK: Cambridge University Press.

Paxton, P. (1999). Is social capital declining in the United States? A multiple indicator assessment. *American Journal of Sociology,* 105(1), 88–127.

Safran, C., Helic, C., & Gutl, C. (2007). E-Learning practices and Web 2.0. *Proceedings of ICL 2007* (pp 1–8). Villach, Austria.

Shirkey, C. (2003). A group is its own worst enemy. Retrieved from http://www.shirky.com/writings/group_enemy.html

Shapira, N., Barak, A., & Gal, I. (2007). Promoting older adults' well-being through Internet training and use. *Aging & Mental Health,* 11(5), 477–484.

Sigman, A. (2009). Well connected? The biological implications of social networking. *Biologist,* 56(1), 14–21.

Speake, S. (2008). Cyberspace and the OD Profession. *OD Practitioner,* 40(4), 60–61.

Steinfield, N., & Lampe, C. (2007). Spatially bounded online social networks and social capital. *Journal of Computer-Mediated Communication,* 12(4).

About the Contributors

Larry Ackerman is a leading authority on organizational and personal identity. He is the founder of The Identity Circle, a strategic consulting and coaching firm, and the author of two groundbreaking books: *Identity Is Destiny: Leadership and the Roots of Value Creation,* and *The Identity Code: The 8 Essential Questions for Finding Your Purpose and Place in the World.* He can be reached at lackerman@ theidentitycircle.com

Dean Anderson, MA, Co-Founder and President of Being First, Inc., specializes in developing executives and consultants into conscious and competent change leaders. Working with Fortune 1000 businesses, government organizations, and nonprofits, he assists clients to build integrated change strategies. As an advocate of co-creating, he works with senior executives using a high performance model, a way of being and relating to individuals to produce win-win solutions that serve both the organization and the individuals. He earned his Masters and Bachelors degree at Stanford University. He can be reached at beingfirst@beingfirst.com.

Linda Ackerman Anderson, MA, Co-Founder and Vice President of Being First, Inc., specializes in facilitating transformational change in Fortune 1000 businesses, government organizations, and nonprofits. During the past thirty years her practice has focused on strategy development for major organizational change using Being First's Nine-Phase Model for leading conscious transformation. As a coach to senior executives and change leaders, she encourages personal modeling of the changes they seek to create in their organizations. She earned her Masters degree at Columbia University's Teachers College. She can be reached at beingfirst@beingfirst.com.

Philip Anderson is the Director, Change Management/ Business Transformation at ManpowerGroup North America. Prior to his position at ManpowerGroup, he held global director positions at Johnson-Diversey, Inc., and Abbott Laboratories. His work has appeared in a number of publications in the OD field. He currently serves on the Advisory Board for the Center for Values-Based Leadership and the Editorial Board for the *OD Practitioner.* He can be reached at Philip.Anderson@manpowergroup.com.

Matthew Auron is a Director on DaVita, Inc.'s award winning Wisdom Team, responsible for OD, training, and coaching work on multiple levels of the organization. Prior to his work with DaVita, he was an Organizational Effectiveness Specialist with Los Angeles Universal Preschool (LAUP) as well as leadership coach and consultant under his own name. He holds a Master of Science in Organization Development from Pepperdine University. He can be reached at Matthew.Auron@davita.com.

Robert C. Barnett, PhD, is a Senior Fellow at MDA Leadership Consulting in Minneapolis, which he joined in 1985. As a consultant, he focuses on organizational development and change, M&A integration, team development, and executive assessment. Barnett has worked with organizations in a variety of industries including manufacturing, pharmaceuticals, healthcare, specialty chemicals, telecommunications, government, and education. He earned his BA and PhD from the University of Minnesota, and an MS in Organization Development from Pepperdine University. He can be reached at BBarnett@mdaleadership .com.

Jean-Pierre Beaulieu, MBA, is president of J-P- Beaulieu, Conseil en Gestion Inc. In his projects, Jean-Pierre favors the active involvement of internal and external partners in order to reap the benefits of the knowledge and experience available to the organization. He uses novel processes, which are adapted to today's organization demands and uses his long experience in large group dynamics. He is coauthor of *Mobiliser l'organisation face à son venir,* Gaëtan Morin 2000. He can be reached at: jpbeaulieu @sympatico.ca.

William Becker, MA, is the CEO of Strategic Business Resources in New York City with over 30 years of domestic and international experience in a range of industries, with medium sized companies to Fortune 500 corporations. He is a founding member of Future Search Network, an association promoting the application of Future Search Conferences. His OD practitioner experience spawned his book, *How to OD . . . And Live to Tell About It,* as well as articles appearing in the Manchester School of Business *Creativity and Innovation Management, M-World Resource Center* publications, the OD Network's *OD Practitioner* and on-line publication *Practicing*. He holds an MA from UCLA, was trained at NTL, and taught as an adjunct professor at three New York universities. He can be reached at wfbecker @verizon.net.

Geoff Bellman has been an OD consultant for almost all of his professional life, working inside and outside corporate America. He is one of the founders of the Community Consulting Project, a group of Seattle area consultants and learners who give their time to nonprofit organizations. Bellman is the author of six books on organizations, leadership, teams, change, and life. He is perhaps best known in OD for his book, *The Consultant's Calling: Bringing Who You Are to What You Do,* Jossey-Bass, 2nd edition, 2002. He can be reached at geoffbellman @gmail.com.

Michael Brazzel, PhD, CPCC, ACC, is an executive coach, organization development, and diversity consultant, economist, former manager in U.S. government agencies, and university educator-researcher. As an internal and external consultant, he has provided organization development and diversity/social justice services to organizations for more than 25 years. Brazzel is a member of the NTL Institute for Applied Behavioral Science, coeditor of *The NTL Handbook of Organization Development and Change: Principles, Practices, and Perspectives* (2006) and the *NTL Reading Book for Human Relations Training* (1999), and co-founder of NTL's Diversity Practitioner Certificate Program. His life's work is based in the values: respect for human differences, racial and social justice, and life-long learning. He can be reached at Brazzel@aol.com.

David S. Bright, PhD, is a professor at Wright State University in Dayton, Ohio, and he holds a PhD in Organizational Behavior from Case Western Reserve University. His research and consulting practices focus on Appreciative Inquiry, virtue based change, and emergent organizing. He can be reached at david.bright@wright.edu.

Gervase R. Bushe, PhD, is at the Beedie School of Business, Simon Fraser University and is an associate with the Centre for Creative Leadership as well as European and Asian Consulting Firms. His passion is planned, transformational change. In the last few years he's been working to transform public education in western Canada through appreciative inquiry, and the health care system in British Columbia through Clear Leadership. He's now working on a process for performance amplification in large businesses that's resulted in transformation in financial and HR outcomes in two different industries. Bushe earned his doctorate at Case Western Reserve. He can be reached at bushe@sfu.ca.

Leon E. Butler, PhD, is the CEO of the Delphi Network Inc. and Internal OD Consultant at the University of Maryland, Baltimore. Butler's work has included the design and implementation of change in public and private

systems, domestic and foreign. His practice includes strategic planning, diversity, conflict resolution, executive coaching and change management interventions. He received his doctorate from the State University of New York at Buffalo, and is a member of NTL Institute. He can be reached at delphinet@comcast.net.

Emile J. Carrière MS (USA, Canada), a former executive with organizations in Canada and the Middle East, leads consulting projects focused on establishing strategic direction and the management of implementation processes. He has an MS in Organizational Development from Pepperdine University, and is co-author of *"La Démarche Prospective."* He can be reached at EJCarrier@aol.com.

Veronica Hopper Carter, PhD brings experience as a psychotherapist to her work as a trainer of organizational consultants, emphasizing all levels of system. With over 20 years experience in the practice of Raj Yoga, she integrates spiritual principles, Gestalt theory and practice, and systems thinking into a base for her teaching. She is an associate of John D. Carter & Associates. She can be reached at VHCarter@aol.com.

John Conbere, EdD, is Professor and Director of the Doctoral Program in OD, Department of Organizational Learning & Development, College of Applied Professional Studies, the University of St. Thomas, Minneapolis, Minnesota. He can be reached at jpconbere@stthomas.edu.

Mark A. Chesler, PhD, is Professor Emeritus of Sociology at the University of Michigan and Executive Director of Community Resources Ltd. in Ann Arbor, Michigan. He is an activist scholar conducting research, teaching, consulting, and organizing on issues of personal/organizational change around social privilege and oppression. He can be reached at mchesler@umich.edu.

David L. Cooperrider, PhD, is the Fairmount Minerals Professor of Social Entrepreneurship at the Weatherhead School of Management, Case Western Reserve University where he is faculty director of the Fowler Center for Sustainable Value http://weatherhead.case.edu/centers/fowler. He is best known for his foundational theory on Appreciative Inquiry and has served as advisor to senior executives in business and societal leadership roles, including projects with five Presidents and Nobel Laureates. He is editor of both the *Journal of Corporate Citizenship* with Ron Fry and the research series for *Advances for Appreciative Inquiry,* with Michel Avital. In 2010 he was awarded the Peter F. Drucker Distinguished Fellow by the Drucker School of Management —a designation recognizing his contribution to management thought. His books include *Appreciative Inquiry: A Positive Revolution in Change* (with Diana Whitney); *The Organization Dimensions of Global Change* (with Jane Dutton); *Organizational Courage and Executive Wisdom* (with Suresh Srivastva). For more on Appreciative Inquiry see http://appreciativeinquiry.case .edu/ and www.davidcooperrider.com.

Barry Dym has founded four organizations, beginning with the Family Institute of Cambridge and, currently, the Institute for Nonprofit Management and Leadership (INML), housed at Boston University's School of Management. He is the author of four books, most recently, *Leadership in Nonprofit Organizations* and *Managing Leadership Transitions*. For over forty years, he has practiced organization development consulting, executive coaching, and psychotherapy. He can be reached at bdym@work-wise.org.

Adrienne Eaton, PhD, is Professor of Labor Studies and Employment Relations and Director of Labor Extension at Rutgers University's School of Management and Labor Relations. She holds graduate degrees from Ohio State University and University of Wisconsin. Her research on labor-management partnerships and worker participation has been published in *Industrial and Labor Relations Review, Labor Studies Journal, Advances in Industrial and Labor Relations,* and several book chapters. She has worked as a research consultant for the Coalition for Kaiser Permanente Unions focused on evaluation of the KP Labor Management Partnership since 1998. She can be reached at eaton@smlr.rutgers.edu.

Sue Eklund, EdD, is Principal Advisor, Change Integration Agency and Adjunct Professor, University of St. Thomas. Her background includes 25 years of human resource development and organization development. She has worked in education, nonprofit and spent several years in leadership positions in corporate training, global leadership and learning, and organization development in Dayton Hudson, Seagate Technology, and Ecolab. She has MA in Education Leadership from MN State University, and a doctorate in OD from the University of St. Thomas. She has served on community Board of Directors including the Webster Groves Chamber of Commerce, the College School, and the St. Louis Center. She is past Sustainer Board President for the Jr. League of Minneapolis and Advisor for Free Arts MN. She can be reached at sue.klund@gmail.com.

Sanyani Edwards, TLLP, is currently seeking a doctoral degree in Clinical Psychology (Psy.D.) from the Michigan School of Professional Psychology. He obtained a MBA and Organization Development degree from Bowling Green State University. He has served as a psychotherapist for several nonprofit organizations in the metropolitan area of Detroit, MI. He is currently an associate at Health Care Associates offering pro-bono services to practitioners facing biased Health Care fraud litigation. He also provides training and presentations to inform the health care community about unfair tactics used by the government to further a hostile agenda against doctors and other health care practitioners. He can be reached at sanyani@sbcglobal.net

Arthur M. Freedman, MBA, PhD, is a consulting organizational psychologist who has received many national and international awards for his contributions to the discipline. He is a founder and board member of the *World Institute of Action Learning*. He consults to public and private sector organizations throughout the globe. He is an Adjunct Professor at the *Carey Business School, Johns Hopkins University*. His many publications include *Action Learning for developing leaders and organizations,* co-authored with Michael Marquardt, Skipton Leonard, and Cori Hill (2009). He can be reached at arthurf@aol.com.

Connie A. Freeman is a passionate and committed senior leader with 20 years of HR/OD/LD experience who has consulted with both public and private sector organizations—including financial services, consumer products, pharmaceuticals, manufacturing, government, healthcare and education. Freeman is currently Senior Vice President, Consulting Solutions for Morehead Associates, where she is consulting with healthcare organizations on the impact of employee and physician engagement on organizational success. She earned her MA in Organization Communication from the University of Illinois and has achieved ABD status toward a Ph.D. She is currently on the Board of the new Strategic Leadership Forum—Carolinas. She can be reached at Connie.Freeman@moreheadassociates.com.

Judith Gail has worked in the applied behavioral sciences as an OD and Change Management practitioner for 18 years. She holds a Master of Science Degree specializing in Organization Development (MSOD), from The American University/NTL Institute for Applied Behavioral Science, in Washington DC. She also holds a BBA in Business Administration. Judith is currently writing a children's book that focuses on elementary age students and the personal dimensions of diversity. She lives in DC with her partner and is dedicated to experiences that make her laugh. She can be reached at judithbryant@consultant.com.

Stephen K. Garcia, EdD, is a Partner at Philosophy IB, a management consulting group that brings strategy to life by changing the way people work. He holds a BA and MBA from the University of Virginia and an EdD in Adult learning from North Carolina State University where his research focused on social networks, innovation and change. He can be reached at sgarcia@philosophyib.com.

Steve Gens has 25 years of business experience in the global biopharmaceutical and healthcare industries working with global virtual teams on critical strategic initiatives. He has a Master of Science in Organization Development with distinction for his field work, and is certificated in Organizational Change Management from the NTL Institute. He can be reached at sgens@gens-associates.com, or www.gens-associates.com.

Robert Goldberg was a Management Development Consultant with Ebasco Services Incorporated in New York.

Laurence J. Gould, PhD, was professor of Psychology and Director of the Psychological Center in the Clinical

Psychological Doctoral Program at the City University of New York. He received his PhD in psychology (1965) from the University of Connecticut. He was a National Institute of Mental Health post-doctoral fellow in psychology at Yale University (1966). He is a founding Director of the Program in Organizational Development and Consultation at The William Alanson White Psychoanalytic Institute; a founding member of the International Society for the Psychoanalytic Study of Organizations; past president and fellow of the A.K.Rice Institute; a principal of the firm Gould Krantz White, Organizational Consultation and Senior Consultant at the ACCEL Group, Inc.

David Grant, PhD, is Professor of Organizational Studies at the University of Sydney Business School, Australia. His research interests focus on organizational discourse theory and analysis, especially where these relate to leadership and organizational change. Grant has worked on research and consultancy projects in Europe, Australia, and Asia. He can be reached at david.grant@sydney.edu.au.

Matt Griffin, PhD, is an Organization Development practitioner with over 15 years experience in providing OD consulting expertise to help organizations improve effectiveness through strategic and cultural change. He currently serves on the OD team at Providence Health & Services, a large nonprofit health care system in the Western US, and as a volunteer consulting team leader with Community Consulting Partnership in Seattle. He can be reached at Matt.Griffin@providence.org.

Kakuta Ole Ole Maimai Hamisi, MA, is Founder and Managing Director of The Maasai Association, a community-based non-profit organization and NGO based in Bellevue, WA and Kajiado Central District of Kenya. The purpose of the Association is preserving the Maasai way of life while becoming participants in the technological age. A Maasai Elder and Warrior, Kakuta earned his Masters Degree in International Relations from The School for International Studies. He divides his time between Seattle and his beloved Merrueshi, the Maasai community deep in the bush of Kenya. For more about Kakuta's community development work go to www.maasai-association.org.

Dave Hanna is a principal with the RBL Group, a global professional services firm committed to creating value through the effective management of people and organizations. He has worked with Global 500 clients in every region of the world and is the author of two books and several articles on leadership and organization effectiveness. His latest book, *The Organizational Survival Code,* is in production. He can be reached at dhanna@rbl.net.

Thomas C. Head, PhD, is a Professor of Management and the Director of Accreditation for Roosevelt University's W. E. Heller College of Business. He is a prolific author with 17 books and over 75 journal articles to his credit on a wide variety of topics. His current interests lie primarily with global organization development and related practices. He has served on the boards of the Academy of Management's Management Consulting Division, The Midwest Academy of Management and Pro-Change International. He has served as the editor for both *The Journal of Pro-Change International* and *The Organization Development Journal.* He earned his PhD in Business Administration from Texas A&M University. He can be reached at thead@roosevelt.edu.

Alla Heorhiadi, PhD, EdD, is Distinguished Service Professor in the Department of Organizational Learning & Development, College of Applied Professional Studies, and Director of the Energetics Institute, the University of St. Thomas, Minneapolis, Minnesota. She can be reached at aheorhiadi@stthomas.edu.

Gina Hinrichs, PhD, worked for John Deere for over twenty years. She was the Quality Manager for Worldwide Harvesting before starting her OD Consulting business in the Midwest, U.S. in 2001. She earned an MBA from Northwestern University before earning her PhD from Benedictine University. Hinrichs is a professor for Capella, Benedictine, and Lawrence Technological University's online and resident programs. She can be reached at ghinrichs517@gmail.com

Larry Hirschhorn is a principal with CFAR, a management-consulting firm with offices in Philadelphia, PA, and Cambridge, MA. He also teaches at the University of Pennsylvania and Fielding Graduate University. He works with clients at the intersection of strategy and organization development. He is the author of several books including, *Managing in the New Team Environment, The Workplace Within,* and *Reworking Authority.* He is a founder and past president of the International Society for the Psychoanalytic Study of Organizations. He writes a blog about the intersection of business and psychology; http://learningfromexperiencelarryhirschhorn.blogspot.com/

Chris Hoffman, MEd, MBA, is a senior OD consultant at Xcel Energy Corporation. He is the author of several professional articles as well as a book on ecopsychology, *The Hoop and the Tree: A Compass for Finding a Deeper Relationship with All Life,* and a book of poetry, *Cairns.* Hoffman earned his MEd at Northeastern University, Boston, MA and his MBA from the University of Colorado. He can be reached at Chris.Hoffman@XcelEnergy.com.

Shana Hormann, PhD, has been working with nonprofit organizations, tribes, and universities in Washington and Alaska since 1975. She has provided training and consultation to nonprofit leaders and staff members, law enforcement officials, educators, medical personnel, and social service professionals throughout the U.S. and Canada about child sexual abuse, family violence, Native education, and juvenile offenders. For the past ten years she has focused her research, writing, and training on organizational trauma. She is on faculty at Antioch University Seattle and currently serves as Associate Academic Dean and Dean of Students. She can be reached at shormann@antioch.edu or shanahormann@gmail.com.

Maya Hu-Chan, MA, President, Global Leadership Associates, is an international management consultant, executive coach, public speaker, and author. She was rated *Top 100 Thought Leaders in Management & Leadership* (2008-2011) by Leadership Excellence Magazine. She specializes in global leadership, executive coaching and cross-cultural business skills. Harvard Business School has chosen her book *Global Leadership: The Next Generation* to be one of their Working Knowledge recommended books. Born and raised in Taiwan and residing in San Diego, California, She has a Masters degree from the University of Pennsylvania. She can be reached at mayahuchan@gmail.com

Harry Hutson. PhD is Vice President, Human Resources at Global Knowledge Network, an information technology education provider. Previously, he was Vice President, Leadership Development at Avery Dennison Corporation, and a Director of Personnel at Cummins Engine Company; for nineteen years, he has focused his work in human development and organization change while performing in human resource management roles within multinational companies. Hutson's professional practice includes consulting with nonprofits, delivering conference workshops, and writing occasional articles for publication. He can be contacted at harry@harryhutson.com.

Kathleen Iverson, PhD, is Associate Professor of Training and Development at Roosevelt University located in Chicago, Illinois, where she teaches graduate level courses in organization development, cultural diversity, research methodology, e learning, training foundations, consulting, and evaluation. She holds a PhD from Loyola University Chicago in Training and Organization Development with a minor in Quantitative Research Methods. Her publications include books and research articles that address e learning, organization strategy, instructional design, and human resource management. She can be reached at kiverson@roosevelt.edu.

Jeffrey Jackson, MBA, is principal of The Vallarta Institute, a consulting, coaching and evaluation firm for foundations and nonprofits with offices in Oakland, CA and a retreat center in Puerto Vallarta, Mexico. He has worked for 11 years at healthcare giant Kaiser Permanente as Manager of Community Relations, Operations/Finance Director for the Labor-Management Partnership, and Director of Consulting Services with The Permanente Medical Group. He can be reached at jeff.jackson@vallartainstitute.com.

Judith H. Katz, EdD, has helped Fortune 100 companies address systemic barriers, foster inclusive interactions through the 12 Inclusive Behaviors, leverage diversity, and foster strategic culture change. As Executive Vice President for The Kaleel Jamison Consulting Group, Inc., Judith has created numerous breakthrough concepts in organization development and transformation, including (with Frederick A. Miller) Inclusion as the *HOW*® as a foundational mindset for higher performance. The author of the landmark book *White Awareness: Handbook for Anti-Racism Training*, she has also co-authored three books with Frederick A. Miller: *The Inclusion Breakthrough: Unleashing the Real Power of Diversity; Be BIG: Step Up, Step Out, Be Bold;* and (forthcoming March 2013) *Opening Doors to Teamwork and Collaboration: 4 Keys That Change EVERYTHING*. In 2007, *Profiles in Diversity Journal* named her one of 40 Pioneers of Diversity, and in 2012 she was honored as one of the Legends of Diversity by the International Society of Diversity and Inclusion Professionals. She can be reached at JudithKatz@kjcg.com

Art Kleiner is the editor-in-chief of strategy+business, the award-winning management magazine published by Booz & Company: www.strategy-business.com. He is also the editorial director of the Fifth Discipline Fieldbook series, the coauthor of Schools That Learn with Peter Senge, et al. (second edition, Random House, 2012), and the author of The Age of Heretics (Jossey-Bass, 2008) and Who Really Matters (Doubleday, 2003). He is on the faculty of New York University's Interactive Telecommunications Program. He can be reached at kleiner_art@bah.com

Adam S. Kling, PhD, is the Global Practice Leader, Executive Selection and Integration at RHR International, LLP. In this role he is responsible for the development and management of the firm's services that address the considerable risks associated with C-level hiring and promotion decisions. He also works with CEOS and executive teams when undergoing significant structural, process, and strategic change. He can be reached at akling@rhrinternational.com.

David Kolb, PhD, is Professor of Organizational Behavior at the Weatherhead School of Management, Case Western Reserve University. He is best known for his research on experiential learning and learning styles described in *Experiential Learning: Experience as the Source of Learning and Development*. Current research activities include assessment of learning flexibility, studies of team learning, research on the cultural determinants of learning style, and research on experiential learning in conversation.

Anne H. Litwin, PhD, has been a consultant to organizations and coach to senior leaders for over 30 years in the United States and internationally. She has been the CEO of her family retail business, is a professional member and past-Chair of the Board of Directors of the NTL Institute. Litwin also conducts research and writes about women in organizations. She can be reached at: www.annelitwin.com.

Jeremy S. Lurey, PhD, is the CEO and Chief Architect of Plus Delta Consulting, LLC. With nearly 20 years of progressive experience as a management consultant, he serves as a trusted business advisor for his clients and partners with them to improve performance and implement positive changes in their organizations. Lurey has particular expertise in strategic planning, executive and management development, change management, business process improvement, and virtual team effectiveness. He can be reached at jslurey@plusdelta.net.

Harold Mack was an internal consultant with Southern New England Telephone Co.

Charles Mallue is Manager, Organization Development for Walt Disney Parks & Resorts. He consults with global leadership teams on the implementation of strategy, the organization of work and people, and the impacts of change. His previous experience includes external consulting and senior level HR positions with NCR, Lexis-Nexis, and Exxon-Mobil. He is a member of the OD Network. He holds an MBA from Youngstown University and certificates from Columbia University's PPOD program and the Gestalt Institute of Cleveland's IOSD program. Mallue can be reached at Charles.Mallue@disney.com.

Robert J. Marshak, PhD, is Senior Scholar in Residence for the AU/NTL MSOD Program at American University, Washington, DC and maintains a global consulting practice. His current interests include discourse-based change processes and dialogic OD. Marshak is a recipient of the Organization Development Network's Lifetime Achievement Award. He can be contacted at marshak@american.edu.

Paul M. Mastrangelo has more than 20 years experience in organization development, organizational research, and adult education. At CEB Valtera he collaborates with leaders from multi-national companies to design, administer, and interpret organizational assessments for change management. He has over 25 professional publications and maintains a professional online presence on LinkedIn, Twitter @paulmastrangelo, and the blog The First Domino. He received his PhD in Organizational Psychology from Ohio University in 1993. He can be reached at pmastrangelo@executiveboard.com.

Hona Matthews, MA, is Director of Organization Effectiveness for ARAMARK Healthcare at a major hospital system in Central Texas. She's a skilled practitioner with 15 years of experience in patient and employee satisfaction, performance management, change management, executive coaching, and curriculum development for the learning organization. She has a vested interest in helping build world class organizations by integrating organization development systems and processes within crucial business operations. She can be reached at matthewshona@aramark.com.

Michael F. McGovern has been a practicing Human Resources, Leadership Development, and Organization De-

velopment professional for more than 25 years and has worked as an internal consultant/professional in both the public, nonprofit and for-profit sectors for companies such as Abbott Labs, BP/Amoco, and the Chicago Transit Authority. He has also been and is currently the Principal of his own consulting firm: Turn-Key Performance Solutions. He has a masters degree in Organization Development from Loyola University of Chicago and a bachelors degree in Education from DePaul University. He currently resides in Park Ridge, Illinois with his wife Susan and their son Michael. McGovern can be reached at michaelfmcgovern@gmail.com.

Frederick A. Miller, serves as CEO of The Kaleel Jamison Consulting Group, Inc. With more than 30 years in organization development and transformation, he specializes in using Inclusion as the *HOW™*—a foundational transformation mindset he co-created with Judith H. Katz—to accelerate results and achieve higher operational performance in Fortune 100 companies and other organizations. He has co-authored three books with Judith H. Katz: *Be BIG: Step Up, Step Out, Be Bold; The Inclusion Breakthrough: Unleashing the Real Power of Diversity;* and (forthcoming March 2013) *Opening Doors to Teamwork and Collaboration: 4 Keys That Change EVERYTHING.* He has served on the boards of Ben & Jerry's Homemade, Day & Zimmermann, and many other organizations. Fred has received many honors during his career: in 2007, *Profiles in Diversity Journal* named him one of 40 Pioneers of Diversity, and he became the youngest person ever to win the OD Network's Lifetime Achievement Award. In 2012 he was honored as one of the Legends of Diversity by the International Society of Diversity and Inclusion Professionals. He can be reached at FrederickMiller@kjcg.com.

Mary T. Miller successfully worked in the automotive industry challenging and supporting employees, at all levels, to develop their individual strengths while positively impacting the bottom line. As a manager in Human Resources at GM/Delphi Corporation, Mary focused her strengths to create organizational effectiveness through individual talent alignment and development. Mary, a Professional Certified Coach, founded her own coaching practice, MTM Transformation Coaching, following her automotive career.

Karon R. Moore has over 28 years of Human Resources experience including 18 years of management experience and 8 years working specifically on a large scale culture change initiative. She recently retired from The Hartford as Assistant Vice President, Diversity and Inclusion, and from the position of Vice-Chair of The Conference Board's Diversity and Inclusion Council. Moore is also a member of Workforce Opportunity Network and an officer on The CT Council for the Advancement of Diversity. She can be reached at: KaronRMoore@aol.com.

Jane Moosbruker, PhD, has over 30 years experience consulting to organizations in the private and public sector, including health care and education. Her focus has included managing changes in structure, technology and leadership, team development, conflict utilization and process consulting or leadership. She has taught in the Psychology Department at Boston College, the Harvard School of Dental Medicine, and American University's MSOD Program. She has over 20 publications in professional books and journals. She has been a member of National Training Laboratories Institute of Applied Behavioral Science since 1968. She obtained her PhD in Social Psychology from Harvard University. She can be reached at jamoos@earthlink.net

Mambo G. Mupepi, PhD, is associated with Global Scholars Program, University of Michigan and Grand Valley State University and is an international organization development and change consultant. He has worked in both the private and public sectors in the UK, USA, and Southern Africa in various positions including Executive Director of Morewear Engineering Ltd (1989-1991) and Director of the Management Training Bureau in the Ministry of Higher Education (1991–1995), before moving to the USA. He completed his Master's degrees in Business Technology and Administration from Eastern Michigan University (1999) and PhD in Organization Development from Benedictine University, Lisle-Chicago (2005). He has published numerous articles and books and can be reached at gmmupepi@gmail.com

Sylvia C. Mupepi, PhD, is an Associate Professor at Grand Valley State University. Prior to coming to the U.S. on a Kellogg Foundation Fellowship, she was the national director of nursing education in Zimbabwe. She has worked with international organizations including the World Health Organization. She holds a PhD from the University of Michigan, undergraduate and graduate nursing diplomas from London and Wolverhampton Universities and an MA from the University of Zimbabwe. She can be contacted at mupepis@gvsu.edu.

Wendell Nekoranec EdD, MBA works as a strategist, change agent, management consultant, educator, speaker, and writer. Consulting work includes large-scale change management, strategic planning, mergers & acquisitions, and process improvement. In addition, he teaches at California State University Long Beach and online for the University of Nebraska. He can be reached at wnekoranec@gmail.com.

Peter F. Norlin, PhD, Principal of *Peter Norlin Δ Change Guides*, and formerly the Executive Director of the OD Network, has spent over 30 years in the field of OD, serving a range of customers from two-person partnerships to Fortune 100 companies. His teaching experience includes faculty appointments at Vanderbilt University, Johns Hopkins University, and Georgetown University. Based in Ann Arbor, Michigan, he is also a professional member of the NTL Institute. He can be reached at pfnorlin@earthlink.net.

Debra Orr is a scholar-practitioner and an Associate Professor/Program Director in Organizational Leadership at Roosevelt University. She is published in the Journal of Nursing Administration, Organization Development Practitioner, Organization Development Journal, and Revue Gestion de Science. Orr serves as President of the Midwest Academy of Management as of October of 2012. An award-winning writer and consultant, on-going researcher and frequent academic presenter, Orr concentrates her efforts on bringing the newest academic research to life within the context of organizations. She can be reached at dorr@roosevelt.edu<mailto:dorr@roosevelt.edu>

Naomi Raab has over 20 years of consulting experience working with leaders who are experiencing growth, change, and sometimes conflict in their organizations. Combining the fields of psychology, management, and organizational dynamics, Raab has assisted people to lead more dynamically and creatively. Raab offers an integrated set of services encompassing organizational, group, and individual aspects of functioning. She can be reached at naomi@raab.com.au.

Maria C. Ramos, EdD, is President of Ramos Associates LLC, an OD consulting firm focused on large systems change, Diversity and inclusion, training and development, and executive coaching in corporations and nonprofit organizations. Recently, she has taught at George Washington University, Syracuse University, and Goddard College. Ramos is a member of the NTL Institute for Applied Behavioral Science. She is reachable at maria@ramosassociates.com.

Mary Ann Rainey, PhD, is an organizational effectiveness consultant and executive coach with a global client roster. Her leadership experience includes corporate Vice President and Vice City Manager. She is co-chairperson of the Gestalt International Organization & Systems Development (OSD) Program and a founding member of the Ghana OSD Program. She has collaborated with David A. Kolb on the application of experiential learning theory to leadership development. She has taught at Case Western Reserve University and Benedictine University and authored several articles. She has served on Boards of Director of NTL Institute of Applied Behavioral Science and the Academy of Management Association. She holds a PhD in Organizational Behavior from Case Western Reserve University and lives in Chicago, Illinois USA. She can be reached at maryarainey@aol.com.

Neil D. Samuels' 23 years of consulting experience span six continents and businesses ranging from Cruise Lines, Architecture, R&D, and Energy Production, to the US Geological Survey, Trading Compliance, and Education. His work builds on a foundation of strengths and Appreciative Inquiry to engage entire organizations in fundamentally changing their conversations to bring about lasting change. Samuels holds an MSOD from Pepperdine University where he served as adjunct faculty in the Graziadio School of Business and Management. He can be reached at neil@profoundconversations.com

David Schechtman is the founder and president of Tru Progress Consulting based in Los Angeles. His experience includes work with Fortune 500 companies in the financial services, healthcare, travel, and telecom industries. His main focus is helping clients transform adversities into victories. He helps his clients navigate difficult circumstances, identify golden learning opportunities, and establish straight-forward action plans for success. His education includes a MS in Organization Development from Pepperdine University. He can be reached at david@truprogress.com.

Edgar H. Schein, PhD, is the Sloan Fellows Professor of Management Emeritus from the MIT Sloan School of Management where he taught from 1956 to 2004. He received his PhD in Social Psychology from Harvard in 1952 and has applied this field to the understanding of career development, organizational culture, process consultation, and the dynamics of interpersonal relations in organizations. He can be reached at scheine@comcast.net.

John J. Scherer, BA, MDiv, LHD, is an international consultant, speaker, and change facilitator with the world's best-known organizations and their leaders. A former Combat Officer in the US Navy, Lutheran Chaplain at Cornell University, Gestalt-oriented Family Systems Therapist, and Co-creator of the first competency-based graduate program in applied behavioral science. Author of many print, audio, video and other on-line resources. His mission: *transforming the world at work™*. He can be reached at www.SchererCenter.com.

Christopher Schoch is the founding partner of MDLS Associates, and has over twenty years of international experience in executive and organizational development. He has worked extensively in Europe, West Africa, the Middle East, and India. Christopher lectures in executive development programs in Europe and the United States including the MIB program of "Ecole Nationale de Ponts et Chausées," and the Antioch University Graduate Management Program in Seattle. He regularly contributes articles to professional journals. He can be reached at: Mdlschoch@aol.com.

Patricia Shafer, MSc, MBA, MA, is president of Compel Organizational Excellence Alliance Ltd., a U.S.-based international consulting and research practice focused on inspiring leaders, mentoring multinationals, empowering women and transforming technology. She is also co-founder of The Change Leaders, an international network of consultants and coaches in the human dynamics of change headquartered in the UK. She holds an MSc., Consulting and Coaching for Change, a joint venture of Oxford University, UK, and HEC, France; an MBA, Northwestern University J.L. Kellogg Graduate School of Management; and certifications in numerous organiza-

tional and leadership assessments. She can be reached at pshafer@compelconsulting.com.

Herbert Allen Shepard, PhD made a significant contribution to Organization Development. He held faculty posts at several universities including M.I.T., where he received his doctorate in Industrial Economics. He founded and directed the first doctoral program in Organization Development at Case Western Reserve; developed a residency in administrative psychiatry at Yale University School of Medicine, and was also President of The Gestalt Institute of Cleveland and The Professional Development Institute. Shepard conducted the first large-scale experiments in Organization Development, while at Esso in the late fifties, and served as principal consultant to TRW Systems in the applications of behavioral science to organizations and teams. His research opened the way for further developments in the psychology of teams, leadership and interpersonal compatibility; cognitive behavior therapy, social cognitive theory (educational psychology); choice theory; principled negotiation, positive psychology and organization development.

Edward Shin is a consultant at Philosophy IB where he applies social network analysis on training and development, change management, and process design projects. His interest in network analysis grew out of his undergraduate work in Molecular Biology at Princeton where he explored the networks of genetic interactions in stem cells. He can be reached at eshin@philosophyib.com.

Peter F. Sorensen, PhD, is Professor and Director of the OD PhD Program and MSMOB programs at Benedictine University. He is Past Chair of the ODC Division of the Academy of Management, and is currently on the executive board of AOM's Management Consulting Division. He has authored over 200 articles, books, and best papers. He was Guest Editor for the New Millennium issues for *OD Journal* and *OD Practitioner.* Sorensen's recent book is *Strategic Organization Development* with Therese Yaeger. He can be reached at psorensen@ben.edu.

Nancy L. Southern, EdD, is Chair of the MA and PhD programs in Organizational Systems at Saybrook University. Her work is focused on creating cultures of collaboration in public, private, and non-profit organizations and local and global communities. She works with senior and mid-management teams to build their capacity to engage in meaningful conversations and dialogue incorporating appreciative and critical inquiry to address their challenges and create their desired change. She can be reached at Nlsouthern@aol.com.

Nicole Stragalas is an external OD consultant in Phoenix, AZ specializing in leadership development and employee engagement. She has developed national programs in service, sales, and quality assurance in the healthcare and banking industries. She has her SPHR certification and is a Six Sigma Green Belt. Her dual Masters degrees were earned at the University of Florida; currently, she's working on her PhD in I/O Psychology through the University of Phoenix. She can be reached at ncstragalas@ mac.com.

Heather Butler Taylor, MSOD, is the President and founder of H. B. Taylor Associates. She specializes in the design and facilitation of diversity awareness interventions, executive and personal coaching, strategic planning, team building, conflict management, organizational consulting and change management in the US and internationally. Taylor holds a MS degree in Organizational Development and a graduate certificate in change management from The Johns Hopkins University, and is a member of NTL Institute. She can be reached at hbtaylor @verizon.net.

Ramkrishnan (Ram) V. Tenkasi, PhD, is Professor of Organizational Change with the PhD program in OD at Benedictine University. His research on institutional and organizational change, knowledge, learning, technology, and innovation has been funded by multiple federal agencies such as the National Science Foundation, Department of Defense, the National Institutes of Health, and private corporations such as Motorola, Texas Instruments, Hewlett Packard, Lucent Technologies, Pfizer, etc. His more than 60 articles and chapters have appeared in leading journals such as *Organization Science, Journal of Applied Behavioral Sciences, Journal of Organizational Change Management, Journal of Engineering and Technology Management, ACM Transactions on Computer Supported Cooperative Work,* and research volumes such as *Research in Organization Development and Change.* He is also Division Chair of the Organization Development and Change Division of the Academy of Management. He can be reached at rtenkasi@ben.edu.

Deb Torchia is a performance-driven organizational consultant with expertise in organizational dynamics and over 20 years of extensive management experience. Career accomplishments include successfully motivating and leading cross-functional global teams, facilitating organizational change, and defining and implementing strategic business plans. She has a MS in Organization Development (MSOD) from American University in Washington, D.C. where she was awarded a distinction for her field work. She can be reached at debtorchia@torchiaandassociates.com.

Dudley Tower has a PhD in Human and Organizational Systems from the Fielding Institute, and is CEO of the Evergreen Institute for Complex Human Systems. He has worked as an Automotive Industry executive, psychotherapist, organizational consultant, and has recently finished his first book, *A Few Simple Rules,* on the application of CAS theory to human systems. He can be reached at dtower@evergreeninstitute.org.

Amanda Trosten-Bloom, Principal with Corporation for Positive Change, was one of the first OD consultants to use

Appreciative Inquiry for whole system culture change in a business setting. Her work focuses primarily on promoting positive change in mid-sized organizations. In these settings, she facilitates AI-based culture transformation, strategic planning, leadership development, and business process improvement. Trosten-Bloom can be reached at: amanda@positivechange.org.

Peter Vaill, PhD, is currently University Professor of Management at Antioch University in Yellow Springs, Ohio. He is internationally known for his innovative approaches to organizational behavior, and has written extensively, including the well-known *Managing as a Performing Art; New Ideas for a World of Chaotic Change; Learning as a Way of Being; Strategies for Survival in a World of Permanent White Water;* and *Spirited Leading and Learning: Process Wisdom for a New Age.* He can be reached at learning being@centurylink.net.

Greg Vaughan, MA, has 20 years experience in organization development consulting and training. He earned his Master of Counseling degree from Arizona State and completed doctoral studies at the University of Nebraska. He took advanced training in open systems design and large group interventions with the Fred Emery Institute. He is president of The Vaughan Consulting Group in Scottsdale, Arizona and can be reached at greg@vaughanconsulting.com.

Michael H. Vinitsky, PhD, is a senior consultant with PDI Ninth House, a leadership solutions consulting firm. He has over 30 years of experience as an internal and external consultant working with leaders to successfully implement large scale change. His work also includes leadership assessment and development and coaching executives to enhance their impact as leaders. He earned his PhD from the University of Minnesota. He can be reached at mvinitsky@dc.rr.com.

Pat Vivian, MA, after working for 15 years as a clinician and manager in nonprofit organizations in New York City and Seattle, started her own consultation practice in 1982. Since then she has worked with hundreds of nonprofit organizations in Washington State and across the U.S. For the past ten years she has focused her consulting, training, writing, and research on organizational trauma. She recently retired from her thirty-year teaching career at Antioch University Seattle. Together with Geoff Bellman and others she co-founded in 1995 the Community Consulting Partnership (CCP), which combines a mission of learning and service through its pro bono team consultation with Washington State nonprofits that cannot afford to pay for OD services. She earned her Masters degree at Antioch University Seattle. She can be reached at p.vivian@att.net.

George Vukotich, Ph.D., is Chair of the Graduate Program in Training and Development at Roosevelt University. He has over 20 years experience working in corporate, consulting, military and educational environments with clients in the finance, telecommunications, manufacturing, retailing, healthcare, and government industries. Some of the organizations he has worked with include; Andersen Consulting, IBM, Booz, Allen and Hamilton, McKinsey, Motorola, Exelon and BP-Amoco. He holds a PhD in organization development from Loyola University along with an MBA in Finance and an undergraduate degree in Computer Science. He can be reached at gvukotich @roosevelt.edu.

Don Warrick is an award winning educator, consultant, and author who specializes in developing and coaching leaders and in organization development, change, and transformation. His latest books are *Lessons In Leadership* (2011), *Lessons In Leading Change* (2012), and *Lessons In Changing Cultures* (Late 2012). He is Professor of Management and Organization Change at the University of Colorado at Colorado Springs where he holds the life time title of President's Teaching Scholar and has received the university's highest award, the Chancellor's Award, as well as the Outstanding University Teacher Award, the Outstanding Faculty Member for the College of Business Award, and many College of Business Teaching Awards. Warrick has been a consultant to Fortune 500 companies, international companies, government agencies, universities, and mid-size and smaller organizations. He received his BBA and MBA degrees from the University of Oklahoma and doctorate from the University of Southern California. He can be reached at Ddwarrick@aol.com.

Marvin Weisbord is co-director of Future Search Network, an international non-profit community service organization. He was for 20 years a partner in the pioneer OD consulting firm Block Petrella Weisbord, where he consulted with corporations, medical schools and hospitals. For many years he ran NTL laboratories in consulting skills, organizational diagnosis, and teambuilding. OD Network gave him a lifetime achievement award in 2004, and its members named his book *Productive Workplaces* one of the most influential of the previous 40 years. He is a resource faculty member in the Organization Systems Renewal Program at Seattle University and an elected fellow of the World Academy of Productivity Science. He is the author of *Organizational Diagnosis* (Addison-Wesley, 1978), *Productive Workplaces* (Jossey-Bass, 1987), *Discovering Common Ground* (Berrett-Koehler, 1992), *Productive Workplaces Revisited* (Jossey-Bass/Wiley 2004), and co-author with Sandra Janoff of *Future Search*, 3rd edition (Berrett-Koehler, 2010) and *Don't Just Do Something, Stand There!* (Berrett-Koehler, 2007).

Margaret Wheatley, EdD, is a well-respected writer, speaker, and teacher. She has written six books: *Walk Out Walk On* (with Deborah Frieze, 2011); *Perseverance* (2010); *Leadership and the New Science; Turning to One Another: Simple Conversations to Restore Hope to the Future; A Simpler Way* (with Myron Rogers); and *Finding Our Way: Leadership for an Uncertain Time*. She is co-founder and President emerita of The Berkana Institute, which works in partnership with a rich diversity of people and communities around the world,

especially in the Global South. Her articles appear in both professional and popular journals and may be downloaded free from her website: www.margaretwheatley.com. Wheatley received her doctorate in Organizational Behavior and Change from Harvard University, and a Masters in Media Ecology from New York University. She's been an organizational consultant since 1973, a global citizen since her youth, a professor in two graduate business programs, a prolific writer, and a happy mother and grandmother.

Diana Whitney, PhD, is the President of Corporation for Positive Change, a consulting firm offering Appreciative Inquiry to businesses and social profit organizations around the globe. She is an internationally recognized consultant, speaker, and thought leader on the subjects of Appreciative Inquiry, Positive Change, and Spirituality at Work. Her consulting practice focuses on the use of Appreciative Inquiry for corporate culture change. Whitney can be reached at: diana@positivechange.org.

Victor Wooddell, PhD, served as an internal organization development consultant to the City of Detroit from 1999 to 2006. He earned his doctorate in Social and Organizational Psychology from Wayne State University. He is now an Associate Professor at Oakland University in Rochester, Michigan, where he teaches courses in human resources development. Wooddell can be reached at wooddellv@ yahoo.com.

Therese F. Yaeger, PhD, is Associate Professor, Benedictine University Organization Development (OD) and Master of Science in Management and Organizational Behavior programs. She is Editorial Board Member of *OD Practitioner*, and has authored numerous papers and books, including *Strategic Organization Development: Managing Change for Success* (2009). Yaeger is Division Chair of the Management Consulting Division of Academy of Management, and Past President of the Midwest Academy of Management. She can be reached at tyaeger@ben.edu.

Bauback Yeganeh, PhD, is the Founder of B.Y. Consulting (www. byconsulting.org) which focuses on leadership development and organizational strategy, and Everidian (www .everidian.com), an eco-advantage consulting group. Yeganeh's work focuses on leadership development, strategy, and eco-advantage. He has consulted to organizations in The Americas, Europe, and Asia including The World Bank, United Nations, FIEP Brazil, Alcatel Lucent, and Progressive Insurance. He can be reached at by@byconsulting .org or byeganeh@everidian.com.

Nadya Zhexembayeva serves as a Director of Inquiry and Knowledge Management for the Business as Agent of World Benefit Inquiry. A native of Kazakhstan, she works on creating the Organization Development Consortium of Central Asia, while continuing her graduate study of Organizational Behavior at Case Western Reserve University. Zhexembayeva can be reached at: ntz@weatherhead.cwru .edu.

INDEX

653